R. Gupta's®

POPULAR MASTER GUIDE

DSSSB–TEACHERS

PGT

POLITICAL SCIENCE

Recruitment Exam

by

RPH Editorial Board

2026
EDITION

RAMESH PUBLISHING HOUSE, NEW DELHI

Published by

O.P. Gupta *for* Ramesh Publishing House

Admin. Office

12-H, New Daryaganj Road, Opp. Officers' Mess,
New Delhi-110002 ☏ 23275224, 23245124

E-mail: info@rameshpublishinghouse.com
For Online Shopping: www.rameshpublishinghouse.com

Showroom

- Balaji Market, Nai Sarak, Delhi-110006 ☏ 23282525 📱 9354373464
- 4457, Nai Sarak, Delhi-110006

Book Code: R-1317

ISBN: 978-93-5012-016-3

Price: ₹ 330

Printed at: Deepak Offset, Delhi

CONTENTS

Scheme of Examination

DSSSB will conduct **One Tier Exam** for PGT posts having two section:

Section-I

S.No.	Subject	Questions	Marks
1.	Mental Ability and Reasoning Ability	20	20
2.	General Awareness	20	20
3.	English Language & Comprehension	20	20
4.	Hindi Language & Comprehension	20	20
5.	Numerical Aptitude & Data Interpretation	20	20
	Total	**100**	**100**

Section-II

S.No.	Subject	Questions	Marks
1.	MCQs pertaining to Post-Graduation qualification and teaching methodology required for the post.	**200**	**200**

Previous Years' Paper

Delhi Subordinate Services Selection Board (DSSSB)

PGT (Political Science) Recruitment Exam, 2025

(Exam held on 14-07-2025)

Subject Knowledge – Political Science & Teaching Methodology

1. Which of the following statements most accurately distinguishes the legislative powers in a presidential system from those in a parliamentary system?

1. In presidential systems, a separation of powers limits the legislature's ability to directly control the executive.
2. In presidential systems, legislatures can dissolve the executive at will.
3. In parliamentary systems, a legislature has no role in law-making.
4. In parliamentary systems, legislatures are strictly ceremonial and do not influence rule-making.

2. Which of the following best characterizes traditional political theory?

1. It is strictly empirical and value-neutral
2. It is normative and concerned with how political life ought to be
3. It emphasizes the scientific study of behaviour
4. It focuses on statistical models and data interpretation

3. Which institution in India facilitated system's efforts to regulate and control its environment?

1. Military 2. Intelligence
3. Guild system 4. Bureaucracy

4. Which of the following is a common feature of a judiciary that lacks independence?

1. Fair trials and due process
2. Protection of minority rights
3. Decisions favouring the ruling government
4. Judicial review over legislation

5. How does the Weberian bureaucratic model relate to the executive's rule-application function?

1. It prioritises charismatic authority in implementation.
2. It emphasises rational-legal authority and hierarchical organisation.
3. It relies on personal loyalty and discretion.
4. It limits executive power through judicial review.

6. 'Man is born free, but everywhere he is in chains'
Who among the following made this statement?

1. John Rawls 2. John Locke
3. Thomas Hobbes 4. Rousseau

7. Which of the following institutions acts as a check on executive excesses?

1. Bureaucracy 2. Judiciary
3. Military 4. Legislature

8. What best distinguishes political theory from ideology?

1. Both Political theory and ideology are manipulative in nature.
2. Political theory uses emotional appeal, while ideology rests on reason.
3. Political theory provides normative orientation, while ideology has speculative intent.
4. Political theory gives the fullest reason possible for a certain standpoint, while ideology often short-circuits reason and reduces principles to formulae.

9. Comparative Political Analysis primarily involves the study of:

1. A single country's political system
2. Political leaders only
3. Similarities and differences between political systems
4. Military strategies and warfare

10. The scope of political theory includes the study of:

1. economic theories and market policies
2. religious beliefs and theological doctrines
3. government machinery and institutional frameworks only
4. fundamental political concepts like liberty, justice, equality, rights, and democracy

11. The behavioral revolution in political science is associated with:

1. the application of empirical and quantitative methods
2. a shift towards normative philosophy
3. a focus on constitutional law exclusively
4. the abandonment of social sciences

12. Which of the following statements regarding the philosophical approach to the study of politics is NOT true?

1. Philosophical approach denotes efforts to arrive at truth through the use of reason.
2. Philosophical approach provides standards of right and wrong for the critical evaluation of the existing institutions.
3. Philosophical approach seeks to clarify about ends and means in studying the subject.
4. Philosophical approach does not seek to clarify thought about the nature of the subject.

13. Post-behavioralism in political theory emerged primarily as a critique of:

1. Marxist economic determinism
2. traditional historical analysis
3. normative and philosophical approaches
4. empirical and quantitative behavioral methods lacking normative relevance

14. Which of the following is a key feature of constitutionalism?

1. Centralised executive dominance
2. Limited government under law
3. Rule by decree
4. Unlimited powers of the state

15. One of the key features of modern political theory is:

1. avoidance of empirical methods
2. focus on classical texts
3. value neutrality
4. rejection of scientific methods

16. Which of the following institutions is involved in interest articulation?

1. The army
2. Political parties
3. The judiciary
4. The civil service

17. Who is associated with the political system theory in modern political science?

1. Gabriel Almond
2. Robert Dahl
3. David Easton
4. Harold Lasswell

18. Which political institution is primarily responsible for the rule-making function in a democracy?

1. Judiciary
2. Bureaucracy
3. Legislature
4. Executive

19. Modern political theory primarily focuses on:

1. normative questions about ideal states only
2. mythological explanations of politics
3. purely philosophical reflections without practical implications
4. empirical analysis of political behaviour and institutions

20. What distinguishes post-modern political theory from traditional theory?

1. Emphasis on elite rule
2. Acceptance of a singular truth
3. Belief in moral universals
4. Deconstruction and identity politics

21. Who among the following highlighted the importance of informal organisation within formal structures?

1. Frederick Taylor
2. Chester Barnard
3. Elton Mayo
4. Max Weber

22. Which of the following is NOT a characteristic of Weberian bureaucracy criticised by feminists?

1. Gender neutrality
2. Rigidity
3. Flexibility
4. Impersonality

23. Who among the following introduced the 'bounded rationality' concept in administrative decision-making?

1. Herbert Simon 2. Luther Gulick
3. Max Weber 4. Woodrow Wilson

24. Which Constitutional provision allows States to promote justice for backward social groups specific to their regions?

1. Directive Principles
2. Article 21
3. Article 15(4)
4. Article 17

25. Which of the following options most accurately defines the concept of Public Administration?

1. Managing private enterprises
2. Implementing government policies and managing public programmes
3. Conducting political campaigns
4. Studying ancient civilisations

26. What major constitutional issue arose as a result of land reform laws like the abolition of zamindari?

1. Absence of local governance
2. Conflict between Fundamental Rights and Directive Principles
3. Disregard for economic development
4. Abuse of federal powers

27. Who is recognised as the father of Scientific Management?

1. Charles Babbage
2. Frederick Taylor
3. Henry R Towne
4. Frederick Halsey

28. What is the primary role of the State in protecting individual freedom as per the Indian Constitution?

1. To enforce religious customs
2. To act on majority sentiment without checks
3. To ensure freedom through constitutional limits and guarantees
4. To permit absolute freedom without limits

29. Who wrote the book 'Gender Images in Public Administration' published in 1993?

1. Camilla Stivers 2. Kathy E Ferguson
3. Gerda Lerner 4. Martha Nussbaum

30. Feminist theory in Public Administration DOES NOT seek to focus on:

1. exclusive presence in public sphere
2. empowering women
3. criticising dominance of male in public administration
4. gender equality

31. Who is accredited with writing an article — 'The Study of Public Administration' to emphasise Public Administration as a discipline?

1. Abraham Maslow
2. Dogulas M McGregor
3. Chris Argyris
4. Woodrow Wilson

32. Yogendra Yadav introduced a concept of Third Electoral System to analyse the transformation of Indian electoral politics. Which of the following features is NOT associated with this concept?

1. Democratic Upsurge
2. Strengthening of elite control
3. Political Fragmentation
4. Post-Congress Polity

33. Which institution is responsible for recognising political parties in India?

1. The Supreme Court
2. The Union Cabinet
3. The Parliament
4. The Election Commission of India

34. Which of the following best represents a recent trend in social movements?

1. Hashtag activism and online petitions
2. Armed revolutions
3. Use of print media
4. Underground political resistance

35. Which commission was established to address the demands and ensure justice related to regional imbalances in India?

1. Election Commission
2. Mandal Commission
3. Finance Commission
4. States Reorganisation Commission

36. Which of the following best illustrates the shift in strategy among recent social movements in India as compared to traditional movements?

1. Exclusive reliance on party-based mobilization
2. Abandonment of legal channels in favor of armed resistance
3. Greater emphasis on intersectional identities and decentralized leadership
4. Full integration into state apparatus through electoral alliances

37. What percentage of seats are reserved for women in Panchayati Raj Institutions?

1. 50% 2. 33%
3. 25% 4. 40%

38. Which of the following concepts emphasises that organisations must maintain cooperation among members?

1. Scientific management
2. Theory of cooperation
3. Bureaucratic structure
4. Zone of indifference

39. Which one of the following is NOT a function of political parties?

1. Rule adjudication
2. Political Recruitment
3. Political Socialisation
4. Coordination

40. Who among the following introduced the concept of 'span of control' in management?

1. Henri Fayol 2. Max Weber
3. Luther Gulick 4. Chester Barnard

41. Which of the following thinkers emphasised the importance of community and decentralised governance in Indian Political Thought?

1. BR Ambedkar 2. Mahatma Gandhi
3. Kautilya 4. Jawaharlal Nehru

42. The concept of 'Strategic Autonomy' in Indian foreign policy refers to which of the following?

1. Maintaining freedom in making foreign policy decisions
2. Military neutrality only
3. Economic independence from WTO
4. Isolationism in world politics

43. Democratic knowledge practices in India are increasingly associated with which of the following educational approaches?

1. Silent reading methods
2. Critical pedagogy
3. Textbook-centered recitation
4. Standardised testing

44. Which of the following is NOT a feature of federalism in India?

1. Supremacy of the Constitution
2. Supremacy of the Governor in the State
3. Vertical separation of powers
4. Written Constitution

45. Feminist interventions in Indian political theory have highlighted:

1. the importance of defense policy in gender studies
2. the need to study the state through gendered lenses and question male-dominated knowledge systems
3. that women are absent from political movements
4. only the economic roles of women

46. Which constitutional provision protects the cultural and educational rights of minorities in India?

1. Article 19
2. Article 14
3. Article 17
4. Articles 29 and 30

47. India's engagement with ASEAN is part of which broader foreign policy initiative?

1. Look East Policy (now Act East Policy)
2. Indo-Pacific Doctrine
3. Non-Alignment Movement
4. South-South Cooperation

48. India became a founding member of which international financial institution in 1944?

1. BRICS Bank
2. Asian Development Bank
3. World Trade Organization
4. International Monetary Fund

49. Which major strategic partnership symbolized India's growing ties with the United States in the post-Cold War era?

1. South Asian Association for Regional Cooperation (SAARC)
2. Indo-Soviet Treaty of Peace
3. Indo-US Civil Nuclear Agreement (2008)
4. Shanghai Cooperation Organization (SCO)

50. According to Gandhi, the ideal Indian state is one that:

1. centralises power in the capital
2. is based on self-sufficient villages
3. promotes industrial capitalism
4. controls the economy

51. Which Indian personality floated the concept of 'Chiti' which encompasses individual consciousness, national consciousness and cosmic consciousness?

1. Sri Aurobindo
2. Veer Savarkar
3. Pandit Deen Dayal Upadhyaya
4. Rammohan Roy

52. What does the acronym I2U2 stand for in the context of international cooperation?

1. Iran–Iraq–UAE–USA
2. India–Israel–UAE–United States
3. India–Indonesia–UAE–United States
4. India–Israel–UK–USA

53. According to Mahatma Gandhi, knowledge is rooted in:

1. state authority
2. experiential truth
3. textbook-based education
4. capital accumulation

54. What is the primary role of the executive in the Indian Political System?

1. Creating laws through legislative debates
2. Conducting national elections
3. Implementing and enforcing laws and policies
4. Interpreting laws through judicial review

55. Which of the following doctrines emphasized India's unilateral efforts to improve relations with its neighbors without expecting reciprocity?

1. Non-Alignment Doctrine
2. Look East Policy
3. Gujral Doctrine
4. Nehru Doctrine

56. India's foreign policy underwent a major shift toward economic diplomacy and global integration beginning in:

1. 1965
2. 1991
3. 2004
4. 1947

57. Which of the following is India's principal external intelligence agency?

1. RAW
2. NIA
3. IB
4. CBI

58. Which of the following best characterizes nationalism in Indian political thought during the independence movement?

1. A movement for self-governance and unity despite diverse cultural back-grounds
2. A rejection of all cultural identities
3. A call for military rule
4. A focus on economic policies only

59. Which of the following is a direct outcome of pluralism in a democracy?

1. Suppression of dissent
2. One-size-fits-all policy
3. Tolerance and dialogue
4. Cultural uniformity

60. Who did NOT accept nationalism (by observing conflicting claims of nations in Europe) as the highest sentiment in human beings?

1. Madan Mohan Malviya
2. BG Tilak
3. Subhas Chandra Bose
4. Rabindranath Tagore

61. How many autonomous district councils exist in the four north-eastern states of India?

1. Nine
2. Eleven
3. Ten
4. Thirteen

62. The Democratic Peace Theory argues that:

1. democracy hinders foreign policy efficiency
2. democracies are more likely to go to war
3. democracies prefer unilateralism
4. democracies rarely fight each other

63. According to Plato, which class should govern the ideal state?

1. Philosopher-kings
2. Soldiers
3. Merchants
4. Common citizens

64. Which body is responsible for delimiting the constituencies for elections in India?

1. Union Ministry of Law and Justice
2. Delimitation Commission
3. Parliament of India
4. Election Commission of India

65. The G77 was established to:

1. represent Global South interests
2. promote nuclear deterrence
3. oversee development loans
4. co-ordinate UN military peacekeeping missions

66. What distinguishes alternative approaches in International Relations from mainstream theories?

1. They prioritize only balance of power calculations
2. They focus only on Western military alliances
3. They incorporate marginal voices, norms, and identity into global analysis
4. They ignore political economy

67. Political culture refers to:
1. the economic system in a political society
2. the ideology of political parties
3. the attitudes, beliefs and values of people towards the political system
4. the structure of political institutions

68. Lokpal and Lokayuktas aim to promote:
1. political reservations during elections
2. accountability in public services
3. communal harmony among the citizens
4. judicial independence at all levels

69. A Money Bill in India can only be introduced in (the):
1. either Houses of Parliament
2. Joint sitting of both Houses
3. Lok Sabha with prior recommendation of the President
4. Rajya Sabha

70. Which realism variant most closely engages with foreign policy analysis at the individual or state level?
1. Neoclassical realism
2. Classical realism
3. Offensive realism
4. Structural realism

71. A jurisdiction under Article 131 is described as:
1. appellate
2. concurrent with High Courts
3. advisory
4. original and exclusive

72. According to the realist theory, why do international organisations such as the UN fail to prevent war?
1. They lack enforcement capability.
2. They avoid interference in human rights.
3. They are non-political actors.
4. They are neutral.

73. Which alternative approach in IR emphasizes the role of identity, norms, and social constructs in shaping state behavior, rather than focusing solely on material power or economic interests?
1. Realism
2. Marxism
3. Constructivism
4. Neoliberalism

74. A dispute between two States over the use of a river would be adjudicated under:
1. Article 172
2. Article 262
3. Article 166
4. Article 162

75. Who was NOT a part of the Neo-realist approach to International Relations?
1. Hans J Morgenthau
2. Kenneth Waltz
3. John Mearsheimer
4. Stephen Walt

76. Who is authorised to make rules and regulations regarding the number of members in the Union Public Service Commission?
1. President of India
2. Prime Minister of India
3. PMO
4. Attorney General of India

77. According to Aristotle, which of the following is a corrupt form of monarchy?
1. Polity
2. Tyranny
3. Oligarchy
4. Democracy

78. The Green Theory of international relations focuses on which of the following?
1. Ecological justice
2. Internet governance and surveillance
3. Humanitarian law enforcement
4. Global military alliances

79. What is a central assumption shared by all variants of realism in International Relations?
1. States cooperate for mutual benefit
2. Cultural values shape global politics
3. States prioritize power and survival in an anarchic system
4. International institutions drive state behaviour

80. How does the legislature exercise oversight over the executive in India?

1. By controlling judicial appointments
2. By implementing policies independently
3. By directly appointing the Prime Minister
4. Through mechanisms like Question Hour and No-Confidence Motions

81. Which institution recommends disqualification of MPs and MLAs under the anti-defection law?

1. Election Commission
2. Speaker or Chairman of the House
3. President of India
4. Supreme Court

82. Which Constitutional Amendment Act introduced the three-tier Panchayati Raj system in India?

1. 73rd Amendment
2. 52nd Amendment
3. 93rd Amendment
4. 42nd Amendment

83. Which of the following options about the Council of Ministers is true?

1. The President selects ministers independently
2. Collectively responsible to the Lok Sabha
3. Ministers are appointed by the Chief Justice
4. Ministers answerable only to the Prime Minister

84. The Twelfth Schedule of the Constitution contains how many functional items for Municipalities?

1. 20 2. 16
3. 18 4. 14

85. Which Constitutional Amendment gave constitutional status to Panchayati Raj institutions in India?

1. 73rd Constitutional Amendment
2. 86th Constitutional Amendment
3. 52nd Constitutional Amendment
4. 42nd Constitutional Amendment

86. Which of the following is NOT a key theme of New Public Administration?

1. Political neutrality
2. Social equity
3. Change and innovation
4. Relevance

87. Which Fundamental Right guarantees that no one can be deprived of life or personal liberty except according to the procedure established by law?

1. Right to Education
2. Right to Equality
3. Right to Life and Personal Liberty
4. Right to Property

88. Which Article of the Indian Constitution guarantees the 'Right to Equality before Law'?

1. Article 14 2. Article 21
3. Article 19 4. Article 32

89. Which of the following is NOT a subject listed under the State List in the Indian Constitution?

1. Police 2. Public health
3. Foreign trade 4. Agriculture

90. The Right to Form Associations, under which civil society groups are legitimised, is guaranteed by which Article of the Indian Constitution?

1. Article 19(1)(a) 2. Article 19(1)(b)
3. Article 19(1)(c) 4. Article 19(2)

91. A major criticism of traditional public administration is that it:

1. emphasises democratic responsiveness
2. is rigid and resistant to change
3. encourages innovation
4. focusses on citizen participation

92. The book 'Politics and Administration' is written by:

1. Frank Goodnow
2. Robert Dahl
3. Woodrow Wilson
4. LD White

93. Which of the following is a challenge unique to public administration in many developing countries?

1. Oversupply of infrastructure
2. Excessive citizen participation
3. Capacity constraints in service delivery
4. Redundancy of government agencies

94. Which of the following is the flagship scheme of the Government of India that promotes micro-irrigation under the motto 'Per Drop More Crop'?

1. Paramparagat Krishi Vikas Yojana
2. Pradhan Mantri Krishi Sinchai Yojana
3. Rashtriya Krishi Vikas Yojana
4. Pradhan Mantri Fasal Bima Yojana

95. Traditional public administration is most closely associated with which of the following features?

1. Decentralised decision-making
2. Hierarchical structure
3. Collective wisdom
4. Market-based reforms

96. Rational choice theory in public administration is most closely associated with which of the following concepts?

1. Incrementalism
2. Network governance
3. Economic man (homo economicus)
4. Bounded rationality

97. Which of the following reflects the correct institutional coordination under the SVAMITVA Scheme?

1. Ministry of Panchayati Raj - Survey of India - State Revenue Departments
2. Ministry of Home Affairs - Election Commission - DRDO
3. Ministry of Agriculture - NITI Aayog - NABARD
4. Ministry of Finance - UIDAI - RBI

98. Which of the following scholars is associated with the New Public Administration?

1. Dwight Waldo
2. Fredrick Taylor
3. Woodrow Wilson
4. Max Weber

99. According to Andre Gunder Frank, what is the reason for persistent underdevelopment in Latin American countries?

1. Continued dependency on and exploitation by the developed capitalist economies
2. Harsh climatic conditions
3. Lack of natural resources
4. Inadequate human resources

100. Match List I with List II.

List-I	List-II
(*a*) Public Accounts Committee	(*i*) Oldest financial committee
(*b*) Estimate Committee	(*ii*) Continuous Economic Committee
(*c*) Business Advisory Committee	(*iii*) Allocation of time
(*d*) Joint committee on office of profit	(*iv*) Related to Article 102 of the Indian Constitution

1. (*a*)-(*iv*), (*b*)-(*i*), (*c*)-(*iii*), (*d*)-(*ii*)
2. (*a*)-(*i*), (*b*)-(*ii*), (*c*)-(*iii*), (*d*)-(*iv*)
3. (*a*)-(*ii*), (*b*)-(*i*), (*c*)-(*iv*), (*d*)-(*iii*)
4. (*a*)-(*iv*), (*b*)-(*ii*), (*c*)-(*iii*), (*d*)-(*i*)

101. What is the primary focus of ethical decision-making in public administration?

1. Maximising publicity
2. Reducing budget deficits
3. Ensuring fairness and integrity in administrative decisions
4. Promoting individual business interests

102. The act of whistleblowing can be considered enactment of citizenship because it:

1. engages the state through moral dissent
2. seeks to migrate under economic pressure
3. refuses any form of public accountability
4. operates secretly under criminal cover

103. Under the Citizenship Amendment Act, 2019, which of the following combinations of criteria must be fulfilled by an applicant to be eligible for Indian citizenship?

1. Hindu from Pakistan + entered before 31 December 2014 + exempted under Passport (Entry into India) Act, 1920
2. Muslim from Bangladesh + entered before 31 December 2014 + holds valid visa
3. Christian from Myanmar + entered after 31 December 2014
4. Sikh from Sri Lanka + entered before 31 December 2014 + holds Aadhaar card

104. The CAA-NRC debate in India has been critiqued as an instance where citizenship is being redefined based on:

1. judicial activism and economic class
2. Uniform Civil Code implementation debates
3. a shift from territorial to cultural - religious ontology
4. tax compliance and Aadhaar enrolment

105. Which of the following concepts challenges the idea of borders as rigid and static?

1. State sovereignty
2. Territorial integrity
3. Nationalism
4. Social constructivism

106. The Protection of Human Rights Act, 1993, provides for the establishment of:

1. Lokpal
2. National Commission for Women
3. National Human Rights Commission (NHRC)
4. National Green Tribunal

107. The phrase 'making space' refers to:

1. producing spatial meaning through policy
2. expanding rural land for agricultural use
3. redrawing national boundaries with force
4. constructing homes in border territories

108. Under the Digital Personal Data Protection Act (DPDPA), 2023, which of the following provisions raises concerns about the potential dilution of privacy protections?

1. Complete ban on cross-border data transfers
2. Mandatory biometric verification for all citizens
3. Exemption of State instrumentalities from key obligations in the name of national interest
4. Prohibition of data sharing with judicial bodies without consent

109. In contemporary India, identity-based politics, such as caste and religion, has:

1. continued to shape electoral behaviour and party strategies
2. been banned under the Constitution
3. declined with the rise of technology
4. been entirely replaced by class-based politics

110. Which of the following is NOT a condition for a political party to be recognised as a national party by the Election Commission of India?

1. Securing at least 6% of valid votes in four or more states in a general election to Lok Sabha or Legislative Assembly, and winning four Lok Sabha seats
2. Winning at least 2% of Lok Sabha seats from three different states
3. Being active for more than 25 years
4. Recognition as a state party in at least four states

111. Who was the founder of the Dravida Munnetra Kazhagam (DMK)?

1. K Kamaraj
2. J Jayalalithaa
3. M Karunanidhi
4. C.N. Annadurai

112. Which constitutional provision in India defines citizenship?

1. Article 370
2. Article 5 to 11
3. Article 21
4. Article 324

113. Consider the following statements and choose the correct answer from the options given below:

Statement I: Cosmopolitanism has its philosophical roots in the ideas of Immanual Kant

Statement II: Cosmopolitanism argue that citizenship should be limited to the membership of a particular nation

Statement III: Cosmopolitanism argues that there is a contradiction between assertion of rights and responsibilities at the global and national level.

Statement IV: The process of globalization has intensified the cosmopolitan view of citizenship.

1. Only statement I and statement II are correct
2. Only statement II and statement III are correct
3. Only statement I and statement IV are correct
4. Only statement III and statement IV are correct

114. Which of the following features is NOT of the Indian party system?

1. Multiparty competition
2. Federal structure with state-based parties
3. Coalition governments
4. Pure two-party dominance

115. Which of the following is a key principle of data privacy?

1. Automatic sharing with third parties
2. Consent of the individual
3. Adhering security protocols
4. Unlimited data retention

116. Who said political parties are inevitable in a democracy?

1. Clement H Dodd
2. Harold J Laski
3. George Washington
4. Adam Smith

117. What is a primary characteristic of border cities in political geography?

1. They are always capitals of countries.
2. They serve as points of interaction between different nations and cultures.
3. They are isolated from international trade.
4. They have no political significance.

118. The United Nations designated 27 January as International Holocaust Remembrance Day to commemorate:

1. the end of the Nuremberg Trials
2. the fall of Nazi Germany
3. the liberation of the Auschwitz-Birkenau concentration camp
4. the signing of the Universal Declaration of Human Rights

119. Which of the following rights are typically included under citizenship?

1. Only economic rights
2. Political, social and economic rights
3. None of the given options
4. Only political rights

120. In critical border studies, what does the concept of 'performing the border' primarily signify?

1. Military enforcement of territorial boundaries
2. The drawing of physical maps by surveyors
3. The symbolic and everyday practices that constitute and reproduce borders
4. The use of drones in border patrol

121. A key feature of environmental governance is:

1. monopolisation of riverbanks for farming
2. inclusion of multiple actors and institutions
3. focussing on conservation areas
4. closure of all industrial zones globally

122. Which SDG aims to achieve gender equality?

1. SDG 5
2. SDG 7
3. SDG 1
4. SDG 10

123. Regional parties in India primarily emerge due to:
1. regional identity, language, ethnicity and localised socio-political issues
2. globalisation and foreign influence
3. decline of bureaucracy
4. lack of central leadership

124. Global value chains (GVCs) describe:
1. compilation of global census data by regions
2. structured pricing of international stock exchanges
3. religious hierarchies in cross-border ethics
4. sequential production stages across countries

125. The concept of 'sustainable development' was popularised globally by which major report?
1. The Kyoto Protocol
2. The Stockholm Declaration
3. The Brundtland Report (1987)
4. The Rio Declaration

126. The concept of intersectionality, which helps understand the overlapping effects of caste, religion and gender, was first introduced by:
1. Simone de Beauvoir
2. Kimberle Crenshaw
3. BR Ambedkar
4. Judith Butler

127. Which of the following international agreements is aimed at climate change?
1. The North American Free Trade Agreement (NAFTA)
2. The Kyoto Protocol
3. The European Union's Common Agricultural Policy
4. The United Nations Security Council Resolution

128. Which of the following organisations is an example of a transnational advocacy network?
1. NATO
2. WTO
3. OPEC
4. Greenpeace

129. Who did NOT favour the state to use its power to increase wealth?
1. Mun
2. Jonathan Edwards
3. Hamilton
4. Colbert

130. Which wave of feminism is primarily associated with the struggle for women's suffrage and legal rights?
1. Postmodern feminism
2. Second-wave feminism
3. First-wave feminism
4. Third-wave feminism

131. Which of the following statements is true regarding the governance of the IMF and World Bank?
1. Voting power is based on the principle of one-country-one-vote.
2. All member countries have equal voting power.
3. Decisions are made by the UN Security Council.
4. Voting power is proportional to a country's financial contribution (quota).

132. Which approach focuses on transforming the development process itself to address women's roles?
1. Modernisation Theory
2. WID
3. Gender and Development (GAD)
4. WAD

133. Who talked about four types of political parties which are based on economic ideology, communist ideology, communal ideology and local parties?
1. Subhas Chandra Bose
2. Mahatma Gandhi
3. Jawaharlal Nehru
4. BG Tilak

134. According to Heywood, what role does global civil society play in international relations?
1. Check and hold states and corporations accountable
2. Enforce state sovereignty
3. Regulate trade agreements
4. Promote military alliances

135. The Uruguay Round of trade negotiations led to the formation of:
1. General Agreement on Tariffs and Trade (GATT)
2. World Trade Organisation (WTO)
3. International Monetary Fund (IMF)
4. World Bank

136. Who said that civil society emerged from the development of an independent commercial order?
1. Alfred Marshall
2. Adam Smith
3. Samuel P Huntington
4. TR Malthus

137. The global social movement discussed by Andrew Heywood is:
1. The anti-globalisation movement
2. The rise of national political parties
3. Economic trade liberalisation
4. The spread of global consumer culture

138. In the context of International Political Economy (IPE), what does the concept of global citizenship emphasise?
1. A passive identity without political or legal obligations
2. A shared sense of rights, duties, and participation beyond national boundaries
3. Loyalty limited strictly to one's own country and its interests
4. Limiting cross-border movement and access to labour rights

139. Which of the following is a criterion for a political party to be recognised as a national party in India?
1. Securing at least 6% of valid votes in four or more states in a general election
2. Registering with the Election Commission
3. Winning a majority in state elections
4. Having a presence in only one state

140. The 1992 Earth Summit held in Rio de Janeiro led to the creation of which major environmental governance agreement?
1. UN Convention on the Law of the Sea
2. Agenda 21
3. The Paris Agreement
4. The Montreal Protocol

141. Which authority is associated with leadership by personal qualities?
1. Traditional authority
2. Bureaucratic authority
3. Charismatic authority
4. Legal-rational authority

142. Robert Nozick's theory of justice emphasises:
1. collective ownership of property
2. historical entitlement and minimal state intervention
3. redistribution of wealth
4. equality of outcome

143. According to OP Gauba, which authority is based on established laws and procedures?
1. Coercive authority
2. Traditional authority
3. Legal-rational authority
4. Charismatic authority

144. What principle in Rawls' theory allows for social and economic inequalities?
1. Principle of utility
2. Principle of liberty
3. Egalitarian principle
4. Difference principle

145. Economic freedom of the states were NOT adversely affected by:
1. Presetorika and Glasnost
2. the Bretton Woods system in 1950s
3. the military hegemony of the US in 1950s
4. the Dominant US Economic power in 1950s

146. What is a key criticism of cosmopolitanism in global politics?

1. Undermines the state sovereignty
2. Rejects global governance
3. Ignores human rights
4. Supports exclusive nationalism

147. Who talked about a kind of mono-national state for the success of democracy?

1. John Stuart Mill 2. Earnest Barker
3. Harold J Laski 4. Jeremy Bentham

148. Which of the following best defines the core idea of democracy?

1. Rule by the people through participation, representation and accountability
2. Rule by military consensus
3. Rule by a hereditary elite
4. Rule by the wealthiest

149. Which authority is inherited and maintained through customs and traditions?

1. Charismatic authority
2. Legal-rational authority
3. Traditional authority
4. Coercive authority

150. Who defined freedom as being free from dominating power?

1. Marxists 2. Republicans
3. Hegelians 4. Ultra-rightists

151. Which of the following economists is associated with the development of the capabilities approach?

1. Amartya Sen 2. John Rawls
3. Karl Marx 4. Milton Friedman

152. Who objected to the concept of natural rights?

1. T.H. Green 2. J Locke
3. J.S. Mill 4. J Bentham

153. What differentiates global social movements from traditional political movements?

1. Focus on local issues
2. Avoid any form of protest
3. Sponsored exclusively by governments
4. Address transnational issues

154. Which of the following is a central debate concerning liberty in political theory?

1. Whether freedom should be absolute or limited by laws
2. Whether freedom should exclude individual rights
3. Whether freedom applies only to economic systems
4. Whether freedom is only for political leaders

155. According to Amartya Sen, the problem of poverty should be addressed through:

1. enhancing individual capabilities and freedoms
2. centralised state control of markets
3. increasing GDP alone
4. military interventions in failed states

156. Which country in Asia made progress in closing the gender pay gap as per the 2024 report?

1. Japan 2. Saudi Arabia
3. India 4. Philippines

157. According to natural rights theory, rights are:

1. inalienable and inherent to human beings
2. earned through citizenship only
3. dependent on political ideology
4. granted by the state

158. Negative rights impose what kind of obligation on others?

1. Promote equality
2. Offer financial support
3. Refrain from interference
4. Provide goods and services

159. Which principle ensures that no one is above the law?

1. Popular sovereignty
2. Divine right
3. Political realism
4. Rule of law

160. Which Amendment to the U.S. Constitution granted women the right to vote?

1. 19th Amendment
2. 15th Amendment
3. 11th Amendment
4. 18th Amendment

161. According to Christophe Jaffrelot, Hindu nationalism is rooted in the ideology of:

1. economic populism
2. liberal multiculturalism
3. secular federalism
4. cultural homogenisation and majoritarianism

162. Who is the author of the book 'Indian Philosophy and Philosophy of Science'?

1. Sundar Sarukkai
2. Gopal Guru
3. Basant Kumar Lal
4. Richard Garbe

163. According to Dr. BR Ambedkar, caste is:

1. a system to preserve racial superiority
2. a flexible tool for religious harmony
3. a necessary evil in village traditions
4. a division of labour and of labourers

164. Who is known for challenging Western universalism and emphasising the need for 'contextual' or 'local' epistemologies?

1. JC Bose
2. BK Matilal
3. DP Chattopadhyaya
4. Ashis Nandy

165. Which leader is associated with reforms that led to the collapse of the Soviet Union?

1. Nikita Khrushchev
2. Mikhail Gorbachev
3. Boris Yeltsin
4. Joseph Stalin

166. What is the primary focus of feminist political theory?

1. Gender equality and challenging patriarchal structures
2. Military strategies and defence policies
3. Promotion of state sovereignty
4. Economic development strategies

167. Which concept best describes the use of violence as a tool to achieve political representation for marginalised groups?

1. Politics of recognition through resistance
2. Structural functionalism
3. State monopoly on violence
4. Liberal pacifism

168. Which of the following statements is INCORRECT for Consociationalism?

1. It aims to restructure the entire political system around the principle of corporate decentralisation.
2. Its central premise is that cleavages between communities in plural societies run so deep that constitutional tinkering with majoritarian democracy is not enough.
3. The most celebrated proponent of this idea is Arend Lijphart.
4. It promotes majority rule by a single ethnic group to ensure stable governance

169. One of the key challenges to contemporary democracy, as highlighted by Colin Crouch, is:

1. increasing voter turnout globally
2. the dominance of corporate and technocratic elites in democratic processes
3. a return to feudal systems
4. rising support for communism

170. The age below which consent is not legally valid under Section 375 IPC, even if voluntarily given, is ______.

1. 25 years
2. 21 years
3. 20 years
4. 18 years

171. Which concept best describes India's approach to maintaining good relations with all countries without aligning with any major power bloc during the Cold War?

1. Economic sanctions
2. Collective security
3. Proxy warfare
4. Non-alignment

172. What was a significant shift in India's foreign policy after the Cold War?

1. Joining military alliances
2. Expansion of colonial territories
3. Strengthening economic liberalization and global engagement
4. Isolation from global affairs

173. According to Neerja Gopal, which factor poses a challenge to traditional identity-based politics in India?

1. Technological modernisation
2. Judicial activism
3. International treaties
4. Economic liberalisation and urbanisation

174. The Indian Ocean Policy includes partnerships with which group of countries?

1. Southeast Asian and east African countries
2. South American countries
3. Middle eastern countries
4. Pacific island nations

175. Identity politics in India often revolves around which of the following?

1. Geological resources
2. Sports and entertainment
3. Language and ethnicity
4. Trade policies

176. The Constitution guarantees an arrested person the right to be informed of the grounds for arrest; to not be denied the right to consult and be represented by a counsel of her choice; and to be produced before the nearest magistrate within twenty-four hours of being arrested under which Article of the Indian Constitution?

1. Article 32
2. Article 20
3. Article 22
4. Article 21

177. Which of the following scholars proposed the 'Clash of Civilizations' thesis?

1. Samuel P Huntington
2. Olivier Roy
3. Scott Appleby
4. Charles Taylor

178. India's Look East Policy, later renamed as Act East Policy, primarily aims to strengthen relations with:

1. southeast Asian and east Asian countries
2. the Middle East and north Africa
3. South American nations
4. Russia and central Asia

179. An informal group named 'Committee on State Politics in India', under the auspices of the Association for Asian Studies, was organised by:

1. Paul Wallace
2. G Ram Reddy
3. Myron Weiner
4. Iqbal Narain

180. Peace theory armament is a slogan of:

1. Total disarmament
2. International Brotherhood
3. Deterrence
4. International Law

181. In the context of assessment, what is meant by 'construct validity'?

1. The extent to which an assessment measures what it is designed to measure
2. The consistency of assessment results over time
3. The ability of the assessment to compare student performance
4. The practicality of conducting the assessment

182. What does the term 'gender socialisation' refer to?

1. The process by which individuals learn and internalise gender roles
2. The celebration of gender diversity
3. The process of choosing a career
4. A biological process determining one's sex

183. Which of the following are the four fundamental skills of language learning?

1. Listening, writing, memorising and reading
2. Listening, speaking, reading and writing
3. Speaking, memorising, reading and writing
4. Listening, memorising, reading and speaking

184. The experiential learning theory emphasises the importance of which of the following elements?

1. Fixed intelligence
2. Passive reception
3. Standardised testing
4. Hands-on activities

185. Which of the following comes under micro planning?

1. Summative assessment
2. Year plan
3. Unit plan
4. Lesson plan

186. How does aesthetic education contribute to emotional development?

1. By encouraging students to express and understand emotions through artistic activities
2. By minimising emotional engagement
3. By emphasising cognitive skills only
4. By focusing on physical activities

187. In the context of curriculum construction, what does 'scope' refer to?

1. The difficulty level of the material
2. The number of students in a class
3. The range and depth of content covered
4. The teaching methods employed

188. What is the primary goal of inclusive education?

1. Focus exclusively on students with disabilities
2. Ensure all students, regardless of their abilities, learn together
3. Create separate curricula for different groups
4. Segregate students based on abilities

189. In the context of curriculum development, what is the main focus of the 'transdisciplinary approach'?

1. Focusing solely on one discipline at a time
2. Strict adherence to traditional subject boundaries
3. Integrating knowledge across multiple disciplines to address complex real-world issues
4. Avoiding the integration of different subjects

190. ______ is a certain kind of experience when a conviction of certainty comes upon quite suddenly like a flash.

1. Knowledge through Reason
2. Knowledge through Tenacity
3. Knowledge through Intuition
4. Knowledge through Authority

191. Which of the following best defines 'growth'?

1. The ability to adapt to environmental changes
2. An increase in size, height, weight or mass
3. A continuous process of change and progression throughout the lifespan
4. The acquisition of skills and abilities

192. Which of the following does not promote positive and healthy cognitive development in adolescents?

1. Helping them review their wrong decisions
2. Helping them set their goals
3. Helping them get enough sleep
4. Helping them fanaticism

193. Which of the following refers to a systematic procedure for collecting information that can be used to make inferences about the characteristics of people or objectives?

1. Assessment 2. Examination
3. Evaluation 4. Measurement

194. What does the term 'gender socialisation' refer to?

1. The process by which individuals learn and internalise gender roles
2. A biological process determining one's sex
3. The process of choosing a career
4. The celebration of gender diversity

195. In inclusive education, what is the least important trait for a teacher to have?

1. Being sensitive to children
2. Teacher's social and economic status
3. Knowledge of students with disabilities
4. Patience and love for students

196. Which of the following is the most suitable definition of Knowledge?

1. Training on one's own thought
2. Data used in a context and with some relevance
3. A self control of behaviour
4. A set of understanding in a particular domain or a field

197. A student following the deep approach of learning has the following characteristics, EXCEPT:

1. they see the different aspects or parts of the task as unrelated to other tasks
2. they are interested in the academic task and derive enjoyment from carrying it out
3. they search for the meaning inherent in the task
4. they integrate aspects or parts of the task into a whole

198. According to the preparation process, how can stray lesson plan and unit plan be differentiated?

1. A stray lesson plan is always longer than a unit plan.
2. A unit plan does not include assessments, while a stray lesson plan does.
3. A stray lesson plan focuses on a single lesson, while a unit plan covers a series of lessons around a common theme.
4. A stray lesson plan is less detailed than a unit plan.

199. Which perspective of learning emphasises the role of stimuli and responses?

1. Humanistic
2. Constructivist
3. Behaviouristic
4. Cognitive

200. Which of the following domains has Response Chain and Movement Co-ordination as its characteristics?

1. Evaluation 2. Cognitive
3. Affective 4. Psychomotor

ANSWERS

1	2	3	4	5	6	7	8	9	10
1	2	4	3	2	4	2	4	3	4
11	**12**	**13**	**14**	**15**	**16**	**17**	**18**	**19**	**20**
1	4	4	2	3	2	3	3	4	4
21	**22**	**23**	**24**	**25**	**26**	**27**	**28**	**29**	**30**
3	3	1	3	2	2	2	3	1	1

31	**32**	**33**	**34**	**35**	**36**	**37**	**38**	**39**	**40**
4	2	4	1	4	3	2	2	1	3
41	**42**	**43**	**44**	**45**	**46**	**47**	**48**	**49**	**50**
2	1	2	2	2	4	1	4	3	2
51	**52**	**53**	**54**	**55**	**56**	**57**	**58**	**59**	**60**
3	2	2	3	3	2	1	1	3	4
61	**62**	**63**	**64**	**65**	**66**	**67**	**68**	**69**	**70**
3	4	1	2	1	3	3	2	3	1
71	**72**	**73**	**74**	**75**	**76**	**77**	**78**	**79**	**80**
4	1	3	2	1	1	2	1	3	4
81	**82**	**83**	**84**	**85**	**86**	**87**	**88**	**89**	**90**
2	1	2	3	1	1	3	1	3	3
91	**92**	**93**	**94**	**95**	**96**	**97**	**98**	**99**	**100**
2	1	3	2	2	3	1	1	1	2
101	**102**	**103**	**104**	**105**	**106**	**107**	**108**	**109**	**110**
3	1	1	3	4	3	1	3	1	3
111	**112**	**113**	**114**	**115**	**116**	**117**	**118**	**119**	**120**
4	2	3	4	2	2	2	3	2	3
121	**122**	**123**	**124**	**125**	**126**	**127**	**128**	**129**	**130**
2	1	1	4	3	2	2	4	2	3
131	**132**	**133**	**134**	**135**	**136**	**137**	**138**	**139**	**140**
4	3	3	1	2	2	1	2	1	2
141	**142**	**143**	**144**	**145**	**146**	**147**	**148**	**149**	**150**
3	2	3	4	1	1	1	1	3	2
151	**152**	**153**	**154**	**155**	**156**	**157**	**158**	**159**	**160**
1	4	4	1	1	4	1	3	4	1
161	**162**	**163**	**164**	**165**	**166**	**167**	**168**	**169**	**170**
4	1	4	4	2	1	1	4	2	4
171	**172**	**173**	**174**	**175**	**176**	**177**	**178**	**179**	**180**
4	3	4	1	3	3	1	1	3	3
181	**182**	**183**	**184**	**185**	**186**	**187**	**188**	**189**	**190**
1	1	2	4	4	1	3	2	3	3
191	**192**	**193**	**194**	**195**	**196**	**197**	**198**	**199**	**200**
2	4	1	1	2	4	1	3	3	4

EXPLANATORY ANSWERS

1. In a presidential system, there is a strict separation of powers between the legislature and the executive. This means that the legislature cannot directly remove the executive except through extraordinary processes such as impeachment. By contrast, in a parliamentary system, the executive (Prime Minister and Cabinet) is drawn from and dependent upon the legislature, which can dissolve the executive through a vote of no confidence.

2. Traditional political theory is primarily normative—it deals with ideas about how politics and governance ought to be organized and justified. Rather than focusing purely on data or behaviour, it evaluates values such as justice, liberty, and authority. Modern political science shifted toward empirical and behavioural approaches, but traditional theory remains normative.

3. In India, the bureaucracy has been the central institution through which the state regulates, administers, and controls its environment. The bureaucracy facilitates governance by implementing laws, overseeing administration, and ensuring continuity of state functions.

4. A judiciary lacking independence tends to issue decisions that favour the ruling government, since it is subject to political influence rather than impartiality. Independent judiciaries are characterized by checks on government, protection of rights, and fair trials.

5. The Weberian bureaucratic model emphasizes rational-legal authority, impersonal rules, and hierarchical organisation. This directly supports the executive's role in implementing laws in a structured, rule-based manner, minimizing personal discretion and ensuring predictability.

6. The statement "Man is born free, but everywhere he is in chains" was made by Jean-Jacques Rousseau in his seminal work The Social Contract (1762). He highlighted the tension between natural freedom and the constraints imposed by social and political institutions, advocating for legitimate authority based on the general will.

7. Among the listed institutions, the judiciary is the one that acts as the most important check on executive excesses. Through judicial review, courts ensure that the executive functions within constitutional and legal boundaries, protecting citizens from misuse of power.

8. The distinction lies in the role of reason. Political theory seeks to provide the fullest rational explanation for a standpoint, engaging deeply with arguments and principles. Ideology, on the other hand, tends to simplify and reduce reasoning into fixed formulae, often serving mobilization rather than critical inquiry.

9. Comparative Political Analysis studies similarities and differences between political systems across countries or regions. Its aim is to understand patterns, causes, and consequences of political behaviour and institutions in a comparative framework.

10. The scope of political theory is broad and includes the study of fundamental political concepts such as liberty, justice, equality, rights, democracy, and authority. It is not confined to machinery or policies but addresses deeper normative and conceptual issues of political life.

11. The behavioral revolution in political science (1940s–1960s) was marked by the application of empirical and quantitative methods. It emphasized observable behavior of political actors, statistical analysis, and scientific rigor over normative or purely philosophical inquiry.

12. The philosophical approach is rooted in reason, moral evaluation, and clarification of political concepts, ends, and means. The statement that is NOT true is that the philosophical approach "does not seek to clarify thought about the nature of the subject". In reality, clarifying thought is one of its core objectives.

13. Post-behavioralism (1960s–70s) emerged as a critique of behavioralism's overemphasis on empirical and quantitative methods while neglecting normative concerns and real-world relevance. It called for a balance between scientific rigor and social responsibility.

14. A central feature of constitutionalism is the idea of limited government under law. It ensures that the powers of the state are restrained by a constitution, protecting rights and preventing arbitrary rule.

15. Modern political theory emphasizes value neutrality, drawing from scientific methods and empirical inquiry, while striving to separate facts from values. This distinguishes it from traditional normative theory.

16. Interest articulation refers to the process by which individuals and groups express their needs, demands, and interests in the political system. Among the given options, political parties are primarily responsible for interest articulation, as they aggregate and represent the demands of society in the political arena.

17. The political system theory in modern political science, which views politics as a system of inputs (demands and supports), processes, and outputs, is associated with David Easton. He emphasized systems analysis in understanding political dynamics.

18. In a democracy, the legislature is the institution primarily responsible for the rule-making function, i.e., making laws that govern society. While the executive enforces, and judiciary interprets, the legislature makes the rules.

19. Modern political theory primarily focuses on empirical analysis of political behaviour and institutions, drawing on scientific methods and data-driven approaches rather than purely normative or speculative questions.

20. Post-modern political theory distinguishes itself by rejecting universal truths and grand narratives, emphasizing deconstruction, identity politics, and plural perspectives. It critiques the essentialism of traditional theory.

21. The importance of informal organisation within formal structures was highlighted by Elton Mayo through the famous Hawthorne Studies (1920s–1930s). His research demonstrated that worker productivity is influenced not only by formal rules and economic incentives but also by social relations, group dynamics, and informal networks within the workplace. This marked the birth of the Human Relations School in organizational theory.

22. Feminists criticized Weberian bureaucracy for its rigidity, impersonality, and claim of gender neutrality (which often masked male dominance). The one that is NOT a characteristic criticized is flexibility, since Weberian bureaucracy is not known for flexibility.

23. The concept of bounded rationality in administrative decision-making was introduced by Herbert Simon. He argued that human decision-makers operate under limits of information, time, and cognitive capacity, preventing "perfect rationality."

24. The Constitutional provision that allows States to make special provisions for the advancement of socially and educationally backward classes is Article 15(4). It was added through the First Amendment (1951).

25. Public Administration is most accurately defined as the discipline and practice concerned with implementing government policies and managing public programmes. It involves both the study of administrative processes and the actual functioning of public institutions.

26. The major constitutional issue that arose from land reform laws like the abolition of zamindari was the conflict between Fundamental Rights and Directive Principles. Land reforms were aimed at implementing social justice (Directive Principles), but they clashed with the right to property under Fundamental Rights, leading to several constitutional amendments and judicial battles.

27. The father of Scientific Management is Frederick Taylor. He emphasized time-and-motion studies, task specialization, and efficiency, laying the foundation for modern management practices.

28. Under the Indian Constitution, the State's role in protecting individual freedom is to ensure freedom through constitutional limits and guarantees. This means safeguarding rights through Fundamental Rights, judicial review, and checks on government authority, rather than allowing unchecked or absolute freedom.

29. The book "Gender Images in Public Administration" (1993) was written by Camilla Stivers. She highlighted how gender perspectives shape administrative theory and practice, critiquing the male-centric assumptions of public administration.

30. Feminist theory in Public Administration seeks to empower women, promote gender equality, and critique male dominance in administrative systems. It does NOT seek to focus on the idea of exclusive presence in the public sphere, since inclusivity and equality are its goals rather than exclusivity.

31. The article "The Study of Public Administration" (1887) was written by Woodrow Wilson, often regarded as the father of Public Administration as a distinct discipline. His essay emphasized the separation of politics and administration.

32. Political scientist Yogendra Yadav introduced the concept of the Third Electoral System (post-1989) to explain shifts in Indian politics. It is associated with democratic upsurge, political fragmentation, and a post-Congress polity. However, it is NOT associated with strengthening of elite control, since the phase reflected increasing participation of backward classes and marginalized groups.

33. In India, the authority to recognise political parties lies with the Election Commission of India. It registers parties, accords them recognition as national or state parties, and allots election symbols.

34. A recent trend in social movements is the use of digital activism, such as hashtag campaigns and online petitions, which leverage social media to mobilize support quickly and globally.

35. To address regional imbalances and reorganize states based on linguistic and administrative considerations, the States Reorganisation Commission (1953–55) was established. Its recommendations led to the States Reorganisation Act of 1956.

36. Recent social movements in India differ from traditional movements by placing a greater emphasis on intersectional identities (such as caste, gender, class, environment) and decentralized leadership, instead of centralized party-led mobilization. This reflects a shift toward inclusivity and grassroots activism.

37. In Panchayati Raj Institutions, the 73rd Constitutional Amendment Act (1992) mandated that 33% (one-third) of the seats be reserved for women. Later, some states voluntarily extended this to 50%, but constitutionally it remains 33%.

38. The concept that emphasizes organizations must maintain cooperation among members is Chester Barnard's Theory of Cooperation. He highlighted that the effectiveness of organizations depends on the willingness of individuals to cooperate.

39. Political parties perform multiple functions such as political recruitment, political socialisation, and coordination. However, rule adjudication is the function of the judiciary, not political parties.

40. The concept of 'span of control'—the number of subordinates a manager can effectively supervise—was introduced by Luther Gulick, a key contributor to classical management and administrative theory.

41. Among Indian thinkers, Mahatma Gandhi emphasized community and decentralised governance through his idea of Gram Swaraj (village self-rule). He envisioned self-sufficient village communities as the foundation of democracy.

42. The concept of Strategic Autonomy in Indian foreign policy refers to maintaining freedom in making foreign policy decisions, without being tied down to any single power bloc, while retaining flexibility to cooperate internationally.

43. Democratic knowledge practices in India are increasingly associated with Critical Pedagogy, which emphasizes dialogue, questioning authority, participatory learning, and empowering marginalized voices, rather than rote memorization or rigid testing.

44. Federalism in India is characterized by a written constitution, supremacy of the constitution, and vertical separation of powers between Union and States. However, supremacy of the Governor in the State is NOT a feature of Indian federalism; governors are constitutional heads, not supreme authorities.

45. Feminist interventions in Indian political theory emphasize the need to study the state through gendered lenses and challenge male-dominated knowledge systems, making women's experiences central to political analysis.

46. The cultural and educational rights of minorities in India are protected under Articles 29 and 30 of the Constitution. These ensure minorities can conserve their culture and establish/manage their own educational institutions.

47. India's engagement with ASEAN is part of the Look East Policy, which was later upgraded to the Act East Policy to strengthen economic, strategic, and cultural ties with East and Southeast Asia.

48. In 1944, India became a founding member of the International Monetary Fund (IMF) (and also the World Bank). This was before independence but with representation as British India.

49. The Indo-US Civil Nuclear Agreement (2008) symbolized India's growing ties with the United States in the post-Cold War era. It marked India's entry into global nuclear commerce despite not being an NPT signatory.

50. According to Mahatma Gandhi, the ideal Indian state would be based on self-sufficient villages (Gram Swaraj), where decentralized governance and community cooperation would guide political and economic life.

51. The idea of 'Chiti' was developed by Pandit Deen Dayal Upadhyaya in his philosophy of Integral Humanism. It refers to the inner consciousness of an individual, the collective national spirit, and a connection to cosmic order—guiding social and political life in harmony with cultural identity.

52. The I2U2 initiative is a strategic grouping of India, Israel, UAE, and the United States. Formed in 2021, it focuses on cooperation in food security, clean energy, technology, and infrastructure, symbolizing India's growing role in West Asia and the Indo-Pacific.

53. For Mahatma Gandhi, knowledge was not confined to books but rooted in experiential truth. Through his concept of Nai Talim (Basic Education), he emphasized learning by doing, moral development, and truth as the foundation of knowledge.

54. In the Indian political system, the executive is tasked with implementing and enforcing laws and policies made by the legislature. It consists of the President, Prime Minister, and Council of Ministers at the Union level, ensuring day-to-day governance.

55. The Gujral Doctrine, propounded by Prime Minister I.K. Gujral in the 1990s, stressed unilateral goodwill towards India's neighbors. It promoted cooperation without expecting reciprocity, aiming to build trust and regional stability in South Asia.

56. India's foreign policy took a major shift in 1991 after the economic crisis, with liberalization and globalization reforms. This period marked a focus on economic diplomacy, global trade, and integration into the world economy, moving beyond Cold War-era isolation.

57. India's principal external intelligence agency is the Research and Analysis Wing (RAW). Established in 1968, RAW handles foreign intelligence, counter-terrorism, and monitoring strategic threats abroad, complementing IB (domestic intelligence).

58. Nationalism in Indian political thought during the independence movement was primarily a struggle for self-governance and unity across cultural, linguistic, and religious diversity. Leaders like Gandhi, Nehru, and Tagore envisioned a collective identity that embraced pluralism while rejecting colonial domination.

59. A direct outcome of pluralism in a democracy is the promotion of tolerance and dialogue. It ensures that multiple voices, identities, and opinions are accommodated, strengthening democratic consensus-building instead of imposing uniformity.

60. Rabindranath Tagore did not accept nationalism as the highest sentiment. Observing Europe's wars and aggressive nationalism, he criticized narrow nationalism and emphasized universal humanism and internationalism as superior ideals.

61. Under the Sixth Schedule of the Indian Constitution, there are ten Autonomous District Councils (ADCs) across the four northeastern states—Assam, Meghalaya, Mizoram, and Tripura. These councils provide self-governance to tribal communities.

62. The Democratic Peace Theory in international relations argues that democracies rarely, if ever, go to war with one another. It suggests that democratic norms, institutions, and interdependence promote peaceful conflict resolution.

63. According to Plato's political philosophy in The Republic, the ideal state should be governed by Philosopher-Kings. They possess wisdom, knowledge, and rationality, making them best suited to rule justly.

64. The Delimitation Commission of India, an independent body, is responsible for redrawing the boundaries of constituencies for parliamentary and state assembly elections to ensure fair representation.

65. The Group of 77 (G77) was established in 1964 within the United Nations framework to represent the collective economic interests of developing countries (Global South) and enhance their bargaining power in international negotiations.

66. Alternative approaches in International Relations (like feminism, post-colonialism, and constructivism) differ from mainstream theories by incorporating marginal voices, norms, identity, and culture into global analysis, rather than focusing only on power and security.

67. Political culture refers to the attitudes, beliefs, and values of people toward the political system, including trust in institutions, participation, and legitimacy of authority. It shapes political behaviour in a society.

68. The Lokpal (national) and Lokayuktas (state) are anti-corruption bodies designed to promote accountability in public services by investigating complaints of corruption against government officials and public servants.

69. In India, a Money Bill can only be introduced in the Lok Sabha, and that too with the prior recommendation of the President. The Rajya Sabha can only give recommendations but cannot reject it.

70. Neoclassical realism is the variant of realism that most closely engages with foreign policy analysis at the individual or state level, combining systemic pressures with domestic factors like leadership, state structure, and perceptions.

71. Article 131 of the Constitution grants the Supreme Court original and exclusive jurisdiction over disputes between the Union and States or between States. This means such disputes bypass lower courts and directly go to the Supreme Court.

72. Realists argue that organisations like the UN fail to prevent wars because they lack enforcement capability. States act in pursuit of their own survival and interests, often ignoring UN authority when power politics dominate.

73. Constructivism is an alternative IR approach that emphasizes the role of identity, norms, and shared ideas in shaping state behaviour. Unlike realism and neoliberalism, it argues that interests are socially constructed, not fixed.

74. Inter-state water disputes are addressed under Article 262 of the Constitution. It allows Parliament to establish tribunals for river disputes and can even exclude the jurisdiction of courts in such matters.

75. Hans J. Morgenthau was a leading scholar of classical realism, focusing on human nature and the pursuit of power. Neo-realism, or structural realism, was developed later by Kenneth Waltz and extended by thinkers like John Mearsheimer and Stephen Walt.

76. The President of India has the authority under Article 318 of the Constitution to make rules regarding the conditions of service and the number of members of the Union Public Service Commission (UPSC). This ensures flexibility in determining the composition and functioning of UPSC as required. The Prime Minister or any other body cannot independently fix the number of members.

77. According to Aristotle, monarchy is a good form of government when the ruler governs in the interest of all. However, its corrupt form is tyranny, where one person rules in their own selfish interest, often oppressing people. Tyranny was considered the worst deviation of monarchy as it destroyed justice and common good.

78. The Green Theory of International Relations focuses on ecological justice and environmental sustainability. It argues that global politics cannot be understood only in terms of power or economy but must also consider ecological survival. It critiques traditional theories like realism and liberalism for ignoring environmental issues such as climate change.

79. All variants of realism in International Relations agree on the assumption that the international system is anarchic, meaning no central authority exists above states. Therefore, states must prioritize power and survival above all else. Even cooperation is temporary and conditional on serving national interests.

80. In India, the legislature oversees the executive through multiple parliamentary mechanisms such as Question Hour, Zero Hour, budget debates, and No-Confidence Motions. These instruments ensure that the executive remains answerable to the legislature. If the executive loses majority support, it is forced to resign.

81. The anti-defection law under the Tenth Schedule empowers the Speaker of the Lok Sabha/State Assembly or the Chairman of the Rajya Sabha/Legislative Council to decide on disqualification of members. This ensures party discipline but has been debated for concentrating power in the presiding officer. The decision, however, is subject to judicial review.

82. The 73rd Constitutional Amendment Act, 1992 gave constitutional recognition to the three-tier Panchayati Raj system: Gram Panchayat, Panchayat Samiti, and Zila Parishad. It made regular elections, reservations for women and weaker sections, and devolution of powers mandatory. It came into effect in April 1993.

83. The Council of Ministers, headed by the Prime Minister, is collectively responsible to the Lok Sabha. This means they must enjoy the confidence of the majority of the Lok Sabha members. If the Lok Sabha passes a No-Confidence Motion, the entire Council of Ministers must resign, ensuring executive accountability.

84. The Twelfth Schedule was added to the Constitution by the 74th Constitutional Amendment Act, 1992. It contains 18 functional items for Municipalities, including urban planning, public health, sanitation, solid waste management, and slum improvement. These empower urban local bodies for effective self-governance.

85. The 73rd Constitutional Amendment Act, 1992 gave constitutional status to Panchayati Raj Institutions. It inserted Part IX in the Constitution, covering Gram Sabha, structure of Panchayats, elections, reservation, powers, and responsibilities. This amendment strengthened grassroots democracy in rural India.

86. New Public Administration (NPA) emerged in the late 1960s as a response to traditional bureaucracy. It emphasized relevance, social equity, values, and change/innovation in public administration. What it rejected was political neutrality, since NPA argued administrators must actively pursue justice and equity.

87. The Right to Life and Personal Liberty under Article 21 guarantees that no person can be deprived of life or personal liberty except according to the procedure established by law. The Supreme Court has interpreted it broadly to include rights such as dignity, livelihood, privacy, and clean environment.

88. Article 14 of the Indian Constitution guarantees the Right to Equality before Law and equal protection of the laws. It ensures that no individual is above the law and that the state cannot deny equality to any person within India's territory.

89. The State List under the Constitution contains subjects on which state legislatures can make laws, such as police, public health, and agriculture. However, foreign trade falls under the Union List, making it not part of the State List.

90. The Right to Form Associations and Unions, which legitimizes civil society groups, is guaranteed under Article 19(1)(c) of the Constitution. This right enables citizens to collectively pursue social, political, and cultural interests, subject to reasonable restrictions.

91. A major criticism of traditional public administration is that it is rigid, hierarchical, and resistant to change. It overemphasizes rules and procedures, often at the cost of efficiency, innovation, and responsiveness to citizens' needs. This led to calls for reforms like New Public Administration and New Public Management.

92. The book "Politics and Administration" was written by Frank Goodnow in 1900. He distinguished between politics (policy-making) and administration (policy implementation), laying the foundation for the study of public administration as a separate discipline.

93. In many developing countries, a unique challenge in public administration is capacity constraints in service delivery. Limited resources, weak infrastructure, and shortage of skilled personnel often hinder effective governance and implementation of policies.

94. The flagship scheme of the Government of India that promotes micro-irrigation under the motto 'Per Drop More Crop' is the Pradhan Mantri Krishi Sinchai Yojana (PMKSY). It focuses on water-use efficiency, sustainable irrigation, and enhancing agricultural productivity.

95. Traditional public administration is most closely associated with a hierarchical structure. Based on Max Weber's bureaucracy, it stresses top-down authority, clear rules, and chain of command to maintain discipline and efficiency.

96. Rational choice theory in public administration is based on the concept of the economic man (homo economicus), who makes decisions to maximize self-interest and utility. It applies economic principles to explain administrative behaviour, assuming individuals act rationally to achieve their goals.

97. The SVAMITVA Scheme (Survey of Villages and Mapping with Improvised Technology in Village Areas) ensures property cards for rural households. It involves coordination between the Ministry of Panchayati Raj, the Survey of India, and the State Revenue Departments, ensuring accurate mapping and land record modernization.

98. Dwight Waldo is one of the leading scholars associated with New Public Administration (NPA). He emphasized relevance, social equity, values, and responsiveness, shifting focus from rigid bureaucracy to a more human-centered and justice-oriented administration.

99. According to Andre Gunder Frank and the dependency theory, underdevelopment in Latin American countries is due to their continued dependency on and exploitation by developed capitalist economies. He argued that integration into the global capitalist system perpetuates inequality and dependency.

100. (*a*) Public Accounts Committee → (*i*) Oldest financial committee

The PAC is the oldest and most important financial committee of Parliament. It scrutinises government expenditure and CAG reports to ensure accountability.

(*b*) Estimates Committee → (*ii*) Continuous Economic Committee

The Estimates Committee examines the budget estimates and suggests reforms for efficiency. It is continuous in nature and focuses on economic planning.

(*c*) Business Advisory Committee → (*iii*) Allocation of time

This committee schedules and allocates time for discussions, debates, and legislative business in the House.

(*d*) Joint Committee on Office of Profit → (*iv*) Related to Article 102 of the Indian Constitution

This committee deals with the disqualification of MPs for holding an office of profit, as mentioned in Article 102.

Correct matching: (*a*)-(*i*), (*b*)-(*ii*), (*c*)-(*iii*), (*d*)-(*iv*)

101. In public administration, the primary focus of ethical decision-making is to ensure fairness, integrity, and accountability in administrative actions. It involves applying moral values, upholding transparency, and protecting citizens' rights while delivering public services. Ethics ensures that administrators act in the public interest, not personal gain.

102. Whistleblowing refers to exposing corruption, malpractice, or abuse of authority within an organization. It is considered an enactment of citizenship because it engages the state through moral dissent, holding institutions accountable to democratic values. It strengthens public trust by demanding ethical governance.

103. Under the Citizenship Amendment Act, 2019, Indian citizenship can be granted to Hindus, Sikhs, Buddhists, Jains, Parsis, and Christians from Pakistan, Afghanistan, and Bangladesh who entered India on or before 31 December 2014 and were exempted under the Passport (Entry into India) Act, 1920.

104. The CAA–NRC debate has been critiqued for redefining citizenship on cultural and religious lines rather than purely territorial residence. Critics argue this marks a shift from the principle of territorial ontology of citizenship to a cultural–religious ontology, impacting India's secular framework.

105. The concept of Social Constructivism in International Relations challenges the idea of borders as rigid and static. It views borders as socially constructed and subject to change based on identities, norms, and historical contexts, rather than permanent, natural divisions.

106. The Protection of Human Rights Act, 1993 led to the establishment of the National Human Rights Commission (NHRC). It is an independent body tasked with protecting and promoting human rights, investigating violations, and advising the government on policy reforms. State Human Rights Commissions were also provided for under the Act.

107. The phrase 'making space' refers to the idea of producing spatial meaning through policy and governance. It highlights how governments, institutions, and social groups construct spaces by defining their purpose, regulation, and cultural meaning, rather than just physical boundaries.

108. The Digital Personal Data Protection Act (DPDPA), 2023 raises concerns about dilution of privacy protections because it exempts State instrumentalities from many obligations in the name of national interest. Critics argue this creates wide discretionary powers for the government, potentially undermining citizens' privacy rights.

109. In contemporary India, identity-based politics continues to be central in shaping electoral behaviour and party strategies. Caste, religion, and community identities still influence voter alignments, candidate selection, and coalition-building, despite modernization and technology-driven campaigns.

110. To be recognised as a national party, conditions include securing 6% valid votes in four or more states and 4 Lok Sabha seats, or winning 2% Lok Sabha seats from 3 states, or recognition as a state party in 4 states. However, being active for more than 25 years is not a condition.

111. The Dravida Munnetra Kazhagam (DMK) was founded by C.N. Annadurai in 1949 after splitting from the Dravidar Kazhagam led by Periyar E.V. Ramasamy. Annadurai shaped DMK as a political force advocating Tamil pride, social justice, and opposition to Hindi imposition. The party went on to dominate Tamil Nadu politics.

112. The constitutional provisions regarding citizenship in India are laid down in Articles 5 to 11 under Part II of the Constitution. These articles define citizenship at the commencement of the Constitution and empower Parliament to make laws regarding acquisition and termination of citizenship.

113. Cosmopolitanism has its philosophical roots in Immanuel Kant's ideas of universal moral community. It does not restrict citizenship to nations but advocates global citizenship. It also argues that globalization has intensified cosmopolitan views of rights and responsibilities beyond the nation-state. Hence, Statements I and IV are correct.

114. The Indian party system is known for multiparty competition, federalism with state-based parties, and the prevalence of coalition governments since the late 20th century. What India does not have is pure two-party dominance, which is typical of systems like the US.

115. A key principle of data privacy is that data should be collected, processed, and shared only with the consent of the individual. This ensures autonomy and protection against misuse of personal data. Automatic sharing or unlimited retention would violate this principle.

116. Harold J. Laski, a noted political theorist, argued that political parties are inevitable in a democracy. He emphasized that democracy requires organized representation of diverse interests, and political parties are the instruments that aggregate opinions and provide channels for political participation.

117. In political geography, border cities are significant because they act as points of interaction between nations and cultures. They often serve as hubs of trade, migration, and cultural exchange, reflecting both cooperation and tension between neighboring states.

118. The United Nations designated 27 January as International Holocaust Remembrance Day to commemorate the liberation of the Auschwitz-Birkenau concentration camp in 1945. It honors the victims of the Holocaust and reaffirms the global commitment against anti-Semitism and genocide.

119. Citizenship typically includes a bundle of political, social, and economic rights. These rights ensure active political participation, access to welfare and justice, and the ability to pursue livelihoods, all forming the basis of equal citizenship in a democracy.

120. In critical border studies, the concept of 'performing the border' refers to the symbolic and everyday practices—such as identity checks, cultural rituals, or economic exchanges—that create and reproduce the meaning of borders beyond just physical lines.

121. A key feature of environmental governance is the inclusion of multiple actors and institutions—governments, international bodies, NGOs, corporations, and local communities. It recognizes that addressing environmental challenges like climate change and biodiversity loss requires collaborative, multi-level decision-making.

122. Sustainable Development Goal (SDG) 5 specifically aims to achieve gender equality and empower all women and girls. It includes targets such as ending discrimination, eliminating violence, ensuring equal participation, and providing access to education and healthcare.

123. Regional parties in India primarily emerge from regional identity, language, ethnicity, and localized socio-political issues. They represent specific state or community interests and often influence coalition politics at the national level, reflecting India's diversity.

124. Global Value Chains (GVCs) describe how goods and services are produced in sequential stages across multiple countries. For example, design may occur in one country, components in another, and assembly in a third. GVCs highlight interconnected global production systems.

125. The concept of sustainable development was globally popularised by the Brundtland Report (1987), officially titled Our Common Future. It defined sustainable development as meeting present needs without compromising the ability of future generations to meet theirs, shaping global environmental policy.

126. The concept of intersectionality was introduced by Kimberlé Crenshaw in 1989. It highlights how overlapping identities such as caste, gender, class, and religion interact to create unique forms of discrimination and disadvantage, especially for marginalized groups.

127. The Kyoto Protocol (1997) is an international agreement under the United Nations Framework Convention on Climate Change (UNFCCC). It was the first treaty to set legally binding targets for reducing greenhouse gas emissions among developed countries.

128. Transnational advocacy networks are coalitions of activists and organizations working across borders to influence policy and promote rights. Greenpeace, an environmental NGO, is a key example, advocating for climate action and sustainable practices worldwide.

129. Unlike mercantilists such as Thomas Mun, Alexander Hamilton, and Jean-Baptiste Colbert, who favored state intervention to increase wealth, Jonathan Edwards, a theologian, did not focus on economic nationalism or state-led economic expansion.

130. First-wave feminism (19th–early 20th century) was primarily concerned with women's suffrage and legal rights. Activists fought for voting rights, property rights, and equal legal status, laying the foundation for later feminist movements.

131. In the governance of the IMF and World Bank, voting power is proportional to a country's financial contribution (quota). Wealthier countries with higher contributions, like the US, hold greater influence, while smaller economies have limited say in decision-making. This often draws criticism regarding fairness.

132. The Gender and Development (GAD) approach focuses on transforming the development process itself by addressing women's roles and questioning existing gender relations. Unlike WID (Women in Development), which integrates women into existing frameworks, GAD aims at restructuring power relations.

133. Jawaharlal Nehru classified political parties into four types: economic ideology-based parties, communist ideology-based parties, communal ideology-based parties, and local parties. His classification reflected the diversity of political forces shaping Indian democracy.

134. According to Andrew Heywood, global civil society acts as a check on states and corporations by promoting accountability, human rights, and environmental protection. It includes NGOs, advocacy groups, and grassroots movements working across borders.

135. The Uruguay Round of trade negotiations (1986–1994) concluded with the formation of the World Trade Organisation (WTO) in 1995. The WTO replaced GATT and expanded rules to cover services, intellectual property, and stronger dispute settlement mechanisms.

136. Adam Smith argued that civil society emerged from the development of an independent commercial order. He believed that commerce and markets fostered voluntary associations, contracts, and cooperation outside the direct control of the state, laying the foundation for civil society.

137. According to Andrew Heywood, the most prominent global social movement is the anti-globalisation movement. It critiques the negative effects of economic globalisation, such as inequality, environmental degradation, and cultural homogenisation, while advocating for fair trade and sustainable alternatives.

138. In International Political Economy (IPE), the concept of global citizenship emphasizes a shared sense of rights, duties, and participation beyond national boundaries. It envisions individuals as members of a global community, responsible for justice, sustainability, and cooperation across nations.

139. To be recognised as a national party in India, one criterion is securing at least 6% of valid votes in four or more states in a general election

(to Lok Sabha or Legislative Assemblies) and winning at least four Lok Sabha seats. This ensures national representation.

140. The 1992 Earth Summit held in Rio de Janeiro produced Agenda 21, a comprehensive action plan for sustainable development. It outlined strategies for governments, international organisations, and communities to combat environmental problems and promote sustainability into the 21st century.

141. Charismatic authority, as explained by Max Weber, is based on the personal qualities and extraordinary leadership of an individual. Leaders are followed because of their charisma, vision, or heroic character, rather than laws or traditions. Examples include Mahatma Gandhi and Martin Luther King Jr.

142. Robert Nozick's theory of justice, outlined in Anarchy, State, and Utopia, emphasises historical entitlement and minimal state intervention. He argued that as long as property is justly acquired and transferred, redistribution is unjust, supporting a libertarian framework.

143. According to O.P. Gauba, legal-rational authority is based on established laws, rules, and procedures. It is impersonal and institutional in nature, ensuring legitimacy comes from adherence to legal systems rather than tradition or personal charisma.

144. In John Rawls' theory of justice, the difference principle allows for social and economic inequalities only if they benefit the least advantaged members of society. This ensures fairness while accepting that inequalities can exist under justifiable conditions.

145. The economic freedom of states in the 1950s was undermined by the Bretton Woods system, US military hegemony, and dominant US economic power. However, Perestroika and Glasnost, introduced by Gorbachev in the USSR during the 1980s, were unrelated to this period.

146. A key criticism of cosmopolitanism in global politics is that it undermines state sovereignty. By emphasizing global citizenship and universal moral obligations, it weakens the authority of nation-states to control their own affairs and prioritize their citizens' interests.

147. John Stuart Mill argued that the success of democracy is easier in a mono-national state, where people share common identity, culture, and language. He believed diversity might complicate democratic consensus, though later thinkers highlighted pluralism as equally important.

148. The core idea of democracy is rule by the people exercised through participation, representation, and accountability. It ensures citizens have a voice in governance, representatives act on their behalf, and institutions remain answerable to the public.

149. Traditional authority, as identified by Max Weber, is inherited and maintained through customs, traditions, and long-established practices. People obey because "it has always been so," often linked with monarchies and hereditary rule.

150. Republicans define freedom as being free from dominating power, emphasizing non-domination rather than mere non-interference. They argue true liberty exists only when individuals are not subject to arbitrary control by others or by the state.

151. The capabilities approach was developed by Amartya Sen, focusing on what individuals are actually able to do and be, rather than just on resources or income. It highlights freedom of choice, opportunities, and well-being as measures of development.

152. Jeremy Bentham objected to the concept of natural rights, famously calling them "nonsense upon stilts." As a utilitarian, he argued that rights are created by law for collective happiness, not inherent or natural to human beings.

153. Global social movements differ from traditional political movements as they address transnational issues such as climate change, human rights, and anti-globalisation. They operate across borders, uniting diverse groups around global concerns rather than just local or national ones.

154. A central debate on liberty in political theory is whether freedom should be absolute or limited by laws. While absolute liberty risks chaos, regulated liberty balances individual rights with social order and justice. Thinkers like John Stuart Mill supported limited liberty with harm principles.

155. According to Amartya Sen, poverty should be tackled by enhancing individual capabilities and freedoms, not merely by raising GDP. This means expanding access to education, healthcare, and opportunities so people can fully develop and exercise their potential.

156. According to the Global Gender Gap Report 2024, the Philippines made progress in closing the gender pay gap. Despite its overall global ranking dropping, the Philippines achieved the highest score in the Eastern Asia and Pacific region for economic participation and opportunity, which covers wage equality and earned income. In contrast, Japan still faces a large gap, Saudi Arabia improved female employment but struggles in leadership and pay, and India continues to rank low in economic parity.

157. In natural rights theory, rights are seen as inalienable and inherent to human beings, not granted by the state or conditioned on citizenship. Thinkers like John Locke argued that such rights—life, liberty, property—are universal and pre-political in nature.

158. Negative rights require others to refrain from interference rather than offer support. Rights like freedom of speech or religion impose a duty on others—especially the state—to abstain from intervening, thereby creating a protected zone of personal liberty.

159. The principle of the Rule of Law ensures that no one is above the law, meaning all individuals and institutions, including the government, are subject to legal constraints and equal application of justice. It upholds accountability, fairness, and legal certainty.

160. The 19th Amendment to the U.S. Constitution, ratified in 1920, granted women the right to vote nationwide. It marked a pivotal victory in the women's suffrage movement, prohibiting voter discrimination based on sex.

161. According to Christophe Jaffrelot, Hindu nationalism is rooted in cultural homogenisation and majoritarianism. It seeks to unify India under a dominant Hindu cultural identity, often at the cost of pluralism and diversity, shaping politics through majority-based cultural nationalism.

162. The book "Indian Philosophy and Philosophy of Science" was authored by Sundar Sarukkai. He explores how Indian philosophical traditions intersect with the philosophy of science, addressing issues of knowledge, truth, and methods of inquiry in a comparative framework.

163. For Dr. B.R. Ambedkar, caste was not merely a division of labour but a division of labourers, a rigid system that institutionalized hierarchy and inequality. He criticized caste as a mechanism of oppression that denied social mobility and perpetuated discrimination.

164. Ashis Nandy is known for challenging Western universalism and emphasizing the need for contextual or local epistemologies. He argued that knowledge systems must reflect cultural and social contexts, questioning the dominance of Western categories in understanding Indian society.

165. Mikhail Gorbachev introduced reforms like Glasnost (openness) and Perestroika (restructuring) in the 1980s. While aimed at revitalizing the Soviet Union, they inadvertently weakened central control, triggered dissent, and eventually contributed to the collapse of the USSR.

166. The primary focus of feminist political theory is to achieve gender equality by challenging patriarchal structures that dominate politics, society, and institutions. It seeks to highlight women's experiences, question male-centric knowledge systems, and push for inclusive political participation.

167. The use of violence as a tool for political representation by marginalized groups is best described as the politics of recognition through resistance. It arises when marginalized communities resort to resistance, including violence, to demand visibility, justice, and rights in the political system.

168. Consociationalism, developed by Arend Lijphart, is designed for plural societies with deep cleavages. It seeks power-sharing arrangements and decentralization rather than majority rule. The incorrect statement is that it promotes majority rule by a single ethnic group, which goes against its inclusive power-sharing principle.

169. According to Colin Crouch, a key challenge to democracy today is the dominance of corporate and technocratic elites. He argues that decision-making is increasingly controlled by powerful economic interests, reducing genuine citizen participation—what he terms "post-democracy."

170. Under Section 375 of the Indian Penal Code, sexual consent is not legally valid if the woman is below 18 years of age, even if given voluntarily. This provision ensures protection against exploitation of minors and establishes the age of consent at 18.

171. During the Cold War, India followed the policy of Non-Alignment, refusing to formally align with either the US-led Western bloc or the Soviet bloc. This approach, championed by leaders like Nehru, sought to maintain independence in foreign policy while promoting peace and cooperation globally.

172. A significant post–Cold War shift in India's foreign policy was its focus on economic liberalisation and global engagement. After 1991, India opened its economy, pursued strategic partnerships, integrated into global markets, and prioritized economic diplomacy alongside traditional political interests.

173. According to Neerja Gopal, economic liberalisation and urbanisation challenge traditional identity-based politics in India. As people migrate to cities and markets expand, class and occupational identities increasingly intersect with caste and community-based politics, reshaping electoral behaviour.

174. India's Indian Ocean Policy emphasizes building partnerships with Southeast Asian and East African countries. This approach enhances maritime security, trade, energy cooperation, and geopolitical influence, reflecting India's strategic interests in the Indian Ocean region.

175. In India, identity politics often revolves around language and ethnicity, along with caste and religion. These markers of identity strongly influence political mobilization, party support, and demands for recognition and autonomy.

176. The rights of an arrested person—to be informed of the grounds of arrest, to consult legal counsel, and to be produced before a magistrate within 24 hours—are guaranteed under Article 22 of the Indian Constitution. This Article provides essential safeguards against arbitrary arrest and detention.

177. The 'Clash of Civilizations' thesis was proposed by Samuel P. Huntington. He argued that post–Cold War conflicts would be driven not by ideology or economics, but by cultural and civilizational differences, particularly between the West and non-Western civilizations.

178. India's Look East Policy, later renamed the Act East Policy, aims to deepen ties with Southeast Asian and East Asian countries. The policy enhances economic, strategic, and cultural cooperation, reinforcing India's role in the Asia-Pacific and Indo-Pacific regions.

179. The informal 'Committee on State Politics in India', organized under the Association for Asian Studies, was led by Myron Weiner. It focused on studying state-level politics in India, marking an important shift in political science research toward regional dynamics.

180. The slogan "Peace through armament" is associated with the idea of deterrence. It suggests that maintaining strong military capabilities prevents war by discouraging adversaries from initiating conflict, a concept central to Cold War-era strategic thinking.

181. Construct validity in assessment refers to the extent to which an assessment actually measures what it is designed to measure. For example, if a test claims to measure critical thinking, construct validity ensures it truly captures that skill and not just memorization.

182. Gender socialisation is the process by which individuals learn and internalise gender roles through family, education, media, and society. It shapes how people behave, what is expected of them, and their identity based on cultural definitions of masculinity and femininity.

183. The four fundamental skills of language learning are listening, speaking, reading, and writing. These skills build upon each other and are essential for communication, comprehension, and literacy development in any language.

184. Experiential learning theory, developed by David Kolb, stresses the importance of hands-on activities in the learning process. Learners actively engage in experiences, reflect on them, and apply the insights to new contexts, making learning deeper and more practical.

185. Micro planning in education refers to short-term, detailed planning for instruction. A lesson plan is the best example, as it structures daily teaching activities, learning objectives, and methods, unlike broader frameworks such as unit or year plans.

186. Aesthetic education contributes to emotional development by encouraging students to express and understand emotions through artistic activities such as music, painting, theatre, or dance. It nurtures creativity, empathy, and sensitivity, helping learners process and communicate emotions effectively.

187. In curriculum construction, scope refers to the range and depth of content covered in a subject or program. It outlines what topics will be taught, how detailed they will be, and ensures balance between breadth of knowledge and depth of understanding.

188. The primary goal of inclusive education is to ensure all students, regardless of their abilities or disabilities, learn together in the same classroom. It promotes equity, acceptance, and opportunities for every learner while reducing segregation.

189. The transdisciplinary approach in curriculum development focuses on integrating knowledge across multiple disciplines to solve real-world issues. It breaks subject boundaries, fostering holistic learning by connecting concepts from science, arts, humanities, and social studies.

190. Knowledge through intuition is a type of experience when a conviction of certainty arises suddenly, almost like a flash. It is immediate and does not rely on logical reasoning or step-by-step analysis, often linked with creativity and deep insight.

191. Growth is best defined as an increase in size, height, weight, or mass. It is a quantitative physical change in the body, unlike development which is qualitative and includes emotional, social, and cognitive progress.

192. Healthy cognitive development in adolescents involves guidance, goal setting, and proper rest. However, radicalizing adolescents negatively impacts their mental growth and critical thinking, steering them away from constructive and positive decision-making.

193. The correct answer is Assessment, which refers to a systematic procedure for collecting information that can be used to make inferences about the characteristics of people or objects. It is broader than just tests and includes observations, quizzes, projects, and feedback.

- Examination → a formal, often standardized type of assessment.
- Evaluation → judging or determining worth based on assessment data.
- Measurement → assigning numerical values to traits, forming part of the assessment process.

194. Gender socialisation is the process by which individuals learn and internalise gender roles from family, peers, education, and media. It shapes expectations about how males and females should behave in a given society.

195. In inclusive education, traits like sensitivity, knowledge of diverse learners, patience, and love are crucial. A teacher's social and economic status is the least important factor, since inclusion depends on attitude, empathy, and teaching skills rather than personal background.

196. The most suitable definition of knowledge is a set of understanding in a particular domain or field. It goes beyond raw data or information and involves structured comprehension that can be applied in reasoning, problem-solving, and decision-making.

197. A student using a deep approach to learning seeks meaning, integrates parts into a whole, and finds intrinsic enjoyment in tasks. The exception is when they see parts of the task as unrelated—this describes a surface learning approach.

198. A stray lesson plan is designed for a single lesson, focusing on one objective or topic, while a unit plan covers a series of lessons around a common theme, integrating broader objectives and multiple activities.

199. The behaviouristic perspective of learning emphasises the role of stimuli and responses. Rooted in the work of Pavlov, Skinner, and Watson, it views learning as a process of conditioning where behaviour is shaped by reinforcement and environment.

200. The psychomotor domain involves physical skills, coordination, and movement. Characteristics like Response Chain and Movement Coordination reflect this domain, as it emphasizes performing actions with precision and developing motor skills through practice.

Previous Paper (Solved)

Delhi Subordinate Services Selection Board (DSSSB)

PGT (Political Science) Recruitment Exam, 2021*

Post Specific Subject-Related Questions

1. Which of the following was suggested by Ambedkar to maintain community bond?
1. He suggested inter-caste marriage.
2. He suggested to eat inter-caste food.
3. He argued that the scriptures protecting 'Varnashrama Dharma' should be discarded as they are just and legitimize the graded organization of society.

A. Only 1 and 2 B. Only 1 and 3
C. 1, 2 and 3 D. Only 2 and 3

2. Raktakorabi and Muktadhara are the works of which among the following Indians?
A. Rammohan Roy
B. Sri Aurobindo
C. Swami Vivekananda
D. Rabindranath Tagore

3. In 1936, B.R. Ambedkar formed a political party to contest 17 seats in the elections of Bombay province. What was the name of the political party?
A. Backwards People Association
B. Backward Bloc
C. Independent Dalit Movement
D. Independent Labour Party

4. Which of the following kind of liberty is not one of the specific liberties that J.S. Mill advocated in his book 'On Liberty'?
A. Liberty to acquire private property
B. The Liberty of Thought and Expression
C. The Liberty of Association
D. The Liberty of Action

5. In which of the following ways did B.R. Ambedkar denounce Marxism?
1. He decried the strategy of violence as a means to seize power and called for resolute mass action to bring about-a good society.
2. He argued that the economic interpretation of history which does not acknowledge the crucial role that political and ideological institutions play and the conception of the withering away of the state.
3. He argued that There is no conflict between classes and class-struggle is writ large in social relations.
4. He argued that a good society demands extensive private ownership of the means of production.

Select the correct answer from the code given:
A. 1 and 2 B. 1, 2, 3 and 4
C. 3 and 4 D. 2 and 4

6. There are three dimensions to Marxian dialectical materialism. Which of the following is ***not*** one of them?
A. The law of unity of opposites (contradiction)
B. The law of transformation of quantity into quality. It means that quantitative changes lead to qualitative revolutionary situation.
C. The law that the material and ideal are same and constitute a unity
D. The law of negation of negation (thesis-antithesis and synthesis).

7. Who among the following said that "the king should initiate action against the leaders of the rebellion because they are the same leaders who lead the rebellion. Under no circumstances should he use force against a crowd of people as it may lead to widespread bloodshed?"
A. Kautilya B. Machiavelli
C. John Locke D. Confucius

*Exam held on 04-07-2021.

8. Match the List-I (Work) and List-II (year) in which Ambedkar published his works.

List-I (Work)	List-II (Year)
(*a*) Annihilation of Caste	1. 1923
(*b*) The Problem of Rupee	2. 1946
(*c*) What Congress and Gandhi have done to the Untouchables	3. 1945
(*d*) Who were the Sudras?	4. 1936

Codes:

	(*a*)	(*b*)	(*c*)	(*d*)
A.	3	2	1	4
B.	1	2	3	4
C.	4	1	3	2
D.	2	4	3	1

9. Who among the following has written the essay "what is the origin of inequality among men, and is it authorised by natural law?"

A. Alexis De Tocqueville
B. Jean Jacques Rousseau
C. Edmund Burke
D. Immanuel Kant

10. Who among the following called Lala Lajpat Rai as "a bourgeois politician with sympathy for Socialism"?

A. Dadabhai Naoroji
B. Netaji Subhash Chandra Bose
C. M.N. Roy
D. C.R. Das

11. Match the List-I (Books) and List-II (Authors) and select the correct answer from the code given below:

List-I (Books)	List-II (Authors)
(*a*) An Essay concerning human understanding	1. Aristotle
(*b*) Leviathan	2. John Locke
(*c*) Discourses on the First Ten Books of Titus Livius	3. Niccolo Machiavelli
(*d*) Politics	4. Thomas Hobbes

Codes:

	(*a*)	(*b*)	(*c*)	(*d*)
A.	1	2	3	4
B.	2	4	3	1
C.	3	2	1	4
D.	3	1	4	2

12. Consider the following regarding to Rousseau's Conception of General Will:

1. Rousseau first wrote about the concept of General Will in his Discourse on Political Economy
2. He asserts that the generality of the will is not so much a matter of numbers as of intrinsic quality and goodness.
3. By making the General Will sovereign and individuals as participants in the General Will, Rousseau reconciled authority with freedom.
4. He asserted that General will aims always at the public good and is different from the will of all.

Select the correct answer from the code given:

A. 1, 2, 3 and 4 B. Only 4
C. 1 and 4 D. 1 and 3

13. Given below are two statements, one labelled as Assertion (A) and other as Reason (R): Select the correct answer from the code given below:

Assertion (A) : In his book Socialism: Utopian and Scientific, Engels defined historical materialism as a theory which holds that the ultimate cause which determines the whole course of human history is the economic development of society.

Reason (R) : The whole course of human history is explained in terms of changes occurring in the modes of production and exchange.

A. (A) is true, but (R) is false.
B. Both (A) and (R) are true and (R) is the correct explanation of (A).
C. Both (A) and (R) are true, but (R) is not the correct explanation of (A).
D. (A) is false, but (R) is true.

14. Given below are two statements, one labelled as Assertion (A) and other as Reason (R): Select the correct answer from the code given below:

Assertion (A) : The 'carrot and stick' policy is a dual policy, which aims at driving a wedge between the moderate and extremist elements in the opposition.

Reason (R) : The government can offer rewards and concessions to the moderates but at the same time, it can continue its military operations against the extremists.

A. Both (A) and (R) are true and (R) is the correct explanation of (A).
B. (A) is false, but (R) is true.
C. (A) is true, but (R) is false.
D. Both (A) and (R) are true, but (R) is not the correct explanation of (A).

15. The classical political theory consists of which of the following?

1. Classical political theory aimed at acquiring reliable knowledge about matters concerning the people, a philosophical pursuit to establish a rational basis for belief; a politically inspired pursuit to establish a rational basis for action.
2. It sought to identify the political with the public, the common: the Greek polis, the Roman res publica, and the medieval age usage of commonwealth – all denoted a sharing of what was common among the people as partners.
3. Relating itself to the political whole, the classical political theory laid emphasis on order, balance, equilibrium, stability and harmony. That is why, it, in the process, dwelt on terms such as conflicts, anarchy, instability and revolution

A. Only 1 and 3 B. Only 2 and 3
C. 1, 2 and 3 D. Only 1 and 2

16. Which among the following credited the Bentham's Panopticon as a new technology of power?

A. John Rawls B. J.S. Mill
C. Michael Foucault D. Kymlicka

17. Which of the following is not one of the inconveniences in the state of nature, according to John Locke?

A. want of a legislature authority to declare law
B. It is constantly in the state of war.
C. lack of an impersonal executioner of the law
D. of an impartial judge to decide cases of violation of law

18. Which of the following Indian political thinkers stated that "the essence of socialism, lies in the control by the state of the means of production"?

A. Sardar Patel B. Jawaharlal Nehru
C. Mahatma Gandhi D. B.R. Ambedkar

19. Who among the following is not a proponent of Political theory as a Science?

A. George Catlin B. Robert Dahl
C. Leo Strauss D. David Easton

20. Given below are two statements, one labelled as Assertion (A) and other as Reason (R): Select the correct answer from the code given below:

Assertion (A) : For Plato, a state is a system of relationships in which everyone does his own business and where the job of the state is to maintain, and promote such relationships.

Reason (R) : Furthermore, Plato asserted that it is the job of the government, to help people live a complete life.

A. (A) is false, but (R) is true.
B. Both (A) and (R) are true, but (R) is not the correct explanation of (A).
C. (A) is true, but (R) is false.
D. Both (A) and (R) are true and (R) is the correct explanation of (A).

21. Consider the following statements:

(*a*) Lord Acton and Alexis de Tocqueville insisted that equality and liberty were antithetical.

(*b*) Rule of law means that the law is sovereign and no person, no matter how great he is or thinks he is, can declare himself above the law because that would be tantamount to arbitrary rule.

(*c*) In the Marxist tradition, it is claimed that all human beings are defined by praxis, that is all human beings are knowledgeable, conscious and practical agents.

(*d*) Positive equality is associated with 'the end of privilege', while Negative equality, means 'the availability of opportunity'.

Choose the correct statements from the code given:

A. (*a*), (*b*), (*c*) and (*d*)
B. (*b*) and (*d*)
C. (*a*), (*b*) and (*c*)
D. (*c*), (*d*) and (*b*)

22. Which of the following is not a component of Social movement?

A. Programmes B. Objectives
C. Ideology D. Education

23. Who among the following asserted, "The parliamentary form of government, as a political institutional device, has proved to be inadequate to continue or expand concrete democratic rights of the people?"

A. M.N. Roy B. Leo Panitch
C. Marion Kozak D. A.R. Desai

24. All India Scheduled Caste Federation (AISCF) was formed in which year?

A. 1951 B. 1935
C. 1947 D. 1942

25. Which of the following is true regarding Resource Mobilisation Theory?

I. It is an outcome of rational choice theory.
II. It is based on the assumption that individuals' actions are motivated randomly not by any preference.
III. The theory purported to show that the success of a movement depended on the resources available to be used.

A. Both II and III are correct
B. Only II is correct
C. Both I and II are correct
D. Both I and III are correct.

26. Who among the following defined 'being free' as "not being interfered with by others"?

A. Isaiah Berlin B. J.S. Mill
C. Jeremy Bentham D. J.J. Rousseau

27. The Book "Hindu Society at Cross Road" was written by:

A. Sarvepali Radhakrishnan
B. Jyotiba Phule
C. K.M. Pannikar
D. V.P Menon

28. Which of the following pair is not correctly matched with respect to the event and its year?

A. Mandal controversy - 1981
B. Loktantra bachao slogan - 1977
C. Bofors scandal - 1989
D. Garibi hatao slogan - 1971

29. Which one of the following contentions does Isaiah Berlin make to defend Negative Liberty?

A. Berlin argued that the principle of liberty brooked no interference with the sphere of one's self-regarding action.
B. Berlin argued that a free man is he that in those things which by his strength and wit he is able to do, is not hindered to do what he has a will to.
C. Berlin argued that the human faculties of perception, judgement, discriminative feeling, mental activity, and even moral preference, are exercised only in making a choice
D. Berlin contended that liberty in its negative sense is principally concerned with the area of control, not with its source.

30. Which of the following is ***not correct*** regarding Political parties and party system in India?

A. The party system in India before 1967 has been a system of Congress dominance.
B. The party system changed from one party dominant system to multi - party system at the national level.

C. Political parties are capitalist in nature after 1967.
D. Party system in India emerged and developed at the state level since independence.

31. Who among the following is the proponent of the Social Theory of Justice?
A. William Maitland B. T.H. Green
C. Stephen Barker D. John Rawls

32. A socio – political movement Nav Nirman Andolan of 1974 was organised in which state of India?
A. Orissa B. Gujarat
C. Rajasthan D. West Bengal

33. Which of the following best describes the Directive Theory of Rights?
A. It believes that rights are conditions of social welfare.
B. It is understood with reference to the economic system in a particular period of history.
C. It treats the state as the product of a long historical process.
D. It means that rights are granted by the state, in the form of a claim in respect of rights which the power of the state grants to the people.

34. The line "Class domination can never be purely 'economic', or purely 'cultural' "is said by:
A. Ralph Miliband B. Karl Marx
C. A.R. Desai D. G.S. Ghurye

35. Writing "State Against the People" is written by:
A. Rajni Kothari B. V.K. Ramaswami
C. P.N. Bhagwati D. Morris Jones

36. Which of the following is ***not correct*** regarding Relative Deprivation Theory?
1. Relative deprivation is defined as actors' perception of discrepancy between their value expectations and their environment's apparent value capabilities.
2. Relative deprivation model describes the situation where the expectations are stable but capabilities decline.
3. Relative deprivation is a necessary but not a sufficient condition for protest movements.

A. Only 1 and 2 B. Only 2
C. Only 2 and 3 D. 1, 2 and 3

37. Robert Nozick's libertarian conception of Justice is a defence of which of the following?
A. It is a defence of a socialist society
B. It is a defence of a people led communist
C. It is a defence of free-market capitalism
D. It is a defence of a Marxist regime.

38. Cauvery water dispute is between which two states in India?
A. Tamil Nadu and Kerala
B. Tamil Nadu and Karnataka
C. Kerala and Karnataka
D. Andhra Pradesh and Karnataka

39. From which of the following does John Rawls draw inspiration in his criticism and alternative to Utilitarianism?
A. From Immanuel Kant's moral idea of liberty and equality of every human being
B. Montesquieu
C. From Robert Nozick's Arguments on Freedom as the Paramount View of Man
D. T.H. Green's idea of negative equality

40. Which one of the following statements about politics in India by L.I. Rudolph and S.H. Rudolph is ***not correct***?
A. Politics in India is centrist politics.
B. Politics in India is not a class politics.
C. The state as an autonomous body negotiates between labor and capital.
D. The Indian state as a 'capitalist state' called for 'capitalism' in pursuit of the public sector and state planning.

41. Which one of the following assumptions is correct regarding the theory of resource mobilization by Rajendra Singh?
1. Social movements should be understood as conflict models of collective action.
2. Both institutional and non-institutional collective actions have conflicts of interest built into the system of institutional power relations.

3. Social movements involve the rational pursuit of interests by competing groups.

A. Both 2 and 3 B. Both 1 and 3
C. Both 1 and 2 D. 1, 2 and 3

42. Which of the following definition is correct regarding "Social Movement"?

I. A deliberate collective endeavour to promote change in any direction and by any means, not excluding violence, illegality, revolution or withdrawal into 'utopian' community.

II. Social movements can be viewed as collective enterprises to establish a new order of life.

III. Social movements are those organized efforts, on the part of excluded groups, to promote or resist changes in the structure of society that involve recourse to noninstitutional forms of political participation.

A. I, II and III
B. Only I is correct
C. Only III is correct
D. Both II and III are correct

43. Which of following scholars, first worked on the 'Cultivation Theory'?

A. Dorina Miron B. Donald Shaw
C. George Gerbner D. Jennings Bryant

44. Vohra Committee Report studied the:

A. Machinery of Government of India
B. Training and recruitment of the higher Civil Services
C. Multi-tier bureaucratic authority
D. Nexus between criminals, politicians and bureaucrats in India

45. Which of the following movement is ***not*** related to Environment?

A. Abolitionist Movement
B. Appiko Movement
C. Narmada Bachao Andolan (NBA)
D. Chipko Movement

46. In which year was the Council of Europe established?

A. 1949 B. 1952
C. 1951 D. 1950

47. Scholars Melvin de Fleur and Sandra Ball-Rokeztch gave which of the following theory?

A. Agenda Setting Theory
B. Spiral of Silence Theory
C. Development Communication Theory
D. Media System Dependency Theory

48. Which of the following pair is ***not*** correctly matched?

A. Fascist movement - Vietnam
B. Islamic movement - Middle East
C. Nazi movement - Germany
D. Tamilian movement - Sri Lanka

49. The Rise and Decline of Nations: Economic Growth, Stagflation, and Social Rigidities, 1982 has been written by:

A. Samuel P. Huntington
B. Harold Lasswell
C. Mancur Olson
D. George Bernard Shaw

50. Which of the following is correct regarding Marxist approach of social movement?

A. Biasness is the central core of social movements.
B. Conflict is the central core of social movements.
C. Love is the central core of social movements.
D. Freedom is the central core of social movements.

51. Consider the following statements with regard to Mandal Commission:

(*a*) The Mandal Commission is officially known as the Socially and Economically Backward Classes Commission (SEBC).

(*b*) The commission developed 11 criteria to identify the backward classes who were called "Other Backward Classes" or OBCs. The criteria are classified as social, economic and educational.

(*c*) The Commission was chaired by a Member of Parliament, D P Mandal.

(*d*) The Commission submitted its report to the President on 31st December 1980.

A. (*a*) and (*d*) B. Only (*c*)
C. (*a*), (*b*) and (*c*) D. Only (*d*)

52. Given below are two statements, one labeled as Assertion (A) and other as Reason (R): Select the correct answer from the code given below:

Assertion (A) : The Indian polity is governed by vertical mobilization by the dominant castes and horizontal alliances in the name of jati and varna.

Reason (R) : The establishment of a formal democracy guarantees that all citizens will enjoy equal access and participation in the political processes.

A. (A) is true, but (R) is false.
B. (A) is false, but (R) is true
C. Both (A) and (R) are true, but (R) is not the correct explanation of (A).
D. Both (A) and (R) are true and (R) is the correct explanation of (A).

53. Who calls Gandhi's method as "dialogical resistance?"

A. David Bayley
B. Karl Marx
C. Lord Mountbatten
D. David Hardiman

54. Given below are two statements, one labeled as Assertion (A) and other as Reason (R): Select the correct answer from the code given below:

Assertion (A) : The modern judiciary in India derives its sources from the Constitution, and acts as a check on the arbitrary decisions of the legislature and the executive.

Reason (R) : A working democracy requires an independent judiciary well-coordinated by an effective executive and a responsible legislature.

A. Both (A) and (R) are true, but (R) is not the correct explanation of (A).
B. (A) is true, but (R) is false.
C. Both (A) and (R) are true and (R) is the correct explanation of (A).
D. (A) is false, but (R) is true.

55. The book titled 'Homo-Hierarchicus on the Indian Caste System' is written by?

A. Louis Dumont B. Nicholas Dirks
C. Kancha Ilaiah D. Gerald Berreman

56. Consider the following statements with regard to Public Interest Litigation (PIL):

(*a*) It is a socio-economic movement generated by the judiciary to reach justice specially to the weaker sections of the society.
(*b*) The purpose of PIL is the enforcement of the right of one person against the other.
(*c*) The granting of the right to PIL has led to plethora of litigations in the courts, indicative of the development of democratic rights by the judiciary.
(*d*) The idea came from 'atio popularis' of the Roman jurisprudence, which allowed court access to every citizen in matters of public wrongs.

Select the ***incorrect*** statements from the code given below:

A. Only (*b*) B. (*a*) and (*b*)
C. Only (*d*) D. (*a*) and (*d*)

57. Given below are two statements, one labeled as Assertion (A) and other as Reason (R). Select the correct answer from the code given below:

Assertion (A) : In a democracy, the civil service has to modify its behaviour and style of functioning to complement the needs of democracy.

Reason (R) : The establishment of the Panchayati Raj institutions on a country-wide basis and the transfer of some of the traditional functions of the civil service system to these newly established institutions constitute a new policy trend in the civil service system.

A. (A) is false, but (R) is true.
B. Both (A) and (R) are true and (R) is the correct explanation of (A).
C. (A) is true, but (R) is false.
D. Both (A) and (R) are true, but (R) is not the correct explanation of (A).

58. 'The Paradoxical Prime Minister: Narendra Modi And His India' is a book authored by:

A. Rajdeep Sardesai B. Rahul Gandhi
C. Burkha Dutt D. Shashi Tharoor

59. Which of the following is the correct importance of social movement?

I. To increase production in the factories and industries.
II. To oppose the 'present' political regime
III. To establish the system which they consider 'ideal' and perfect capable to resolve the problems of society

A. Both I and III are correct
B. Only I is correct
C. I, II and III
D. Both II and III are correct

60. Which among the following is the author of the book 'System and Process in International Politics'?

A. Gordon Anderson B. Morton Kaplan
C. Suson Eaton D. David Easton

61. Apartheid is related to which country?

A. Italy B. India
C. France D. South Africa

62. The book "Transnational Relations and World Politics" is written by:

A. Mathew Evangelista
B. Robert O. Keohane
C. Riddel-Dixon
D. Kegley Jr.

63. Which of the following is *not* correct regarding treaties of nuclear explosions?

A. The 1963 Partial Test Ban Treaty
B. The 1972 Threshold Test Ban Treaty
C. The 1976 Peaceful Nuclear Explosions Treaty
D. The 1996 Comprehensive Test Ban Treaty.

64. Terrorists are trained in one country to operate in more than one country is called:

1. Cross Border Terrorism
2. International Terrorism

A. Only 2 B. Both 1 and 2
C. Only 1 D. Neither 1 nor 2

65. The term "refugee" as defined by the United Nations Convention Relating of 1951 is any person who:

1. was a victim of events in Europe occurring before 1 January 1951.
2. was outside the country of his origin (home country of which he is a national)
3. could not go back to his home country of origin due to a well founded fear of persecution

A. Only 2 and 3 B. Only 1 and 2
C. 1, 2 and 3 D. Only 1 and 3

66. Which of the following shows the Impact of Science and Technology on Military Affairs?

I. Long range missiles, aircraft and submarines have reduced the significance of physical location as a determinant of the vulnerability of a nation.
II. It provides a striking demonstration of the effort of changes in military technology on international relations.
III. It increases the friendship between two nations.

A. Both II and III are correct
B. Both I and III are correct
C. Both I and II are correct
D. I, II and III are correct

67. Which of the following is ***not correctly*** paired?

A. The Lebanese Conflict – 1958
B. The Congolese Conflict – 1968
C. Indo-Pak Conflict – 1965
D. Suez Canal Crisis – 1956

68. Which of the following is ***not correct*** about Nuclear Non-Proliferation Treaty?

A. The treaty divides the signatories into two categories: those who possess the nuclear weapons and those who did not.
B. Earlier focus had mostly been on weapons systems, strategic parity and corresponding geostrategic considerations.
C. The NPT was the second step to the construction of an effective international regime designed to halt the proliferation of nuclear weapons after ABM treaty.
D. It commits the non-weapon states to inspection of their holdings of nuclear materials.

69. About China, who had once said: "It is a sleeping giant, let it sleep for if it wakes it would shake the world"?
A. Lord Litton
B. Jawaharlal Nehru
C. Napoleon
D. Alexander I. Czar

70. To look at international relations not from the viewpoint of nation states but from the perspective of the security of the individual is known as
A. Human Benefits B. Human Rights
C. Human Duties D. Human Threat

71. Which of the following is correct regarding People's Liberation Army of China?
1. The PLA was formed in the year 1927.
2. The name PLA was given to it after the Japanese attacked China in 1937.
3. Zhu De and Mao Zedong were the main founders of PLA.

A. Only 2 and 3 B. Only 1 and 3
C. Only 1 and 2 D. 1, 2 and 3

72. Which one of the following is ***incorrect*** with regards to the concept of the self-determination?
A. It is obvious that the concept, along with that of nationalism played a significant role in the process of de-colonisation.
B. Freedom to the colonies mark the end of the role of the principle of Self-determination
C. The concept of Self-determination makes no provision for identifying the bases for defining the territorial limits.
D. It is the application of the principle of Self-determination within multi-cultural societies that is most complex.

73. Which of the following is ***not*** the elements of the UN Activities in the area of self-determination?
A. Racial equality in South Africa and Rhodesia
B. De-colonialism
C. Military action to free Goa from the Portuguese Rule
D. Trusteeship System

74. Which of the following is not one of the defensive alliances formed by the capitalist or free market nations post the second world war?
A. Warsaw Pact
B. SEATO
C. CENTO
D. NATO

75. Which of the following pair is ***not*** correctly matched about formation year of organisation?
A. United Nation (UN) - 1945
B. International Covenant on Civil and Political Rights (ICCPR) - 1966
C. International Covenant on Economic, Social and Cultural Rights (ICESCR) - 1956
D. Universal Declaration of Human Rights (UDHR) - 1948

76. Which of the following is not true about the Idealist school of philosophy in India?
1. Kautilya was an advocate of idealist school of philosophy.
2. The Upanishads give us the basis of the theory of non-violence which becomes the basis of idealist tradition.
3. This idealist method had its limitations as India discovered to its cost during the action in Goa in 1961, the Chinese invasion in 1962, and the Pakistani aggressions of 1965, 1971 and 1999.

A. Only 3 B. Only 1
C. 1, 2 and 3 D. Only 2

77. Which of the following is ***not*** the major cause of Inequality among nations?
A. Uneven International Economic System.
B. Trade among developed and developing nations.
C. Emerging Labour Markets and Skill Differentials.
D. The power game in international politics.

78. In which of the following year Shimla Agreement was signed between India and Pakistan?
A. 1972 B. 1965
C. 1991 D. 1971

79. Consider the following about the early foreign policy of India towards Tibet:

1. In continuation of the policy of Indo-Chinese friendship, India signed the Sino-Tibetan Agreement on May 23, 1951, which sealed Tibet's fate permanently.
2. In 1954 Nehru had conceded the Chinese claim over Tibet by accepting its suzerainty over it, when India signed an agreement for trade with the "Tibetan region of China."
3. To pacify the Chinese, Nehru concluded the Panchsheel (Five Principles) Agreement with Chou En-lai in 1954, based on the principles of mutual respect for territorial integrity and sovereignty, non-aggression, non-interference in internal affairs, equality and peaceful coexistence.

Choose the correct from the following code:

A. 1 and 2 B. Only 1
C. Only 3 D. 1, 2 and 3

80. Who strongly said that "Man is a Political Animal"?

A. Socrates B. Chanakya
C. Plato D. Aristotle

81. As human person becomes more and more conscious of himself as human – as an individual and as a social being:

A. he/she becomes more conscious of his/her first principles and of his/her rights and duties as a human person
B. he/she becomes more conscious of his/her moral consciousness and of his/her rights and duties as a human person
C. he/she becomes more conscious of his/her human moral precepts and of his/her rights and duties as a human person
D. he/she becomes more conscious of his/her human inter-relatedness and of his/her rights and duties as a human person

82. Who among the following said, "The state represents violence in concentrated and organised form. The individual has a soul but the state is a soulless machine; it can never wean from violence to which it owes its very existence."?

A. Herald Laski B. B.R. Ambedkar
C. Karl Marx D. M.K. Gandhi

83. What is the immediate ontological foundation of the moral order?

A. Moral precepts
B. Human interrelatedness
C. Love
D. Salient moments

84. Karel Vasak has sought to classify the historical development of human rights according to the French revolutionary slogan:

A. Justice, Liberty and Equality
B. Liberty, Equality and Fraternity
C. Liberty, Equality and Secular
D. Sovereign, Socialist and Secular

85. In the 1860s, the USA witnessed a civil war between the northern and the southern states on which of the following issue?

A. Gun control laws
B. Abolition of slavery
C. Secession
D. Rights of women

86. Which of the following observed that "During the emergency the executive, for its political ends, has used the police"?

A. Shah Commission
B. National Police Commission
C. Ribeiro Committee
D. Malimath Committee

87. Who among the following gave the Structural Framework Approach?

A. Max Weber B. William Mitchell
C. Gabriel Almond D. Talcott Parsons

88. Hyperglobalist define globalisation as which among the following?

A. A new epoch of history in which traditional nation-states have become 'unnatural, even impossible business units in a global economy'.
B. Globalisation is 'transforming' the world and see it as a driving force behind the rapid social, political and economic changes that are reshaping modern societies and a world order.

C. The forces of globalisation are themselves dependent upon the regulatory power of national governments to make states globalise, liberalise and privatise
D. A new form of Imperialism, they see it as an extension of the neo-liberal conservative policies practiced by the advanced western countries to put their own economies in order as well as overcome global depression following the oil crisis of the 1970s and 80s.

89. Which of the following theories is credited to have changed the apologetic view of capitalism into a pragmatic one?
A. Competitive Market Advantage Theory
B. Labour Theory of Value
C. Comparative Cost Advantage Theory
D. General Theory of Employment, Interest and Money.

90. Which of the following is not paired correctly with regards to the theory of Origin of State?
A. Rousseau – Democratic State
B. John Locke – Limited State
C. Frederick Engels – Product of Natural Social Development
D. Thomas Hobbes – Omnipotent State

91. What is the reason behind the human consciousness becoming moral?
1. He/she has been continuously asking himself the question what he is?
2. Because he becomes more aware of himself as a human person.
3. Because the more human person becomes himself/herself the more he she becomes conscious of what he/she should be.

A. Only 2 B. Only 1
C. 1, 2 and 3 D. Only 3

92. "Legal relations as well as forms of state could neither be understood by themselves, nor explained by the so-called general progress of the human mind, but that they are rooted in the conditions of life." Who among the following said this?
A. Irving Fisher
B. Peter Kropotkin
C. Karl Marx
D. John Maynard Keynes

93. Which of the following was not the goal of the World Conference on Human Rights held at Vienna in 1993?
A. Widely hoped co-ordination of efforts of the individual and nongovernmental organizations under the spearheading leadership of the UNO.
B. Establishment of equal validity for social and economic rights along with civil and political rights and the right to development.
C. Confirmation of universality of Human Right.
D. Expansion of the sphere of accountability of the sovereign state.

94. Ethics is the philosophical treatise which studies human behaviour and tries to determine what is right or wrong behaviour. It is also called?
A. Moral philosophy
B. Critical Ontology
C. Behavioural philosophy
D. Empirical Knowledge

95. "The Study of the Problem of Discrimination against Indigenous Populations" was reported by?
A. Riddel-Dixon B. MA Conroy
C. Robert O. Keohane D. Jose R. Martinez

96. Which of the following statements is ***incorrect***?
A. The Congress supported the United Front Government
B. The Left supported the United Front Government
C. The United Front Government came to power in 1989
D. The BJP did not support the United Front Government

97. In which year did China annex Tibet?
A. 1955 B. 1958
C. 1949 D. 1950

98. India entered into the nuclear club as the sixth member with the testing of a nuclear device in which year?
A. 1996 B. 1991
C. 1998 D. 1974

99. Who among the following said that "Life, the continuation of the body in time, and liberty, the unhindered movement of the body, became two of the highest moral values"?

A. Upendra Baxi
B. Ramin Jahanbegloo
C. Bhikhu Parekh
D. Robert Benewick

100. According to Thomas Aquinas, a general principle such as 'serious promises should not be lightly broken' is an example of which of the following?

A. Fist principles B. Self-Evident
C. Self-deduction D. Logical deduction

101. In which year was the Backward and Minority Communities Employees Federation (BAMCEF) formed?

A. 1976 B. 1972
C. 1978 D. 1974

102. Which of the following was the first of the 15 Soviet republics to declare its independence?

A. Latvia B. Tajikistan
C. Lithuania D. Estonia

103. Which of the following is the first major reform that brought in democracy in Britain?

A. Reforms Act, 1852
B. Reforms Act, 1822
C. Reforms Act, 1842
D. Reforms Act, 1832

104. Bias towards party interest is attributable to which of the following kinds of bureaucracy?

A. Guardian bureaucracy
B. Merit bureaucracy
C. Caste bureaucracy
D. Patronage bureaucracy

105. In 1977, the Government of India appointed Ashok Mehta Committee for which of the following reasons?

A. Introduction of Panchayati Raj System
B. Revive and strengthen the Panchayati Raj System
C. For regular elections of Panchayati Raj
D. To analyse the development at the grass root level

106. Given below are two statements, one labeled as Assertion (A) and other as Reason (R): Select the correct answer from the code given below:

Assertion (A) : Political parties have continued to remain in the centre of Indian politics.

Reason (R) : Opinion polls in India have repeatedly shown that people generally vote more for the party than for the candidate

A. (A) is true, but (R) is false.
B. (A) is false, but (R) is true.
C. Both (A) and (R) are true and (R) is the correct explanation of (A).
D. Both (A) and (R) are true, but (R) is not the correct explanation of (A).

107. The Convention on Wetlands of international importance especially as waterfowl habitat was ratified in which year?

A. 1973 B. 1972
C. 1974 D. 1971

108. Which of the following personalities founded Self-Employed Women's Association (SEWA) in the year 1972? She also worked with the Gandhian women trade union called Textile Labour Association.

A. Susheela Gopalan B. C.K. Janu
C. Raghubir Kaur D. Ela Bhatt

109. Which of the following is not one of the advantages of British rule in India?

A. Bringing entire India under one administrative umbrella.
B. Laying of railways
C. Encouraging social reforms
D. Encouraging Jobs under British government

110. The Telangana Agitation started in the year:

A. 1943 B. 1945
C. 1947 D. 1969

111. Consider the following statements with regard to Political Processes:

(*a*) Political processes can be reduced to the preferences or behaviour of individuals, but are also conditioned by group actions and interactions.

(*b*) These groups-their solidarities and their conflict-make independent contributions to determining political outcomes.

(*c*) "Representation" is the exclusive key relationship between such groups and the making of authoritative decisions.

(*d*) This relationship is increasingly structured through specialised, "legally constituted" organisations with identifiable and reproducible boundaries.

Select the correct statement from the code given below:

A. (*b*) and (*c*) B. (*b*) and (*d*)
C. Only (*d*) D. Only (*a*)

112. Who led the Narmada Bachao Andolan movement?

A. Sunderlal Bahuguna
B. Rajendra Singh
C. Baba Amte
D. Medha Patkar

113. In which year was the first summit of NAM held?

A. 1972 B. 1961
C. 1978 D. 1966

114. Which of the following has written the book titled 'Women's Role in Economic Development'?

A. Ester Boserup
B. Thomas Robert Malthus
C. Olivia S. Mitchell
D. Elinor Ostrom

115. Bentham started and financed the Westminster in ....

A. 1823 B. 1822
C. 1820 D. 1824

116. Consider the following statements with regard to Public Policy:

(*a*) Public policy is an action which employs governmental authority to commit resources in support of a preferred value.

(*b*) It is a strategy for achieving public goals through the management and allocation of power, rights, resources, information, and inducements.

(*c*) In democratic forms of government, the major part of public policies are made in the parliament through legislative processes.

(*d*) The domain of public policy is very limited and it includes only those matters that concerns defence, agriculture and health.

Select the ***incorrect*** answer from the code given below:

A. Only (*b*) B. (*b*) and (*c*)
C. (*c*) and (*d*) D. Only (*d*)

117. The book titled 'The Bureaucratisation of the World' is written by:

A. Bruno Rizzi B. Harriet Martineau
C. Michel Foucault D. Herbert Spencer

118. Consider the following statements with regard to Communist Parties:

(*a*) Initially, European communist parties were organised on the pattern of socialist parties, but after 1924, they followed the pattern of Soviet Communist Party.

(*b*) Communist parties follow the principle of 'democratic Centralism', which implies democratic participation of members in party structure, but centralised decision making and supervision.

(*c*) At different levels in the party, discussion does take place, but directions of the leadership can never be violated or defied.

(*d*) No other party anywhere in the world, except perhaps the Fascist parties, is so rigidly based on ideology as the communist parties are.

Select the correct statement from the code given below:

A. Only (*c*) B. (*a*) and (*b*)
C. (*a*), (*b*), (*c*), (*d*) D. (*a*) and (*d*)

119. Which amendment introduced the third tier of government in the Indian Democracy?

A. 74th Amendment
B. Both 73rd & 74th Amendments
C. 73th Amendment
D. 67th Amendment

120. Who has written the book titled 'Politics in India'?
A. Rajni Kothari B. Sanjib Baruah
C. Louis Dumont D. Atul Kohli

121. Which of the following statements is not correct about the Directive Principles of State Policy?
A. The courts, while interpreting the Constitution, including the Fundamental Rights, are to be guided by them.
B. The Constitution enjoins the state to regard them as fundamental in governance and to apply them when making laws.
C. A more direct activist role of the state in bringing forth socio-economic transformation was assigned by the Constitution of India through Directive Principles of State Policy.
D. These principles are directly enforceable by the law courts.

122. In early 1947, Hindustan Mazdoor Sevak Sangh was set up with the
A. Bombay Textile Workers
B. Calcutta Textile Workers
C. Ahmedabad Textile Workers
D. Sabarmati Textile Workers

123. An American general, Norman Schwarzkopf, led the UN coalition against Iraq in which of the following UN Operation?
A. Operation Iraq Freedom
B. Operation Desert Strom
C. Operation Terror Freedom
D. Operation Black Commando

124. The president addresses both the Houses of Parliament assembled together:
A. every session
B. first session after each general election and the first session of each year
C. during emergency session summoned for the purpose
D. any session

125. Expand UNFCCC?
A. United Nations Framework Convention on Climate Change
B. United Nations Framework Counter on Climate Change
C. United Nations Framework Convention on Climate Call
D. United Nations Fast Convention on Climate Change

126. When was Meghalaya carved out of Assam?
A. 1972 B. 1971
C. 1973 D. 1970

127. The Idea of five year plan was adopted in India from?
A. The United States of America
B. Japan
C. United Soviet socialist republics
D. Australia

128. Which of the following is not a kind of Sovereignty?
A. Implicit and Explicit Sovereignty
B. Dejure and Defacto Sovereignty
C. Legal and Political Sovereignty
D. Real and Titular Sovereignty

129. In the state of ___________, the Communist Party came to power in 1957. This was the first time in the world, a Communist party government had come to power through democratic elections.
A. Kerala B. Karnataka
C. Punjab D. West Bengal

130. Who was the finance minister of the Interim Government post war in 1946?
A. Zulfikar Ali Bhutto
B. Liaquat Ali Khan
C. John Mathai
D. Maulana Abul Kalam Azad

131. Which of the following statements is not correct about Austin's Concept of Sovereignty?
A. Sovereign is the supreme power in the state. He is the source of all authority in the state. His authority is unlimited and absolute. He does not take commands from any one as nobody has a right to command him.
B. Sovereignty has to be determinate. It resides in a person or a body of persons. State is a legal order in which the sovereignty can be located very clearly.

C. The rights and liberties of the individual also culminate from the sovereign and do not restrict the operation of the individuals' sovereignty.
D. Sovereignty is necessary for the state. Sovereignty is one of the four elements of the state. There cannot be a state without sovereignty.

132. Under which Article of the Constitution, every resident, adult citizen of sound mind, and not legally barred on grounds of crime, corruption or illegal practice, is entitled to be registered as a voter?
A. Article 225 B. Article 224
C. Article 326 D. Article 329

133. Marx in his history of ideas puts three main explainations of how the human societies have developed over the years. Which of the following is not one of them?
A. Realist Interpretation
B. Idealist Interpretation
C. Spiritualist Interpretation
D. Materialist Interpretation

134. India's first major science policy, the Scientific Policy Resolution (SPR) was drafted in which year?
A. 1983 B. 1958
C. 1971 D. 1964

135. Which Article states that the state shall endeavour to develop agriculture and industry along modern scientific lines?
A. Article 114 B. Article 148
C. Article 48 D. Article 39

136. Who argued that sovereignty is the creation of a social contract and the sovereign is that individual or assembly who is authorised to will for the general purpose?
A. Thomas Hobbes
B. Jean-Jacques Rousseau
C. David Held
D. Jean Bodin

137. The state shall, within the limits of its economic capacity and development, make effective provision for securing the right to work, to education and to public assistance in case of unemployment, old age, sickness and disablement, and in other cases of undeserved want. This is as per which article?
A. Article 47 B. Article 41
C. Article 44 D. Article 40

138. Indira Gandhi got the Congress Working Committee to adopt the ten-point programme in ________
A. May 1967 B. April 1967
C. June 1967 D. July1967

139. The socialist model of development was related to:
A. Pakistan B. The USA
C. USSR D. Europe

140. A legal proceeding during which an individual's right to hold an office or governmental privilege is challenged is called:
A. Writ of mandamus
B. Writ of quo warranto
C. Writ certiorari
D. Writ of prohibition

141. Parties act as a check against the tendency of absolutism which is also known as:
1. Caesarism
2. Bonapartism
3. Multi-partisan
A. Only 1 B. Only 2
C. 1, 2 and 3 D. Only 3

142. In America, when the President's post falls vacant (resignation, death, impeachment, etc) then who of the following takes over as President?
A. Vice President
B. The Chief of Defence
C. The Governor of the state of Washington
D. The Judge of Supreme Court

143. Trygve Lie was the first secretary general of UN. He was from which of the following countries?
A. Germany B. Italy
C. Norway D. France

144. How many members are there in Public Accounts Committee?
A. 22 B. 20
C. 18 D. 24

145. Which country in central Asia witnessed a civil war that went on for Ten years?
A. Tajikistan B. Azerbaijan
C. Turkmenistan D. Uzbekistan

146. By which Article of the Constitution can the Rajya Sabha pass a bill with 2/3rd majority and establish one or more all India services?
A. Article 256 B. Article 96
C. Article 356 D. Article 312

147. Swatantra Party was formed in which of the following years?
A. 1952 B. 1961
C. 1959 D. 1955

148. The Indian leader who is the first recipient of Bharat Ratna award is:
A. Rajagopalachari B. K.M. Munshi
C. Balraj Madhok D. B.R. Ambedkar

149. On 19 March 2003, the US launched its invasion of Iraq under the code name:
A. Operation Red
B. Operation Terror Freedom
C. Operation War On Terrorism
D. Operation Iraqi Freedom

150. By which year had India completely started using EVMs in elections?
A. 1992 B. 2004
C. 1984 D. 2010

151. Which among the following Prime Minister of India led the first coalition government of India?
A. Indira Gandhi B. Morarji Desai
C. Charan Singh D. Chandra Shekhar

152. The Vice President of India is:
A. The de facto President of the National Human Rights Commission
B. The de facto representative of India to the UN General Assembly
C. Ex-Officio Chairman/Chairperson of the Rajya Sabha
D. The Speaker of the Lok Sabha

153. Which of the following does not come under the purview of Civil Case?
A. Divorce between Husband and Wife
B. Property
C. Breach of Contract
D. Robbery

154. ______ theory in political analysis assumes that individuals tend to use actions that bring them the best results.
A. Grey Theory B, Game Theory
C. Race Theory D. Damp Theory

155. The railway strike of 1974 was called by George Fernandes when he was the President of:
A. All India Railwaymen's Federation
B. Railway Employees' Union
C. Rail Mazdoor Sangh
D. Bharatiya Kamgar Sena

156. Which party dominates the political affairs of Maldives?
A. Maldivian socialist party
B. Maldivian Communist party
C. Maldivian republic party
D. Maldivian democratic party

157. The Red Empire (USSR) was disintegrated in which of the following years?
A. 1991 B. 1989
C. 1992 D. 1993

158. In the year 1997, Mr. Indra Kumar Gujral, elected as Prime Minister was a Member of __________
A. State Legislature for Gujarat
B. Lok Sabha
C. State Legislature for Kerala
D. Rajya Sabha

159. When was Rajeev Gandhi assassinated?
A. 21st June, 1992 B. 20th May, 1990
C. 30th May, 1991 D. 21st May, 1991

160. Easton's conceptual framework evolved in _____ phases
A. 4 B. 5
C. 2 D. 3

161. Which of the following theories is not regarding origin of States?
A. force theory B. Marxian theory
C. Braid theory D. Divine theory

162. Once a Budget has been presented in the Parliament, the government has to get all money bills related to the union budget passed within ______?

A. 30 Days B. 60 Days

C. 75 Days D. 90 Days

163. A trans-national state is known for having a ....

A. Divided Power

B. Sole Centre of power

C. United power

D. Divided sovereignty

164. Which among the following are the three types of services envisaged in the Constitution of India?

A. Civil Service, Military Service and Paramilitary Service

B. All-India services, Central services and State services

C. Navy Service, Air force Service and Army Service

D. First Grade Service, Second Grade Service and Third Grade Services

165. Nicomachus was a court physician to king __________.

A. Xenocrates B. Amyntas III

C. Alexander D. Syracuse

166. The full form of MFN is:

A. Most Favoured Nation

B. Most Favourite Nation

C. Most Forward Nation

D. Multi Favoured Nations

167. Who is writer of the book "Who were Shudras"?

A. Atal Bihari Vajpayee

B. APJ Abdul Kalam

C. B.R. Ambedkar

D. Salman Khurshid

168. By welfare state, citizens should be given the guarantee of minimal ....

A. Wealth B. Land

C. House D. Standard of living

169. According to Marxists the main test of the injustice in society is:

A. Richness B. Poverty

C. Exploitation D. Mode of Production

170. Locke's first Treatise was written during ....

A. 1680–1681 B. 1683–1684

C. 1679–1680 D. 1685–1686

171. Objective Resolution was moved in the first session of the Constituent Assembly on 13 December, _____ by Jawahar Lal Nehru.

A. 1945 B. 1948

C. 1946 D. 1947

172. _____ said, Mill is a messenger of "Hollow Liberty".

A. Barker B. Auguste Comte

C. Aristotle D. Georg Simme

173. Supreme court and High Court have:

1. Judicial review power
2. Impeachment power
3. Power of removing Governor

A. Only 3 B. 1, 2 and 3

C. Only 1 D. Only 2

174. Which Case normally does not come across Lok Adalat?

A. Marriage Cases

B. Compensation Cased pertaining to Motor Accidents

C. Labourer Compensation Cases

D. Murder Cases

175. Friedrich Wilhelm Nietzsche characterised Platonism as the intellectual side of ....

A. Farzi B. Yahudi

C. Christianity D. Islam

176. The book "Reasonableness of Christianity" was published in ....

A. 1692 B. 1660

C. 1695 D. 1690

177. In which among the following cases, the Supreme Court of India propounded the theory of basic structure of the Constitution?

A. Golak Nath

B. Keshvanand Bharati

C. Gopalan vs. State of Madras

D. Minerva Mills

178. Who wrote "The Indian Constitution: Cornerstone of a Nation"?

A. Hobbes B. John Rawls

C. Amartya Sen D. Granville Austin

179. Which of the following is not in the ten principles of social justice?
A. Solidarity
B. Promotion of peace
C. Human Dignity
D. Promotion of political ideology

180. Aristotle was born at __________ in Northern Greece.
A. Chalcis B. Athens
C. Macedon D. Stagira

181. Our Education experts always have given enough emphasis on Activity Based Learning. These Activity based questions make Social Science lessons:
A. Sorrowful B. Non lengthy
C. Joyful D. Comprehensive

182. As an upper primary level teacher, which one of the following is not taken into account while designing an examination with special reference to Political Science?
A. object
B. subject knowledge
C. instructional objective
D. time of teaching

183. A teacher should always inculcate good behaviors and manners among his/her students. Which from the following should be used to increase correct responses and appropriate behaviour?
A. Bet B. Praise
C. Reward D. Arrogance

184. According to John Dewey, schools must prepare students for
A. present life B. political career
C. entrepreneurship D. future life

185. A Teacher is supposed to be the Friend Philosopher and Guide. He should plan his evaluation while keeping in mind all types of learning aspects. As a teacher of Political Science, according to you what type of evaluation identifies learning deficiencies and difficulties of the learners?
A. Summative B. Diagnostic
C. Formative D. Assertive

186. A teacher always should prepare a proper lesson planning and keep a record of it every time. You should plan your lesson always keeping the linkage area of the child's life at school. The suggestion of National Curriculum Framework (2005) is that Social Science must link a child's life at school with:
A. expectation of teacher
B. life inside the orthodox classroom
C. only bookish knowledge
D. life outside the orthodox classroom

187. Which of the following statement is not true in case of MCQs?
A. Only one of the choices is the correct answer
B. All choices appear to be plausible
C. Even an inexperienced teacher can prepare the questions easily
D. Error-free and quick evaluation is possible by computer

188. Which of the of the followings indicates child's physical growth?
A. Negative B. Comparative
C. Positive D. Quantitative

189. Which of the following is not the tool for Formative Assessment in scholastic domain?
A. MCQs
B. Oral Questions
C. Communication Skill
D. Project Works

190. In the preliminary and primary level the fundamental subject is EVS, which is the combination of Science and Social Science, but at the upper primary level it has been distributed in various subjects among them which of the following subjects is not included?
A. Geography B. Psychology
C. History D. Political Science

191. From the ancient ages we have heard from many stories the thoughts like "Failure is the Pillar of Success" , "Man made mistakes" etc A similar statement is "Individual learns from his own mistakes" This based on which learning theory according to you?

A. Instrumental conditioning
B. Insight of the Out side
C. Classical conditioning
D. Trial & Error

192. Which of the following statements is not true?
A. Education is a goal-oriented process
B. Development is a quantitative process
C. Learning is a process of behavioral changes
D. Growth is a biological process

193. As people grow older, the __________ of learning __________.
A. quality, declines B. speed, declines
C. fluently, declines D. quantity, declines

194. A good teacher always needs to use various kinds of Teaching Aids to make the teaching procedure more and more fruitful. According to you which type of teaching aids are most useful in the learning Social Science?
A. Drawing Tools B. Clay
C. Audio-visual aids D. Museum

195. The suggestion of National Curriculum Framework (2005) is for the upgradation of Education Policy to make it most effective and Positive. What according to you is the best method to study growth and development of the child?
A. Social Method
B. Developmental Method
C. Qualitive Method
D. Psychoanalytic Method

196. As a teacher you are given two choices one to teach EVS at the primary level and another to teach Social Science at the upper primary level. You have opted for Social Science. What according to you the classroom processes involving in Social Science helps in developing:
A. Skill, knowledge and expression
B. Knowledge
C. Expression
D. Skill

197. A modern man first need to learn past for the better learning of the present. According to you the study of Social Science and EVS is necessary for
1. The development of infra-structure facilities
2. The understanding of educational problems
3. The understanding of the socio-cultural structure and its relation with environment

A. Only 2 B. 1, 2 and 3
C. Only 3 D. Only 1

198. According to you as a teacher of Political Science which of the following approaches have been considered while developing social and political life textbooks for the upper primary and Secondary level?
1. Learning through retention based on facts and data.
2. Learning through use of concrete examples and experiences.

A. Only 1
B. Only 2
C. Both 1 and 2
D. Neither 1 nor 2

199. The Expert Child Psychologists are working day and night for inventing better educational policy for our child, PSRN is also a part of this invention. Term PSRN in child development implies:
A. Perceptual skill only
B. Problem solving, reasoning and numeracy
C. Problem solving relationship and numeracy
D. Perceptual skill, reasoning and numeracy

200. Every time the situation takes under the scanner at the time of teaching debatable and controversial. According to you while teaching controversial issues in Social Science class, one should always:
A. Take them up occasionally
B. Conduct brief discussions
C. Completely avoid confrontations
D. Take them up with proper planning to initiate a dignified discussion

ANSWERS

1	2	3	4	5	6	7	8	9	10
C	D	D	A	A	C	A	C	B	C
11	12	13	14	15	16	17	18	19	20
B	A	B	D	C	C	B	B	C	B
21	22	23	24	25	26	27	28	29	30
C	D	D	D	D	A	C	A	D	C
31	32	33	34	35	36	37	38	39	40
D	B	C	A	A	B	C	B	A	D
41	42	43	44	45	46	47	48	49	50
D	A	C	D	A	A	D	A	C	B
51	52	53	54	55	56	57	58	59	60
C	A	D	A	A	A	D	D	D	B
61	62	63	64	65	66	67	68	69	70
D	B	B	A	C	C	B	C	C	B
71	72	73	74	75	76	77	78	79	80
D	B	C	A	C	B	B	A	D	D
81	82	83	84	85	86	87	88	89	90
D	D	B	B	B	A	C	A	D	C
91	92	93	94	95	96	97	98	99	100
B	C	A	A	D	C	D	D	C	B
101	102	103	104	105	106	107	108	109	110
C	C	D	D	B	D	D	D	D	D
111	112	113	114	115	116	117	118	119	120
B	D	B	A	D	D	A	C	B	A
121	122	123	124	125	126	127	128	129	130
D	C	B	B	A	A	C	A	A	B
131	132	133	134	135	136	137	138	139	140
C	C	A	B	C	A	B	A	C	B
141	142	143	144	145	146	147	148	149	150
D	A	C	A	A	D	C	A	D	B
151	152	153	154	155	156	157	158	159	160
B	C	D	B	A	D	A	D	B	D
161	162	163	164	165	166	167	168	169	170
C	C	D	B	B	A	C	D	C	C
171	172	173	174	175	176	177	178	179	180
C	A	C	D	C	C	B	D	D	D
181	182	183	184	185	186	187	188	189	190
C	D	B	A	B	D	C	D	D	B
191	192	193	194	195	196	197	198	199	200
D	B	B	C	B	A	C	B	D	D

Previous Paper (Solved)

Delhi Subordinate Services Selection Board (DSSSB)

PGT (Political Science) Teacher Recruitment Exam, 2018*

Post Specific Subject-Related Questions

1. In traditional autocratic system, the manager would specify both the standards for performance and the methods for achieving them. In a participative management system, which of the following is specified by a manager?

A. Only the methods for achieving the standards of performance
B. Neither the standards of performance nor the methods for achieving them
C. Both the standards of performance and the methods for achieving them
D. Only the standards of performance

2. Which one of the following is NOT the characteristic of Max Weber's Model of bureaucracy?

A. Offices are arranged in the form of hierarchy
B. All organizational members are to be selected on the basis of technical qualifications
C. Control in the bureaucratic organization is based on personally applied rules
D. Officials pursue, their careers within the organisation

3. Which of the following is NOT a basic of behaviouralism according to David Easton?

A. Discoverable informalities in human behaviour
B. Value commitment
C. Inter-disciplinary focus
D. Systematization

4. Which of the following elements is ignored in the classical theory?

A. Formal structure
B. Managerial structure
C. Informal patterns
D. Principles of organisation

5. Who among the following revised the Human Relations approach of Prof. E. Mayo into a New Human Relations Model of Management?

A. Fritz Roethlisberger
B. Rensis Likert
C. James MacGregor
D. Mary Parker Follett

6. Which among the following are the features ot participative management?

1. Overlapping
2. Cross functional linkages
3. Multi-directional communication
4. Effective man-to-man relationship

Select the correct answer using the codes given below:

A. 1 and 2 B. 2 and 3
C. 1, 2 and 3 D. 1 and 4

7. Which of the following does NOT consist of the ideal characteristic of bureaucracy as propounded by Max Weber?

A. Impersonal order B. Monocratic type
C. Hierarchy D. Informal methods

8. Which one of the following does NOT constitute the human relations movement of Elton Mayo?

A. The first inquiry
B. Hawthorne Studies
C. Shop Management
D. The great illumination

*Exam held on 05-08-2018.

9. Which one of the following approaches emphasizes more on social and psychological factors at the workplace which in turn determine the workers' satisfaction and organizational output?
A. System approach
B. Behavioural approach
C. Classical approach
D. Human Relations approach

10. Which one of the following is not a significant feature of the Hawthorne research?
A. Emphasis on rules
B. Informal organization
C. Human Relations approach
D. Man's social nature

11. An organization system is concerned primarily with
A. Defined sets of interactions
B. A set of connected parts
C. The roles that individuals play
D. Interdependent parts and their interactions

12. Which of the following is NOT correct about system approach?
A. A system is more than sum of its parts
B. A system can be considered to be either closed or open
C. Boundaries in a system are NOT rigid, impenetrable or closed
D. If a system is to achieve dynamic equilibrium, it must not have interactions with its environment

13. Consider the following statements in respect of bureaucratic form of organizational design
1. The primary strength of the bureaucracy lies in its ability to perform non-standardized activities in a highly efficient manner.
2. In bureaucracy, there is little need for innovative and experienced decision makers, below the level of senior executives
3. The pervasiveness of rules and regulations substitutes for managerial discretion.

Which of the statements given above is/are correct?
A. 2 only C. 2 and 3
B. 1 and 3 D. 1, 2 and 3

14. The term 'Gang Plank', used by Henry Fayol refers to:
A. Need for level jumping
B. Conformity to hierarchy
C. Emphasis on formalism
D. Defeat of objectives

15. Which among the following is/are the basis of Herbert Simon's decisionmaking theory?
1. The need to take administrative principles seriously.
2. Preferences and social conditioning of the administrator.
3. Orders of superior.

Select the correct answer using the codes given below:
A. 1 only B. 1 and 2
C. 2 only D. 3 only

16. The principle of anonymity of civil servants goes with:
A. The principle of neutrality
B. The principle of ministerial responsibility
C. The principle of committed bureaucracy
D. The principle of rational bureaucracy

17. Political neutrality is:
A. Absence of political bias in Civil Services
B. Absence of extra-party activities
C. Supporting every policy of the government
D. Absence of political influences on Civil Services and loyalty to government

18. Identify the trend which is NOT visible in Civil Services of many countries in modern times.
A. Growth of diversification by employment of more and more technical personnel and specialists
B. Continuous extension of powers of the Civil Service
C. Change in the Concept of Civil Services neutrality
D. Less Emphasis on moral and professional standards

19. Who among the following regards politics as ethics writ large?
A. Aristotle B. Machiavelli
C. Ivor Brown D. Bluntschli

20. Which of the following approaches combines the institutional approach emphasizing on democratic form of government and representative bodies of legislatures with the empirical analyses of the behavioural approach?
A. Structuralism approach
B. Developmentalism approach
C. Pluralism approach
D. None of the above

21. Which approach bases its study of explaining political phenomena with the use of numerical and statistical data like tables, graphs, particularly in analysing electoral behaviour of voters and the parties, election surveys, etc?
A. Systems theory approach
B. Quantitative or statistical approach
C. Behaviourlism approach
D. Simulation approach

22. The structural-functional approach and the input-output approach have been derived from:
A. The political simulation approach
B. The quantitative approach
C. The general systems theory approach
D. The sociologoical approach

23. Derived from the political stimulation approach this theory studies the characteristics of decision making on individuals or groups who may influence the decision makers though they may not be in the capacity of taking decision themselves:
A. Political stimulation approach
B. Game theory approach
C. Decision making approach
D. Political communication approach

24. Which of the following propounded the theory of separation of powers?
A. Jeans Bodin
B. Montesquieu
C. Thomas Hobbes
D. George Washington

25. In recent times in most of the federal countries:
A. The centre has become very powerful
B. The units have become very powerful
C. The centre has become very weak
D. The states and centre have become very powerful

26. The Parliamentary form of Government was first developed in:
A. Britain B. France
C. Greece D. Switzerland

27. Which of the following is an essential feature of a totalitarian system?
A. A weak legislature
B. A unitary Constitution
C. Absence of legally recognized opposition
D. Centralised economic planning

28. In the Presidential form of Government, the head of the government:
A. Is elected by the legislature
B. Takes part in the discussion of the legislature
C. Casts the deciding votes in a no-confidence motion
D. Remains aloof from the legislature

29. A confederation differs from a federation in so far as:
A. It is an alliance between independent and sovereign States
B. It has a common centre
C. Its member cannot withdraw from confederation
D. Its member retain sovereign authority

30. A telling example of a fusion of the Presidential and Parliamentary forms of Government is provided by:
A. Switzerland B. Canada
C. France D. Germany

31. Which of the following is pre-requisite for constitutionalism?
A. Limited Government
B. A Written Constitution

C. Guarantee of Fundamental Rights
D. Division of Powers

32. Which one of the following defines correctly the term 'Government'?
A. The administrative system of a State and distinguished from political executive, legislature and judiciary
B. Organisation of political executive and administrators
C. The political executive, legislature and judiciary
D. The complex system comprising all elements - political executive, administration, legislature and judiciary

33. The post-war epoch has seen the transformation of the Cabinet Government into:
A. Bureaucratic depotism
B. One party dominant rule
C. The Prime Ministerial Government
D. Judicial supremacy

34. Which one of the following principles distinguished the Cabinet system from the Presidential system?
A. Fixed tenure of Government
B. Judicial Review
C. The relationship of the legislature with the executive
D. The concentration or division of governmental powers

35. Pressure Groups differ from political parties in so far as:
A. They have larger membership
B. They contest elections
C. They pursue broader objectives
D. Their field of operation is very limited

36. A political party has been defined as "an association organized in support of some principles or policy which by constitutional means endeavours to make the determinant of Government" by:
A. MacIver B. Barker
C. Bryce D. Machiavelli

37. Which one of the following is an apt description of Bodin's theory of sovereignty?
A. Absolute sovereignty
B. Limited sovereignty
C. Political sovereignty
D. Popular sovereignty

38. Who among the following thinkers criticized the Austenian theory of sovereignty on the ground that law is not the command of the sovereign but an expression of the community's sense of right?
A. Laski B. Krabbe
C. Duguit D. Gierke

39. Associations are not persona ficta but real persons existing prior to the State. This view was propounded by:
A. Hobbes B. Hegel
C. Duguit D. Gierke

40. About which of the following thinkers it has been said that his theory of the State is "an incongruous mixture of natural rights and physiological metaphor"'?
A. Bradley
B. Spencer
C. Bluntschli
D. Burke

41. Match List-I with List-II and select the correct.

List-I	*List-II*
(*a*) The State is the soul writ large	1. Hegel
(*b*) The State is coordinating and adjusting	2. Weber
(*c*) The State has the monopoly of legitimate physical force	3. Ernest Barker
(*d*) The State is the self-realizing and self-actualizing individual	4. Plato

Codes:

	(*a*)	(*b*)	(*c*)	(*d*)
A.	4	3	2	1
B.	3	2	1	4
C.	1	3	2	4
D.	4	2	3	1

42. The idea of social contract has been recently revived under a new form by:
A. Nozick B. Rawls
C. Oakshott D. Hannah Arendt

43. The theory of Social Contract primarily seeks
A. to explore the historical origin of the State
B. to explain the basis of political obligation
C. to justify the status quo
D. to bring out a radical transformation

44. Which one of the following statements about Rousseau is correct?
A. He perfected the theory of Social Contract
B. He repudiated the theory of Contract alltogether.
C. He transformed the theory of Contract into an idealist mode of political discourse.
D. He added nothing to the theories of Hobbes and Locke beyond combining their views.

45. The Historical Theory of the Origin of the State was propounded by:
A. Sir Henry Maine B. Triestske
C. Oppenheimer D. Durkheim

46. Which one of the following theories held that the State is a product and manifestation of the irreconcilability of class antagonisms?
A. Evolutionary Theory
B. Anarchist Theory
C. Marxist-Leninist Theory
D. Guild-Socialist Theory

47. What is the correct order of primacy of the following layers of social structure according to the Materialistic Interpretation History?
1. Relations of production
2. Ideology
3. Forces of production
4. Legal and Political organizations

Select the correct answer using the codes given below:
A. 1, 3, 2, 4 B. 3, 1, 4, 2
C. 3, 4, 1, 2 D. 2,3,4, 1

48. Which one of the following political thinkers was the first exponent of the liberal theory of States?
A. John Locke
B. T.H. Green
C. Jean Jacques Rousseau
D. Hobbes

49. "By liberty I mean the eager maintenance of that atmosphere in which men have the opportunity to be their best selves." Laski. Which one of the following expresses the view implied in the above statement?
A. Liberty is the absence of restraint
B. Liberty is what the law permits
C. Liberty is the ability to do what one desires
D. Liberty is the maintenance of conditions for the growth of human personality

50. Which one of the following statements about the Welfare State is correct?
A. A Welfare State is the same as a Socialist State
B. The Welfare State is based on the principles of classical liberalism
C. The Welfare State is Collectivist State
D. The Welfare State embodies the principles of neoliberalism

51. Who among the following thinkers held that "Human consciousness postulates liberty, liberty involves rights and rights demand the State"?
A. Hegel B. Green
C. Bosanquet D. Laski

52. "Rights properly so called are creations of law properly so called."
This definition of rights is associated with:
A. Hobbes B. Hegel
C. Bentham D. Laski

53. The essence of Natural Rights is that:
A. they are derived from a historical state to nature
B. they existed in the state of nature and are not existent in civil society
C. they are the products of nature conceived as concatenatus of physical forces
D. they are in conformity with universal principles of justice and morality

54. Who among the following used the expression "forced to be free" in connection with the notion of liberty of the individual?

A. Rousseau B. Locke
C. Green D. Hobhouse

55. Article ______ of the Constitution speaks of the need to organise Village Panchayats.

A. 15 B. 55
C. 40 D. 48

56. The 73rd Amendment Act came into force from:

A. January, 1980 B. April, 1991
C. April, 1993 D. April 24, 1993

57. Who is to conduct the elections to the Panchayats and Municipalities?

A. State Government
B. Central Government
C. State Election Commission
D. Central Election Commission

58. Which of the following is correct in respect of financial powers of Local Government in India?

A. Local Governments have constitutionally earmarked taxation power.
B. Local Governments are empowered to levy such tax as are permitted under the law.
C. Local Governments are empowered to levy charges all times within their share of activities.
D. Local Governments are empowered to levy taxes with the permission of the department concerned

59. Which of the following stands at the apex of the three-tier structure?

A. Panchayat Samiti B. Gram Panchayat
C. Zilla Panchayat D. None of the above

60. Local-Self Government are included in the:

A. State list
B. Union List
C. Concurrent list
D. Both State and Union list with centre having the final say

61. How many types of emergencies have been envisaged under the Indian Constitution?

A. Four C. Five
B. Six D. Three

62. The Constitution of India draws its authority from:

A. The Constituent Assembly which represented all sections of society
B. The Indian Independence Act, 1947
C. The people of India
D. The President

63. The Finance Commission makes recommendations about:

A. Distribution of net proceeds of taxes between the Centre and the States
B. Economy in expenditure
C. Grants-in-aid including determination of the principles governing them
D. Both B and C

64. The Comptroller and Auditor General exercises control over State Finances through its power to"

A. Recommend allocation of Grant-in-aid to the States
B. Prescribe the forms in which the account etc. of the State have to be maintained
C. Make suggestions for affecting economies in expenditure of the State
D. Re-allocation of revenues between the Centre and the States from time to time

65. In the matter of distribution of revenue between the Centre and the States, the Constitution has largely followed the:

A. Canadian Constitution
B. American Constitution
C. Government of India Act, 1935
D. Swiss Constitution

66. Who said that the Constitution of India established a unitary State with subsidiary federal features rather than a federal State with subsidiary unitary features?

A. K. Santhanami
B. K. C. Wheare
C. Sir Ivor Jennings
D. K. M. Panikkar

67. Which one of the following incidents prompted Vinobha Bhave to initiate the Bhoodan Movement in India?
A. Nalgonda incident
B. Srikakulam incident
C. Naxalbari incident
D. Madhubani incident

68. Judicial control over local bodies aims at:
A. Ensuring that they are discharging their obligations within the limit of the statute
B. Prevention of undue interference by the executive in the working of local bodies
C. Ensuring non-intervention by political parties in local affairs
D. None of the above

69. A Judge of the High Court may be removed from office during his tenure by:
A. The Governor, if State Legislature passes a resolution to this effect by two-thirds majority
B. The President, on, the basis of a resolution passed by the Parliament by two-thirds majority
C. The Chief Justice of the Supreme Court, on the recommendation of the Parliament
D. None of the above

70. The Judicial Review in the Indian Constitution is based on:
A. Procedure established by law
B. Due process of law
C. Rule of law
D. Precedents and Conventions

71. Sarkaria Commission was set up to review the relations between:
A. The Prime Minister and the President
B. Executive and the Judiciary
C. Legislature and the Executive
D. Centre and the States

72. Violation of the "Rule of Law" arises mostly from:
A. Limited Franchise
B. Delegated Legislation
C. Lack of checks and balances
D. None of the above

73. The correct sequence in Game theory is:
A. game - choice - player - equilibrium
B. payoffs - strategies - system - game
C. payoffs- choice- player- game
D. systems - equilibrium - game - player

74. Which one of the following statements is not correct?
A. Diplomacy is an instrument of foreign policy
B. Major international agreements are usually negotiated by Foreign Ministers
C. Diplomats do not play now as great a role in international negotiations as they once did
D. Diplomats now get greater latitude than they enjoyed 19th Century

75. Which one does not contribute to the formation of International Government?
A. Expansion of international trade
B. Establishment of international organization
C. Inter-state rivalry
D. Means of communication

76. In his realistic theory of International Politics Morgenthau's autonomy of political sphere denotes:
A. autonomy of the State in international sphere
B. autonomy of the decision-makers vis-a vis-the legislature
C. autonomy of the political action in complete disregard to other standards of thought
D. autonomy of the policy-makers vis-a vis other agencies or organs of the government

77. The Marxists perceive international politics as:
A. A struggle for power between the Bourgeois and Socialist systems with the hope of inevitable triumph of international proletarianism
B. A struggle for power between two nations or group of nations that can be managed by maintaining balances of power

C. Interactions among States that can be peacefully
D. Interactions among States guided and molded by leaders of those States

78. Decision making theorist's focus on:
A. Foreign policy decisions made by a State
B. Impact of domestic politics on foreign policy decisions
C. Specific decisions makers who speak and act in the name of a State
D. Actual or objective environment that influence foreign policy decisions

79. Who among the following is the pioneer of the theory of neo-realism?
A. Kenneth Waltz
B. Hans Morgenthau
C. Barry Buzari
D. Raul Prebish

80. In the positive-sum game:
A. what one actor wins, the other losses
B. gains and losses are not necessarily equal and both the sides may gain
C. gains and losses are necessarily equal and both the sides may gain
D. both the actors lose

81. Schelling's concepts of, 'mixed-motive game' richly embodies:
A. political and economic points of view
B. cultural and ideological points of view
C. psychological and sociological points of view
D. strategic and military points of view

82. Central feature of Immanuel Wallerstein's work is:
A. world system
B. nation
C. regional systems
D. underdevelopment

83. Which among the following scholars propounded the systems approach towards the study of international relations?
A. David Easton B. Gabriel Almond
C. C. McClelland D. J.W. Burton

84. Match List-I with List-II and select the correct answer using the code given below.

List-I (Scholar)	***List-II (Theory/Approach)***
(*a*) Morgenthau	1. Systems Theory
(*b*) Bernard Cohen	2. Game Theory
(*c*) Merton Kaplan	3. Decision making approach
(*d*) Emile Berd	4. Realist School

Codes:

	(*a*)	(*b*)	(*c*)	(*d*)
A.	4	3	1	2
B.	2	1	3	4
C.	4	1	3	2
D.	2	3	1	4

85. Which one of the following approaches or modest of international politics does not give importance to the role of state as an actor?
A. Dependency model
B. Realist model
C. Nee-realist model
D. Interdependence pluralist model

86. Which country was appointed the first Chairman of the Decolonization Committee of the United Nations?
A. USA B. Sweden
C. India D. Japan

87. Consider the following statements in respect of the general systems theory:
1. The general systems theory is highly attractive from the standpoint an empirical research.
2. The theory has been criticized for falling to adequately cater for concept such as political power and influence.

Which of the statement given above is/are correct?
A. 1 only B. 2 only
C. Both 1 and 2 D. Neither 1 nor 2

88. What is the model that deals with a conflict situation where all the rivals are to benefit in different degrees, described as?
A. Malign - conflict situation
B. Benign - conflict situation.
C. Zero - sum situation
D. Non-zero - sum situation

89. The Work Essays on Nationalism is authored by:
A. Herry Hart B. Hal Fisher
C. C. J. Hayes D. None of the above

90. According to Morgenthau the best means of preserving peace in a society of sovereign nation is:
A. National Interest B. Diplomacy
C. Foreign Trade D. Autonomy

91. The term 'City State' is generally associated with:
A. Ancient Egypt B. Ancient Greece
C. Ancient China D. None of the three

92. The statement that the State is an ethical institution which is indispensable for the full moral development of man is attributed to:
A. Idealists B. Marxists
C. Anarchists D. Individualists

93. The view that the State is a necessary evil is associated with:
A. Marxists B. Sophists
C. Anarchists D. Individualists

94. The concept of 'legal sovereignty' was for the first time propounded by:
A. Locke B. T. H. Green
C. Rousseau D. Hobbes

95. "If sovereignty is not absolute, no State exists"—Who said this?
A. Hobbes B. John Locke
C. Jean Bodin D. John Austin

96. De-jure sovereign refers to:
A. A person in whom the entire authority is vested by the Constitution but does not make use of the power
B. The constitutional ruler of State
C. A person who is authorised by Parliament to rule the country
D. A person who has legal right govern and command obedience

97. Under democratic system of Government the popular sovereignty resides in:
A. Popularly elected representative body
B. The electorate
C. The people
D. All the above

98. According to Hobbes the State of nature was a period of:
A. Peace and scarcity
B. Religious dominance
C. Constant warfare
D. Peace and plenty

99. "Man is born free and every where he is in chains" was said by:
A. Rousseau B. Locke
C. Marx D. Aristotle

100. Who asserted that the State would ultimately wither away?
A. Aristotle B. Gandhi
C. Marx D. Kant

101. The Parliament and the Constitution are instruments of:
A. Economic justice B. Social justice
C. Political justice D. Legal justice

102. The proposal of which plan established the Constituent Assembly?
A. The Cripps Mission Plan
B. The Cabinet Mission Plan
C. The Mount Batten Plan
D. None of these

103. Which of the following is not treated as part of the Constitution?
A. Pressure groups
B. Fundamental duties
C. Fundamental Rights
D. Preamble

104. Total number of Schedules in the Indian Constitution are:
A. 11 B. 12
C. 6 D. 4

105. Which Part of the Indian Constitution deals with the Fundamental Rights?
A. Part Ill B. Part V
C. Part II D. Part I

106. The Human Rights Day is observed every year on:
A. 10th December
B. 10th November
C. 30th December
D. 2oth January

107. Hot line facilities for victims of human rights are available for
A. 18 Hours B. 22 Hours
C. 24 Hours D. 20 Hours

108. "Arthashastra" was written by:
A. Kautilya B. T. H. Green
C. Plato D. Aristotle

109. Which among the following is the meaning of 'Polis'?
A. City-State B. Village
C. State D. Country

110. Which among the following is an element of State?
A. Army B. King
C. Treasury D. Sovereignty

111. Theory of Separation of Power was propounded by:
A. Carl Fedrich B. J. S. Mill
C. Montesquieu D. Aristotle

112. Democracy is a system of Government in which the final power rests with:
A. The Politicians B. The Civil Service
C. The People D. The Mob

113. Which is consider as fourth estate of the Government?
A. Political parties B. Pressure groups
C. Public opinion D. Newspaper

114. Who appoints the Ambassadors?
A. President
B. Defence Minister
C. External Affairs Minister
D. P.M.

115. Which among the following is a permanent member of Security Council of U.N.?
A. U.K. B. Brazil
C. Taiwan D. India

116. "My Experiment with Truth" is written by:
A. J.P. B. Patel
C. M. K. Gandhi D. V. P. Singh

117. In India, the first Municipal Corporation was set up in which one among the following?
A. Bombay B. Delhi
C. Madras D. Calcutta

118. Who is the Head of the Cabinet?
A. Home Minister B. Prime Minister
C. Finance Minister D. President

119. National Human Rights Commission was established in the year:
A. 1945 B. 1993
C. 1950 D. 1948

120. Under single transferable vote system each voter can:
A. Indicate one preference less than the seats to be filled up
B. Indicate as many preferences as there are candidates etc., be elected
C. Indicate only one preference
D. Indicate only two preferences

121. The rights provided by Constitution are called
A. Economic Right
B. Optional Right
C. Governmental Right
D. Fundamental Right

122. The most important aspect of Secularism is its ______ of religion from State:
A. Include B. Separation
C. Both A and B D. None of these

123. History provides many examples of discrimination, exclusion and persecution on the ground of:
A. Caste B. Law
C. Religion D. Exclusion

124. A group of people who come close to each other to attain their common aim of power is known as:
A. Factional Group
B. Interest Group
C. Political Party
D. Political Leadership

125. Which of these is the main component of Political Party?
A. Leaders B. Active members
C. The followers D. All of these

126. UPA stands for:
A. United Progressive Alliance
B. Union Progressive Alliance

C. United Progressive Allowance
D. Union Protested Alliance

127. When several parties in a multi-party system join hands for the purpose of contesting elections and winning power, it is called:
A. Group B. Alliance
C. Uni-party system D. None of these

128. Who among the following is known as "The Father of the Indian Renaissance"?
A. Swami Dayanand Saraswati
B. Swami Vivekananda
C. Ishwar Chandra Vidyasagar
D. Rajaram Mohan Roy

129. Separation of same religion from the State in democratic societies is because of:
A. To interrupt religious teaching
B. To protect the freedom of Individual exit from their religion
C. Both A and B
D. None of these

130. How many essentials are required to constitute a State?
A. Three B. Six
C. Five D. Four

131. Materialistic interpretation of history was propounded by:
A. Mensheviks B. Lenin
C. Bolsheviks D. None of these

132. Which political theory propounded that State will ultimately disappear?
A. Syndacatism B. Communism
C. Fascism D. Fabian socialism

133. A voluntary union of sovereign and independent States is called:
A. Confederation B. Unitary State
C. Federation D. None of these

134. Which of the political philosophers was more admitted by the American Founding Fathers and his thoughts on the importance of private property were reflected in the drafting and historical development of the American Constitution?
A. Rousseau B. Thomas Hobbes
C. John Locke D. None of these

135. "An essay concerning Human Understanding" is written by:
A. J. J. Rousseau B. Thomas Hobbes
C. John Locke D. None of these

136. Constitution classified as rigid and flexible in a book titled "Studies in History and Jurisprudence" was written by:
A. T. H. Green B. Gilchrist
C. Lord Bryce D. None of these

137. Which of these books represents the scheme of Plato's Philosophy?
A. The Republic B. The Laws
C. The Politics D. None of these

138. Law is "the body of Principles recognized and applied by the State in the administration of justice" is said by:
A. Salmond B. Holland
C. Green D. None of these

139. The ideas of Aristotle are more acceptable to the West than Plato's because he propagated:
A. Tyranny B. Democracy
C. Rule of law D. None of these

140. Who was named the first leader of the opposition in Ayub Khan's constituted first national assembly?
A. MaulanaTamizuddin Khan
B. Yousaf Khattak
C. Mumtaz Daultana
D. Sardar Bahadur Khan

141. Who was the Governor General of India during the 1st Indo Pakistan conflict over Kashmir in 1948?
A. Mahatama Gandhi B. Lord Mountbatten
C. Zahir Hussain D. Krishna Menon

142. According to John Locke, the best form of Government is:
A. Aristocracy B. Monarchy
C. Democracy D. None of these

143. The Fascism of Plato got birth in 4th Century BC, whereas the modern Fascism in the Product of early:
A. 20th Century B. 18th Century
C. 19th Century D. None of these

144. The turning point in the life of Plato came when he was:
A. 28 years B. 24 years
C. 26 years D. None of these

145. Karl Marx is known for his theory of:
A. Materialistic Interpretation of history
B. Force as the Basis of State
C. Dialectical Spiritualism
D. None of these

146. "Justice as treating equals equally and unequals unequally" who said this:
A. J.S. Mill B. T.H. Green
C. Aristotle D. None of these

147. The concept of "legal sovereignty" was for the first time given by:
A. Locke B. Bentham
C. Hobbes D. None of these

148. Number of lists of subjects for law making in 1973 Constitution is:
A. One B. Two
C. Three D. None of these

149. The doctrine which is a curious blend of German Idealism, English economics and French revolutionary and social thoughts is known as:
A. Fascism B. Communism
C. Socialism D. None of these

150. A form of closure under which a bill is divided into compartments, groups of which must be completely deal with each day is called:
A. Guillotine closure B. Simple closure
C. Kangroo closure D. None of these

151. A necessary normal code for conducting the business of the State is called:
A. Constitution B. Ordinance
C. Convention D. None of these

152. "Power tends to corruption and absolute power corrupts absolutely" is the famous quotation by:
A. Lord Curzon
B. Lord Acton
C. Winston Churchill
D. Nond of these

153. As per Marx in the stage of communism the governing principle will be:
A. Every one is equal, but some are more equal than others
B. From each according to his ability to each according to his work
C. From each according to his ability to each according to his needs
D. None of these

154. A ______ is a type of sovereign State characterized by a union of partially self-governing States or regions united by a Central Government.
A. Confederation B. Federation
C. Unitary State D. None of these

155. Those who are active against the very existence of State are known as:
A. Anarchists B. Fascists
C. Socialists D. None of these

156. "Political Science begins and ends with the State" is said by:
A. Professor Garner
B. Paul Janet
C. Stephen Leacock
D. None of these

157. A discourse on the origin of inequality and the social contract was presented by:
A. Rousseau B. Hobbes
C. John Locke D. None of these

158. "Introduction to the Principles of Morals and Legislation (1789)" was written by:
A. John Locke B. Jeremy Bentham
C. J.S. Mill D. None of these

159. "The cause of sedition is always to be found in inequality" is said by:
A. Machiavelli B. Aristotle
C. Plato D. None of these

160. Which one of the following is not a common feature of federalism in U.S.A and India?
A. Two sets of judicial organizations
B. The existence of the Supreme Court
C. Distribution of powers between the Union and the States
D. Written Constitution

161. One of the chief defects of Universal Adult Franchise is:
A. It lays emphasis on the principle of equality
B. It leads to rule by ignorants
C. It protects the right of minorities
D. It gives chance to a common man to be associated with the decisions of the government

162. Which one of the following is the most important feature of elections?
A. Peaceful change of government
B. Removal of bottlenecks in the working of democracy
C. Helping citizens maintain their rights
D. Elimination of multi-party system

163. The political parties are helpful to poor people in so far as they:
A. Render them legal assistance
B. Help them to contest elections
C. Provide free education to their children
D. Provide them the basic amenities of life

164. Political parties contribute to the proper working of parliamentary government by
A. By maintaining peace in the country
B. By educating the public about the various problems facing the country
C. By providing organized majority to back the Council of Ministers
D. Assisting poor candidates with finances to contest the election

165. Political parties are undemocratic in so far as:
A. They try to implement their programme once they come into power
B. They do not permit their members to express their views independently
C. They criticize the policies of the government
D. They try to contest elections and capture power

166. The pressure groups try to promote the interests of their members by exerting pressure on:
A. The legislature B. The executive
C. The judiciary D. All the above

167. Amongst the agencies of public opinion the press plays an important role. Press can be an effective agency of public opinion only if:
A. It supports the cause of the weaker sections
B. It is highly critical of government policies
C. It is free and Impartial
D. It is committed to the policies of the government

168. Which one of the following statements is correct?
A. Blackstone, an English Jurist, did not consider censorship as a restraint on freedom of speech
B. The French philosophers of the nineteenth century did not çonsider censorship as restraint on freedom of the speech
C. The U.S. courts have not regarded prior censorship as a restriction on freedom of speech
D. All the above considered censorship as restriction of freedom of speech

169. Modern liberalism differs from classical liberalism in so far as:
A. It pleads for free enterprise
B. It stands for a world free from all forms of tyranny and exploitation
C. It is against democratic institutions
D. It does not support individual liberty

170. The modern individualism, which arose as a reaction against extreme collectivism, differs from nineteenth century individualism is so far as:
A. It pleads for maximum function for the state
B. It pleads for absolute freedom for individual
C. It pleads for abolishing the state
D. It focuses attention on group rather than the individual

171. Utilitarianism, which is another theory of liberalism is associated with the name of:
A. Locke B. Green
C. Bentham D. Hegel

172. Evolutionary Socialism believes:
A. In bringing about changes through peaceful methods
B. In bringing changes through revolutionary methods
C. In status quo viz. maintaining the present situation
D. None of the above

173. The Socialists favour nationalization of natural resources with a view:
A. To avoid exploitation
B. To ensure their full utilization
C. To increase production
D. To reduce the cost of production

174. Which one of the followings is not an evolutionary brand of Socialism?
A. Fabianism
B. Guild Socialism
C. State Socialism
D. Communism

175. According to Marx, history is the product of:
A. Political forces
B. Combination of material, religious and political forces
C. Religious forces
D. Material forces

176. According to Marx, a revolution in the Capitalist society takes place.
A. Due to growing antagonism between the haves and havenots
B. Because of dissatisfaction of the educated people with the system
C. Due to increasing importance of political elites
D. Due to foreign interference

177. Communism which was propounded by Marx and Engels and modified by subsequent philosophers believes in:
A. State ownership of all the means of production
B. Complete freedom in the economic sphere
C. Mixed-economy with only key industries under state control
D. None of the above

178. Which one of the following statement has been wrongly attributed to Marx?
A. The state uses force for the protection and promotion of the interests of the ruling class
B. All the phenomena of human society have their origin in material conditions of life
C. The state uses force for the protection and promotion of interests of the poor people
D. State is the executive committee of the bourgeoisie

179. In the political sphere the Fascists stood for:
A. Bi-party system
B. Multi-party system
C. Single party government
D. Partyless government

180. The Fascists were opposed democracy on account of various reasons. Which one of the following reasons has been wrongly listed:
A. Because they believed human inequality
B. Because majority consists of fools
C. Because they felt that the masses were not competent govern themselves
D. Because they did not believe the inherent worth of man

181. "Education is something which makes man self-reliant and selfless". This definition of education is given by:
A. Upanishad B. Rig Veda
C. Bhagavad Gita D. Gandhiji

182. One of the notable schemes of UGC for nurturing social equity for various beneficiary categories in India is:
A. PWD Act, 1995
B. Post-Doctoral Fellowship
C. SET Examination
D. SSA

183. The Literary rate of Female Dalit of Bihar according to 2011 census is:
A. 38.5% B. 44.6%
C. 83% D. 62%

184. Hoy's definition of school culture is the ______ of an organization.
A. Belief B. Intellectual
C. Emotional D. Environmental

185. Studies of teacher identity and its impact on instruction consists of 3 broad types of inquiry. Which of the following is not the part of these:
A. Identity formation
B. Physical altitude
C. Characteristics of teacher identity
D. Identity narratives

186. In addition to discourses regarding student demographics and perseverance teachers use the discourse of _____ to define the performance of effective teacher.
A. Perseverance
B. Nurturing
C. Student demographics
D. Perfomance

187. Teacher identity is viewed through the lens of _____ which is closely linked to school culture.
A. Cultural identity
B. Student parameters
C. Classroom environmental
D. Community practice

188. If schools can develop a _______ school culture, they can be more successful.
A. Negative B. Positive
C. Translative D. Re-active

189. Effects of technology on different processes does not include:
A. Industrialization B. Urbanization
C. Modernization D. Liberalization

190. As of the International Schools Consultancy's List of January 2015, how many International Schools does India have?
A. 1340 B. 410
C. 820 D. 1000

191. Whose directives State, qualifying ages for candidates who wish to take board exams?
A. KSEEB, UGC, CBSE
B. KSERT, NCERT, KSEEB
C. UGC, NCERT and CBSE
D. KGC, UGC, NCTE

192. School culture is touted as a _____ strategy.
A. Perform C. Reform
B. Civic D. Critic

193. Which management can be a predictive of school culture?
A. Friendship B. Entertainment
C. Leadership D. Risk

194. Actual learning phase step in the process of learning emphasises on:
A. A goal
B. A motive
C. Learning situation
D. A block to achievement of goal

195. Which of the following is not a factor that influences learning?
A. Environmental and other factors
B. Individual difference of learners
C. Learning is a monotonous process
D. Teachers enthusiasm in classroom learning

196. Cognitive characteristics of learners are related to:
A. Learner's personal life
B. Academic performance of the learner
C. Social and emotional perceptive of learners
D. Skills of learner concerned to brain

197. _____ refers to neither influence nor obstruction of previously learned knowledge skill to a new learning situation.
A. Positive transfer B. Negative transfer
C. Lateral transfer D. Zero transfer

198. CPD in pedagogy and practice stands for
A. Continuing Professional Development
B. Classroom Learning Programme Description
C. Competitive Perspective Deterioration
D. Cognitive Pulse Development

199. The follow-up review should be conducted once there has been time and other tasks identified in the action plan:
A. To encourage the review
B. To complete the study unit
C. To evaluate the content
D. To re-consider the objectives

200. How many criterias of successful praise are listed?
A. 10 B. 8
C. 6 D. 18

ANSWERS

1	2	3	4	5	6	7	8	9	10
D	C	B	C	B	D	D	C	D	A
11	12	13	14	15	16	17	18	19	20
D	D	D	A	B	A	D	B	C	B
21	22	23	24	25	26	27	28	29	30
C	C	C	B	A	A	C	D	D	C
31	32	33	34	35	36	37	38	39	40
B	D	C	C	C	A	A	B	D	B
41	42	43	44	45	46	47	48	49	50
A	B	A	C	A	C	B	A	D	A
51	52	53	54	55	56	57	58	59	60
B	C	A	A	C	D	C	C	C	A
61	62	63	64	65	66	67	68	69	70
D	C	*	B	C	B	A	A	B	A
71	72	73	74	75	76	77	78	79	80
D	C	A	D	C	C	A	D	A	B
81	82	83	84	85	86	87	88	89	90
C	A	C	A	A	C	C	C	D	A
91	92	93	94	95	96	97	98	99	100
B	A	D	D	D	D	C	C	A	C
101	102	103	104	105	106	107	108	109	110
*	B	A	B	A	A	C	A	A	D
111	112	113	114	115	116	117	118	119	120
C	C	D	A	A	C	C	B	B	B
121	122	123	124	125	126	127	128	129	130
D	B	C	C	D	A	B	D	*	D
131	132	133	134	135	136	137	138	139	140
D	B	A	C	C	C	A	A	C	D
141	142	143	144	145	146	147	148	149	150
B	C	A	A	A	C	B	*	C	A
151	152	153	154	155	156	157	158	159	160
A	B	C	B	A	A	A	B	B	A
161	162	163	164	165	166	167	168	169	170
B	A	D	B	B	D	C	D	B	D
171	172	173	174	175	176	177	178	179	180
C	A	A	D	D	A	A	C	C	D
181	182	183	184	185	186	187	188	189	190
B	B	B	D	B	B	D	B	D	B
191	192	193	194	195	196	197	198	199	200
C	A	C	C	C	D	D	A	D	C

Previous Paper (Solved)

Delhi Subordinate Services Selection Board

DSSSB–PGT (Political Science) Recruitment Exam, 2015

SECTION-II

Post Specific Subject-Related Questions

1. The term 'City State' is generally associated with

A. Ancient Egypt
B. Ancient Greece
C. Ancient China
D. None of the three

2. Plato fixed the population of an ideal state at

A. 1,900 persons
B. 5,040 persons
C. 10,000 persons
D. 1,00,000 persons

3. According to Aristotle

A. State is a divine institution
B. State is an artificial creation
C. State is a creation of force
D. State is natural Institution

4. The Marxists hold that

A. The state is a class structure
B. State represents only the workers
C. State represents the entire community
D. State is a power system

5. The statement that the state is an ethical institution which is indispensable for the full moral development of man is attributed to

A. Individualists
B. Anarchists
C. Idealists
D. Marxists

6. Who said 'Man is a social animal'?

A. Aristotle B. Plato
C. Rousseau D. Laski

7. The view that the state is a necessary evil is associated with

A. Individualists B. Anarchists
C. Marxists D. Sophists

8. Who said that state is expansion of family?

A. Plato B. Aristotle
C. Locke D. Newton

9. Who said "I am the State"?

A. James II of England
B. Napoleon I of France
C. Louis XIV of France
D. Hitler of Germany

10. The term Sovereignty has been drawn from the Latin term

A. Supranus B. Supreme
C. Soviet D. Statute

11. Who said that sovereignty was the fullness of state?

A. The Greeks
B. The English
C. The Romans
D. The Indians

12. The concept of 'legal sovereignty' was for the first time profounded by

A. Hobbes B. Rousseau
C. Locke D. T.H. Green

13. The pluralists believes in

A. Legal sovereignty
B. Political sovereignty
C. Nominal sovereignty
D. Absolute sovereignty

14. "If sovereignty is not absolute, no state exists" — Who said this?
A. John Austin B. Jean Bodin
C. Hobbes D. John Locke

15. In India the legal sovereignty lies in
A. Parliament B. Supreme Court
C. President D. Electorate

16. De-jure sovereign refers to
A. A person who has legal right to govern and command obedience
B. A person who is authorised by Parliament to rule the country
C. A person in whom the entire authority is vested by the Constitution but does not make use of the power
D. The constitutional rule of state

17. Under democratic system of government the popular, sovereignty resides in
A. Popularly elected representative body
B. The electorate
C. The people
D. All the above

18. According to Laski the state is
A. Master of society and association
B. Servant of society
C. Identical with society
D. None of the above

19. In modern times the Force Theory found a strong advocate in
A. Lenin
B. Hitler
C. Winston Churchill
D. Mahatma Gandhi

20. According to the Matriarchal Theory the head of the family was
A. The eldest male member
B. The eldest female member
C. Nominated by the king
D. Nominated by the Chief Priest

21. The three most prominent exponents of Social Contract Theory were
A. Austin, Bodin, Hobbes
B. Hobbes, Locke, Rousseau
C. Mac Iyer, Laski, Hobbes
D. J. S. Mill, Smith, Hobbes

22. The Social Contract Theory is based on
A. Nationalism
B. Constitutionalism
C. Individualism
D. Socialism

23. Social Contract Theory deals with
A. The nature of state
B. The functions of state
C. The purpose of state
D. The origin of state

24. According to Hobbes the state of nature was a period of
A. Peace and plenty
B. Constant warfare
C. Peace and scarcity
D. Religious dominance

25. According to Locke people in the state of nature enjoyed only
A. Divine Rights
B. Natural Rights
C. Legal Rights
D. Religious Rights

26. Rousseau hailed from
A. Britain B. Germany
C. France D. Russia

27. Who said that "Man is born free, and every where he is in chains"?
A. Aristotle B. Marx
C. Rousseau D. Locke

28. The modern state is described as
A. Police state
B. A welfare state
C. A laissez faire state
D. Autocratic state

29. Feudalism was a dominant feature of
A. The City States
B. The Roman Empire
C. The Holy Roman Empire
D. All the three

30. Who asserted that the state would ultimately wither away?
A. Kant B. Marx
C. Aristotle D. Gandhi

31. Who said that "The state is nothing more than a machine"?
A. Marx B. Lenin
C. Stalin D. Engels

32. The Marxist Theory has advocated
A. Capitalism
B. Communism
C. Feudalism
D. Communalism

33. Surplus value means
A. Excessive value
B. Low price
C. High profit
D. Difference between wages and proceeds of sales

34. The Parliament and the Constitution are instruments of
A. Legal justice
B. Political justice
C. Economic justice
D. Social justice

35. Constitution is
A. The fundamental law of the land
B. A historical document
C. A socio-economic document
D. None of these

36. The Indian Constitution was enacted by
A. Dr. B. R. Ambedkar
B. Jawaharlal Nehru
C. Mahatma Gandhi
D. The Constituent Assembly

37. The proposal of which plan established the Constituent Assembly?
A. The Cripps Mission Plan
B. The Cabinet Mission Plan
C. The Mount Batten Plan
D. None of these

38. The Constitution of India is
A. Rigid
B. Flexible
C. Very rigid
D. Partly rigid and partly flexible

39. The first meeting of the Constituent Assembly of India was held on
A. 26th January, 1950
B. 26th November, 1949
C. 9th December, 1946
D. 9th December, 1949

40. Who acted as the Provisional President of the Constituent Assembly?
A. Dr. Rajendra Prasad
B. Dr. B.R. Ambedkar
C. Dr. Sachidananda Sinha
D. Mahatma Gandhi

41. Who is regarded as the 'Architect of the Indian Constitution'?
A. Dr. Rajendra Prasad
B. Dr. B.R. Ambedkar
C. B.N. Rao
D. Mahatma Gandhi

42. The Constitution of India came into force on
A. 15th August, 1947
B. 26th November, 1949
C. 26th January, 1950
D. 9th December, 1946

43. Art. 1 of the Indian Constitution describes India as a
A. Quazi federal state
B. Federal state
C. Unitary state
D. Union of states

44. Which of the following is not treated as part of the Constitution?
A. Preamble
B. Fundamental Rights
C. Pressure groups
D. Fundamental duties

45. Total number of Schedules in the Indian Constitution are

A. 4 B. 6
C. 11 D. 12

46. Who is the present Vice President of India?
A. Dr. Hamid Ansari
B. Prathibha Patil
C. Pranab Mukherjee
D. Rajanath Singh

47. Total number of Fundamental Rights enjoyed by the citizens of India are
A. 5 B. 6
C. 7 D. 8

48. Which part of the Indian Constitution deals with the Fundamental Rights?
A. Part I B. Part II
C. Part III D. Part V

49. The Human Rights Day is observed every year on
A. 20th January
B. 30th December
C. 10th December
D. 10th November

50. Which rights are regarded as 2nd generation rights?
A. Economic, social and cultural rights
B. Fundamental rights
C. Civil and political rights
D. Human rights

51. The first world conference on Human Rights was held at
A. Senegal
B. New Delhi
C. Vienna
D. San Jose in Costa Rica

52. Hot line facilities for victims of human rights are available for
A. 20 Hrs. B. 24 Hrs.
C. 18 Hrs. D. 22 Hrs.

53. Genocide means
A. Mass killing
B. Suicide
C. Killing children
D. Killing females

54. Govt. of India passed the Prevention of Food Adulteration Act in
A. 1934 B. 1944
C. 1954 D. 1964

55. Expand IPC.
A. Indian People's Court
B. Indian Penal Court
C. Indian Penal Code
D. Indian Postal Code

56. PIL means
A. Public Interest Litigation
B. Police Investigation Limited
C. Personal Information Limited
D. Public Information Limited

57. Who is the father of Public Administration?
A. L.D. White
B. Woodrow Wilson
C. Luther Gullick
D. Simon

58. Who coined the term 'POSDCORB'?
A. J.D. Millet
B. Piffiner
C. Luther Gullick
D. L.D. White

59. "Arthashastra" was written by
A. Aristotle B. Plato
C. Kautilya D. T.H. Green

60. The devices of direct democracy are found in
A. Switzerland B. France
C. England D. America

61. Which among the following is the meaning of 'Polis'?
A. Country B. State
C. City-state D. Village

62. Political Science is a branch of
A. Physical Science
B. Natural Science
C. Pure Science
D. Social Science

63. Mahatma Gandhi believed in
A. Power-Politics

B. Purity of means
C. State monopoly
D. Planning and heavy industries

64. Political Science deals with
A. Political power
B. Economic power
C. Social power
D. Cultural power

65. Who was the author of the book 'Politics'?
A. Hegal B. Socrates
C. Aristotle D. J.S. Mill

66. Which among the following is an element of state?
A. Sovereignty B. Treasury
C. Army D. King

67. Who advocated communism of wives?
A. Plato B. Aristotle
C. Socrates D. Karl Marx

68. Who wrote the book 'Leviathan'?
A. Locke B. Rousseau
C. Hobbes D. St. Thomas

69. Theory of Separation of Power was profounded by
A. Aristotle
B. Montesquieu
C. Carl Fedrich
D. J.S. Mill

70. Which of the following Hitler advocated?
A. Nazism B. Fascism
C. Democracy D. Anarchism

71. Who among the following practised Satyagraha?
A. Nehru B. Gandhiji
C. Ambedkar D. Patel

72. Democracy is a system of government in which the final power rests with
A. The Mob
B. The People
C. The Politicians
D. The Civil Service

73. Who profounded Panchasheela?
A. Shastri B. Indira Gandhi
C. Ambedkar D. Nehru

74. Lal Bahadur Shastri National Academy of Administration is at
A. Delhi B. Bangalore
C. Mangalore D. Mussorie

75. Which is the recruiting agency of I.A.S.?
A. KPSC B. BPSC
C. UPSC D. MPSC

76. The function of line agency is
A. To serve B. To execute
C. To train D. None of these

77. Who is responsible for Budget approval?
A. The Parliament
B. The Executive
C. The Judiciary
D. The President

78. The Budget is prepared by
A. P.M.
B. Finance Minister
C. Defence Minister
D. Home Minister

79. Who is the first citizen of Karnataka?
A. Governor
B. Chief Minister
C. President
D. Chief Secretary

80. Which is consider as fourth estate of the Government?
A. Newspaper
B. Public opinion
C. Political parties
D. Pressure groups

81. Who appoints the Ambassadors?
A. P.M.
B. External Affairs Minister
C. President
D. Defence Minister

82. International relations is referred to
A. Foreign Policy

B. Economic Policy
C. Social Policy
D. Domestic Policy

83. Who was the Architect of NAM?
A. Nehru B. Gandhi
C. Patel D. Jinnah

84. Where is the Head Quarters of U.N.O.?
A. Washington B. New York
C. The Hague D. Japan

85. Where is the Head Quarters of SAARC?
A. Dhaka B. Delhi
C. Kathmandu D. Colombo

86. When did U.N.O. came into existence?
A. 1945 B. 1946
C. 1947 D. 1948

87. Which among the following is a permanent member of Security Council of U.N.?
A. India B. Taiwan
C. U.K. D. Brazil

88. Who wrote 'Hind-Swaraj'?
A. Nehru
B. Gandhiji
C. Ambedkar
D. Indira Gandhi

89. Which among the following is the upper house of U.K.?
A. House of Commons
B. Rajya Sabha
C. House of Lords
D. Senate

90. Who wrote "My Experiment with Truth"?
A. V.P. Singh B. M.K. Gandhi
C. J.P. D. Patel

91. Which one of the following was elected President of India unopposed?
A. Dr. Rajendra Prasad
B. Dr. Radhakrishnan
C. Neelam Sanjiva Reddy
D. K.R. Narayanan

92. Which one of the following writs literally means 'What is your authority'?
A. Habeas Corpus
B. Certiorari
C. Quo Warranto
D. Prohibition

93. In India, the first Municipal Corporation was set up in which one among the following?
A. Calcutta B. Madras
C. Bombay D. Delhi

94. Who is the head of the Cabinet?
A. President
B. Finance Minister
C. Home Minister
D. Prime Minister

95. Who is the author of the book "Who are Shudras"?
A. Dr. B.R. Ambedkar
B. Mahatma Gandhi
C. Devaraj Urs
D. Jaya Prakash Narayan

96. Expand UDHR.
A. Universal Declaration of Human Right
B. Universal Declaration of Home Right
C. United Declaration of Human Right
D. Universal Decision on Human Right

97. Magna Carta was passed in the year
A. 1210 B. 1215
C. 1315 D. 1415

98. National Human Rights Commission was established in the year
A. 1948 B. 1950
C. 1945 D. 1993

99. National Voters Day celebrated every year on
A. January 26
B. August 15
C. November 14
D. January 25

100. Who was the first Speaker of Lok Sabha?
A. Sanjeeva Reddy
B. Balayogi
C. G.V. Mavalankar
D. B.D. Jatti

ANSWERS

1	2	3	4	5	6	7	8	9	10
B	B	D	D	C	A	A	B	C	A
11	**12**	**13**	**14**	**15**	**16**	**17**	**18**	**19**	**20**
C	A	B	A	A	A	C	B	B	B
21	**22**	**23**	**24**	**25**	**26**	**27**	**28**	**29**	**30**
B	C	D	B	B	C	C	B	C	B
31	**32**	**33**	**34**	**35**	**36**	**37**	**38**	**39**	**40**
D	B	D	A	A	D	B	D	B	C
41	**42**	**43**	**44**	**45**	**46**	**47**	**48**	**49**	**50**
B	C	D	C	D	A	B	C	C	A
51	**52**	**53**	**54**	**55**	**56**	**57**	**58**	**59**	**60**
D	B	A	C	C	A	A	C	C	A
61	**62**	**63**	**64**	**65**	**66**	**67**	**68**	**69**	**70**
C	D	B	A	C	A	A	C	B	A
71	**72**	**73**	**74**	**75**	**76**	**77**	**78**	**79**	**80**
B	B	D	D	C	B	A	B	A	A
81	**82**	**83**	**84**	**85**	**86**	**87**	**88**	**89**	**90**
C	A	A	B	C	A	C	B	C	B
91	**92**	**93**	**94**	**95**	**96**	**97**	**98**	**99**	**100**
C	C	B	D	A	A	B	D	D	C

Political Science

1

MEANING OF POLITICAL SCIENCE

MEANING OF POLITICAL SCIENCE

Political Science is that part of social science which deals with the foundations of the state and the principles of the government. According to J W Garner, "Politics begins and ends with the state." Similarly, R G Gettel wrote that Politics is the "study of the state in the past, present and future". Harold J Laski stated in the same vein that the study of Politics concerns itself with the life of men and women in relation to organized state. Thus as a social science, Political Science deals with those aspects of individuals in society which relate to their activities and organizations devoted to seeking of power, resolution of conflicts and all these, within an overall framework of the rule and law as laid down by the state.

According to Catlin, politics means either activities of political life or the study of those activities, which are generally treated as activities of the various organs of government.

According to R.N. Gilchrist, political science deals with general problems of the state and government. The great Greek political philosopher, Aristotle (384 – 322 B.C.) was the first thinker to use the term 'politics'.

SCOPE OF POLITICAL SCIENCE

The term 'scope' refers to the subject matter or the boundaries of political science.

Broadly speaking, the scope of political science may be divided into three parts:

1. Scope of political science concerning the state.
2. Scope of political science with reference to human rights.
3. Scope of political science in relation to government.

1. Scope of political science concerning the state :

Scope of Political Science

Present Form of the state	Historical Form of the state	Ideal Form of the state

In political science, we study the present form of the state Its aims and objectives and the means adopted by the state to achieve its objectives. This aspect of the study of political science has been termed by Gettell as the analytical study of the state.

The present form of the state is the result of its historical development. Political science makes a historical analysis of the origin of the state and the theories of the state.

The study of political science has to predict the future of the state that is how it ought to be. According to Gettell political science is a historical investigation of what the state has been, an analytical study of what the state is and a politico – ethical discussion of what the state should be.

2. Scope of political science with reference to human rights

The citizens have their civil, political and economic rights. These rights have to be preserved and protected by the State for the welfare of its citizens.

3. Scope of political science in relation to government

Stephen Leacock said that, political science deals with government. A state cannot exist without government. Government is the working agency of the state. The different forms of government, various organs of government, political parties, local self-government, judiciary, and internationalism are covered by the political science.

GROWTH OF THE DISCIPLINE OF POLITICAL SCIENCE

Systematic study of Politics started with the Greeks in the fourth century BC. Philosophers like Plato and Aristotle used it in the most comprehensive sense. Aristotle called Politics a "master science". For him, it comprised of not only the institutions of state or government but also family, property and other social institutions. Politics, for the Greeks, was an allencompassing activity.

The ancient Greek view about Political Science was mainly ethical. In contrast, the ancient Romans considered the legal aspect of Politics more important for their governance. Individual and the State During the Middle Ages, Political Science became a branch of religious order of the Church. Political authority was, then, subordinated to the authority of the Church.

Normally a lay man associates Politics with party politics. But as students of Political Science, we know that Politics is much larger than that: it is systematic study of state and power.

As the state grew in size and became more complex, Political Science acquired a realistic and secular (non-religious) approach. After the Industrial Revolution, the role of the State, which was limited to maintenance of law and order and providing defence against external aggression, underwent considerable changes with the emergence of the new economic system called capitalism.

In the twentieth century, after the Second World War, the 'behavioural approach' offered a new dimension of Political Science. The behavioural movement in American Political Science in the 1950s and the 1960s placed a lot of emphasis on the 'science' part of Politics. It wanted to model Politics after the methods followed by natural sciences like Physics, Botany, etc.

The behaviouralists built theory inductively from empirical propositions. Those who follow inductive method would come to the conclusion after study, observation and experiment. For example, when some behaviouralists saw African-Americans (Blacks) of the southern United States of America (USA) voted for the Democratic Party of the United States, they came to the conclusion that the African-Americans do vote for the Democrats.

This behavioural approach shifted the focus of its study from political institutions and structures to their functions. It placed stress on political activity and the behaviour of men and women who control these institutions. It replaced the study of ideas by the study of facts, evidence and behaviour. It considered political activity manifested in behaviour as the true subject of Political Science.

A political activity may be in the form of an individual contesting an election. It may be the activity of a group seeking the adoption of a particular policy in its favour by the government. As different people pursue different interests, such activities tend to generate disagreement, competition and conflict. But the distinctive quality of Politics is that it includes physical coercion or force by the government. It may and usually does involve the persuasive influence and effort of the government to resolve conflicts through its balanced policy decisions.

Politics is also viewed as a process whereby individuals, groups or communities seek to achieve their specific but conflicting goals. Politics, as the process, seeks to allocate resources (Easton calls it, values) authoritatively.

Politics, as the study of structures, institutions, processes and activities, recognizes the possibility of the use of power. The Marxist approach, which is derived from the writings of the nineteenth century German philosopher Karl Marx, views Politics as a study of irreconcilable conflicts between the two classes 'haves' (those who have private property, or simply the rich) and the 'have-nots' (those who do not have any private property, or simply the poor); in other words, the exploiters and the exploited. The emancipation of the havenots will come only through a revolution which would put an end to the institution of private property, thus changing the class society to the classless society. But Politics, as against the Marxist view, has another view also, the liberal view, according to which Individual and the State Politics is considered as an as effort for conciliation and accommodation to bring about rule of order and Justice. Incidentally, the Marxist view of politics comes as a reaction to the liberal view of politics.

DISTINCTION BETWEEN POLITICAL SCIENCE AND POLITICS

The terms 'Political Science' and 'Politics' are often used interchangeably. However, the distinction between the two needs to be understood. Some scholars define Politics to be "the science and art of government." But this is only a part of the total explanation of the subject of Political Science. Now-a-days the term Politics is used to mean the problems of the citizens interacting with the instrument of political power in one form or the other. Sometimes, Politics was and still is used as the technique of compromise or the method to capture power and retain it.

According to many political scientists, the study of Political Science comprises theory of the state, concept of sovereign power, forms and functions of government, making and execution of laws, elections, political parities, rights and duties of citizens, policy functions and study of welfare activities of the State and government.

There is another aspect of Politics that needs to be emphasised. Politics, many a time, implies practical politics. Practising politics is different from studying it. Practical politics includes actual formation of government, the working of government, administration, laws and legislation. It also includes international politics including matters such as peace and war, international trade and economic order, protection of rights, etc. All these also comprise the subject matter of the study of Politics.

While the knowledge of Political Science as a discipline is acquired through study, the skill of practical politics is acquired through politicking or manipulations and craftiness or by exploiting caste and regional loyalties and religious sentiments. Practical politics is often described as the 'dirty game' and a 'corrupting' process in the common people's mind.

But we find that there are hardly any human groupings or societies, which are free from 'politics' and hardly any individual who does not know the implications of the "game of politics".

Practical Politics also has many positive aspects. In this era of welfare state many positive programmes such as removal of untouchability, land reforms, release of bonded labourers, prohibition of trafficking in human beings and begar (forced labour), introduction of minimum wages, employment generation programmes, empowerment of the other backward classes are all examples of positive aspects of practical politics.

'Politics' refers to the process of actual happenings in society and in institutions, which Political Science refers to its understand in a systematic manner.

POLITICAL SCIENCE AND OTHER SOCIAL AND HUMAN SCIENCES

Social science are those sciences, which discuss about the things connected with the affairs of individuals living in society, political science, economics, history, geography are some of the important social sciences.

Political science is immensely benefited from other social sciences. It is essentially connected and related to other social sciences. As a matter of fact, all social sciences are interrelated and interdependent.

Political Science and History

There is closed and intimate relatioship between political science and history. The relatioship between political science and history is beautifully explained by John Seeley.

"History without political science has no fruit and politicalscience without history has no root".

To quote the same author again,

"Politics is vulgar when not liberalized by history and history fades into mere literature when it loses sight of its relation to politics".

According to Freeman,

"History is past politics and politics is present history ".

They are complementary to each other. Montesquieu and Bryce made use of historical marterials to study political science.

Lord Bryce claims that,

political science stands midway between history and politics, between the past and the present.

It has drawn its materials from the one; it has to apply them to the other.

History deals with past events, movements revolutions, national struggles etc. and gives information about the origin and development of political institutions and thought. When various issues, concepts and terms, ideologies, are discussed in political science, their historicaldevelopment is also taken into consideration.

Political Science and Economics

Political science and economics are very closely related. In the past, economics has been regarded as a branch of political science. Adam smith the father of economics in his book "An Enquiry into the Nature and Courses of Wealth of Nations" also considered economics as an important branch of political science. It was called political economy.

Now the two social sciences namely political science and economics have their individuality and identification. Economics is a social science dealing with the production, distribution, exchange and consumption of wealth in the society. All economic activity is carried on within the state on conditions and stipulations laid down by the state.

Political science and economics are concerned with such matters, as formulation of five year plans, the socialistic pattern of society economic and welfare activities of government.

The political conditions of a country are greatly affected by its economic conditions. Healthy economy depends on a strong, effective and efficient administration of a country.

Political Science and Geography

Political science is also related to geography. Geo means earth and graphy means description and geography is the description of the earth. Geography is the study of the earth's surface, physical features, natural and political divisions, climatic conditions, population, etc.

It helps us to understand the impact and influence of geographical conditions of the political institutions of a country. Political geography is known as geopolitics, a new branch of study in modern times. Montesquieu stressed the influence of physical environments on the forms of government and liberty of the people. As territory is an essential element of a state, geo-political factors influence political environment. According to Rousseau, there is a link between the climatic conditions and form of government. Warm climates are conducive to despots, cold climates to barbarism and moderate climate to a good polity.

Political Science and Sociology

Sociology is the root of all social sciences. Auguste Comte is the father of sociology. Sociology is the study of Society. Political science and sociology are inter-related political scientists and sociologists contribute mutually for the benefit of whole society.

For example, the institution of marriage and related problems after that, namely divorce are within the domain of sociology. How to solve these problems in a harmonious way for better standard of life is within the competence of political science.

What was once a sub-field of sociology has now takes the form of "political sociology" which is now a legitimate subfield of political science.

2

STATE

DEFINITIONS

The state is the most universal and most powerful of all social institutions. The state is a natural institution. Aristotle said man is a social animal and by nature he is a political being. To him, to live in the state and to be a man were indentical. The modern term "state" is derived from the word "status". It was Niccolo Machiavelli (1469 – 1527) who first used the term "state" in his writings. His important work is titled as "Prince". The state is the highest form of human association. It is necessary because it comes into existence out of the basic needs of life. It continues to remain for the sake of good life. The aims, desires and aspirations of human beings are translated into action through the state. Although the state is a necessary institution, no two writers agree on its definition.

Some of the definitions of the concept of State are as follows:

"The State is the politically organized people of a definite territory". —***Bluntschli***

State is "a community of persons, more or less numerous, permanently occupying a definite portion of territory, independent, or nearly so, of external control, and possessing an organized government to which the great body of inhabitants render habitual obedience." —***Garner***

State is "a territorial society divided into governments and subjects, whether individuals or associations of individuals, whose relationships are determined by the exercise of this supreme coercive power." —***Laski***

State "is a people organized for law within a definite territory". —***Woodrow Wilson***

"The State is a concept of political science, and a moral reality which exists where a number of people, living on a definite territory, are unified under a government which in internal matters is the organ of expressing their sovereignty, and in external matters is independent of other governments." —***Gilchrist***

ELEMENTS

From the above definitions, it is clear that the following are the elements of the state:

1. Population
2. Territory
3. Government
4. Sovereignty

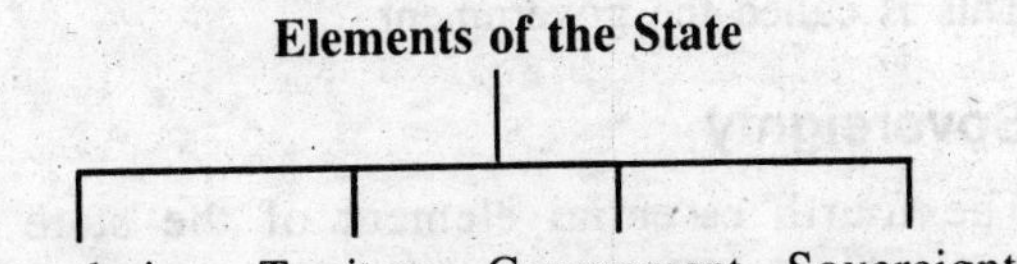

Population

It is the people who make the state. Population is essential for the state. Greek thinkers were of the view that the population should neither be too big nor too small. According to Plato the ideal number would be 5040. According to Aristotle, the number should be neither too large nor too small. It should be large enough to be self–sufficing and small enough to be well governed. Rousseau determined 10,000 to be an ideal number for a state. Greek thinkers like Plato and Aristotle thinking on the number was based on small city – states like Athens and Sparta. Modern states vary in population.

Territory

There can be no state without a fixed territory. People need territory to live and organize themselves socially and politically. It may be remembered that the territory of the state includes land, water and air – space. The modern states differ in their sizes. Territory is necessary for citizenship. As in the case of population, no definite size with regard to extent of area of the state can be fixed. There are small and big states. In the words of Prof. Elliott "territorial sovereignty or the Superiority of state overall within its boundaries and complete freedom from external control has been a fundamental principle of the modern state life".

Government

Government is the third element of the state. There can be no state without government. Government is the working agency of the state. It is the political organization of the state. Prof. Appadorai defined government as the agency through which the will of the State is formulated, expressed and realized. According to C.F. Strong, in order to make and enforce laws the state must have supreme authority. This is called the government.

Sovereignty

The fourth essential element of the state is sovereignty. The word 'sovereignty" means supreme and final legal authority above and beyond which no legal power exists. The concept of "sovereignty" was developed in conjunction with the rise of the modern state. The term Sovereignty is derived from the Latin word superanus which means supreme. the father of modern theory of sovereignty was Jean Bodin (1530 – 1597) a French political thinker. Sovereignty has two aspects :

1. Internal sovereignty
2. External sovereignty

Internal sovereignty means that the State is supreme over all its citizens, and associations. External sovereignty means that the state is independent and free from foreign or outside control.

According to Harold J. Laski, "It is by possession of sovereignty that the state is distinguished from all other forms of human association.

DISTINCTION BETWEEN STATE AND SOCIETY

The distinction between the state and the society can be explained as under:

(a) Strictly speaking, the state is a political organization; it is society politically organized. Society, on the other hand, is a social organization and has within it, all types of associations (social, economic, religious, political, cultural and the like). Society is both broader as well as narrower than the state. It is broader when it is used to describe the whole community of mankind; it is narrower when it is used to describe a small group of a village.

(b) In terms of origin, society is prior to the state. Society may be said to have been born the day the human life must have begun. But the state did not begin with the society; it must have started at a later stage of social development. Human beings are social being first and then political beings.

(c) Being prior to the state, society is clearly a natural and therefore, an instinctive institution. The state, on the other hand, is artificial, a created institution; its was made when it was needed. That is one reason that we see the state as a formal and legal organization with its body, its structure. The society, too, is a body, an organization; it is not as formal an organization as the state is.

(d) The state exists for the society in the same way as a means exists for its end. The state is, therefore, a means and the society is an end. It is always the means that exists for the end; the end never exists for the means.

(e) The state is sovereign: no sovereignty means no state; the society is not sovereign; it exists without being sovereign. As sovereign, the state is supreme over all other organizations, institutions and individuals within its boundaries; as sovereign, the state is independent of all other like states; sovereignity gives the state a separate and independent existence.

(f) The state has to have a definite territory. Definite territory is an essential element of the state. It is, therefore, a territorial organization in so far as it stays on the definite portion of territory: its territorial boundaries are fixed, definite and permanent. Society does have a territory but its territory is not permanent; its place of operation may extend or may get limited. The Islamic society, for example, transcends national boundaries. So does the Free Mason Brotherhood.

(g) The state has general rules of conduct called the laws; the society, too, has general rules of conduct but they are called rituals, norms, habits and the like. Laws of the state are written, definite and clear; those of the society, are unwritten, indefinite and vague.

(h) The state's laws have a binding sanction. The violation of the laws of the state is followed by punishment: physical or otherwise or both. The rules of the society, if violated, lead to social boycott, i.e. social exclusion. The area of the state, we may say, is the area of that of taking action in case of disobedience; it has power is force. The area of society, on the other hand, is the area of voluntary cooperation and its power is goodwill; its method is its flexibility.

Inspite of these distinctions, society and state are closely inter-connected and interdependent. Social conduct and the structure of the society must conform to the laws of the state. The state, on the other hand, must be responsive to the will of the society.

STATE AND NATION

By nation, as you know, we mean a historically constituted stable community of people formed on the basis of a common language, territory, economic life and physhological make up manifested in a common culture. Nation, Bluntschilli says, is "a union of masses of men bound together specially by language and customs into common civilization which gives them a sense of unity". A nation is a culturally homogeneous social group.

The state, as we know, is a people organized for law within a definite territory; it is always sovereign-supreme internally and independent externally. The nation is a group of people psychologically bound together while sharing common joys and sorrows. The distinction between state and nation can be explained as under:

(a) Nation and state are distinct entities. A nation may not be always a state; India was not a state before August, 1947. A state may not always be a nation. Austria-Hungary was a state but not a nation before World War I because the heterogeneous people did not form a culturally homogeneous people.

(b) The state is a state because it is sovereign. The nation is not a state if it is not sovereign. Sovereignty is the chief characteristic of a state; it is not a feature of the nation. A nation becomes a nation-state when the nation attains statehood.

(c) The state is a political concept while the nation is a cultural, and a psychological body. Hayes says, "Nation is primarily cultural, and only incidentally political". What it means is that nation is not a political concept, it is only spiritual.

(d) Laws bind the people together in a state; sentiments and emotions bind the people in a nation. The unity of the state is always external; the unity of the nation is eternal. In the case of the state, unity is imposed; it comes from above through laws. In the case of nation, unity comes from within, through emotions.

(e) There is an element of force connected with the state. The state's laws are binding. There is a coercion exercised by the state if its authority is defied. In the case of the nation, there is the element of persuasion.

(f) The elements of the state are definite:

population, fixed territory, government and sovereignty. The elements of a nation are not definite. Somewhere common language helps constitute a nation, somewhere else, common race makes a nation. Common religion, for example, was a factor in making Pakistan as a nation; it was common language in the case of the United States as a nation whereas it was common heritage that made India a nation.

(g) A state may be larger than a nation. The former USSR had, within it, more than a hundred nationalities. Conversely, a nation may be larger than a state; a nationality may spread over two states. The Korean nationality is spread over two states: North Korea and South Korea.

STATE AND GOVERNMENT

The government, is one element of the state. It is the agency through which laws are made, enforced and those who violate laws, are punished. It is the visible manifestation of state authority. It consists of all the persons, institutions and agencies through which the will of the state is expressed and carried out. Though the state speaks through the government, it is proper to differentiate between the two.

(a) The state has authority inherent in itself whereas the government has no inherent powers. The government gets its structure, authority and power from the Constitution of the State.

The Constitution being the collection of basic rules, is the fundamental law according to which the government of a state is organized.

(b) The state is a larger entity that includes all the citizens; the government is, relatively a smaller unit that includes only those who are employed to perform its functions. We are all citizens of the state, but we are all not functionaries of the government. Garner writes: "The government is an essential organ or agency of the state but it is no more than the state itself than the board of directors of a corporation is itself the corporation."

(c) The idea of state is quite abstract. The government is the concretization of the idea of the state. We see the government, not the state.

(d) The state is a near permanent institution; it is so because it does not die unless it is attacked and made a part of the other state. The government is temporary; it is so because it may change: today's rulers may not be tomorrow's rulers. To put it the other way, the state may be the same everywhere whereas, the government may vary from one state to another. India, the United States, Great Britain and France for example, are all states. But the governments which work in these states may not be of the same type. In India and Great Britian there is a parliamentary government, whereas in the United States of America there is presidential government.

Parliamentary Government is a system of government where the legislative organ of the government is closely related to its executive organ; the cabinet is taken from the legislature and is responsible to it, especially to the lower house of the legislature.

Presidential government is a system of government where the legislative organ of the government is independent of the executive organ; the executive exists separately from the legislature and is not responsible to it.

(e) The sovereign powers lay with the state; it is the state which is sovereign. The government only exercises power. The government's powers are delegated and derivative; the state's powers are real and original.

(f) The opposition to the state is different from the opposition of the government. We criticize the government; we never condemn the state. The criticism of the state is a revolt; the criticism of the government is not a rebellion. We would never hear from an Indian that India is bad; but we would usually hear that the policies of the Indian Government headed by a political party or a multitude of political parties are bad. It is a crime to condemn one's state; it is a duty, in fact it is a right to criticise one's government.

(g) The government is merely an element of the state. Accordingly, it is one part of the state. It is a part of the whole (of the state). As a part, the government is not greater than the whole. When we talk of the state, we talk of the population, the definite territory, the government and sovereignty. But when we talk of the government, we talk of one part, one element of the state.

(h) The state's territory is always definite. It remains unchanged. Its boundaries remain where they are. The government's territory is never permanent. Muhammad Tughlaq had changed his capital to a place called Daulatabad. Many governments had changed their capitals to London during the World War II, fearing the German attack.

BRANCHES OF GOVERNMENT

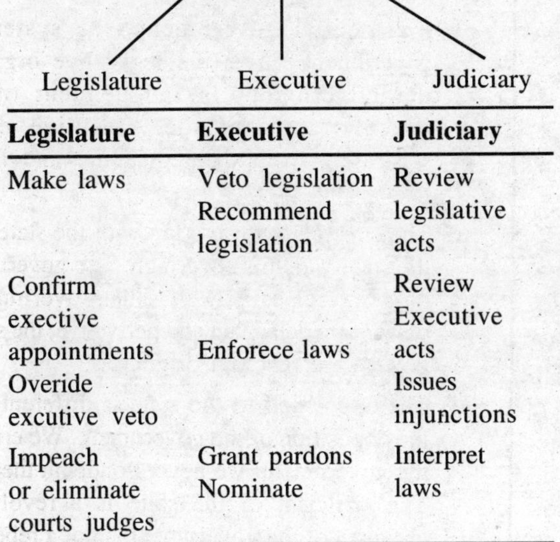

Legislature	Executive	Judiciary
Make laws	Veto legislation Recommend legislation	Review legislative acts
Confirm exective appointments	Enforece laws	Review Executive acts
Overide excutive veto		Issues injunctions
Impeach or eliminate courts judges	Grant pardons Nominate	Interpret laws

Executive

It is one of the three branches of government as given above. State functions through the executive, the namely the government. It is the duty of the executive or enforce the laws passed by the legislature. The executive who exercise real power is the real executive. The executive who has nominal power is the normal executive. The President of India is the nominal executive. The union council of ministers led by the Prime Minister of India is the real executive. Parliamentary executive is chosen from the legislature and is responsible to the legislature. The executive in India is parliamentary in its character.

Powers and functions of executive are :

1. Enforcing law
2. Maintaining peace and order.
3. Repelling aggression.
4. Building friendly relations with other states
5. When necessary to wage war to protect the country.
6. Making appointments to higher posts.
7. Raising money and spending them.
8. Convening the sessions of the legislature and conducting business.
9. Issues ordinances whenever the legislature is to in session.
10. Implement schemes and projects to improve he social and economic conditions of the people.
11. Power to grant pardon, reprieve or remission of punishment.

Legislature

The legislature is the law making branch. The legislature has an important role in the amendment of the constitution. The legislature is a deliberative body where matters of social, economic and political concerns are discussed, debated and decided. The British parliament is said to be "the mother of parliaments". It is the oldest legislature in the world. According to Prof. Laski, law- making is not the only function of the legislature but its real function is to watch the process of administration to safeguard the liberties of private citizens. The legislature of the union is called the parliament in India. It consists of two chambers.

1. The House of the People or the Lok Sabha as the Lower House.
2. The Council of State or the Rajya Sabha as the Upper House.

The functions of legislature are

(a) Enact laws

(b) Oversee administration

(c) Pass the budget

(d) Hear public grieveances.

(e) Discuss subjects like

1. Development plans
2. National policies
3. International relations.

Judiciary

Judiciary is the third important organ of the government machinery. Its main function is to interrupter laws and administer justice. Lord Bryce has said that there is to better test of excellence of government than the efficiency of its judicial system.The welfare of citizens depends to a larger extent upon the judiciary. Judiciary is one of the pillars of democracy. Its interpretation ensures justice, equality and liberty to all its citizens. An independent and impartial judiciary is an essential feature of a democratic setup. The Supreme Court of India consists of a Chief Justice and other judges. The Supreme Court has its permanent seat in Delhi. According to Justice Hughes, "we are under a constitution, but the constitution is what the judges say it is".

Functions of Judiciary

1. Administration of justice.
2. To determine what is law and what is the cope and meaning of it.
3. To give advisory opinion on matters referred to it.
4. To issue orders or writs for the purpose of preventing violation of rights and laws.
5. To acts as guardian of the constitution.

3

ORIGIN OF THE STATE

Among the many theories which are concerned with the origin of the state the following are explained in this chapter.

1. Theory of Divine
2. Social Contract Theory
3. Matriarchal Theory
4. Force Theory
5. Evolutionary Theory

THEORY OF DIVINE

The theory of divine origin is the oldest among all theories. According to this theory state is established and governed by God himself. God may rule the state directly or indirectly through some ruler who is regarded as an agent of God. The trace of divine origin is seen in the epic Mahabarat. According to the Mahabarat there was anarchy in the beginning in the society and the people prayed to God to come to their rescue.

The rise of Christianity and the growth of the power of the church in the medieval period led to a conflict between church and state and an active discussion of the divine origin of political power. All were agreed that the ultimate source of authority was divine but the supporters of the church say that Pope alone received his power directly from God. Kings are breathing images of God upon earth. Even if the king be wicked, the subject has no right to rebel against him. To rebel against the king is to rebel against God himself for the God's chosen Vassal. The main points in the doctrine of the divine right of kings may thus be summed up.

1. Monarchy is divinely ordained and the king draws his authority from God.
2. Monarchy is hereditary and it is the divine right of a king that it should pass from father to son.
3. The king is answerable to God alone; and
4. Resistance to the lawful authority of a king is a sin.

The theory of divine origin was popular for a long time but later on it began to decline on account of many factors.

Criticism

The theory of divine origin has been criticised on many grounds.

To say that God selects this or that man as ruler is contrary to experience and common sense. God cannot be expected to do such worldly things for human beings. The theory is dangerous because it pinpoints the unlimited and arbitrary power of the kings.

The theory of divine origin of the state advocates only monarchical form of government. The monarchical form of government is practically disappearing from the world. No wonder the theory of divine origin also does not find its supporters in modern times.

We all believe in the theory of evolution. Everything in the world has grown up by slow degrees and consequently the same must have been the case with the state. It is too much to believe that one day God thought of creating the state and created one.

The theory put emphasis on revelation and not reason. In modern times we attribute everything to reason and hence it is not accepted today.

Although the theory has many defects and is no longer accepted today, it cannot be denied that it had its utility.

The theory of social contract with its emphasis on consent, was a great deadlock to the theory of divine origin. It was maintained that state was created by individuals by means of a contract and not by God. The separation of the church from the state was also partly responsible for the decline of the theory.

SOCIAL CONTRACT THEORY

The substance of this theory is that state is the result of an agreement entered into by men who originally had no governmental organisation. In the first period there was no government and no law. The people lived in a state of nature. After some time they decided to set up a state. That they did by means of a contract. The social contract theory described the original condition of men as the "state of nature". To escape from the condition of the state of nature man made a social contract. To some writers the contract was pre-social and to others it was pre-political.

Writers on this theory are agreed on the point that the state of nature preceded the establishment of government there was no organised life in the state of nature. Each lived according to his own wish and fancies. No man made laws were there to control man. The law known to men living in the state of nature was the law of nature or natural law. There was none to interpret the law or adjudicate. Hence men lived under uncertain conditions. When men felt the need to escape from this type of life he did so by common agreement or contract. As a result of this, a civil society was created. Thus creation of civil society preceded the emergence of the state.

In the sixteenth and seventeenth centuries the supporters of the social contract theory multiplied and there was more or less universal acceptance of the doctrine. Hooker was the first scientific writer who gave a logical exposition of the theory of social contract. The theory found real support in the writings of Thomas Hobbes, John Locke, Jean Jacques Rousseau who are known as contractualists.

Comparison of Social Contract Theories of Hobbes, Locke and Rousseau

Hobbes	Locke	Rousseau
1. Principal works		
Leviathan (1651)	**Civil government (1690)**	**Social contract (1762)**
2. The State of Nature		
Man egoistic moved by fear, power glory political equality of all no question of right or wrong. Just or unjust war of all against all, life, nasty, brutish and short.	A state of good will, mutual existence and preservation state of peace not war governed by law of nature but state became necessary to have one standardized interpretation of law of nature.	Men in state of nature equal self sufficient and contended, lived life of idyllic, happiness man actuated by impulse and not reason, origin of property creates inequality necessity of state.
3. Law of nature		
In state of nature there was no civil law, law of nature was regulative of human action, law of nature conceived differently by Hobbes to mean different things on different occasions i.e. (a) it was dicate of right reason for preservation of life. (b) It was based on prudence which dictated that	Law of nature does not represent natural impulse but a moral law based upon reason to regulate human conduct.	Law of nature based on instinct sociability resulting from feeling and not from reason.

everybody should try to secure peace by sacrificing natural right by convenants and it must be respected.		
4. Natural Right		
Natural right depends upon ones might	Right inherent in man by nature; natural rights of man are to life, liberty and property.	Man is free in the state of nature and enjoys all rights incidental to his person.
5. Social Contract		
The individual gives up all his rights expect on ie right of defence and self preservation to a common sovereign, social contract creates a common wealth and a sover-eign (one, few, or many) contract unilateral and not binding on sovereign.	Men enter into social contract that is create a state to have a common agency for interpretation and execution of the law of nature. Individuals surrender some but not all the rights. Not clear whether locke an contract creates civil society or only government. Government limited in authority and not absolute.	State results from a contract between individuals in their personal capacity and individuals in their corporate capacity. A, B, C and D etc. in their individual capacity surrender all rights to A+B+C+D etc as a corporate whole.
6. Sovereignty		
Hobbesian sovereignty is unlimited, indivisible, inalienable, absolute above law, source of law, justice, property above state and church has no right of revolution against sovereign.	Locke does not conceive of a sovereign state. His government is limited to performance of its duties. The inherent right of man to life, liberty and property, represents a limitation on government. Locke conceives of popular and not legal sovereignty.	The corporate whole that is people as a whole are sovereign. Thus Rousseau believes in popular sovereignty. People are the legal sovereign. Sovereignty resides in the 'general will'of the people. The characteristics of this sovereignty are its unity, individuality, permanencies, in alienability and its absolute and unrepresentable character. The government is dependent on the sovereign of the people. Rousseau distinguish between the sovereign state and subordinate government.
7. Liberty		
In the state of nature liberty depends upon the state and is guaranteed by the state. It is a gift of the state and can be abrogated by the state. It cannot be quoted against the authority of the state.	A man has certain rights inherent in him ie rights to life, liberty and property which the state cannot deprive him of	In the civil state individual liberty is a gift of the sovereign state. It must be reconciled with the absolute authority of the state and cannot be quoted against the same.

8. Individual and the state

The Hobbesian individual owes everything i.e. rights peace and law to the state and is therefore best in the state. He must obey the sovereign and pay taxes. Individual has some kind of liberty even in the civil state i.e.

(a) Liberty not to kill himself if asked to do so by the sovereign.

(b) Liberty to life which enables him to resist the sovereign if the latter attacks his life.

(c) Liberty to refuse allegiance to a sovereign who cannot save his life or to a deposed sovereign.

9. State and Government

Hobbes does not distinguish between state and Government or between dejure and defacto sovereign.

Locke distinguishes between state and government and state and society. His theory loads to limited constitutional government.

Rousseau distinguish between state which is sovereign and government which is subordinate creature of the state.

Rousseau compared with Hobbes and Locke

Rousseau had drawn something from Hobbes and something from Locke. In fact he began with the method of Locke and ended with those of Hobbes. Both Rousseau and Locke agreed that man in the state of nature was free and happy. Formation of civil society by means of a contract was deemed the only way out. Both Locke and Rousseau made the distinction between the state and government though Rousseau maintained that the institution of government was not the results of contract. Both believed that the contract did not remove the supreme power from the people. Rousseau's voice is the voice of Locke but the hands are those of Hobbes.

Evaluation of Social Contract Theory

The social contract theory as expounded by Hobbes, Locke and Rousseau does not explain the origin of the state. There is no evidence to support this theory. The contention of these philosophers is not borne out by facts. What was contributed by Hobbes to political philosophy was absolutism. Locke gave recognition to the concept of limited government. Rousseau popularised the idea of popular sovereignty.

Criticism

The doctrine that the state originated in a contract was a favourite home of political speculation during the seventeenth and eighteenth centuries.

Historically the theory is a mere fiction. There is nothing in the whole range of history to show that the state has ever been deliberately created as a result of voluntary agreement. Primitive man did not posses that maturity of outlook which the making of social contract presupposes.

The social contract theory is unhistorical. It is merely a fiction. The social contract theory is also attacked on legal grounds. It is contended that a legally sound contract implies the prior existence of some authority and its sanction before the contract implies the contract is entered into. In the case of social contract theory there was neither the authority nor the sanction before the contract was concluded. The social contract theory is also criticised on philosophical grounds. The social contract theory is criticised as bad history, bad law and bad philosophy. It is bad philosophy, because it looks upon the state as an artificial contrivance and not a natural process of growth.

MATRIARCHAL THEORY

Mclennan, Morgan and Jenks are the notable exponents of matriarchal theory. The matriarchal system was prior to the patriarchal system and tribe. There was no permanent institution of marriage. A woman had more than one husband and because of the uncertainty of male parentage kinship was reckoned through woman that is from mother to daughters. In the place of a family consisting of a man his wife and children there was a large and loosely connected group called a horde or pack organised for matrimonial purposes. The matriarchal family developed as indicated below.

1. First there was a tribe and it was the oldest and primary social group.
2. In course of time a tribe breaks into clans.
3. Clans in their turn give place to households.
4. Atlast comes the modern family.

Criticism

The matriarchal theory is more sociological than political. It seeks to explain the origin of family and not that of the state. There is no adequate proof in support of the matriarchal system as the universal and necessary beginning of society.

PATRIARCHAL THEORY

The Patriarchal theory explains that the state originated from the patriarchal family or the family in which the pater or father was the head. State is an enlargement of the family. Originally the family consisted of a man, his wife and children. The father was the head of the family and his control and authority was complete in all respects over all its members. When his children married there was expansion in the original family and it led to the establishment of new families. But the authority of the father and head of the original family remained as before, and it was duly acknowledged by all his descendants. This constituted the patriarchal family. The chief exponent of the patriarchal theory is Sir Henry Maine. The following important points may be noted in Maine's Patriarchal theory.

1. In the Patriarchal family the element of paternity was the chief fact.
2. Descent was traced not only through males and from the same ancestor. None of the descendants of a female was included in the primitive notion of family relationship. Kinship was accordingly, purely negative.
3. Permanent marriage was the rule whether monogamy or polygamy
4. The Head of the family was the basis of all authority, and his power was unqualified over his children and their houses and other relations of all descendants. howsoever numerous.
5. He controlled not only the business affairs of the group which he headed but its religion and its conduct.

The family was the primal unit of political society, "the seed led of all larger growths of governments, "as Woodrow Wilson calls it. The single family had developed into several families; yet all of them were fully conscious of their ultimate kinship. Bound together by ties of common anchestors, they associated in a wider common fellowship group, the gens, owing allegiance to some elected elder - perhaps the oldest living ascendent or the most capable. Similarly, the gens broadened into the tribe. The pastoral pursuits gave way to agriculture and settled life on a definite land became a matter of necessity; land tribes united to form the state.

In support of his statement, Sir Henry Maine cited the patriarchs of the old testament "families" and "brotherhood" of Athens, the patriapotestos in Rome and the Hindu Joint family system in India.

Criticism of Matriarchal and Patriarchal Theory

Modern theories show that the patriarchal family was not universal, the patriarchal theory was subjected to severe attacks. Patriarchal and matriarchal theories are in essence sociological rather than political theories. Stephen Leacock says nonetheless, both the theories sufficiently establish that family is the original link in the evolution of the state.

Both these theories do not satisfactorily explain the origin of the state. Matriarchal and patriarchal could have been prevalent in certain early societies. But it is wrong to assume that the creation of state was occasioned by these systems. There was not substantial proof to support the universal validity of these theories.

FORCE THEORY

According to this theory, the state originated due to force exerted by the strong over the weak. The idea contained in the statement is that "war begat the king". The same view is expressed by Hume, Oppenheim, Jenks-Bernhardy and Trietschke are the exponents of force theory. A number of rulers also believed in this theory. The powerful conquered the weak state is the outcome of the process of aggressive exploitation of the weaker by the stronger. Might without right is antagonist to individual liberty.

Criticism

The theory of force unduly emphasis the principle of the survival of the fittest. It means that might is right and those who are physically weak should go to the wall. It is dangerous to employ such a principle in the internal existence of the state. Every state will be at perpetual war with the rest. This is a condition of chaos, pure and simple endangering the peace and security of the world. The attention and efforts of every state will be directed towards war preparedness and to win the war if it comes. War which is an alias for murder, glorifies brute process, suppressing the moral forces. This is the mean self of man and not his real self. This theory justifies despotism. It is opposed to the idea of freedom. It is too much to believe that the state is created and maintained by sheer force and the spiritual and moral values have absolutely no place in life.

EVOLUTIONARY THEORY

It explains the state is the product of growth, a slow and steady evolution extending over a long period of time and ultimately shaping itself into the complex structure of a modern state. This theory is more scientific. The state is neither the handiwork of God, nor the result of superior physical force, nor the creation of evolution or convention, nor a mere expansion of the family. The state is not a mere artificial mechanical creation but an institution of natural growth or historical evolution says professor Garner.

There were a number of factors which helped the evolution of the state. They were kinship, religion, war, migration economic activities and political consciousness. The important factors which contributed to the growth of the state are

1. Kinship
2. Religion
3. Property and defence
4. Force
5. Political consciousness

4

SOVEREIGNTY

MEANING

The term sovereignty is derived from the Latin word 'Superanus' meaning supreme. It is basically a legal concept. It denotes supremacy of state. To understand the term sovereignty, it is desirable to look into some definitions of the given by some political thinkers. **Jean Bodin** defined sovereignty as "absolute and perpetual power of commanding in a state. It is supreme power over citizens and subjects unrestrained by law". **Pollock** says that "Sovereignty is that power which is neither temporary nor delegated nor subject to particular rules, which it cannot alter, nor answerable to any other power on the earth." **Burgers** described sovereignty as "original absolute unlimited power over the undivided subjects and over all associations of subjects. It is the underived and independent power to command and compel obedience."

D.F Russell defines sovereignty as "the strongest power and supreme authority within a state, which is unlimited by law or anything else."

According to **Laski** sovereign is "legally supreme over any individual or group. It possesses supreme coercive power."

The above definitions may differ from each other but one thing is very clear and there is no doubt about the superior authority of sovereignty.

The basic idea is that the sovereignty is able to declare law, issue commands and take political decisions, which are binding on individuals and associations within his jurisdiction.

Characteristics

Sovereignty has the following characteristics:

1. Sovereignty is absolute from the legal point of view.
2. Sovereignty is permanent. It lasts as long as he state. Change in Government does not end sovereignty but only transfers it to the next bearer.
3. Sovereignty of the state is universal. It extends to all within its territory.
4. Sovereignty is inalienable. Sovereignty of the state cannot be given away without destroying the state.
5. Sovereignty cannot be divided between or shared by a plurality. To Gettell – "If sovereignty is not absolute no state exists; if sovereignty is divided more than one state exists; but with the emergence of the concept of federalism, the idea of dual sovereignty was provided by Tocqueville, Wheaton and Halleck.
6. Sovereignty is exclusive. State alone has the sovereign authority and legitimate power to make citizens obey its dictates. It is again important to note that all these characteristics of sovereignty are peculiar to the legal notion of sovereignty. They are best represented by an absolute monarchy.

In the actual working of the state – especially in the case of democratic, federal, pluralist and constitutional government – it becomes extremely difficult to discover the seat or real character of sovereignty.

KINDS OF SOVEREIGNTY

Sovereignty can be classified into different kinds.

Titular Sovereignty

By titular sovereignty we mean sovereignty by the title only. It refers to the sovereign powers of the king or monarch who has ceased to exercise any real authority. In theory he may still posses all the powers but in practice sovereign power is enjoyed by some other person or body of persons.Titular sovereign is only a symbol of authority, a legacy of past. Britain presents a good example of titular sovereign. The king is the titular head and he does not enjoy any real powers. Actual powers are enjoyed by council of ministers and parliament. In India president is a titular sovereign and the cabinet is a real sovereign.

De Facto and De Jure Sovereignty

De facto sovereignty indicates to a sovereign who without legal support or constitutional support enjoys sovereign power. De jure sovereign is recognized by law or the constitution, but not in position to practice its power. In case of revolutions, that is a successful overthrow of the existing regime in a state tree may be de facto and de jure sovereigns. For example when Mussolini came to power in Italy in 1922, de facto sovereignty passed into his hands although Victor Emmanual was the de jure sovereign. The military dictatorship of the present world, established after a coup d'etate also represents de facto sovereignty until it evolves suitable means to legitimize its authority.

Legal and Political Sovereignty

Legal sovereign grants rights to its citizens and there can be no rights against him. It means rights of citizens depend on the will of legal sovereign and any time he can take away. Legal sovereign has following characteristics:

1. The legal sovereignty is always definite and determinate.
2. Legal sovereignty may reside either in one person or in a body of persons.
3. It is definitely organized, precise and known to law.
4. Rights of citizen are gift of legal sovereign.
5. The will of state is expressed by the legal sovereign only.
6. Legal sovereignty is absolute. It cannot be question.

But behind the legal sovereignty there is another power, which is unknown to law. It is political sovereignty. In practice absolute and unlimited authority of the legal sovereignty does not exist anywhere. Even a dictator cannot act independently and exclusively. The will of legal sovereignty is actually sharpened by many influences, which are unknown to law. All these influences are the real power behind the legal sovereign; and this is called political sovereignty. As **Professor Gilchrist** says- "The political sovereign is the sum total of the influences in the state which lie behind the law." The political sovereignty is not known to law. In modern representative democracies the political sovereignty is very often identified with either the whole mass of he people or with electorate or with public opinion. The legal sovereign cannot act against the will of political sovereign. **Dicey** says that "body is politically sovereign which the lawyers recognize there is another sovereign to whom the legal sovereign bow- that body is political sovereignty; that which is ultimately obeyed by the citizens of the state."

A lot of confusion arises when we attempt the exact definition of political sovereignty. It is a vague and indeterminate and cannot be located with exactness. It is suggested by some writers that there is no justification for making a distinction between legal and political sovereignty, as that involves the division of sovereignty, which is not possible.

Popular Sovereignty

When the sovereignty resides in the people of he state it is called as popular sovereignty. This theory was expounded by Rousseau, when later became the slogan of French Revolution.

The doctrine of popular sovereignty regards people as the supreme authority. It is people who decide right or wrong. People are not bound by any natural or divine law. Government exists only as a tool for the good of the people. It should be held directly responsible to the people. It can exercise authority only on the basis of the law of land.

THEORY OF SOVEREIGNTY

AUSTIN'S THEORY OF SOVEREIGNTY (MONISTIC VIEW)

Austin's theory of sovereignty depends mainly upon his view on nature of law. According to Austin "Law is a command given by a superior to inferior". the main tenets of Austin's theory of sovereignty are as follows:

1. Sovereign power is essential in every political society.
2. Sovereignty is a person or body of persons. It is not necessary that sovereign should be a single person. Sovereignty may reside in many persons also. Austin explains that a "Sovereign is not necessarily a single person, in the modern western world he is rarely so; but he must have so much of the attributes of a single person as to be a determinate."

   To Austin state is a legal order, in which there is a supreme authority, which is source of all powers. Sovereignty is concerned with man, and every state must have human superior who can issue commands and create laws. Human laws are the proper subjects of state activity.
3. Sovereign power is indivisible. Division of sovereignty leads to its destruction. It cannot be divided.
4. The command of sovereignty is superior to over all individuals and associations. Sovereign is not bound to obey anyone's order. His will is supreme. There is no question of right or wrong, just or unjust, all his commands are to be obeyed.
5. Austin's theory says that the obedience to sovereign must be habitual. It means that obedience should be continuous. He also includes that is not necessary that obedience should come from the whole society. It is sufficient, if it comes from the lay majority of people. Obedience should come from bulk of the society otherwise there is no sovereign.

   In brief we can say that sovereignty according to Austin is supreme, indivisible and unquestionable.

Criticism

Like all other theories of sovereignty Austin's theory is also not free from criticism. The first criticism is regarding sovereignty residing in a determinate superior. Even sovereign's acts are shaped by so many other influences, such as morals, values and customs of the society. **Sir Henry Maine** gives the example of Maharaja Ranjit Singh. He pointed out that the Maharaja "could have commanded anything. The smallest disobedience to his command would have been followed by death or mutilation." In spite of this, the Maharaja never "once in all his life issued a command which Austin could call a law. The rules which regulated the life of his subjects were derived from their immemorial usage."

Secondly Austin says that the sovereign is possessed of unlimited powers, which is again not acceptable. It is possible only in theory not in practice. Laski points out that "no sovereign has anywhere possessed unlimited power and attempt to exert it has always resulted in the establishment of safeguards."

Thirdly Austin says that sovereign is indivisible. All powers Must be centered in the hands of one person or a body of persons called sovereign. But this has been also disproved by Federal system of governments. It is characteristic of federal state that power must be divided between the federal government and its units.

Austin's theory is criticized further on the grounds of his definition of law. Austin defines law as "command given b a superior to inferior". This is also not true. No sovereign can ignore the existence of customary law, which has grown through usage in every country. It seems to be that Austin's theory may not be accepted as valid for political philosophy. His legal theory of sovereign.

narrows down "the meaning of vital terms." It should, however be admitted that as an analysis of strictly legal nature of sovereignty. Austin's theory is clear and logical.

PLURALIST THEORY OF SOVEREIGNTY

The pluralist theory of sovereignty was a reaction to monistic or legal theory of sovereignty. To monistic theory state is supreme association and all other associations are he creation of state and their existence depends on the will of the sovereign power.

The pluralist theory rejects this and tries to establish that there is no single source of authority that is all competent and comprehensive.

Laski says that sovereignty is neither absolute nor a unity. It is pluralist, constitutional and responsible. State has no superior claim to an individual's allegiance. It can justify itself as a public service corporation. State exists to coordinate functions of human association in the best interest. Another exponent of pluralist theory Robert M.MacIver propounds that state is one of the several human associations, although it exercises unique functions. Important feature of the state is supremacy of law.

Pluralists believe that state enjoys a privileged position because of its wider jurisdiction, which covers all the individuals and associations within its boundary. This does not mean that it is superior to other associations. It is also true that state has power to punish those who defy its command but that does not mean that it is absolute. The state must justify the exercise of its special powers. Pluralist is divided and limited. The pluralist demand that the same must justify its claim to allegiance on moral grounds. Actually to them the management and control of society must be shared by various associations in proportion to their contribution to the common goods. This theory stands for the decentralization of authority.

The pluralist also rejects the distinction between state and government. They insist on a realistic political science and consider the distinction between two as artificial. The pluralists are not against the state but would discard sovereign state with its absolute and indivisible power. The chief tenets of pluralist theory of sovereignty are as follows.

(a) Pluralist sovereignty deals with political aspects of sovereignty.

(b) State is one of the several human associations catering to various interests of the individuals.

(c) State is arbiter over conflicting interests of different associations.

(d) State should compete with other human associations to claim superior authority.

(e) State was not absolute or supreme legally.

(f) State is not the only source of legislation or law.

(g) Law is very antithesis of command.

(h) The state is both the child and parent of law.

(i) He root of obedience of law isn't coercion but the will to obey.

(j) State and government are not different.

Criticism

The pluralist theory of sovereignty is also not free from criticism. Critics maintain that without establishment of a classless society, sovereignty can neither be divided nor be limited. In order to limit the sovereignty of the state there must be a classless society.

The demands for freedom from different associations also are criticized. Division of sovereignty among different associations is not only impossible but also improper. The pluralist view will lead to political anarchy and social instability.

The pluralist limits the sovereignty in order to maintain independence of individuals and other associations, however in order to maintain the rights of the individuals and associations, the state must have sovereign power. The interest of individuals and associations, will conflict and the state will be helpless if it does not posses sovereign power.

Inspite of all these criticism it cannot be denied that the pluralist theory of sovereignty protested the rigid and dogmatic legalism of the Austin's theory of sovereignty. It supports humanist and democratic ideas. It challenged the concept of unlimited sovereignty.

This theory also pointed out the importance of other associations. Only state is not important but in a society there are also many other associations, which play important role in its development. At last we can say that the greatest contribution of this theory is that it gave state a human face, and checked it from being a threat to the liberty.

5

POLITICAL THEORY

LIBERALISM

IDEA

Liberalism comprises a set of ideas and practices governing collective life in any society. Liberalism is a distinctly modern phenomenon. It emerged out of the enlightenment, the Glorious Revolution in England and the French Revolution. John Lock is waived as the father of liberalism. It is closely wedded to individualism. Its central theme is that the individuals are embodiment of reason who know what is good and bad for them. While classical liberals conceived of state as hinderance of hinderances, contemporary liberals acknowledge concerns that go beyond pure individualism. However, it should not have been observed as a single comprehensive doctrine, rather there have arisen a number of off shoots.

Origin and Evolution

The word liberalism has latin root liber which means liberty. But as a word, first it was used to refer a political party in Spain. Perhaps the best illustration of historical role of liberalism is given by Harold J. Laski, in his State in Theory and Practice, has significantly observed : "The birth of the Liberal tradition can only be explained by the shift in the residence of economic power which accompanied it. At bottom it was a way of justifying the transfer of political authority from a land-owning aristocracy to a commercial middle class, and, like all philosophies which seek to justify such a transfer, it stated its principles in terms of a logic wider in theory than it was prepared to admit in practice."

It played a crucial role in particular historical setting. It was an ideology of the newly emerged class who wanted an economic system of free trade based on the principle of laissez-faire in place of mercantilism. In place of absolute monarchy and factual patronages, they sought supremacy of Parliament.

However with the passage of time it moved from purely laissez-faire individualistic premiers to welfare and even interventional state. It sought to incorporate principles and principles for development of individual personalities.

David G. Smith : 'Liberalism is the belief in and commitment to a set of methods and policies that have as their common aim greater freedom for individual men.

L.T. Hobhouse, in his Liberalism

Liberalism is the belief that society can safely be founded on self directing power of personality, that its only on it his foundation that a true community can be built, and that so established its foundations are so deep and so wide that there is no limit that we can place to the extent of the building.

Grimes : "Liberalism represents a system of ideas that aims the realization of pluralist society, forcing diversity in politics, economy, religion and our cultural life."

Basic Feature

1. Man as the embodiment of reason.
2. Man is capable of deciding his good and bad.
3. Primacy of procedure.
4. Contract as mechanism of social relations.

5. No incompatibility between individual interest and social good.

6. Upholder of civil and political liberties.

7. Emphasis on toleration.

8. Conceive of civil society as the arena of realization of freedom.

MODERN AND CLASSICAL LIBERALISM

Broadly, two trends can be in liberalism :

1. Classical liberalism
2. Modern liberalism

Classical Liberalism

- Also called Negative Liberalism.
- Theoretical formulation in the words of
  - — Locke : Two Treatise on Civil Govt.
  - — Montesquieu : The Spirit of Laws
  - — Bentham : Fragments on Government
  - — Smith : Wealth of Nations
  - — Spencer : The Man versus the State
- Market to be chief motivating force for the pursuit of all values.
- Politics was conceived as autonomous capable of rising above narrow, vested interests.
- State was a necessary evil. To Bentham 'The best Govt. was the one that governed the least'.
- The doctrine of liberty was tied to doctrine of equality.
- Claim to equality was only a political claim and in other sphere it meant equality of opportunity.

Modern Liberalism

- Also described as positive liberalism.
- Abandoning the policy of laissez-faire and adopting the policy of welfare and interventionist state.
- Emphasised by Mill and Green and developed by Hobshouse, Laski and Tawney.
- Sought to extend the sphere of equality to the realm economy.
- Economic equality implied a more equitable distribution of the national income through higher wages and larger social benefits and service financed by heavy taxation on high income of individuals and corporations.
- They discarded the concept of free market as the guarantor of economic efficiency.
- If had its economic implication in the work of Keynes report of Lord Beveridge (U.K.).

Varieties of Liberalism

Different schools within the liberal tradition can be categorised as

1. Individualism
2. Utilitarianism
3. Neo-liberalism or Libertarianism

INDIVIDUALISM

Thomas Hobbes and John Locke are regarded as the originator of individualism.

The political theory of the individualism places high value on the individual. It regards the human individual as an end in itself and considers political, economic and social institutions as mere means to that end. It regards the state as a necessary evil and limits its scope to provide security to its citizens.

According to the individualist theorists, the people have their natural or pre-political freedoms. In pursuing their interests, the individuals should not be restrained by the society or by the state except to prevent them from invading or cheating other individuals.

The government which governs the least is considered to be the best government. The individualists maintain that the state should only perform the protective or law-and-order functions for its citizens; beyond those functions, the state should not intervene in the social and economic spheres. The individualists laid stress on the aspect of liberty, interpreted in terms of absence of restraint enjoyed primarily in the realm of civil society.

The individualists were inspired by a french school of economic thought called Physiocrats who paved the way for laissez-faire individualism.

Laissez-faire

It is a French word which means 'leave alone'. It signified non-intervention by the state in the economic activities. It forms a part of liberal political theory in the sense that it regards the property right of individual as a necessary condition of liberty and seeks to set limit on government to regulate the socio-economic domain. It regards state as a necessary evil because it curtails freedom but can only safeguard it in case of its encroachment by others.

It was led by burghers, the tradesmen, the money-lenders and the small manufactures of France and England in the eighteenth century who had felt terribly restrained by the controls and regulations of the mercantilist state.

It flourished as a social and political theory form the middle of the 18th century till about the middle of the 19th century. It was advocated by the French physiocratic political economists (Francois Quesnay and Victor de Riqueis; Marquis de Mirabeau), the English classical political economists (Adam Smith, David Ricardo, Thomas Malthus, and John Stuart Mill) and by Herbert Spencer. In India, the individualistic view of the ideology of Laissez-faire is chiefly a characteristic of early phase of capitalism (after merchantile one).

Mercantilist policies were pursued by the state of England, France and Germany in the 17th and early part of the 18th centuries. Through the policies of mercantilism, each country sought to obtain a favourable balance of trade against its international or foreign rivals.

There mercantilist system was a system of state regulations and controls over the economy, aimed at increasing national power and wealth. It was directed not only against foreign states and their economies, but also against the internal or domestic sources of challenge. Factory replace form as unit of production.

The wealth accumulated in this phase gave rise to a new middle class, who pressed for reform and loosening state control.

Different Views : Adam Smith, John Stuart Mill and Herbert Spencer were the major theorists of individualism and laissez-faire. Their theories have been discussed as under.

Adam Smith : Adam Smith in his "An Inquiry into the Nature and Causes of the Wealth of Nations (1776)", offered an economic argument for laissez-faire individualism. He attacked the mercantilist system of controls and regulations, which, he said prevented the division of labour from yielding its fruits. He also attacked the state's rights to grant monopoly privileges to firms and companies which thereby receive unfair and unproductive protection from competition. He was greatly influenced by the ideas of French physiocrats.

According to Smith, economic growth depends on exploitation of nature, division of labour, expansion of markets, free trade, capital accumulation and economic competitor. The free or unfettered pursuit of self-interest by the individuals under competitive conditions would, according to him lead to greater productivity and the increase of wealth, the benefits of which would get diffused throughout the society. In this way, there would come about a "system of natural liberty and perfect justice." The competitive market, he said, is self-regulating and harmonious. He pins faith in visible hand that will bring about the harmony of individual interests through the self-adjustment of the forces of supply and demand.

Smith espoused the political manifestation of economic laissez-faire, in terms of natural liberty of individuals. Consequently, states role was confined to

— protect the nation
— protect the individual
— maintain certain public work departments.

Herbert Spencer : Spencer wrote three works, viz, "The Proper Sphere of Government, Social Statics" and "Man versus State" to advance an extreme form of laissez-faire individualism, inspired by the Darwinian notion of the survival of the fittest and the law of natural selection, he says "State exists so Long as Crime exist in Society."

He says that society should allow those who are fit and well-adjusted to survive and flourish, while those who are unfit and maladjusted to their environment should be left to perish.

In his view, the only legitimate functions of the state are the maintenance of order and the administration of justice, and their purpose is "simply to defend the rural rights of man to protect person and property.'' Beyond these, the state, says Spencer, should not interfere with the natural, self-adjusting laws of society. He denies to the state any role in regulating currency, running the postal services, regulating trade and commerce or aiding the poor.

He drew a distinction between the ''military state,'' in which the individuals are mere meant to the realization of the ends of the state, and the ''industrial state'', in which the individuals constitute the supreme end of government. The rights of the individual, he says, proceed the state and are inalienable. Even popular majorities would not interfere with those inalienable rights. Aim of liberalism, ''was that of putting a limit to the power of kings. The function of true Liberalism in the future will be that of putting limit to the powers of parliament.'' States intervention in society hampers individual initiative and retards the progress of society.

J.S. Mill : Mill in his works; viz; ''On Liberty'' ''Principles of Political Economy'' ''Considerations on Representative Government'', ''The subjugation of women,'' started with defence of laissez-faire individualism but sought to remedy it with positive functions of the state. In fact he was a champion of negative liberty and positive state. While Smith and Spencer sought to promote the individualistic doctrine in instrumental terms, Mill gave it a moral orientation, this case for individual liberty was conceived as an essential ingredient of qualitative life. In particular, he emphasised on liberty of thought and expression as well as liberty of conduct.

Mill makes a distinction between 'self-regarding actions' and 'other regarding actions.' An individual is granted complete freedom in all matters not affecting the community. However, in 'other regarding actions', he grants the right to the community.

His opposition to the interventionist state is based on the assumption that things are better done by the concerned individuals than by government officials. The second reason is that self-governing activities by the individuals are a ''means to their own mental education a mode of strengthening their active faculties, exercising their judgement and giving them a fair knowledge of the subjects with which they are thus left to deal.'' Mill argues, in other words, that we can develop ourselves by doing many things which we normally leave to the Government to do for us. Even if certain things can be better done by the Government than by ourselves. Mill says, we should still do them ourselves as they will have an educative and developmental impact on us.

Elaborating upon his ethical grounds for opposing the state's compulsion of the individual, Mill writes: ''A state which dwarfs its men, in order that they may be docile instruments in its hands even for beneficial purposes-will find that with small men no great thing can really be accomplished.''

In contemporary period moral individualism has been emphasized by Rawls; economic (laissez-faire) individualism by Triedman, Lozick and Hayek; methodological individualism by Karl Popper in his theory of incremental change.

Criticism of Individualism

1. Utilitarians point out at the contradiction between individual good and aggregate good. To them aggregate good need not account for good of each individual.
2. Laissez-faire individualism resulted in recurring economic crisis and depressions. It led to retrenchment of labour and increase in unemployment.
3. C.B. Mackpherson in his ''Political Theory of Possessive Individualism'' accuses individualists of conceiving individuals as the proprietor of his own person or capacities, owing nothing to the society.
4. It gave rise to monopolists degrading the status of worker and petty bourgeois classes.
5. It provided ideological base to the flourishing of capitalist mode of production.
6. Most derogatory aspect has been comparison of social life with biological law of natural selection. As Mahatma Gandhi observed ''Man is higher than the brute in his moral

instincts and moral institutions. The law of nature as applied to the one is different from the law of nature and free will as it is.''

But, it can not be denied that individualistic view had a major role in liberating societies from courage of religious wars in Europe, feudal bottlenecks and promoting democratic sentiments. It paved way for higher productivity. But it had serious lacunae which were sought to be overcome in other versions of liberalism.

UTILITARIANISM

Utilitarianism is a theory about nature and motives of human conduct and standard of moral judgement. It is essentially an ethical theory whose founder was Jermy Bentham. J.S. Mill came to revise the basic tenets of utilitarianism. Henry Sidgwick is another exponent of this tradition.

Bentham's well known works are ''Fragment on Government'' and ''Introduction to the principles of moral and legislation''. He conceived man as a sensual being who acts so as to enjoy pleasure and avoid pain. He observes ''Nature has placed mankind under the governance of two sovereign masters, pain and pleasure. It is for them above to point out what we ought to do, as well as to determine what we shall do. On the one hand the standard of right and wrong, on the other the chain of the causes are fastened to their throne. They govern us in all we say, in all we think; every effort we can make to throw off our subjection will serve but to demonstrate and confirm it.'' As a consequence, they insisted that all measures and institutions be judged in terms of their contribution towards enjoyment of pleasure and avoidance of pain. They coined hedonistic calculus to measure pleasure and pain. The purpose to state being ''Greatest happiness of greatest number'' where ''everyone was to count for one and no one to be move than one.'' So, ''a good government is one which governs the heart.''

Criticism

1. Utilitarianism does not see qualitative difference between pleasures. This aspect was overcome by J.S. Mill. He rejects Benthamite premise that quantity of pleasure being equal, pushpin is as good as poetry. Rather, he holds that as a source of pleasure poetry is much higher than pushpin or any other game. As he observes ''it is better to be a human being dissatisfied than a pig satisfied: better to be a Socrates dissatisfied than a fool satisfied.''
2. C.B. Macpherson points at the contradiction in this view. There is tension between man as a desirer of utility and man as enjoyer or developer of his powers.
3. John Rawls criticises it on grounds of fairness. While calculating the aggregate good, it neglects the good of the least advantaged. As a result, utilitarianism treats some individual only as means towards end of others. It is incompatible with the conception of social cooperation among free and equal individuals for mutual advantage and with the idea of reciprocity implicit in a well ordered society.
4. In its practical connotation, utilitarianism and its hedonistic calculus received serious set backs. The appalling miseries and contradictions in societies saved way for welfare, interventionist state as espoused by T.W. Green and Lord Keynes.

Even though the liberal democratic societies adopted welfare model, its effects were not very optimistic. Growing economic burden and political apathy failed to deliver results. The regulation of property hampered private initiative and enterprise. As a result, a new school of thought emerged in the liberal tradition, known as Libertarianism or Neo-Liberalism.

NEO-LIBERALISM

An extreme form of laissez-faire individualism that developed in the writings of Hayek, Friedman and Nozick. They are also referred to as libertarians. They draw on the natural rights tradition of John Locke and champions full autonomy and freedom of the individual. They decry welfare policies of the state and supports a minimal state. Some of them even accords to market, the role to perform the economic functions including the defence of person and property through a private form. In essence, they support full autonomy and freedom of the individual; it seeks his 'liberation' from all institutions which tend to restrict his vision of the world, including the institutions of religions, family and customs of social conformity apart from political institutions. Philosophically it repudiates the deterministic outlook of human life, treats man as maker of his destiny. In the political sphere, libertarianism particularly insists that man's economic activity must be actively liberated from all restrictions to enable him to achieve true progress and prosperity.

Libertarianism holds that certain rights of the individual which precede his political life, are indefensible and these cannot be surrendered in favour of the collectivity. It particularly defends the right to acquire and hold property and freedom of contract. These rights are by no means product of the state itself, hence the state cannot be allowed to intervene for any artificial balancing of rights. It even condemns taxation of the rich for the benefit of the poor. It argues that taxation for welfare of certain sections of society involves the forced transfer of fruit of one man's labour to another, which serves as a disincentive to the individual. On the contrary, if all individuals are free from it.

F.A. Hayek

Hayek in his 'The Road of Serfdom' exhorts that the growth of state will lead inexorably to totalitarianism. To him, socialism, planning and collectivism are a tool to curtail individual freedom. He supports free market economy. It is not concerned with distribution. But, he advocates state provision of a minimum income.

In his "Constitution of Liberty" Hayek defines liberty as the "State in which a man is not subject to thé coercion by the arbitrary will of another. It is purely a legal conception and not a political one. In fact, law, liberty and property are intricately intertwined in his scheme. A liberal social order is necessary for its realization.

Robert Nozick

Nozick in his "Anardy, State and Utopia" holds the view that the welfare state is minimal to individual freedom. He defends the market and a minimal "nightwatchman" state. To him, the state comes into existence for the maintenance of property rights of the individuals. It has no legitimate powers beyond the functions of protection, justice and defence. It can not redistribute property or income. He argues that inequalities at the level of production should not be rectified at the level of distribution.

Milton Friedman

Friedman condemns the welfare state by observing that "not all means are justified simply by reference to the ends, how so ever noble they are. In his "Capitalism and Freedom" he sees an inevitable link between capitalism and enjoyment of freedom, consequently, he supports state intervention only in those sphere which can not be handled by market. It has no role beyond and above sustaining and supplementing a market society.

Criticism

1. The Libertarians have been dubbed as philosophers of the bourgeoisie interested primarily in the maintenance of status quo.
2. The renewed emphasis is on negative liberty and minimal state neglects the egalitarian agenda which every genuine political theory should serve.
3. It paves way for renewed emphasis on the biological law of natural selection and survival of the fittest syndrome.
4. It neglects the claims of disadvantaged and discriminated sections of society.

NEW THEMES

Isaiah Berlin

In his two concepts of liberty Berlin reconciles individual freedom with value pluralism. To him, "good life can be lived in several ways and no idea can claim mastery over the another". Freedom is the freedom to choose from an indefinite number of values. He rejects reason as an arbiter among inherently rivalrous and incommensurable goods. He accepts the reality of cultural community memberships but sees it as being shaped by the free play of individuality. Such comprehensive is his scheme that John Gray remarked that "Berlin marks a departure point for theorisation of idea of pluralism and freedom.

John Rawls

The works of John Rawls goes beyond the laissez-faire principles of individualistic liberalism. In his 'A Theory of Justice' he tries to evolve a working principle for social cooperation in liberal democratic societies by basing it on a justificatory base of reciprocal exchange. He takes cognizance of inequalities in a market society and adequately responds to it. The underlying assumption of his theory is that if basic structures of society are fair, most of the problem as regards the stability of a system can be solved.

In his 'Political Liberalism', Rawls seeks to orient liberal occupation with diversity, difference and community. He clings to the public-private dichotomy by responsing a public conception of justice arrived at through overlapping consensus of reasonable comprehensive doctrines.

In his 'The Laws of People' Rawls presents a procedural theory of Justice at the global level.

Critical Evaluation

The political theories of liberalism have received mounting challenges. While, earlier it was believed that it faces fierce opposition only from the Marxists, today there have arisen new schools of thought questioning liberalism on a number of points. These include :

1. Marxist accuse liberals of providing ideological apparatus to the capitalist mode of production, hiding inequalities and exploitation of workers and perpetuating status quo.
2. Communitarians have questioned the notion of disembodied self. They hold that an individual is deeply embedden in a social matrix which is vital part of his identity.
3. Postmodernists have questioned the enlightenment predicaments that liberalism is accused of serving. They deny the relevance of universal categories and grand theories. Instead they hold, that social experience are contingent. There is nothing certain and final. In essence, they emphasize fragmented nature of social world.
4. Multiculturalists have attacked the uniformity popularized by liberal institutions. They question the relevance of individual right allocated to the citizens without taking into account of his linguistic, ethnic or other such connections.
5. Feminists have attacked the division of social life into public and private sphere. They hold that the notion of neutral public sphere is biased and reflects the male presuppositions.

Ever since its genesis in the turmoil in Europe, Liberalism had suited the genesis of time. It replaced traditional conservation and orthodoxy by modern rationalism. Perhaps because of its efficacy and pragmation, more and more country's are getting lured towards liberal democratic institution. The triumph of liberal democracy as a final form of government may be decried in some quarters, but as Stephen Eric Bronner argues "a replacement to liberal democratic state no longer exists." However it will have to be sensitive as regards contradictions of economic relations in the society. It will have to buttress itself with egalitarian elements of socialism and cultural connectiveness of multiculturalism.

MARXISM

IDEA

Marxism comprises a set of idea and practice about man and society that originated in the writings of Marx and Engles and developed by Lenin and Mao. Like Liberalism, it is a distinctively modern doctrine. Surprisingly, Marxism was unknown at the time of Marx who said "All I know is that I am not a Marxist." G.V. Plekhnov, a Russian Marxist announced that "Marxism is a world view". Perhaps, its revolutionary tactics and unanticipatory claims remain a unique feature and continue to inspire millions of people worldwide. There are people like David McLellan who seems to believe in Marxism even before Marx. His three volumes

1. Marxism before Marx
2. Karl Marx-His life and Thought
3. Marxism after Marx : An Introduction, speaks for it.

Origin : Marxism originated in response to havoc which the early civilization had brought about. It continues because it contains tools to penetrate the opaque side of capitalism. Its scientific rigour, humanist hinge and optimism with communism remains as relevant as ever. As Harry W. Laidler in "Social Economic Movements" has observed "The Communist Manifesto, issued in the revolutionary year 1848 at the behest of a small international workingmen's organization, was at once an interpretation of the role of the working class in past and future history and a clarion call to labour to unite for the purpose of securing its emancipation and, through that emancipation, the freedom of all mankind. It marked the advent of Marxian or 'scientific' socialism, a social philosophy which has exerted such a powerful influence on the political, social, economic, and cultural thought of the last half century and which seems destined to play still larger role in future historical developments."

Main Works : By Marx and Engles

— The Class Struggles in France

— The 18th Brumaire of Louis Bonaparte

— The Civil War in France.

— Introduction to a Contribution to the Critique of Hegel's Philosophy of Right

— Manifesto of the Communist Party

— Critique of the Gotha Programme

— Das Capital

Lenin

— What is to be Done

— State and Revolution

— Imperialism : The Highest Stage of Capitalism

CLASSICAL AND NEO-MARXISM

The original tenets of Marxism-as a scientific system of thought are identified as Classical Marxism. The wider implications of Marxism, including humanist thought of the Young Marx, are broadly identified as Neo-Marxism.

Marxism begins with the simple observation that in order to survive, man must produce food and material objects. In doing so he enters into social relationship with other men. From the simple hunting band to the complex industrial state, production is a social enterprise. Production also involves a technical component known as the forces of production which includes the technology, raw materials and scientific knowledge employed in the process of production. Each major state in the development of the forces of production will correspond with a particular form of the social relationships of production. Thus the forces of production in a hunting economy will correspond with a particular set of social relationships. Taken together, the force of production and the social relationships of production form the economic base or infrastructure of society. The other aspects of society, known as the superstructure, are largely shaped by the infrastructure. Thus the political legal and educational institutions, the belief and value systems are primarily determined by economic factors. A major change in the infrastructure will therefore produce a corresponding change in the superstructure. Marx maintained that, with the possible exception of the societies of prehistory, all historical societies contain basic contradictions which means that they cannot survive forever in their existing form. These contradictions involve the exploitation of one social group by another. For example in feudal society, lords exploit their serfs, in capitalist society, employers exploit their employees. This creates a fundamental conflict of interest between social groups since one gains at the expense of another. This conflict of interest leads to replacement of one mode of production by another one and transforming the superstructure as well. It will finally usher a communist society.

Neo-Marxism on the other hand, seeks to analyse the subtle aspects of the phenomenon of dominance, and dependence, distortions in contemporary civilization and the possible ways to human emancipation. Theme of alienation is repeatedly evident in these writings. Herbert Marcuse is an outstanding Neo-Marxist.

FREEDOM IN MARXIST THEORY

Although Marx and Engels never wrote systematically about the concept of freedom, its implications are sound enough to attract readers. In fact, it was seen in opposition to alienation that the capitalist mode of production had generated. As Rowcke in his work "The Problem of Freedom in Marxist Thought" observes "The notion of freedom plays a central role in the thought of Karl Marx...his notion of freedom often figures significantly in the background which gives meaning to his more specific and immediate concerns... the notion of freedom lurks behind the critique of religion and the whole description of the forms of alienation...the theme of the freedom of men has a pervasiveness and extent in the long development of his thought which marks it as one of those basic themes providing continuity to his work." Nevertheless, he accepts that capitalism was more beneficial in extending freedom than the earlier modes of production because it threw career open to talent and unleashed production forces of greater extent.

Marxist conception of freedom sees an interdependent relationship between liberty and equality. It means self-realization and self-determination. It is not to be confused with satisfaction of material wants. It signifies a condition where each human being endowed with their creative potential can exercise them. It can not be realized in a capitalist system of production characterized by necessity. Rather, true freedom can be realised in a rational system of production. This means the destruction of capitalism and the creation of a communist society that embodies collective control, collective individuality and personal freedom. As Gellner has observed "For the Marxists civil society is a fraud. The idea of plurality of institutions-both opposing and balancing the state and in turn controlled and protected by the state-is, in the Marxist view, merely the provision of a facade for a hidden and a maleffіcent domination."

PROPERTY IN MARXIST THEORY

One of the most distinctive feature of Marxism has been a scatching critique of the institution of private property. Perhaps it would not be incorrect to say that their critique of capitalist mode of production is primarily based on their analysis of the institution of private property.

According to Marxists, the institution of property did not enjoy the same status in different epoch of the history. They point out that there was no notion of private property under the primitive communist society. It arose with changes in the mode of production. There emerged different forms of private property in different mode of production, while in the slave society a slave was the private property of his master, feudalism was marked by private property in land ownership. However, it became a dominant form of economic organization with the arrival of commodity production under Capitalism.

The Marxists see division of labour as the principal cause for the emergence of private property. In the undeveloped stage of production of the primitive communal society the people directly depend on the nature. They live by hunting, fishing, cattle rearing etc. With the development of productive forces and resulting division of labour in the large state there arises slave system characterised by the existence of private property in the workmen themselves. When the large-scale agriculture becomes the chief mode of production, in the feudal period, the chief forms of property consist of landed property with serf labour claimed to it. The surplus value appropriated by the dominant class and instruments of primitive accumulation paved way for industrial revolution and the mechanized production pave way for the capitalist system.

Under the Capitalist system, the means of production are privately owned and the worker is forced to sell his labour power as a commodity in the market. The surplus value accumulated by the capitalist further the exploitation of working class. However, Marxists are optimistic with bourgeois in forms of property as it helps in creating working class as a class for itself. They will rebel against the existing class relations, which justify the bourgeois system of property.

Marx, Engels and Lenin held the view that the proletarian revolution would put to an end commodity production and also private property in the means of production. The property in these countries will be in the form of state property or collective property. It would finally disappear even in the sphere of consumption with the establishment of a classless communist society.

STATE IN MARXIST THEORY

Main Works

Antonio Gramsci	: Prison Notebooks.
Ralph Miliband	: The State in Capitalist Society
Nicos Poulantzas	: Political Power and Social Classes
N. Bobbio	: Which Socialism?: Marxism, Socialism and Democracy
Lenin	: State and Revolution
Engels	: Socialism: Utopian and Scientific, The origin of the Family, Private Property and the State

Different Views

Marx

1. ''An executive committee for managing the common affairs of the whole bourgeoisie.''
2. ''National power of capital over labour.''
3. ''An engine of class despotism.''
4. ''Political power, properly so called, is merely the organised power of one class for oppressing another.''

Engels

1. ''An organization of a particular class to forcibly keep the exploited class in the conditions of oppression.''
2. ''Essentially a capitalist machine.''

View of Marx and Engels

Karl Marx and Frederick Engels wrote extensively. They developed a scientific theory of society explaining how the present social order had come about, and how it would be transformed into a better one in the course of history. They made attempt to discover laws of historical changes. Wherein they showed that social development was inevitably moving in the direction of social revolution which would ultimately lead to the establishment of a communist society. But, what is most surprising is that they do not offer a clear cut theory of state. Their ideas are sketchy. It is fragmented and unsystematic one. Same is true of other classical Marxists such as Lenin, Trotseky and Gramci. As Bob Jessop observes ''Although they offer various acute observations on the state in general, specific historical causes and the nature of ideological domination, they do not confront the crucial questions of the differential forms of the capitalist state and their adequacy to continued accumulation in different situations.''

Marx's view on the state are largely determined by his perceptions and analyses of the French State, the Revolution of 1848 and Coup d' etat of Napoleon III, he wrote extensively in Rheinische Zetung'' against the authoritarian state. In the Eighteenth Drumaire of Louis Bonaparte, he denounced the bureaucratic and all powerful state.

Marx and Engels present a class theory of state. So to them ''History of all hitherto society is the history of class struggle'' (with the exception of primitive communism). In every class divided society there are two class, viz; a dominant and a dependent or oppressor and a oppressed class while the dominant class own the private property in the means of production; the dependent classes are closely clung with property relation.

Class in itself and Class for itself

It expresses the historical role for the proletariat in Marxist scheme of thing. A class in itself means that the working class in capitalist societies are aware of the need for co-operative effort to promote their own interest. They work together and realize that they constitute a particular segment of the society. They also become conscious of their conflicting interests with that of the bourgeoisie or the capitalist. However, a class can become a class for itself only when it becomes aware of its historic role and revolutionary potential. It realizes that it has an additional mission of transforming the present set up i.e. the capitalist mode of production through a proletarian revolution, paving way for classless society.

Origin and Forms

Marx and Engels reject the liberal view that the state is a natural institution and that it exists to promote the well-being of all the people. Rather, they hold that the state is a product of society at a certain stage of its development. It is a historical entity. It emerged out of the class division of the society and out of the need to hold the class antagonism in check. State has not been there in the primitive society, where the institutions of law, government and politics were totally absent.

Engels in his "The Origin of the Family, Private Property and the State" remarks that "The State...has not existed from all eternity. There have been societies that did without it, that had no idea of the state and state power. At a certain stage of economic development, which was necessarily bound up with the split of society into classes, the state became a necessity owing to this split."

In the early societies of primitive communal life, the relations of production were those of co-operation as their material basis were largely dependent upon hunting, fishing, fruit gathering and cattle-grazing. Thus, societies existed prior to the state.

They maintain that the institution of state originated for the first time as a result of the dissolution of the primitive communities. It gradually evolved when certain changes took place in the early economic forms of primitive society. State was actually necessitated at a particular stage of economic development when certain members of the society acquired control over the productive forces. This development in the field of economic production inevitably led to the division of society into classes—those who owned and controlled the means of production and those who did not.

Lenin in his State and Revolution, says "The State is product and manifestation of irreconcilability of class antagonisms. The state arises where, when and insofar as class antagonisms objectively cannot be reconciled."

State thus, originated out of the class division between the 'haves' and the 'havenots.' It came into existence in order to serve the interests of the former and continues to exist as an instrument for the exploitation of the latter.

Accordingly, different mode of production corresponds to a different form of state. There exists five different modes of production in Marxists scheme of things.

Primitive Communism

Also referred to as Stateless Societies or prestate societies. According to Marx and Engels, the primitive tribal societies existed much before the origin of the state. The groups were organised on the basis of blood relationship, common language and traditions. Though there was no established authority in terms of law, some rudiments of power did exist there. The primitive communal body generally functioned on the basis of full co-operation of its members as there was no clash or competition among them.

Tools were held in common ownership and things were produced by common labour. There was no surplus since men could produce only for the subsistence of each member of the community. There was no private property and no exploitation of man by man. The common affairs were managed collectively or entrusted to the elders. There was no distinction between ruler and the subjects. Hence, there was no need for a special apparatus of the state.

The change in the material basis and the development of productive forces on account of settled agriculture led to new division of labour and gave way to new socio-economic formations.

The Slave System

It is characterised by private ownership not only in the means of production but even workers are treated as property of their master. It arises with the emergence of private property and division of labour, is new and more complex socio-economic formations. As Engels describes it, "the break up of tribal authority involves a change in the system of property, and this transformation is accompanied by the rise of groups with reconciliable interests."

The society split up into two antagonistic classes–slaves and slave owners; the former as producers and the latter as non-producers who owned former's production conditions. The slaves were regarded as a form of property on the ground that they belonged wholly to the master. They had no social or legal existence independent of their masters. Their own labour power was an important factor of production, but the fruits of their labour wholly went to the master. Thus, in the slave mode of production, slaves stood in opposition to the slave owning classes. Subsequently, large-scale agriculture becomes chief mode of production, giving way to another system.

Feudal System

In the medieval feudal society, land was the sole source of economic life. The landlords, therefore, enjoyed certain special status, privileges, authority and political rights. The relations between the primary producer and the landlord were such that the former remained subordinate to the latter, and the latter's superior position and authority were an established fact of living. The society was divided into the landlord and serfs.

With the mechanized production Marx and Engels say : "the factory system began to develop alongside the guild structure; but the primitive factory where one man hired a dozen or so helpers and worked alongside them on his own premises, was only a beginning".

Capitalist System

It is characterized by the private ownership of the means of production in few hands. The society is split into two classes capitalists and workers (proletariat). The hallmark of this system is freedom of contract, that creates impression of a free society. However, it is marked by exploitation of workers.

Workers who do not own the means of production, only sell their labour power to the capitalists for wages. The means of production are owned by the capitalists who alone regulate the labour process. The labour produces surplus values because the worker is paid only a part of his produce as wages and the rest of the labour which remains unpaid is wholly appropriated by the capitalists. In such a society, the capitalists being the dominant economic class, influence the political and social system in numerous forms.

Ralph Miliband in his Marxism and Politics, has identified four functions of capitalist state.

1. Repressive : by maintaining law and order.
2. Ideological : Cultural :- to secure legitimacy
3. Economic : by developing capitalism
4. International: by serving ruling classes across the borders.

Socialist System

This system is also referred to as crude communism. It is coterminus with the dictatorship of the proletariat and an interim stage of transition to Communism. Marx says, Socialism "is the declaration of the permanence of the revolution, the class dictatorship of the proletariat, as the necessary transition stage to the abolition of all class distinctions, the abolition of all conditions of production which correspond to those condition of production." The bourgeoises state is still retained but without bourgeoisie, as Lenin observes "only the guns are turned to the opposite direction." It will be governed by the principle, "from each according to his ability and to each according to his work."

Marx and Engels held the view that the communist society is the final goal of Socialist revolution. Wherein, the State will either away. The guiding principle of social interaction will be voluntary association of individuals. The industrial technology would be put to maximum use and the forces of production and the relations of production will remain in perfect harmony.

Contemporary View

Bob Jessop in his "Marxist theory of state identifies" six approaches through which classical Marxists deal with the state :

Firstly, Treating state as a parasite institution that play an important role in production and reproduction activity. Modern State was an expression of the irreconcilable conflicts rooted in the egoism of civil society. Its officials oppress and exploit civil society on behalf of a particular sectional group. As Marx argues that the corporate organisation enables the bourgeoise and modern craftsmen to defend their material interests, the state becomes the private property of officials in their struggle for self advancement.

Secondly, Treating state and state power as epiphenomena (i.e. simple surface reflections) of the system of property relations and the resulting economic class struggles.

Thirdly, Treating state as the factor of cohesion in a given society. Engles views the state as an institution that emerges with economic exploitation. Its function is to regulate the struggle between antagonistic classes through repression and concession and thus moderate class conflict without undermining the continued domination of the ruling class and reproduction of the dominant mode of production.

Fourthly, Treating state as an instrument of class rule. This is the most common approach.

Fifthly, Treating state as a set of institutions without making some general assumption about its class character. The state is seen as a public power that develops at a certain stage in the division of labour and that involves the emergence of a distinct system of government which is monopolised by officials who specialize in administration.

Sixthly, Treating state as a system of political domination with specific effects on the class struggle. As more or less adequate to securing a balance of class forces that is favourable for a class.''

The socialist state was brought into existence after proletariat revolution in erstwhile Soviet Union, was guided by Lenin. He was Marxist in approach. He used state as an instrument for the suppression of bourgeois class. This change was sought to be brought about by the vanguard of the proletariat, the workers party.

Mao, dealing with a comparatively different mode of production in China, espoused a different version of class struggle. He talked about permanent revolution so as to consolidate the gains of socialist revolution. In his opinion the state will have major cultural function and dismantle the capitalist political and ideological structure and put in new ones.

Autonio Gramsci concedes the autonomy of state, politics and ideology. It explained way the capitalist state has survived for so long in western societies. In particular he emphasised on the role of civil society in generating beliefs and thought conducive to the existence of capitalist state. He explained in terms of conception of ideological hegemony. As Bob Jessop remarks ''the ability of the power bloc to maintain its hegemony depends on its success in articulating 'popular democratic struggles' into an ideology that sustains the power of the dominant classes and functions, rather than working to reinforce the revolutionary movement.''

The debate raged between **Ralph Milliband and Nicolas Ponlantzas** in 1969 brought out a new impression of Marxist view on state. While Milliband concedes the classical Marxist notion of political power as handmaiden of economic power, Ponlantzas supports the notion of relative autonomy of state. While Milliband sees unity between state power and class power, Ponlantzas treats state as a forum of class struggle. It performs many functions that could not be simply relegated as class functions.

Criticism

1. Contrary to assumptions of Marxists that there will be polarization of society into two class, there has emerged a powerful middle class playing significant role in the political process.
2. The optimistic vision of Marxism Socialism has failed and 'there is no escape' as ''Fukuyama argues from liberal democracy.''
3. The dictatorship of the proletariat has no democratic institutional mechanisms. It is party rule and bureaucratic centrism. This point has been highlighted by Rosa Luxamberg.
4. The conception of socialist state is ambiguous and incomplete. That is why

Milovan Djlas points out Marxism does not offer a theory of political liberty.

RELEVANCE OF MARXISM

A serious question mark has been raised against the relevance of Marxism in the contemporary times. It has been alleged that Marxism as a political theory has failed. The critics have clung to demise of Soviet Union as a point of reference.

In fact the rivalry between Marxism and its rival liberalism is not new. It has been a relatively old one. But, what is new in these attacks is the label of triumph of liberal democracy. The following points have been put forth in order to decry the relevance of Marxism.

Firstly : It has been alleged that Marxism is essentially based on class analysis. But, today there are complex, multiple and even overlapping identities that demands tools and techniques beyond those offered by Marxism. These points have been raised by genesis of post-structuralist/post modernist framework of political analysis. They decry the ideal of universalism and foundationalism having a epic of history. Rather they emphasize fragmentation and contingency as the basis of every social experience. It has been hinted that political theory can no longer have grand vision culminating in the realization of a communist or other society but different arrangements may be devised by people to suit their requirements. This line of thinking is accruing out anti-universalistic thrust advocated by post modernists.

Secondly, Francis Fukayama points out that the collapse of communism in Soviet Union and move towards market economy in China marked the "triumph of liberal democracy as the only nobler form of government. It has been alleged that if anything, Marxism does not present a viable future in an ever changing world. Its bureaucratic centralism has been dubbed as a form of totalitarianism.

Thirdly, The economic determinism of Marxism neglect the autonomous role of politics and culture in collective life. Perhaps it fails to show as to why people respond differently to similar situations of crisis and upheaval.

Fourthly, The revolutionary tinge of Marxism is the cause of contention. Many believe that it destroys the achievement of history in a single stroke of violence. Rather, peaceful transfer of power has become an accepted norm throughout the world.

Fifthly, The rigidity and formalism inherent in Marxist predisposition render it difficult to deal with changes that one inherently local and expedient. High degree of centralization and control creates apathy among masses.

Despite, its failure and crisis Marxism continues to inspire millions of people throughout the globe. The reasons are :

Firstly, Class analysis continues to offer the most viable and pragmatic tool of analysis in a highly in egalitarian social world. Perhaps none can deny that the world continues to be divided among 'haves' and 'have-nots'. Though there are other interests and categories but any broad categorization in the political analysis inevitably involves the issues relating to class.

Secondly, The revolutionary potential of Marx continues to inspire people who have not benefited from capitalist ventures. The mechanism of rising expectations is being sought to be achieved through method devised by Marx.

Thirdly, The highly egalitarian tinge of Marxism remains the only best alternative to liberalism. Regimes not benefiting from the capitalist modernization may get lured to doctrines that they may find more viable and attractive. As such, both people and the leadership in the developing world seek to interpret Marxism in their own way to suit their local milieu.

Fourthly, The global economic integration in its longer turn is bound to produce, situations of scarcity and inequality wherein the deprived and isolated people would look to Marxism.

IDEOLOGY

Ideology denotes a belief system. In its political connotation, it refers to a set of comprehensive belief about politics that seek to condemn or justify an existing system. Generally, it is action oriented. Mark N. Hagopian in his "Regimes, Movements and Ideologies" characterises it as "a programmatic and rhetorical application of some grandiose philosophical system, which arose men to political action and may provide strategic guidance for that action." Marxism, Nazism, Fascism are prominent political ideologies.

Different Views on Ideology

Karl Marx : Equated Ideology with "false consciousness". In his analysis of the capitalist mode of production, he came to the conclusion that every dominant class at a given stage of production makes its use to maintain itself in power.

Lenin : saw it in neutral terms. He grasps its practicality and held that even proletariat can have an ideology.

Lukacs : labelled Marxism itself as an ideology.

K. Mannheim : Contrasted ideology with utopia, while the former is concerned with conservation, the latter is associated with change. He also labelled Marxism to be an ideology.

A. Gramsci : talked about the ideological hegemony of the bourgeoise and explained the continuance of capitalist system in west.

Components of Ideology

Ray and Bhattacharya in their work 'Political Theory' lists following structural components of Ideology

1. its linkage with a grand philosophical system
2. its programme content derived from its philosophy
3. its strategy of achieving the programmatic goal
4. the coverage of its following (What groups or how much of the population subscribes to it).

Functions of Ideology

1. provides tools to action
2. helps in securing legitimacy of political regimes
3. evaluates and influence the political systems
4. helps in exercising controlling political process
5. help in channelling collective will
6. helps in mobilizing masses towards collective goal.

End of Ideology

Most of ideologies, according to Alan R. Ball "are mainly consequences of an interactions to the French Revolution of 1789 and the industrial revolutions that dominated the nineteenth century." But, immediately after the end of second world war, a debate 'the end of ideology' raged the western intellectual circle.

The debate started with a conference on "The Future of Freedom" held in Milan, Italy (1955). A series of work followed this conference and all of them emphasised on unidimensional approach to political issues. Most noteworthy was the association of some of the erstwhile Marxists and sharing their views.

Important Works

Edward Shils	: "The End of Ideology" (a report)
Daniel Bell	: End of Ideology
Ralph Dawendor	: Class and Class Conflict in Industrial Society
S.M. Lipset	: Political Man
J.K. Galbraith	: The New Industrial State
W.W. Rustow	: The Stages of Economic Growth : A Non-communist Manifesto.

The views outlined by these writers include

Daniel Bell : Daniel Bell argued that ideologies are exhausted and we have reached a post industrial society. They are prone to similar developments. What ever differences and problems exist between them are purely of technical nature and do not require remedies in the doses of ideologies.

Ralph Dahrendorf : Ralph Dahrendorf advocated a conception of post-capitalist society where the class structure has substantially undergone modification.

S.M. Lipset : S.M. Lipset described the division between idelogies of right and left. The problems are not so profound in western democracies that require existence of ideology. Instead, problems are such that they can be better dealt with administrative and technical innovations.

J.K. Galbraith : J.K. Galbraith located a bureaucratic and technocratic organization in the structures of power. They are not capitalists.

Critical Evaluation

However, these themes received reversal at the hands of C. Wright Mills, Macpherson, Alisdair MacIntyre and Richard Titnus. It has been alleged that the notion 'End of Ideology' itself is an ideology and are an attempt to mark subtle closure to other mode of politics. It has also been alleged that it was aimed at marking triumph of liberalism over revolutionary politics of Marxism. Most lucid statement comes from MacIntyre, who observes that 'End of Ideology' theorists failed to entertain one crucial alternative possibility; namely, that the end of ideology far from making the end of ideology was itself a key expression of the ideology of the time and place where it arose.''

End of History : From 'End of Ideology' debate we have come at a new end. In recent times, Francis Fukuyama in his work ''The End of History and the Last Man'' (1992) announced the triumph of liberal democratic state. He was a deputy director of the state department's policy planning staff and former analyst at the RAND corporation, USA.

Theoretical Basis : Fukuyama proceeds on Kojeve's interpretation of Hegel's philosophy of History. For Hegel, history progresses with the contest of ideas reaching its termination in the establishment of nation state symbolized as the ''march of god on earth''. In his opinion, the demise of communist Russia and liberal market economy in China has led to the universalisation of western liberal democracy as the final epoch of human government. It provides best response to human natures inbuilt struggle for individual recognition.

Critical Evaluation : He meted resistance from Piore Hassner, Gertrude Himmefard, Irving Krispol. J. MacCarney in his ''Shaping Ends : Reflections on Fukuyama'' serious doubts his case.

INDIVIDUAL AND SOCIAL JUSTICE

Concept of Justice has remained a perennial concern with which political theory has been associated since the time of Plato. Consequently, the term has undergone multiple construction with the passage of time. With the growing influence of ideal of democracy and socialism, the concept has been thoroughly transformed. The significance of conception of justice can be simply analyzed from the fact that almost all noble virtues and egalitarian claims are justified in reference to it. History speaks volumes for the changing concept of justice from the interest of the stronger to evolve a social order where working basis for social cooperation is based on grounds of fairness.

Different Views

Sophists : "Justice is the interest of the stronger."

Plato : "Harmonious operation of the three elements of human soul (wisdom, courage and temperance)."

Aristotle : "Justice consists in treating equals equally and unequals unequally."

St. Augustine : "The essence of justice is the relation between man and God from which right relation between man and man follows."

Thomas Hobbes : "Justice consists in working according to the law."

John Locke : "Justice implies right distribution of goods."

Marx : "Justice is achieved with the elimination of class society and establishment of classless society."

Radbruch : "Justice is equality."

Individual Justice

The concept of individual justice primarily indicates a viewpoint that places individual at the centre of political philosophy. As such, the remains a pivotal contribution of liberal—individualism. It says stress on enabling individuals to develop their personal faculties wherein the role of state is to be of a minimal interfere. John Locke, Adam Smith, Herbert Spencer, Jeremy Bentham were the fore runners of this conception. In contemporary times, Issiah Berlin, Milton Friedman, Robert Nozick and Hayek are main proponents of individuals justice. "It has been alleged by these theorists that if people are left free to themselves, individual justice can be achieved in the society.

View of Locke : In his "Two Treatises On Civil Government (1689) visualizes government as a trust whose function is only to secure the natural right to life, liberty and property.

View of Adam Smith : In his "Wealth of Nations" (1776) locates a natural attributes of trade and commerce in human beings. He believes that individuals self interest automatically promotes common interest. As such, he assigns three role to the state : (1) Protection (2) Justice (3) Policy decisions.

View of Bentham : In his "Introduction to the principles of Morals and Legislation" (1789) says that every policy must ensure "Greatest number". For this purpose, the Government's main function is to make those laws that do not interfere in free activity of individuals.

View of Spencer : Contrasts political life with Darwinian notion of natural selection. In his opinion, states welfare measures are an obstacles in the social evolution to see contradiction between social justice and the individual justice.

View of Berlin : In his "Two Concepts of Liberty" holds that if justice is to be achieved in a society, the individuals should be left to their own discretion. The availability or non-availability of means is entirely the individual's concern and that the state has no responsibility of making the required means available to him.

View of Hayek : In his "Law, Legislation and Liberty" (1976) holds that the Conception of Social Justice is meaningless. Justice implies non-interference of state. As he says "individuals differ in their talents and skills, and their equality before the law is bound to create inequality in their actual position in terms of their material status".

View of Friedman : In his "Capitalism and Freedom" holds that any society should be judged by the extent of freedom enjoyed by family and individuals. The "Government should take upon itself, only those functions which can not be tackled by the state or which incur heavy expenditure". Its work is to sustain the market and not to control it.

View of Nozick : In his "Anarchy, State and Utopia" (1974) bases his view on those of Lockes. He says "acquisition or transfer of property without Force or Fraud is just, but not otherwise". To him, the inequalities of wealth and power are the product of individual differences in talents and efforts and that it would not be just to remove or reduce these inequalities by transferring property.

Social Justice

The concept of social justice may be traced to Plato's "Republic". But, it remained absent till the industrial revolution in the nineteenth century. The liberal thinkers like T.M. Green and J.S. Mill espoused the positive functions of the state which gave way to the welfare state in the twentieth century.

As opposed to liberalism, Marxism is primarily committed to a conception of social justice. To Marxists, economic equality is the basis of social justice. Which can be achieved only in a classless society. Its vision of classless society is marked by common ownership of property guided by the principle "from each according to his ability and to each according to his need".

It will abolish the private ownership of the means of production and establish an egalitarian society.

In recent times, John Rawls has articulated a conception of social justice within Liberal framework. To him,

1. The problem of justice is the right distribution of public good, viz., income, wealth, rights, basis of self-respect etc.
2. Justice is the first virtue of social institution. If the institutions are just, their control would be just and thus justice in society would prevail.

THEORY OF SOCIAL CHANGE

Of the different theories of social change, Marxism-Leninism is the most celebrated one. Such celebrations are partly on account of its revolutionary tactics and partly reflects its vision of a classless society. While Marx and Engels provided theoretical impetus to the theory of social change, Lenin helped in actualizing the idea. He reinterpreted Marxism to suit primarily Russian conditions. However, in doing so, he gave a complete conception of revolutionary organization.

LENIN

Vladimir Ilyich Lenin was born on April 10, 1870 in the town of Simbirsk, situated on the banks of river Volga. The tyrannical rule of the Tsarist government and oppression of the workers and peasants by the capitalists shaped his life. Consequently Lenin dedicated himself to the cause of the revolution of the working class from his early youth. He regarded Marxism as a guide to action and accordingly shaped the future of Russia.

Lenin fully believed in the economic interpretation of history. In his opinion capitalism had not collapsed because it was still in the highest stage. He observed that ''Imperialism is capitalism at that stage of development at which the dominance of monopolies and finance capital is established; in which the export of capital has acquired pronounced importance, in which the division of the world among the international trusts has begun; in which the division of all territories of the globe among the biggest capitalist powers has been completed.'' In his work ''Imperialism : The Highest Stage of Capitalism,'' he held the view that it was the last stage of capitalism. This stage is characterised by a monopoly and finance phase of capitalism. The capital itself becomes a commodity of export and two world becomes enslaved to a few financiers. On this basis, he characterised first world war as war between financial groups for control of colonies.

Lenin puts faith in revolution and observes ''The Proletariat needs state power, the centralized organization of force, the organization of violence, both for the purpose of crushing the resistance of the exploiters and for the purpose of guiding the great mass of the population... in the work of organizing the Socialist economy. By educating a worker's party. Marxism educated the vanguard of the proletariat capable of directing and organizing the new order, or being a teacher, guide and leader of all toiling and exploited in the task of building up their social life without the bourgeoisie and against the bourgeoisie.''

However, Lenin saw in these changes a new epoch of national liberation movements in colonial countries led by the oppressed and dependent peoples and the proletariat of the capitalist countries themselves. It was in this context, Lenin welcomed the defeat of his own nation under Stay.

Lenin conceived capitalist expansion in its global manifestations. But, the nations can have social change without being fully developed capitalist economy. However, his theory has implication mainly in the context of Soviet Union. For his programme and policies were instrumental in Soviet conditions.

Lenin had complete faith in theory of class, struggle and regarded ''dictatorship of the proletariat'' as the most important ingredient of Marxist thought. ''The State and Revolution'' deals with his revolutionary transformation. He devised the institution of the Vanguard party or the workers party to lead the revolution. It was to seize power and build a government. The members of the party would be trained in the art of revolutionary tactics. They would form the core of revolutionaries. His justification for a single party is observed in the following lines ''in the U.S.S.R, there are only two classes, workers and peasants, whose interests far from being hostile–are, on the contrary, friendly. Hence, there is no ground in the U.S.S.R. for the existence of serveral parties, and consequently, for freedom for those parties.''

According to Lenin, the new state brought about by the revolution will be used for oppressing and dismantling vestiges of capitalism. It will either way only when communism is established. Meanwhile, the party would create conditions for the realization of communism. It was entrusted to reinterpret the Marxist-Leninist theory in its organization. It was not accountable to anyone and could not be questioned for its acts of omission or commission. He opposed decentralization as a principle for organization of party. Rather, we favoured a hierarchical organization with strict centralized machinery. These tenets of Lenin's theory have been popularized under the notion of "democratic centralism." Representative system and parliamentary institutions were completely opposed in his scheme of things.

Criticism

1. Kantsky and Bernstein does not favour Lenin's democratic centralism or rule by party. In particular, Kantsky favours Parliamentary institutions and democratic procedure of elections.
2. Rosa Luxemburg is apprehensive of Lenin's Vanguard party. Instead she believes that it will become handmaiden of the central committee geared to serve their interests.
3. Leo Trotsky says that minority revolution led by the Vanguard party is against the basic premises of Marxism.

MAO-TSE-TUNG

Mao played a vital role in propagating communism in China. He combined Marxism-Leninism with the socio-economic structure of China. While Marx had predicted socialist revolution in capitalist societies, Mao brought it in a predominantly agrarian society. It showed that class need not always be the crucial element of revolutionary change.

Mao was a member of the Chinese Communist Party. He was deeply displeased by the conditions of the peasants. To guide the socialist revolution is relied on following tactics.

1. **Armed Struggle and Guerilla Tactics** : Mao held that no revolution could be brought about without armed struggle and guerilla activities. The revolutionaries will have to be trained in these arts and the peasants have a major role to play in it.
2. **Workers Leadership** : Even though Mao emphasized on the role of peasantry, he was convinced that only the workers could provide effective leadership.
3. **Role of Village and Peasants** : Since the revolutionaries predominantly living in villages were weak, Mao laid stress on them. As regards the role of peasants, he observed "The gigantic struggles of the peasants—the peasants uprisings and wars–alone formed the real motive force of historical development in China's feudal society."
4. **Autonomy of Political Will** : Mao did not believe that only economic conditions can bring about a leap from one mode of production to another. Rather he believed that a political will is necessary for social change.
5. **Emphasis on War** : Mao was convinced that only through a war that capitalist structures could be dismantled and communism could be installed. Perhaps, he favoured war to peace because he saw the latter as the continuation of present system of capitalism.
6. **Transform Society** : For Mao revolution is not an instrument of power but to transform the society. It would change both; the feudal and capitalist structures and install a socialist system.
7. **Collaboration among peasant, worker, petty bourgeoisie and national bourgeoisie:**

Mao thought that complete social change could not be achieved without the joint efforts of the different segments of society. Consequently, he favours role of workers, peasants, petty bourgeoisie and national bourgeoisie.

Permanent Revolution : Mao believed that the socialist revolution was to be an ongoing affair. It was to last as long as there remained differences and distinction. Its motto was to abolish all class divisions.

6

POLITICAL THOUGHT

POLITICAL THOUGHT

PLATO

Life and Time

According to Ernest Barker, "political thought begins with the Greeks. Its origin is connected with the clear and calm rationalism of Greek mind". They were the first to challenge supremacy of religion and curious to know everything.

Plato, the disciple of Socrates and the teacher of Aristotle is one of the greatest political thinkers produced by ancient Greece. He adopted the method of dialogues (dialectic) and lectures to propound his philosophy.

Plato was born in 427 B.C. in a noble Athenian family, some four years after the outbreak of the Peloponnesian war and just over a year after the death of Perides. His period (427 B.C. to 347 B.C.) was an era of great historical importance. The important developments of his life time were the defeat of Athens in wars against Spartas, the establishment of tyrannical rule of reactionaries, execution of his master (Socrate) by reactionaries. The prevailing condition in the society was inhuman and unsatisfactory.

He grew up in a city at war: "The Peloponnesian war", which began just before his birth and lasted untill he was twenty three. It ended in defeat and humiliation of Athens and in the break up of the confederation.

IMPACTS

Schools Prior to Plato : Prior to Plato, there existed some school of thought which had profound impact on Plato's thinking.

The Sophists

They were a group of teachers who gave practical education and left a deep impact on the history and thought of the Greeks. They believed in the selfishness of man and considered state as an artificial contrivance. They completely ignored the moral considerations. They held that force was the basis of all political authority and the political authority was justified in being selfish and even tyrannical.

Socrates

Plato's association with Socrates was the outstanding fact of his life. It was from Socrates that Plato derived what remained the central focus of his thought—the idea that virtue is knowledge. He saw a close relationship between ethics and politics.

Socrates sentence to death at the age of 70 on the charge of corrupting the youth was turning point in Plato's life. The family took decision to abandon a political career that was most suited to him.

Socrates deductive and dialectical reason together with following three doctrines were adopted by Plato.

1. Socrates dictum that virtue is knowledge
2. His theory of Reality
3. His theory of knowledge

From his theory of knowledge, Plato built up his whole structure of rule of philosophy, his ideal state and philosopher king. From Socrates doctrine of reality came the concept of "idealism" in philosophy and political thought. The outwardly things are merely the superficial appearance of things.

They are not real and permanent but ephesmal and phenomenal in nature. According to Socrates 'Beauty exists without a beautiful thing—its outward manifestation. From Socrates idea, he thinks of an ideal state "city in Heaven". By the theory of knowledge Socrates meant real knowledge, i.e. permanent, scientific, mathe-matically true and based on reason. For Plato it is the philosophers, the embodiment of real knowledge and not the slaves of opinions and superstitions, who have the commanding position in his ideal state.

Pythagoras

Plato's visit (388-387 B.C.) to Italy proved to be a factor of crucial importance. From him, Plato imbibed the spirit of mathematic as a philosophic discipline.

Thus, the prevailing state of anarchy in Athenian society had profound impact on Plato. Similarly, teaching of sophists and his meeting with pythagorian thinkers influenced his outlook. But, it was Plato's association with Socrates and execution of his master that substantially moulded his life. Perhaps it won't be unfair to say that in essence many of stances are Socratic. Barker acknowledges "the image of his teacher never faded from his mind and he actually represents the greatest legacy bequeathed by Socrates to mankind".

Plato's Works : The Republic
The Statesman
The Laws.

THEORY OF JUSTICE

Like many other concepts in political science, the concept of justice has been one greatest contribution of ancient Greece. Plato, one of the greatest political philosopher has made a significant contribution to the development of notion of justice. His work 'Republic' has been titled as "on concerning justice". The impact of his work is such that most often scholars aims to imbibe the spirit of this classic in developing their own notion of justice.

To Plato : "*Justice is having and doing what is one's own*", and

"*A just man is a man just in the right place doing his best and giving full equivalent of what he receives*".

Critique of Prevailing Theories

To develop his own theory of justice, Plato discusses the prevailing theories of justice. Three of them are :

1. **Theory of Cephalus: Traditional:** Cephalus considers justice as speaking the truth and paying what was due to gods and men. This discussion assumes that justice is an art which gives good to friends and evil to enemies instead.

   Plato holds that true justice means "doing good to all and harm to none". Furthermore he says that it is not always possible to distinguish between the enemies and the friends. Plato argues that theory of Cephalus treats justice individualistic, rather than a social concept. Instead, concept of justice should have an universal application. By treating justice as an art, it is made an instrument of those wielding power.
2. **Theory of Thrasyachus: Radical:** Thrasyachus represents the outlook of radical sophists. According to him,

   "Justice is the interest of stronger".

   It believes in the prince, "might is right".

   Plato rejects it outrightly and holds that justice can never be the interest of stronger. The government is an art and it aims at perfection of only act. Moreover, justice is always better than injustice and a just man is wiser, stronger and happier than an unjust man because he also knows his limitations.
3. **Theory of Glaucon: Pragmatic :** He treats justice as an artificial thing—a product of social convention. This theory is the precursor of the social contract theory. In the state of nature there was no justice, or state. Many weaknesses combined together and created the state. Justice is the child of fear and is based on the necessity of the weaker and not the interest of the stronger. Plato criticises it on the ground that it considers justice as something external or an

importation. He holds that justice is rooted in human mind. Though it is located in both, the individual and the state, but encompasses it in larger quantity and in visible form.

Plato's Theory of Justice

As a perfect dialectician, Plato contrasts the three elements of state, viz., rulers, soldiers and farmers with three elements of human mind, viz., reason, spirit and appetite. Each representing the three attributes of human mind. This led Prof. Barker to remark "this triplicity of the soul, whatever its source is the foundation of much of the republic".

How it can be Achieved

Justice for the society can be realised if each group performs the function, it is best suited to perform without interfering in the affairs of others. Thus justice implies a sort of specialisation and the principle of non-interference and harmony. Justice is the bond which holds a society together, a harmonious union of individuals, each of whom has found his life work in accordance with his natural fitness and his training. It is both a Public and Private virtue because the highest good both at the state and its members is hereby conserved.

Basic principle of theory of Justice :

1. It means functional specialisation. In it each component of the state performs the functions, it is best suited to perform, justice can be ensured in the society.
2. It implies non-interference. Only when no component of the state interferes with the sphere of other's duty that unity can be ensured. Moreover, only by doing so a society can benefit from the work of an individual.
3. It implies a principle of harmony. Three human virtue, viz., wisdom, courage and temperance representing three classes are harmonised by the justice.

THEORY OF EDUCATION

Plato is known for his concept of justice not only because he outlined a novel philosophical scheme of justice but, he also envisaged a comprehensive scheme by which ends of justice can be achieved. He advocated two kinds of means—positive and spiritual method of education and temporal method of communism of property and wives. However, of the two, he attaches more importance to education.

In the words of Barker, it is "an attempt to cure a mental malady by mental medicine". Plato felt that the various evils playing in the society could be rooted out by proper education and regards it as spiritual remedy. The importance which Plato attached to education in his ideal state is evident from the fact that he devoted a good portion of the second book of Republic to this topic. Rousseau remarked that "Republic is hardly a political work at all, but is finest treatise an education that ever was written." Commenting on the importance of Plato's theory of Education, Sabine says, "So striking is the part played in Plato's ideal state by education that some consider it to be the chief topic of Republic."

Link with Theory of Justice

It is closely interlinked with his concept of justice, to him, there are two dimensions of education. Individual and Social. While on the one hand it helps individual realise "virtue is knowledge' on the other hand it infused unity in society by enabling the individuals to perform the duties of their respective stations.

FEATURES OF PLATONIC EDUCATION

1. **State controlled system of compulsory education :** He does not favour the idea of leaving education in the hands of parents. He considered education as positive means by which the ruler could mould the character of the people and promote spirit of unselfish devotion towards their duties. By making it compulsory, he thought that all citizens would develop their mental faculties and become valuable unit of state.
2. **Favour education, both for men and women :** He was in favour women holding public offices like men. It is for this step of his, that he is regarded as a revolutionary.
3. **Meant for artisans as well as peasants :**

Though Plato does not make a clear mention in this regard, it is quite implied from his statement that "Men of copper can be made into men of silver and even of gold, if they possess their attributes."

4. **Strict censorship of all literary and artistic works :** He wanted any right type of literature should reach the hands of the youth. The ultimate authority to judge the righteous or otherwise of the literature was the ruler imbued with wisdom.
5. **Aimed at moral as well as physical development of the child :** He held that a healthy mind could reside only in a healthy body and it was essential that education should develop both these faculties.
6. **Produce philosopher king :** It was the chief objective of his scheme of education. The philosophers were expected to govern the masses only through rigorous programme of education.

EDUCATIONAL CURRICULUM

Comprised two stages—Elementary stage and Higher stage. This scheme is comprehensive one.

Elementary Stage

Further divided into three sub-stages :

— First stage lasted from birth to age of 6 years. At this stage, both girls and boys were to be given education in language, basic facts of religion and religious institutions, truth and morality.

— Second stage lasted from 7 years to age of 18 years. At this stage education was imparted in music, gymnastics and elementary mathematics. Plato held that music was essential for the development of the soul and gymnastics was for healthy body.

— Third stage extended from 18 to 20 years of age. At this stage, both the men and women were given compulsory military education to create qualities, courage, endurance and discipline.

HIGHER STAGE

At the age of 20 there was to be a test and those showing aptitude for science and philosophy were to be given further education. The scheme of higher education was to make the recipient wise and practically trained. This scheme was described by Sabine as "Most original as well as most characteristic proposal of the Republic". It was sub divided as

— First stage covers the period of 21 years to 30 years. During this phase the selected students were given knowledge in the field of logic Metaphysics, higher mathematics and special studies of warfare and Public Administration.

— Second stage covers the period of age 30 years to 35 years to selected few. Emphasis was laid on dialectics because according to Plato dialectic was the only system of knowledge through which highest reality could be achieved. The stage was essentially meant to create the philosopher king.

— Third stage ends at age of 50 years. At age of 35 years philosophers start ruling and continue upto 50 yrs. at which they retire and resume study in the contemplation of God. Such a study they continue upto the end of their life. Hence Plato's education is a life long process for the philosopher king.

COMMUNISM OF PROPERTY

Communism essentially means a systematic arrangement wherein society controls the production and distribution. The classes are related with their economic conditions. Both in Athens and Sparta some sort of communism existed in the form of state controlled private property and the produce was put to common use by the community. But Plato deserves the credit for communism of wives and property. He does so on these grounds. Firstly, he assumes that the existence of three classes in his ideal state i.e. philosophers, soldiers and farmers. Now, Justice according to Plato is fulfilment of its specific duties by each class. Secondly, if the philosophers and soldiers are to act according to justice they must have nothing to do with 'Property' which is the outward manifestation of "Appetite" which in turn is the element assigned to the farmer class. For their sustenance the guardians should depend on the peasant class. Thirdly, he believes that the most significant factor that leads to corruption and degradation in a state is the combination of economic power with political power. Therefore, he pleads that those who exercise political power should have no economic motives and those who are engaged in economic activities should have no share in political power. According to Barker, "Plato starts from practical considerations and in this sense his communism is the most practical feature of his ideal state".

Plato's purpose in envisaging communism is to produce the greatest degree of unity in the state. Private property was a stumbling block in the way of such unity. Hence Plato would like to abolish the property itself. Plato's communism of property is only a secondary method of bringing about unity in the state. The primary method is his scheme of education.

Plato feared that the possession of private property would give rise to selfish considerations and deviate the attention of the philosopher rulers from public service. He therefore deprived the two ruling classes of the right to property. In the words of Sabine, Plato felt that "To cure the greed of rulers there is no way short of denying them the right to call anything their own". For Plato the rulers should live in barracks and have meals at a common table. They should not possess private property because it was bound to undermine the value of virtue, which was the most important ingredient of the ruling class. He repeatedly insists that his communism is meant only for the guardian class. Thus, says Barker "Platonic communism is ascetic and just for that reason it is also aristocratic." It is imposed on the best and only the best.

COMMUNISM OF WIVES

According to Plato, justice implies fulfilment of specific duties by each class. If the philosophers and soldiers are to act according to justice, they must have nothing to do with 'property'. Therefore he pleads that those who exercise political power should have no economic motive and those who are engaged in economic activities should not have any share in political power. According to Prof. Barker "Plato starts from practical considerations and in this sense his communism is the most practical feature of his ideal state".

Plato's concept of communism of wives is a step ahead in his scheme of communism of property. In his opinion the abolition of the institution of private property without the abolition of the family would result in the failure of his scheme. Hence, Plato laid greater emphasis on communism of wives. Barker says rightly "The abolition of family life among the Guardians is thus inevitable corollary of their renunciation of private property. Plato recognises that property and the family are interdependent facts".

Features of Plato's Communism of Wives

Firstly, Communism of wives applies only to the guardian class i.e. the rulers and the soldiers; not to producing class.

Secondly, The family life is serious and powerful rival to loyalty to the state. Communism of wives was aimed to curb the sentiments of selfishness and emancipate the woman to enable them to devote to the service of state.

Thirdly, No system of permanent wedding. All the women are to be common to all men of guardian class.

Fourthly, All guardians; (both men and women) are to live together in common barracks managed by state.

Fifthly, State is to arrange a temporary mating between the best of men and best women for one year keeping in mind the population of the city state.

Sixthly, The responsibility for rearing of children was to be entrusted to state nurses.

Seventhly, The children born in a particular season were to be treated as brothers and sisters.

Eighthly, The weak and disfigured children were to be killed soon after their birth so that they may not prove to be a burden for the state in the long run.

Ninthly, Common ownership of women by the guardian class. Unlike it, the communism of property which insisted on common renunciation of property by the guardian class.

Reasons for Communism of Wives

Plato suggests communism of wives in order to fulfil three purposes.

1. Major aim of Plato is to create Unity in the State. To him, family was the stumbling block in this attainment because family affection was a patent rival of loyalty to the state. As Prof. Barker points out "he may be said to wish to import the family into the state. He would make the state—or rather the rulers of the state—a family and the family a state".
2. He wants to emancipate the Athenian women from bondage of family. Plato wanted that talents of women should be utilised for the benefit of society.
3. He was convinced that by introducing this system a better and more intelligent race could be raised. The best among women within a certain age limit should be united to the best among men within a certain age limit for one year. Sabine has said Plato held that "the improvement of race demands a more controlled and more selective type of union".

PHILOSOPHER KING

Plato's concept of ideal state depicted a model of what state ought to be. The elements which constituted his ideal state are identified as Justice, Education, Philosopher king and Communism of wives and property.

Plato's concept of Philosopher rulers is the direct result of his basic assumptions with which he starts.

Firstly, He contrasts three elements of state viz., rulers, auxiliaries and peasants with three elements of human mind viz., reason, spirit and appetite.

Secondly, Socratic dictum "Virtue is knowledge". According to Plato virtuous are wise people. He held that the affairs of the state could be set right only if wise people, after getting due training ruled. His dictum is "The wise shall rule and the ignorant shall follow". Plato's thinking is pragmatic as he tries to remedy the then practices in all city-states. He believed that only competent, wise and efficient people should have the right to govern.

FEATURES OF PHILOSOPHER KING

The concept is described by Prof. Foster as "the most profoundly original conception in the entire political thought of Plato" has some distinct feature.

1. Plato denounced democratic system as a government of ignorant. Instead suggested some novel and unprecedented institution which resembled almost tyranny. So, he thought of a unlimited government of a philosopher Ruler for his ideal state.
2. He favoured the concept of government by elite. Those who possess the capacity should rule over those many who do not.
3. Plato's conception of Philosopher is one who is the lover of wisdom and passionate seeker of truth. So, he is in a better position to determine what is in the interest of the community than an ordinary person.
4. Plato's philosopher ruler's are the product of comprehensive and rigorous training and education.
5. Philosopher rulers are assigned absolute powers. They are not accountable to public opinion or bound by customs or written laws. According to Plato, since philosophers are the embodiment of virtue and knowledge, there is no logic for Public control over their actions. The Philosopher rulers through the use of their wisdom can give to every person what he deserves, no short, it is expedient to have the government of philosopher rulers.
6. Plato imposes a restraint on their power by insisting that they
   - must watch against the excessive inflow of property and wealth in the state.
   - should keep the size of the state consistent with the unity and self sufficiency.

- must ensure due performance of allotted duties by each citizen.
- must ensure that no change is made in the education system.

PLATO'S COMMUNISM AND MARX'S COMMUNISM : A COMPARISON

Modern Communism as practised in erstwhile Soviet Union and China has been a collective philosophical predicament expounded by Karl Marx and modified by Lenin and Stalin in Soviet Union and Mao in China. Historically it owes its genesis to the ill-effects of nineteenth century industrial revolution.

In essence, Communists hold a materialist view of history. Whosoever controls the means of production controls the whole society. Thus society is divided into two classes, 'haves' and 'have nots'. To Marx, "History of all hitherto society is the History of class struggle". They believe that final goal of class struggle will overthrow the capitalist system and establish the dictatorship of the proletariat. In course of time, a classless society will emerge and the state will wither away.

A comparison between Platonic Communism and Modern Communism reveals more dissimilarities than similarities.

Similarities

1. Both make the individual good as interdependent on common good.
2. Both are against the institution of private property, modern communism applies to all the sections of society. But, for Plato only guardians are debarred from holding property.
3. Both believe in division of society into classes while Plato thinks of three classes, viz., rulers, warriors and peasants, Marx espouses the existence of only two classes the haves and havenots.
4. Both intend to build unity and solidarity by removing causes of stress and tension.
5. Both want to evolve a society organized on the basis of social service.

Differences

1. Plato's communism is the outcome of conditions of Athens in the 4th century B.C. But, Modern communism is the result of the most complex conditions arising due to the industrial revolution in the Nineteenth Century Europe.
2. Plato's communism does not want total transformation of society. The producing class remains intact. It is applied only to the Guardian class. But, Marxist communism is mainly concerned with alteration of economic structure of the society. It aims at abolition of private ownership of the means of production. All economic resources are centralised by the machinery of communist party.

   This led Barker to remark that "Plato's communism was aristocratic; it is a way of surrender; and it is a surrender imposed on the best. It exists for the sake of the whole society, but not for the whole society."
3. While Plato's communism concerned prohibition of things that enabled Guardians to discharge their function, modern communism is concerned with common ownership of the means of production.
4. Plato's scheme of communism covered both; communism of property as well as wives. On the contrary, modern communism is concerned only with means of production.
5. Plato's communism aimed at making the Greek city state, a self sufficient properly governed unit. But, modern communism espoused a global vision to bring about a world revolution to usher in a communist society.
6. While Plato's communism was aristocratic; modern one is 'Proletarian'.
7. Plato's communism had high degree of abstraction with great philosophical rigour. Modern communism is more realistic combined with scientific rigour.

PLATO AND FASCISM/TOTALITARIANISM: A COMPARISON

Plato entitled "Republic" to be "an Justice", but in subsequent centuries fascist theorists claimed that Plato was a fascist : the rule of philosopher king, communism of wives and property and submission of individual to the state resemble fascism of 20th century. But many other theorists, particularly C.E.M. Joad in his "Guide to Philosophy of Morals and Politics" refuses to accept such claims in total.

There are similarities as well as differences between Fascists and Plato.

Resemblances between Plato and Fascists

1. Both subordinate the individual to at the outer of state. Plato's communism is best manifestation of totalitarianism. For, even purely private affairs like marriage and mating is brought within the purview of state. Similarly Mussolini is saying "Everything within the state, nothing against the state, nothing outside the state" denies distinction between private and public domain.
2. Both believe in the natural inequality among human beings. According to them nature ordains that superior shall rule over inferiors. To the Nazi's "out of all races, the Aryan race is superior, out of the Aryan race, the Germans are superior out of them elite are superior and out of elite the Fuehrer (the leader) is the superior most". Similarly Plato championed Greek superiority.
3. Both have no faith in democracy. Plato denounces democracy as the rule of ignorant people. The fascist denounce democracy, as a stupid, corrupt, slow moving, impractical and inefficient form of Government.
4. Both Platonism and Fascism views dictatorship of one man as best form. Plato thinks of a philosopher king in whom all the powers of government are concentrated. For the Fascists, it is Fuehrer who is omnipotent and omnicompetent.
5. Both make the individual as means to an end. The state is made an end.
6. Both deny the importance of public opinion and people's right to change the government. The government is based not on the consent of the governed but some over arching good of society championed by elite.
7. They are more interesting in laying emphasis on duties rather than on rights.

Differences between Plato and Fascists

1. Contextually, the two are different. Moreover there is a gap of more than 2,300 years between them while Platonism was a response to the prevailing state of anarchy in small city state of ancient Greece, Fascism is a modern doctrine linked with the idea of nation state.
2. Plato's ideas comprise complete philosophy, based on certain basic assumptions on the other hand, fascists ideas are scattered and unorganized. In fact, ideas of Nietzsche, Hegel, Mussolini and Hitler are exhorted to justify Fascist state. Thus says Sabine, "It is a body of ideas taken from various sources and put together to fit the exigencies of the situation.".
3. The tendency of Platonic Republic and Fascist glamour for war are poles apart while Plato intended to make "polis" a self sufficient unit, fascists exhort that "expansion is the sign of life".
4. Platonism represents political idealism because Plato's state never came into experience. Fascism stands for political realism because it was in operation for more than 2 decades and was a factor of crucial significance for the outbreak of second world war.
5. While Plato prefers ethics over politics, the fascists subordinates ethics to politics.

As C.E.M. Joad points out, "the end for which government is exercised in Platonic state is the well being of the community as a whole through the medium of justice on the other hand the object for which rule is exercised in the Fascist state is enhancement of the power of the few, many being regarded merely as the raw material over which the power of the few is exercised and the means through which it is achieved.

ARISTOTLE

LIFE AND TIME

Aristotle was born at Stagira on the Aegean Sea in 384 B.C.

His father was a physician to the King of Macedon. This gave him an opportunity to acquire first-hand information about the royal court. It also gave him understanding of the working of the state. It helped Aristotle to develop an analytical and scientific bent of mind. He came to Athens at the age of eighteen and joined Plato's academy where he stayed for twenty years till the death of Plato in 347 B.C. In 342 B.C. he was called to Macedonia to become the tutor of young Alexander. After the death of Alexander he fled to Chalcis and died the same year.

Aristotle studied under Plato for 20 years from the age of 17 to 37. This association was "the factor most important in the shaping of his philosophy-political and other." Prof. Roster says "Aristotle is the greatest of all Platonists. He is permeated by Platonism to a degree in which perhaps no great philosopher besides him has been permeated by the thought of another".

INFLUENCES

Aristotle was influenced by Plato in his following ideas :

1. Social nature of human beings
2. State as a natural institution
3. Aristocratic nature of government
4. Denouncing democracy
5. Idealized the city state
6. Commensurability of interests between individual and state.
7. Interdependence between ethics and politics.

In addition to it, Aristotle was greatly influenced by

1. His father who was a biologist, this led Aristotle to compare state with organism and individuals with organs.
2. The turbulent state of affairs led Aristotle to believe that rulers were idealist. If political actualities could be examined, the prevailing state of affairs could be improved.
3. Personal experience of a happy married life.
4. Preconceived Greek notions and myth of Greek superiority. His justification of slavery and notion of citizenship confirms his biases.

POSITION OF ARISTOTLE

Aristotle, the ablest of Plato's disciple is novel in many respect. Unlike his master, Aristotle devotes his attention to political realities and can be rightly hailed as father of science of politics.

Aristotle's Work : The Politics

STATE AS A NATURAL INSTITUTION

Aristotle, a disciple of Plato imbibed a few teaching of his master. One such similarity in the political philosophy of the two thinkers is to treat state as a natural institution, possessing moral authority. The state aims at moral perfection of men who can achieve self sufficiently only in the state.

Natural character of the state is justified by Aristotle on following grounds :

Firstly, Aristotle insists that the two primary instincts of reproduction and self preservation force the men to associate with family is the first step in such direction and state is the union of several villages which is a union of several families.

Secondly, According to Aristotle, state exemplifies the real character of man. They can realize themselves only in the state. Being a rational creature man can develop their rational faculties only through membership of state.

Thirdly, Aristotle stresses that the state is an organism and individuals are its part.

Fourthly, Aristotle's dictum "man is political animal" and "state is natural" reinforces each other.

FUNCTIONS OF THE STATE

The state, for Aristotle is a plurality, where people associate for the satisfaction of their common needs by exchange of goods and services. To him, "The state is the union of families and villages in a perfect and self-sufficing life". Whereas, the family and village exist essentially for the preservation of life and the comforts of companionship, "the state exists for the good life and not for the sake of life only".

Unlike the individualists who insist on protection of individual rights, Aristotle wants state to create essential conditions for moral, mental and physical development of the people. It is not a mere Kinonia for war and trade.

IDEAL STATE

Aristotle widely regarded as a realist, outlined his ideal state in book II, III, VIII of his "Politics". A comparison between idealism of Plato and Aristotle is best illustrated by Sabine, "What Aristotle calls the ideal state is always Plato's second best". While Plato hails his ideal state to be good for all times to come, Aristotle accepts limitations of his ideal state. Moreover, Aristotle like his master prefers monarchy. But, he insists on the primacy of law not a philosopher king.

Features of the Ideal State

Following features can be outlined about Aristotle's ideal state.

1. There is supremacy of law in his ideal state. He favours impersonal rule of law which represents the wisdom of community since the ages.
2. It is an ethical institution to develop the moral qualities of the citizens to promote good and happy life of everyone.
3. Private ownership but common use of property.
4. Aristotle's ideal state is marked by division of labour where slaves are engaged in agriculture residents in commerce and citizens in political activities.
5. Aristotle's ideal state is the city state of the moderate size. Population should be manageable.
6. It should be self-sufficient, without any aggressive design against foreign countries.
7. There should be six classes, viz., agriculture, artisans, a war like class, leisured class, priests and administrators. Only the later four are entitled for citizenship.
8. There is a predominance of middle class that provide stability because it possess twin qualities of obedience and command.

Best Attainable State or Polity

A great realist, as Aristotle was realised limitation of his ideal state. This leads him to outline a best attainable state. It avoids the extremes of democracy and oligarchy, described as Polity. It represents the "golden mean".

According to Aristotle, there are mainly two kinds of state, viz., Democracy and Oligarchy that are in operation. But, they are themselves plagued by certain drawbacks. While, in oligarchy power is either concentrated in few hand or a single person, democratic rule is marked by rule of money. The real problem is that the oligarchs oppress the majority and democratic means fail to provide intelligible administration. This leads Aristotle to favour a middle class rule.

Aristotle's favour for polity is based on following assumptions :

1. Neither extremely rich nor extremely poor persons are competent to rule. While the former only knows how to rule, the latter do not know how to rule.
2. A middle class knows how to rule and be ruled in turn. It is an embodiment of attributes that shed the attributes of extremely rich and extremely poor.
3. The middle class should at least be larger than either the extremely rich or the extremely poor.
4. A state with predominant middle class population remain safe from revolutions.
5. Polity is a golden mean, a mixed constitution that combines the elements of both; democracy and oligarchy avoiding their extremes.

CITIZENSHIP

Aristotle's views on citizenship are coloured by his conservative stance. He wanted to rationalize the situation in Athens and was opposed to radical transformation.

Citizens in the "polis" were privileged class of people who enjoyed complete monopoly in political affairs. Property was an important qualification for being a citizen. It was based on heredity. The bulk of the population comprising the slaves, metics (resident aliens) and women were debarred from citizenship status.

Who is a Citizen?

According to Aristotle, a citizen is a person who participates in the administration of justice and in legislation, as a member of the deliberative Assembly. A person can not claim status of citizenship exclusively on following grounds :

- Residence in a particular place.
- Enjoyment on legal rights.
- Descent from a citizen.

Criteria for Citizenship

These three aspects could be considered for citizenship only if a person participates in administration of justice and legislation. In other words, a citizen must possess the essential attribute of ruling and being ruled, at the same time. In his scheme, "leisure" remains an essential condition of citizenship because without it none can cultivate virtue and devote themselves to the affairs of the state.

Aristotle excludes women, old people and children from the category of citizens because they are intellectually inferior; physically unfit and politically immature.

REVOLUTION

Aristotle after his study of 158 constitutions comes out with a detailed analysis of causes of revolution and ways to prevent them. Perhaps, his concept of Revolution is most potent testimony of his scientific rigour and empirical enquiry.

What is Revolution?

Aristotle, in Part V of 'Politics', offers two-fold meaning of revolution.

Firstly, A revolution means any major or minor change in the constitution.

Secondly, A revolution is also said to have occurred if ruling power has been transferred, even if the constitution remains the same.

Form of Government	Causes of Revolution	Means to Prevent Revolutions
Democracy	– Excessive use of power – unwarranted condemnation of rich by the poor	– allowing rich to participate in the administration
Oligarchy	– Rivalry among the ruling oligarchs themselves	– Fair treatment of the poor – Prohibiting individual or group to wield too much power
Aristocracy	– Conferring honour only to a few	– same as above
Polity	– Defective balance of different element in the constitution	– By mixing oligarchic and democratic means
Monarchy	– Oppressive rule	– Espionage system – Intellectual and material development
Tyranny	– Interference of foreign state	– Creating an awe in minds of people – Expansion of Territory

Causes of Revolution

Aristotle attempts a detailed analysis of the causes of revolution which can be broadly classified as

1. General causes
2. Revolutions in a particular kind of state

General causes of revolution includes the desire of the people to be treated as equal. The states which are marked by greater extent of equality will be more stable. This explains the reason behind Aristotle's favour for a state in which middle class predominates. Thus, to Aristotle, lesser the inequality lesser will be chances of revolution.

The general causes of Revolution, in Aristotle's opinion can be tackled by

1. Inculcating habit of law abidingness among citizens.
2. Treating various classes with consideration.
3. Educating the citizens in spirit of constitution.
4. Awarding political offices on temporary basis.
5. Ensuring dispersal of political power in more individuals.
6. Rewarding people as much as possible.
7. Limiting foreigners from holding public offices.

Aristotle also diagnoses the revolution in particular kind of state and outlines remedies to check them :

CONTRIBUTION OF ARISTOTLE

Aristotle, one of the great disciples of Plato has been hailed as father of political science. His ideas on politics, viz., social nature of man, rule of law, revolution, citizenship and constitutionalism have remained a matter of considerable significance to political scientists. For, he made the first systematic attempt to base his conclusions on facts, figures and data.

The contribution of Aristotle can be studied under following heads.

1. **Comparative Method :** Though the comparative approach to politics is of recent origin, it was greatness of Aristotle to use it to study 158 constitutions.
2. **Primacy of Law :** According to Prof. Ebenstein, "The concept of rule of law and the constitutional state is perhaps the most important legacy. Aristotle has bequeathed to posterity". The significance of impersonal nature of law and its efficacy to resolve political conflicts is as pragmatic as ever. In this aspect he greatly influenced Aquinas, Hooker and Locke.
3. **Theory of Origin of State :** Aristotle dictum that "Man is a political animal" and his view of natural origin of state have been widely acclaimed to be scientific.
4. **Positive Functions of the State :** By saying "state exists not only for the sake of life but also for the sake of good life", Aristotle wants the state to take care of material as well as moral development of individual. Such view is novel in the sense that even in today's world states are entrusted with almost the same task.
5. **Conservative Thinker :** Aristotle's favour for retaining the existing institutions continues to influence conservatives.
6. **Role of Middle Class :** Aristotle's analysis of role of the middle class in sustaining political issues in contemporary period.
7. **Private Property :** Aristotle's plea for private ownership but common use has come to be accepted as most viable solution to problem of social justice.
8. **Autonomy of Politics :** Aristotle remains the first to make an attempt to separate politics from ethics by use of scientific methods to analyze political issue.

PLATO AND ARISTOTLE : A COMPARISON

Though Aristotle is influenced by his master Plato, under whom he spent some crucial period of his life, yet he is not a blind follower of Plato. He criticizes Plato on a number of points. The significant points of differences between Plato and Aristotle are as follows :

Firstly, while Plato is an idealist and radical, Aristotle is realist and conservative. Aristotle stood for the idea of "individual self-sufficiency, unlike the philosophical absolution of Plato. Greatly influenced by scientific profession of his father Aristotle remains the first scientist.

Secondly, Aristotle dubs Plato's scheme of ideal state and rule by philosopher king as neglecting the common experience of changes. While Plato wanted to build new institutions, Aristotle was interested in retaining the existing institutions.

Thirdly, Against the Platonic predisposition with the ideal of unity in the society, Aristotle hints that there exists diversity in society. He is against Plato's scheme of functional specialisation and holds that instead of creating unity, it would lead to disunity.

Fourthly, Plato's envision a scheme of communism to achieve the idea of justice. But, Aristotle is against communism of wives and property. Instead he believes that it is natural for human beings to own property and marry. Moreover, they are essential for fullest development of human being.

Fifthly, Aristotle does not pin faith in the rule of philosopher king. Rather, he upholds the primacy of law.

Sixthly, Aristotle's study of 158 constitutions was a pragmatic one. Through it he outlined a scheme for classification of government and sketched the relation between ruler and ruled. But, Plato leaves the administration entirely in the hands of philosopher king without defining the relation between rulers and the ruled.

MACHIAVELLI

An Epitome of His Time

Although it is difficult to draw a clear line of demarcation between medieval and modern period, Niccolo Machiavelli has been hailed as father of modern political theory. The period of events that occurred in Europe between fourteenth to sixteenth centuries influenced him to a great extent.

Machiavelli was born in Florence (Italy) in 1469 and studied under his father who was a jurist. He produced 'Prince' (1513), 'Discourses' (1521) and his life reflects that he was more a practical politician than a political philosopher. There are significant factors that influenced his thinking.

1. **Contemporary Situation in Italy :** Divided Italian principalities and constant situation of war amongst them greatly affected Machiavelli. He was led to convince that unless unity was restored, nothing fruitful can be done.
2. **Association with Cesare Borgia :** Cesare Borgia, Duke of Valentine, the superbly endowed son of Pope Alexander VI was a decisive factor in shaping his thought.
3. **Political Turmoil and Upheavals :** Machiavelli's sentence for life on charges of plotting against Medici family, political corruption and undue interference of Pope affected him. It was because of such state of affairs that his age was called age of 'Bardards and Adventurers'.
4. **Renaissance :** This movement which stood for revival of ancient art, cultures and values brought man at the centre of political life. God was relegated to the background. It is with such an spirit and outlook Machiavelli proceeded in his 'Prince'. His individualism is direct descendent of Renaissance.
5. **Political Thinkers :** Apart from contemporary situation, Machiavelli was greatly influenced by people like Aristotle and Marsilio of Padna. From Aristotle, he imbibed empirical outlook and Marsilio influenced him in his secular ideas. His works include Prince and Discourses.

Method

Though Machiavelli was influenced by some of the eminent political thinkers of the preceding period, his method is original in its rigour and content. Morley says "Machiavelli's merit in the history of political literature is his method". Similarly Allen remarks "What was most new and original in the work of Machiavelli was perhaps his method of his manner of approaching problems of politics".

FATHER OF MODERN POLITICAL THOUGHT

Niccolo Machiavelli has been an enigma throughout the ages. Whatever he wrote on politics are in the form of pamphlets and scattered. But, later on it was discovered, mainly by Quentin Skinner that he made tremendous contribution to the growth of political thought. He was original in many of his ideas and laid the foundations of modern political thought.

1. Machiavelli's discussion of a territorial, national and sovereign state is the hallmark of modern period. He was the first to use the term state in modern connotation which becomes the main topic of discussion in the hands of subsequent writers.
2. Machiavelli's separation of politics from ethics and assigning it an autonomous sphere is another contribution. Prior to him politics was considered the hand maid of ethics.
3. Machiavelli is the first to bring the aspect of realism in politics. Prior to him normativism dominated the political thinking.
4. Machiavelli's advocacy of power politics is another contribution that has been followed widely in the realm of international relations. Perhaps no nation can afford to rely exclusively on idealism.
5. Machiavelli's method of history combined with commonsense observation has remained pragmatic till now.
6. Machiavelli's denouncement of Church and its interference in the state places him as the first secular thinker.
7. Machiavelli's analysis of role of the state to offer security of its citizens remains pragmatic as ever.
8. Machiavelli's republican spirit (service to the nation) has been celebrated by nationalists of all ranks.
9. Machiavelli's suggestion to the prince signifies an eyesight of political psychologist. Every theorist in modern time seeks to base his argument on the basis of motivation and orientation of human beings towards political objects.

SEPARATION OF ETHICS AND POLITICS

Despite an attempt by Aristotle, politics remained a hand maid of ethics from Greek period onwards. It was Machiavelli who attempted this task with a commitment. To him, politics and ethics were two different sciences whose dominions were altogether separate. While politics deals with rules of conduct of state; ethics deals with rules of conduct of individuals. Not only this, he even placed politics above the ethics.

Influenced by the state of affairs of his native state and intellectual cross currents of his time, Machiavelli advocates that 'end justifies the means'. In his own words, "When the safety of our country is absolutely at stake, there need be no question of what is just or unjust, merciful or cruel, praiseworthy or disgraceful; but all other considerations set aside, that course alone is to be taken which may save our country and maintain its liberty". But, it is not to be followed by individuals in private realm. Only state can opt for such a strategy because it acts for all. The rulers are allowed to break promises and violate principles if it is at the stake of state.

Machiavelli thought of the state as a morally isolated being whose main aim is to acquire and maintain power. He is neither moralist nor immoral but unmoral and acts as a physician of the state to diagnose the ills and provide remedies.

STATECRAFT OF MACHIAVELLI

Machiavelli was a practical politician who was greatly disturbed by the conditions of his native state. He never claimed to be political philosopher. His 'Prince' contains the tips given to the fictional prince. The 'Prince' as mainly a handbook on the art of ruling and maintaining oneself in power. In his advice; he is mainly concerned with the actual state of his time without bothering about its origin, nature, functions etc. Allen says "The Prince was written of a Prince, for a Prince and for no one else"?

However in subsequent period, his ideas were concretized to develop a systematic whole. The following are the various ideas of Machiavelli on state that can be said to have formed into a systematic political theory.

1. For Machiavelli, state has its origin in the calculating self interest on the part of individuals. For, human beings are selfish, egoistic and ambitious, but weak and fickle.
2. The state for Machiavelli is an artificial creation.
3. Machiavelli identifies three kinds of state, viz., monarchy, aristocracy and republic. He neglected aristocracy, hailed republic as best but favoured monarchy in Italy which was plagued by many problems.
4. State exists only on account of interplay of material interests. Likewise, he makes the Church subservient to the state.
5. Machiavelli supports the constitution of state by citizens with spirit of probity, law abidingness, trustworthiness in the performance of public duties.
6. Machiavelli puts faith in the reality of power politics. For him, there remains an inherent tendency in states to expand and continue. To quote him, "All free governments have two principal ends—one of which is to preserve their liberties and the other to enlarge their dominions".
7. Machiavelli is in favour of maintaining a national army without which a state can not survive for longer period, so he advocates military training for citizens between the age of 17 and 40.
8. Though, Machiavelli considered force and fear as important ingredient in administration, he does not relegate the significance of law. He regards it as an important aspect in inculcating 'virtue' among citizens.

SUGGESTIONS TO THE PRINCE

From above, one can come to the conclusion that Machiavelli is more concerned with instrumental dimension of the state, than with its origin, evolution or development. His works, Prince and Discourse are essentially a work on the art of government, rather than a theory of the state. It was intended to help the prince in his day to day administrative work and to keep himself in power. They are as follows :

1. Most important advise to the prince is to 'use the force ruthlessly' to maintain and strengthen his authority.
2. Machiavelli advises the Prince to use the methods of propaganda and religion and act as both; fox and lion. For, force can not only bring the fruitful result.
3. In his opinion, a prince should be competent enough to take firm decisions because loosing initiative and delay are more dangerous than doing wrong.
4. He wants the rulers to maintain a well trained, regular national army of his own soldiers to defend the state and make it powerful.
5. For Machiavelli, a prince should be well versed in the art of war and maintain arms and ammunition of best quality.
6. Machiavelli exhorts that "a Prince should retain the affection of his people, otherwise in any crisis, he has no remedy.
7. According to Machiavelli, a prince should be better feared than loved, but should not be hated.
8. He warns the ruler not to intervene in the property and conjugal relations of its subjects, "A person will more readily forgive the murder of his father than the confiscation of his patrimony".
9. Machiavelli urges the rulers to create public spirit and virtue among the subjects by the means of education, religion and propaganda.
10. In dealing with administration, the ruler should try to maintain utmost secrecy. Otherwise, his orders will become ineffective and may endanger the security of state.
11. For Machiavelli 'end justifies the means'. He advises the ruler to act as fox and lion to achieve the end.
12. A ruler in Machiavelli's opinion, should be an opportunist because there are no permanent friends or foes.
13. A ruler should show and present himself as kind hearted, generous, sincere, humane, brave etc.; even though he is not exactly so.
14. A ruler should possess virtue i.e. combination of will and intelligence that sees things as they are.

15. A ruler must embark on expansionist policy because failure to expand the state shall lead to stagnation and ultimate decline of the state.

16. A ruler should avoid flatters and form his opinion on his own.

17. In a newly conquered territory, a ruler should destroy liberty because people accustomed to freedom can never be reconciled the loss of it.

HOBBES

Life and Time

Thomas Hobbes was born in the family of an Anglican Clergyman in 1588. He was educated at Malmesbusy and at Oxford. Later, he was appointed as a tutor to heir of William Cavendish and maintained a life long connection with this distinguished family. Came into personal contact with great minds like Ben Jonson, Baccon and Galileo. He was a witness to the civil war in England between the supporters of monarchy and republicanism and sided with the king. Charles I was beheaded and monarchy was abolished.

Influences on Hobbes

Like any thinker, Hobbes was influenced by contemporary situation in England and intellectual cross currents of his time. In particular:

1. Civil war in England convinced him of brutish nature of human beings that can be only tackled by a strong and stable government. He favoured monarchy because he believed that the state of war can be transformed into a civilized life only through it.
2. He was influenced by Plato and Hobbes in his idea of social contract that is acknowledged in all quarters.
3. His concept of sovereignty was borrowed from Bodin. But, he developed it further with improvement.
4. Galileo's mechanics influenced Hobbes to accept the mechanical nature of world.
5. He applied the study of geometry to the realm of politics under the influence of Euclid.
6. He was influenced by Machiavelli in his views on human nature.

Works : Leviathan, De Corpse and Dechive

Methodology of Hobbes

Hobbesian method was the geometrical method, the only scientific method in his opinion. It is a deductive method where conclusions are derived from assumptions or already established truths.

Hobbes believed in the mechanical nature of the world. To him, everything in the universe, even man and political institutions is a movement of particles. "Whatever phenomenon takes place in the world is the result of motion of particles''. It underlined following ideas.

1. There is nothing such a spirit or soul but everything is the resultant of motion of particles.
2. Materialist methodology rejected medieval apprehensions with the state and emphasised that it was a step forward. For it free men from endless struggles.
3. The individual remains the pivot round which his methodology revolves. In this way became the forerunners of middle class liberalism.

However, following criticism are levelled against him.

1. Prof. Jones pointed out "Hobbes utterly failed to deduce either his psychological theory or his sociological theory from the laws of motion as he proposed to do".
2. His deductive method can not hold good in all cases. Political life is full of contingencies and complexities.

HOBBES ON HUMAN NATURE

Rightly said "all political philosophers have begun the study of state with the study of man", but this is more true of Hobbes. In his scheme of thing, it is the individual around which the whole edifice of his thinking revolves.

Hobbes's concept of human nature is closely intertwined with his mechanistic outlook. For him, motion of particles creates sensation in human mind.

Sensations give rise to perception, imagination, memory, prudence and realson.

For Hobbes, reason is artificial creation of human mind. But, emotion and passion are natural and inborn attribute of human mind.

Further, he holds that emotion can be good or bad. The movement of mind which accompanies good is called pleasure and the movement of mind which accompanies bad or evil or aversion is called pain.

In his own words "the end of every man is continued success in obtaining those things which he desires", in life there exists a perpetual and restless desire of power because it helps in getting pleasure and avoiding pain.

Since all men desire more or less the same thing and are roughly equal in strength and cunning, there is bound to be what, he calls "war of every man against every man". Thus, man is essentially selfish, altruistic, non-rational, impulsive and self-centred. Such a nature is transformed while entering into contract and forming a state.

HOBBES ON STATE OF NATURE

Hobbes's concept of state of nature denotes a period preceding the formation of Leviatham. In essence, it is a conceptual device to denote a pre political period after which state is created through a contract.

Hobbes's view on state of Nature is a natural outgrowth of his views on human nature. The existence of numerous self-interested, egoistic individual makes them psychologically isolated but physically surrounded by his fellow beings who are also his competitors.

The competition becomes essential not only accidental. Equality of powers coupled with equality of fear and equality of hope will induce every man to endeavour to outwit his fellow beings. The result is an open conflict the war of all against all. The hand of each is at every others throat. Men in the state of nature of the concept of Hobbes live in a condition of perpetual fear, of cut-throat competition and war. Unless there is a common sovereign power to regulate the behaviour of individuals, says Hobbes, they are all in "that condition which is called Warse : and such a warse is of every man against every man. Life of man is solitary, poor, hasty, brutish and short.

From above, the chief characteristics of Hobbesian state of nature can be discerned as follows :

Firstly, It is governed by no rules or laws. Men are engaged in fierce but ceaseless battle for blind passions. Which can not be judged by any standards.

Secondly, Every individual has natural right to everything that can be obtained by power in competition with fellow beings.

Thirdly, There is no conception of justice or injustice because justice for Hobbes is by-product of law.

Fourthly, There is no place for "industry, because the fruit thereof is uncertain", and consequently no culture of the earth, no navigation, nor use of the commodities that may be imported by sea, no commodious building, knowledge of the face of earth, no account of time, no letters, no society".

HOBBES ON LAWS OF NATURE

Laws of nature or 'dictates of reason', borrowed from Grotius plays a crucial role in establishing a Leviathan. It shows the individuals, a way out of state of nature characterised by war of everyman against everyman. In essence, laws of nature "lex naturales" are a sort of restriction on the power of individuals in the state of nature to inhibit the exercise of natural rights".

Contrary to subsequent writers like Locke who thinks of law of nature as instrumental in exercise of natural rights, Hobbes links it to limit the natural rights.

There are several ingredients in law of nature.

1. It is a logical outcome of Hobbesian mechanistic psychology. For, condition prevailing in state of nature can not bring peace and harmony.
2. It provides a common yardstick in the form of Leviathan to regulate the political life of

individuals. For, in the absence of an all powerful sovereign authority, anti-social impulses can not be kept in check.

3. Reason has a regulative, not a emotive force as it does not give any motive force to human minds. It enlightens the narrow selfishness to form a civilized society.

The important laws of nature laid down by Hobbes are as follow :

1. Aristotle of peace or laws of nature hints that men should seek and observe peace. The state of nature is not conducive to achievement of self preservation. They should follow the laws that abandon the war like situation and strive to live in peace with his fellow-beings.
2. Every individual should abandon his natural right to all things. This abandonment should be general and reciprocal. It is at this stage that individuals enters into a compact i.e. the "mutual transfer of rights" more commonly known as contract. It is by this dictate of reason that the artificial person, the state, the Great Leviathan, that mortal God on Earth, to whom the individuals owe their liberty in society and peace in life, is created.
3. Men should abide by the terms and conditions of the contract made among themselves. The very fact that individuals are not disciplined, the creation of all powerful sovereign with all means of coercion at his command is absolutely necessary.
4. One should have a sense of gratitude so that the benefactors does not have "reasonable cause to repent him on his goodwill".
5. "Every man strive to accommodate himself to the rest".
6. Men should pardon the offices of the repentant fellow-being.
7. No man by deed, word, countenance or gesture, declare hatred or contempt of another.
8. At the entrance into conditions of peace, no man requires to reserve to himself any sight, which he is not content should be reserved to everyone of the rest.
9. If man be trusted to judge between man and man, it is a precept of law of nature that he deals equally between them.
10. Such things as can not be divided, be enjoyed in common if it can be; and if the quality of the thing permits, without stinct.
11. They that are controversy, submit their right to the judgement of an Arbitrator.

SOCIAL CONTRACT OF HOBBES

Hobbes in his political philosophy mainly proceeds on the essential wickedness of human nature. Even though the law of nature shows the way out of state of nature, it does not ensure harmony. To ward off such apprehension, he supports an all powerful sovereign authority to enforce the laws of nature. For "'covenants' without sword are butt words" and of no strength to secure a man at all.

Why Contract?

To end the state of nature, every individual enter into, what Hobbes calls 'contract' with each individual. Through contract :

individuals undertake not "to will their own will"

individuals "accept to undertake limitation on their will"

they "submit the wills of all to the will of one".

Social contract is the basis of Hobbes's state whereby individuals of their own impulse, unite and execute a contract among themselves without the ruler or sovereign being party to it. The origin of state lies in the transfer of all the natural rights of individuals (except the right to life). The individuals agree to institute a third party—a common recipient—who himself is not a party has to protect the right to life. The contract creates one common superior out of the equally placed individuals. It represents the sum total of all the powers of individuals.

Features of Contract

Chief features of contract are :

Firstly, individuals are the basis of contract. They are endowed with equal natural rights in the state of nature. It is neither a contract among groups, nor is a contract among unequals. Moreover, it is a contract resulting from the prudential calculations of individuals and not from fear.

Secondly, the sovereign is not a part but apart from and above the participants. However, it can never make a breach of the contract.

Sovereign can not be unjust because 'justice lies in adherence to the contract'.

Thirdly, the contract is irrevocable and finite. The individuals have no right without the consent of the sovereign.

Fourthly, the minority has no right to object to the dictates of the majority in selecting a sovereign.

Fifthly, although sovereign may be one person, two or many, but his preference is for monarchy.

Sixthly, the main motto of the contract is protection of life of individuals. Though the sovereign is supreme in all aspects, he can not encroach upon lives of individuals.

Seventhly, there is no distinction between state and society and between state and government. For, it is the sovereign power which creates civiiized political society out primitive state of nature.

HOBBES' CONCEPTION OF SOVEREIGNTY

Sovereignty is the unrestrained power of the state backed by coercive force over all individuals and institutions lying within its allotted physical area. Sovereignty in the modern sense of the term may be defined as the unrestricted and supreme authority of the state of frame and administer law with all the coercive force behind it. State power and sovereignty are considered identical terms.

Even though the credit for initiation of the term 'sovereignty' goes to Jean Bodin, it was Hobbes who properly laid the foundation of modern sovereign states.

Who is Sovereign : Hobbes's sovereign is created by a contract among individuals with one another. The underlying idea was that the state of nature exhibited a state of war with maximum uncertainty, particularly with respect to life.

Desire for self preservation (the greatest of all) suggests men to follow the dictates of reason to constitute an impartial sovereign. It is to be noted, that, sovereign is the representative of each individual, distinct from the natural person.

According to Hobbes, the "essence of sovereignty lies in the power to determine on behalf of the entire community. What should be done to maintain peace and order". It implies that sovereignty lies in the power to make laws binding on all the subjects.

Characteristics of Sovereign

1. Sovereign enjoys the absolute power to make laws. He is not only the chief source of all laws but also their sole interpreter.
2. Sovereign is the sole source of distinction between right and wrong, good and bad, moral and immoral. For, there did not exist any such agency in state of nature where every man was at war with every another.
3. Sovereign is the source of all powers; executive, judicial, legislate and can declare war and peace. There is no notion of separation of power in Hobbes's scheme.
4. Sovereign is endowed with indivisible, inseparable, absolute powers. Moreover, he is neither accountable, nor can be replaced by another. However, it lasts as long as life of the subjects is not threatened.
5. Sovereign is entrusted with duty to be successful so as to prove its worth. It should make laws that are equitable and commensurate with prospects for peace. Hobbes's Leviathan is a policeman, not an instructor because it is concerned only with preservation of natural right to life.
6. Sovereign is the creator of both; the state and the society.
7. Hobbes has preference for a monarch as sovereign.

CONTRIBUTION OF HOBBES

Despite a lot of hue and cry shown towards the absolutist case in Leviathan, writers like Sabine,

Oakeshott, Wayper, Jones and Maxey have regarded Hobbes as one of the political thinkers in the history of political thought. According to Sabine, "Hobbes is probably the greatest writer of political philosophy that the English speaking people have produced". Similarly, Oakeshott says "Leviathan is the greatest, perhaps the sole master-piece of political philosophy in the English language". Maxey goes to the extent of saying Hobbes as "one of the greatest political thinkers of the English race".

Significant contributions of Thomas Hobbes are as under :

1. His Theory of absolute sovereignty.
2. His Individualism.
3. First to view state as conciliator of interests.
4. His Utilitarianism.
5. His Materialism.
6. His scientific method.
7. Father of Empiricism.
8. Contract among equals was novel one.
9. Concept of positive law.

LOCKE

Life and Time

John Locke, one of the eminent political thinker of England was born in 1632. His father was a lawyer. He was a physician by profession.

Work : Treatise on Civil Government.

On Toleration.

Essays Concerning Human Understanding.

Influences on Locke

1. Association with Lord Ashley as physician and confidential secretary.
2. Witness of Glorious Revolution (1688) that led to replacement of absolute monarchy by responsible government.
3. Philosophers like Filmer and Hobbes.
4. Sydney whose "Discourses Concerning Government" emphasised sovereignty of the people.
5. From Hobbes, Locke borrowed the theory of consent and contract.

On Human Nature

Locke's concept of human nature is expounded in his "Essays Concerning Human Understanding", but is not as systematic as Hobbes. In this opinion, human beings are social creatures, decent and have attributes of ruling themselves. They are moral and rational. They are equal in the sense that they possess the tool of reason. They enjoy the natural right to life, liberty and property by virtue of being human. Locke explains the motive. Force behind all human action in terms of pleasure and pain. According to him "the object of all human action is to substitute pleasure for pain". Moreover "What has an aptness to produce pleasure, is called good and what is apt to produce pain is called evil".

Locke on State of Nature

Locke, being a contractarian conceives of a situation prior to the formation of state. But his views are opposite to his predecessor Hobbes.

Firstly, While Hobbes state of nature is a pre-social phenomenon; Locke conceives of it as a pre-political rather than presocial phenomenon.

Secondly, While Hobbes's state of nature is marked by fear, fraud and constant anarchy; Locke's state of nature is an organized society in which peace and reason prevail.

According to Locke, even prior to the formation of state, there existed an organised society. For reason teaches men to live in a spirit of brotherhood. The individuals enjoy their natural rights.

ON LAW OF NATURE

According to Locke, law of nature is in the form of prescription. It does not describe how men behave, but as to how they ought to behave. It is concerned with conducts of men.

The basic interpreter of Law of nature is the tool of 'reason' held equally by everyone. It follows that if there occurs a violation of law of nature a man can punish the transgressor by the instrumentality of reason.

While Hobbes's Law of nature is significant only for transference of state of nature into civil society, Locke's Law of nature operate in the state of nature and remains in operation even after civil state comes into existence.

Locke explains the reason of contract with respect to some inconsistencies in the law of nature. He says that even though there is peace and order in the state of nature, individuals enter into contract.

- Towards off confusion and uncertainty arising out of nature, content and interpreter of the law of nature.
- To establish a common agency for interpreting and executing the laws of nature.

While in Hobbes, individuals enter into contract as it was prime necessity to pressure their lives, Locke's individuals enter into contract to tide over certain difficulties in the state of nature.

Though Locke fails to provide a convincing argument as regards his basic assumptions, he lucidly fit together a number of political ideas. His concept of human nature, law of nature and reason went a long way in ushering individualism.

LOCKE ON PROPERTY

Locke's views on property are coloured by his individuals stance. According to him, there was common ownership of property in the state of Nature. Apart from it, every individual possesses the property of labour. A person by mixing his labour with an object makes it his own private property. He does not put any limitation on the amount of property an individual could accumulate.

LOCKE'S VIEW ON STATE

Locke's view on state are outcome of his concept of human nature. According to Prof. Vaughan "everything in Locke's system revolves round the individual; everything is disposed so as to ensure the sovereignty of the individual". He expounds a mechanical state whose prime raison-de-etre is to protect the natural rights to life, liberty and property. In fact the state is secondary and natural rights are of primary importance in his scheme.

INDIVIDUALIST

Locke, a great individualist advocated a negative conception of the state. Its role is limited to prevent the subjects from infringing one another's rights. The moment it fails to live upto its expectations, it forfeit the right to rule and can be legitimately over thrown. The state is limited to no more than a limited liability company.

According to Locke, law of nature has primacy over laws of state. In fact all laws made by the state must commensurate with law of nature.

Locke's government is based on the consent of individual. In its absence, the government may become absolute and people may not obey the state laws. He makes division of power so as to ensure that it fulfils the paramount requirement of preservation of individual freedom.

CONTRIBUTION OF LOCKE

John Locke, one of the outstanding figures in the realm of politics was the perpetrator of American and French Revolutions. Perhaps his influence has been so immense that all liberals hail him as godfather. The contribution of Locke can be studied under following heads.

1. One of major contributions of Locke has been the principle of Limited Government. He drew distinction between state, society and government. While society is primary, state comes into existence only for some convenience. Government is agency of state to exercise powers as its trustee.
2. Locke's conception of natural right to life, liberty and property has remained a doctrine of preeminence. Perhaps, it was for the first time that so much moral sanctity was attached to the natural rights of individuals.
3. Locke's view on right to revolt inspired the revolutionaries influence and America.
4. By conceiving mechanical nature of state, he becomes the forerunner of liberal thought. He passed the government on the consent of people who are endowed with reason and are best judge of themselves. It owed existence as long as it served its purpose.

5. Locke helped in development of the idea of a democratic state based on popular institutions and constitutional government. The principle of majority that underlines the democratic mechanisms are Locke's contribution.
6. Lockè reacted against divine right theory and linked state with the world by affairs.
7. Locke laid great emphasis on the principle of toleration and secularism.

SOCIAL CONTRACT OF LOCKE

Locke's love for private property leads him to envisage a scheme of social contract. His individuals enter into the contract to preserve their property, which includes three natural rights, viz.; life, liberty and property. To him, "The chief aim of man's uniting into commonwealth is the preservation of their property".

Property which includes three natural rights are of primary importance and are prior to state and government. These rights are "attributes of the individual person born with him, and hence indefeasible claims upon both; society and government". The salient features of his contract are:

1. **Political, not Social :** By Lockean contract only state is created, not the society or government.
2. **Limited and Specific :** Commonwealth is created for protection of three natural rights. Individual retain substantial power.
3. **Consent :** Lockean commonwealth is created not out of fear but based on consent of everyone for better life.
4. **Irrevocable :** Similar to Hobbes, Locke makes contract irrevocable.
5. **Law of Nature :** Even after contract, Law of nature is retained.
6. **Trust :** Commonwealth is handed over power and rights to discharge its functions properly. By doing so, both; the individual and community benefits.

HOBBES AND LOCKE : A COMPARISON

Among the earliest political philosopher-thinkers of England, Hobbes and Locke are prominent ones. While Hobbes was witness of civil war, Locke saw the Glorious Revolution (1688). These instances greatly moulded their character and evident in their thinking. Although Locke was influenced by his predecessor, Hobbes; but he leaves no stone unearthed to refute the claim of his master. There are very few similarities between them.

Similarities

1. To them, contract is the source of state and is based on consent of individual.
2. Both conceive of a minimal-negative state concerned with maintenance of individual rights.
3. In their scheme, reason plays a vital role. While for Hobbes laws of nature are 'dictates of reason, for Locke it interprets the law of nature.
4. Generally speaking, both of them emphasize on permanent nature of contract.

Differences

1. The approach of two thinkers is different. While Hobbes bases his philosophy on mechanics, Locke is no where clear in his approach. He compiles different ideas into a coherent whole.
2. In their concept of human nature, there is striking difference between the two thinkers. Hobbes believes that human beings are egoistic, selfish and quarrelsome. Locke, on the other hand, believes that they are selfless, peace loving and good creature.
3. While Hobbesian state of nature is a state of war of every man with every other, state of nature in Locke is a state of peace, goodwill and mutual assistance.
4. As regards the nature of contract there are differences. While Hobbes creates an all powerful, inalienable sovereign, Locke limits the power of sovereign only to interpret and enforce the law of nature for protection of natural rights.
5. There is no right to rebel in Hobbes's scheme, but Locke grants this right to the individual.

The government is a trust which can be overthrown the moment it violates their trust.

ROUSSEAU

Life and Time

J.J. Rousseau stands as one of the most famous contractualist of the modern times. But, the most contrasting aspect of his thought has been his opposition to enlightenment and notion of popular sovereignty. His view became a more potent factor in preparing the way for the great French Revolution. Taken in the context of his time, he paved the way for a new democratic order. According to Gettell **"History of Political Thought"**, "He is more dogmatic than Hobbes and more popular and eloquent than Locke, this work inspite of its inaccuracies and inconsistencies, exerted a tremendous influence upon the period following its appearance".

Rousseau was born in 1712 in Geneva. His father was a watchmaker and mother died while giving birth. At the age of 10, his father left Geneva leaving Rousseau in the case of a person. For a long time he roamed as a vagabond and failed to make friends due to his egoism and bad manners. In the year 1749, he wrote thesis on contribution of Science and Arts. In later years he went to England and came into contact of Burke and Hume. But, the friendships could not last long on account of his sceptical attitude.

Influences on Rousseau

Firstly, Rousseau was greatly influenced by the Republican heritage of Geneva. As Watkin observes "As an obscure but enfranchised member of a sovereign community he had been brought up in the tradition of a society where active participation in politics was the right of all free men. At a time when most intellectuals were willing to regard themselves as the loyal and obedient subjects of absolute monarchs, Rousseau was never able to accept the idea that men should be anything less than active and responsible members of a sovereign political community."

Secondly, Rousseau's family life convinced him of the bad social institutions. His experience at the hands of guardians convinced him of the evil in human nature. Much it, his thoughts were unnatural and human inventions.

Works of Rousseau

1. Discourses on the Moral Effects of Arts and Sciences.
2. Discourses on the Origin of Inequality.
3. An Introduction to Political Economy.
4. The New Heloise
5. The Social Contract.
6. Emile.

Methodology of Rousseau

According to Maxey "Rousseau's methodology is one of great thinking and he uses facts only to prove his philosophical assumptions". Though Rousseau was greatly inspired by other thinkers but much of his thinking is original in content and spirit. His ability to see contradictions of science and art in an age where these were hailed as the paramount virtue, eloquently testifies to it.

ROUSSEAU'S IDEA OF NATURE

According to Rousseau "Man is born free, and everywhere he is in chains. Many a one believes himself the master of others, and yet he is a greater slave than they. Consequently, he aims at devising principles of social and political life that will enable people to enjoy the fruits of freedom.

In Rousseau's opinion, the development of art and science have severed people's ties with the nature. He therefore pleaded for abandonment of these things as it obstructed the fulfilment of men's true nature.

Unlike Hobbes, Rousseau held that the man is inherently good. Consequently, the role of right art should be to promote the goodness of every human being. The evil, corruption and wickedness were nothing but creations of social institutions.

Rousseau locates two instinct in men with which they are originally endowed. The first one is self-love or the instinct of self-presentation. The second is sympathy on the gregarious instinct, or instinct of mutual aid. However, they are not evenly balanced and may come into conflict. Consequently a new instinct of conscience comes out to reconcile the two instincts. He attaches more importance to conscience than to reason because it is not nature and simply guides individuals and does not enable him to do things. As Wayper observes "he sees safety only in a perfect union in which sentiment and reason mutually check and control each other—in which sentiment urges reasons to the right path and in which reason leads us along it towards perfection.

According to Rousseau the problem arises when men allow self-love to be trumped by pride. Pride signifies quest for things that is not natural. As Wright observes "we can give up pride we can cease from all comparison with other men and simply go about our destiny. We can renounce a host of imaginary desires and hold fast to the true things needful, cast away a world of illusion and rediscover our own self. We can be meek and inherit our soul. In a word, we can return to nature?

LIBERTY IN ROUSSEAU'S THOUGHT

According to Rousseau liberty is natural to man. But, the liberty which men enjoy in the civic state is very different from the liberty as independence, they possess in the hypothetical pre-civic state. A higher form of liberty i.e. moral one can be realised only when they acquire such control over personal desire that only one desire is left; namely, the desire to be one with reason. It can be realised only when men submit themselves to the nature.

KARL MARX

Life and Time

Karl Marx was born in 1818 in Tier (Rheinish province of Prussia). His father, Heinrich Marx was a lawyer. During his student years at the University of Bonn and later at Berlin, Karl Marx made a profound study of history, literature, philosophy and law. In 1842 he became a editor of 'Rheinische Zetung'. But soon after went to France, when the newspaper was banned. In 1847 he organized Communist League in London. He lived in Germany for some time and died in England.

Works : The Poverty of Philosophy (1847)
The Communist Manifesto (1848)
The Critique of Political Economy
Civil War in France
Das Capital

Influences

1. German Idealist particularly Hegel's logic of Dialectic provided basis for his entire philosophy.
2. The Classical British Political Economists, particularly Adam Smith provided basis for labour theory and theory of surplus value.
3. French socialists influenced his theory of state and revolution.
4. Marx's association with his life-long friend and a collaborator had immense impact on his philosophy.

Main Contribution

Main contribution of Marx are as under :

1. Dialectical Materialism
2. Historical Materialism
3. Theory of Surplus Value
4. Theory of Revolution
5. Alienation Theory
6. Class Struggle

DIALECTICAL MATERIALISM

Marx's concept of dialectical materialism constitutes the foundation on which entire Marxist thought is based. He borrowed the concept "Dialectic" from Hegel and gave it a materialist twist.

According to Issac Kramnic and F.M. Watkins "the word dialectical originally referred to the process whereby ideas are formed and clarified in the course of debate". Hegel used it as a philosophy of history. To him, ideas are basic to all human activity which develops in a zig-zag manner following the formula of thesis, antithesis and synthesis. The social institutions are merely manifestation of ideas. He conceived of nation state as highest stage of social evolution.

Karl Marx appreciated Hegelian conception but he replaced dialectical idealism with dialectical materialism. Unlike Hegel, he believed that the social institutions are shaped by material conditions of life, which are determined by the economic mode of production.

According to Marx, the world by its very nature is material and the various phenomenon of the world constitute different forms of matter in motion. In his own words, "it is not the consciousness of men that determines their being, but on the contrary their social being that determines their consciousness".

THREE LAWS OF DIALECTICS

Dialectical method is based on three laws which are as follows :

1. **The law of transformation of quantity into quality and vice versa :** It means that changes are qualitative till a certain point after which its form is changed. For example, capitalism to socialism.
2. **The law of unity of opposites :** It implies that everything within itself contains contradictory but interdependent elements. For example, Capitalism contains both, bourgeoisie and proletariats.
3. **The law of negation of negation :** Thesis, antithesis and synthesis are connected in a chain which develops by negating other.

Through this process, Marx explains the history from primitive communism to world communism.

HISTORICAL MATERIALISM

Historical materialism or the materialist interpretation of history implies that all phenomenon of history are dependent on economic factors.

According to Marx, production is the most fundamental of all human activities. Society is the outcome of men's cooperation to produce for the satisfaction of human needs. But, changing needs, defective mode of production and limited knowledge continue to put strain on any given system of production.

Marx in his "Preface of the contribution to the Critique of Political Economy" holds that "In the social production of their life men enter into definite relations that are indispensable and independent of their will; relations of production which correspond to a definite stage of development of their material productive forces. The sum total of these relations of production constitutes the economic structure, the real basis on which rises a legal and political structure".

Marx adds that, "at a certain stage of their development, the material productive forces of society comes into conflict with existing relations of production. Every society contains the seeds of its own destruction. The contradictions between forces of production and relations of production lead to breakdown of the existing mode of production and its superstructure."

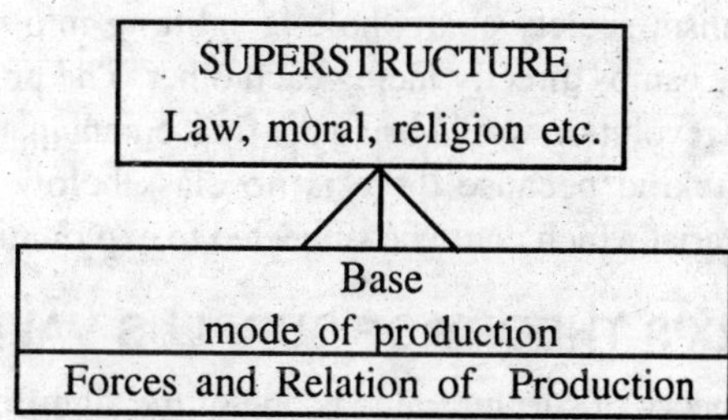

Base Superstructure Model

Stages of Historical Development

It is through this logic that Marx identified five stages in historical development:

(1) Primitive Communism (2) Ancient Society (3) Feudal Society (4) Capitalist Society (5) Communist Society.

The communist society is the final epoch in historical development. It would be a society without distinctions of social class and a true beginning of history as a record of full human self-realization.

MARX'S CONCEPTION OF CLASS STRUGGLE

Marx's theory of class struggle is a logical corollary of his concept of historical materialism. The opening line of the Communist Manifesto says "The history of all hitherto existing society is the history of class struggle". It results in the elimination of the existing class structure and its replacement by a now one, corresponding to the new mode of production.

According to Marx except the primitive communist society, all the societies have been characterized by clear cut class divisions. Freeman and Slave, Lord and Serf, bourgeoisie and proletariat; in a word, oppressor and oppressed, haves and havenots stood in constant opposition to each other. Those who owns the means of production, control not only the economic life but also the political life. Those who possess economic power also possess political power.

In his analysis of the capitalist society, Marx says "of all the classes, the proletariat alone is a really revolutionary class". He observed that under capitalism society as a whole is splitting into two hostile camps directly facing each other. The proletarian revolution would bring the final emancipation of mankind because there is no class below the proletariat which could be subjected to exploitation.

MARX'S THEORY OF SURPLUS VALUE

The theory of surplus value is one of the significant contribution of Karl Marx to political science. It is discussed in his monument work "Das Capital" which showed the opaque side of capitalism and is ample testimony of worker's exploitation in capitalist society. His theory is based upon the labour theory of value as Sabine remarks "the theory of surplus value was professedly an extension of the labour theory of value already stated by Ricardo and the classical economists".

According to Marx, of the four elements of production viz., land, labour, capital and organization; only labour is the source of value. Every commodity was exchange value represented by price. However, workers get much less than what he produces. Much of it is appropriated by the capitalist. This difference between the exchange value of the manufactured commodity and the price paid to the worker for his labour is called surplus value.

Under the socialist system the value of labour would be paid to the worker. Moreover, Marx emphasizés that "He who does not work, neither shall eat".

MARX'S VIEW ON REVOLUTION

Karl Marx, one of the great revolutionaries and political philosopher held that "the philosophers have always interpreted the world. What matters however is to change". His commitment to change led him to synthesize the political and economic outcome of the French and Industrial revolutions and create a coherent system of thought that led to revolutions after his death. Speaking about the relevance of Marxist concept of revolution Lawrence Kaplan says "because Marxism does not merely interpret the world but also seeks to change it, almost every revolution in the twentieth century has been carried out in his name". It is concentrated expression of his view of historical development.

What is Revolution?

According to Marx revolution means seizure of political power by the oppressed class by use of force. They are inevitable in class divided societies. To him, "In the social production of their life, men enter into definite relations that are indispensable and independent of their will, correspond to a definite stage of development of their material productive forces.... At a certain stage of development, the material forces of production in the society come into conflict with the existing relations of production leading to a new mode of production".

Revolution in Capitalist Societies

Marx notes that while revolutions in the past were accomplished by a minority, proletarian revolution would be a revolution of the majority. Moreover, its aim is not to win power exploiting another class. Rather, its aim is to end the system of exploitation itself. Although he believes that "of all the instruments of production, the greatest productive force is the revolutionary class itself", but he advises them to become a "class for itself" by developing class consciousness.

According to Marx, Proletarian revolution would be the final revolution in the history of mankind. It will replace capitalism by socialism and establish dictatorship of the proletariat in the intervening period between socialism and communism. State is retained but with difference. It is a state majority of propertyless for the liquidation of private property along with its ideology and culture. Slowly and gradually there will emerge a classless society and withering away of the state.

CONCEPT OF ALIENATION IN MARX'S THOUGHT

Marx's concept of Alienation has been a relatively new entrant in the domain of politics. For, it is compiled in "Economic and Philosophic Manuscripts" (1844) that were published in 1932. It contains humanist elements in Marxism evident in the writings of young Marx. This aspect has received, considerable attention in the writings of neo-Marxists. Marx's concept of alienation is dependent on his analysis of capitalism, mainly for its dehumanizing effects.

What is Alienation

According to Marx, alienation is a material process by which man creates things out of nature and comes to be dominated by those creations. The creative potential is fundamental to human beings. They continually create the world. But, they lose control of their own creations and become subject to them. It is externalization of human creativity into forms which not only obscured but denied their human, creative origin.

Causes of Alienation

The chief cause of alienation is the institution of private property. Marx would ask "If I wish to play tennis or golf do I need to own to court and so exclude others before I can pursue that objective", he identifies four told alienation.

1. Alienation from product
2. Alienation from labour
3. Alienation from other men
4. Alienation from himself

Alienation from product

This happens in two ways : Firstly, a product does not belong to a person who creates it. Secondly, the profit from his product goes on to increase the capital investment and increase the control of capital over labour.

Alienation from labour

It is the major form of alienation whereby the worker is alienated from his own nature. It can be illustrated by the saying "the worker works in order to live, he does not see his work as fulfilling his life, but simply as something to be got through in order to live".

Alienation from other men

The competitive character of economic system is subject to the laws of supply and demand without considering the human consequences. Some are thrown out, some are made to work for long hours.

Alienation from himself

The three forms of alienation reduces himself to the level of an animal existence where he has no interest for art, literature, music, etc.

How can it be overcome

Marx holds that the condition of man's alienation can be overcome only under communist system. There will not be commodity production and private property. The work will be allocated by a principle through which an individual can engaged himself in creative activities.

J.S. MILL

Life and Time

John Stuart Mill, one of the respected figures in British political circle was the eldest son of James Mill, a close associate of Bentham. From his childhood he was subjected to rigorous training with books. He studied Greek, French and Latin languages. He was the last of the utilitarians and foremost of the individualists.

Influences

1. Dialectic method of Plato used in his masterpiece Republic.
2. Benthamite Utilitarianism laying stress on pleasure-pain theory.
3. Philosophers like Coleridge and Wordsworth also influenced Mill.
4. His wife Mrs. Taylor who was part of all his discussion on political issues.

Works : On Liberty

Considerations on Representative Government

Principles of Political Economy

MODIFICATION OF UTILITARIANISM

Being son of James Mill, it was natural for J.S. Mill to imbibe the spirit of utilitarianism. At the age of 16, he founded the utilitarian society and sought to propagate Benthamite Principle of Utility. However, in view of scathing critiques, he started writing in defence of utilitarianism. Knowingly or unknowingly as Wayper says, "in his doctrine to safeguard utilitarianism from the reapproaches levelled against it, Mill goes towards overthrowing the whole utilitarian position".

His defence of utilitarianism marked following changes in Benthamite utilitarianism:

1. For Bentham man is a pleasure seeking being devoid of moral responsibilities.Being devoid of moral responsibilities will replace self interest with self sacrifice.
2. Mill made qualitative difference between different kinds of pleasures. He modifies Bentham's thesis on quantity being more important and holds that poetry is superior and preferable to pushpin or any other game.
3. He abandoned the hedonistic "felicitous calculus". To him, pleasure or pain is only a subjective sensation that can not be objectively measured.
4. Instead of pleasure, he makes dignity as final end of human life. To him, a sense of dignity is natural for human beings.
5. He envisaged a positive function for the state while Bentham outlines states role to increase pleasure and decrease pain, will want it to promote virtue among the individuals.
6. While Bentham subordinates liberty to the utility, Mill acknowledges liberty as amend in itself.
7. In place of Bentham's theory of "Everyone to count for one and no one for more than one", Mill supports plural voting. In fact, he recog-nizes the concerns of minority groups also.

DEMOCRACY

Representative Government in Mill's Philosophy

Even though J.S. Mill started as a defender of utilitarianism, his attempt to reform it outlined many novel features. One such feature was positive functions of the state. In his "considerations on Representative Government", Mill is mainly concerned with institutional reform in the government so as to make it a responsible and representative institution. So, impressive is his view that even some of the contemporary theorists of Democracy, like C.B. Macpherson and Carole Pateman claim to imbibe Mills spirit.

According to Mill the best form of government is the representative government. It safeguards freedom, right of self-determination. It encourages free discussion which is necessary for the emergence of truth. It reconciles the individual freedom with political equality.

Conditions for Success

In view of his optimism with representative democracy, Mill lays down several conditions for its success.

1. A scheme of individual rights which adequately safeguard the minorities against the will of elected majority.

2. Universal education to enable the citizens to become aware of their rights and obligations.
3. Active, self helping character of the citizenry.
4. Proportional representation (Hare system) to ensure minorities representation in proportion to their strength.
5. Voting by open of public ballot.
6. Equal voting right for all irrespective of sex or colour. In "Subjection of Women" he analyzes reasons for giving suffrage to women.
7. Indirect election.
8. State funding of election.
9. Institution of second chamber to safeguard the interests of those sections which would otherwise not be adequately represented in the popular assembly.
10. No voting rights to moral deviants, legally bankrupts and those unable to pay local taxes.

MILL'S THOUGHT ON INDIVIDUAL LIBERTY

J.S. Mill was a staunch proponent of individual liberty. His essay "On Liberty" remains one of the finest treatises ever written on the idea of freedom. Liberty for him is the life breath of society.

Threats to Liberty

Mill identifies threat to liberty mainly from two sources one, state laws that could restrict freedom and two, society which expresses the general but unorganized opinion. But, he accepts reasonable interference to individual liberty to prevent harm to other people.

Kinds of Liberty

Mill discusses liberty broadly under three heads. They are as follow :

Firstly, The liberty to thought and expression.

Secondly, Liberty of tastes and pursuits.

Thirdly, Freedom of Association.

Mill's discussion of the liberty of thought and expression is the most classic part of his essay 'on liberty'. It is essential not only for the development of the individual personality but also for the health and vigour of the society. It is not necessary for its instrumentality in ensuring effective government, but is good for its intrinsic worth. Moreover, it helps in establishing the truth.

MOHANDAS KARAM CHAND GANDHI

M.K. Gandhi, popularly known as Mahatma Gandhi was born on 2 October, 1869 at a place, Porbandar in Gujarat. His father Karam Chand Gandhi was a Dewan of the State. His mother was a religious minded lady who influenced the Mahatma, more than his father. He was married at the age of twelve. At the age of 19 years, he was sent to England. Soon after his return from England in 1891, he went to Abdullah, a Gujarati merchant. He was deeply displeased by the ill treatment meted out to Indians. From 1904 to 1914, he launched Satyagraha. Soon after, he returned to India and played a major role in India's freedom struggle. He died on January 30, 1948 from an injury caused by bullet fired from close range by Nathu Ram Godse.

Activities in India

— established Sabarmati Ashram on May 25, 1916
— joined Indian National Congress in 1916
— started Non-Cooperation Movement in 1921
— started Civil Disobedience Movement in 1930
— attended Second Round Table Conference in 1931
— revived Civil Disobedience Movement in 1932
— launched Quit India Movement in 1942

Main works

— Hind Swaraj
— Young India
— Harijan
— My Experiments with Truth

Influences on Gandhi

— Jesus Christ's message of love and non-violence

— John Ruskins view about goodness of human nature. His work is 'Unto This Last' gave him respect for manual labour.
— Works of Edward Carpenter "Civilization and its Cause and Curve" and Maxnardow "Paradoxis of Civilization".
— Thought of British political philosophies T.H. Green.
— Like Plato and Aristotle considered state as an enlarged embodiment of individual.
— Like Thorean, Gandhi considered state as essentially based on violence, Civil Disobedience and non-payment of taxes.
— Work of Leo Tolstoy, viz., The Kingdom of the God is within you, the Gospel in Brief, The letter to a Hindu.
— Like Tolstoy, Gandhi was a philosophical anarchist. In particular, he was influenced by Tolstoy's path of non-violence. His famous "Kingdom of God is within you" led Gandhi in non-cooperation.
— Gandhi was also influenced by Rousseau's dictum "back to the nature". In fact his view on Panchayat was greatly in fluenced by Rousseau.
— Teaching of Mao Tse and Confucianism also influenced Gandhiji.

NON-VIOLENCE

"Gandhi was neither a politician nor a political thinker", says Prof. S.P. Verma "he was a seeker after truth". He saw a close relation between means and end. So Gandhi came to accept that truth could be realized only through ahimsa. He saw truth and non-violence "as the two sides of the same coin". He considered it be "not a mere philosophical principle, it is the rule and breath of my life.... It is a matter not of the intellect but of the heart."

Gandhi used non-violence in broader terms. It is not used in negative sense of non-killing of human or animal life. Rather, it was something positive in action and deed. He observed "Non-violence is the law of our species as violence is the law of brute. The spirit lies dormant in the brute and he knows no law but that of physical force. The dignity of men requires obedience to a higher law—the struggle of the spirit. Non-violence is a perfect state. It is the goal towards which all mankind moves naturally, though unconsciously".

Gandhi's technique of non-violence was aimed at promoting social change. He opined that "It is a soul force or truth force or truth-seeking force. It is in short satyagraha which means resistance to evil with the moral and spiritual force or firmness in the indication of Truth".

However, Gandhi did not foreclose the option of violence. If one is caught in between inflicting violence and acting in cowardly manner, Gandhi favoured the use of violence. To him "It is better to be a soldier than to be a coward". He also cautioned that non-violence was to be used only by those who were capable of using violence effectively but they deliberately restrained from doing so.

CRITIQUE OF MODERN CIVILIZATION

Gandhi's "Hind Swaraj" written in a discursive format presents an alternative to the challenging sway of science and technology in human life. He analyzes the practical questions confronting Indian society and presents a moral solutions to them.

According to Gandhi, much of the appalling conditions of contemporary times are product of European enlightenment. The crude materialism as standard of life and prevalence of immorality in the name of morality have been brought about by modern civilization. To him, British parliament is a "sterile woman" and party politics is pity politics which aims at securing individual interest at the cost of social or general interest.

Civilization to Gandhi, is a mode of conduct which gives them a sense of duty. Duty is inseparably dependent on morality. He points out how our criteria of judgement get confined to our own notion of good. For "good to be of universal significance must be backed by morality".

Gandhi denounces the way of modern means of communication like railways and professionalization of occupation as crippling human minds and degenerating their potentialities. He holds that treating religion as superstition has further complicated the situation. On the contrary, we points out that religion remains the everyday aspect of life unifying humanity.

AUROBINDO GHOSH

Life and Time

Aurobindo was born on 15 Aug. 1872 at Calcutta. His father Dr. Krishandhan Ghose was a medical man who was educated from Aberdeen University, England. It was natural for his son to be educated in westen system of education. In his later years, the man proved himself to be a great mystic, a poet, a profound thinker and above all an ardent patriot. With an outstanding personality and foresight to visualize the past and future, the man continues to influence millions of his countrymen.

Different Views on Aurobindo

To Romain Rolland : He was the highest synthesis of the genius of the east and the west and the prince among the Indian thinkers.

Dr. Radhakrishnan hailed him as the most accomplished of modern Indian political thinker.

Rabindranath Tagore (a nobel laureate) was so impressed by his abilities that he is the one who can propagate the message of India.

Fredrics, an American educationist saw him as the 'guiding star of our earth and prophet of our age'.

Aurobindo remained in England for fourteen years and studied Greek and Latin classics and works of great European thinkers. It was in England that he took pledge to liberate his motherland from the imperial yoke. He began by organizing a secret society called 'Lotus and Dagger' for the uplift of his nation. Despite being qualified for I.C.S., he could not make it due to riding test. This further accentuated hatred against the British rule. Soon afterwards, his father who was at once reluctant to inculcate Indian ethos in his son injected national feelings.

Participation/Active Role

— Took active part in Indian politics from 1905 to 1911.
— He belonged to the Extremist camp.
— Edited the 'Bande Matram'.
— Put behind bar in Alipur Conspiracy Case.
— Withdrew from active politics at the age of 38 years.
— Died at Pondicherry in 1950.

Main Works of Aurobindo

— Life Divine
— Essays on Gita
— Synthesis of Yoga
— Renaissance of India
— Basis of Yoga
— Ideal of Human Unity
— Defence of Indian Culture
— Riddles of the World
— The Super Man

SPIRITUAL NATIONALISM

Aurobindo gave a new conception of Indian Nationalism. To him, it is not simply a political programme. Rather, he saw the manifestation of good in the nation. India, in his opinion is unique in herself and a genius par-excellence.

According to Aurobindo India is a divine power and an embodiment of spirituality. To fight for nation is to show love for mother. He exhorts "Nationalism is a religion that has come from God. Nationalism is a creed which you shall have to love. If you are going to be a nationalist, you must do it, in the religious spirit. Nationalism survives in the strength of God and it is not possible to crush it whatever weapons are brought against it. Nationalism is immortal."

Aurobindo wanted India to play a leading role in the world's quest towards spirituality. But, she could fulfil her task only when she attains complete independence. "In the ideal of Nationalism which India will set before the world, there will be an essential equality between man and man irrespective of caste, creed, religion or economic status. Nation is a **Virat Purush** or a magnified image of man and all the individuals are an integral part of the personality which is symbolized by the nation".

Aurobindo's conception of Nationalism was not sectarian. But, rather cosmopolitan where India was destined to play a bigger role and spearhead the case for one humanity.

PURNA SWARAJ

Aurobindo was a great nationalist who had great pride in the culture and traditions of his motherland. He believed that only a national government can rejuvenate the capacity and energy of India. It was due to these assumptions that Aurobindo considered Purna Swaraj to be the main objective of Indian nationalism.

Aurobindo considered the efforts of moderates as ineffective and fruitless. While, he accepted that their attempts can bring about reforms in the legislature or Indianization of civil service, they can not be helpful in creating a responsible constitutional government. While they were significant, they could not be realized under conditions prevalent at that time.

According to Aurobindo foreign rule was the main culprit for the ill plight of Indians. He believed that a subject nation can not use its own capacity and energy. Slowly and steadily it loses all its powers. The solution that he favoured was national independence. It will not only ensure individual development but also ensure full development of the national strength.

VIOLENT RESISTANCE

The Partition of Bengal (1905) had a deep impact on Aurobindo Ghosh and he was led to believe that a violent resistance could be a better political alternative for the sake of national liberation. He favoured violent resistance only if the objective could be gained quickly and the masses must acknowledge whether the violent resistance is feasible under the existing circumstances. He accepted that though there are suffering in such efforts, but he believed that armed revolt was the quickest and thorough in results.

However Aurobindo was fully aware of the existing environment. Lack of thorough unity and proper organization, made him to accept the usefulness of passive resistance as the best device for getting rid of the British domination.

PASSIVE RESISTANCE

In broader terms, passive resistance implies abstaining from doing something by which the opponent would otherwise be helped. In the context of British rule, it included boycott of foreign goods, institutions, etc.

Aurobindo highlights certain qualifications for passive resistance. Those include

(*a*) disobeying just coercive laws.
(*b*) defy unjust executive orders.
(*c*) refuse to pay taxes.
(*d*) social ex-communication against those who are traitors and hamper the activities of freedom fighters.

According to Aurobindo "so long as the action of the executive is peaceful and within the rules of the fight, the passive resister scrupulously maintains his attitude of passivity but he is not bound to do so a moment beyond. To submit to illegal or violent methods of coercion, to accept outrage and hooliganism as the legal procedure of the country is to be guilty of cowardice and dwarfing national manhood, to sin against the divinity within ourselves and the dignity in our motherland". He allowed the resister to use violence if the opponent uses it. A passive resistance must be supplemented with active resistance. In the opinion of J.K. Ray "Aurobindo was confident that passive resistance if applied to different departments of Administration will cut the ground from under the feet of foreign bureaucrats, render their existence anachronistic and useless and pave the way to national emancipation".

M.N. ROY

Life and Time

Manvendra Nath Roy was born in 1886, in 24 Parganas district of Bengal. Soon after receiving his education at Calcutta, he developed close contact with revolutionaries. He was an active member of Yugantar group, a revolutionary organization mainly active in Bengal. His association with Jatin Mukherjee was another factor of crucial importance in his revolutionary activities. In view of growing governmental pressure and attack on revolutionaries, he went to Java, Philippines, Korea Manchuria and USA. He deeply studied the tenets of Marxism Socialism and was invited by Lenin to visit Russia in 1920, in 1926 he went to China as the chief representative of the communist international. Soon after he severed ties with the communist international so as to avoid back lash with Stalin. He returned to India in 1936 and was arrested in the Kanpur conspiracy case. Later on, he organized a 'League of Radical Congressmen' and the Radical Democratic Party.

Roy's life is broadly divided into three different phase

I—spanning upto 1919—as a revolutionary

II—spanning upto 1929—as a Marxist

III—till death—as Radical Humanist.

Main works

1. India in Transition (1922)
2. Indian Problem and its Solution (1922)
3. One Year of Non-Cooperation
4. The Future of Indian Politics (1926)
5. Revolution and Counter Revolution in China (1930)
6. Materialism (1934)
7. New Orientation
8. Beyond Communism to Humanism
9. New Humanism and Politics.

RADICAL HUMANISM

Roy started his political activities as a revolutionary by participating in the activities of Yugantar Group. Later on, he studied Marxism and was deeply inspired by its basic tenets. In his opinion "Marxism is the outcome of the development of thought from dawn of history, therefore it is the heritage of humanity, it is the ideological equipment belonging to every body for "a better world". But in view of dogmatic interpretations of Marxism by Russian tyrants, he moved on to outline, what he termed as Radical Humanism.

Roy's radical Humanism is not simply a reaction against Stalin's interpretation of Marx but instead it represents his vision of freedom and well being. As he says, 'radical humanism is a philosophy of freedom based on modern scientific knowledge. It aimed at infusing and re-invigorating ethical or moral outlook in the man.

There are following grounds on which Roy opposed Marxism.

Firstly, He did not pin faith in the Marxism theory of surplus value. Rather he believed that surplus provided one of the basis for society's progress.

Secondly, He did not approve of economic deterministic outlook of man. As Dr. V.D. Varma observes "in place of the Marxist thesis which interpret ethical norms in terms of class struggle, Roy accepts that there is something permanent in ethical values". Roy also said "Philosophically, the materialist conception of history must recognize the creative role of intelligence. Materialism can not deny the objective reality of ideas".

Thirdly, Roy had strong praise for individualism.

Fourthly, Roy was not convinced with the Marxism notion of "history of all hitherto existing societies is history of class struggle". Rather, he believed that conflict cooperation are part of social life. Moreover, the contemporary reality did not expressed Marx's ideas.

Fifthly, Roy was highly critical of the dictatorship of the proletariat. On the contrary, we believed that the real "conflict was between totalitarianism and democracy, between all-devouring collective ego-nation or class and the individual struggling for freedom". A revolution through education was the most suitable method for change. In his opinion, revolutions and the resulting dictatorship of the proletariat lead to totalitarianism of one or the other kind.

NEW HUMANISM

Roy changed his view from radical to New Humanism. It was marked by as Vishnoo Bhagwan observes "He found in the European renaissance enriched by the discoveries of present day sciences the basis of a new social order. Hence it is rightly contended that Roy's humanistic elements of thoughts are traceable to several schools and epochs of western philosophy. He craves for New Humanism based upon natural reason and secular conscience".

Roy made a novel connection between the means and ends. As he said "It is very doubtful if a moral object can ever be attained by immoral means". But, his conclusions draw a totally different picture than Gandhi's Ram Rajya. He was convinced of the usefulness of European rationalism. He advocated use of physical sciences in the service of mankind.

The basis of Roy's "New Humanism" was cosmopolitan. It transcended natural as well as political boundaries. As he observed "New Humanism is cosmopolitan commonwealth of spiritually free men would not be limited by the boundaries of national states. Which will gradually disappear under the 20th century renaissance of man". The role of education was of pivotal importance in Roy's scheme of things.

Roy's conception of New Humanism was basically a conception of individual freedom based on reason and morality. It was to be a tool for social progress. As he observed "The quest for freedom is the continuation of biological struggle for existence at the emotional and cognitional level". His love for individual freedom and social progress is expressed in his following word. "A brotherhood of men attracted by the adventure of ideas, keenly conscious of the urge for freedom fired with the vision of a free society of free man and motivated by the will to remake the world so as to restore the individual in his position of primary and dignity will show the way out of the contemporary crisis of modern civilization.

POLITICAL AND ECONOMIC IDEAS

Roy's love for individual freedom led him to outline a broader framework that could be most conducive to its realization. Being witness to the fate of centralized society (Soviet Union), he favoured decentralization of power in the political as well as economic realm. The villages and local units must be the tool of social change and it should not be brought about by the political parties. As Vishnoo Bhagwan observes "Like J.P. Narayan, we strongly advocated partyless democracy".

Roy did not favour the prevailing systems of representative democracy. According to Dr. V.P. Verma "He stood for a social system, where social technology and the pooled powers of human reasons and engineering would be applied to the reconciliation of individual freedom and social good and progress". He labelled this model as 'organized democracy' resembling Rousseau's theory of direct democracy. He said "To be real, democracy must be direct, government must be under the direct control of the people".

However, in view of its impracticability in the contemporary world, Roy made certain modifications. These included an institution of council of state whose members were to be elected as well as selected by professional groups. The council will mainly concern itself with the planning and guiding the execution of plan.

Roy neither favoured laissez faire capitalism, nor did he precised collectivism of Soviet type. As he said "The concept of the economic man negatives the liberation doctrine of individualism. The economic man is bound to be a slave or a slave holder". In the same vein he said "State control of the means of production and planned economy do not by themselves end exploitation of labour nor lead to an equal distribution of wealth". Moreover, he was totally against any use of state power in economy, speaking about welfare state, he remarked "Money is taken out of the pocket of the worker and put into his other pocket in the form of benefits, in the process, the money loses about 20-25 per cent of its value".

Roy favoured a cooperative economy based on twin-principle of decentralization and cooperation geared towards serving human ends. These economic units must use technology on substantial scale to industrialize itself. As he said "Machine should not be the Frankenstein of modern civilization. Created by man, it must subserve man's purpose—contribute to his freedom.

COMPARATIVE POLITICS AND POLITICAL ANALYSIS

WHAT IS COMPARATIVE POLITICS?

The growth of Comparative Politics has been a recent phenomenon (particularly post second world war period). It is a systematic outcome of realization within the circle of political scientist to study political reality with the use of new methods and techniques to evolve what may be called a science of politics. Moreover, widespread scepticism and disenchantment with the traditional approaches provided impetus to this trend.

Contemporary manifestation comparative politics is aimed at studying politics as a dynamic affair—as an activity, a process and power relations. While 'comparative government' is concerned with the study of different political system with respect to the institutions and their functions, comparative politics is concerned with study of institution, functions and also the study of non state actors. It has wider focus and as Sidney Werba points out "look beyond description to more theoretically relevant problems; look beyond the formal institutions of government to political processes and political functions, and look beyond the countries of Western Europe to new nations of Asia, Africa and Latin America."

Main Concerns

Some of the main points of Comparative Politics include.

1. Change in focus from purely normative to empirical enquiry.
2. Focus on all those factors having impact on politics.
3. Their approach is interdisciplinary.
4. Attempts to build value free political theory.
5. Most of these works concentrate on the study of developing societies (third world countries).

Thus the study of comparative politics has enormously influenced the expanding horizon of political science. It has attempted to encompass all those factors which it considers affects the politics of the day. It also expresses a kind of intellectual rigour towards the analysis of developing countries.

APPROACHES TO THE STUDY OF COMPARATIVE POLITICS

They are of two kinds : Traditional and Modern

TRADITIONAL APPROACHES

1. **Philosophical**
   — Oldest approach
   — Identified with names and preferences
   — Contemporary exponent is Leo Strauss, Lindsay
2. **Historical**
   — used in two senses
1. Arriving at laws through analysis of events of past as found in writings of Hegel, Marx.
2. Attempts at understanding politics through historical account of political thought of the past—Sabine.
   — Popular in last quarter of 19th century.
   — Seeks to understand state and institution in process of change.

- Exponent are Sabine, Dunning, McIlwain, Burgess, K. Sceley, Carlyle, Carlin, Aristotle and Machiavelli
- Criticised by behaviouralist like Easton.

3. Legal

- Focusses on legal and const. framework in which different organs of Government have to function and inquires into their legal position, power and procedure which makes their action legally valid.
- Proponents of this approach are Bodin, Hobbes, Bentham, Austin and A.V. Dicey.

4. Institutional

- Popular in first quarter of 20th century.
- Closely related to legal approach, yet different
- Exponents-Bagehot, James Bryce, Giovani Sartori
- Amongst traditional approaches it alone gives an independent identity to the systematic study of politics
- Emphasis of facts so exemplifies a shift from normative to empirical approach. However relies heavily on description rather than explanation.
- It is assimilated into the behavioural approach and is still important. For it draws attention to the role of formal rules and institutions.

MODERN/CONTEMPORARY APPROACH

Attempt to establish separate identity of Political Science to try to understand politics in its totality comprises : behavioural, post behavioural approach :

- Power approach
- Some models.

Power

- Machiavelli, Hobbes, Nietzche, Marx Weber, Catlin, Laswell, Kaplan, Watkins, Trietschke, Morgenthau.
- Emphasis on format as well as informed centre.
- Even Marxists emphasis but differ from liberals under location of the centres of power.

BEHAVIOURALISM

- Believes that observing the outward behaviour of political outer and political institutions and analysing their behaviour by scientific method can acquire the knowledge of political system.
- Draws heavily from sociology and psychology.

Factors Responsible

1. Concept of General System Theory of Ludvig Von Bert pioneered at unification of sciences (Biologists).
2. Logical positivism popularly known as Vienna circle in 1920's — everything that was over and beyond experience.
3. Linguistic philosophy -T.D. Weldons 'Vocabulary of Politics, Peter Laslett, Bertrand Russell, A.N. Whitsheed. Only those statements or propositions which could be conclusively verified or falsified by empirical means could be regarded as genuine.

Origin is traced to :

- **Graham Wales**—Human Nature in Politics 1942
- **Arthur Benthey**—The process of Government, 1908.
- **Charles Merriam** is regarded as intellectual god father of behavioural political science.

Present state of the Study of Politics—APSR (1921)

New Aspects of Politics—1925 :

- Merriam emphasized renewed scientific endeavour and need for a policy science by using quantitative techniques already developed in Psychology and Sociology.

— **G.E.G. Catlin**—Science and Method of Politics (1927) advanced case produce see pure science.

— **Laswells**—Politics: who gets what, when, how? Proved a Landmark in empirical approach to politics as study and analysis of power.

— **To Eulan** the root is man.

— **To Kirkpatrik**, behaviouralism is a revolution

— **To Easton** it called for methodological rigour and empirical theory.

— **To Dahl** it manifests a mood which calls for greater unity between empirical political studies and concern for general theory.

By second half of 1960's behaviouralism became an accepted face.

Its focus is individual person, rather than the group or the political system but it necessarily takes account of the influences of the growth on the individual's behaviour, (Sociological and Psychological)

They advocates a new method. They insist on survey research.

Their method is interdisciplinary.

Major Tenets

Easton has identified eight major tenets which he regarded as 'intellectual foundation stones' on which movement is constructed :

1. **Regularities :** discoverable uniformities that can be expressed in theory like statements for expectation and prediction.
2. **Verification :** each generalisation must be testable by observation.
3. **Techniques :** self-conscious selection, refined and validated mean. For observing, recording and analysing pet behaviour.
4. **Quantification :** unless it is done, it would be impossible to obtain precise and accurate knowledge.
5. **Values :** Objective scientific inquiry has to be value free or value neutral.
6. **Systematization :** research must be theory oriented and theory directed.
7. **Pure Science :** Knowledge would be utilized in the solution of urgent practical problems of society.
8. **Integration :** to them man is a social animal, so political research was to take into account the findings of other disciplines.

Behaviouralist achievement by the theory building and techniques of research (greatest in sample survey).

Focussed on micro level situations rather than attempting macro level generalizations.

It is poorer. When it comes to institutions and processes whose data can not be quantified.

In place of state they coined the term political system consisting of all things associated with political process.

Critics of Behaviouralism

Leo Stranes in 'what is political philosophy' (Journal of Politics 1957) argued that the rise of behaviouralism was symptomatic of a crisis in D.T. because of its failure to come to grips with the normative issues.

Sheldon Wolin in 'Political Theory as Vocation' APSR, 1969 declared that preoccupation of Political Science with method signifies an abdication of true vocation of Political Theory.

Thomas Kuhnis 'The Structure of Scientific Revolution' (1962) had promoted the view that significance of scientific method lies in its capacity of problem solving and crisis management, not in methodological sophistication.

By 1960s end, even exponents undivided that strict adherence to pure science was meeting failures.

POST-BEHAVIOURALISM

In 1969 Easton announced a new revolution that represented a shift of focus from strict methodological issues to a greater concern with public responsibilities. It stood for no complete departure from behaviouralism rather it stood for consolidating its gains and applying them for problem solving and crisis management.

Relevance and action are major bases of his approach.

To Easton, it was future oriented seeking to propel Political Science in new directions. He equated it with a movement of an intellectual tendency.

Major Tenets

Easton came out with seven major traits of post-behaviouralism and described them as credo of relevance or 'a distillation of maximal image'.

1. Substance must come before technique, to the slogan raised by the behaviouralists that it was better to be wrong than vague. Post behaviouralist raised country sogan that it was better to be vague than non-relevantly precise.
2. Place main emphasis on social change, not social preservation as behaviouralists seemed to be doing.
3. To reach out to the real needs of mankind.
4. That values played an important role in politics and research in the name of science, could not be permitted to know them out of political studies. If knowledge was to be used for right goals, value had to be restored to the central position.
5. Political scientists, being intellectual of society had a major role to play. They had to protect human values of civilization.
6. Knowledge must be put to work. A sense of commitment and action must permeate and colour entire research in Political Science.
7. Politicisation of the Profession—of all professional associated as well as universities.

SYSTEM APPROACH

What is a System? : It is defined as bounded region in space time, involving energy interchange among their parts which are associated in functional relationships with their environments.

Purpose : The purpose of general systems theory, is to reduce multiplication of efforts by integrating all knowledge and treating all systems as interrelated.

Every discipline is like to sub-system of general system besides being a system in itself.

Not only that, since every system has its own structures and substructures which function with the help of infants : withinputs, throughputs, outputs and feedbacks, so two more approaches have emerged as derivates of the systems approach.

1. Structural functional approach lays emphasis on the structures and functions of every part and subpart of a system and its functional aspect.
2. Input output analysis lays emphasis on certain forces that come from the environment and play their part in the decision making process, while decision taken by men in authority roled one called outputs.

Origin : System analysis was introduced due to the realisation of Easton, Almond and Mortan A. Kaplan who have reacted against the traditional tendency of rigid compartmentalisation of social sciences. They have realised that unidimensional studies in social sciences have not only caused duplication, triplication and even multiplication of efforts but also impeded the patterns of a scientific analysis of creating conditions hostile to the tendency of unification of all knowledge. They have drawn inspiration from the contribution of Ludvig Von Bartaranfy who pioneered the movement of unification of all natural sciences.

Easton's Contribution

Easton's monumental work 'A system analysis of political life' published in 1965, set out to develop a theory that would help to explain behavioural reality in as much as political is but a symbolic system useful for understanding concrete or empirical political analysis.

Characteristics of Theory : The empirical political theory of Easton has following characteristics :

1. Easton is for a unified theory of knowledge—same categories and propositions could be applied to all kinds of political activities.
2. Easton is concerned with the issue of survival or persistence of political system.

3. Easton is critical of equilibrium analysis that stops at the point of analysing factor that creates stability or instability in political system.
4. Easton's purpose is to study political system in both theoretical and applied perspective.
5. Easton aims at keeping the study of politics at an autonomous level.
6. Easton seeks to study political systems in their abstract or theoretical as well as concrete or applied aspects.

Characteristics of Political System : Main characteristics of political system :

1. A political system is a set of intersections abstracted from the totality of social behaviour, through which values are allocated for a society.
2. There are certain properties common to both natural and social systems. Like natural systems, social systems possess properties that enable them to cope with the words—types of disturbances to which they may be subjected.

   Like a living system the political system has 'responding' and 'self regulating' mechanisms by which it can change, correct and readjust its processes and structures in the face of activity which threatens to disrupt its own activity.
3. Political system is not a static but a dynamic affair.

   It is on account of the feedback mechanism that the system persists even though everything associated with it may change continuously and radically.
4. Political system is an open system amenable to the influence of environmental factors. It can be distinguished from other systems by boundary lines.

   Outside and beyond the political system there are other systems or environments that may be distinguished from each other.
5. The environment of a political system may be intra societal as well as extra-societal.
6. A political system always remains subject to challenges from forces operating in the environment, which is required to cope with. Easton calls such forces as stresses that constitute the response mechanism of the political system.

   The stresses are of two kinds—demand stress and support stress.
7. Political system may be in a steady state if there is proper balance between inputs and outputs.

MODEL OF SYSTEMS APPROACH

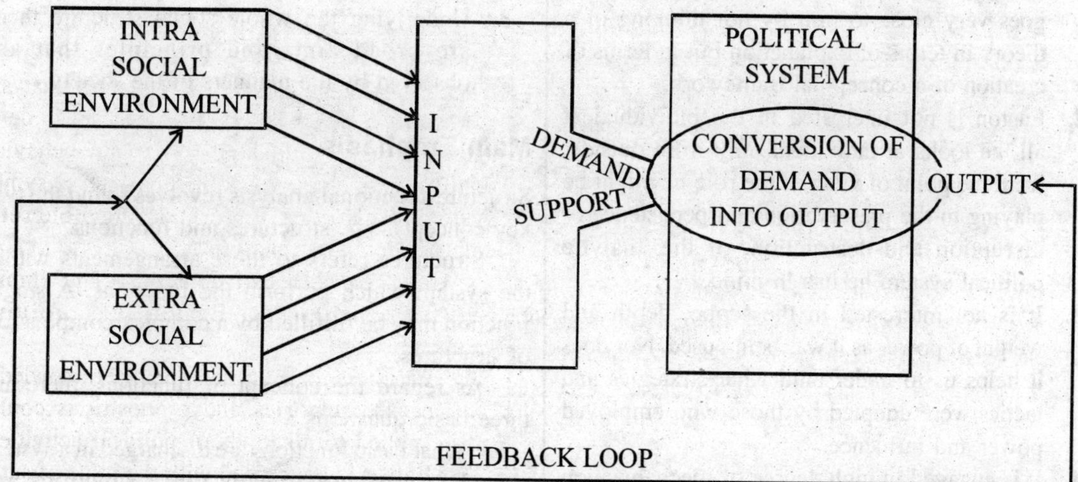

Source : J.C Johari

Inputs are demands made upon the political system and the support of the system itself;
Supports are those processes or structures which give it the capacity to cope with the demands made upon it.
Outputs are the results of the processing of demands.
There may be withinputs as the demands made by the political elites themselves.

8. A political system lives in a critical range—inputs have an overload.
9. The survival of a political system requires certain structural bases that may be in the form of institutional arrangements like electoral machinery and political parties and non institutional arrangements in the form of political beliefs and attitudes of the people.
10. The political system, apart from being a system in itself, consists of subsystem (mediating groups) involved in the decision making process, what Easton calls para political system.

Criticism

1. Easton's definition of terms like politics and political-system are so vague that one fails to apply the time of demarcation between an abstract and a concrete political system. Even though he criticises Talcott Parsons, Easton goes very close to him by not thinking of a theory in terms of explanation but in terms of creation of a conceptual framework.
2. Easton is not interested in the individual at all, he looks at individual only from outside, from the point of view of the role he might be playing in the preservation and persistence or disruption and destruction, of the analytic political system he has in mind.
3. It is not interested in the scope, depth and weight of power as it was being used. Nor does it helps us to understand what strategies and tactics were adopted by those who employed power and influence.
4. It is engaged in high degree of mechanization and abstractions.

STRUCTURAL FUNCTIONALISM

System analysis has two important derivatives : Structure functional and input-output analysis also called approaches.

Structural functionalism is a tool of investigation which perform the task of explaining what political structures perform what basic functions in the political system.

The concept of system analysis in the realm of political science lays stress on the relation of political to the society.

Scholars subscribing and structural functional approach lays emphasis on the point that, indeed, the society can survive or develop unless it has a political system performing such a function.

Chief Features : The chief points are as :

1. It takes the society as a single inter-connected system each element of which performs a specific function aiming at maintenance of equilibrium.
   Thus it seeks to understand a behaviour pattern as a socio-cultural institution in terms of the role it plays in keeping the given system in proper order and thus maintaining it as a going concern.
2. A social system has a dominant tendency towards stability that is maintained by virtue of built in mechanism.
   Thus change in social system is not sudden as revolutionary but gradual and adjustive.
3. Underlying the whole social structure there are broad aims and principles that are observed by the manners of the society.

Main Emphasis

Structure-functional analysis revolves round the two key concepts, viz. structures and functions.

Structures refers to those arrangements within the system which perform the functions. A single function may be fulfilled by a complex combination of structures.

As regard the concept of functions, there are three basic questions :

1. What basic functions are discharged in a system
2. By what instruments those functions are performed

3. Under what condition performance of these functions is done

As a model adopted from natural sciences functionalism accepts the organismic analogy—that a social or political unit will have certain adoptive qualities—in consult to a lybenatic is mechanistic analogy.

Characteristics

According to Almond, a political system has four characteristics that may be called 'legitimate patterns of interaction'.

1. Every political system has its structures some of which may be more specialised performing more functions, while others may be less specialised, performing less functions in it.
2. Whatever differences may be between the system and its structures, the same political functions are performed in all political systems.
3. Political structures and multifunctional.
4. All political system beings parts of the society as a whole have a culture of their own fact is always a mixture of the traditional and the modern.

This approach is inclined to emphasise the search for processes that maintain the stability of the system.

INPUT-OUTPUT ANALYSIS

In Border Forms : It is framework for organising, conceptualising, codifying and manipulating data.

If political system is a set of interactions having structures, each part of which performs its 'functions' in order to keep it like an ongoing concern, it is also a set of processes routinely converting inputs into outputs.

Chief Characteristics

1. Focus is on the system as a basic unit of analysis and on the intra-system and inter-system behaviour of various systems as principal areas of research.
2. Its refers to the analytic system (abstractions with focus on selected elements of human behaviour) existing and operating within an overall social system.
3. This approach treats all political systems as both open and adaptive. Its most salient focus is on the nature of exchanges and transactions that take place between politial systems and its environment.
4. There exist a very strong and underlying concern with questions relating to persistence of the system, the sources of stresses and modes of processes of regulating all tensions and threats that utter challenge to the stability.
5. It does not reject the issue of change, it cleverly interprets the process of accommodating change that is invariably slow, peaceful and gradual but that by no means threatens the very stability and maintenance of the political system.

The political system is seen as a conversion process performing work, producing outputs, and outering its environment with a continuous exchange between a political system and its environment based on the steady operation of the dynamic processes.

The approach focusses mainly on changes whose principal results are only to modify or streamline the system.

Key Concepts

1. Inputs : It refers to demand made by people who contribute their role in the political system—called environment.

Demand :

ex : demand for allocation of goods and services
demand for regulation of behaviour
demands for participation in political system
demand for communication and information.

Support :

ex : material support
obedience to laws and regulation
particularly support
attention paid to governmental communication

A proper balance should be maintained between the demands and support for smooth running of the political system.

2. Outputs : are authoritative decision and actions of the systems leaders that bear on the allocation of values for the system.

Outputs are the result of the conversion process acting upon a great variety of demands and supports.

They are primarily means of generating specific support for a political system as they, according to Easton 'may help to maintain a minimum level of support for the various political objects. Further, to Easton it is the aspect of output that tends to be neglected in theoretical enquiry and which lies at the heart of this part of enquiry.'

3. Feedbacks : It is this aspect that completes the cycle of political system and that makes it a dynamic and regenerative operation.

Main Features :

- — helps system receive information concerning the position of the goal and concerning its own distance from it.
- — helps system to response to this information, by further changes into its own position or behaviour.

It is essentially a regulative element.

4. Capabilities : It refers to the extent to which the system can cope with inputs in a successful manner.

It may be extractive, regulative, distributive.

CONSTITUTIONALISM IN THEORY AND PRACTICE

The study of political constitutionalism occupies a significant place in the sphere of comparative politics in view of the fact that it is the constitution that, as Dicey said, directly or indirectly affects the sovereign power of the state.

Constitutionalism is a modern concept that desires a political order governed by laws and regulations. It stands for the supremacy of law and not of the individuals; it imbibes the principles of nationalism, democracy and limited government. Constitutionalism in a formal sense, denotes the principle and practice under which a community is governed by a constitution.

Karl Freidrich says, constitutionalism is both a theory and a practice about politics according to rule of the game. Rules of the game is needed to restraint the government. It is a system of restraint of government. Constitutionalism is based on the belief in a limited government and in the use of constitution to impose these limitations.

Constitutionalism in the proper sense of the term is still in the process of evolution. According to Karl Loe Wenstein, the ancient great empires—Egypt, Babylonia, Persia had no constitutional process, instead evolved what he called transcendental constitutionalism where the ruler and the ruled were all subject to divine law pronounced by prophets.

However, the true origin of this concept is found in ancient Greeks thinkers who challenged mythological legitimisation of power. Subsequently Roman constitutionalism also came into being and after the decline of the Roman empire, medieval constitutionalism sought to invoke natural law, sometimes identified it with divine law. But all these were partly sedimentary forms of constitutionalism. It was only towards the end of middle ages that significant advance was made in the direction of modern constitutionalism.

THEORIES OF CONSTITUTIONALISM

Conservative Theory

— Greek, Roman and Medieval

Greek and Roman : Both were more practice than theory. Both had certain value preferences. This value preference was stability and strength as systems. Both had preference for restraints.

Roman constitutionalism is known to us through polibious. The Roman constitutional according to Polibious consisted of—Rules supported by laws which in turn were supported by Religion.

In the Medieval period, the role of Church is important. Church restricts the monarch from becoming a tyrant. According to Christiandom 'only those laws are good which have their base in religion.' Political thinkers followed the trend set by St. Augustine and St. Thomas in making secular authority subsequent to the authority of the Church. This baleful mate of affairs could not be remedied until after a period of about 800 years. The national monarchs raised their heads to overthrow the discredited hold of the papacy.

Liberal Theory

Hobbes rejected the idea of constitutionalism. He was in favour of unrestricted power in the hand of Leviathan. Thomas Harrington was in favour of government of laws. He was against government of men.

Locke favoured constitutionalism, limited government, people have right to give themselves a constitution. He talks about natural rights. It restricts the government. He was in favour of division of law making power. This was an attempt to put restriction.

Western writers like Thomas Saine, James Bryce, Harold J. Laski, Herman Rines, Charles H. McIiawain, C.F. Strong, Carl J. Friedrich etc. have taken a view that constitutionalism is both an end and a means; it is both value free and value ladden, it has normative and empirical dimension.

Whether the constitution is in the form of a document made at a particular time of history as the American constitution was made by the Philadelphia Convention in 1787, or it is in the form of numerous laws, institutions, and conventions. Western concept of constitutionalism lays stress on this point that the basic laws of the land should be such that the difference between the government of the people and the constitution of the state is discernible. The constitution is more important than the government.

The western concept of constitutionalism desires a constitutional state with a well acknowledged body of laws and conventions. It has a legislature, an executive, and judiciary, all required to work within the prescribed framework by following the defined procedure. If there is a change, it should be peaceful and orderly so that the political system is not subjected to violent stresses and strains. There is the rule of law ensuring liberty and equality to all; there is the freedom of the press to act as the Fourth estate, there is a plural society having freedom for all interests to seek the corridors of power, there is a system that strives to promote international peace, security and justice.

Marxist Theory

The Marxists begin their theory by criticising liberal theory. According to them liberal constitutional theory is status quoist. Socialist constitutionalism aims at socialist transformation. The constitutionalism is not an end in itself, it is just a means to implement the ideology of scientific socialism. It is a tool in the hands of the dictatorship of the proletariat that seeks to establish classless society that would eventually turn into a stateless condition of life. The purpose of having the constitution is not to limit the powers of the government but to make them so vast and comprehensive that the ideal of workers state is realised and a new type of state comes into being. The real aim of the constitution in such a country is not to ensure liberty and equality, rights and justice for all but to see that the enemies of socialism are destroyed and the new system is firmly consolidated.

The Marxist concept of constitutionalism is based on the principles of a particular ideology of Marxism-Leninism according to which the state is viewed as a class institution whose raison d'etre is to act as an instrument of exploitation and oppression by one class over another. What the constitution of the state but the policy of communist party is supreme. State and thus constitutionalism is seen to have class character. It incorporates rights.

PRACTICE OF CONSTITUTIONALISM

Constitutionalism in Developing Countries

It is very difficult to suggest the precise feature of the concept of constitutionalism in poor and backward countries of the Afro-Asian world that have recently emerged as sovereign nation-states and are struggling hard for achieving the ideal of a social welfare state. It appears that they are between the poles imitating the system of some European country under which they remained for a sufficiently long period of colonial domination on the one hand and going for a better and more workable system having much of the indigenous elements coupled with something of the socialist systems of the world on the other. It is also found that several developing countries are experimenting with the imported constitutional arrangements and trying to establish a synthesis between the ideals of the liberal democratic constitutional state on the one side and the demands and aspirations of the people on the other. It is for this reason that countries like Pakistan and Bangladesh (also be found involved in alternating from parliamentary to Presidential systems and vice versa.)

Constitutionalism in Post-colonial countries, as **Carl Freidrich** says "became a factor of considerable importance" because constitutionalism in post-colonial countries was symbolic, it was a symbol of their newly acquired independence. Only few of them followed Marxist paradigm, most of them went for liberal values of US and UK because of the fact that :

1. The political orientations of the political elites of post colonial countries towards liberal values, most of whom were educated in liberal western tradition. They thought that constitutionalism can be a means for political modernisation.
2. Most of the newly independent countries were familiar with liberal political institutions.
3. They inherited an administrative structure from their western colonial rulers so it was pragmatic to make use of it.
4. Political elites had a liking for civic and political rights.
5. Geographical vastness/cultural plurality—Federalism (liberal definition of federalism).
6. Liberal constitutionalism was only an alternative to anarchy or Authoritarianism in the opinion of political elites.
7. Liberal constitutionalism provides an opportunity to downtrodden to join the ranks of elites.

Most of the post-colonial countries imported the institutions and ideas, which in most of the cases was away from the political reality (Theory and practice). So, in most of the post-colonial countries constitutionalism do not express the practical reality.

Lowenstein : Constitutions of most of the colonial countries are nominal constitutions because they do not express the political reality.

A nominal constitution is a blue print :

— formally accepted
— legally valid, but
— not fully effective.

He says that there are certain normative constitutions also—formally accepted, legally valid and fully effective.

No constitution can be 100% normative. A normative constitution is only relatively normative.

REASONS FOR GAP IN THEORY AND PRACTICE

Constitutional theory in developing countries is intricately bound to colonial legacy. The body of knowledge about constitutions have been derived from the west. Therefore

1. Constitutional Theory is a derivative theory derived from the colonial institutions as well as colonial knowledge about politics of west
2. There has been institutional carryover from colonial era—policy, bureaucracy etc.
3. There have been attempt at indigenous roots of democracy, after a great deal of self-reflections especially in the 1970's.
4. Some countries have tried to justify alternative to liberal constitutions notably through
   — Military rule
   — Emergency (India)
   — Cultural Revolution (China)
   — There has been upsurge of social movements in third world—Human right, women, Environment protection, ethnic right etc. All these groups pointed out the

inadequacies of the constitution. There were demands for constitutional change.

5. Pressure from external factors—Globalisation, terrorism and conflicts were the cause for this gap.

VIEW OF EMINENT THEORISTS

C.B. Macpherson : in this work "The Real World of Democracy" (1978), says the politics of Third World is a variety of democracy different from the liberal and communist notions of democracy. In the post colonial countries which adopted liberal constitutions, comparative Market Society is absent. In a comparative market society there is a competition of political ideas and in such society only the liberal ideas and liberal state flourish. Whatever competition was there, it was imposed from above. In such countries individual freedom is less important but equality within the community is more important. In such countries where community was more important than the individual, there is not much chance of survival of liberal ideas and constitution.

Carl Freidrich : says that liberal constitution has generally failed in most of the post-colonial countries. The restraint exercised by the people is not so effective (lack of willingness of thought on the part of the people).

Mehran Kamrava : Constitutionalism has become unworkable—Indigenous political and social conditions were not taken into account. For example, in Africa attention was not paid to a communalism, tribal loyalties. It led to the breakdown of important feudal institutions and ideas. It failed to contain or control centrifugal tendencies.

Sources of Strain in Constitutionalism

1. Threats to political stability and integrity.

In most post colonial countries there is plurality of one or the other kind in the aspect of life. Plurality of race, religion, language, culture. Moreover, the socio economic condition behind the working of plurality is under-development.

Most of the post colonial countries opted for democratic politics but it has degenerated into electoral politics. Identities are politicised and the result is conflict. There threats can be real or a threat but it is mishandling of the plurality that is the cause of stability and integrity.

Response : either constitutionalism is ended or suspended or distorted.

2. Mass Poverty : It never goes above but goes along other evils—poor health, illiteracy, relative lack of communication and mobility. It is socio-economic condition that keeps the poor busy in struggle for survival. Poor are not aware of their roles and constitutionalism is threatened.
3. Sharpening of class contradictions : The demand for better wages by have nots and the political elites interpret it as a threat to law and order or harmful to national production.
4. Dependence on Foreign Aid : Neo-colonialism or Globalisation : in such a situation, foreign-interests are accommodated and foundations of the constitutional government are eroded.
5. Personalismo (Personality Cult) : person is more important than the institutions.
6. Corruption at higher places
7. Military intervention
8. Extra-Constitutional Machinery : Pressure group politics (approaching decision makers personality, privately), lobbying.
9. Communication Network : If there is private ownership of means of communication, information reaching masses at times being tailored to suit the political elites and serves somebody else's interest.
10. The Market processes
11. Intelligence operation
12. Management of threat of Military attacks

Conclusion

In the end it must be noted that everchanging completely of contemporary political life often draw attention towards states withdrawl from constitutional. However it must be realised that eradicating conditions of starvation, famine, disease, poverty etc. require discretionary action from the state. Moreover, in third world countries the principle of constitutionalism must incorporate the principle of nationalism. It must reflect the democratic values and imbibe socialistic aspirations whereby it may balance values and divergent interests and classes and society. It must recognize the efficacy of new international order, ideals of international law and justice and renounce policies and programmes of war or irrational protectionism.

EXECUTIVE, LEGISLATURE AND JUDICIARY WITH SPECIAL REFERENCE TO UK, USA AND SWITZERLAND

UNITED KINGDOM

WORKS ON BRITISH POLITICAL SYSTEM

1. Walter Bagehot : The English Constitution
2. A.V. Dicey : Law of the Constitution
3. H. Finer : Government of Greater European Powers
4. W.I. Jennings : Cabinet Government
5. W.I. Jennings : The Law and the Constitution
6. H.J. Laski : Parliamentary Government in England
7. H.J. Laski : Reflections on the Constitution
8. A.L. Lowell : Government of England
9. Herbert Morrison : British Parliamentary Democracy
10. Ramsay Muir : How Britain is Governed
11. K.C. Wheare : Modern Constitutions
12. Ernest Barker : Essays on Government
13. James Bryce : Modern Democracies

NATURE OF THE CONSTITUTION

- unwritten Constitution
- product of history
- involved with time
- Ivor Jennings in his 'The Law of the Constitution says "the British Constitution has not been made but has grown and there is no paper"
- Streachey has labelled British Constitution as 'Child of Wisdom and Chance"
- based on custom, conventions, statutes, charters etc.
- Thomas Paine and De Tocquiville does not consider British having a Constitution

SOURCES OF THE CONSTITUTION

- Charters, Statutes etc. It includes Magna Carta (1215), the Petition of Rights (1628), Bill of Rights
- Decisions of the judges. The Parliamentary sovereignty was established in Brand laugh Gossett (1884)
- Common Law
- Usage or Conventions
- Commentaries by Writers A.V. Dicey's Law of the Constitution is important one

FEATURES OF THE CONSTITUTION

1. Mostly an unwritten Constitution.
2. Parliamentary Supremacy.
3. A flexible Constitution Parliament is empowered to make or unmake a law and it does not require special procedure for this purpose.
4. A Unitary Constitution.
5. Two Party System.
6. Hereditary Character.
7. Rule of Law and Civil Liberties.

THE KING AND THE CROWN

The history of British political system is one of gradual transfer of power from hereditary monarch to the democratically elected Parliament. Till the Glorious Revolution (1688), the king ruled as well as reigned. But now the King reigns but does not rule.

King is a person while Crown is an institution, to whom the power of the King have been continuously transferred. The Crown is an abstract concept which has assumed the powers and rights of the King. It is a association of King, Ministers and Parliament. The distinction between King and the Crown evolved with King John.

Powers of the Crown

The powers of the Crown are nominally powers of the king but exercised by the Ministers who are responsible to the Parliament.

Executive Power

- Crown is the executive head
- Directs the administration of Britain
- Appoints higher officials
- Supervises the works of local government (boroughs and Counties)
- Has Supreme command over armed establishments.

Legislative Power

- Crown is an integral part of the Parliament
- Summons, prorogues, dissolves the Parliament
- Each opening session is greeted by speech from the throne

Judicial Power

- Judges are appointed by Crown
- A member of Cabinet (Lord Chancellor) exercises supervision over them.
- Grants pardon to persons convicted on Criminal charges

PRIVY COUNCIL

- A descendent of the King's council, the Curia Regis
- In earlier days kings consist of advisors.
- With passage of time, it has given way for Cabinet
- Cabinet is an inner committee of the Privy Council
- It consists of Cabinet Ministers of the past as well as present, Prince of Wales and the Royal Punkes, the Archbishop and Bishop of London and a number of distinguished persons.
- Its member enjoy life long tenure.
- It provides form for interaction to various committees.

MINISTRY

It consists of following elements :

Cabinet

- A closer and small body within the ministry which carries out the affairs of the country.
- It meets as a collective body.
- Usually every member is head of one or more departments.
- They head the government.
- A Committee of the ministry.

Ministers of Cabinet Rank

- came into existence in Attlee's government
- not members of the Cabinet
- head administrative department
- accorded the status of Cabinet minister
- attend the meeting of the Cabinet not in their own right, but only when invited by the Prime Minister.

Minister of State

- usually does not head department
- they are deputy ministers.

Parliamentary Secretaries

- members of the Parliament
- do not have any power
- help their senior ministers in parliamentary proceedings and departmental activities.

Strength : Upto ninety one ministers can be from House of Commons. Any increase in their member would require inclusion of peers.

THE CABINET

- Bagehot label it as a "hyphen that joins, the buckle that binds the executive and legislature departments together."
- Barker says "co-ordinates and controls the whole of the executive government, and integrates and guides the work of the Legislature.
- A.L. Lowell "Keystone of the Political arch."
- Marriot "the pivot round which the whole political machinery revolves."
- Ivor Jennings "provides unity to the British system of government."
- Ramsay Muir "the steering wheel of the ship of the state."

Development : The beginning of the Cabinet system is traced from the Wing Junto of 1696. In 1714 King did not participate in Cabinet meetings. George I did not attend Cabinet meetings because he did not understand English. As a consequence, the members started seeking unanimity in their decisions which was conveyed to the King. Later on there developed the principle of ministerial responsibility. Strafford was the first minister to answer to parliament. However, the Cabinet system in its present form came into existence in the reign of Queen Victoria.

Features

- not enjoy a legal status
- consists of most active people within the party
- a small body
- marked by unity of purpose and speedy delivery
- works under leadership of the Prime Minister
- support of Party ensures majority in the Parliament
- works on the principle of collective responsibility
- it functions secretly and its secrecy is safeguarded by law and convention

Working

- Usually meets at the official Residence of the Prime Minister.
- During sessions of the Parliament, it meets twice and once a week otherwise.
- Cabinet Secretariat prepares the agenda of the Cabinet meeting.
- Issues are decided unanimously.
- There is no voting.
- Work through Committees.
- Committees of the Cabinet can include non-cabinet members also.

Functions

- Determines policies.
- Deliberates in the Parliament.
- Controls the legislation.
- Directs the functioning of different departments.
- Acts as co-ordinator between the various departments.
- Ensures implementation of policies.
- Spends government money and raises revenue for its programmes.
- Appoints officials at home and abroad.

Cabinet Dictatorship

The terminology of Cabinet Dictatorship has gained ascendance on account of ability of Cabinet to get all its measures passed by the legislature. The disciplined two party system has enormously empowered the Cabinet. The influence of party ship is no where as enormous as in Britain. Moreover the growth of delegated legislation is seen as threat to Rule of Law and liberty of citizens.

However, these fear need not threaten as long as franchise remain the weapon in the hands of people. The governments that hope to assume authoritarian terms, can do so only at the cost of losing power. Moreover, the changing socio-economic conditions and problems have led to increase in power of the executive all over the world. There should not be any scepticism with it, so long as it threatens the fundamental law of the land or people's expectations from the government.

THE PRIME MINISTER

- Most powerful person.
- Greaves says "is the master of the country and master of the government.

- Morley "keystone of the Cabinet arch."
- For the first time office of the PM is recognized by Ministers of the Crown Act, 1937.
- Must be a member of either house of the Parliament.
- Powers are derived from conventions.

Powers

- Head of the government.
- Selects ministers.
- Presides over Cabinet meetings
- Ask for resignation of ministers.
- Advice dismissal of a minister.
- Leader of majority party.
- Co-ordinates the work of several departments.
- Initiates and intervenes in all debates of general importance.
- Can ask for dissolution of the Lower House.
- Acts as channel of communication between the Ministry and the Crown.
- Acts as the Chief advisor of the King.

Position

Lord Morely described him as the first among equals. But Ramsay Muir in his "How Britain is Governed" holds than he wields too much power, even more than the President of United States.

Ogg and Zink in their "Modern Foreign Governments" compares him to "inter stellas luna minores" or a moon among lesser stars. But, Ivor Jennings in his "Cabinet Government" considers him a sun around which planets revolve. However, it is because of disciplined two party system and his own personality and prestige that any Prime Minister can hope to retain the stature that have been outlined above. That explains why people like Mrs. Thatcher and Mr. Attlee were different. Prime Ministers B.E. Carter in his "The office of the Prime Minister" is of the opinion that the power of the Prime Minister and his senior colleagues is substantially greater than that of the American President. But he is not the wholesole man and accountable to the electorate, party, his team and others.

PARLIAMENT

A deliberative and legislative body where people talk about the affairs of the nation. In British political system, its origin is traced to need of money by the king. The first Parliament is supposed to be summoned by Simon de Montford in (1265). But Glorious Revolution (1688) led to supremacy of Parliament. Then followed the period of gradual democratization of the parliament which still continues.

Supremacy of the Parliament

According to A.V. Dicey "under the British constitution the Parliament enjoys the right to make and unmake any law whatever and no person or body is recognised by the law as having a right to override and set aside the legislation of Parliament." There does not exist any distinction between constitutional and other laws in England.

The Parliament consists of the King and the two Houses, viz; House of Lords and House of Commons.

House of Lords

- Also called upper chamber.
- G.H. Adams in his "Constitutional History of Britain" points out that bicameralism became evident by the end of Edward-III reign.
- Organised on the principle of heredity.
- Lord Chancellor is the Presiding Officer.
- Lord Chancellor is the minister of the Cabinet.

Powers

1. Influence Governmental policies.
2. Delay legislation except financial ones (for one year).
3. Participates in impeachment cases.
4. Act as Supreme Court of Appeal in Civil cases.

Proposal for Reform

- Introduction of limited system of election of members.
- Doing away with exclusive insistence on heredity.

- Including women.
- Provision for disqualification of members not participating regularly or being absent without a genuine cause.

House of Commons

- Lower Chamber
- An elective body
- Total seats—650
  - 543 England
  - 32 Wales
  - 57 Scotland
  - 18 Northern Ireland
- Normal tenure is for 5 years
- Must meet once a year.
- Speaker is most important official.

SPEAKER

- Elected official
- Presides over the meetings
- Sir Peter de la Mare was first speaker
- Unanimously elected
- Belongs to party in power
- Expected to be impartial
- Once elected, continues in office for the whole life of Parliament
- Continues in office even after new Parliament, if he so desires
- Re-elected unopposed
- Acts as link between the House and the King.
- Keeps the house and members in order and select the speaker in debate
- Does not vote except in case of a tie.

Decline of Parliament

There has been a criticism of Parliaments inability to check the growing encroachment by executive and other agencies. Such apprehensions have arisen due to following factors.

- Delegated legislation
- Well established party system
- Complexity of administration and technical nature of modern legislation
- Emergence of Social Service State

However, it must be noted that Parliamentary system is more democratic as it makes the government accountable to elected representatives of the people.

UNITED STATES OF AMERICA

IMPORTANT WORKS

M.E. Dimock	:	American Government in Action
J.W. Garner	:	Government of the United States
W.B. Munro	:	Government of the United States
Burn & Peltason	:	Government by the people
Ernest Griffih	:	The American system of Government
H.J. Laski	:	The American Presidency The American Democracy

CONSTITUTION

- Drafted at Philadelphia Convention
- A written document
- Oldest written Constitution
- To Gladstone it is "the most wonderful work ever struck off at a given time by the brain and purpose of man."
- A federal constitution
- Based on separation of power and check and balances
- Presidential form of executive
- Rigid Constitution which warrants participation of both sets of government.
- Judicial Review

THE PRESIDENT

- Is the real executive
- Wields enormous power and influence
- Must be a natural born citizen, 35 years of age, a resident of U.S.A. for 14 years
- Tenure of 4 years
- Eligible for re-election
- Cannot be elected more than twice
- President Roosevelt was elected four times
- Elected by indirect election
- Removed from office by impeachment on grounds of treason, bribery or other high crimes

- In case of Impeachment, the charges are initiated by the House of Representatives and Senate acts as Court of trial
- Chief Justice of the Supreme Court presides over trial
- Article II deals with the office of the President

POWERS : Most of the provisions regarding powers of the President are general in terms. As a consequence, it all depends on his personality as to how he deems it fit to carry the administration of the country.

Executive Powers

1. Ensures the observance, enforcement of laws, treaties and decisions of court and acts as chief Administrator.
2. Nominates and appoints the ambassadors, ministers, consuls, judges of the Supreme Court and other officers.
3. He is the Commander-in-Chief of army and navy and the State Militia.
4. He can grant reprieves and pardons for offences against the United States except in case of impeachment.
5. He is the Chief foreign policy maker and accredited official spokesman of U.S.A. in international relations.

Legislative Power

1. Informs the Congress and recommends measures for consideration.
2. He may convene either of both the Houses of Congress in extraordinary circumstances.
3. Submits the Budget to the Congress.
4. Empowered to issue ordinances.
5. Enjoys the Veto power over legislation passed by the Congress.

CONGRESS : Article I of the American Constitution vests all legislative powers in the hands of the Congress.

It consists of two Houses, viz; House of Representatives and the Senate.

House of Representatives

- Also called Lower House
- Organized on the basis of population
- Normal tenure is of 2 years
- A member must not be less than 25 years old, must be citizen of USA, stayed in U.S.A for 7 years and a native of state from which he is elected
- Exemption from legal cases
- A special session can be called by the President
- Speaker is the presiding officer of the House

Speaker

- Elected from majority party
- Acts as leader of the party to which he belongs
- Can not punish a member
- Decides the speaker in debates
- His rulings are not final
- Enjoys the same right to participate in debate and vote, as other members
- Usually he does not vote except when the House is voting by ballot or when there is a tie

The Senate

- Upper House
- Most powerful upper chamber in the World
- Small body with only one hundred members
- Two members are elected from each state
- Each member is elected for a term of six years, one third retiring every two years
- A permanent body
- A member must not be less than 35 years of age, an inhabitant of State from where he is elected and a citizen of USA for 9 years
- They are elected by the people of the state.
- In case of vacancy, a temporary appointment may be made by the Governor of the State
- Vice President of the USA is the Presiding officer
- Vice President votes only in case of a tie

FILIBUSTERING : A senatorial device by which measures are delayed by members by participating in debate for longer period.

Functions

1. Senate confirms the appointments made by the President. It does so by simple majority.
2. All treaties entered into by the American President require ratification from the Senate and a two-thirds vote is necessary.
3. Senate acts as the court of trial for impeachment. Two-thirds vote of the senate is required for conviction.
4. Senate enjoys co-equal power with House of Representative in the matter of legislation.
5. Senate has wide ranging investigative functions.

The disagreement between two Houses are resolved through a Conference Committee.

AMERICAN SUPREME COURT

- Apex Court
- Mentioned in Article III of the Constitution
- Consists of one Chief Justice and eight other judges
- Judges are appointed by the President with Senatorial Consent
- No prescribed qualification for the judges
- Judges continue to hold office for life or during good behaviour
- Meets in Washington
- Special session can be called by the Chief Justice.

Jurisdiction

(I) Original Jurisdiction

- Very limited
- Covers cases involving foreign ambassador, minister or consul
- also covers cases involving one or more states

(II) Appellate Jurisdiction

- Much wider
- Regulated by Congress
- it covers
  (*a*) Cases coming from the highest State Courts where a federal question is presented, namely, when the State Court has held that a federal law violates the Constitution.
  (*b*) Cases from the Lower Federal Courts, mainly from the Courts of Appeal.

SWITZERLAND

IMPORTANT WORKS

E. Bonjour	:	Real Democracy in operation
C. Hughes	:	The Federal Constitution of Switzerland
Erich Grunner	:	The Political System of Switzerland
H. Finer	:	The Theory and Practice of Modern Government

SWISS CONSTITUTION

1. A federal one; Although the term Confederation is used in Constitution.
2. A detailed and lengthy document.
3. Republican spirit.
4. Rigid but not as complicated as U.S.A. Constitution.
5. A living/dynamic Constitution.

FEDERAL EXECUTIVE

- Article 95 provides for a Collegiate Executive
- Executive authority is exercised by a Commission of seven men.
- Committee is known as Bundesrat or Federal Council.
- Members are chosen for 4 years by Federal Assembly.
- Article 96(2) provides that the term Federal Council coincides with that the National Council.
- Any Swiss citizen, eligible to be elected to the National Council can be chosen for Federal Council.
- Not more than one person can be chosen from each canton.
- Members are not representatives of party.
- Modesty remains a high political value in Switzerland.

- Federal Council is subordinate to the Federal Assembly.
- Most of the old members are usually reelected.
- Dicey compares the Swiss Federal Council to a Board of Directors of a Joint Stock Company.
- Work is divided into seven departments but decisions are taken by the Council as a body.
- Deliberations of Council are secret.
- Council has corporate character.

PRESIDENT

The Federal Assembly chooses one member from amongst the councillors to the rank of President for a period of one year.

- Based on the principle of rotation
- His position is not exalted or superior to his colleagues
- Acts as Chairman of the Council
- Casts his vote in case of a tie

Functions of the Federal Council

1. To conduct the affairs of the state with the provisions of the Constitution.
2. To supervise the 'guarantee' of constitutions of the Cantons.
3. To initiate the legislation process.
4. To reply to Federal Assembly on matters of given debate under right of interpellation.
5. To issue direction for execution of law.
6. To supervise the military affairs of the confederation.
7. To prepare budget.
8. To submit to the Assembly, a report of its working.
9. To maintain peace and order.
10. To conduct foreign relations and ensure neutrality and independence.
11. To appoint federal officials.
12. To supervise the branches of administration in Cantons.

Position of Federal Council

The executive in Switzerland, is not an independent or co-ordinate branch of government. It is neither Parliamentary nor Presidential type. Rather there exists an executive which is a collegial body of seven members. According to Bryce it ''stands outside party, is not chosen to do party work, does not determine party policy, yet is not wholly without some party colour.'' It reflects the presence of all the major political parties.

Advantages

- Promotes mutual confidence and cooperation
- It represents a government of all by all and for all
- Provides political stability
- Promotes public spirit

In recent times, there has been a continuous growth in the power of Council vis-a-vis the Assembly. The world wide trend toward centralization has influenced the Swiss executive as well. It has what Andre Seigfied calls ''gradually came to wield a quasi-absolute power.''

THE FEDERAL ASSEMBLY

There exists a bicameral legislature in Switzerland. The two chambers include Council of States and the National Council.

Supremacy : Article 71 provides ''subject to the rights of the people and of the Cantons. The Supreme power of the Confederation shall be exercised by the Federal Assembly.''

However, the voters of Switzerland are empowered with the weapon of referendum to Veto Bill.

The Council of States

- Represents the units of Confederation
- Two members are drawn from Cantons and one from half canton
- Total Members are 46
- Modalities of election, tenure, allowances of members are decided by the Cantons itself
- Cantons follow the methods of both; direct and indirect elections
- Article 81 debars the members of Federal Council to become member of National Council

- A special session may be called by Federal Council or members ¼ of National Council or of five Cantons
- The Chairman and Vice Chairman are elected out on the basis of circulation
- It is a weaker chamber as compared to the National Council

The National Council

- Fixed membership-200
- Elected by proportional representation
- Clergies are excluded from membership of the National Council
- Seats are allotted on the basis of population
- Tenure is of 4 years
- Cannot be dissolved
- Every elector can be elected
- Following people are excluded from being elected
  (a) Executive and Administrative Servants
  (b) Members of Council of States
  (c) Federal Councillors
- Chairman & Vice Chairman are elected for one session at a time.
- There is followed the procedure of rotation of office.
- Chairman does not enjoy wide powers.
- To elect the Federal Councillors, the Federal Court, the General of Federal Army and the Chancellor votes.
- All sessions in a year count as a single session.
- A special session can be called on by Federal Council or on request of ¼ of its own members or members of five cantons.
- According to Andre Siegfried, "the sessions of the National Council are more like meetings of an administrative body affecting only indirectly those who are not immediately concerned-but what an efficient administration."
- Three official languages are French, German and Italian.
- Absolute majority Constitutes the quorum.
- There does not exist any official opposition.

Provision of Joint Sitting : There are 3 cases for holding joint sitting

Firstly, To select Federal Councillors.

Secondly, To grant pardon for individual offences.

Thirdly, To resolve jurisdictional conflicts.

FEDERAL COURT

- Created in 1874 and first met in 1875
- Members are elected by the Federal Assembly
- Members are so elected that the three official languages are represented
- Members of Federal Council and Federal Assembly can not become its members
- A member of Federal Court can not hold any other office
- No prescribed qualification
- Number of judges is 26 and there are 11 to 13 substitutes
- Judges are elected for 6 years period
- Judges are re-elected

Jurisdiction

- Relates to cases of Civil and Criminal nature and questions of public law
- No power of judicial Review
- Has wide ranging civil jurisdiction
- Enjoy Criminal Jurisdiction as well
- Enjoy Constitutional jurisdiction in case of conflict between federal and Cantonal authorities. It can also adjudicate dispute between contons as regards rights of citizens or violation of treaties or agreements.

Swiss Court is a single Court. It does not have subordinate Courts (like the U.S.A.). It depends on the Federal Council for the enforcement of its decisions. It has no power of Judicial Review and in case of disagreement or conflicts it is bound to apply the law passed by the Federal Assembly.

PARTY SYSTEM

The political parties have become an indispensable part of modern representative forms of government. In the democratic forms of government they not only provide the link between government and the citizen but also help in change and transformation. They ensure peaceful transfer of power. That is why

Munro equates Democratic system with the party system. Almost a similar opinion has been expressed by Smith who hailed Political Party as the vanguard of democracy.

A political party is a voluntary organization joined by persons more or less sharing common aims and objectives who seek to gain control of the governmental apparatus with a view of furthering their interests.

They have become a universal aspect of contemporary political life.

Party politics is a new phenomena. The founding fathers of U.S.A. described the influence of parties and even Bluntschli's comprehensive theory of state paid no reference to party government.

Definitions : They are product of nineteenth century.

Sigmund Neuman : Political parties are the life line of modern politics.

Barker : Compares them to the conduit that carries the process of social thought of society into the area of government.

Said : Under a regime of universal suffrage, they are inevitable like the tides of the Ocean.

Schumpeter : Whenever universal suffrage was delayed the political party on its most advanced democratic forms was late in the appearing.

In England

Tories and Whigs were not party but political groups in the House of Commons.

Modern political parties first appeared on the U.S. precisely because of prevalence of adult franchise.

Burke : Political party is a body of men united for promoting up their joint endeavours in the national interest upon some particular principles in which they all agree not wholly true.

Weber : Political party is a voluntary society of propaganda and agitation seeking to acquire power to realise objective, aims or personal advantages or both.

Schumpeter : The first and foremost aim of each political party is to prevail over the others in order to get into power or to stay in it.

Duverger : Groups organised for the purposes of achieving and exercising power within a political system.

It is a community with a particular structure. They are distinguished by the nature of organization.

Field : A political party is rather like a comet, which has a solid nucleur at the head and a long gaseous tail which follows it.

Robert Michels : The cause or the growth of oligarchy in the democratic parties is to be found in the technical indispensability of leadership in his book 'Political Parties' contradicted by Lipson.

Lenin : A small compact care, consisting of reliable, experienced and hardened workers, with responsible agents in the principal districts and connected by all the rules of strict secrecy with the organization of revolutions, with the wide support of the masses and without an elaborate set of rules.

NATURE OF POLITICAL PARTIES

Political parties are groups with some degree of organization and permanency.

They are specialised associations.

They have definite aims and objectives.

Their central concern is to capture power.

A tool to ensure responsibility.

It is present even in the non-democratic regimes.

Origin of Political Parties

Political parties had their beginning with the system of Parliamentary politics and electoral system.

Political Parties and Pressure Group : A Comparison

Political Party	Pressure Group
Formal	Informal
Interest Aggregation	Interest Articulation
Direct involvement	Indirect participation
more durable	guided by expediency
To Neumann	
Heterogeneous group has integrative function of diverse forces	Homogeneous group concerned with a specific purpose

Proponderance of leadership is an inseparable part of party system.

The framers of American Constitution : Washington and Hamilton regarded that all parties are evils.

Major Determinants of Political Parties

The determinants of party system can be classified as

1. **Historical :** Parties are the product of modern political process of their emergence presupposes a certain degree of urbanisation and development of mass communication.
2. **Level of Economic Development :** In a liberal democratic state parties with a totalitarian structure may hardly find a congenial place to live in and operate.
3. **Ideology :** However it is not necessary that every political party is committed to common ideology.

The political parties of the U.S. have nothing like ideological commitments for which reasons they have been described by James Bryce as two bottles of wine, liquor being the same but different labels.

Jean Paul Sartre, one of the last surviving ideologises, is reported to have advised young men in France to go to Africa to pursue their ideology as Western Europe as well as its political parties had no ideology to offer.

Role of Political Parties

1. The parties unite, simplify and stabilize the political process. Provide coherence.
2. Form order out of chaos.
   Though the interest articulation function is performed by the pressure groups, the work of interest aggregation is done by the parties.
3. Provide a link between the government and its people. They seek to educate, instruct and activate the electorate. That is, they perform the job of political mobilisation, secularisation and recruitment.
4. They present issues, they set value goals for the society.
   Though American political parties have, what Dahl says 'ideological similarity and issue conflict,' they have no disagreement on the fundamental goals of the society. To Bryce, they are two bottles of wine with different labels.
   The two parties of Ireland (Finna Fail and Fine Gael) are prototype of two parties of U.S.
5. They do the task of political modernisation.
6. They also perform social welfare functions.

CLASSIFICATION OF POLITICAL PARTIES

Classification : Duverger

A french political scientist suggested a novel but traditional classification of political parties in his work political parties.

1. One of the basis of leaders-single members-usually members of traditionally respected and powerful families.
2. Divided as interior and exterior on the basis of their Parliamentary role.
3. On the basis of structure :
   (*a*) Caucus
   (*b*) Branch
   (*c*) Cell
   (*d*) Militia

Caucus Type

Also called Committee type.
Avoids mass membership.
Emphasis on quality rather than quantity.
Virtually remain inactive between elections.
With the extension of franchise and expanding mass base, caucus suffers natural decline.
American parties fit this description

Branch Type

Mass party with open membership and hierarchical structure dominated by a Central leadership delegates are elected by branches to Central body.

Central body represents the highest policy-making body.

German Social Democratic Party.
British Labour Party.

Cell Type

A communist invention
Smaller and more cohesive than branch type.
Organised on the basis of place of work.
Secretive and Highly disciplined.
Their area of interest is more than winning election.
They have wider political interest in changing society.

Militia Type

Modelled on the army command and control pattern.
Organisation is hierarchical.
Expects complete allegiance of members to Leader.
Kufler's Storm troopers.
Muslim's fascist milita.

But none of these pure types can be found in reality. Party's actual functions will always be having mixed structures.

In fact his model focuses on four types of parties.

Caucus	:	American
Branch	:	West European
Cell	:	Communist
Militia	:	Fascist-Nazi

Characteristics of Single Party Model

1. **Monopolistic :** If political power is wielded by one party alone and no other party is permitted to exist at all.
   (a) **Totalitarian :** Wercieve, only official ideology.
   (b) **Authoritarian :** Some autonomy, ideology is weak.
   (c) **Pragmatic :** Hold of ideology is irrelevant.
2. **Hegemonic position :** Although existence of other parties is allowed, only one party counts more than all.
   Other parties are like Satellites. Other parties are not permitted to compete with the hegemonic party in antagonistic terms and on an equal basis.
   Ideological : Communist party of Poland
   Pragmatic : PRI (Institutional Rev. Party of Mexico)
3. **Predominant Party :** One party governs alone as long as it continue to win absolute majority in the elections India, Japan, Turkey.

The two and multi party systems of society embody the common characteristic of polarised pluralism.

Characteristics of Polarised Pluralism

1. Different parties exist and operate, including anti-system; not revolutionary character.
2. Oppositions.
3. A Centre party.
4. The degree of ideological distance may be discovered between different parties.
5. Centrifugal drives prevail over centripetal ones.
6. Existence of different parties differing not only in policies but more importantly on principal fundamentals.
7. Existence of irresponsible opposition.
8. The ruling party or other ones may cause inflationary disequillibrium by making tall promises to the voters.

A Biparty system is one where the existence of third party does not prevent the two major parties from governing alone, and therefore coalitions are unnecessary.

Sartori has included the case of countries having stable coalition systems in this category (Germany, Belgium, Switzerland, Denmark).

Sartori has excluded the case of United States from this model on the plea that this applies to a country having Cabinet Government, not a presidential Government.

Multi or atomised party system leads to the existence of highly fluid party politics.

A coalition party is fragmented by leaders with very small groups revolving around each leader.

But in practice, it creates a problems lack of cohesion in coalitional form of government, reading to precaurios instability.

But experiences in countries like Switzerland, Sweden, Denmark and Germany with long tradition of multiparty system have shown stable and successful governments.

Almond : Almond classified on the basis of

1. **Organisation :** Authoritative dominant, non-authoritative, competitive two-party or competitive multi party.
2. **Style :** Secular pragmatic bargaining, idelogical or absolute value oriented particularistic or traditional.

Conclusion

Where as Bryce sums up the value of party as 'The parties keep a nation's mind alive as the rise and fall of the sweeping tide freshens the water of long ocean inlets; Leacok says 'A different parties remain in a state of wilful inconvincibility with individual judgement frozen tight in the shape of the party would.' It creates factionalism as it tends to make the political life of a country machine like or artificial.

The idea of partyless democracy had its root in the philosophy of George Washington James Madison and Gandhi, Roy, Vinoba Bhave and J.P.

POLITICAL PARTIES IN GREAT BRITAIN, U.S.A. AND SWITZERLAND : A COMPARISON

GREAT BRITAIN (U.K.)

1. Political parties have evolved with the evolution of democratic institutions. As such the conventional Tories and Whigs (Charles II) became Liberal and Conservative parties only in the nineteenth century. Labour Party came into existence in the twentieth century.
2. Even though the political parties of Great Britain have acquired constitutional status, they are primarily based on customs and conventions.
3. Due to unitary structure of government and strong nationalistic spirit, the political parties primarily focus on the common issues that have nationwide appeal.
4. There exists strong, clear cut ideological differences between the political parties. The conservative focus on cutting down government expenditure on social sectors, the labour party advocates welfare policies. As such their social bases are also different.
5. Britain has a two party system. Even though other parties exist, they are insignificant in the political process. For example, Labour Party's birth led to decline of liberal party.
6. Political parties in Britain are more powerful than their counterpart in Presidential System because it is based on the principle of collective responsibility of Council of Ministers to the Parliament.
7. There exists strict discipline in the ranks of Party members. They never vote on any issue to which the party objects.
8. There is high degree of political maturity and sensitiveness among the rank of the parties with regard to political issues. Most of its members are educated ones and of high moral status.

AMERICA (U.S.A.)

1. There exists biparty system in America. While earlier Federalist and antifederalists were two parties, today there exist the Republican and the Democratic parties. Bi-party spirit is more strong than U.K.
2. The ideological differences between the two political parties is not so striking as in the case of U.K. That is why Prof. Bryce dubs American political parties as two bottles of wine with different labels.
3. Political parties are active only during the election.
4. Political parties focus on local issues that may be championed to obtain votes.
5. Political parties are not influential in the affairs of the state (as compared to U.K.) because the system is Presidential one with separation of powers.
6. In terms of their bases the American Political parties rely on regional forces.
7. The members of the political party are often observed as voting against the general opinion of the party. Moreover, there are no setbacks

due to these endeavours because government of the day is hardly destabilized as in U.K.

8. There exists a number of professional politicians in the ranks of political party. They are recruited to work in extra-governmental environment.
9. There has been an increase in the instances of corruption in which political parties are involved.

SWITZERLAND

1. There exists low degree of party politics as compared to US or UK.
2. There is multiparty system in Switzerland.
3. Like U.S.A, the political parties are mainly concerned with putting up candidates for political posts, organizing and enlightening public opinion.
4. In spite of multiparty system there hardly has arisen a situation of political instability.
5. Some of the important political parties are : Liberal Party, Radical Party, Catholic Liberal Party, Social Democratic Party and Peasant Party.
6. There is loosely organized party system in Switzerland. Most of the elected members of the Union Legislature decide about the party membership only after general elections.
7. Every party has three main parts, viz; Diet, Central Committee and Working Committee.
8. There exist high degree of cooperation among the various political parties.
9. Usually there is absence of a single leader in the party.
10. Political parties are not very important in the political system and there is lack of party spirit.
11. Political parties do not enjoy any constitutional status (same as USA).

DEMOCRATIC AND TOTALITARIAN PARTY : A COMPARISON

Democratic model allows elements of opposition leading to the existence of a big or multiparty system.

Totalitarian model signifies the existence and leading role of a single political party.

In Democratic model parties operate within a constitutional framework to that party and government becomes different institutions.

In totalitarian model party and government become identical and the latter becomes the shadow of the former. To Apter totalitarian party is coterminus with the state itself.

AMERICAN AND BRITISH PARTY : A COMPARISON

(Republican and Democratic) (Labour and Conservative)

Both are models of biparty system. But, while the American political parties lack rigid organisational discipline and clear cut ideological commitments, English party system exhibit cohesion, effective organisation and specific ideological commitments. They are more nationalistic in spirit but American political parties focus on local issues as well.

In underdeveloped or developing countries, parties are a product of historical circumstances. Parties come into existence not for the sake of running the government but for the sake of fighting for national liberation.

ROLE OF OPPOSITION IN DEMOCRACY

Though, a radical statesman John Hobhouse said it was not until 1937 that the opposition was recognised officially.

The institution was officially recognised in

Canada	:	1905
Australia	:	1920
South Africa	:	1946

In the British Westminster model, the official opposition has been recognised as vital and integral as the Cabinet itself.

Sir Ivor Jennings says : 'If there is no opposition, there is no democracy.'

A.L. Lowell says : The constant pressure of a recognized opposition is an obstacle to despotism... is a wok against the tyranny not only of a despot but also of a fanatical majority.

In the case of several Asian and African countries nationalist parties often found it relatively easy to establish one party system and place extraordinary restrictions on civil liberties precisely because no organised group with any measure of popular support was committed to maintenance of a competitive frame works.

ELECTORAL SYSTEM

Adult Franchise is the basis of election. To Victor Hugo suffrage had crowned man as a citizen.

Norway was the first country to do so. In another countries it started as :

Germany	:	1919
U.S.A.	:	1919
Sweden	:	1920
Britain	:	1928
U.S.S.R.	:	1936
France	:	1945
Italy	:	1948
Switzerland	:	1973

Voting Age

Japan	:	25
Denmark	:	25
Norway	:	23
Germany	:	20
India	:	18
U.K.	:	21
U.S.A.	:	18

DIFFERENT VIEWS

To Mill : Universal teaching must precede universal enfranchisement.

To Laski : Exclusion from power means, exclusion from the benefits of power.

Compulsory Voting : Belgium, Rumania, Argentina, Netherland, some of Swiss Cantons.

CRITERIA OF REPRESENTATION

There are two known criteria of general representation :

1. Territorial
2. Functional

Territorial Representation

Under this the whole country is divided into geographical areas of heavy equal population called constituencies.

Gerrymandering a malpractice is vague in U.S. wherein manipulation of delimitation of the boundaries of constituencies is done to help party in power to capture few more votes.

Functional Representation

Representation on the basis of economic functions or occupational interests.

The Guild Socialists, Syndicalists and Italian Fascists were its advocates. Indeed the system was tried by Mussolini in his corporate state of Italy.

Laski is critical of functional representation.

CRITERIA OF ELECTORAL SYSTEMS

To Laski a good electoral system ought to satisfy four general considerations.

1. It should so constitute the legislature that the vital issues of public policy. The legislature must reflect the opinions of the majority and the minority.
2. The constituencies should be small enough to develop the personal relation between the elected representative and the electorate.
3. It should reflect the changing opinion of the major issues by methods like elections.
4. It should assure that the voters as far as possible remain directly in contact with the government in power.

KINDS OF ELECTORAL SYSTEM

The result of voting is determined according to the prevailing electoral systems.

Broadly one can identify three electoral systems under democratic systems.

1. Plurality or first past the post
2. Majoritarian
3. Proportional representation

First Past the Post

Also called simple majority system.

The principle of first past the post is applied.

A candidate who receives the highest number of votes, may be less than even half the votes polled, is declared a winner.

This practice is widely followed :

Demerit : The plurality system undermines the legitimacy of government in so far as government only often enjoys only minority support less than 50%.

Minorities may remain under represented.

Merit : The champions, contend that this system promotes two party system.

Prevent separatist tendencies among minorities.

Provides for a relatively stable and effective government.

Majoritarian

A candidate is usually required to obtain an absolute majority 50% of valid votes cast.

When there are three or more contestants it is assured by

1. Second Ballot System
2. Alternative Vote

Single Candidate Constituencies

A voter can vote for only one candidate.

If no candidate gets a first ballot majority, a second run off ballot is held between the leading two candidates.

This system is popular in France.

In Alternative vote system there are single members constituencies.

There are preferential voting : 1, 2, 3 and 4 so on. Winning candidate needs to get 50% of the votes cast. Votes are counted according to the first preference. If no candidate gets absolute majority of the first preference votes, the candidate who gets the least number of first preferences is eliminated and the next preferences of his or her voters are added to first preference of those candidates.

Alternative vote system is followed in the election to the Lower House in Australian, American and Indian Presidents.

To Finer 'the majority produced by the systems of the second ballot or the alternative vote is a kind of second best, not whole hearted first choice.'

Proportional Representation

Proportional representation was favoured by J.S. Mill. It is claimed that under this system any party, interest or group would secure representation in proportion to the support it has among the electors. There are multi member constituencies.

The main idea is to ensure by distributing votes rather than voters, that the number of seats won by a political party in the legislature shall be approximately proportionate to the votes cast for that party.

There are two main schemes in proportionate representation.

1. The Hare system
2. The List system

Hare System

Hare system is also called single transferable vote system.

Devised by Thomas Hare in Pamphlet called Machinery of representation, hailed by Mill as the greatest improvement yet made in the theory and practice of government.

Multi member constituencies never less than three electors vote preferentially.

Candidate are elected if they achieve a Quota.

Quota is usually equal to the total number of valid votes divided by one more than the number of seats available plus one vote.

$$= \frac{\text{Total number of valid votes polled}}{\text{Total number of seats to be filled}} + 1$$

Votes are counted according to first preference.

An elected candidate's surplus votes are redistributed.

The candidate obtaining least number of first preferences is eliminated and the next preferences of his or her voters are added to the first preferences of other candidates.

This system of redistribution is repeated till the number of candidates securing electoral quota equals the number of seats available.

The Hare system is used in the election to Municipal Council in U.S. and Canada.

Both Houses of Parliament in Northern Ireland
Lower House of Parliament in Peru and Malta
Rajya Sabha and Legislative Council in India.

List System

Under this system, the entire country is treated as a single constituency or it is divided into a large multimember constituencies.

Ballots contain separate lists of candidates of different political parties.

Electors vote for the parties not for candidate.

Parties are allocated seats in direct proportion to the votes they gain in the election.

In Switzerland, voter has the right even to write additional names to determine his own preference.

Followed in Germany, Legislatures of Finland, Knesset of Israel, Switzerland.

The list system is the only potentially pure system of proportional representation and is therefore fair to all parties.

The system of proportional representation has unique advantage of giving representation to all types of groups. But its disadvantages are unstability and fissiparous tendencies.

METHODS OF MINORITY REPRESENTATION

Methods of Minority representation are :

Cumulative Vote System

Involves with member constituencies.

A voter has as many votes as the number of seats.

A voter has the right to the option of either giving his votes to all, to a few or even to concentrate all his votes just for one candidate.

A well organised minority has an opportunity to get at least one of its representatives elected by cumulating all its votes in favour of its own candidate.

It used in educational institutions and for local bodies in Great Britain and U.S.

Limited Vote System

Involves multi member constituencies : Voter has certain number of votes which is less than the number of seats to be filled.

This system acts as a check on the monopolisation of representation in a constituency by a single political body and helps minority to get at least one seat.

Communal Representation

Separate electorate for separate communities.

A second method is reservation of seats in joint electorate : the voter may cast votes for the candidates of communities other than their own. But in deciding the result, a member of community who gets the highest number of votes among candidates of that community will be elected.

Instructed Represenation

Advocated by Bentham & James Mill

To them unless the legislators elected by the poorer classes be bound to their wishes by a pledge, the interests and demands of the poorer classes will never be fairly represented.

J.S. Mill however completely discarded the idea and agreed with Burke.

Concurrent Majority

Advocated by John, C. Calhoun

It means that any decision should be treated as valid only when due concurrence of all the important sectional interests affected by it has been obtained.

Its implications are veto power in UN and EEC.

Coalitional Democracy

It is regarded particularly suitable for the governance of the societies which are deeply divided by religious, ideological, linguistic, regional etc. differences.

It involves four basic principles, which are of primary importance.

1. Executive power sharing : means grand coalition of the representatives of all significant segments.
2. Greater autonomy to different segments : federalism.

3. Proportionality : allocation of political offices, administrative appointments and public funds on the basis of population of each segment.
4. Exercise of veto by minority.

SEPARATION OF POWERS

The theory of separation of power deals with functional organization of the government. It gives an idea about the organization of rule making, rule application and rule adjudicating departments. This theory is mainly associated with the name of famous French Philosopher, Montesquieu.

The traces of recognizing the need to evolve some mechanism for separation of power could be traced to earlier times (Aristotle Polybins and Cicero, Marsiglio of Padua, Bodin, Locke Madison etc.). But, a systematic effort was made by Montesquieu. He propounded his theory in his work 'Spirit of the laws' had decisive impact on founding fathers of American political system. He evolved his analysis by a close analysis of the British political system.

The most significant point of the theory is that it bases itself on the preservation of political liberty. According to Montesquieu ''individual liberty is certainly endangered when two organs of the government are combined. It is to be found only in moderate governments.'' His chief contention is that the three organs of the government should work independently. In other words, the legislative, the executive and the judicial branches should not intervene in the works of one another. So, he holds that the three organs of the government should be organized in such a way that each organ performs differently and remain independent and supreme within its own sphere.

However, this theory has not been applied in its entirely. The increasing complexity of the socio-economic life has rendered it impossible for clear cut separation of power. Moreover, the three organs of the government must be seen in connection. They have certain goal and objective that deem it necessary to interact with one another. On the contrary, it may lead to isolation and disharmony. As MacIver observes ''What is needed, in fact is not the separation of functions but their proper articulation; only thus can responsibility be wedded to efficiency.''

Application of the Theory of Separation of Power

U.S.A.

Separation of power is mainly a hallmarks of President system. American political system stands as the model in this respect. As Herman Finer says ''the American constitution was consciously and elaborately made an essay in the separation of powers and is today the most important policy in the world which operates upon that principle.'' However, this provision is implicity stated in the Constitution. In Kilbourn Vs. Thomson (1880) the American Supreme Court observed that ''It is believed to be one of the chief merits of the American system of written constitutional law that all powers entrusted to government whether state or national, are divided into three general departments, the executive, the legislature and the judicial. It is also essential to the successful working of the system that the persons entrusted with the power in any of these branches shall not be permitted to encroach upon the powers confided to others, but that each shall by the law of its creation be limited to the exercise of the powers appropriate to its own department and no other.''

The prominent implications of the theory are

1. American President is given wide range of powers viz; appointment of officials, policy making etc. In these respect there is no interference by the legislature or judiciary.
2. American President is not responsible to the Congress for his acts of omission or commission. He can not be removed by the Congress except through impeachment.
3. The Congress discusses and decides a large number of issues pertaining to policy measures and questions of national or international importance. The President does not interfere in these aspects.
4. American President neither summons nor can dissolve the Congress.

5. The American Supreme Court remains independent in its sphere of action.

However, to ward off the problems resulting from clear cut separation of power, there is provision of checks and balances. By this principles, each organ of the governments in spite of being separate and integral in itself, controls each other. These include

1. Many of appointments made by and treaties entered into by the President need ratification on the Senate. Only then, they can become a law.
2. American President enjoys the Veto power over bills passed by the Congress.

BRITAIN

The British has a Parliamentary system of government where in the Council of Ministers form an integral part of the Parliament. They are collectively responsible to the lower House of the parliament. Moreover, the upper house (House of Lords) acts as the highest Court of appeal. There is no Supreme Court in Britain.

Thus, there exists concentration rather than separation of powers in the British political system. Organised party system and pressure of public opinion acts as antidotes to the governmental tyranny.

INDIA

India has a Parliamentary system of government which operates on principle of collective responsibilility. The Ministers are drawn from the Parliament. The President is elected by members of the Parliament. Ordinance making power of the President corresponds to the law made by the Parliament. Thus, there is no separation of power between legislature and executive.

Article 50 of the Constitution provides for separating judiciary from executive. This has been a hallmark of Indian Constitution. Judges are free from executive control, hold office during good behaviour and their salaries could not be altered to their disadvantage.

Conclusion

Thus, the way different political system adopts to the theory of separation of power reflects their normative predispositions. It also reflects their socio-economic milieu that warrants variation in a theoretical predicament. While American political system has been able to continue with the principle of separation of power with check and balances, the British have more attention for strong government. The Indian Constitution follows a "middle of the road" course. It follows concentration of power as regards relationship between executive and legislature and separation of power as regards organisation of the judiciary.

RULE OF LAW

Rule of Law is the cornerstone of the British Constitution. The principal exponent of the principle is Prof. A.V. Dicey. According to him, it implies three things

Firstly, "no man is punishable or can be lawfully made to suffer in body or goods except for a distinct breach of law established in the ordinary legal manner before the ordinary courts of the land." It implies that no person can be deprived of his life, liberty and property except through trial in a duly constituted court of law.

Secondly, "Not only with us is no man above the law, but every man, whatever be his rank or condition, is subject to the ordinary law of the realm and amenable to the jurisdiction of the ordinary tribunals." It establishes the legal equity. "Every official from the Prime Minister to constable or a collector of taxes is under the same responsibility for every act done without legal justification as any other citizen."

Finally, it implies that "the general principles of the constitution are ... the result of judicial decisions determining the rights of private persons in particular cases brought before the courts." The rights are not listed in the Constitution and this avoids any miscarriage of limiting them.

According to Dicey the principle of rule of law is best antidote to governments tyranny. In his opinion, there exists liberty in Britain only because there was the Rule of Law.

However, there are serious drawbacks in Dicey's conception of Rule of Law.

Firstly, It is meaningless in societies marked by wide inequalities. It will have to buttress itself with certain elements of egalitarianism by which legal equality can be meaningful.

Secondly, I. Jennings in his "The Law and the Constitution" observes that "the growth of the new functions of the state has made much of his analysis irrelevant." The growing complexity of governmental functions and resulting phenomenon of delegated legislation has restricted crude observance of the Rule of Law.

Thirdly, The growth of administrative laws to tackle the social welfare functions of the state has further minimized the scope of Rule of Law.

Fourthly, Immunities granted to persons and property of diplomats limit the scope of Rule of Law.

JUDICIAL REVIEW

The power of Judicial Review is an important Constituent of American political system by which the Supreme Court enjoys wide ranging power. It may be defined as the power of the court to declare any law null and void, if it transgresses or is inconsistent with any provision of the constitution. It enables the courts to examine the action of legislature, executive and administration and ensure their conformity to the provisions of the constitution. Though every court in U.S.A. is empowered to review a law or an executive action, but the Supreme Court's decision is the final one.

Application of Judicial Review

U.S.A.

The power of Judicial Review is implicit in the American Constitution. It has nowhere been dealt in detail. The two provisions are :

Article VI which provides that the "Constitution, and the laws of the United States which shall be made in pursuance thereof; and all Treaties made, or which shall be made, under the authority of the United States, shall be the supreme law of the land" and Article III, Sec. 2, provides that "the judicial power shall extend to all cases, in land and equity, arising under this constitution, the law of the United States, and treaties made or which shall be made, under their authority.

However the issue was made clear is Marbury Vs Madison (1803) case, it underlined the view that the Judicial Review is a part of Constitutional Law. There are following implications of Justice Marshall's decisions.

Firstly, the constitution is a written document which clearly defines and limit the power of government.

Secondly, the constitution is a fundamental law and is superior to the ordinary law passed by Congress

Thirdly, the Act of Congress which is contrary to and violation of the fundamental law is void and cannot bind the courts.

Fourthly, the Judicial power obligation to uphold the oath, render it necessary for the courts to declare unconstitutional those acts of Congress which contravene the fundamental law.

It must be emphasised in this connection that the courts are not concerned with policy, wisdom or expediency but only with constitutionality of legislation. In the opinion of Supreme Court, "it neither approves, nor condemns any legislative policy. Its delicate and difficult office is to ascertain and declare whether the legislation is in accordance with, or in controvention of, the provisions of the Constitution and having done that, its duty ends."

However, the critics have accused the Supreme Court of becoming a non-elective super-legislature. The judgements have wide ranging consequences. Issues of public policy are severely affected by a minority of American society sitting in the judicial branch of government. Of late, there has been a change and Supreme Court has undergone modernization and there has been a substantial change in its functioning.

INDIA

The power of judicial review is not explicitly stated in the Constitution. According to Article 13 : 'any action of the legislature or the executive in contravention of the provisions of the chapter of Fundamental Rights shall be declared void.'' While the Courts in U.S.A. proceed on ''due process of law,'' India follows ''procedure established by law.'' While procedure established by law enquires into the legality of any legislative or executive action, the purase 'due process' also examines the malafide intention of the law giver.

In addition, the Indian constitution attempts to strike a balance between Parliamentary sovereignty and judicial supremacy. The Parliament may make law to avoid deadlocks by Courts.

8

CONSTITUTIONALISM

Every state must have a constitution. Without a constitution it is difficult to govern a state. History tells that since the origin of the state there had been some kinds of rules and regulations in some form to maintain the order and harmony in the state. In every state be it a democratic or despotic it is essential that such rules must be accepted which would decide the role and organization of political institutions in order to save the society from anarchy. In modern states these rules find expression in the form of a constitution.

MEANING AND DEFINITION

A constitution is a basic design, which deals with the structure and powers of the government. It also includes rights and duties of citizens. Very often 'constitution' is understood as a document which has been written and accepted at a particular time, but this is not the true meaning of constitution, constitution may be written or may be unwritten. Sometimes it is found in an established body of rules, maxims, traditions and practices in accordance with which its government is organized and its powers and exercised. Many political thinkers have tried to define the term 'constitution'.

For Aristotle "constitution is the way in which, citizens who are the component parts of the state are arranged in relation to one another".

According to Woolsey, a constitution "the collection of principal according to which he powers of the government rights of the government and relations between the two are adjusted."

Bryce defines it as "the aggregate of laws and customs under which the life of state goes on the complex totality of laws embodying the principles and rules whereby the community is organized, governed and held together".

Herman Finer says, - "the state is a human grouping in which rules a certain power relationship between its individuals and associated constituents. This power relationship is embodied in political institutions. The system of fundamental political institutions is the constitution the autobiography of the power relationship."

Bouncier defines a constitution as "the fundamental law of a state directing the principles upon which the government is founded and regulating the exercise of the sovereign powers, directly to what bodies of persons thee powers shall be confined and the manner of their exercise.

George Cornewell Lewis describes the constitution as "the arrangement and distribution of sovereign power in the community or the form of the government".

Charles Baregeaud says – "A constitution is the fundamental law according to which the relations of individuals or normal persons to the community are determined. It may be a written instrument, a precise text or series of text enacted at a given time by a sovereign power or it may be the more or less definite results of a series of legislative acts, ordinances, judicial decisions, precedents and customs of diverse origin and of unequal and importance".

Sir James Mackintosh says "By the constitution of a state, mean the body of those written or unwritten fundamental laws which regulate the most important rights of the higher magistrates the most essential privileges of the subjects.

According to Leacock - "Constitution is the form of government". Austin has defined constitution saying, "that it fixes the structure of supreme government."On the basis of above definitions we can say that a constitution is

- The fundamental law of the land
- May be written or unwritten
- Deals with the composition and power of the government.
- Deals with the rights of citizens.
- Deals with the relationship between the government and governed.
- It is supreme law that must be followed?

CONTENTS OF THE CONSTITUTION

A constitution must have the following provisions in it

1. Organization and form of administration of the state
2. Functions of different organs of the government their powers and mutual relations.
3. Mention of fundamental rights of the citizens
4. The relation of the government with the people.
5. The procedure of the government of the constitution

NEED FOR FUNDAMENTAL RIGHTS

The provision of fundamental rights in constitution is considered essential for it imposes definite limitations on the powers of the government. It is a declaration that no government can tamper with these rights of individuals. It establishes a limited and free government. Fundamental rights are the lifelines of democracy. Almost all the written constitution of the world contains Fundamental rights. In the constitution of India part III (Arts 12-35 fundamental rights) are included. The state cannot make a law, which takes away, or abridges any of the rights of the citizens guaranteed in Part III of the constitution. If it passes such law, it may be declared unconstitutional by the courts. The people of he United States of America attach a great sanctity to the rights. But fundamental rights are not absolute.

They are subjected to limitations in order to secure or Promote the greater interests of the community or the state. If there is no binding on fundamental rights it may lead to anarchy. Restrictions are necessary. Many constitutions provide for such Restrictions.

CONSTITUTION OF GOVERNMENT

Second essential content of a constitution is composition and powers of government. The main objective of the constitution is to provide outlines for the structures and powers of the government. A great portion of constitution is devoted to serve this particular purpose. How should the government be organized? How should it work? These questions are answered in the constitution. In wider sense the organization of government includes:

1. Division of powers amongst various departments.
2. Organisation of particular agencies through which state manifests itself.
3. The extent and duration of their authority
4. The modes of appointment or election of public functionaries.
5. The constitution of the electorate.

Some constitutions give a detailed and specific description of composition and powers of the government and there are some constitutions, which are very general and short in displaying government.

AMENDMENT OF CONSTITUTION

It indicates towards the procedure of amendment of the constitution. A written constitution must have procedure for amending the constitution and it is regarded as an essential part of every written constitution.

The method of amendment only guarantees application and sanctity of the constitution. It is upon the method of amendments that guarantees of individuals liberty and the adaptability of the constitution depends.

The method of amendment may be simple or may be a Complex and difficult procedure. It is simple and enables the political sovereign to express its will, there can be no conflict between the actual conditions and legal organization. But an easy method of amendment may lead to instability. If the constitution is having difficult method of amendment it may result in one of the two things.

First there may grow up extra legal institutions fully supported by public opinion.

Secondly, if such extra-legal institutions are not allowed to grow, the consequence may be a revolt.

The method of amendment must be such which should neither give instability nor generate revolution.

As Jennings says "A constitution has to work not only in the environment in which it was drafted but also centuries later. It must therefore be capable of adoption to new conditions as they rise."

All the above-discussed contents are essential for a written as well as unwritten constitution. The difference is that in a written constitution they find more clear and definite place whereas in unwritten constitution they are little vague.

REQUISITES OF A GOOD CONSTITUTION

A good constitution must have the following qualities.

1. **Clarity or definiteness:** Every clause of the constitution should be written in simple language. It should express its meaning clearly without leaving any scope for confusion.
2. **Brevity:** The constitutions should not be lengthy. It should contain only important things and unimportant things should be left out. But the brevity should not lead to gap in Constitution having some issues unexplained.
3. **Comprehensiveness:** The constitution should be applicable to the whole country. If it is a federation then it must say the structure and power of the center and provincial government.
4. **Flexibility:** The constitution should not be too rigid to hinder the process of amendment when needed.
5. **Declaration of rights:** A good constitution must contain the fundamental rights of the people. In the constitution of countries like India, Russia, China, America and Japan such declaration have been made.
6. **Independence of judiciary:** Independence of judiciary is another quality of a good constitution. The judiciary should function freely and act as the guardian of the fundamental rights of the people without favour or fear.
7. **Directive Principles of State Policy:** In a good constitution mention must be made of the directive Principles of he State Policy because, it helps the establishment of a welfare state. These principles also serve as a boon for the government.

ARISTOTLE'S CLASSIFICATION OF CONSTITUTIONS

Aristotle for the first time adopted a scientific method to classify the constitution.

His classification is based on the study of 158 constitutions of the ancient world. He has classified the constitution on the basis of location of sovereign power and end or purpose towards which the power was directed. States which seed the good life of all are true or normal states. Those which deviate from that end are perverted states. His classification is illustrated by the following table.

Aristotle's Classification of Constitutions

Rule/Form of Constitution	Pure Form seeking the common welfare	Perverted form common welfare ignored
Rule by one	Monarchy	Tyranny
Rule by few	Aristocracy	Oligarchy
Rule by many	Polity	Democracy

From the table one can understand Aristotle's classification of constitution was mainly based on location of sovereign power and end of the state.

Though the classification given by Aristotle is more realistic and scientific, it does not provide a clear picture. Critics point out that Aristotle's classification is not sound because it does not rest upon any scientific principle by which government can be distinguished from the another. It is arithmetical rather than organic, quantitative rather than qualitative in character. Aristotle gave a wrong meaning to the term democracy.

Sir John Seely criticized it on the ground that it was not applicable to the modern governments. He pointed out that Aristotle knew only city-states and they were not like the "country-states" of modern times.

In Aristotle's classifications there is not place for limited monarchy, a presidential form of government, a parliamentary form of government, a unitary government and federal government. There is no guarantee that governments change in order indicated by Aristotle.

After Aristotle several other political thinkers have tried to classify the constitution. Among them the most scientific and acceptable to modern states is that of Leacock.

Modern constitutions are classified in the following manner.

1. Written and unwritten constitutions.
2. Rigid and flexible constitutions.

EVOLVED AND ENACTED CONSTITUTIONS

An evolved constitution is the result of the growth of rules, which have been developed with the time, added one by one as and when the need was felt.

It is the product of accumulated material, which has moulded and shaped the political institution of the country. Such a constitution is not made, it grows with its roots in the past, it is nothing but, a collection and continuation of customs, usages, traditions, principles and judicial decisions.

The enacted constitution is the result of the deliberate effort of man. It is consciously made. It may be made by a constituent assembly or by the command of sovereign authority, king or parliament. The features of an enacted constitution are embodied in a document or in a series of documents.

Constitutions are now divided into written and unwritten instead of evolved and enacted.

WRITTEN CONSTITUTION

A written constitution is normally supposed to mean a document or a collection of documents in which the basic rules regarding the main organs and institutions of government are clearly laid down. A written constitution is a deliberate creation. It is a consciously planned system. It may be created by a constituent assembly or a convention. The constitution of India was formulated and adopted by the constituent assembly.

The constitution of USA was drafted by a special convention of delegates, presides over by George Washington. This constitutions emerged out of the Philadelphia convention on September 17,1787, and was referred to the States for their ratification.

A written constitution may be single document having one date. Such is the case of India, Myanmar and United states. It may be in a series of documents bearing different dates. This is the case with France, Australia etc. The French constitution under the Third Republic was fragmentary and did not consist of one single document. It was composed of three constitutional laws passed on February 24, February 26 and July 26, 1874. Whenever there is a written constitution in a country, a distinction is made between constitutional law and ordinary laws. The constitutional law is supposed to be the will of the sovereign and it should not be altered by the ordinary legislative process. The statutory law has to limits itself within the framework of constitutional law. If they conflict with constitutional law they are termed as ultra vires.

Merits

1. The most important merit of a written constitution is that it is very definite. There is not uncertainty. The constitution provides all fundamental principles in written and people can refer to it as and when they want.

2. As written constitution is drawn with great care and after long deliberation. It means it is the result of experience and knowledge. There is no place for he temporary emotions and hasty decision.
3. A written constitution protects the rights of the individuals. Rights are incorporated in it making them superior to the ordinary law and saving them from being change by different government from as they wished.
4. It checks the constitution from being twisted and turned according to popular whims and emotions this giving a guarantee of stability.
5. A written constitution is stable and guides through difficult situations. It is more suitable for emergency period.
6. For a federal government written constitution is more suitable because there is provision for the central and state power separately.

Demerits

1. Generally, written constitutions are difficult to amend, thus introducing rigidity and conservatism.
2. In a written constitution judiciary is quite conservative an interpretations are merely to see whether a law conforms to the constitution or not. This might strangle a nation, which needs to change according to the times.
3. It tries to encompass all rules and ideals o a nation, which may not be suitable for all the ages. Thus the future growth may be neglected.
4. It sometimes becomes too exhaustive leading to legal jugglery.

UNWRITTEN CONSTITUTION

An unwritten constitution reflects the evolutionary nature of free documentation of the rules and regulations. First they are practiced and by a continuous practice, they become part of the construction. They constitution of Britain is he best example of an written constitution. An written constitution is the result of long process and natural growth of political constitutions of the country. There is no single document or documents, which contain it though many sources may be found which describe it.

Merits

1. They are quite easily adaptable to changing circumstances. Law can be added as and when required. There is no limitation of any pre-documented constitutional law. Thus they are progressive.
2. They are flexible and people can bring about changes without undertaking revolutions. As these constitutions evolve themselves with the changing time, public opinion finds suitable place in constitution and it terminates possibility of revolution.
3. Unwritten constitution can undergo changes, with out basic framework being sidelined. This is useful especially in case of unforeseen situation.
4. Historically they seem to stand the test of times and keep up the traditions of a nation state as it is said about the British constitution that it has unbroken history. It's a continuous process of development.

Demerits

1. The serious defect of an unwritten constitution is that it is vague and indefinite. Common man may not understand the constitutional system of the country. He cannot refer to any document in which he can find all that he requires to understand the structure of the government of his country. An unwritten constitution requires a very high degree of political consciousness among the people to understand it's spirit, and ordinarily that is not easy to find.
2. Some times unwritten constitutions are quite unstable.
3. The judiciary may play more role than is warranted. It becomes the playthings of judicial tribunals. The judiciary can interpret the unwritten laws as it suited to its desire and will.

4. It also contended that an unwritten constitution is not suited to democracies. The massed need a well- defined document under which they have to live. They may be suited for aristocratic societies but not for democracies.

FLEXIBLE AND RIGID CONSTITUTION

Bryce has suggested that the classification of the constitution should be based on the method of amendment to the constitution and its relation to the ordinary or statutory law. Under this scheme there are two types of constitution.-flexible and rigid.

FLEXIBLE CONSTITUTION

In a flexible constitution there is no distinction between ordinary law and constitutional law. Both the enacted in the same way and their source is also same. Constitution may be written or largely based on conventions. They are amended in the same way. No special procedure is required for amending the ordinary or constitutional law. The constitution of Britain is a classic example of a flexible constitution. Parliament in Britain is sovereign.

1. There is no law which parliament cannot make.
2. There is no law which parliament can not unmake and there is no law English constitution no marked or clear distinction between law, which are fundamental or constitutional, and laws, which are not.

In Britain constitutional changes can be made by following the same way as an ordinary law is enacted. The courts have no authority of review. They cannot nullify any enactment of parliament.

Merits

1. A flexible constitution can be amended with the same ease and facility with which ordinary laws are altered. It makes possible the adjustment of the constitution to the ne and the changing needs of the society.
2. A flexible constitution can easily adopt the needs of people with the change of time because of its elasticity. When the demands of people are fulfilled by the constitution there is hardly any change of revolution. It is the flexible character of the British constitution, which has saved Britain on so many occasions for the danger of revolution. The transfer from a monarchy to parliamentary system also was free from violence. Whereas France, which is very close to Britain experienced a revolution and so far five constitutions have been enacted because of revolutions and odd circumstances.
3. A flexible constitution is very useful for developing a country, because it is a great expression of its development. It does not hinder progress due to it's adaptability. At the same time it protects the basic principles of the constitution. A flexible constitution is based on the sound assumption of some sociopolitical change and premise that there cannot be a perfect constitution for all times, to tackle the socio-political changes.
4. Flexible constitution is moulded by the conventions of national life. It represents the historical continuity of the nation's life and incorporates within it the changes as and when the need arises. A flexible constitution can, thus, claim to feel the pulse of public opinion. It represents the minds of people. Judge Cooley had said that "of all the constitutions, which may come into existence for the government of the people, the most excellent is obviously that which is the natural out growth of the national life, and which having grown and expanded as the nation has matured, is likely at any particular time to express the prevailing sentiment regarding government and the accepted principles of civil and political liberty."

Demerits

1. Due to its flexible nature the constitution keeps on changing. The constitution may be changed just to satisfy the people who are in majority ignoring the welfare of minority. It

fails to provide a stable system in administration, which results in the poor performance of the government.

2. When the procedure of amendment is simple and easy, it is liable to be seriously affected by ever changing popular passion. And popular passions are guided by emotions, not by reasons. Decisions, which are based on emotions, not by reasons. Decisions, which are based on emotions, may disturb the harmony and balance of a nation. It may divide the society and there may be a possible threat to the integration of the nation itself.

Flexible constitution is not suitable for a federal system, because the rights of constituent units are not guaranteed due to flexible nature of the constitution. There are two possibilities if a federation is having flexible constitution.

1. The units may lose their independence and freedom and centre may become more powerful, which is against the spirit of federal system.
2. The units may act very independently without respecting the constitution, as it is not stable.

As the constitution can be changed by following a simple procedure, there is no guarantee that fundamental rights will not be disturbed. Any government can very easily change the provision of fundamental rights or even may delete it from the constitution.

RIGID CONSTITUTION

Rigid constitutions are those, which require a special procedure for the amendment. The constitutions of USA, Australia and Switzerland are the example of a rigid constitution.

The rigid constitution is above the ordinary law and can be changed by a procedure, which is different from the procedure of ordinary law, thus making it difficult to change.

The objective is to emphasize that the constitutional law embodies the will of the sovereign, and it should be treated as sacred document.

American constitution is the best example of a rigid constitution. The American congress cannot make any law contrary to the constitution.

The American Supreme Court acts as the guardian of the constitution and it has right to declare any law of the congress null and void. The constitution of India is neither so flexible as the British constitution not so rigid as the American constitution.

Merits

1. A rigid constitution possesses the qualities of stability and performance. 'A rigid constitutions is essentially a written constitution which is the creation of experienced and learned people. Thus it is the symbol of national efficiency. People regard it as a sacred document and they are ready to work according to its provisions'.
2. A rigid constitution safeguards legislative encroachment, Constitution should not be a plaything in the hands of legislatures.
3. A rigid constitution safeguards fundamental rights effectively. Fundamental rights are part of constitution.

No legislature can tamper them, because they are superior to ordinary law.

1. A rigid constitution protects the rights of minority. Minorities cannot be expected to agree to their rights being imperiled by a majority action. If the majority ventures it, the judges perform their function of guardianship.
2. A rigid constitution is free from dangers of temporary popular passion. Because of complex amendment procedure the constitution may not be swept away by the emotions of the people which in most of the cases are not based on wisdom and reasoning.
3. A federal set up of government essentially needs a rigid constitution for the safty of the rights of the units as well as for the strength and integration of the federation. Under rigid constitution units of a federation feel secure

and at the same time there is a check on their activities also in order to stop them from violating each other's jurisdictions.

Demerits

1. Sometimes changes in the constitution become inevitable but a rigid constitution cannot be amended easily.
2. The framers of constitution is not hardly foresee the future. A rigid constitution is not suitable for a progressive nation where changes take place frequently.
3. Under the rigid constitution, the main concern of the judiciary is to see whether the law conforms to the provisions of the constitution or not.

FORMS OF GOVERNMENT

Government is one of the essential elements of the State. It is the working agency of the State. The importance of the Government in modern times is highly felt. Attempts have been made from time to time to classify the various forms of Government.

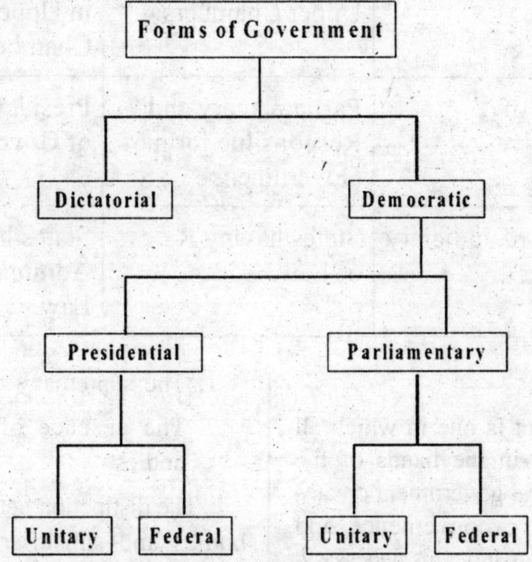

The classification of Governments as explained by C.F.Strong may be represented through the following table:

Sl. No.	Source of Classification	A	B
I.	Jurisdiction of governmental powers	Democracy	Dictatorship
II.	(a) Nature of the State	Unitary State	Federal State
	(b) Nature of the Constitution	Flexible	Rigid

	(c) Nature of Constituency	(i) State having universal franchise system	(i) States having limited voting system
		(ii) States having single-member constituencies	(ii) States having multi-members constituencies
III.	(a) Nature of Legislature	States having Bicameralism	States having Unicameralism.
	(b) Structure of the Legislature	States having Elected Members in Upper Chambers	States having no elected Members in Upper Chambers
IV.	Nature of Executive	Parliamentary and Responsible form of Government	Presidential form of Government
V.	Nature of Judiciary	States having Rule of Law.	States having Administrative Law.

UNITARY

A unitary form of government is one in which all the powers are concentrated in the hands of the central government. The central government creates local units for administrative convenience and delegates to them such power as it deems necessary. These local units are called local governments.

England, France, Japan, SriLanka are examples of Unitary governments.

Definition

Some leading writers defined unitary government as follows:

GARNER: "Where the whole power of government is conferred by the constitution upon a single central organ"

A.V.DICEY: "Habitual exercise of supreme legislative authority is by one central power"

C.F.STRONG mentions two important qualities of the Unitary Government. They are:

1. The supremacy of the central government;
2. The absence of the subsidiary sovereign bodies.

The distinction between subsidiary law-making bodies and subsidiary sovereign bodies is the distinction between the local authorities in a unitary state and state authorities in a federal state.

Merits

1. There is unity, uniformity of law, policy and administration.
2. There is no conflict of authority and responsibility.
3. A unitary government will make prompt decisions and take speedy action.
4. A unitary government is less expensive.
5. Amendments to the constitution are easy.
6. Suitable for small countries.

Demerits

1. The concentration of powers may pave way for the despotism of the central government.
2. The central government will have to tackle so many complex problems that they have no adequate time to devote to local affairs.
3. The central government will not be acquainted with local problems, local interest and initiative.
4. It is not suitable for big countries.

FEDERAL

The term "Federation" is derived from the Latin word "foedus" meaning treaty or agreement – that is agreement between central government (federal government) and the state governments. Prof. Dicey defines federalism as a political contrivance intended to reconcile national unity with the maintenance of state rights.

Federalism is the theory or advocacy of federal political order, where final authority is divided between sub-units and a centre. Unlike a unitary state, sovereignty is constitutionally split between at least two territorial levels so that units at each level have formal authority and can act independently of the others in some area. Citizens thus have political obligations to two authorities. The allocation of authority between the sub-units and centre may vary, typically the centre has powers regarding defence and foreign policy, but sub-units may also have international roles. The sub-units may also participate in central decision-making bodies. Much recent philosophical attention is spurred by renewed political interest in federalism, coupled with empirical findings concerning the requisite and legitimate basis for stability and trust among citizens in federations.

FEATURES OF THE FEDERAL GOVERNMENT

1. The supremacy of the constitution.
2. The division of powers between the central government and state governments.
3. The rigidity of the constitution.
4. The independent judiciary.

PARLIAMENTARY

A parliamentary form of government is that in which the executive is responsible to the legislature. It is also called the cabinet government or responsible government. **Example:** India, United Kingdom (U.K)

Essential features

1. The executive has two types of functions. One is the nominal and the other is the real. The nominal head represents the state. The real head represents the government. In Britain, head of the state is the king or queen. The head of government is the prime minister. Legally all the powers are vested with the nominal head. **Example:** President of India. In practice, all the powers are exercised by the real head Example, cabinet under the leadership of the prime minister of India.
2. The ruling party should have a clear and stable majority in the legislature. In the event of a "hung parliament" a coalition government can also be formed. For example in India during the prime ministership of Mr. Deva Gowda (1996) Mr. I.K. Gujral (1998) we had hung parliament.
3. Head of a cabinet is the leader of the majority party in the legislature. He is the prime minister.
4. The prime minister and the cabinet ministers are selected from among members of parliament.
5. Each minister is responsible to the legislature for the acts of omission and commission of his own department. Likewise, all ministers are collectively responsible to the legislature for the collective policy of the ministry in power.

Merits

1. The most important merit in a parliamentary form of government is the harmony and co-operation between the legislature and the executive.

2. It is flexible and elastic. Whenever there is a crisis, smooth change of government is possible without revolution.
3. Opposition political party offers a constructive criticism of governmental policies.
4. It is responsive to public opinion.

Demerits

1. It is against the theory of separation of powers. When the executive and legislature functions are combined together, there is every likelihood of prime minister becoming more powerful.
2. In the absence of majority, coalition is the only alternative. Coalition government is a weak form of government and may result in political instability.
3. If ruling party resigns from the government or defeated in the elections, the opposition party assumes office of governance. It will reverse all the decisions of the previous government. It means that there is no continuity in policy matters.

PRESIDENTIAL

The presidential form of government is that in which the executive is not responsible to the legislature. **Example:** United States of America (U.S.A)

Essential features

1. The president is the real executive. There is no nominal or ceremonial executive. All the powers are vested in the hands of the president.
2. The powers of the three organs namely, legislature, executive and judiciary are separated and vested in different persons.
3. Though the three organs of the government are kept apart, they are also connected by the system of checks and balances. Each organ of government exercises checks on the other two organs so that a sort of balance is established.
4. The tenure of the president is fixed. The tenure of office cannot be lessened or increased under any circumstances. President can be removed by the legislature only by a process of impeachment.

Merits

1. Stable government is possible.
2. Under a presidential form of government, experts are appointed as heads of the departments without consideration of their party affiliations. The president may appoint persons who belong to the opposition parties.
3. There is continuous and consistent policy.
4. Highly suitable during the period of national crisis.
5. There is no chance for concentration of powers.

Demerits

1. The executive is not responsible to the legislature and can do whatever it pleases.
2. There is always the possibility of deadlocks between the legislature and the executive.
3. It is not flexible form of government.
4. The Presidential executive finds it difficult to follow a vigorous foreign policy, as there is no harmonious relationship between the executive and the legislature. The executive may follow a policy which may not be acceptable to the legislature.

COLLEGIATE

The collegiate or plural executive is one in which the authority is exercised by two or more individuals having co-equal authority. It is a system of government which adopts the merits and discards the defects of both the parliamentary and presidential systems of government. **Example:** Switzerland

The collegiate executive of Switzerland is called the Federal Council. It consists of seven members called councillors. These councillors are elected for a fixed term of four years by the two Houses of the Legislature (Federal Assembly) at a joint sitting. Swiss Government has seven departments and each department is under the control of a councillor. After being elected as the councillor they have to resign their membership in the Federal Assembly. They can be re-elected as many times as possible. The office of the President and the Vice-President of the Federal Council are shared among the councillors on a rotation basis for a one year term. No president can hold office for more than one year.

Merits

1. The collegiate executive of Switzerland is characterized by stability and responsibility.
2. There is no possibility of concentration of powers in a single individual.
3. This type of executive avoids tyranny and dictatorship.
4. The collegiate executive of Switzerland is representative of all opinions and all areas of the country.
5. This type of executive paves the way for continuity and permits traditions to be formed.

Demerits

1. Since the collegiate executive consists of seven members belonging to different political parties, there is unnecessary delay in taking decisions.
2. The members of the federal council belong to various parties. Hence it is difficult to ensure secrecy which is essential for proper functioning of the executive.
3. In this system of government speedy action is possible during emergencies.
4. The executive is organized on plural principle. Hence it is not compatible with unity and independence.

MODERN DICTATORSHIP

The term dictator has been borrowed from ancient Rome. Dictatorship is a form of government. Dictatorship is against democracy. While democracy upholds liberty, dictatorship suppresses liberty. F.NEUMANN says "By dictatorship, we understand the rule of a person, a group of persons who arrogate to themselves and monopolize power in the state, exercising it without restraint."

Features of modern dictatorship

1. Modern dictatorship is one man rule and authoritarian.
2. One party rule – Example: Communist Party–China
3. No individual freedom for people.
4. Wide gulf between dictator and people based on fear and force.

Merits

1. Dictators show a singleness of purpose resulting in efficiency and quick decisions.
2. Cost of administration is low.
3. Dictatorship implies one party, one leader and one programme. National unity and solidarity is the contribution of dictatorship.

Demerits

1. Dictatorship is based on force and fear.
2. People have no rights.
3. Dictators use their energy to realize their selfish aims. The interest of the people will not be taken into consideration.
4. Dictators are for bringing about revolutionary changes.

PUBLIC ADMINISTRATION

GROWTH OF PUBLIC ADMINISTRATION

Public administration has been an integral aspect of civilization since the ages. However, as a discipline, it is of recent origin. About its origin as **Peter Self** points out : ''developed as an offshoot of Political Science or Public Law and until recently, administration as an academic subject was the very plain step-sister of these older discipline.''

Definitions

The term Public Administration has been defined differently by a number of people.

F. Willoughby : "The term administration may be employed in Political Science in two senses. In its broadest sense it denotes the work involved in the actual conduct of governmental affairs, regardless of the particular branch of government concerned. In its narrowest sense, it denotes the operations of the administrative branch only."

D. Waldo : "Public Administration is the art and science of management as applied to the affairs of the State."

M.E. Dimock : "Administration is concerned with 'what' and 'how' of the government. The 'what' is the subject matter, the technical knowledge of a field which enables the administrator to perform his tasks. The 'how' is the technique of management, the principles according to which cooperative programmes are carried to success. Each is indispensable; together they form the synthesis called administration."

John A. Veig : "Administration signifies the organisation, personnel, practices and procedures essential to effective perform of civilian functions entrusted to the executive branch of the government".

P. McQueen : "Public Administration is administration related to the operations of Government whether central or local."

Merson : ''The science of Public Administration is an enquiry as to how policies may best be carried into operation."

Corson and Ham's : "Public Administration is the action part of the government, the means by which the purposes and goals of the government are realized."

F.A. Nigro : "Public Administration (i) is cooperative group effort in a public setting; (ii) covers all the three branches—executive, legislative and judicial, and their inter-relationship; (iii) has an important role in the formulation of public policy and is thus part of the political process; (iv) is different in significant ways from private administration; and (v) is closely associated with numerous private groups and individuals in providing services to the community."

Woodrow Wilson : "Public Administration is detailed and systematic execution of law. Every particular application of law is an act of administration."

L.D. White : "Public Administration consists of all those operations having for their purpose the fulfilment or enforcement of public policy."

Luther Gulick : "Public Administration is that part of the science of administration which has to do with government and thus concerns itself primarily with the executive branch where the work of government is done."

Simon : "By Public Administration is meant in common usage, the activities of the executive branches of the national, state and local government."

J.M. Pfiffner : ''Public Administration consists

of getting the work of government done by coordinating the efforts of the people so that they can work together to accomplish their set tasks."

E.N. Gladden : "Public Administration is concerned with the administration of the government."

H. Walker : "The work which the government does to give effect to a law is called Public Administration."

M. Marc : "Public Administration has come to signify primarily the organization, personnel, practices and procedures essential to effective performance of the civilian functions entrusted to the executive branch of the government."

Origin and Evolution

As an academic discipline it has its origin in the work of Dr. Woodrow Wilson of U.S.A who published an article entitled "The study of Administration" (1887). However, soon after a tortuous and unending debate started on its disciplinary character. It has taken several strides in the form of scientific management movement followed by Human Relations approach of Elton Mayo, decision making approach of Herbert Simon as well as system and structural functional approaches. But Public Administration has been retaining the dynamism with need of the hour. The sources of dynamism have been the actual changes in the real world of governance under the sweeping social changes and the effort of scholars for new conceptual and methodological tools in the discipline. The instances have been such that to some Public Administration is dead and to some the discipline is now full blown and autonomous. For a student of discipline it is logical to analyse the stages of its growth.

PHASES OF EVOLUTION

Broadly speaking there are six phases of its development.

FIRST PHASE—1887–1926

Prof. Woodrow Wilson is said to be the father of discipline. In his article entitled "*The Study of Administration (1887)*", he emphasised the need for a separate study of Public Administration as a distinct from Political Science. He thus initiated Politics-Administration dichotomy which dominated the scene for quite some time. In 1900 Goodnow published his work '*Politics of Administration*' in which he developed this idea further. He said that Politics has to be concerned with the laying down of the policies which administration has to execute. In 1914 American Political Science Association published a report recognising Public Administration as an important sub-area of Political Science. In 1926, L.D. White wrote the first text book on the subject by '*Introduction to the Study of Public Administration.*' It stressed the point that politics and administration are two different activities and the latter has to emphasize efficiency and economy in executing policies.

SECOND PHASE—1927-1937

The dominant theme of the period was principles of Public Administration. The main belief was that there are certain principles of administration and the main thrust was to try to discover them and apply them. In 1927, W.F. Willoughby wrote '*Principle of Administration*' followed by a number of publications, e.g. H. Fayol's '*Industrial and General Management*'; Mooney and Reiley's '*Principles of Organisation*', Mary Parker Foulet's '*Creative Experience*', Gullick and Urwick published '*Papers on Science and Administration*' (1937), they coined the acronym POSDCORB.

Scientific management to efficiently manage the business of administration was emphasized. Politics as practised by politicians became irrelevant structure and process of organisation were put to rigorous analysis.

This period is called the Golden Age of Principles and in this period Public administration achieved high degree of respectability. Its products were in great demand.

THIRD PHASE—1938–1947

The universality of the principles of administration was soon challenged. It was a period of continuous and mounting challenge and questioning.

Chester I. Bernard in his '*The Functions of the Executive*' (1938) did not uphold the stand taken by earlier writers.

Herbert Simon '*The Proverbs of (article) Administration*' (1946) '*Administration Behaviour*' (1947) held that there is no such thing as principles of administration, what have been taken as to be such principles are in fact Proverbs of administration.

In 1947 Robert Dahl also challenged the proposition that Public administration is a science on following grounds :

(a) Science is value-free, but administration can not be so
(b) Human personalities differ
(c) Social framework differ

FOURTH PHASE—1947–1970

This period had been one of crises for the public administration. The brave new world promised by the thinkers of the 'Principles' era stood shattered and future appeared to be little uncertain. The rise of new nations added to the problem.

Many scholars wanted to return to the fold of the mother science viz., Political Science but found that there was domination of Political Science over Administration. They also felt that the political science not only discouraged the appearance of the Public administration as a separate discipline but did not encourage the growth and development of the discipline within its own fold.

Public Administration however enhanced its relation with other disciplines and outcome was

Comparative Public Administration—1952
Development Public Administration—1953

FIFTH PHASE—1970-1990

The scientific or logical positivist approaches robbed public administration of its goal making, welfare and social justice available to the man, woman, children in the course of achieving overall socio-economic development. Outcome was Minnow brook conference in 1968 and the birth of New Public Administration. It was also thought that the generation gap between the practitioner of the Public Administration was also creating a lag.

The term New Public Administration gained greater currency with two publications in 1971, namely.

- "Towards a New Public Administration : Minnowbrook Perspective", edited by **Frank Marini** (1971)
- "Public Administration in a time of Turbulence" edited by **Duright Waldo** (1971)

However, the seeds of these publications can be located in

1. The **Honey Report** of Higher Education for Public Service 1967.
2. The Conference on the Theory and Practice of Public Administration 1967

Chief Features of the New Public Administration : The chief characteristics of New Public Administration are

1. **Relevance :** There had been renewed emphasis on being sensitive to the societal problems. The scholars were of the opinion that Public Administration can not be instrumental in vacuum. Instead it should actively engage itself in the problem confronting society.
2. **Values :** New Public Administration brought values back into the realm of Public Administration. It emphasised on achieving right things in the right way through right techniques.
3. **Equity :** The performance of public administration was to be judged not in terms of growth but it had to be sensitive to the aspect of equity. It had to see that no one was left behind in the affairs tackled by administration.
4. **Change :** As opposed to status quo, the new Public Administration emphasized change. It included reorientation of policy issues and decisions, affecting citizens.

The concept of cutback management was ushered with emphasis on terminating unneeded or ineffective organisation.

An active and participative citizenry is recognised as the benchmark for effective public Administration.

George Frederickson in '*New Public Administration*', 1980 points out "organisations function fundamentally in the realm of values", The New Public Administration was concerned with client 'needs as expectations' as well as assessment of impact of program's effects. This required involvement of values in the policy making process.

Freedom and individual dignity were to be protected through administration.

SIXTH PHASE—1991–TILL TODAY

However the so called NPA movement, which had triggered hopes and aspirations of the Negroes and feminists in America, proved to be monstrously unsuccessful in catering to the expectations of the socially deprived class. At the **Boston Annual Conference** (1987) of the American Society of Public Administration, it was decided to hold Minnowbrook conference II in 1985 to facilitate a general examination of the future of Public Administration and to determine whether important discipline differences exist between people who entered Public Administration in 1960's and those who entered in the 1980's.

Watergate Scandal increased the already existing cyculcism towards government, and propelled the students to think in terms of 'less of government' moves to cut out waste corruption and control over bureaucracy were emphasised. The concept of positive state started giving way to regulatory state.

More privatisation, contracting out more voluntarism, more third party government became watchwords.

In 1994 a conference of **Common Association for Public Administration and Management** in Canada synthesized the foundation of **New Public Management**. It seeks to reorient the public administration to suit the changing dynamics brought about by liberalisation and Globalization. The theoretical formulations of New Public Management were concretized in work of J.V. Ostram "Calculus of a Concept" etc.

THEORIES OF ORGANIZATION

Avasthi and Maheshwari in their work 'Public Administration' holds that "there are three theories of organization.

1. The Classical Theory of Organisation : it includes (a) The Scientific Management Theory (b) The Bureaucratic Theory (c) The Formal Organisation Theory.
2. The Human Relations Theory
3. The Bureaucratic Theory."

THE SCIENTIFIC MANAGEMENT THEORY : F.W. TAYLOR

The Scientific Management Theory is the first systematic theory of organization. It is developed by Fredrick Winslow Taylor (1856-1915) who carried out a well planned research in industrial management.

Prevailing State of Affairs

Taylor found administration or management in his time in a highly unsatisfactory state of development, no better than a haphzard set of **rules of thumb**. There was no standardization of work. The workers were left entirely to themselves. They followed their own method and brought their own equipments. The work in the factory was completely unplanned.

Taylor felt the need for the management to discharge their additional responsibilities and do the work for which it was best suited, such as planning, organising, controlling, determining and co-ordinating.

Taylor is regarded as the father of Scientific Management, for it was he who first advocated the systematic adoption of method of science to the problems of management.

His contribution to the theory has been outlined in following works

- A Piece Rate System (1895)
- Shop Management (1903)
- The Art of Cutting Metals (1906)
- The Principles of Scientific Management (1911)

Philosophy of Management

Taylor's philosophy of Management is based on four basic principles :

1. the development of true science of work;
2. the scientific selection of the workmen;
3. scientific education and development of workmen;
4. intimate and friendly co-operation between the management and the man.

Methods of Research

These principles are accompanied by following methods.

1. **Time and Speed :** Micro analysis of each work.
2. **Functional Foremanship :** Divided working system into 'shop' and 'office' each divided into four parts.
3. **Piece Rate System :** Paying work, not positions.
4. **Standardization of Machines, Work and Procedures :** Use of charts, graphs and direction manuals etc.

Mental Revolution

The goal of scientific management can be achieved only if it is accompanied by a complete 'Mental Revolution.' It includes

1. Take the attention of the work force away from the amount of surplus and go on increasing that amount.
2. Instead of individual judgement/opinion in all matters relating to work, the decision should draw upon the scientifically arrived views.
3. Friendly cooperation between management and work force.

Criticism

1. An efficiency and initiative oriented theory with an overall emphasis on output, it made man a machine in the factory system.
2. In neglects the impact of informal organisation on workers and work environment.
3. Simon in his "Organisation" accuses Taylor of emphasising physiological need only.
4. It has insufficient scientific basis. For, its analysis lacks complete analysis of an enterprise. Rather, it is limited to the level of shop floor activity.
5. According to Marxists, the workers are reduced to be part of factors of production, 'a cog in a wheel.'

Influence and Significance

1. Its emphasis on efficiency as a primarily goal of administration and management has been acknowledged widely.
2. Provided theoretical base for future studies.
3. Its method and techniques were used extensively by Germany, England, France, USSR, Japan in their period of growth.
4. Its values and methods are commensurate with idea for reforms in government and administration.
5. Helped in minimising wastage of resources.

HUMAN RELATION THEORY : ELTON MAYO

The Scientific Management theory emphasised the aspect of efficiency, economy and productivity but lacked analysis of human aspects of the organisation. This aspect was taken care by Human Relation School led by Elton Mayo.

Elton Mayo (1880-1949) is among the foremost administrative thinkers of our time and had enormous influence in the development of industrial sociology and psychology. An Australian by birth, he studied medicine. His work took him to Scotland from where, he returned to his native place, Australia. His most productive period began in 1926 when he accepted associate professorship at the Harward Business School in USA.

In 1927 Mayo launched his famous Hawthorne researches. He spent the evening of his life in England where he died in 1949 at the age of sixty nine.

The term human relations mostly refers to relations between workers and employers which are not regulated by legal norms. These relations are connected with moral and psychological rather than legal factors.

Works : Works of Mayo are

1. *The Human Problems of an Industrial Civilization (1933)*
2. *The Social Problems of Industrial Civilization (1945)*
3. *The Political Problems of Industrial Civilization (1947)*

Hawthorne Experiment

This theory emerged from a number of set of extended experiments conducted by Elton Mayo, Fritz Roethlisberger and others at the Hawthorne plant of the Western Electric Company in Chicago from 1927-32. In all his research programmes Mayo focussed his attention on the behaviour of the workers and their production capacity, keeping in view physiological, physical economic and psychological aspects. He called this approach as **Clinical Method**. The outcome was ably discussed in ''**Management and Workers**'' by Reothlisberger and Dickson (1939).

Findings of Hawthorne Experiment : From the Howthorne experiments following conclusions were drawn

(i) Productivity is affected not by physical stamina and strength but by social and psychological factors.
(ii) Non-Economic regards and sanctions are significant determinants of the employee's motivation and job satisfaction.
(iii) Basing division of work too stringently on specialisation is not necessarily the most efficient approach.
(iv) Employees may react to the management and work itself as members of the formal organization rather than as individuals.

Mayo's Concerns

Mayo's central concern is to treat workers as human beings. The results of the experiment indicated that when great attention was paid to the employees as a human beings, it increased his self-esteem driving him to work more. It proved further that the employees socialise with one another and formed groups which Mayo called '**Informal Organisations.**'

The Hawthorne experiment proved that men are not inert and isolated creature. On the contrary, they react in their own way. These studies proved that an organisation was also a social systems, a group of people behaving.

Criticism

1. Loren Baritz and others have criticized Mayo and Human Relationists for being anti-union and pro-management.
2. Peter Drucker attacked Human Relationists for their lack of awareness of economic dimension.
3. Daniel Shell dubbed the methodology of Human Relationists as defective. ''They displayed a lack of awareness of larger social and technical systems.''
4. W.H. Whyte accuses Mayo for encouraging employers to interfere in the private lives of individual workers.

Influence/Significance of Human Relations Theory

1. Mayo emphasises that non-economic rewards and sanctions are significant determinants of workers motivation and job satisfaction has been accepted in many quarters.
2. His contention that socio-psychological factors influence productivity can not be denied.
3. Informal organisation of workers have crucial bearing on the relationship between management and work force is illuminating aspect in administrative studies.

MAYO AND TAYLOR : A COMPARISON

F.W. Taylor and Elton Mayo who represent the two schools of thought to solve the industrial problems shared some attributes but differed in others.

Similarities

1. Both saw cooperation as a medium to resolve the conflict between workers and management.
2. Both laid emphasis on higher productivity.
3. Both believe in the capacity of elite to bring harmony and increase production.
4. Both were interested in efficiency and increased production. So they discovered the causes of obstruction and ways to overcome it.
5. Both approach the aspect of management with the tool of Science.

Differences :

Taylor	Mayo
1. Focussed on individual as a worker	1. Focussed on worker as a group member
2. Not concerned with interpersonal relations	2. Mayoists were more concerned with the interpersonal relations
3. Neglected the psychological and social variable of organizational behaviour	3. Psychological and social variables are the cornerstone of Human Relation Theory
4. Regarded economic reward as the crucial motivating factor	4. Discouraged the lure of money and stressed group membership
5. Regarded worker as completely hostile to management	5. Did not think so.

FORMAL THEORY : FAYOL AND OTHERS

Henri Fayol (1841-1925) has been the main advocate of Formal Theory, also known as the Mechanistic Theory or the Structural theory of Organization. He started his career as a French mining engineer and for some time acted as a Chief Executive. He was awarded **Nobel Prize in 1921.** His famous work is "*General and Industrial Management* (1916)."

Elements of Organization

According to Fayol there are six elements in an organization.

1. Technical (Manufacture/Production)
2. Commercial (Buying and Selling)
3. Financial (Provision of Capital)
4. Security (Safeguarding/protection of property)
5. Accounts (including statistics)
6. Management (planning, organizing, commanding, coordinating and controlling)

But, he laid emphasis on the Managerial activity as the most important activity in the organisation.

Principles of Organization

Fayol listed fourteen principles of organization that are as follows :

1. **Division of Work :** It promotes specialization and enables a person to acquire an ability and accuracy by which he can do more work with the same effort.
2. **Authority and Responsibility :** According to Fayol authority and the responsibility go hand in hand. Authority is not to be conceived apart from responsibility and wherever authority is exercised responsibility arises.
3. **Discipline :** It involves obedience by employees. To Henri Fayol, discipline constituted one of the significant principles for an organization. The disciplinary attitude of the workers in their work, helps in reducing time for the completion of work i.e. it increases efficiency as well as the quality of the work. It depends upon good supervision, clear and free agreements, and judicious application of penalties.
4. **Unity of Command :** Every subordinate should receive orders and be accountable to only one superior. Dual or multiple command is a perpetual source of conflict. It undermines authority, puts discipline in jeopardy.
5. **Unity of Direction :** According to this, each group of activity having same objective must have one head and one plan. This principle, seeks to ensure unity of action. It refers to the functioning of the corporate department.
6. **Subordination of Individual Interest :** Although it is true that individual interest can never be sacrificed, but for Fayol they should be minimised and should not prevail over the

interest of the organization as it hampers the growth and success of the organisation in every possible way. Group interest should be subordinated to the common good.

7. **Remuneration of Personnel :** The amount of remuneration and the methods of payment should be just and fair and should provide maximum possible satisfaction to both employees and employers.
8. **Centralisation :** For Fayol, there should be centralisation in an organization. Its objective is to promote the optimum utilisation of all faculties of the personnel.
9. **Scalar Chain :** Henri Fayol, favoured the idea of scaler chain in a organization. According to him, division of authority should follow hierarchical structure.
10. **Order :** There should be order and peace in an organisation as it ensures an environment where workers can perform their task most efficiently and effectively in an organisation, there should be a place for everything and everyone. This kind of order requires precise knowledge of human requirements and resources of the concern so that balance may be created between them.
11. **Equity :** It implies that employees should be treated with justice and kindness. Administrators should be fair and impartial in their dealings with subordinates. They should adopts sympathetic and unbiased attitude towards workers. It helps to create cordial relation between Administration and workers.
12. **Stability of Tenure of Personnel :** The tenure of a personnel should be stable if not fixed as it creates a feeling of responsibility in them. Moreover, if the personnel are removed from their post more frequently, it destabilises the whole organisational set up. An employee can never render worthwhile service if he is removed from the job before he gets accustomed.
13. **E-spirit-de-corps :** This refers to the harmony and mutual understanding among the members of an organisation. Administration should maintain team spirit and co-operation among employees. Unity among the personnel can be developed through proper communication and coordination.
14. **Initiative :** It refers to the freedom to think for one-self and use of discretion in doing work. It develops the interest of employees in their job and provides job satisfaction to them.

To facilitate his idea of principles to be adopted by various organisations, Fayol stressed the need for the management teaching and training in schools and universities.

Henri Fayol described certain qualities of good managers :

1. Physical Fitness (health, vigour, address)
2. Mental Alertness (Judgement, adaptability)
3. Moral part of character (loyalty, tact willingness to accept responsibility)
4. General education
5. Special Knowledge
6. Experience

Other Contribution to Formal Theory of Organizations

Later on contributions came from other thinkers like Mooney, Urwick and Luther Gullick. Mooney in his books "*Onward Industry.*" "*The principles of Management*" described various principles of Administration but is different from Urwick.

A significant contribution to the classical theory was made by Luther Gullick and L. Urwick in their "Papers on the Science of Administration" (1937). They considered organization as a machine. In their quest to find out universal principles of administration, they outlined seven such principles widely known by acronym POSDCORB. It includes

Planning : outlining things to be done and methods to achieve the purpose of the organization.

Organization : arranging work through the use of formal authority.

Staffing : recruiting and training the staff.

Directing : framing general rules and implementing them as leader.

Coordinating : interrelating the various parts of work.

Reporting : informing the subordinates.

Budgeting : fiscal planning, accounting and control.

TAYLOR & FAYOL : A COMPARISON

Taylor	Fayol
1. His analysis was mainly concerned with the shop floor management	Mainly interested in the management or the top level of the Organization
2. More concerned with inventing methods and tools to increase the efficiency and productivity	More concerned with outlining general principles of Management
3. Study was based on scientific observation	Study was based on commonsense and personal experience
4. Contributes for micro level	Contributes at Macro level

Criticism

1. The theory holds a mechanistic view of organization. Wherein individual is like a cog in the organisational machine.
2. It is atomistic and ignores the environment and role of group lives in shaping individual motivations.
3. Some of the principles are contradictory in themselves. The principle of unity of command conflict with principle of Division of Work.
4. It does not take note of any non-economic incentive.

BUREAUCRATIC THEORY

The word 'Bureaucracy' was coined by **Mr. Vincent de Gournay** (1712-59), an eminent French economist. But, a systematic treatment of the term was done by **Gaetano Mosca**, '*The Ruling class.*' He regarded Bureaucracy as fundamental to all great empires and classified political systems either as feudal or bureaucratic. Later on Karl Marx, Roberto Michels and Max Weber widened use of the term 'Bureaucracy.'

Definition of Bureaucracy

According to Weber "**bureaucracy is a sociological concept meant for the rationalistic organization of collective life.**"

Influences on Weber : He was influenced by following events.

1. Unification of Germany
2. Rapid Industrialization
3. Expansion of state activities in welfare provisions

However, Weber saw it as a universal phenomenon. To him, "with the growing complexity of the modern life, there is only one form of organization and that is bureaucracy. There can be no escape from it."

Characteristics of Bureaucracy

1. **Impersonality :** The official staff members are personally free, observing only the impersonal duties of their offices.
2. **Hierarchy :** There is a clear hierarchy of offices. The functions of the offices are clearly specified.
3. **Permanence :** The officials are appointed on the basis of a contract.
4. **Expertise :** The officials are selected on the basis of contract qualifications, ideally substantiated by a diploma gained through competitive examination.
5. **Money Salaries :** They have a money salary and usually pension rights. The salary is graded according to position in the hierarchy.
6. **Rules :** The official can always leave the past and under certain circumstances can also be terminated if violates the terms of contract.
7. **Exclusiveness :** The officials post is his role or major occupation.
8. **Career System :** There is a career structure, and promotion is possible either by seniority or merit, and according to the judgement of superiors.
9. **Discipline and Control :** The official may appropriate neither the post nor the resources that go with it. He is subject to unified control and disciplinary system.

Criticism

1. Robert K. Merton accuses Weber of making ''rules more important than the game.'' This leads to rigidity, formalism and even ritualism.
2. Michel Crozier, ''The Bureaucratic Phenomenon'' characterized bureaucracy as a rigid organization that can not correct its behaviour by learning from its errors.
3. David Beetham ''Max Weber and The Theory of Modern Politics'' points out that Weber concept of bureaucracy :
   Firstly, is only a technical instrument and nothing more.
   Secondly, has inherent tendency to usurp the goal setting function which belongs to area of politics.
   Thirdly, reflects the class structure of the society.
4. Robert Presthms holds that Weberian model is a product of alien culture, not suitable for the developing societies.
5. F.W. Riggs said that Weber's ''Ideal type'' construct of Bureaucracy assumes a relatively autonomous system. This is not suitable for developing societies because here administrative structures are intricately dependent on the social structure.
6. Carl Friedrich holds that ''Weber sets forth his ideal types as mental construct which are neither derived from a process of deductive rationalisation from higher concepts, nor built up from empirical data by relevant inference, non-demonstrably developed as working hypotheses from such data.''

Influence/Significance of Bureaucratic Theory

1. Aspect of universality has been proved.
2. Its aspect of selection/recruitment through merit, technical qualifications, impersonality have been widely appreciated and implemented.
3. Present day bureaucracy reflects almost all chief characteristics of Weberian model.
4. Provide theoretic base for future enquiry in the realm of administration.

PRINCIPLES OF ORGANISATION

Despite lack of agreement on the relative importance of different principles of organization, various writers agree that there are certain fundamental principles underlining the organizational lives.

Definitions

Pfiffner : "Organisation consists of the relationship of individual to individuals and of group to groups which are so related to bring about an orderly division of labour."

L.D. White : "Organisation is the arrangement of personnel for facilitating the accomplishment of some agreed purpose through allocation of functions and responsibilities."

Chester Barnard : "Organisation is a system of consciously coordinated activities or forces of two or more persons."

J.M. Gaus : "Organisation is the relating of efforts and capacities of individuals and groups engaged upon a common task in such a way as to secure the desired objective with the least friction and the most satisfaction for whom the task is done and the engaged in the enterprise."

Mooney : "Organisation is the form of every human association for the attainment of a common purpose."

Simon : "By organisation we mean a planned system of cooperative effort in which each participant has a recognised role to play and duties and tasks to perform."

Gulick : "Organisation is the formal structure of authority through which work sub-divisions are arranged, defined and coordinated for the defined objective."

Gladden : "Organisation is concerned with the pattern of relationships between persons in an enterprise, so constructed as to fulfil the enterpriser's function."

What are Principles?

In essence, the principles are not fixed laws but inductive generalizations drawn from a large number of administrative phenomenon. They have become inevitable in studies on administration. There are various reasons for their continued importance. Koontz and O'Donell give following reasons :

- To increase organizational efficiency
- To crystallize the nature of organizations job
- To improve research in organization
- To attain social goals

Different Views

According to Gullick and Urwick, Fayol, Willoughby and others "there are some general principles which can be taken as more or less proven truths."

Simon held that principles are nothing but proverbs of administration.

L.D. White felt that they are only working rules with wide experience seem to have validated.

Different Principles : Some of the important principles of organization are, Hierarchy, Span of Control, Unity of Command, Integration and Disintegration, Authority and Responsibility, etc.

HIERARCHY : As a Principle of Organization

Hierarchy has been a hallmark of all organizations in modern age. According to L.D. White "Hierarchy consists in the universal application of the superior-subordinate relationship through a number of levels of responsibility reaching from the top to the bottom of structure." It means the control of higher over the lower. Mooney also calls it a "Scalar Principle of Organisation."

Chief Features :

Features of hierarchy are

Firstly, exhibit division of administration into units and sub-units.

Secondly, pyramidal structure with wide base, tapering towards the top.

Thirdly, flow of command and authority from top to bottom.

It can be depicted as

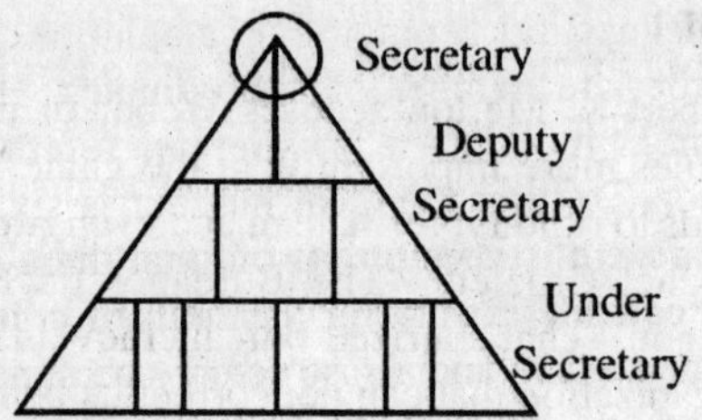

Merits

Advantages of Hierarchy are

1. Replaces chaos by order and consensus.
2. Provides channel of communication.
3. Makes clear cut division of authority and responsibility.
4. Promotes specialization and division of labour.
5. Facilitates smooth delegation of authority.

Demerits

Disadvantage of Hierarchy are

1. Creates rigidity and formalism not sensitive to dynamic aspect.
2. Plagued by Rep-tapism.
3. Ill feelings of Superior and subordinates.

SPAN OF CONTROL : As a Principle of Organization

Span of control is a necessary corollary to the principle of Hierarchy. It simply means the number of subordinates that an administrator can personally direct. According to Dimock, "the span of control is the number and range of direct, habitual communication contacts between the chief executive of an enterprise and his fellow officers." However, there is no unanimity among the scholars as regards the length of the span or the number of subordinates an individual can direct.

Different Views

For Urvey—Five

Hamilton—Six

J.C. Worthy—Twenty

Dale—Sixteen

Graicunas did geometrical calculations to find the appropriate number of subordinates. He gave the formula in ($2^{n-1}+n^{-1}$) where n refers to the supervisor. To him, the ideal number is six.

The recent studies points out that there can not be clear cut rule governing the span of control. In fact, organization and its structure, personality of supervisor and his function has crucial bearing in this respect.

The revolution in the realm of science and technology and new communication and media networks have facilitated the greater span of control. Similarly, new methods of techniques of persuasion, bargaining, threat of penalty are increasingly being used. The growth of managerial sciences have also facilitated this trend.

UNITY OF COMMAND : As a Principle of Organization

The principle of unity of command is a tool to underline everyone's responsibility in the organization. It addresses the issue of confusion and conflict by clearly outlining the command system. Pfiffner and Presthus hold that "The concept of unity of command requires that every member of an organisation should report to one and only one leader." Fayol points out that the principle of unity of command means that "an employee in the organization should receive orders from one superior only."

Different Views

Henri Fayol is the **staunch advocate** of the principle of unity of command. A violation of the principle results in uneasiness in the organization. The principle of dual control can not be effective. If things are done otherwise, either the dual control is removed or the organization suffers.

F.W. Taylor preferred the principle of dual or multiple supervision. He favoured a worker's supervision by eight persons.

Contemporary Reality

The reality of duality and multiplicity command is often found in operation. Seckler and Hudson point out that "...the old concept of one single boss for each person is seldom found...the administrator in government has many bosses and he can neglect none of them. From one he may receive policy orders; from another, personnel; from third, budget; from the fourth, supplies and equipments."

Perhaps the best view is summed up by Herbert Simon. Though, he recognized the need of dual supervision, he favoured unity of common. For, it would resolve the conflict arising out of duality.

The contemporary realities are in favour of multiplicity of common. Its best example is the office of collector. This need not threaten the organization as long as a worker does not receive dual or multiple command on the same subject.

INTEGRATION AND DISINTEGRATION : As a Principle of Organization

Integration means unification of different parts. An integrated administrative system is one where a single person wields all executive authority. On the other hand, a disintegrated administrative system is marked by distribution of executive authority.

Contemporary Reality

Administrative system of all shades exhibits the characteristics of both; integration and disintegration. The difference between the two is of degree rather than of kind. While India offers a good example of integrated system, United States has a disintegrated administrative system.

Merits

However, the integrated system has certain advantages that are summed up by Willoughby

1. correlates various services into one.
2. provides effective administration.
3. makes authority and responsibility clear.
4. helps in achieving cooperation among those working in the same field.
5. helps in eliminating duplication of efforts.
6. facilitates standardization of all administrative processes.

7. furnishes means by which conflicts of jurisdiction may be avoided or adjusted.

Growth of administration together with continued stress on administrative machinery demands unified efforts. For, independent agencies, it created, may be more interested in catering to vested interest, the aspect of performance and reforms.

THE CHIEF EXECUTIVE

All nations are governed by administrative system wherein chief executive remains at the top of the hierarchy.

Form of government : there are two types: one is chief executive (real and titular) and other is presidential system marked by a single executive vested with all executive powers.

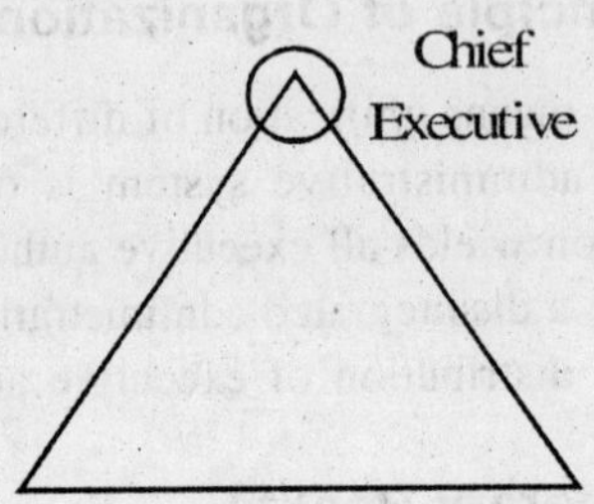

Collegiate Type of Chief Executive operators in Switzerland is a mix of parliamentary and Presidential model, wherein seven members of the Federal council executive function on rotation basis.

Functions of Chief Executive

The major functions of the Chief Executive in the area of administration are as follows (mainly as listed by L.D. White).

1. Formulation of Policies :- Besides being master of most the policy issues in the legislature (as in parliamentary system) or influencing the members of Congress (as in Presidential System), the process of delegated legislation has enormously increased the function of Chief Executive.
2. Create Organizations and Outline its Structure:- While Presidential Chief Executive has feeble power of creating smaller agencies and merge them with others, cabinet wields more power in this respect.
3. Personnel Administration: All administrative officials are appointed and dismissed by the Chief Executive, President of U.S.A. has more power than cabinet of Parliamentary system. In Parliamentary system there are constitutional arrangement for appointment and removal of some public officials.
4. Commands Administration: A number of directives, proclamations, orders are bound to comply with the statutory enactments.
5. Investigation and Enquiries: In order to check abuse of power and malpractices of administration, a number of attempts are undertaken by the Chief Executive.
6. Budgetary responsibilities: In Parliamentary system the titular head causes the budget to be laid before the Parliament. But, in Presidential System Congress had the budgetary responsibility.
7. Coordination: In order to ensure efficient and effective functioning of the administrative structure, the Chief Executive has vital task of coordinating activities of various department.

Luther Gullick: has used the acronym 'POSDCORB' to describe the administrative functions of the Chief Executive.

1. P= Planning-It means that the Chief Executive will select objectives and the actions to achieve them.
2. O=Organizing-It involves establishing structures for administrative tasks. His aim is to create an environment for human performance.
3. S=Staffing-It involves recruitment, training appraising of personnel and creating congenial environment for their working.
4. D=Directing-It involves leadership role on the part of Chief Executive to see that the work is done in sure with the expectations of the plan.
5. CO=Cordinating-It involves reconciliatory task so as to avoid confrontation, duplication of efforts. It is the essence of administration.

6. R=Reporting- It involves regular appraisal of works through research and supervision.
7. B= Budgeting-It involves a crude financial functions wherein he/she is directly involved.

Evaluation of the Role of Chief Executive

Thus, a lot of functions have been entrusted in the hands of the Chief Executive. The dynamics of his functions have become more complex in recent times. He discharges these functions aptly with a large number of officials. In this way the Administrative Organization has the counting functions. Nevertheless there always remains tough tasks before the Chief Executive because he does not simply have to administer but also to see new others to administer.

Suggestion to the Chief Executive

Donald C. Stone in "New Horizons in Public Administration. A symposium " provides a list of suggestions to the Chief Executive. These include.

Firstly, To create an environment conducive to convert effort in pursuing the objectives of the organization.

Secondly, No interference of the heads in decision making at lower levels of the organization for which different officials are responsible,

Thirdly, Act in economical fashion even if they have a large grant of legal authority,

Fourthly, He should be aware of activities in the organization and to be in position to act on the issues which require his personal attention

Fifthly, To act predominantly as a catalyst in the works of the department.

Sixthly, To have sufficient knowledge of the programmes so as to command the loyalty and respect of the specialists and lead them together as a team.

L. D. Lipson in an article "Being an Executive" recommends following attributes on the part of an executive.

Firstly, Being objective and broadminded,

Secondly, keeping the lives of authority straight,

Thirdly, having people who are smarter than him

Fourthly, Avoid handling details by himself.

R.S. Dawar in his "Creative Leadership" has listed following qualities of a successful executive. They are :

1. Courageous: It signifies "readiness to do a thing because he believes it to be right, without paying much attention to the consequences"
2. Will Power:
3. Emotional stability:
4. Independent:
5. Knowledge:
6. Decisiveness and Initiative:

Different Kind of Chief Executive

Parliamentary	Presidential
1. Real Chief Executive is the Prime Minister.	1. Single Chief Executive is the President.
2. Members of the Cabinet are colleagues of the P.M.	2. Secretaries of respective (fourteen) departments are subordinates of the President. There is spoil system in America.
3. Operates on the principle of collective responsibility of ministers to the Lower House of the Parliament.	3. Secretaries are appointed and can be removed by the President.
4. Chief Executive is drawn from the Parliament.	4. President is elected separately (from the members of legislature.
5. Operates on the system of fusion of power between the executive and legislature	5. Operates on the principle of separation of power.

LINE, STAFF & AUXILIARY AGENCY

Though the administration of every country is carried on by the Chief Executive, he is assisted by a number of subordinates. The Chief Executive delegates his powers to team who carry out the function under his name. Nevertheless, the supreme power of supervision, direction and control remains in the hands of the Chief Executive.

The organizational system of government consists of the line, staff of the Auxiliary agencies. The concept of line and Staff originated in the realm of military Services. The line is directly linked with administrative programmes. The Staff provides specialized advice but does not command. Auxiliary Staff provides service to both, the line and Staff. The line agencies are central elements of any administrative system; Staff and auxiliary agencies are necessary in a large and complex organization, but they are secondary.

The Line

They are the backbone of administrative machinery. It signifies an unbroken vertical line through which authority flows from the top to the bottom of organization.

L.D. White in his "Introduction to the Study of Public Administration" has outlined following essential functions of line agencies

1. Making decisions.
2. Taking responsibility.
3. Interesting and depending policy and operations
4. Planning.
5. Maintaining production while seeking both, economy and efficiency.

Features of the Line Agencies

1. Associated with primary functions.
2. Vertical organization.
3. Reduction of authority from top to bottom.
4. Concerned with decision making.
5. Issues commands.
6. Close personal contacts between officials.
7. Every person is in the direct claim of command.
8. Delegation of authority from top to bottom.

Types of Line Agencies

1. **The Department:** An homogeneous unit where work is concentrated. It is a division, branch or regiment immediately below the Chief Executive into which entire work of the government is divided.

   U.S.A. : There are 13 departments headed by a Secretary.

   U.K. : The number of department is not fixed. It is coterminons with ministry.
2. **The Public Corporation:** A statutory body created for the purpose of effective organization. As Marshall E. Dimock defines, "Public corporation is a public owned enterprise that has been chartered under federal, State or local law for a particular business or financial purpose". Its rise is closely connected with the growing complexity of modern governments. However there remains a problem of concern 'Autonomy' and 'Control' of public corporations.
3. **The Independent Regulatory Commissions:** A body created to assist the heads of administration which remains relatively autonomous. They perform both; quasi-legislative and quasi-Judicial functions and remain independent from the executive control. They are a peculiar feature of the American Administrative System.

The Staff

The Staff comprises those agencies of the administrative system that support the line agencies. They do not initiate or decide the matter. It is essentially the extension of the Chief Executive himself, carrying on for him those functions which he would do himself, if he had the time.

Features of the Staff

1. Assist rather than command.
2. No power of decision making.
3. Secondary functions.
4. No direct dealings, remains in the background.
5. Purely advisory character.
6. Always attached to the line.

Kinds of Staff

A.R. Tyagi in his 'Public Administration' categorises following staff agencies:

1. General Staff.
2. Technical Staff.
3. Auxiliary Staff.

U.S.A. : White House, National Security Council.

U.K.: Cabinet Office, Civil Service Department under-PMO, Planning Commission.

The Auxiliary: They are the operating agencies concerned mainly with the maintenance of an existing organization. While Staff agencies are concerned with thinking, planning and advisory functions, auxiliary agencies are not concerned with the major substantive functions.

Willoughby called them "house keeping services".

Differences between Line & Staff Agencies

Line	Staff
1. Decide and Command	1. Does not command, only assist and advice.
2. Primary agencies.	2. Secondary agencies.
3. Directly involved	3. Involved in assistance
4. Act	4. Thinks
5. Functional agency	5. Institutional agency.
6. Follow clear cut organization of authority from top to bottom.	6. Organization is not in a straight line.
7. Responsible.	7. Not responsible.

CONTROL OVER ADMINISTRATION

Every form of democratic government have envisaged scheme/mechanisms to exercise control over administration. The task of administration remains in the hand of executive branch. The legislative and judicial branch have developed tools to ensure that the administration is accountable. The growth of administrative functions has made the aspect of control more complex and interesting. For, in place of erstwhile self-sufficient rural communities, today government is called upon to perform a number of functions connected with providing say, birth registration to death certificate.

LEGISLATIVE CONTROL OVER ADMINISTRATION

The basic principle underlying modern democracies is the sovereignty of the people. But, in real practice the representatives are elected by the people to safeguard their interests. The representatives compose the legislature. So, the measure of legislative control over administrative has democratic sentiment and is more effective.

In a Parliamentary democracy, the Executive is drawn from the Parliament. In the Presidential form, there is clear cut separation of Executive and legislative branch. Thus, the exercise of control is more warranted in Parliamentary system.

Measures of Legislative Control

Some of the important measures of legislative control are as follows :

1. **Control of Administrative Policy :** Legislation is the most important function of legislature. By laying down rules through legislative enactments, the legislatures limit as well as influence the authority and policies of the government.
2. **Control of Appropriations :** The executive is at the mercy of legislature for all aspects of revenue and expenditure. No revenue can be levied nor can any expenditure incurred without the sanction of the legislature. Moreover, the budgetary discussion provides opportunity to the representatives of the people to criticize the government on aspects that are unwarranted.

   It is the most effective means of legislative control over executive.
3. **Audit and Report :** In India, the report of CAG (Comptroller and Auditor General) of India helps exercising legislative control. CAG audits all government accounts to ensure that the money has been spent on items for which it was granted and does not exceed the sanctioned amount.

4. **Parliamentary Questions :** The proceeding of the Parliament start with one hour duration question answer session. Wherein the minister of respective department gives reply to query of members. The effectiveness of this measure is highlighted by Mr. Atlee, who observes that "I always consider that question time in the house is one of the finest examples of real democracy."
5. **Zero hour discussion :** Zero hour discussion is an extra regular method that is entirely an Indian innovation since 1962. It is invoked after question hour (with the consent of presiding officer) to incite opinions on matter of public importance which have not been listed in days business.
6. **Calling Attention Motion :** This device is used to bring the matters of urgent importance on the floor of the house.
7. **Short Notice Discussion :** Short notice discussion is a discretion of the speaker in case of matters which does not satisfy a member's question. It is resorted only with the consent of the government, not otherwise.
8. **Adjournment Motion :** A device to raise discussion on any specific question of an urgent nature. However, this device is usually not preferred by the speaker.
9. **Debates and Discussion :** Apart from the measures cited above, there are a number instances that provide opportunity to members to discuss and debate on government policies.
   - inaugural speech of the President
   - budget speech of the Finance Minister
   - general discussion on the budget
   - full scale discussion of Government policies.
10. **Parliamentary Committees :** There are a number of committees that help exercise legislative control over executive. They are as follows :

- Public Accounts Committee (PAC)
  - examines report of CAG
  - submits its report to the lower House
- Estimates Committee
  - scrutinizes the government expenditure before they are included in the budget.
  - carries its examination throughout the year and helps in checking extravagance.

Besides these two, there are other committees which help the legislature in exercising control over administration.

Limitations Highlighted by Appleby

Appleby observed that these measures are not so effective in exercising proper control over administration. He supports his view on following grounds.

- Report of CAG is of no relevance because it is merely concerned with technical aspect of financial irregulary.
- Influence of rich businessmen.
- Discussion are mainly against civil servants which does not inculcate healthy habits in them.

Other Limitations

1. Delegated Legislation
2. Decreasing private members bill
3. Party politics
4. Cabinet dictatorship
5. Lack of technical knowledge on the part of representatives as regards financial administration.

JUDICIAL CONTROL OVER ADMINISTRATION

The judicial control over administration is exercised mainly with view to ensure legality of administrative acts. In this way, it helps in protecting citizens and their right which may otherwise be in danger or prone to encroachment.

Methods of Judicial Control

The judicial control may take following forms.

1. **Judicial Review :** The Judicial system of different countries show variance in the realm of judicial review. While in U.S.A. judiciary is supreme and has absolute power of judicial review, in the United Kingdom the power of judicial review is very limited. In India, the courts do not intervene with administrative

acts as long as it is ultra-vires of its scope and form.

2. **Statutory Appeals :** Statutes are legal enactments of the legislature. They authorize an institution (Court or Tribunal) to intervene in particular cases of administrative acts. Under this provision an appeal shall lie to the concerned authority if the violation as said to have occurred.
3. **Suits against Government :** According to Article 300 of the Indian Constitution provides that the state is enable.
4. **Suits against Public officials :** President and Governors are conferred immunity in exercise of their power and duties. Almost similar is the case with judicial officials. As regards other officials, there is provision of two months notice in civil proceedings and previous sanction of the President or Governor in Criminal proceedings is to be obtained.
5. **Extraordinary Remedies :** The Constitution empowers the courts to provide extraordinary remedies in case of violation of administrative acts and misuse of office by way Writ Jurisdiction. Such powers are conferred on the Supreme Court by Article 32(2) and on the High Courts by Article 226.

Habeas Corpus

It means 'You shall produce the body.' It is an order issued to a person detaining another and commanding him to produce the body of the prisoner at a certain time and place. The purpose is to determine whether the person seeking remedy is denailed legally or illegaly. They are mainly directed to safeguard and put an end to arbitrary imprisonment.

Mandamus : 'Command'

Used for compelling Public officials and Judicial bodies to carry out their legal duties. Issued also against inferior court and quasi-judicial bodies.

Prohibition : Issued by a Superior Court to an inferior court, preventing the latter from usurping jurisdiction which the law does not endow it with. Helps in controlling tribunals.

Certiorari : 'To be certified' Issued only against some judicial act. The main difference between centiorari and prohibition is that the former is both negative and positive, whereas the latter is only preventive.

Quo-Warranto : 'What warrant or authority.' It is an ancient law writ. Its purpose is to usurps from public office. It can be issued by a petitioner who has certain interest.

However, it is to be observed that the writ jurisdiction of High Court is wider than the Supreme Court. The former can issue writs for legal rights as well, which is not under the competence of the Supreme Court.

Limitations

1. Court intervene only after the damage has been done.
2. Very costly involving technicalities
3. Court can not intervene on their own.

BUREAUCRACY

Bureaucracy is an important ingredient of contemporary public life. It refers to an administrative organization which is concerned with execution of governmental programmes and policies. The growth and complexity of governmental function has contributed to the rise of bureaucracy. To a large extent, it has become a universal phenomenon.

Definitions

Max Weber : "Bureaucracy is a sociological concept meant for the rationalistic organization of collective life."

Harold Laski : "is a system of government, the control of which is completely in the hands of officials that jeopardizes the liberty of ordinary citizens."

Carl J. Friedrick : "is a form of organization marked by hierarchy, specialization of roles and a high level of competence displayed by incumbents trained to feel these roles".

Morstein Marx : "...has several unmistakable characteristics. They include as principal factors hierarchy, jurisdiction, specialization, professional training, fixed compensation and performance."

Gladden : Bureaucracy is "the government by officers."

MacIver : Bureaucracy is "a system of administration characterised by the lack of expertise, impartiality and humanism."

Arthur K. Davis : An "integrated hierarchy of specialised offices defined by the systematic rules-an impersonal routinised structure where legitimatised authority rests in the office and not in the person of the incumbents."

Peter M. Blau and Marshal W. Mayer : "Organisation designated to accomplish large scale administrative tasks by systematically coordinating the task of many individuals."

The term "bureaucracy" was first coined by **Vincent de Gourney**, a French economist in 1746. As F.M. Marx observes "The term bureaucracy which was first used in the French form 'bureaucratic' by a French minister of Commerce in the eighteenth century to refer to the government in operation, spread to Germany during the nineteenth century as 'Burokratic' and has since found its way into English and many other languages". He also identifies four kinds of bureaucracy, indicating its existence even in earlier times. These are as follows :

1. Guardian Bureaucracy
   (a) Chinese—till the Sung period before 960 A.D.
   (b) Prussian—1640 to 1740 A.D.
2. Cast Democracy
3. Patronage Bureaucracy
4. Merit Bureaucracy

Though the credit for systematic enunciation of the concept of bureaucracy goes to Max Weber, there were others who dealt implicitly with the concept. **Robert Michels** in his work '*Political Parties*' envisioned the possibility of organizations turning oligarchic which essentially signified concentration of power in the hands of a few. Similarly **Gaetand Mosca** in his "*Ruling Class*" identified two kinds of political systems viz., feudal and bureaucratic. To him, bureaucracy is a "class of ruling elites whose power is absolute.

Max Weber identified following causes for the rise of bureaucracy in modern times. These include

1. **Creation of Money Economy :** It ensured a secure and regular salaries to the bureaucrats leading to a permanent organization.
2. **Emergence of Capitalist Economy :** The prime principles of capitalism—rationality—dictates bureaucratic form of organization.
3. **Growth of Population :** It dictates larger organizations having tendency of assuming bureaucratic form.
4. Development of modern means of Communication.
5. **Emergence of Complex administrative problems :** It required expertise and competence in the organization favouring bureaucracy.
6. **Growth of Democratic Institutions :** The downfall of feudal elements and encouragement of merit based system of functional rationality dictated bureaucratic organizations.

Mohit Bhattacharya identifies two set of characteristic of Weberian model. They are

1. Structural—
   (a) division of work.
   (b) hierarchy.
   (c) system of rules.
2. Behavioural—
   (a) rationality.
   (b) impersonality.
   (c) rule orientation.
   (d) neutrality.

Karl Marx developed his views on bureaucracy in his confrontation with the Prussian state. In his 'Rheinische Zetung' he denounced the bureaucracy as a smoke screen between the exploiters and exploited. It served as an instrument of dominant class for the exploitation of the dependent class. It was an instrument of class rule at the hands of the bourgeoisie. He did not favoured its retention in a socialist stage. In the communist society, social and economic inequality will be eliminated, class difference will be resolved and there won't be a need for this institution.

BUREAUCRACY IN THIRD WORLD: ITS SUITABILITY TO DEVELOPMENT ADMINISTRATION

1. It becomes dysfunctional.
2. Weber talks about rule oriented bureaucracy whereas Development Administration demands flexibility and innovativeness.
3. Bureaucracy is the instrument of socio-economic transformation it wields, greater power. Hence, it becomes authoritarian in long run.
4. Written produces hierarchy etc. make the decision making a delatory process.
5. No neutrality, transfers and posting have become means in the hands of politicians to compel the bureaucracy to do something as desired by them and hence neutrality can not be brought about.
6. Over bureaucratisation, state quiest and unnecessary political interference have nullified the very concept of bureaucracy as an instrument of social change.
7. Bureacracy comes from a particular social system and therefore, inherits the basic values of that social system. Therefore, as explained by Riggs, in a prismatic society the bureaucracy gives the impression of corruption, red-tapism, nepotism, favouritism etc.
8. It is a product of western ecologies. Therefore, it becomes dysfunctional in third world countries.
9. The concept of impersonality may bring a rigid rule oriented approach against value based administration.
10. Strict division of labour, mass effectiveness and innovativeness.
11. The criteria of hierarchy is more appropriate to a centerhead administration system than to a democratic decentralised system. It after leads to generalist specialist controversy.
12. Stress should be more on performance rather than procedures and file works in the administration of development projects and programmes.

INDIAN CONSTITUTION

MAKING OF THE INDIAN CONSTITUTION

The Indian Constitution is a systematic outgrowth of following factors.

1. India's subjection to colonial rule and struggle for independence.
2. The ideological and intellectual inputs provided by stalwarts like Gandhi, Nehru, Ambedkar, Rajendra Prasad and others.
3. Socio-economic milieu of Indian society.
4. Liberal democratic ideas of representative government, adult franchise, elected institutions etc. which was more pragmatic and commensurate with Indian ethos.

Apart from the above cited factors many factors have contributed to affect the constitutional provisions and it would be far from truth to accept that Indian Constitution is still in the process of evolution.

CONSTITUTIONAL DEVELOPMENT

The constitution of India was adopted by the Constituent Assembly in 1949, was not absolutely new. It was, to a great extent influenced by the Government of India Act 1935. The foundation of British rule was laid in 1600 through the establishment of East India Company in England under a charter of British Queen Elizabeth. The Company acquired control over Bengal in 1765. The period from 1765 to 1772 is called the period of Dual Government.

The landmarks in the development of the constitution during the British rule are explained below in a chronological order.

Regulating Act of 1773

This was the first step taken by the British Government to control and regulate the affairs of the East India Company in India. It laid the foundations of Central Administration in the following three respects :

1. It designated the Governor of Bengal as the Governor-General of Bengal. The first such Governor-General was Lord Warren Hastings.
2. It subordinated the Governors of Bombay and Madras to the Governor-General of Bengal.
3. It established Supreme Court at Calcutta as the highest court.

Pitts India Act of 1784

It placed the Indian affairs under direct control of the British Government. For that purpose, it established a Board of Control (representing the British Cabinet) over the Court of Directors (the governing body of the East India Company).

The governor-general's position was made stronger. He could over-rule his council on important matters. Presidencies of Bombay and Madras were brought under his authority.

Charter Act, 1813

By the Charter Act, the company's trade monopoly in India was ended, and trade was thrown open to all British subjects. But trade in tea and trade with China remained exclusive to the company. And both the government and the revenues of India continued to be in their hands.

Charter Act of 1833

It made the Governor-General of Bengal as the Governor-General of India. All civil and military powers were vested in him. Also, the Government of Bombay and Madras were deprived of their legislative powers.

This was the final step towards centralisation in British India. The Act created for the first time, the Government of India having authority over the entire territorial area possessed by the British in India. Moreover, the Act also ended the activities of the East India company as a commercial body.

Charter Act of 1853

This Act separated, for the first time, the legislative and executive functions of the Governor General's Council. It also introduced a system of open competition as the basis of recruitment for civil servants of the company and thus, deprived the Directors of their patronage power.

Government of India Act of 1858

This Act transferred the government, territories and revenues of India from the East India Company to the British Crown. In other words, the rule of Company was replaced by the rule of Crown in India. The powers of the British Crown were to be exercised by the Secretary of State for India. Thus, the Board of Control and Court of Directors were replaced by this new office. The secretary of state was a member of the British Cabinet and was assisted by Council of India, having 15 members. He was vested with complete authority and control over Indian administration through Governor-General as his agent, and he was responsible ultimately to the British Parliament.

Indian Councils Act of 1861

The provisions of this Act were :

1. It introduced for the first time the representative institutions in India. It thus provided that Governor-General's Executive Council should have some Indians as non-official members while transacting legislative business.
2. It initiated the process of decentralisation by restoring the legislative powers to the Bombay and Madras Presidencies.
3. It accorded the statutory recognition to the portfolio system.
4. It empowered the Governor-General to frame rules for more convenient transaction of business in the council.

Indian Councils Act of 1892

It introduced the principle of election but in an indirect manner. The Governor-General still had the power of nomination even though the members were indirectly elected. Also, it enlarged the functions of Legislative Councils and gave them the power of discussing the Budget and addressing questions to the Executive.

The main features of the Act were as under :

Indian Council Act 1892 : Sir George Chesney Committee

- The Indian Councils Act of 1892, further increases the number of members of central and provincial legislative councils.
- The non-official members of the central council were to be nominated by calcutta chamber of commerce and Provincial Legislative Councils.
- Non-officials members of Provincial councils were to be nominated by local bodies, such as the Municipal Council's and District Boards.
- The members of the councils were given right to ask questions on matters of public interest.

Indian Councils Act of 1909

This Act is also known as Morley-Minto Reforms. It changed the name of Central Legislative Council to Imperial Legislative Council and retained official majority in it. The provincial legislative Councils, on the other hand, were allowed to have non-official majority. Apart from increasing the size of Legislative Councils, the Act also enlarged their deliberative functions. The Act also introduced a system of communal representation for Muslims by accepting the concept of 'Separate Electorate'. Thus, this act 'Legalised Communalism' and Lord Minto came to be known as the 'Father of Communal Electorate'.

The main features of the Act were as under :

- Expanded the central and provincial Legislative Councils.
- Maintained majority of official members.
- Non official majority in provincial legislature but not of elected ones.
- First attempt of introducing representative and popular element.
- Official majority in Central (Imperial) Legislature.
- Separate electorate for Muslim.
- Members can discuss budget and more resolutions and supplementary question.
- Members can discuss matters of public interest.

The main features of the Act were as under :

Government of India Act of 1919

This act is also known as Montagu-Chelmsford Reforms. It relaxed the central control over the provinces by demarcating and separating the central subjects from that of provincial subjects. The central and provincial legislatures were authorised to make laws on their respective list of subjects.

The Act further divided the provincial subjects into two parts :

1. Transferred
2. Reserved

The transferred subjects were to be administered by the Governor with the aid of ministers responsible to the Legislative Council. The reserved subjects, on the other hand, were to be administered by the Governor and his Executive Council without being responsible to the Legislative Council. This dual scheme of governance was known as 'Dyarchy'. However, this experiment was largely unsuccessful.

The Act introduced, for the first time, bicameralism and direct elections in the country. Thus, the Imperial Legislative Council was replaced by a bicameral legislature consisting of an Upper House (Legislative Assembly). The majority of members of both the Houses were chosen by direct election.

The Act also required that the three of the six members of the Governor-General's Council (other than the commander-in-chief) were to be Indian. The main features of the Act were as under :

Government of India Act 1919

- In fact an amending Act and provided for a Preamble.
- Subjects of administration divided into 2 categories— central and provincial.
- Dyarchy in Provinces–transferred and reserved subjects.
- Ministerial responsibility in limited sphere.
- Elected members constituted 70%.
- Delegation of power between centre and provinces (no federation).
- Introduction of Bicameral legislature at centre first time.
- Each home was to have an elected majority.
- Discretionary power in the hands of Governor General.
- No provision of collective responsibility.
- Budget was divided into two categories — votable, non-votable.
- Maximum limit on Governor General's Executive Council was removed.
- Half of his Executive Council members to be Indians (three).
- Control of Secretary of State was reduced.
- 4 new offices of the High Commissioner of India was created.

The Act of 1919 – Dyarchy in the Provinces

- The Act established in the nine provinces the dual system of Government called Dyarchy.
- According to this system, the provincial subjects were divided into two parts-the Reserved and Transferred.
- Land Revenue, Famine Relief, Irrigation, Law and under, control of news papers etc. were the Reserved Departments to be controlled by the Governor and his Executive Councillors.
- They were not responsible to the Legislative council. The Transferred departments were to be administered by the Governor and the ministers chosen from the elected members of the Provinicial Legislative Council.
- The system of double government did not work satisfactorily and was abolished in 1937.

The Simon Commission-1927

- November 1927, a statutory commission called Simon Commission was appointed by the British government.
- Its main task was to examine the working of the Government of India Act of 1919.
- The commission under the chairmanship of Sir John Simon landed in Mumbai on 3rd February 1928.
- It was boycotted by all parties, because the seven members of it were all British.
- The commission visited many places. The whole country rang with the slogan Simon Go Back in one such demonstration at Lahore Lala Lajpat Rai received lathi blows on his head. He lated died in 1928.

Nehru Report-1928

- While the Simon Commission was carrying on its work without any regard for sentiments of the people of India, the leading Indian political parties tried to lay down a common political programme. In February 1928, an All parties conference appointed a committee under the chairmanship of Moti Lal Nehru to discuss question of framing a new constitution of India.
- The Committee prepared a report which laid down Dominion Status as India's political objective.
- The British government, however, did not accept the report of this committee.
- The committee refused to grant self-government to India within the British empire.

Government of India Act-1935

- Simon Commission report was considered by RTC.
- After 3rd RTC, white paper was issued.
- White paper examined by a Committee of Parliament by Linlithgow.
- The recommendations of joint select committee formed the basis of GOI 1938.
- A comprehensive and declared document-321 sections and 10 schedules.
- Federal Scheme and Provincial autonomy (autonomous units).
- Three Lists : Federal-59, Provincial-54, Concurrent-36.
- Dyarchy at centre
- Received subjects to be administrated by Governor General with Counsellors appointed by him.
- In six provinces legislature was bicameral and unicameral in five.
- Bicameral Legislature at Centre : Council of State and Federal Assembly.
- Direct election for both houses.
- For council of State
- Seats were reserved on the basis of relative rank and importance of the state.
- One third member retire every third year.
- Six member to be nominated by Governor General.
- The Governor at his discretion decided as to what were his discretionary power.
- The Governor General could authorise either federal or provincial legislature to enact a law with respect to any matter not enumerated in lists.

Cripps Mission-1942

- During Second world war the British desperately needed Indian's cooperation in war and to secure it, sent to India in March 1942, a mission headed by a cabinet minister Sir Stafford cripps.
- Cripps came to India on 22 March 1942. After long discussions with Indian leaders he put forward his proposals even baging that:
- India should be given the Dominion Status after the war.
- During the War period, the Defence portfolio would remain in the hands of the viceroy and
- After the termination of the war, a constituent Assembly would be setup to decide the future of India.
- The congress as well as the Muslim League refused the offers and the Cripps Mission ended in complete the failure.

Wavell Plan

- Concerned mainly with the Viceroy's Executive Council.
- Proposed to make Council more representative.
- External affairs to be under Indian Minister.

Simla Conference

- Called to suggest names for Executive Council.
- Conference failed due to Jinnah.

Cabinet Mission

The Cabinet Mission recommended for

(*i*) a Union of India comprising British India and the Indian States.

(*ii*) the federal centre should have control over defence, foreign affairs and the communication.

(*iii*) the division of provinces according to three groups

(*iv*) setting up of a Constituent Assembly to draft a constitution.

(*v*) the establishment of an interim National Government by the constitution of the Viceroy's Executive Council from among the leaders of the different parties.

The Muslim League accepted the proposals but criticised it particularly on the issue of Pakistan.

An interim Government was finally formed by the Congress in September 1946 with the Jawaharlal Nehru heading the Council of Ministers.

Mountbetten Plan-1947

- Lord Louis Mountbatten was sent to India and he assumed office as viceroy in March 1947. On 3 June came the broadcast laying down the method by which power would be transferred to Indian hands. He also advanced the date of withdrawal of the British from India to 15th August 1947.
- It was accepted by the Congress and the League. Pakistan was to comprise Sindh, Baluchistan and Northwest Frontier Province.
- But the provinces of Bengal and Punjab were to be partititoned between India and Pakistan.
- According, on 15th August, India and Pakistan emerged as two independent states.

Indian Independence Act-1947

- Simple and short document consisting of 20 clauses.
- Partition to be effected from Aug 15, 1947 as Independence Day.
- Constituent Assembly to function as Legislative bodies.
- Princely states were free to join either country or remain independent.
- Office of Secretary of State was abolished.
- Governor General and Governor to function as Constitutional heads.
- Partition of Punjab and Bengal.
- Paramountacy of crown over Princely states to lapse.
- First sitting of the Constituent Assembly-9 Dec. 1946.
- Constituent Assembly as a Government body for Dominion of India-14 Aug 1947.
- Meanwhile demand of Pakistan was accepted.
- When the Constituent Assembly reassembled on-31 Oct 1947.

Total Members-299
229-elected
70-nominated

The draft of Constitution prepared in Feb. 1948.

Third sitting was over by 26 Nov. 1949-284 member finally passed sitting on 24 Jan. 1950.

COMMITTEES OF THE ASSEMBLY

	Members	Chairman
Drafting Committee	7	Ambedkar
Union Powers Committee	9	Nehru
Committee on FR and Minorities	54	Patel
Steering Committee	3	K.M. Mushi
Provincial Constitution Committee	25	Patel
Committee on Union Constitution	15	Nehru

B.N. Rao-Advisor to the Constituent Assembly prepared draft.

A 7 member Committee chaired by Sir Alladi Krishnaswami Iyer was set up to examine the draft.

There were more than 30 members who belonged to scheduled castes.

Minorities such as Anglo-Indians and Parsees were represented by Frank Anthony and H.P. Modi respectively.

Mrs. Sarojni Naidu and Mrs. Vijaya Laxmi Pandit were important women members.

It took 3 years to complete its work and Rs. 64 crore were spent on Assembly during the period.

The provisions relating to citizenship, elections, provisional Parliament temporary and transitional provisions were given effect from Nov. 26, 1949 referred to as date of commencement.

Two-thirds of the provisions of the constitution is similar to the Government of India Act 1935.

FACTS ABOUT CONSTITUTION

There were 395 Articles, 22 Parts and 8 Schedules in 1950. But now it contains 470 Articles, 25 Parts, 12 Schedules and 106 Amendments.

SOURCES OF CONSTITUTIONAL PROVISIONS

Great Britain	: Parliamentary form of Government, process of law making, institution of speaker, writ jurisdiction.
America	: Federal structure, supremacy of the constitution, independent judiciary, Judicial review, impeachment, process of ratification of Constitutional amendments by state Legislatures, Fundamental Rights.
Ireland	: Directive Principles, Method of the election of President, nomination of members in the Rajya Sabha.
Canada	: Definition of Indian Federation as an Union of State, Vesting residuary powers to the Union.
Australia	: Concurrent List, Joint Sitting of the two Houses
Japan	: Procedure established by law.
Germany	: Emergency provisions.
USSR	: Fundamental Duties
South Africa	: Constitutional Amendments

MAJOR LANDMARKS IN CONSTITUTIONAL DEVELOPMENT

The enormous task of drafting constitution of independent India was done by an indirectly elected Constituent Assembly. From 9 Dec, 1946 to 26 Nov., 1949. But, there remained significant landmarks in this direction. Some of them are as follows.

- Dec. 1918, At the 33rd session of INC held at Delhi a unanimous resolution proclaimed that ''principles of self-determination should be applied'' to India.
- Jan. 1922, Gandhi writing in Young India declared that Swaraj would not be the gift of British Parliament, but will of people must be expressed through freely chosen representatives.
- May, 1928, All Parties conference held at Bombay appointed an all-parties committee headed by Motilal Nehru to frame a Constitution for an independent India.
- Dec, 1929, Lahore session of the All India Congress Committee passed resolution for complete independence. Soon after demand for a Constituent Assembly was emphasized.
- 1938 Haripura and 1940 Ramgarh Session reiterated claims for a Constituent Assembly.
- 1940, August offer implicitly conceded the demand for Constituent Assembly.
- 1942, Cripps Mission accepted for the first time India's right to independence and her right to frame her own Constitution. But, it failed.
- May, 1946, Cabinet Mission finally conceded the demand for setting up a Constituent Assembly for whole India.

  The Constituent Assembly was to consist of 385 members.

  Members elected from British India-292
Members who were to be representative of native states-93

  Total-385

The Muslim League boycotted the Assembly. When Assembly met at its first meeting on Dec 9, 1946 only 211 members were present. The process of merger and integration of Indian states kept on changing its strength.

After nearly three years of its work, Assembly adopted the Constitution on 26 Nov., 1949. It held 11 sessions, coverings 1,965 days.

The last sitting was held on 24 Jan. 1950.

Number of members was decided on the basis of one representative for a population of ten lakh.

In all, Assembly had 15 committees with 80 members. The Drafting Committee constituted in 1947 under the chairmanship of Dr. Ambedkar consisted of six other members to prepare the draft Constitution. The Draft Constitution was prepared in Feb., 1948.

CHARACTER OF THE ASSEMBLY

1. The members were indirectly elected by only 20 to 24 percent of the total population. Apart from them, there are many nominated members representing native states.
2. About 83 per cent were Hindus, out of which 45 per cent were Brahmins. Altogether 74 per cent belonged to upper castes.
3. Most of the members were elites educated in western, english system.

BASIC FEATURES OF THE CONSTITUTION

The Constitution of a country is the legal document with the help of which a country's affairs are managed. It is a combination of many factors, viz., history, values, traditions, ethos, socio-political milieu and alike. It is a document which establishes the doctrine of limited government and promotes democratic rule. Indian constitution drafted and enacted after a period of struggle and deliberation is among the longest in the world. Though most of it is taken from the Government of India Act 1935, the Indian framers gave it a twist so as to be an instrument of socio-economic justice without compromising the aspect of security, good governance and other aspects.

The following are the basic features of Indian Constitution.

1. One of the longest document in the world. Originally it contained 395 Articles and 8 schedule. Now, it contains 444 Articles and 12 schedules.
2. Indian Constitution is a written Constitution like American, Canadian and French Constitution.
3. India has a federal system with unitary bias. The desire and commitment to preserve the unity without compromising the issue of development of different regions, made this choice inevitable.
4. Independent and impartial judiciary is hallmark of Indian Constitution.
5. Novel features like fundamental rights, fundamental duties and directive principles of state policy in a single document.
6. Parliamentary system of government.
7. Compromise between Parliamentary supremacy and Judicial Review.
8. A democratic Republic, head of the state is elected indirectly. He/she is not hereditary.
9. A mix of rigid and flexible elements the constitution amendment procedure as moderate enough to address the needs of change. But, is also strict in the sense that crucial provisions need special majority.
10. Citizenship is single, everybody fulfilling certain qualification is entitled for citizenship of the country, not of a particular state.

FUNDAMENTAL RIGHTS

The Constitution of India is committed to a fundamental change in the social order so as to ensure more human life of people. Perhaps no part other than on Fundamental Rights and Directive Principles of State policy testifies to this commitment of Indian Constitution.

Fundamental rights are the rights that have been incorporated in the Constitution and are justiciable in court of law. They have been modelled on the basis of U.S. Constitution and are hailed as "Cornerstone of the Indian Constitution." It is to be noted that though all fundamental rights are human rights but not the vice-versa. Most of these rights are worded negative and directed against the state. Some of the rights viz, Article 17 are enforceable against the private individuals as well.

HISTORY OF DEMAND FOR FUNDAMENTAL RIGHT

- Swaraj Bill (1895) by Lokmanya Tilak.
- Congress Resolution in the period of first world war.
- Commonwealth of India Bill by Annie Besant.
- Madras Resolution of Congress (1927).
- Nehru Committee 1928.
- Karachi Session of Congress (1931) adopted a Resolution on Fundamental Right.
- Sapru Committee Report (1945) made distinction between justiciable and non-justiciable rights.

CHIEF CHARACTERISTICS OF FUNDAMENTAL RIGHTS

1. Integral part of the Constitution cannot be altered or taken away by ordinary legislation.
2. They are not absolute. 'Reasonable' restrictions can be imposed in view of sovereignty and integrity of the country or alike on certain grounds.
3. Though most of the rights are worded negatively some are positive rights. For example
   Negative : Article 18
   Positive : Article 16
4. They are justiciable. But, chief feature is that part III dealing with Fundamental Rights is guarantor as well as protector of Fundamental Rights. A remedy under Article 32 is given for enforcement of a Fundamental Rights.

CLASSIFICATION OF FUNDAMENTAL RIGHTS

Fundamental Rights are classified as

1. Right to Equality
2. Right to Freedom
3. Right against Exploitation
4. Right to freedom of Religion
5. Cultural and educational rights
6. Right to Constitutional Remedies

The Original Constitution provided for the Right to property but it has been abolished by the 44th Amendment.

Recently, Right to primary education has been included in Part three under Article 21 A.

1. **Right to Equality :** Article 14 to 18 deals with the Right to Equality.

   Article 14, says that "the state shall not deny to any person equality before the law or the equal protection of the laws within the territory of India.

   - **Equality Before Law :** It is an expression of English common law and is somewhat negative concept implying absence of special privilege on grounds of birth, caste, creed, colour or sex.

     Equality before law is second corrollary from Dicey's concept of the "rule of law." It implies that no one is above the law of land. It is the law no one is supreme. However, exceptions are granted to the office of President and Governor.
   - **Equal Protection of the Law :** It is of American origin and is a more positive concept implying equality of treatment in equal circumstances.

   It provides for protective discrimination.

   Article 15(1), says "the State shall not discriminate against any citizen on grounds only of religion, race, caste, sex, place of birth or any of them.

   Besides these 5 grounds, state can prescribe guidelines say; for job in a particular region.

   Article 15(2) says "No citizen can be denied access to public places only on the ground of caste sex, race, religion, place of birth or any of them."

   This Article is a Corollary to Article 17 (against Untouchability).

   Article 15(3) says that "nothing in this article shall prevent the state from making special provisions for women and children."

   Article 15(4) says that "Nothing in this or in clause (2) of Article 29 shall prevent the state from making any special provision for the advancement of any socially and educationally backward classes of society or for the SCs and STs." This Article was introduced by Ist Amendment.

Article 16(1) provides for equality of opportunity in public employment.

Article 16(2) prohibits discrimination on grounds only of religion, race, sex, descent place of birth or any of them in matters relating to public employment.

Article 16(3) provides for residential qualification in certain category of public employment.

Article 16(4) provides for reservation of seats for the backward classes of citizens in public employment if they are inadequately represented.

Article 16(4A) provides for reservation in promotion for SCs and STs in Government service.

Article 16(5) provides for reservation of seats to officer connected with a religious or dominated institution for members professing the particular religion or belonging to the particular denomination to which the denomination relates.

Article 17 abolishes 'untouchability' and makes its practice, an offence punishable under the law.

In view of this, an act was made by Parliament. Untouchability (offences) Act 1955, which is renamed as Civil Rights Protection Act 1976.

Article 18 abolishes titles and prevents state from conferring title to any person.

2. **Right to Freedom :** Article 19 to 22 deals with the Right to Freedom.

Article 19(1) includes six freedoms.

(*a*) Freedom of Speech and Expression.

(*b*) Freedom of Assembly.

(*c*) Freedom of Association.

(*d*) Freedom of Movement.

(*e*) Freedom of Residence and settlement.

(*f*) Freedom of profession, occupation, trade and business.

(*g*) included freedom 'to acquire hold and dispose of property' which has been abolished by the 44th Amendment.

Freedom of the Press is included under Article 19(1)(a).

Article 20 provides protection against arbitrary and excessive punishment to any person who commits an offence. It can not be suspended during the period of emergency.

Article 21 guarantees right to life and personal liberty. It says that "No person shall be deprived of his life or personal liberty except according to the procedure established by law."

It is the most important Article which has been hailed as backbone of Part III and Part IV of the Constitution by the Supreme Court. It can never be suspended.

Article 21 is the bedrock from which many rights have been inferred by the Supreme Court.

Article 22 provides protection against arbitrary arrest and detention. It includes

- informing the detainee of the cause of his arrest.
- allowing him to consult and be defended by a legal practitioner of his choice.
- producing him before a nearest magistrate within the period of 24 hours.

3. **Right against Exploitation :** There are two Articles : 23 and 24 under it.

Article 23 : it seeks to ban traffic in human beings, begar or any form of forced Labour.

Article 24 it prohibits employment of children below the age of 14 years in any factory or mine or any hazardous condition.

4. **Right to freedom of Religion :** it includes four rights under Article 25, 26, 27, 28.

Article 25 entitles everyone the freedom of conscience and the right to process, practice and propagate a religion of one's choice.

Article 26 grants right to religious denominations to

- establish institutions for practice or propagating their religion.
- manage its own affairs in matters of religion.
- passes and dispose of their immovable property.

Article 27 provides for exempting religious institutions from paying taxes to state for religious purposes.

Article 28 deals with religious instruction to be imparted in educational institutions.

- No religious instruction can be provided in institutions owned and administered by the state.
- Religious instruction may be imparted but pupil may not be compelled to attend them in institutions recognized by the state and receiving aid out of state funds.
- Religious instructions can be imparted and people can be compelled to attend them in educational institutions administered by state established by a religious endowment or religious trust.

5. **Cultural and Educational Rights :** It includes Articles 29 and 30.
   Article 29 provides for criteria for determination of minority.
   Article 30 provides that all minorities shall have the right to establish and administer educational institution of their choice.
6. **Right to Constitutional Remedies :** It has only one Article 32. In the words of Dr. Ambedkar Article 32 is fundamental of all Fundamental Rights. This right makes it constitutionally obligatory on the part of the Supreme Court to enforce the Fundamental Rights.
   It includes five kinds of writ jurisdiction adopted from England.
   - Habeas Corpus
   - Mandamus
   - Certiorari
   - Prohibition
   - Quo Warranto

"Habeas Corpus" is in the nature of an order calling upon the person who has detained another to produce the latter before the court. It literally means 'to have a body.' In addition to aggrieved person; other individual or organization can head for its enforcement.

"Mandamus" means command. It is issued to command a person or a body to do what is his or its duty to do. It is a discretionary remedy at the hands of HC and an aggrieved person can approach the court. It can be issued against public offices as well as inferior courts and judicial bodies.

"Prohibition" issued to an inferior court to keep within limits of their jurisdiction. It is a matter of right for which only aggrieved person can approach the Court.

"Quo Warranto" issued to enquire into the legality of the claim of a public office. It asks 'What is your authority.' Its intention is to see that unlawful claimant does not usurp a public office.

"Certeorari" issued to quash orders passed in excess of jurisdiction of a court.

FUNDAMENTAL DUTIES

In ancient times, it was felt that if everyone performs his duties, then the rights would automatically be safeguarded.

There was no provision of Fundamental Duties in the original Constitution. The Constitution (Forty Second Amendment) Act, 1976 added part IVA and a new Article 51A to the Constitution. It gives a list of Eleven Fundamental Duties. They are as follows:

1. To abide by the Constitution and respect its ideals and institutions, the National flag and the National Anthem.
2. To cherish and follow the noble ideals which inspired our national struggle for freedom.
3. To uphold and proved the sovereignty, unity and integrity of India.
4. To defend the country and render national service when called upon to do so.
5. To promote harmony and spirit of common brotherhood amongst all the people of India transcending religious, linguistic and regional or sectional diversities, to renounce practices derogatory to the dignity of women.
6. To value and preserve the rich heritage of our composite culture.
7. To protect and improve the natural environment including forests, lakes, rivers and wild life and to have compassion for living creatures.
8. To develop the scientific temper, humanism and the spirit of inquiry and reform.
9. To safeguard public property and to abjure violence.

10. To strive towards excellence in all spheres of individual and collective activity so that the nation constantly rises to higher levels of endeavour of achievement.
11. A new fundamental duty was added to the constitution by the 86th Amendment Act, which added right to education with a view to provide individual rights a sense of social responsibility.

DIRECTIVE PRINCIPLES OF STATE POLICY

The Directive Principles of State Policy mentioned in Part IV of the Constitution contain 15 Articles (36-51). They are one of the many novel elements of the Constitution which have been adopted from the Irish Constitution. They are in the nature of certain ideals the state should strive for. They give certain directions to executive and the legislature. They give certain unforcible rights which the state shall aim at securing by its various policies. These features have undergone evolution and represent context and experience of India. They are a combination of socialist ideals, Gandhian perception, Western liberalism and the ideals of India's freedom struggle.

Different Views

According to B.R. Ambedkar "they are like the instruments of instruction to the government."

According to Ivor Jennings "the philosophy underlying most of these provisions is 'Fabian Socialism' without the word 'Socialism', there is only nationalisation of the means of production, distribution and exchange is missing."

Gravinile Austin considers it to be aimed at furthering the goals of the social revolution or to foster his revolution by establishing the conditions necessary for its advancement.

Constitution declares directives to be fundamental in the governance of the country and it shall be the duty of the state to apply these principles in making laws. It spells out the norms of social and economic democracy in the country.

PROVISIONS

The various articles on Directive Principles are as follows.

Article 38 instructs the state to promote the welfare of people by securing and protecting a social order in which justice (socio-economic and political) shall inform all the institutions of national life.

Article 39(a) it talks about state's role in providing adequate means of livelihood to all its citizens.

Article 39(b) provides for state's direction for equitable distribution of resources.

Article 39(c) provides for prevention of concentration of wealth in fewer hands.

Artcile 39(d) provides for equal pay for equal work, for both; men and women.

Article 39(A) provides for equal justice and free legal Aid.

Article 40 says that the state shall organize village Panchayats as units of self-government.

Article 41 provides for right to work, public assistance in case of unemployment, old age, sickness and disablement keeping in view the limitations of economic resources.

Article 42 provides just and humane conditions of work and maternity relief.

Article 43 provides for living wages for worker and a decent standard of life, leisure and social anc' cultural opportunities for people.

Article 43(A) provides for participation of workers in the management of industry and other undertakings. It has been added by 42nd Amendment.

Article 44 provides for a Uniform Civil Code applicable to the entire country.

Article 45 provides free and compulsory education to children till 14 years of age. It has now been made a fundamental right under Article 21A.

Article 46 provides for protection of educational and economic interests of weaker sections of the society and in particular, of the scheduled castes and scheduled tribes.

Article 47 provides for prohibition of consumption of intoxicating liquor and to raise the level of nutrition and five improvement of public health.

Article 48 provides for preserving and improving the breeds and prohibiting the slaughter of cows, calves and other milks and draught cattles.

Article 48A added by 42nd Amendment, provides for protection and improvement of the environment and to safeguard the forests and wild life of the country.

Article 49 provides for protection of monuments of historical and national importance.

Article 50 provides for separation of judiciary from executive.

Article 51 provides for promotion of international peace and security.

RELATION BETWEEN FUNDAMENTAL RIGHTS AND DIRECTIVE PRINCIPLES OF STATE POLICY

Despite being part of the same constitution, a contrast is often made between part III and part IV i.e. between fundamental rights and directive principles. The main reasons are the judicial enforceability of FR and its nature being negative obligation of the state. The directives are non-justiciable and are more in the nature of positive affirmations of the state. However in recent time, some of the directives have been made a part of chapter on Fundamental Rights to be in tune with the requirements of changing polity.

Differences

Fundamental Rights	Directive Principles
1. Negative obligation on the state	positively worded
2. Justiciable	non-justiciable
3. Seeks to establish political democracy	Intends to establish a just socio-economic and political order
4. Have precedence over directive as long as a law does not provide for implementing directive	can take precedence over only through enactment of a complex nature

History

The relationship between the Fundamental Rights and Directive Principles is best illustrated in the Article 37. It provides that Directives are not enforceable in a court of law. But, they are fundamental in the governance of the country and it shall be the duty of the state to apply them in making laws.

In view of such provision, there have arisen certain conflicts between the Directive Principles and Fundamental Rights. But, as of now Article 39(b) and 39(c) can take precedence over Fundamental Right enshrined under Article 14 and Article 19.

A survey of historical development in relationship between Fundamental Rights and Directive Principles are as follows.

- During the initial period from 1950 to 1966 there was emphasis on sacrosanct character of Fundamental rights. The Supreme Court held the view that if two interpretations of a law are possible, the one avoiding conflict should be accepted. But in case of a single interpretation, leading to conflict fundamental right would prevail other directive principles. In this view, constitutionality of I^{st} Amendment Act was hailed as valid.
- In the historic Golak Nath's case, 1967, the Supreme Court emphasised on unamedability of the fundamental rights which have been given a 'transcendental position.'
- The Government passed 24th and 25th Amendment Act 1971.

  The 24th Constitution Amendment Act made it clear that the Parliament has power to amend any provision of the Constitution, including the fundamental Rights.

  The 25th Constitution Amendment Act introduced Article 31(c) which provides that in case of implementing Article 39(b) and (c) if there is a conflict with fundamental right, the law shall not be declared null and void.
- In Keshavananda Bharati case overruled the Golaknath's case but made it clear that courts retained the power to judicial review in case of law giving effect to directives under Article 39(b) and (c). One of the crucial implications of this judgement was 'basic structure' which can not be altered.
- During the period of Emergency Parliament passed the 42nd Amendment Act, 1976 which provided for implementation of directives other than only under Article 39(b) and (c).

- In Minerva Mill's case, 1980 the Supreme Court declared that a balance between Part III and Part IV was a basic feature of the constitution. This abrogated the view of giving precedence to the directives over fundamental rights.

Significance of Directive Principles of State Policy

Firstly, they are intended to usher an egalitarian order, once the limitations or resources is overcome and state is competent enough to fulfil them. For, most of the directives are resource consuming.

Secondly, they have exercised an important check on the government. Rightly remarked by Ambedkar that the directives 'can be the best election manifesto.'

Thirdly, they guide both, the government and the people in the realm of politics and society. They have significant educative value.

Fourthly, they emphasize the goal of welfare state and social justice that are warranted in Indian polity and keep check on elitist or populist measures.

INDIAN CONSTITUTION

THE PRESIDENT

The Constitution makers of India adopted a Parliamentary form of Government based on British westminster model. But, unlike the British model, they opted for a chosen head of state elected indirectly for five years. He occupies a position of pre-eminence in the institutional set of the country and regarded as first citizen of the country.

Qualification : A person should be

1. a citizen of India.
2. must not be less than 35 years.
3. must be qualified to be elected as member of Lok Sabha.
4. must not hold any office of profit under the state.

Election : According to Article 54, the President shall be elected by a electoral college consisting of

- the elected members of both the houses of Parliament.
- the elected members of State Legislative Assemblies and Legislative Assemblies of Union Territory of Delhi and Pondichery.

Article 55 provides for ensuring uniformity in the election of President by

1. maintaining a balance between states as a whole and the Union.
2. population of states and votes of legislators.

Value of Vote of M.L.A.

$$= \frac{\text{Population of state} \times \frac{1}{100}}{\text{total number of elected M.L.A. of the state}}$$

Value of Vot eof M.P.

$$= \frac{\text{Total value of vote of all states}}{\text{Total number of elected M.P.'s}}$$

PRESIDENTS AND THEIR TENURE*

S.No.	Name	Tenure
1.	Dr. Rajendra Prasad	26 Jan. 1950 to 13 May 1962
2.	Dr. S. Radhakrishnan	13 May 1962 to 13 May 1967
3.	Dr. Zakir Hussain	13 May 1967 to 3 May 1969
4.	V.V. Giri	3 May 1969 to 20 July 1969 (Acting)
5.	Justice M. Hidayattullah	20 July 1969 to 24 Aug. 1969 (Acting)
6.	V.V. Giri	24 Aug. 1969 to 24 Aug. 1974
7.	Fakhruddin Ali Ahmed	24 Aug. 1974 to 11 Feb. 1977
8.	B.D. Jatti	11 Feb. 1977 to 25 July 1977 (Acting)
9.	N.S. Reddy	25 July 1977 to 25 July 1982
10.	Gyani Zail Singh	25 July 1982 to 25 July 1987
11.	R. Venkataraman	25 July 1987 to 25 July 1992
12.	Dr. Shankar Dayal Sharma	25 July 1992 to 25 July 1997
13.	Dr. K.R. Narayanan	25 July 1997 to 25 July 2002

*** See appendix for rest list***

The election of President is held in accordance with system of proportional representation by means of single transferable vote.

Term : The term of President's office is five years from the date on which he enters upon his office. However, he is eligible for re-election.

Salary : The President gets emolument of Rs 5,00,000/- per month along with allowances and government accommodation.

Resignation : President may resign his office by writing under his hand addressed to the Vice-President.

Impeachment : The President may be impeached for 'violation of the Constitution' in accordance with the provisions in Article 61 of the Constitution.

Procedure for Impeachments : A motion seeking removal of the President can be introduced in either house of the Parliament by giving a notice signed by not less than 1/4 of the total strength of the house. The resolution can be moved after a fourteen days notice is served on him. If the house passes the resolution by not less than 2/3rd of the total strength of the house, the matter is to be referred to the other house which will investigate the charges. The President however, has the right to defend himself in the other house either by himself or through an attorney. If the second house also passes the resolution by majority of not less than 2/3rd of the total strength of the house, the President is considered removed from his office from the date of passing of such resolution.

Powers and Functions of the President

The Parliamentary form of government depends on principles and practices wherein the President is the formal executive and council of minister headed by the Prime Minister is the real executive. All the actions of government are undertaken in the name of President but only on the advice of ministers chosen by him. According to Article 53 of the Constitution "executive powers of the Union shall be vested in the hands of the President who shall exercise it either directly or through officers subordinate to him in accordance with the provisions of the Constitution."

The powers of the President can be broadly categorized as :

1. Executive Power
2. Legislative Power
3. Military Power
4. Emergency Power
5. Diplomatic Power
6. Judicial Power
7. Financial Power

1. Executive Power : All executive actions are taken in his name. He has power to appoint the Prime Minister, other ministers of the Government of India, Attorney General for India, the Comptroller and Auditor General of India, the Judges of the Supreme Court, the Judges of High Court of States, the Governors of State, Members of Union and Joint Public Service Commission, the members of Finance Commission, the Chief Election Commissioner and members of election commission.

The President shall also have the power to remove ministers, Attorney General, judge of Supreme Court or High Court or Election Commissioner on the advice of Parliament, Chairman and member of Public Service Commission on the report of Supreme Court.

2. Legislative Power : President is an integral part of Indian Parliament. In this respect

- he can prorogue or summon the houses of Parliament, dissolve the Lok Sabha and summon the Joint session of the two houses of Parliament in case of a deadlock.
- he gives his assent to all bills passed by the Parliament to become a law.
- he addresses either or both houses of Parliament, at the first session of the lower house after each general election and at the commencement of first session each year.
- he has power to send messages to either house of Parliament which the House must consider.
- he has power to nominate not more than 12 members to the Rajya Sabha for their contributions towards arts, literature, science and social services. By the 104th Constitutional amendment nomination provision of 2 members belonging to the Anglo-Indian Community to the Lok Sabha has abolished.

- he has power to promulgate an ordinance when the Parliament is not in the session (Article 123). Presidential ordinance has the same force and effect as an Act of Parliament.
- he has power to
  declare his assent to a bill
  declare that he withholds his assent
  return the bill for reconsideration (not money bill)
- The Governor of a state may reserve a bill for President assent, but it is obligatory when the Bill derogates the power of High Court. In cases where a state bill is reserved for Presidential assent, he can declare that he withhold his assent or can give assent.

3. **Military Power :** The President is the Commander-in-Chief of the Defence forces. However, the exercise of his power is to be regulated by law of the Parliament.
4. **Judicial Power :** The President is accorded the power to grant pardon, reprieve, respite, remission of punishment in cases of (a) Court Martial (b) offences against laws made under the Union and Concurrent lists (c) death sentences. He also appoints judges of the Supreme Court and High Courts through an integrated consultative process.
5. **Diplomatic Power :** As the highest constitutional dignitary, the President appoints ambassadors to foreign countries and receives diplomatic delegates of foreign countries.
6. **Financial Power :** It is President who causes to laid before the Parliament, the annual budget. Money Bill can be introduced only with his prior recommendation.
7. **Emergency Power :** President is assigned three kinds of emergency powers under Article 352, 356 and 360.

Under Article 352, called National Emergency

It provides that "The President may proclaim national emergency if he is of the opinion that there exists a grave threat to the security of India or any part thereof; whether by war, external aggression or armed rebellion." Emergency can be declared even in view of imminent threat. It can be imposed only on a written advice from the Cabinet (44th Amendment). Every such proclamation ceases to exist at the expiration of one month of proclamation unless approved by resolution of both the houses of Parliament. The validity period is six month but can be increased by resolution of Parliament (six months at a time). The resolution approving proclamation was to be passed by majority of total membership of the House and not less than two-thirds of members present and voting separately in each House. The President can modify or revoke the emergency by a separate proclamation. It can be withdrawn if Lok Sabha desires. For this a special session of Lok Sabha may be called by the President (if the Lok Sabha is not in Session) or the Speaker if a notice addressed by 1/10th of membership of the House is given to them. A special session must be held within 14 days of receiving of such a notice.

Effects

- Centre can give directions to states
- Parliament can legislate on State list
- Distribution of power is suspended
- Term of Lok Sabha may be extended by law of Parliament for a period not exceeding one year at a time.
- Fundamental freedoms under Article 19 will be suspended automatically (except when the ground is 'armed rebellion'). Other Fundamental rights except Articles 20 and 21 can be suspended by the President.

Uses :

Firstly	1962-1968 (external aggression)
Secondly	1971 (external aggression)
Thirdly	1975-1977 (internal disturbance)

Article 356 called President's Rule in State

"If the President is of the opinion (on the basis of report of Governor or otherwise) that the

Constitutional machinery of the State can not be carried on in accordance with the provisions of the Constitution he can declare President's rule.

In such cases, the President may

- dissolve the State Legislature
- suspend the legislature
- entrust the Parliament to exercise the power of state legislature.
- assume all or any function of the state or direct the Governor to exercise the executive functions.

Any such proclamation ceases to operate after two months unless approved by both the Houses of Parliament by simple majority. It will remain in operation for a period of six months from the last day on which houses pass the resolution approving the same. Such proclamation can be approved for six more months. The maximum duration is three years, but must satisfy two conditions.

(a) A proclamation of emergency is in operation.

(b) Election Commission certifies that such resolution is necessary to hold elections under existing conditions.

Effects

- State Government is dismissed
- Executive power exercised by Governor
- Legislature is suspended or dissolved

In S.R. Bommai Case (1994) SC held that court can enquire into the manner in which President formed his opinion. It may direct reinstallation of the Government.

Uses :

Firstly in Pubjab and since then used many a time.

Article 360 Called Financial Emergency

'If the President is satisfied that a situation has arisen whereby financial stability or credit of India or any part thereof, is threatened' he may proclaim financial emergency.

Such proclamation shall cease to be in operation after 2 months unless approved by the Parliament. Once approved, it shall remain in operation unless revoked by the President.

Effects

- Centre can give directions to state to observe such canons of financial propriety as may be specified in the directions of the President.
- Salaries and allowances of the constitutional functionaries and civil servants may be reduced.
- Governor may reserve all money and financial bill passed by the state legislature for consideration of the President.
- Distribution of financial resources between centre and state may be suspended.

PRESIDENTIAL VETO

It is a device available with the President to check hasty and ill-considered legislation by the Parliament. Veto has been classified in three categories on the basis of its impact, viz, Absolute Veto, Suspensive Veto and Pocket Veto. If the President refuses to sign the bill passed by the Parliament and stops the passage of law, it is known as absolute veto. Actually the President of India can use absolute veto in two cases (i) on private members bill; and (ii) if the Council of Ministers tenders resignation after the bill has been passed by the Parliament and before the President gives his assent. In this case the new Cabinet usually advises the President to reject the bill.

Suspensive veto implies the after the bill is passed by the Parliament it is sent the President for his assent. The President can refer back the bill to Parliament for reconsideration. If the Parliament re-passes the bill, the President has to give his assent. As this type of veto has the impact of suspending the enactment of the law. It is known as suspensive veto.

In pocket Veto the President instead of giving assent to the bill or sending it back to the Parliament for reconsideration, takes no action on the bill. After the lapse of the stipulated period the bill automatically lapses. In short the President can kill a bill by simply pocketing it.

Uses :

Not used so far.

Criticism : of Emergency Powers

1. Destroys federal scheme

2. Inhibits Authoritarian tendencies
3. Erodes Autonomy of State
4. Endangers Fundamental Rights

Position of the President

The issue of Presidential stature has been raged into debate on a number of time by Dr. Rajendra Prasad, K. Subba Rao and V.V. Giri. According to Ambedkar 'the title of functionary reminds one of the Presidents of the United States. But beyond identity of names there is nothing in common between the form of Government prevalent in America and the form of Government proposed under the Draft Constitution. Under the Presidential system of America, the President is the chief head of the executive. Under the Draft Constitution the President occupies the same position as the King/Queen under the British Constitution.'' He further added that ''The President of the Indian Union will be generally bound by the advice of his ministers. He can do nothing contrary to their advice, nor can he do anything without their advice.''

Later on the Supreme Court in following cases

- Ram Jawaya Vs State of Punjab
- R.C. Cooper Vs Govt. of India
- Samsher Singh Vs State of Punjab

Observed that the President is not the real executive. It is the Council of Ministers which is vested with real executive power.

42th Amendment Act (1976) made it binding on the part of President to act on the advice of Council of Ministers. ''There shall be a Council of Ministers with the Prime Minister at the head to aid and advice the President who shall, in the exercise of his functions, acts in accordance with such advice.''

44th Amendment Act (1977) added a provision in Article 76 which now reads, ''There shall be a Council of Ministers with the PM at the head to aid and advice the President who shall, in the exercise of his functions, act in accordance with such advice. Provided that the President may require the Council of Ministers to reconsider such advice, either generally or otherwise, and the President shall act in accordance with the advice tendered after such reconsideration.''

VICE PRESIDENT

Apart from having a President, Indian Constitution provides for a Vice President. But, he does to have any function in his capacity as Vice President. Nevertheless, he remains the second highest Constitutional dignitary.

Election : The Vice President is elected by an electoral college consisting of all the members of Parliament (both the house), including nominated ones.

Election for the post of Vice President is conducted at a joint sitting of both the houses of Parliament. The procedure of joint sitting done away with 11th Amendment Act 1961.

Qualification : Must be 35 years of age qualified to be member of the Rajya Sabha, does not hold any office of profit

Position : Second highest constitutional dignitary.

Tenure : Five years from the date on which he enters upon his office.

Before entering upon his office, the VP is required to take an oath before the President or some person appointed by him.

Salary : 4,00,000 + daily allowances.

The Constitution does not fix any emoluments for the Vice President of India. He is entitled to a salary as the Chairman of the Rajya Sabha. When he 'acts' as President, he is entitled to get the emoluments equivalent to that of the President.

Removal : Article 67(b) called removal because less formal procedure is followed without any charges he can be removed.

The Vice President may be removed from his office by a resolution of the Rajya Sabha passed by effective majority and agreed to by Lok Sabha by simple majority.

However such a resolution can be moved only by giving at least fourteen day's notice.

Functions : The Vice President does not have any function to perform as Vice President of India.

The Vice President acts either as an ex-officio Chairman of the Rajya Sabha or, as an acting President when the office of the President is vaccant by reason of his death, resignation or removal.

As an officiating President when 'the President is unable to discharge his functions due to absence or illness.

As an Ex-Chairman of Rajya Sabha he conducts all its proceedings except when resolution for his removal is under consideration.

Ordinarily, he does not vote but when the house is divided equally on any issue, he exercises casting vote.

Vice Presidents of India*

1. S. Radhakrishnan	1952 - 1962
2. Zakir Hussain	1962 - 1967
3. V.V. Giri	1967 - 1969
4. G.S. Pathak	1969 - 1974
5. B.D. Jatti	1974 - 1979
6. M. Hidayatullah	1979 - 1984
7. R. Venkataraman	1984 - 1987
8. Shankar Dayal Sharma	1987 - 1992
9. K.R. Narayanan	1992 - 1997
10. Krishan Kant	1997 - 2002

See appendix for rest list

THE COUNCIL OF MINISTERS

The basic idea underlying Parliamentary system is that the head of the state is the nominal executive, the real executive power lies with the Council of Ministers. The Council of Ministers are collectively responsible to the lower house of the Parliament. As a consequence of conventions, Indian President is vested with all executive power, but we exercise these power duly on the advice of Council of Ministers. The real Executive is the Council of Ministers headed by the Prime Minister. Their collective responsibility ensures that they remain in office as long as they enjoy the confidence of the Parliament. They swim and sink together.

Appointment of Ministers

While the Prime Minister is selected by the President, the other ministers are appointed by the President on the advice of the Prime Minister [Article 75(i)] and the allocation of portfolios amongst them is also made by him. President's power of dismissing an individual Minister is virtual power at the hands of the Prime Minister. In selecting the Prime Minister, the President must select the leader of the party in majority in the Lok Sabha, or, a person who is in a position to win the confidence of the majority in that House.

A Composite Body

The Constitution does not classify the members of the Council of Ministers into different ranks. All this has been done informally, following the English practice. Salaries and Allowances of Ministers Act, 1952, defines Minister as a "Member of the Council of Ministers, by whatever name called, and includes a Deputy Minister."

Council of Minister consists of 3 different categories of Ministers :

1. Cabinet Minister
2. Minister of State
3. Deputy Minister

The Cabinet rank ministers are the head of their departments. They attend the Cabinet meetings as a matter of right. However, a person can be appointed Cabinet Minister without a portfolio. The 44th Constitution Amendment Act (1978) has conferred Constitutional status on the Cabinet Ministers.

The Ministers of State are formally of Cabinet Status and are paid the same salary as the Cabinet Ministers and they hold independent charge of their departments. But, they attend the Cabinet meeting only when invited.

The Deputy Ministers work under Minister of State and have no separate charge of a department. They get lesser salary than Minister of State or Cabinet Minister. They assist the Minister in charge of a Department or Ministry and takes no part in Cabinet deliberations.

Size of the Council of Minister

The original constitution did not provide for limiting the size of ministry. As a result, it remained the discretion of Prime Minister to increase or decrease the number of Council of Ministers.

Recently, Parliament has limited the size of ministry not to exceed 15% of the effective strength of the lower house in Parliament and Assemblies in States.

Qualification

A Minister must be a member of either House of the Parliament. A non-member can also be appointed as Minister but he must get himself elected to either House of Parliament before the expiry of a period of six months commencing from their appointment.

Collective Responsibility

In essence, Indian Constitution follows in the British Principle except as to the legal responsibility of individual Ministers for acts done by or on behalf of the President.

According to Article 75(3) of the Constitution —"The Council of Ministers shall be collectively responsible to the House of People." So, the Ministry, as a body, shall be under a constitutional obligation to resign as soon as it loses the confidence of the popular House of the Legislature. The collective responsibility is to the House of the People even though some of the Ministers may be members of the Council of States.

Individual Responsibility

The principle of individual responsibility of the head of the State is embodied in Article 75(2)— "The Minister shall hold office during the pleasure of the President." The result is that, though the Ministers are collectively responsible to the Legislature, they shall be individually responsible to the Executive head and shall be liable to dismissal even when they may have the confidence of the Legislature. But since the Prime Minister's advice will be available in the matter of dismissing other Ministers individually, it may be expected that this power of the President will virtually be, as in England, a power of the Prime Minister. Usually, the Prime Minister exercises this power by asking an undesirable colleague to resign, which the latter readily complies with, in order to avoid the odium of a dismissal.

Powers and Functions of the Council of Ministers

The Council of Ministers forms the Government of the Union. It is headed by the Prime Minister, who is the head of the Union Government. Its powers and functions may be discussed as below :

1. **Legislative Functions :** The Council of Ministers controls the legislature of the Union Government, i.e., Parliament. It formulates its policy, submits and explains it to Parliament for approval. Since it holds majority in Parliament, it is always sure of the acceptance of its policy. The entire legislation of importance passed by Parliament is initiated by the Ministers.
2. **Financial Powers :** The Cabinet controls the financial policy of the Union. It is the Finance Minister who submits the budget to Parliament. Parliament approves the budget expenditure and revenue items in its original form with support of a subservient majority.
3. **Executive Powers :** The Council of Ministers is the executive of the Union. The Ministers preside over the various departments of the government and give direction to the administration. The Cabinet brings about co-ordination of policy among various departments and settles their conflicts. The Cabinet formulates foreign and defence policies of the country and executes the five year plans.

CABINET SYSTEM

In a Parliamentary form of government, the Council of Ministers is collectively responsible to the lower house of the Parliament. The Council swims and sinks together. To ensure unanimity and team work, a small but composite body within the Council i.e. Cabinet has grown into significance. With the growing instrumentality of the government, Cabinet today wields more power and is seen with suspicion. The principle of majority rule has enhanced this tendency.

Composition and Structure

The composition of the cabinet reflects a concern for a degree of regional balance and for the representation of important communities—Muslims, Sikhs, SCs, STs and OBCs. They are heads of their departments.

The Cabinet has four major functions; to approve all proposals for the legislative enactment of Government policy, to recommend all major appointments, to settle interdepartmental disputes and to co-ordinate the various activities of the Government and oversee the execution of its policies.

Only members are entitled to attend the weekly meetings of the Cabinet, but ministers of State, Chief Ministers and technical experts may be invited to attend discussions of subjects with which they have special concern. Votes are rarely taken in the Cabinet; decisions usually are reached after discussion by a sense of the meeting. Only major issues are referred to the Cabinet, and frequently even these, such as the preparation of the budget, are decided by the appropriate minister in consultation with the Prime Minister.

Speaking about merit of Cabinet system, Herman Kiner says "on the whole the Cabinet system offers quick, vigorous, thoughtful and responsible leadership."

Rise of Cabinet Dictatorship and Decline of Parliament

In recent times there have been talk of decline of Parliament and rise of cabinet dictatorship. Such tendencies are seen in relation to the disciplined party system and effective majority system. In Parliamentary system, the party or coalition commanding majority in the lower House forms the Government. This ensures the Government commanded by the Cabinet to have virtually all its wishes carried by the Parliament.

While Jawaharlal Nehru promoted free discussions and debate among ministers, Mrs. Indira Gandhi tried to consolidate the position of PM. But post 1989 phase and era of coalition and minority Governments marked some decline in the authoritarian position of Prime Minister.

In India the notion of Cabinet dictatorship is relative and not absolute. Cabinet has not shown tendencies that are contrary to the norms of democracy. Following points support the evidences.

1. **Party System :** The fragmented and increasingly federalized party system with divergent ideologies and programmes have rendered it impossible for a single political party to command absolute majority. Unlike Britain where two party system with disciplined party workers and fixed electoral votes, India has witnessed transformation in her party system from one party dominance system to multiparty coalition politics.
2. Closely connected to fragmented party politics is the politics of coalition which has become more than a reality in Indian context. The members of Cabinet represent different political party, region and socio-economic milieu. Hence, there has arisen a politics of compromise and accommodation. Perhaps no Government can inhibit and promote authoritarian tendencies.
3. There has increased the role and influence of PM as coordinator and leader. He remains first among equals and ensures that Government survives and continues to perform. In this perspective, he exercises restraints and accommodates different perspectives and voices.
4. The role of second chamber in a federal polity like India have also checked cabinet dictatorship. The Government is criticized for its acts of omission and commission. Barring few financial and money matters, the Rajya Sabha enjoys co-equals powers with the Lok Sabha. Similarly Articles 244 and 312 confer it special powers with regard to federal structure.
5. The enlightened public opinion and mass media have enhanced the mechanism of democratic control. Every issue have come to be debated to evolve national consensus and no Government can ignore them.

Despite these optimism, it can not be denied that the powers of the Parliament have been usurped by the Cabinet. Both, the constitutional provisions and the practical reality confirm to such suspicion.

Constitutional Provision : Article 74–which provides that the President shall exercise his powers only with advice of the Council of Ministers. He can return a matter for reconsideration, only once.

In Article 352, a provision was added by the 44 Amendment. It provides that the President can impose national emergency only when the Cabinet recommends it in writing.

Practical Reality : It is a matter of everyday experience wherein one witnesses that the whole business of the Parliament are allocated to affairs of Government for either policy making or its criticism through debates and discussion.

Nevertheless, the powerful position of the Cabinet in India should not be described as its 'dictatorship.' But, one can not refuse to accept that there have been continuous decline in calibre of our Ministers. They have become rubber stamp of vested interests.

PRIME MINISTER

The office of the Prime Minister which remains an integral part of the Parliamentary system is a British contribution to the realm of politics. Indians adopted Parliamentary system with the office of Prime Minister from Britain.

Position : So important is his significance that Morley described him as ''Primus inter pares'' or first among equals. He has also been hailed as ''Inter Stellar Luna Minores'' or little moon among stars and ''key stone of the Cabinet Arch.''

Provision : According to Article 74(1) of the Indian Constitution, ''there shall be a Prime Minister to head the Council of Ministers.'' Hence, without the Prime Minister, the Council can not function. The very fact that he is a Prime Minister means that he is superior to others. That is why Ramsay Muir compared cabinet to the steering wheel of the state

PRIME MINISTERS OF INDIA*

Name	Party	Tenure
Jawaharlal Nehru	Congress	17 Aug., 1947 to 27 May, 1964
Guljarilal Nanda (Acting)	Congress	27 May, 1964 to 9 June, 1964
Lal Bahadur Shastri	Congress	9 June, 1964 to 11 Jan., 1966
Guljarilal Nanda (Acting)	Congress	11 Jan., 1966 to 24 Jan., 1966
Indira Gandhi	Congress	24 Jan., 1966 to 24 March, 1977
Morarji Desai	Janata Party	24 March, 1977 to 28 July, 1979
C.C. Singh	Janata Party	28 July, 1979 to 14 Jan., 1980
Indira Gandhi	Congress	14 Jan., 1980 to 31 Oct., 1984
Rajeev Gandhi	Congress	31 Oct., 1984 to 1 Dec., 1989
V.P. Singh	Janata Dal	2 Dec., 1989 to 10 Nov., 1990
Chandrashekhar	SJD	11 Nov., 1990 to 21 June, 1991
P.V. Narsimha Rao	Congress	21 June, 1991 to 16 May, 1996
A.B. Vajpayee	BJP	16 May, 1996 to 31 May, 1996
H.D. Deve Gowda	Janata Dal	1 June, 1996 to 20 April, 1997
I.K. Gujral	Janata Dal	21 April, 1997 to 18 March, 1998

See appendix for rest list

and the Prime Minister to the 'steers Man.'' Ivor Jennings called him as ''the sun around which the planets revolve'' and Hinton said that the Prime Minister was an ''elected Monarch.''

Powers and Functions

1. **Head of the Government :** While the President is head of the state, the Prime Ministers is head of the Government. In theory all major executive functions are vested in the hands of the President, but exercises them only with aid and advice of the Council of Ministers headed by the Prime Minister.
2. **Leader of the Cabinet :** According to Ivor Jennings, ''he is a sun around which other ministers revolve like planets.'' He selects ministers of his council and distributes portfolio amongst them. He acts as Chairman of the Cabinet. He can ask for resignation of an individual Minister or can get him dismissed by the President.
3. **Leader of the Parliament :** In this capacity, the Prime Minister
   - determines the dates of meeting, as also its programmes for the session.
   - chief spokesperson of the government in the Parliament.
   - announces the major policy decision of the government.
   - can participate and intervene in all debates in the Parliament.
4. **Leader of the Majority Party in the Lok Sabha :** In Parliamentary democracy, usually the leader of majority party in the Lower House is appointed as the Prime Minister. However, in case no party gets majority, the President may appoint a person whom he may deem fit to garner the support of majority.
5. **Chairman of the Planning Commission :** In this capacity he becomes a chairman of super cabinet wherein all chief ministers of states and administrators of Union Territories are represented. It covers all developmental activities undertaken by the centre as well as states.

Prime Ministerial System

The Parliamentary system of government as practised in the United Kingdom and other countries functions on the basis of majority party working under the leadership of the Prime Minister. His position is of pre-eminence and is more powerful than the President in Presidential system. In recent times, there has been increasing use of the term 'Prime Ministerial' as synonymous with 'Parliamentary' Government. This change has occurred due to continuous widening of the powers of the Prime Minister.

So important is the stature of the office, that every Parliamentary elections are the Prime Ministerial elections. Every party puts its leader as probable Prime Ministerial candidate. He is leader of majority party in the Lower House. In his capacity he garners support of his party colleagues on various issues and have his way. The whole system of Government is under his control and he is the real Executive. He is the chairman of the Cabinet which itself is formed on his advice. Apart from these provisions, the practical politics of the day have increased his discretion. The growing instrumentality of government and measures like delegated legislation have also enhanced the power of the executive. There have been instances when the Prime Minister's office resembled the U.S. President's executive office.

However, the politics of coalition, federalized political party, effective opposition and mass media have increasingly transferred the aura of PM's office. He now has to work under a lot of pull and pressure and even resort to accommodation and compromise for survival of the Government. In England the Prime Minister wields a lot of influence because of the disciplined two party system which either forms the government or remain in opposition. On the contrary, Indian polity has been a federal one with a lot of strong regional political parties paving way for era of coalition. And, this trend is likely to survive for some time.

THE PARLIAMENT

To Edmund Burke "Parliament is not a Congress of ambassadors from different and hostile interests, but it is a deliberative assembly of one nation."

The Constitution of India adopts a Parliamentary form of government like the British Westminster model. However, it is not sovereign in the British sense. Instead, it was expected to suit the requirements of federal polity and acts as an instrument of governance, change and social transformation. It is specifically outlined in Part V of the Constitution from Article 79-123.

The Indian Parliament or the Union Legislature in India consists of the President and the two houses viz, the Lok Sabha and the Rajya Sabha. Unlike the Presidential system that is promised on the principle of separation of powers, the Parliamentary system envisage a scheme of interrelationship between executive and legislative branch of government.

Composition

1. The President.
2. The Lok Sabha or the Lower House or the House of People.
3. The Rajya Sabha or the upper house or council of state.

Functions

1. To enact laws for the administration of the country.
2. To reflect federal sentiment of the Indian polity.
3. To exercise control over the government and ensure limited government.
4. To provide forum for deliberation on issues concerning affairs of the polity.
5. To integrate the polity by providing membership to the representatives.

The Lok Sabha

Composition : The members of Lok Sabha are elected directly by people from their respective constituencies. Under the provision of the constitution.

- Not more than 530 members to be chosen from territorial constituencies in the states.
- Not more than 20 members to represent the Union Territories.
- Not more than 2 members to be nominated from the Anglo-Indian community by the President, was abolished in January 2020 by the 104th constitutional amendment act, 2019.

The total strength of the house can not exceed 550. At present it consists of 543 members due to delimitation of constituencies so as to ensure that "the ratio between the number of seats and the population of any state is, as far as possible, same for all states."

Term : The term of Lok Sabha is of 5 years from the date appointed for its first meeting. It may be dissolved before the expiration of its full term by the President if the government loses the confidence of the Lower House and there are no other alternative to form the government. The term of Lok Sabha can be extended (not necessarily). When a proclamation of emergency is in force, for a period not exceeding one year at a time and not exceeding a period of six months after the proclamation of Emergency cease to operate.

Qualifications : To be a member of the Lok Sabha a person should be

- an Indian Citizen
- Completed 25 years of age

Disqualifications : A member of the Lok Sabha can be disqualified if the person

- holds any office of profit under the Government of India or the State.
- is of unsound mind and stands so declared by a competent court.
- is an undischarged insolvent
- is not a citizen of India, or has voluntarily acquired the citizenship of a foreign state.
- is to be disqualified by or under any law made by Parliament.

Sessions : The Lok Sabha is to meet at least twice a year and the interval between two consecutive sessions shall be less than 6 months.

A special session of the Lok Sabha can be called

Representation of States in the Lok Sabha

State	Number of Representative
Andhra Pradesh	25
Telangana	17
Arunachal Pradesh	02
Asom (Assam)	14
Bihar	40
Goa	02
Gujarat	26
Haryana	10
Himachal Pradesh	04
Jammu and Kashmir	05
Ladakh	01
Karnataka	28
Kerala	20
Madhya Pradesh	29
Maharashtra	48
Manipur	02
Meghalaya	02
Mizoram	01
Nagaland	01
Orissa	21
Punjab	13
Rajasthan	25
Sikkim	01
Tamil Nadu	39
Tripura	02
Uttar Pradesh	80
West Bengal	42
Chhattish Garh	11
Jharkhand	14
Uttarakhand	05
Andaman and Nicobar	01
Chandigarh	01
Dadra and Nagar Haveli	01
Delhi	07
Daman & Diu	01
Lakshadweep	01
Puducherry (Pondicherry)	01

if a notice in writing signed by not less than one-tenth of members of the Lok Sabha is given to the Speaker. When such a notice is given to the President he must summon the session within 14 days.

Speaker : The Speaker is the presiding officer of the Lok Sabha who is elected from amongst the members by a simple majority. His office is an office of much dignity, honour and prestige.

Election : Governed by Article 93. Under the influence of convention that has developed in India, a candidate of the ruling party is elected unopposed to the post of speaker of Lok Sabha.

Removal : Article 94. A speaker can be removed only by a resolution passed by effective majority after 14 days notice of moving of such a resolution has been given.

Salary : 3,50,000

Powers and Functions

The speaker is endowed with a wide range of powers. His powers are

1. To see that there is decorum and discipline in the House.
2. To decide who shall hold the floor and speak in deliberations of the House.
3. To safeguard the rights and privileges of the members of the House.
4. To put the motion of the vote to announce the result. He does not vote but in case of a tie, he casts his vote.
5. To act as administrative head of the Lok Sabha Secretariat.
6. To accept resignations sent by members of Lok Sabha.
7. To protect the House from unnecessary executive intrusion.
8. To allot time for each item on the agenda of the House.

Some of his special powers are

9. To certify whether a particular bill is a Money Bill or not (Article 110).
10. To preside over joint sitting of both the houses of the Parliament.
11. To admit a vote of no-confidence against the Government.

Position : In early days the speakers like G.V. Mavalankar (first speaker of Independent India) and M.A.S. Ayangar were highly respected for their act. But, of late party politics is crawling into his office and severely damaged its prestige and honour. Recurring instances of ex-speakers being offered highly prestigious and ceremonial positions has maligned the stature of speaker's position. If Parliamentary democracy is to survive and continue with vigour, speakers need to shed complacency. He need to be impartial in conducting affairs of the House, as his British counterpart.

Besides speaker there is a deputy speaker (usually from opposition party) who presides in the absence of speaker.

PARLIAMENTARY PRIVILEGES

Certain privileges and immunities are granted to members of the Parliament to enable them to work freely and efficiently. They are as follows :

1. Freedom of speech.
2. Freedom from arrest in civil cases for duration of session of Parliament and 40 days before and after.
3. To summon any person to produce documents or to answer charges for contempt of the house.
4. Right to exclude outsiders from the proceedings of the house.
5. Power to punish for breach of privileges committed, mode or outside the Parliament.
6. Right to regulate its own internal proceedings without interference from any executive or judicial authority.

THE RAJYA SABHA

Also called Upper House or Council of States.

Composition : Article 80 of the Constitution outlines that

- Not more than 238 representatives to be sent from States and Union Territories.
- Twelve members to be nominated by the President having special knowledge or practical experience in the field of science, art, literature and social service.

Total = 250

However, the Parliament by law has fixed the total strength of Rajya Sabha to be not more than 245 (233 elected + 12 nominated).

DURATION OF DIFFERENT LOK SABHAS*

Term	DATE	
	From	To
First Lok Sabha	13 May, 1952	4 April, 1957
Second Lok Sabha	10 May, 1957	31 March, 1962
Third Lok Sabha	16 April, 1962	3 March, 1967
Fourth Lok Sabha	16 March, 1967	27 December, 1971
Fifth Lok Sabha	19 March, 1971	18 January, 1977
Sixth Lok Sabha	25 March, 1977	22 August, 1979
Seventh Lok Sabha	21 January, 1980	31 December, 1984
Eighth Lok Sabha	15 March, 1985	27 November, 1989
Ninth Lok Sabha	18 December, 1989	13 March, 1991
Tenth Lok Sabha	9 July, 1991	15 May, 1996
Eleventh Lok Sabha	22 May, 1996	4 December, 1997
Twelfth Lok Sabha	23 March, 1998	26 April, 1999
Thirteenth Lok Sabha	20 October, 1999	February, 2004

**See appendix for rest list*

SPEAKERS OF LOK SABHA*

S.No.	Name	Tenure
1.	G.V. Mavlankar	15 May, 1952 to 27 February, 1956
2.	M.A. S. Ayangar	2 March, 1956 to 10 May, 1957
3.	M.A. S. Ayangar	11 May, 1957 to 16 April, 1962
4.	Hukum Singh	17 April, 1962 to 16 March, 1967
5.	Neelam Sanjeev Reddy	17 March, 1967 to 19 July, 1969
6.	Dr. G.D.S. Dhillon	8 August, 1969 to 19 March, 1971
7.	Dr. G.D.S. Dhillon	20 March, 1971 to 1 December, 1975
8.	Baliram Bhagat	5 January, 1976 to 25 March, 1977
9.	Neelam Sanjeev Reddy	26 March, 1977 to 21 July, 1977
10.	K.S. Hegde	21 July, 1977 to 21 January, 1980
11.	Dr. Balram Jakhad	22 January, 1980 to 15 January, 1985
12.	Dr. Balram Jakhad	15 January, 1985 to 18 December, 1989
13.	Ravi Roy	19 December, 1989 to 9 July, 1991
14.	Shiv Raj Patil	10 July, 1991 to 21 May, 1996
15.	P.A. Sangma	22 May, 1996 to 23 March, 1998
16.	G.M.C. Balayogi	24 March, 1998 to 21 October, 1999
17.	G.M.C. Balayogi	22 October, 1999 to May, 2002

See appendix for rest list

Representation of States and Union Territories in Rajya Sabha

State	Number of Seats	State	Number of Seats
Andhra Pradesh	11	Uttar Pradesh	31
Telangana	07	West Bengal	16
Assam	07	Jammu and Kashmir	04
Bihar	16	Nagaland	01
Goa	01	Himachal Pradesh	03
Gujarat	11	Manipur	01
Haryana	05	Tripura	01
Kerala	09	Meghalaya	01
Madhya Pradesh	13	Sikkim	01
Tamil Nadu	18	Mizoram	01
Maharashtra	19	Arunachal Pradesh	01
Karnataka	12	Delhi	03
Odisha	10	Puducherry (Pondicherry)	01
Punjab	07	Chhattisgarh	03
Rajasthan	10	Jharkhand	06
		Uttarakhand	03

Term : The Rajya Sabha is a permanent body, not subject to dissolution. The term of the members of the house is six years. Nearly one-third of the members of the Rajya Sabha retire after every two years.

Method of Election : Except for a few members (twelve) who are nominated by the President, the members are elected indirectly by proportional representation by means of single transferrable vote. They are elected by an electoral college consisting of elected members of the state Legislative Assemblies. Union Territories elect through the same method by special electoral college.

Qualification : A person seeking membership of Rajya Sabha must be 30 years of age.

Comparison Between Two Houses : The Lok Sabha and Rajya Sabha

The Lok Sabha is represented directly by elected representatives of the people. The Rajya Sabha, on the other hand, consists of 12 nominated and indirectly elected members. They are elected by elected representatives of respective states and similarly by Union Territories. As such have been termed as the House of People and Council of State. This contrast between the two houses is also reflected in the domain of Parliamentary powers and functions.

The contrast between the power of two houses can be studied under following headings.

1. Finance
2. Legislation
3. Control over Executive
4. Election
5. Impeachment
6. Constitutional Amendments
7. Approval of proclamation of Emergency

1. Finance : A money Bill or a Financial Bill can only be introduced in the Lok Sabha. A Money Bill when passed by Lok Sabha is returned from Rajya Sabha with certain recommendations, may or may not be accepted by the Lok Sabha. It can delay Money Bill by 14 days only. Its power is only of advisory character. Speaker of Lok Sabha was the sole power to decide whether a Bill is Money Bill or not.

2. Legislation : As regards ordinary legislation both the houses enjoy co-equal powers. In case of disagreement between the two Houses on ordinary bill, there is provision of joint sitting of both the Houses to resolve the deadlock. However, Rajya Sabha suffers due to numerical strength.

3. Control Over Executive : Article 75(3) provides that "Council of Minister shall be collectively responsible to the Lok Sabha." A vote of censure, no-confidence motion or confidence can be introduced and passed only in the Lok Sabha.

4. Election : Both the houses have co-equal powers in the election of President and Vice President.

5. Impeachment : Both the houses enjoy equal power in the impeachment of President. According to Article 61 of the Constitution the resolution for the removal of the President must be passed by each House by a majority of not less than two-thirds of the total membership of each House separately. But, a resolution seeking removal of Vice President can be introduced only in the Rajya Sabha.

6. Constitutional Amendments : In the realm of amendment of Constitution both the houses have been placed at par. There is no provision of joint sitting in case of deadlock between the two houses. Constitutional Amendment Bill must be passed by both the houses sitting separately.

7. Approval and Disapproval of National Emergency : The two houses have equal power so far as the approval of proclamation of emergency under Article 352, 356 and 360 is concerned. Moreover, if Lok Sabha stands dissolved or is dissolved within the period of proclamation of emergency, a resolution approving the proclamation is passed by the Rajya Sabha, the proclamation would be legally upto a maximum of 30 days from the date on which the Lok Sabha assembles after its reconstitution.

However Article 352 (National Emergency) provides that a resolution seeking disapproval of the continuance of national emergency can be introduced and passed only in the Lower House.

Besides above provisions, there are two other provisions which confer special power upon the

Rajya Sabha to discharge its function of federal character. They are

Firstly, The Rajya Sabha may by a resolution supported by not less than two-thirds of the members present and voting confer the power on the Parliament to legislate on matters cited in State list in view of national interest (Article 249). Such a resolution may be in operation for one year but may be increased for one year at a time by passing separate resolution.

Secondly, Under Article 372 Rajya Sabha by a resolution supported by not less than two-thirds of the members present and voting provide for creation of all Indian services.

Salaries

1.	President	5,00,000
2.	Vice-President	4,00,000
3.	Governor	3,50,000
4.	Speaker of Lok Sabha	3,50,000
5.	Chief Justice of India	2,80,000
6.	Judges of Supreme Court	2,50,000
7.	Chief Justice of High Court	2,50,000
8.	Judges of High Court	2,25,000
9.	CAG (Comptroller and Auditor General)	2,50,000
10.	CEC (Chief Election Commissioner)	2,50,000

Legislation or Law Making in Parliament

The primary function of the parliament is legislation. It has an exclusive power to legislate on the subjects mentioned in the Union list as well as all the residuary subjects.

It shares the power of legislation on subjects in the concurrent list with the state legislature. In case of conflict, the law of parliament prevails to the extent of inconsistency.

It may legislate with respect to any subject in the state list in circumstances when the subject assumes national importance or during emergency.

Ordinary Bill

Provisions regarding ordinary bill are contained in Article 10. It can be introduced in either house of Parliament except bills under Article 3, these bill does not require prior recommendation of the President.

Both houses enjoy equal legislative jurisdiction over ordinary bill. The ordinary bills are passed by simple majority.

In case of deadlock between the two houses, a joint sitting is convened by the President.

President enjoys the right to send the ordinary bill for reconsideration only once.

The draft of the proposed bill has to be sent to the Secretariat of the House. The presiding officer of the house, after consulting the Business Advisory Committee determines the day and time when the Bill is to be moved in the house.

On the appointed day and time after receiving the assent of the presiding officer, the mover reads the title of the bill and gives a short speech highlighting the aims and objectives of the Bill. If there is no opposition from any one, the Bill is supposed to have been passed in the first reading. But when the opposition is not prepared to even consider the Bill, the presiding officer allows a full debate and then the Bill is put to vote. If the house approves it, the Bill is supposed to have been passed in the first reading.

At the second reading (after two days), there is a general discussion and after this there are three alternatives.

1. The house may decide to discuss the Bill in details, clause by clause and also vote each and every clause.
2. The house may decide to circulate the Bill for eliciting the public opinion. Then the Bill is published on the Government Gazette inviting public reactions.

   The gist of the public opinion is there circulated among members. The House discusses the Bill in details in the light of the public opinion and then votes it clause by clause.
3. The House may decide to refer the Bill to a select committee even President can not

convene joint sitting. Other House can delay an ordinary Bill for six months.

Select Committee consisting of such members of the House as may have special interest in the subject. The Presiding officer constitutes such a committee consisting of 20-30 members. The committee makes a thorough scrutiny and submits a report to the House. The House then discusses and votes the Bill clause by clause.

At the third reading, there is only a general discussion and no amendments, excepting some verbal exchanges is permitted. If the House approves the Bill, the Bill goes to the other House.

In the Other House, the Bill undergoes all the stages as in the originating House subsequent to its introduction. It may

(i) Reject the Bill altogether-joint sitting Art 108.
(ii) Pass the Bill with Amendments
If other house accepts-goes to President.
If other house does not accept-joint sitting.
(iii) Not take any action for more than 6 months joint sitting. Article 108

At the joint sitting if the Bill is passed by the majority it is treated to be passed by the two houses.

If President withholds his assent, there is end to Bill. If President returns the Bill for reconsideration and the houses pass the Bill with or without amendments, the President shall have no power to withhold his assent from the Bill.

Money Bill : Provisions are contained in Article 110 : A Bill is money if it deals exclusive only with one or more of money matters mentioned. Under Article 110 of the constitution. They include :

- the imposition, abolition, remission, alternation or regulation of any tax.
- the regulation of borrowing of money by Government.
- the custody of consolidated Fund and the Contingency fund of India deposition and withdrawal.
- appropriation of money out of the consolidated fund of India.
- declaration of any expenditure to be expenditure charged on the consolidated fund or increment in the amount of any such expenditure.
- The receipt of money on account of the consolidated fund of India or the Public Account of India or the custody or issue of such money or the audit of the accounts of the Union of a State or
- any matter incidental to the above mentioned points.

Article 110 also provides that declaration of the Speaker that a Bill is a money Bill, shall be final.

- A money Bill can be introduced only in Lok Sabha with the recommendation of the President. It is passed by simple majority.
- If RS rejects, passes or not acts upon the Bill for 14 days, the Bill is deemed to have been passed by both the houses.
- There can be no deadlock over passage of money Bill in between two houses.
- The President can not withhold his assent in case of a Money Bill.
- In case of deadlock provision of joint sitting.

Annual Financial Statement Or 'Budget' Article 112

- The Budget is a statement of the estimated receipt and expenditure for the coming year.
- It is the duty of the President to cause Annual Financial statement to be brought before the Parliament.
- It is prepared by the Finance Minister.
- It also shows the ways and means of meeting the estimated expenditure.
- Budget has two parts – Revenue part
  – Expenditure part
- The revenue part comes to be known as the Financial Bill.
- The expenditure part comes to be known as the Appropriation Bill.
- Appropriation Bill consists of separately
  –expenditure charged on the Consolidated Fund
  –Sums required to meet other expenditure proposed to be met from consolidated fund of India prepared in the form of demand for grants.

- Charged expenditure can be discussed but not voted upon.
- Demand for grants are put to vote in the Lok Sabha which shall have power to assent to any demand, or to assent to any demand subject to reduction of that amount, refuse to assent to any demand.
- The LS shall have no power to suggest an increase in demand for grants.
- No money can be withdrawn from the consolidated fund except under an Appropriation Act.
- Both, the Appropriation Bill and Financial Bill are passed as money Bill.
- No demand for grant is made without the recommendation of the President.
- Demand for grants are presented under particular heads and voted separately.
- Council of state has no business with Budget beyond the general discussion.

On a stated day the budget is laid before both the Houses. While presenting the budget, the Finance Minister makes an exhaustive explanatory speech clarifying all the important issues involved in the proposals. There is no discussion on the day on which it is presented to the house.

The second stage in regard to the budget is a general discussion on its proposals subsequent to presentation. No item of expenditure is exempted from his general discussion and even items that are charged on the consolidated fund can come within the purview of the criticism of the legislatures. At this stage no motion is moved nor does voting takes place on any item.

After the general discussion, the estimates are submitted to the House of People in the form of demands for grants under particular heads. They are put forward by the Ministries of the respective department. Speeches from members may follow and amends may be moved to refuse or reduce the amount. The Speaker in consultation with the leader of the House, allots in definite number of days for discussion and voting. On the last day-5 O'clock- the Speaker must stop all discussions and put all the remaining demands to a vote of the House which will be at liberty to accept them or to throw them out. It will now have no opportunity to modify them in any way.

After the demand for grants is made, a bill called Appropriation Bill is introduced in the House. The bill like any other Bill must be passed by both houses.

Any amendment as regards fixing quorum in the house can be effected by simple majority.

Amendment Bill

A Constitution is a living document, which has to adapt itself to the changing socio-economic conditions.

I. The constitution makers provided for an easier mode for changing those provisions which did not primarily affect the federal system.

   There are about three dozen articles which can be altered by simple majority and were not to be deemed to be the amendment of the constitution. It could be done by simple process of legislation.

   Under this procedure comes
   (a) Names boundaries of states
   (b) Creation or abolition of Legislative Council
   (c) Codification of Parliamentary privileges
   (d) Fixing quorum in Parliament
   (e) Salaries and allowances of President, Governor, Judges

   The Process of Amendment is prescribed in Article 368.

II. For certain category of constitutional provisions a special majority is required.

   Such an amendment must be passed by each house by a majority (i.e. more than 50%) of the total membership of the House and by a majority of not less than two-thirds of the members of that house present and voting.

   Ratification of States in case of Constitutional amendment bill is must before being presented to the President for his assent.

   24 Amendment Act has made it obligatory for the President to give his assent to Constitution Amendment Bill.

   Under this category comes majority Constitutional provisions.

III. In case of certain amendments, besides the special majority mentioned above, ratification by not less than half of the states is required. This has to be done before presenting the Bill for President's assent.

Under this category comes

(a) procedure for election of the President
(b) executive power of Union and States (Art 73, 162)
(c) SC and HC (Art 241, Ch-IV of Part V, Ch-V of Part VI)
(d) Distribution of legislative power (Chap I Part XI)
(e) any list in seventh schedule
(f) Representation of State in Parliament (Art 80-81)
(g) Provisions of Art 368 itself
   - a bill can be introduced in either House
   - no provision of joint sitting.
   - previous sanction of President is not required.
   - 24th Amendment Act 1971 has made it obligatory on the President to give his assent to a Bill for amendment.

Parliamentary committees are not constitutional bodies but have been brought into existence under the rule making power of Parliament.

PARLIAMENTARY COMMITTEES

- appointed or elected by the House or nominated by the Speaker/Chairman.
- works under the direction of Presiding officer.
- presents its report to the house or presiding officer.
- has a Secretariat provided by the House.
- holds office generally for a year.
- expected to contain representative of all parties in the House.
- enables legislature to work on 'Division of Labour.'
- not constitutional bodies, but mention is formed in Article 88 & 105.
- have been brought into existence under the rule making power of the Parliament.

There are consultative committees attached to serious department and ministries but are not Parliamentary Committees.

The kinds-Ad hoc and Standing Committee

Ad hoc Committees are constituted by the House or the speaker as and when the need arises and cease to exist as soon as they complete the work assigned to them.

Also referred to as select committee.

The number is not fixed.

Ex : The Select or joint committees on Bills - a bill.

Joint Parliamentary Committee - a specific subject.

Ad hoc Committees are also referred to as select committee. Standing Committee are of permanent nature.

Standing Committees are elected by the house or appointed by the Speaker/Chairman every year as from time to time.

Article of permanent nature

Ex : Financial - (1) DAC (2) estimates (C) Com. on public undertaking Dept. related standing committees.

House Committees
Enquiry Committees
Scrutiny Committees
Services Committee

Strength

Business Advisory Committee	—	15
Estimates Committee	—	30 (not RS)
Committee on Public Account	—	22
Committee on Petitions	—	15
Committee on Welfare of SC/ST	—	30

The Chairman of all committees are appointed by Speaker, except that of Joint Committee on salaries and allowances of members of Parliament, who is elected by the Committee itself.

In 1993 Parliament set up 17 standing committees to secure more accountability of Executive to the legislature.

Mainly to Scrutinise Budgets.
Report of Estimates Committee is not debated.

Public Accounts Committee

- Consists of not more than 22 members.
- Elected on the basis of proportional representation.
- 15 from the Lok Sabha and 7 from Rajya Sabha
- Chairman is a member of opposition party.
- Scrutinises appropriation accounts of GOI.
- Scrutinises the report of CAG.
- Ensures that money is spent in accordance with the Parliaments decisions.
- Investigations are in the nature of post mortem.

Estimates Committee

- Committee of House of People.
- Consists of 30 members
- Chairman is appointed by speaker.
- Constituted after presentation of Budget.
- reports on what economies, improvement in Organisational efficiency or administration reform may be effected.
- Scrutinises the expenditure effected by the Government
- report is not debated.
- carries its examination throughout the year.

While DAC has to examine accounts quite some time after the expenditure was actually been incurred.

Committee an estimates is concerned with the working of different ministries during the course of the financial year.

Committee on Public undertakings is mentioned in Fourth schedule and consists of members from both the houses.

Committee on Public Undertakings

- Consists of 22 members.
- 15 members from LS. and 7 from RS.
- elected by system of proportional representation.
- Chairman is appointed by the Speaker.
- mentioned in 4 schedule.
- involve both pre and post expenditure phases.

COMMITTEE SYSTEM HAS HELPED EXERCISE LEGISLATIVE CONTROL OVER EXECUTIVE

Not more than one no-confidence motion can be admitted in one session of the Parliament. But as regards confidence motion, there is no limit on the number of times it can be introduced in one session.

PARLIAMENTARY PROCEDURES

No Confidence Motion

It is

- introduced only in LS by opposition.
- to discuss all acts of Omission or Commission of Government
- when admitted, takes precedence over all pending business of the house.
- if adopted by LS, Govenment is expected to resign.
- not more than one in one session of Parliament.
- wider in scope.
- firstly in 1963.

Confidence Motion

It has emerged as a part of Parliamentary practice in India

- with the formation of minority Government, it has become imperative for the President to direct Government to prove its majority within a specified time period.
- if defeated, Government is obliged to resign.
- no limit on number of times, it can be introduced in one session.
  → First Government to lose confidence motion was V.P. Singh's.

Question Hour

- first item of business in each house, begins at 11 O' clock.
- two types of questions; starred and unstarred.
  → Starred questions are answered by ministers orally.

→ Unstarred questions are meant for written answers for which minister get sufficient time.

CONSOLIDATED FUND OF INDIA

Article 266(1) provides for a constitutional fund.

It is the largest fund

- placed at the disposal of Parliament.
- includes all revenues received, all taxes collected and all loans raised by Government of India.
- each state has a consolidated fund to its own.

CONTINGENCY FUND OF INDIA

Article 267 provides for

- statutory fund called contingency fund.
- Its upper limit is Rs 50 crore.
- It is placed at disposal of President
- to meet unforeseen expenditure by Government

Guillotine : Due to lack of time, if the Lok Sabha accepts demands for grant made by various ministries without any discussion on them is known as application of Guillotine.

Application of Guillotine is passed only in Lok Sabha.

Cut Motions : A legislative device used to exercise financial control over executive when a demand is made by a minister, a cut may be proposed in it by any member.

The motion for cut comes in the form of an amendment and is intended to bring reduction in the expenditure.

National Government : A government formed by all the political parties or almost all the political parties represented in the Parliament.

Shadow Cabinet : It is formed by main opposition party in the Parliament Members are assinged specific portfolio to lead debates

JURISDICTION AND SEAT OF HIGH COURTS

Name	Year	Territorial Jurisdiction	Seat
Allahabad	1866	Uttar Pradesh	Allahabad (Bench at Lucknow)
Andhra Pradesh	2019	Andhra Pradesh	Amaravati
Bombay	1862	Maharashtra, Goa, Dadar and Nagar Haveli and Daman and Diu	Mumbai (Benches at Nagpur, Panaji and Aurangabad)
Calcutta	1862	West Bengal and Andaman & Nicobar	Kolkata (Circuit Bench at Port Blair)
Chhattisgarh	2000	Chhattisgarh	Bilaspur
Delhi	1966	Delhi	Delhi
Guwahati	1948	Assam, Nagaland, Mizoram and Arunachal Pradesh	Guwahati (Benches at Kohima, Aizawl and Itanagar)
Gujarat	1960	Gujarat	Ahmedabad
Himachal Pradosh	1971	Himachal Pradesh	Shimla
Jammu & Kashmir	1928	Jammu & Kashmir	Srinagar and Jammu
Jharkhand	2000	Jharkhand	Ranchi
Karnataka	1884	Karnataka	Bengaluru (Circuit Benches at Dharwar and Gulbarga)
Kerala	1958	Kerala & Lakshadweep	Ernakulam
Madhya Pradesh	1956	Madhya Pradesh	Jabalpur (Benches at Gwalior and Indore)
Madras	1862	Tamil Nadu & Puducherry	Chennai (Bench at Madurai)
Orissa	1948	Odisha	Cuttack
Patna	1916	Bihar	Patna
Punjab and Haryana	1966	Punjab, Haryana and Chandigarh	Chandigarh
Rajasthan	1949	Rajasthan	Jodhpur (Bench at Jaipur)
Sikkim	1975	Sikkim	Gangtok
Uttarakhand	2000	Uttarakhand	Nainital
Tripura	2013	Tripura	Agartala
Meghalaya	2013	Meghalaya	Shillong
Manipur	2013	Manipur	Imphal
Telangana	1954	Telangana	Hyderabad

- it gives an effective opposition
- it trains the M.P's in the art of governance
- also known as Cabinet in waiting.
- functions well when there is two party system in U.K. non-existent in India.
- introduced in LA of Haryana in 2000.

Lame Duck Session : Last session of old Parliament held after the election of new Parliament. Members of old Parliament who could not get elected to the new Parliament are called lame duck M.P's. Lame duck session is not relevant in Indian context. For election to LS takes place only after dissolution of the house. Possible in R.S. where seats to be vacant are elected a month in advance.

Crafter Government : A Government comes into existence only if government loses confidence of LS or PM passes away or resign.

Interim Government : A Government formed during transitional phase.

Minority Government : A Government which does not enjoy the confidence of the Lower House. It survives with outside support of other parties.

Coalition Government : A Government which is formed by coalition of two or more political parties with some common goals to be achieved. Since 1989 we are witnessing an era of coalition government.

Ordinance : They are orders of the President which has the same effect as an act of the Parliament. These orders are issued only when the Parliament is not in the session. It ceases to remain in force, six weeks after Parliament reassembles, unless approved by it.

Delegated Legislation : An informal legislative device by which the executive fills the details of legislative policies, broadly outlined by the legislature. It is comparatively a recent phenomenon that has come into operation with growing complexity of the government. It has severely restricted the power of legislature.

Delimitation : Is an electoral procedure by which electoral constituencies are readjusted in view of changing population in a region. It is done by a Delimitation Commission constituted by an act of Parliament after each census.

Hung Parliament : When no political party or coalition of political parties enjoys the majority in L.S. after a general election. Under such circumstances it becomes difficult for any party to form a government. It paves way for coalition and minority governments.

THE JUDICIARY

Article 233-237 : provides for a single, unified, hierarchically organised judiciary.

One court exercises administrative control over court below and judges of one hierarchy getting elevated and appointed as judges of courts above.

SUPREME COURT

The Constitution makers of India adopted the concept of Supreme Court from the United States of America. However, unlike the U.S.A., the Supreme Court in India is not the sovereign body. It is endowed with vast powers and functions including the power of judicial review. In the last 74 years of its working, the court has helped in strengthening democracy, protecting people's right and checked authoritarianism. It is vested with administrative powers over courts lying below it. Indian constitution provides for a single integrated judiciary with the Supreme Court, at the top of hierarchy.

Composition

The Supreme Court at present consists of Chief Justice and 33 other Judges. In 1950, it had only eight Judges. Parliament was, however, authorised to change the number of its Judges. On account of the increase in its work load, the strength of the Supreme Court judges has been raised from time to time. In 1956, the Parliament passed the Supreme Court Number of Judges Act, which raised the total strength to 11. In 1960, the Supreme Court number of Judges Amendment Act was passed further raising the strength of the Court Judges to 14 including the Chief Justice. Its strength was further increased to 18 in 1977. In 1986 it was increased to 25 and 31 in 2009.

Appointment : Article 124 a judge of the Supreme Court is appointed by the President in consultation with such of the judges of the Supreme Court and of the High Court in the States as the

President may deem necessary for the purpose. In the Case of appointment of a Judge other than the Chief Justice, the Chief Justice of India must be consulted. In practice, the appointment of the Chief Justice of India as well as of the other judges of the Supreme Court is recommended by the Home Ministry and after the matter has been examined by the Appointments Committee of the Indian Cabinet and the decision receives the blessings of the Prime Ministers, it is formalised by the Indian President.

In Supreme Court Advocates on Record Association (SCARA) Versus Union of India 1993, the Supreme Court held the opinion that appointment of Judges is an "Integrated Participatory Consultative Exercise." There must not be any appointment to the higher Judiciary against opinion expressed by Chief Justice of India.

In case of appointment of Chief Justice of India, it is usually the senior most judge who is elevated to the post. But, this convention was broken in 1977 when A.N. Ray superseded three colleagues (J.M. Shelat, K.S. Hedge, A.N. Grover). In 1977 Mirza Hamidullah Beg supreseded H.R. Khanna. However, since 1980 senior most judge is appointed as Chief Justice. An acting CJ may be appointed by President in case a vacancy arises. The Chief Justice of India with the prior consent of President may appoint a Judge of High Court to sit and act as Judge of Supreme Court provided, it the session of the Supreme Court cannot be held or continued for want of a quorum. (Article 127).

Similarly, when there is pending business before the Supreme Court, the Chief Justice, with the consent of the President may request in writing the attendance of a retired Judge of SC to act as Judge of SC.

Salary : Provided in Second Schedule

Chief Justice	:	2,80,000
Other Judges	:	2,50,000 (same of CAG)

In addition, each judge is also entitled to a free House and certain other allowances and privileges. Neither the salary, allowances, and privileges, nor his rights in respect of leave of absence or pension can be varied to his disadvantage after his appointment. However, the salaries of the Judges may be reduced by a law of Parliament during a grave financial emergency proclaimed by the President.

Qualifications : A person shall not be qualified for appointment as a Judge of the Supreme Court unless he is a citizen of India and :

(a) has been for at least five years a Judge of a High Court or of two or more such courts in succession; or

(b) has been worked for at least ten years as an advocate of a High Court or of two or more such courts in succession; or

(c) is, in the opinion of the President, a distinguished jurist.

The inclusion of the last provision which would enable the President to appoint a distinguished jurist on the Supreme Court, even if he did not qualify by a specified number of years of practices at the Bar, was intended to open a wider field of choice.

Tenure

No minimum age is prescribed for appointment as a Judge of the Supreme Court, nor any fixed period office. Once appointed, a Judge of the Supreme Court may cease to be so, on any one of the following grounds (other than death); (a) on attaining the age of 65 years; (b) on resigning his office by writing addressed to the President; (c) on being removed by the President upon an address to that effect being passed by a special majority of each House of Parliament.

Chief Justices of India*

S.No.	*Name*	*Tenure*
1.	Harilal J. Kania	Jan. 26, 1950 – Nov. 6, 1951
2.	M. Patanjali Sastri	Nov. 7, 1951 – Jan. 3, 1954
3.	Mehar Chand Mahajan	Jan. 4, 1954 – Dec. 22, 1954
4.	B.K. Mukherjee	Dec. 23, 1954 – Jan. 31, 1956
5.	S.R. Das	Feb. 1, 1956 – Sept. 30, 1959

S.No.	Name	Tenure
6.	Bhuvaneshwar Prasad Sinha	Oct. 1, 1959, – Jan. 31, 1964
7.	P.B. Gajendragadkar	Feb. 1, 1964 – March 15, 1966
8.	A.K. Sarkar	March 16, 1966 – June 29, 1966
9.	K. Subba Rao	June 30, 1966 – April 11, 1967
10.	K. N. Wanchoo	April 12, 1967 – Feb. 24, 1968
11.	M. Hidayatullah	Feb. 25, 1968 – Dec. 16, 1970
12.	J.C. Shah	Dec. 17, 1970 – Jan. 21, 1971
13.	S.M. Sikri	Jan. 22, 1971 – April 25, 1973
14.	A.N. Roy	April 26, 1973 – January 27, 1977
15.	M.H. Beg	Jan. 28, 1977 – February 21, 1978
16.	Y.V. Chandrachud	Feb. 22, 1978 – July 11, 1985
17.	Prafullachandra Natvarlal Bhagwati	July 12, 1985 – Dec. 20, 1986
18.	R.S. Pathak	Dec. 21, 1986 – June 18, 1989
19.	E.S. Venkataramiah	June 19, 1989 – Dec. 18, 1989
20.	Sabyasachi Mukherjee	Dec. 19, 1989 – Sept. 25, 1990
21.	Ranganath Mishra	Sept. 26, 1990 – Nov. 24, 1991
22.	Kamal Narain Singh	Nov. 25, 1991 – Dec. 12, 1991
23.	M.H. Kania	Dec. 13, 1991 – Nov. 17, 1992
24.	Lalit Mohan Sharma	Nov. 18, 1992 – Feb. 11, 1993
25.	M.N. Venkatachaliah	Feb. 12, 1993 – Oct. 24, 1994
26.	Aziz Mushabber Ahmadi	Oct. 25, 1994 – March 24, 1997
27.	Jagdish Sharan Verma	March 25, 1997 – Jan. 17, 1998
28.	M.M. Punchhi	Jan. 18, 1998 – October 9, 1998
29.	A.S. Anand	Oct. 10, 1998 – Oct. 31, 2001
30.	S.P. Bharucha	Nov. 1, 2001 – May 4, 2002
31.	B.N. Kirpal	May 5, 2002 – Nov. 7, 2002
32.	G.B. Pattanaik	Nov. 8, 2002 – Dec. 18, 2002
33.	V.N. Khare	Dec. 19, 2002 – May 1, 2004
34.	S. Rajendra Babu	May 2, 2004 – June 1, 2004
35.	R.C. Lahoti	June 2, 2004 – Oct. 31, 2005
36.	Yogesh Kumar Sabharwal	Nov. 1, 2005 – Jan. 13, 2007
37.	K.G. Balakrishnan	Jan. 14, 2007– May 11, 2010
38.	S.H. Kapadia	May 12, 2010 – Sept. 28, 2012
39.	Altamas Kabir	Sept. 29, 2012 – July 18, 2013
40.	P. Sathasivam	July 19, 2013 – April 26, 2014

See appendix for rest list

Seat of Supreme Court

The Supreme Court ordinarily shall sit at Delhi but it can sit at such other places as the Chief Justice of India may, with the approval of the President, from time to time decide.

Removal

A Judge of the Supreme Court can be removed from his position only on the ground of proved misbehaviour or incapacity. He can be removed from his office by an order of the President passed after an address from each House of Parliament, supported by a majority of the total membership of that House and by a majority of not less than 2/3rd of the members present and voting.

Procedure for Removal

A resolution seeking removal of a Judge can be introduced in either House of the Parliament. In Lok Sabha it must be supported by not less than 100 and Rajya Sabha not less than 50. An Enquiry Committee consisting of Judges may be constituted by the House to investigate charges. The Report of Committee is not binding on the House. Moreover, it there is no charge against the Judge, further proceedings will not go around. In 1991 proceedings were started for removal of Justice Ramaswami, for alleged financial irregularities and misuse of High Court funds in his capacity as Chief Justice of Punjab and Haryana High Court. Impeachment proceedings were started in 1993 but fell on account of abstention of Congress (I).

INDEPENDENCE OF SUPREME COURT

To ensure the independence of Supreme Court following steps have been undertaken

- Appointment of judges by the President in consultation with CJI and such other judges as he may deem fit.
- Fixed tenure and removal only on ground of proved misbehaviour or incapacity and address by both houses of Parliament by special majority.
- The terms and conditions of Service of a judge can be varied to his disadvantage after his appointment (Article 125).
- The Salaries and allowances of the judges as well as of the staff are charged on the consolidated fund of India and not subjected to vote in Parliament (Art 146).
- No discussion can take place in the Parliament, with respect to conduct of any judge in the discharge of his duties except when a resolution for his removal is under consideration (Article 121).
- No person who has held office as a judge of the Supreme Court can plead or act in any court or before any authority within the territory of India.

Court of Record : Article 129 provides The Supreme Court shall be a Court of record and shall have all powers of such a Court, including the power to punish for contempt itself. A Court of record obviously is one where the acts and Judicial proceedings are kept for memory and testimony. As a court of record the Supreme Court has power to punish those who are adjudged as guilty of contempt of court. The Court has taken up the cases for their contempt.

Jurisdiction of the Supreme Court : Indian Supreme Court enjoys a number of powers evident in its jurisdiction. They are of following kinds:

1. Original; 2. Writ; 3. Appellate; 4. Advisory; 5. Revisory.

1. **Original Jurisdiction :** Article 131 of Indian Constitution provides for original jurisdiction that deals with disputes (i) between the Government of India and one or more States, (ii) between the Government of India and any State or States on the one side and one or more other States on the other, or (iii) between two or more states. However, disputes arising out of the provisions of treaties with the former Indian States or to which any such State is a party are excluded from the Original Jurisdiction of the Supreme Court.
2. **Writ Jurisdiction :** Supreme Court enjoys powers under Article 32 for the enforcement of Fundamental Rights. It is exercised in the nature of writs, viz; Habeas Corpus, Mandamas, Certeorari, Quo Warranto and Prohibition.
3. **Appellate Jurisdiction :** The Supreme Court is the highest court of appeal in all Civil, Criminal and Constitutional cases. Moreover, under ''special leave to Appeal'' provided in Article 136; the Supreme Court has discretionary powers to take cases from High Courts.

   Article 134 of the Constitution for the first time provides for an appeal to the Supreme Court from any judgement, final order or sentence in a criminal proceeding of a High Court, as of right, in two specified classes of cases—(a) where the High Court has on an appeal reversed an order of acquital of an accused person and sentenced him to death; (b) where the High Court has withdrawn for trial before itself any case from any Court subordinate to its authority and has in such trial convicted the accused and sentenced him to death. In these two classes of cases relating to a sentence of death by the High Court, appeal lies to the Supreme Court as of right. Moreover, an appeal may lie to the Supreme Court in any criminal case if the High Court certifies that the case is a fit one for appeal to the Supreme Court.

4. **Advisory Jurisdiction :** Under Article 143 of the Constitution, President can seek advisory opinion of the Supreme Court when it appeals to him that a question of law or fact has arisen, or is likely to arise, which is of such a nature and of such public importance that it is expedient to obtain the opinion of the Supreme Court upon it. The President is not bound to accept the opinion of the Supreme Court. The Court is not bound to give its advice.
5. **Revisory Jurisdiction :** Under Article 137 the Supreme Court can revise its own judgement, order or direction. Besides, Article 138 and Article 139 provides that Parliament by law can extend the jurisdiction of the Supreme Court.

JUDICIAL REVIEW

Judicial review is the power of Supreme Court and High Court to declare a law as unconstitutional and void if it is inconsistent with one or more provisions of the constitution to the extent of such inconsistency. Under this it can examine legislature enactments and their constitutionality. It can examine the validity of any order of the executive or any law of the legislature. It is the Supreme Court to declare what the provisions of the Constitution mean. The Supreme Court has power to review any judgement or order made by it earlier. The power of judicial review is more implicit and traceable to Article 82, 226 and also under Article 13.

Based on Three Principles

- Concept of Limited Government.
- It maintains harmony with different provisions i.e. if two interpretations of law is possible, one leading to validation of Constitutional provision would prevail.
- Ordinarily, the Court shall not interfere with and pronounce the validity of a law until it comes into effect.

Objectives

- maintain Supremacy of Constitution.
- maintain balance between various organs.
- maintain division of power, essential for federation.

PUBLIC INTEREST LITIGATION

Pro bono Public 6

PIL is one of the most potent weapons. The Judiciary, in India has acquired in recent times to enforce legal obligations of executive and legislature. Its objective is Public good, group interest and not individual interest for which FR are provided. It emanates from the power of Judicial review. The Supreme Court through its various decisions has evolved rules governing Public Interest Litigation.

Originated in Australia

A PIL can be filed up by publicity spirited individual or organisation not directly interested in the case. It is the privilege of the court to entertain or not the application for PIL

- has democratised the judiciary.
- Supreme Court has vastly expanded the scope of FR by liberally interpreting Art 32, 226.

LOK ADALATS

— First held in 1985.

— Given statutory status under Legal Service Authorities Act 1987.

— Aims at providing speedy and economical service to poor.

— Eliminate delay and speed up clearance of pending cases.

— Organised by state or district bodies.

— Case goes to LA if two parties make joint application.

— Given powers of Civil Court.

13

STATE GOVERNMENT

STATE EXECUTIVES : THE GOVERNOR

The Constitution provides for a Governor as the **head of the executive** at the state level. But, for a long time the institutional functioning was determined by one party dominant system. A major change occurred after the **fourth General Elections in 1967**. In a number of States, the party in power was different from that of the Union. There occurred fragmentation of political parties and emergence of new regional parties. Unpredictable realignments of political parties and groups took place for the purpose of forming Government. The Governors were called upon to exercise their discretionary powers more frequently. The manner in which they exercised those functions direct affect impact on Union-State relations.

The state executive consists of a Governor with a council of ministers with Chief Minister at its head.

Constitutional Provisions

Article 153-There shall be a Governor for each state.

Article 155-Governor shall be appointed by the President.

After 7th Amendment 1956, the same person can be appointed Governor for more than one state.

Qualification

Must be 35 years of age and must not hold any office of profit, nor be the member of any legislature or parliament.

Normal term of his office is 5 years but may be dismissed or resign. (Article 156)

Salary

Monthly salary of 3,50,000 month + allowances, no pension is given to him.

Oath

Takes an oath to preserve and protect the constitution. In case, he is member of any legislature in India, he will have to resign before taking over charge of his office.

Position

Though he is a constitutional head of the state during normal times, he acts as the agent of the centre during period of emergency in state. Even during normal circumstances, constitution has given certain discretionary powers to the Governor as well.

In Hargovind Pant Vs Raghukul Tilak, it was held by SC that "the office of Governor is not an employment under the Government of India. It is an independent office and is not under the control or subordinate to the Government of India."

Even though, the Governor is merely appointed and not elected, his position is better secured under constitution than the President. He wields both influence and power. His office is equally Ceremonial and equally functional.

Governor enjoys more discretionary powers than the President. If President enjoys discretionary powers, it is accidental (out of compulsion) and not institutional according to the provisions of constitution. However, Governor's discretionary powers are deliberately conferred on him by the constitution. Further, the President can not exercise his executive powers without a council to aid and advice him. Governor does not always require Council of Ministers to aid and advice him.

Governor enjoys move discretionary powers by virtue of weak position of state and the strong position of the union. But in practice his powers are powers of the union vis-a-vis state.

Powers of The Governor

1. **Executive :** All the executive functions in the state are carried on in the name of the Governor. He appoints the Chief Minister and on his advice appoints other Ministers and distribute portfolios among them.

   He also appoints Advocate-General, Chairman and members of State public service commission. Members of the state public service commission cannot be removed by him, they can be removed only by the President on the report of the Supreme Court on reference made by the President.

   He is entitled to be consulted by the President in the matter of appointment of Judges of State High Court. By the 104th Constitutional amendment nomination provision regarding Anglo-Indian Community has abolished. He can nominate 1/6 part of the total members of the Legislative Council.

   In the states of **Odisha, it is the special responsibility** of the Governor to see that a Minister is placed in charge of tribal welfare. **In Assam**, the Governor is given certain **special powers** with respect to the administration of the tribal areas provided in the sixth schedule of the Constitution. In Nagaland, Manipur and Sikkim also the Governor is vested with special responsibilities.

2. **Legislative :** Governor is an integral part of the state legislature. Governor of state enjoys extensive legislative powers. He summons either or both Houses of the State Legislature to meet at a time and at a place as he thinks fit. The only condition is that six months shall not intervene between its last sitting in one session and the date appointed for its first sitting in the next session. He may prorogue either House or dissolve the Legislative Assembly. He may address either House and may send messages to it. It is provided that the Houses to which he send message will consider any matter required by the message to be taken into consideration. The Governor addresses the House or the Houses on the commencement of the first session after general election and at the commencement of the first session on each year. When a bill has been passed by a House or Houses, it must be presented to the Governor. The Governor shall declare that he assents to it or that he withholds his assent or that he reserves the bill for the consideration of the President. The Governor may return a Non-Money bill with a message for reconsideration. He may suggest amendments. The House or Houses must consider his suggestions without delay. If the bill is passed again by the House or Houses without amendment, he cannot with hold his assent.

3. **Judicial : Article 161** empowers Governor to grant pardons, reprieves, respites or remission of punishment or to suspend or commute the sentence of death to any person convicted of any offence against which executive power of state extends. He has **no power to pardon in case of defence of death**. But has the power to suspend, remit a sentence of death. He is entitled to be consulted by the president in appointment of Judges of State High Court.

4. **Emergency :** Governor has the power to make a report to the President whenever he is satisfied that a situation has arisen in which Government of the state cannot be carried on in accordance with the provisions of the constitution [Article 356]. But this power has often been misused as Rajiv Dhawan has indicated.

5. **Financial :** He causes the annual financial statement to be laid before state legislature and reconmmends for introducing money Bill. No demand for grants can be made except on the recommendation of the Governor.

Ordinance Making Power

The Governor can promulgate ordinance only when houses are not in the session. It is not a discretionary power. Ordinance cease to have effect at the expiry of six weeks from the date of reassembly, unless disapproved earlier. He himself is competent to withdraw the ordinance at any time.

Ordinance making power is co-extensive with legislative power of State Legislature. If the provisions of ordinance are repugnant with a union law relating a concurrent subject, the Governor's ordinance will prevail notwithstanding repugnancy, if the ordinance had been made in pursuance of the instructions of the President.

Discretionary Powers

Article 163(1)-(Comparable to 74) 'there shall be a Council of Ministers headed by CM to aid and advice the Governor who shall act in accordance with such advice except in cases where the constitution requires the governor to act in his discretion.'

Article 162(2) 'if any dispute arises whether the power of Governor is his discretionary power or not, his decision shall be final and binding.' This means that whether the power of a governor is his discretionary power or not is itself a discretionary power.

1. **In appointing a Chief Minister :** If there is no clear cut majority of a party or an alliance of parties in the Legislative Assembly and there are two claimants for the post of CM, the Governor can appoint the person to be CM whom he thinks fit to provide a stable Government.
2. **Dissolving the Legislative Assembly :** Similarly, if the party in power has lost majority in the Legislative Assembly and the CM advises the Governor to dissolve the Assembly, the Governor can find alternatives to form the Government without going for dissolution.
3. **As an Administrator :** By a convention as established in England, Governor sends a fortnightly report to the President about affairs of the State administration, Public law and order.
4. **Reserve bill for Consideration of the President :** Under **Article 200**-Governor enjoys the right to reserve a bill for the consideration of President. Even a money Bill can be reserved.

In the case of a money Bill, the President may either declare his assent or withhold his assent. In case of a Bill other than a Money Bill, the President may direct the Governor to return the Bill for reconsideration. The Legislature must reconsider the Bill within 6 months. But it shall not be obligatory upon the President to give his assent in this case too.

Under Article 371 : Special responsibility is conferred on Governor of some states.

In Maharashtra, Gujarat, Nagaland, Mizoram, Orissa, MP and Bihar Governors have special responsibility.

STATE LEGISLATURE

Every state has a legislature consisting of the Governor and the Legislative Assembly. Some states have the second chamber, called Legislative Council.

LEGISLATIVE COUNCIL

- It exists in six states, viz; Bihar, Karnataka, Andhra Pradesh, Telangana, Maharashtra and U.P.
- Under **Article 169**, the Parliament by law, can provide for the creation of Legislative Council in a state or abolition if it exists, provided the Legislative Assembly of the state passes a resolution to that effect (by a majority of the total membership of the Assembly and by a majority of not less than two-thirds of the members present and voting).
- Its total members not to exceed 1/3 of Legislative Assembly.
- The total membership in no case be less than 40.
- Composition
  1/3 elected by Vidhan Sabha
  1/3 elected by Local bodies
  1/12 elected by graduates of three years standing
  1/12 elected by teachers school & colleges
  1/6 elected by Governor (also from co-operative)
  Thus 5/6 elected indirectly elected 1/6 nominated.
- To become, a member a person must be 30 years age.

LEGISLATIVE ASSEMBLY

- It consists of not more than 500 or less than 60.
- Assembly of Mizoram and Goa have 40 members each, while Sikkim has 32 only.
- The member must be 25 years of age.
- Term of the Assembly is 5 year.
- To be elected to Legislative Council or Legislative Assembly, a person must be a elector for any seat in Legislative Assembly in the state.

As regards disqualifications of members, the decision of Governor in consultation with the election commission shall be final.

Constitution provides for joint sitting for only one purpose at the state level : When the Governor adresses the legislature at the beginning of Budget session or immediately after the general election.

The Two House : A comparison

Legislative Council does not enjoy equal Legislative powers with Legislative Assembly. It is a mere advisory chamber.

In the first journey of a bill it can interpose some delay i.e. 3 months. In second journey, the Council shall has no power to withhold the Bill for more than a month. In case of disagreement between two houses there is no provision of joint sitting.

THE STRENGTH OF VIDHAN SABHA IN STATES

S. No.	Name of the State	Strength of Vidhan Sabha
1.	Andhra Pradesh	175
2.	Arunachal Pradesh	60
3.	Asom (Assam)	126
4.	Bihar	243
5.	Goa	40
6.	Gujarat	182
7.	Haryana	90
8.	Himachal Pradesh	68
9.	Karnataka	224
10.	Kerala	140
11.	Madhya Pradesh	230
12.	Maharashtra	288
13.	Manipur	60
14.	Meghalaya	60
15.	Mizoram	40
16.	Nagaland	60
17.	Orissa	147
18.	Punjab	117
19.	Rajasthan	200
20.	Sikkim	32
21.	Tamil Nadu	234
22.	Tripura	60
23.	Uttar Pradesh	403
24.	West Bengal	294
25.	Chhattisgarh	90
26.	Jharkhand	81
27.	Uttarakhand	70
28.	Telangana	119
Union Territories :		
1.	Puducherry (Pondicherry)	30
2.	National Capital Territory of Delhi	70
3.	Jammu and Kashmir	83

Evaluation of State Politics in India : The reality of contemporary state politics in India illustrates that despite being equal units of the Indian federation, there remains great variations in the political trends in all the states. Differences on account of history, needs, social milieu and geographical location have rendered great diversity in their political process. In spite of centralized planning and aspiration of uniform development there remains wide regional disparity. These factors have vibrant repercussions on politics in the state. They have placed the expectation of the people at a crucial juncture. The political leadership and institutional functioning cannot remain aloof from it. Even the task of nation building and political development are showing different trends. The need of the hour is to rejuvenate the hitherto neglected local bodies, local forums, intelligential etc. to play a role in the political process. This will do a lot in enlightening the citizenry and awakening their political consciousness. Democracy can be built and strengthened not only through institution but will

THE CHIEF MINISTER

According to the Constitution of India, the Governor is the nominal head and the Chief Minister is the real head in the state executive. Since the parliamentary form of government exists, we find two types of heads. Thus, the position of the Chief Minister at the state level is anologus to the position of Prime Minister at the Centre. Every state shall have a Council of Ministers headed by the Chief Minister to aid and advise the Governor in the exercise of this powers and functions, except the discretionary ones under Article 163. The Chief Minister is appointed by the Governor. Actually, after the general elections to the state Legislative Assembly are over, the Governor calls the leader of the majority party to form ministry in the state. The Chief Minister shall hold office during the pleasure of the Governor. However, the normal term of office of the Chief Minister is five years. But, he may lose the office due to his resignation and the imposition of state emergency under Article 356.

POWERS OF CHIEF MINISTER

The Chief Minister is the chief of state administration. He has enormous functions and powers. The following are the functions and powers of the Chief Minister.

A. Relating to the council of ministers
B. Relating to the Governor
C. Relating to the State Legislature
D. Other functions and powers.

A. Relating to the Council of Ministers

As the head of the Council of Ministers, the Chief Minister enjoys the following functions and powers.

1. The Chief Minister recommends the persons who can be appointed as ministers by Governor.
2. He allocates the portfolios among the ministers.
3. He shuffles and reshuffles his ministry.
4. He can ask a minister to resign or to advise the Governor to dismiss him in case of difference of opinion.
5. He presides over the meetings of the Council of Ministers and influences its decisions.
6. He can bring about the collapse of the council of ministers by resigning from office; and
7. He guides, directs, controls and coordinates the activities of all the ministers.

B. Relating to the Governor

1. The Chief Minister is the principal channel of communication between the Governor and the Council of Ministers under Article 167, and
2. He advises the Governor in relation to the appointment of the following officials.
   (a) Advocate General
   (b) State Election Commissioner
   (c) Chairman and Members of the State Public Service Commission.
   (d) Chairman and Members of the State Planning Commission
   (e) Chairman and Members of the State Finance Commission.

C. Relating to State Legislature

1. The Chief Minister advises the Governor with regard to the summoning and proroguing the sessions of the state legislature.
2. He announces the government policies on the floor of the house.
3. He can introduce the bills in the Legislative Assembly; and
4. He can recommend for the dissolution of the Legislative Assembly to the Governor anytime.

D. Other function and powers

1. As the leader of the ruling party, the Chief Minister has to control the party and develop the disciplines.
2. As the leader of the state, he has to keenly consider the demands of the different sections of the people.
3. As the political head of the various services, he has to supervise, control and co-ordinate

the secretaries of various departments in the state level.

4. For smooth functioning of the state and for good centre-state relations, he has to develop a rapport with the union government; and
5. The size of the ministry is decided by the Chief Minister. However, only 15 percent of the members of the Legislative Assembly can be made as ministers due to the recent constitutional amendment.

COUNCIL OF MINISTERS

The constitution of India under Article 163 provides that there shall be a Council of Ministers with the Chief Minister as its head to aid and advise the Governor in every state. Accordingly, the Governor is a nominal head and real powers of the state government vests in the Council of Ministers in Tamil Nadu. Though the Governor has discretionary powers, he rarely exercises them. As already stated, the Governor appoints the Chief Minister and on his recommendation other ministers are appointed. There is no fixed term of office prescribed for the ministers and they hold office during the pleasure of the Governor. However, the normal term of office of the minsters is five years. The salaries and allowances of the ministers are determined by the state legislature from time to time.

Since parliamentary form of government is followed in the states as in the Union Government, the ministers are individually and collectively responsible to the state Legislative Assembly in which they are members. As a result, the ministers work as a team. "All for one and one for all" policy works in the functioning of the Council of Ministers. A minister can not separate himself from the collective decision of the ministry. The Council of Ministers remains in power so long as it commands the confidence of the Legislative Assembly. If a no - confidence motion is passed in Legislative Assembly, the Council of Ministers headed by the Chief Minister has to tender resignation. This is known as collective responsibility.

As far as the size of the Council of Ministers is concerned, it is not uniform in all the states in India. The Administrative Reforms Commission (ARC) suggested, "Taking a broad view of the needs of the administration in different states, we consider that big states like Uttar Pradesh, Bihar, Madhya Pradesh and Maharashtra may have about 20 persons in the Council of Ministers. The middle sized states like Madras (now Tamil Nadu), Karnataka and Andhra Pradesh may have 14 to 18 ministers and the small states like Kerala, Haryana and Punjab may have 8 to 12 ministers". However, the size of the Council of Ministers depend on the Chief Minister of the state concerned. But, the number of ministers should not exceed 15 percent of the total members of the state legislative Assembly due to the recent Constitutional Amendment Act. Each minister has to be a member in the state Legislative Assembly. If not, he has to procure this membership within six months.

HIGH COURT

The High Court stands at the head of the Judiciary in Tamil Nadu. It consists of a Chief Justice and several other judges. The Chief Justice is appointed by the President of India. Other judges are appointed by the President after consultation with the Chief Justice of Supreme court, the Governor of the state and the Chief Justice of the High court. Besides, the President has the power to appoint additional judges for a temporary period not exceeding two years, for the clearance of arrears of work in High Court and an acting judge, when a permanent judge of the High Court is temporarily absent or unable to perform his duties or is appointed to act temporarily as Chief Justice. A Judge of High Court shall hold office until the age of 62 years. Every judge permanent, additional or acting, may vacate his office earlier in any of the following ways.

1. By resignation in writing and adressed to the President
2. By being appointed a Judge of the Supreme Court or being transferred to any other High Court, by the president; and
3. By removal of the President on an address of both Houses of Parliament on the ground of proved misbehavior or incapacity.

Qualifications

The qualifications laid down in the constitution for the appointment as a High court Judge are following:

1. He must be a citizen of India
2. He must not be over 62 years of age.
3. He must have held a judicial office in the territory of India. or,
4. He must have been an advocate of a High Court for at least 10 years.

Independence of the Judges

As in the case of the Judges of the Supreme Court, the constitution seeks to maintain the independence of the Judges of the High Courts by the following provisions.

1. The Judges of the High Court are important constitutional authorities.
2. The salaries and allowances of the Judges are charged from the Consolidated Fund of the state.
3. Salaries and allowances payable to a Judge and rights in respect of leave and pension can not be varied by the parliament to his disadvantage after his retirement, except under the Financial Emergency under Article 360.
4. The removal of a Judge is followed by a strict procedure like that of the removal of a Judge of the Supreme Court; and
5. A Judge should not hold any office of profit after his retirement.

Jurisdiction and powers

The High Court of Chennai has the following jurisdiction and powers as per the constitution.

1. **Original Jurisdiction:** The High Courts at the three presidency towns of Bombay, Calcutta and Madras had an original jurisdiction, both civil and criminal, over cases arising within the respective presidency towns. The original criminal jurisdiction of the High Court has, however, been completely taken away by the criminal procedure code, 1973. Though city civil courts have also been set up to try civil cases within the same area, the original civil jurisdiction of these High Courts has not altogether been abolished but retained in respect of actions of higher value.
2. **Appellate Jurisdiction:** The High Court is the highest court in the state of Tamil Nadu. It has appellate jurisdiction in both civil and criminal cases. On the civil side, an appeal from the decision of District Judge and from that of a subordinate Judge in cases of higher value, lie direct to the High Court.
3. **Writ Jurisdiction:** According to B.R. Ambedkar, the Chairman of the Drafting Committee of the Constitution of India, Article 32 is the soul and heart of the constitution, because, it safeguards the rights, liberty and privileges of every citizen of India in terms of writs. As such, the High Court has the writ jurisdiction under Article 226. There are five writs, namely, Habeas Corpus, Mandamus, Prohibition, Certiorari and Quo-warranto.
4. **Power of Superintendence:** The High Court has the power of superintendence over all courts and tribunals throughout its territorial Jurisdiction, except military tribunals. Indeed, it has a wide power.
5. **Head of State Judiciary:** As the head of the state judiciary, the High Court has got an administrative control over the subordinate judiciary in respect of certain matters, besides its appellate and supervisory jurisdiction over them. Thus, the High Court is powerful. Also, it acts as the court of records. Above all, it has the bench jurisdiction in which the most important and burning cases of the state are settled.

DISTRICT ADMINISTRATION

District is the basic unit of administration in India. The Oxford Dictionary defines it as a "territory marked off for special administrative purpose". A district is generally named after the largest town or city of the territorial area of the concerned district Therefore, a district is an administrative unit in the hierarchy of administration which consists of a number of territorial areas, namely, villages, towns and cities. Hence, the word 'District Administration' means the management of the tasks of government as it lies within an area legally recognised as a district. The five types of the district in India are the rural district, urban district, industrial district, backward district and the hill district.

Features of District Administration

Generally, the district administration has the following features.

1. It is at district level that the state government comes into contact with the people.
2. District administration is a field work as opposed to staff or secretariat functions.
3. The problems at the district level are local relating to the district.
4. At district level, policy formulation ends and the implementation begins.
5. The District Officer is the last agent of the state government and the 'man of the spot' for any activity or incidence in the district; and
6. At the district, there is functional aggregation of units. A large number of departments have their field agencies located in the district.

District Level Functionaries

The District Collector is the head of district administration. The office of the collector at first was created by Warren Hastings in 1772 for the dual purpose of collecting revenue and dispensing justice. Strictly speaking, the collector is for the collection of land revenue in the beginning. But, at present, there are enormous functions to the district collector. The general roles and the functions of the district collector are following.

1. As Collector, he has to collect land revenue.
2. As District Magistrate, he has to maintain law and order in the district.
3. As District Officer, he has to deal with the personnel matters like salary, transfer, etc within the district.
4. As Development Officer, he is responsible for the implementation of rual development programmes.
5. As the Returning Officer, he is the chief for the elections to the Parliament, the State Legislative Assembly, and the local government in the district. Hence, he coordinates the election works at the district level.
6. As the District Census Officer, he conducts the census operations once in ten years.
7. As the Chief Protocol Officer, he has to protect the VIPs in their tour and stay in the district.
8. As the coordinator, he supervises the district level other functionaries and departments.
9. He presides over the District Plan Implementation Committee.
10. He acts as the official representative of the state government during the ceremonial functions in the district.
11. He acts as the Public Relations Officer of the state government.
12. He acts as the Crisis Administrator in chief during the natural calamities and other emergencies.
13. He supervises and controls the local government institutions.
14. He handles the work pertaining to civil defence; and
15. He is responsible for civil supplies, food and other essential commodities.

Hence, the District Collector is the multi-functionary in the district level. In fact, the work-load functions are more to a collector due to the welfare state policy in which the government has to implement a large number of programmes for the people. Actually, the office of the District Collector is very much prestigeous. The District Collector is the hero of the district administration. The other important district level functionaries are following.

1. Superintendent of Police
2. District Medical Officer
3. District Health Officer
4. District Forest Officer
5. Assistant Registrar of Cooperative Societies
6. District Agricultural Officer.
7. District Industries Officer
8. District Judges
9. Backward Class Welfare Officer
10. Superintendent of Jails
11. District Labour Officer

14

LOCAL GOVERNMENT

PANCHAYATI RAJ

The term 'Panchayati Raj' in India signifies the system of rural local self-government. It is created in all the states in India by the acts of the state legislatures to establish democracy at the grass roots level. It is entrusted with the duties and responsibilities in the field of rural development. It was constitutionalised through the 73rd Constitutional Amendment Act of 1992. At the central level, the Ministry of Rural Development looks after the matters relating to the Panchayati Raj bodies.

In the scheme of division of powers between the centre and the states in the Indian federal system, the item of *'Local Government'* is given to the states. Thus the fifth entry of the State List of the seventh schedule to the constitution of India deals with 'local government'.

BALWANT RAI MEHTA COMMITTEE

In January 1957, the Government of India appointed a committee to examine the working of the Community Development Programme (1952) and the National Extension Service (1953) and to suggest measures for their better working. The chairman of this committee was Balwantray G. Mehta. The committee submitted its report in November 1957 and recommended the establishment of the scheme of 'democratic decentralisation' which ultimately came to the known as panchayati raj. The specific recommendations made by it are:

1. Establishment of three-tier Panchayati Raj System—Gram Panchayat at the village level, Panchayat Samiti at the block level, and Zila Parishad at the district level. These tiers should be organically linked through a device of indirect elections.
2. The village Panchayat should be constituted with directly elected representatives, whereas the Panchayat Samiti and Zila Parishad should be constituted with indirectly elected members.
3. All planning and developmental activities should be entrusted to these bodies.
4. The Panchayat Samiti should be the executive body while the Zila Parishad should be the advisory, coordinating and supervisory body.
5. The District Collector should be the chairman of the Zila Parishad.
6. There should be a genuine transfer of power and responsibility to these democratic bodies.
7. Adequate resources should be transferred to these bodies to enable them to discharge their functions and fulfil their responsibilities.

These recommendations of the committee were accepted by the National Development Council in January 1958. The council did not insist on a single rigid pattern and left it to the states to evolve their own patterns suitable to local conditions. But the basic principles and broad fundamentals should be identical throughout the country.

Rajasthan was the first state to establish Panchayati Raj : The scheme was inaugurated by the Prime Minister on 2nd october, 1959, in Nagaur district. Rajasthan was followed by Andhra Pradesh which also adopted the system in 1959. Thereafter, most of the states adopted the system.

Though most of the states created Panchayati Raj institutions by mid 1960s, there were differences from one state to another with regard to the number of tiers, relative position of samiti and parishad, their tenure, composition, functions, finances and so on. For example, Rajasthan adopted three-tier system while Tamil Nadu adopted two-tier system West Bengal, on the other hand, adopted four-tier system. Further, in Rajasthan–Andhra Pradesh Pattern, Panchayat Samiti was powerful as the block was the unit of planning and development while in Maharashtra–Gujarat pattern, Zila Parishad was powerful as the district was the unit of planning and development. Some states also established Nyaya Panchayats, that is, judicial panchayats to try petty civil and criminal cases.

STUDY TEAMS AND COMMITTEES

Since 1960, many study teams, committees and working groups were appointed to examine the various aspects of functioning of Panchayati Raj system. They are mentioned below in a chronological Order, along with the names of the Chairmen in bracket.

(*i*) 1960—Committee on Rationalisation of Panchayat Statistics (V.R. Rao)

(*ii*) 1961—Working Group on Panchayats and Cooperatives (S.D. Mishra)

(*iii*) 1961—Study Team on Panchayati Raj Administration (V. Iswaran)

(*iv*) 1962—Study Team on Nyaya Panchayats (G.R. Rajgopal)

(*v*) 1963—Study Team on the Position of Gram Sabha in Panchayati Raj Movement (R.R. Diwakar)

(*vi*) 1963—Study Group on Budgeting and Accounting Procedure of Panchayati Raj Institutions (M. Rama Krishnayya)

(*vii*) 1963—Study Team on Panchayati Raj Finances (K. Santhanam)

(*viii*) 1965—Committee on Panchayati Raj Elections (K. Santhanam)

(*ix*) 1965—Study Team on the Audit and Accounts of Panchayati Raj Bodies (R.K. Khanna)

(*x*) 1966—Committee on Panchayati Raj Training Centres (G. Ramachandran)

(*xi*) 1969—Study Team on Involvement of Community Development Agency and Panchayati Raj Institutions in the Implementation of Baisc Land Reform Measures (V. Ramanathan)

(*xii*) 1972—Working Group for Formulation of Fifth Five year Plan on Community Development and Panchayati Raj (N. Rama krishnayya)

(*xiii*) 1976—Committee on Community Development and Panchayati Raj (Smt. Daya Choubey)

ASHOK MEHTA COMMITTEE

In December 1977, the Janta Government appointed a committee on Panchayati Raj institutions under the chairmanship of Ashok Mehta. It submitted its report in August 1978 and made 132 recommendations to revive and strengthen the declining Panchayati Raj System in the country. Its main recommendations are:

1. The three-tier system of Panchayati Raj should be replaced by the two-tier system, that is, Zila Parishad at the district level, and below it, the Mandal Panchayat consisting of a group of villages covering a population of the 15000 to 20000.
2. A district should be the first point for decentralization under popular supervision below the state level.
3. Zila Parishad should be the executive body and made responsible for planning at the district level.
4. There should be an official participation of political parties at all levels of Panchayat elections.
5. The Panchayati Raj institutions should have compulsory powers of taxation to mobilise their own financial resources.
6. There should be a regular social audit by a district level agency and by a committee of legislators to check whether the funds allotted for the vulnerable social and economic groups are actually spent on them.

7. The state government should not supersede the Panchayati Raj institutions. In case of an imperative supersession, election should be held within six months from the date of supersession.
8. The Chief Electoral Officer of state in consultation with Chief Election Commissioner should organise and conduct the Panchayati Raj elections.
9. Development functions should be transferred to the Zila Parishad and all development staff should work under its control and supervision.
10. A minister for Panchayati Raj should be appointed in the state council of ministers to look after the affairs of the Panchayati Raj institutions.
11. Seats for SC and ST should be reserved on the basis of their population.

Due to the collapse of the Janta Government before the completion of its term, no action could be taken on the recommendations of the Ashok Mehta Committee at the central level.

L.M. SINGHVI COMMITTEE

In 1986, Rajiv Ghandhi government appointed a committee on 'Revitalisation of Panchayati Raj Institutions for Democracy and Development' under the chairmanship of L.M. Singhvi. It made the following recommendations.

(i) The Panchayati Raj institutions should be constitutionally recognised, protected and preserved. For this purpose, a new chapter should be added in the Constitution of India. This will make their identity and integrity reasonably and substantially inviolate. It also suggested constitutional provisions to ensure regular, free and fair elections to the Panchayati Raj bodies.

(ii) Nyaya Panchayats should be established for a cluster of villages.

(iii) The villages should be reorganised to make Gram Panchayats more viable. It also emphasised the importance of the Gram Sabha and called it as the embodiment of direct democracy.

(iv) The village Panchayats should have more financial resources.

(v) The judicial tribunals should be established in each state to adjucate controversies about election to the Panchayati Raj institutions, their dissolution and other matters related to their functioning.

CONSTITUTIONALISATION

64th Amendment Bill : In response to the above recommendations of L.M. Singhvi Committee, Rajiv Gandhi's government introduced the 64th Constitutional Amendment Bill in the Lok Sabha in July 1989 to constitutionalise Panchayati Raj institutions and make them more powerful and broad based. Although, the Lok Sabha passed the Bill in August 1989, it was not approved by the Rajya Sabha. The bill was vehemently opposed by the opposition on the ground that it sought to strengthen centralisation in the federal system.

V.P. Singh Government : The National Front Government, soon after assuming office in November 1989 under the Prime Ministership of V.P. Singh, announced that it would take steps to strengthen the Panchayati Raj institutions. In June 1990, a two-day conference of the state Chief Ministers under the chairmanship of V.P. Singh was held to discuss the issues relating to the strengthening of the Panchayati Raj Bodies. The conference approved the proposals for the introduction of a fresh constitutional amendment bill. Consequently, the Constitutional Amendment Bill was introduced in the Lok Sabha in September 1990. However, the fall of the government resulted in the lapse of the Bill.

Narsimha Rao Government : The Congress Government under the prime ministership of P.V. Narsimha Rao once again considered the matter of the constitutionalisation of Panchayati Raj bodies. It drastically modified the proposals in this regard to delete the controversial aspects. Finally, it introduced the Constitutional Amendment Bill in the Lok Sabha in September 1991. It was passed by the Lok Sabha on December 22, 1992 and by the Rajya Sabha on December 23, 1992. Later, it was approved by the 17 state Assemblies and received the assent of the President of India on 20 April, 1993. Thus it emerged as the 73rd Constitutional Amendment Act, 1992 and came into force on 24 April, 1993.

73rd Amendment Act of 1992 : This act has added Part-IX to the Constitution of India. It is entitled as 'The Panchayats' and consists of provisions from articles 243 to 243-O. In addition, the Act has also added Eleventh schedule to the Constitution. It contains 29 functional items of the Panchayats and deals wih Article 243-G.

The Act has given a practical shape to Article 40 of the Constitution which says that, "The state shall take steps to organise village Panchayats and endow them with such powers and authority as may be necessary to enable them to function as units of self-government." This article forms a part of the Directive Principles of State Policy.

The Act gives a constitutional status to the Panchayati Raj institutions. It has brought them under the purview of the justiciable part of the Constitution. In other words, the state governments are under constitutional obligation to adopt the new Panchayati Raj system in accordance with the provisions of the Act. Consequently, neither the formation of Panchayats nor the holding of elections a regular intervals depends on the will of the state government any more.

The provisions of the Act can be grouped into two categories—compulsory and voluntary. The compulsory provisions of the Act have to be included in the state laws creating the new Panchayati Raj system. The voluntary provisions, on the other hand, may be included at the discretion of the states. Thus the voluntary provisions of the Act ensures the right of the states to take local factors like geographical, politico-administrative, and others, into consideration while adopting the new Panchayati Raj system. In other words, the Act does not disturb the constitutional balance between the centre and the states in the Indian federal system. Though it is a central law on a state subject (*i.e.,* local government is a subject included in the state list under the Seventh schedule of the constitution), the Act does not encroach upon the jurisdiction of the states which are given adequate discretionary powers with regard to the Panchayats.

The Act is a significant landmark in the evolution of grassroot democratic institutions in the country. It transfers the representative democracy into participatory democracy. It is a revolutionary concept to build democracy at the grassroots level in the country.

The salient features of the Act are:

1. **Gram Sabha:** The Act provides for a Gram Sabha as the foundation of the Panchayati Raj system. It is a body consisting of persons registered in the electoral rolls of a village comprised within the area of Panchayat at the village level. Thus, it is a village assembly consisting of all the registered voters in the area of a Panchayat. It shall exercise such powers and perform such functions at the village level as the legislature of a state determines.
2. **Three-Tier System:** The Act provides for a three-tier system of Panchayati Raj in every state, that is Panchayats at the village, intermediate, and district levels. The Act defines all these terms in the following manner.

   A. Panchayat means an institution (by whatever name called) of self-government for rural areas.

   B. Village means, a village specified by the Governor by public notification to be a village for this purpose, and includes a group of villages so specified.

   C. Intermediate level means a level between the village and district levels specified by the Governor by public notification for this purpose.

   D. District means a district in a state.

   Thus, the Act brings about uniformity in the structure of Panchayati Raj throughout the country. However a state having a population not exceeding 20 lakhs may not constitute panchayats at the intermediate level.
3. **Election of Members and Chairpersons:** All the members of Panchayats at the village, intermediate and district levels shall be

elected directly by the people. Further, the chairperson of Panchayats at the intermediate and district levels shall be elected indirectly—by and from amongst the elected members of. However, the chairperson of a Panchayat at the village level shall be elected in such manner as the state legislature determines.

4. **Reservation of seats:** The Act provides for the reservation of seats for scheduled castes and scheduled tribes in every Panchayat in proportion of their population to the total population in the Panchayat area. Further, the state legislature shall provide for the reservation of offices of chairpersons in the Panchayat at the village or any other level for the SC and ST.

   The Act provides for the reservation of not less than one-third of the total number of seats for women. Further, not less than one-third of the total number of offices of chairpersons in the Panchayat at each level shall be reserved for women.

   The Act also authorises the legislature of a state to make any provision for reservation of seats in any Panchayat or offices of chairperson in the Panchayat at any level in favour of backward classes.

5. **Duration of Panchayats:** The Act provides for a five-year term of office to the Panchayat at every level. However, it can be dissolved before the completion of its term. Further, fresh election to constitute a Panchayat shall be completed *(i)* before the expiry of its duration of five years; or *(ii)* in case of dissolution, before the expiry of a period of six months from the date of its dissolution.

6. **Disqualifications:** A person shall be disqualified for being chosen as or for being a member of Panchayat if he is so disqualified *(i)* under any law for the time being in force for the purposes of elections to the legislature of the state concerned, or *(ii)* under any law made by the state legislature. However, no person shall be disqualified on the ground that he is less than 25 years of age if he has attained the age of 21 years. Further, all questions of disqualifications shall be referred to such authority as the state legislature determines.

7. **State Election Commission:** The superintendence,direction and control of the preparation of electoral rolls and the conduct of all elections to the Panchayats shall be vested in the State Election Commission. It consists of a State Election Commissioner to be appointed by the Governor. His conditions of service and tenure of office shall also be determined by the Governor. He shall not be removed from the office except in the manner and on the grounds prescribed for the removal of a judge of the state High Court, and his conditions of service shall not be varied to his disadvantage after his appointment.

8. **Powers and Functions:** The state legislature may endow the Panchayats, with such powers and authority as may be necessary to enable them to function as institutions of self-government. Such a scheme may contain provisions for the devolution of powers and responsibilities upon Panchayats at the appropriate level with respect to *(i)* the preparation of plans for economic development and social justice; *(ii)* the implementation of schemes for economic development and social justice as may be entrusted to them, including those in relation to the 29 matters listed in the Eleventh Schedule.

9. **Finances:** The state legislature may *(i)* authorise a Panchayat to levy, collect and appropriate taxes, duties, tolls and fees; *(ii)* assign to a Panchayat taxes, duties, tolls end fees levied and collected by the state government; *(iii)* provide for making grants-in-aid to the Panchayats from the Consolidated Fund of the state; and *(iv)* provide for constitution of funds crediting all moneys of the panchayats.

10. **Finance Commission:** The Governor of a state shall, after every five years, constitute a Finance Commission to review the financial

position of the Panchayats. If shall make the following recommendations to the Governor.

(*i*) The principles which should govern:

(*a*) The distribution between the state and the Panchayats of the net proceeds of the taxes, duties, tolls and fees levied by the state.

(*b*) The determination of taxes, duties, tolls and fees which may be assigned to the Panchayats.

(*c*) The grant-in-aid to the Panchayats from the consolidated fund of the state.

(*ii*) The measures needed to improve the financial position of the Panchayats.

(*iii*) Any other matter referred to the Finance Commission by the Governor in the interests of sound finance of the Panchayats.

The State Legislature may provide for the composition of the Commission, the required qualifications of its members and the manner of their selection.

The Governor shall place the recommendations of the Commission along with the action taken report before the state legislature.

The Central Finance Commissioner shall also suggest the measures needed to augment the Consolidated Fund of a state supplement the resources of the Panchayats in the states (on the basis of the recommendations made by the Finance Commission of the state).

11. Audit of Accounts: The state legislature may make provisions with respect to the maintenance of accounts by the Panchayats and the auditing of such accounts.

12. Application to Union Territories: The President of India may direct that the provisions of this Act shall apply to any union territory subject to such exceptions and modifications as he may specify.

13. States and Areas Kept Out: The Act does not apply to the state of Jammu and Kashmir, Nagaland, Meghalaya and Mizoram and certain other areas. These area include *(a)* the scheduled areas and the tribal areas referred to in Article 244 of the Indian Constitution; *(b)* the hill area of Manipur for which a District Council exist; *(c)* Darjeeling district of West Bengal for which Darjeeling Gorkha Hill Council exist.

14. Continuance of Existing Laws and Panchayats: All the state laws relating to Panchayats shall continue to be in force until the expiry of one year from the commencement of this Act. In other words, the states have to adopt the new Panchayati Raj system based on this Act within the maximum period of one year from 24th April, 1993, which is the date of the commencement of this Act. However, all the Panchayats existing immediately before the commencement of this Act small continue till the expiry of their term, unless dissolved by the state legislature sooner.

Consequently, majority of states passed the Panchayati Raj acts in 1993 and 1994 to adopt the new system in accordance with the 73rd Constitutional Amendment Act of 1992.

Eleventh Schedule

It contains the following 29 functional items placed within the purview of Panchayats.

1. Agriculture
2. Land improvement, implementation of land reforms, land consolidation and soil conservation
3. Minor irrigation, water management and watershed development
4. Animal husbandry, dairying and poultry
5. Fisheries
6. Social forestry and farm forestry
7. Minor forest produce
8. Small-scale industries, including food processing industries
9. Khadi, village and cottage industries
10. Rural housing
11. Drinking water
12. Fuel and fodder

13. Roads, culverts, bridges, ferries, waterways and other means of communication.
14. Rural electrification, including distribution of electricity
15. Non-conventional energy sources
16. Poverty alleviation programme
17. Education, including primary and secondary schools
18. Technical training and vocational education
19. Adult and non-formal education
20. Libraries
21. Cultural activities
22. Markets and fairs
23. Health and sanitation, including hospitals, primary health centres and dispensaries
24. Family welfare
25. Women and child development
26. Social welfare, including welfare of the handicapped and mentally retarded
27. Welfare of the weaker sections, and in particular, of the scheduled castes and the scheduled tribes
28. Public distribution system
29. Maintenance of community assets.

URBAN LOCAL GOVERNMENT

The term *'Urban Local Government'* in India signifies the governance of an urban area by the people through their elected representatives. The jurisdiction of an urban local government is limited to a specific urban area which is demarcated for this purpose by the state government.

There are eight types of urban local governments in India-Municipal Corporation, Municipality, Notified Area Committee, Town Area Committee, Cantonment Board, Township, Port Trust and Special Purpose Agency. The system of urban government was constitutionalised through the 74th constitutional Amendment Act of 1992. At the central level, the subject of 'urban local government' is dealt with by the following three ministries.

1. Ministry of Urban Development created as a separate ministry in 1985.
2. Ministry of Defence in the case of cantonment boards.
3. Ministry of Home Affairs in the case of Union Territories.

HISTORICAL PERSPECTIVE

The institutions of urban local government originated and developed in modern India during the period of British rule. The major events in this context are:

(*i*) In 1687, the first municipal corporation in India was set up at Madras.

(*ii*) In 1726, the municipal corporations were set up in Bombay and Calcutta.

(*iii*) Lord Mayo's Resolution of 1870 on financial decentralisation visualised the development of local self-government institutions.

(*iv*) Lord Ripon's Resolution of 1882 has been hailed as the 'Magna carta' of local self-government. He is called as the father of local-self government in India.

(*v*) The Royal Commission on decentralisation was appointed in 1907 and it submitted its report in 1909. Its chairman was Hobhouse.

(*vi*) Under the dyarchical scheme introduced in Provinces by the Government of India Act of 1919, local self-government became a transferred subject under the charge of a responsible Indian minister.

(*vii*) In 1924, the Cantonments Act was passed by the Central legislature.

(*viii*) Under the provincial autonomy scheme introduced by the Government of India Act of 1935, local self-government was declared a provincial subject.

74TH AMENDMENT ACT OF 1992

This Act has added Part IX-A to the Constitution of India. It is entitled as "The Municipalities' and consists of provisions from articles 243-P to 243-ZG. In addition, the Act has also added Twelfth Schedule to the Constitution. It contains 18 functional items of municipalities and deals with Article 243-W.

The Act gave constitutional status to the municipalities. It has brought them under the purview of justiciable part of the constitution. In other words, state governments are under constitutional obligation to adopt the new system of municipalities in accordance with the provisions of the Act.

The Act aims at revitalising and strengthening the urban governments so that they function effectively as units of local government.

The salient features of the Act are:

1. **Three Types of Municipalities:** The Act provides for the constitution of the following three types of municipalities in every state.
   (*a*) A Nagar Panchayat (by whatever name called) for a transitional area, that is, an area in transition from a rural area to an urban area.
   (*b*) A Municipality for a smaller urban area.
   (*c*) A Municipal Corporation for a larger urban area.

A transitional area, a smaller urban area or a larger urban area means such area as the Governor may specify by public notification for this purpose with regard to the following factors.

(*a*) Population of the area
(*b*) Density of population
(*c*) Revenue generated for local administration
(*d*) Percentage of employment in non-agricultural activities
(*e*) Economic importance or such other factors as the Governor may deem fit.

2. **Composition:** All the members of a municipality shall be elected directly by the people of the municipal area. For this purpose, each municipal area shall be divided int territorial constituencies to be known as wards. The state legislature may provide the manner of election of the chairperson of a municipality. It may also provide for the representation of the following persons in a municipality.
   I. Persons having special knowledge or experience in municipal administration without the right to vote in the meetings of municipality.
   II. The members of the Lok Sabha and the state legislative Assembly representing constituencies which comprise wholly or partly the municipal area.
   III. The members of the Rajya Sabha and the state legislative council registered as electors with the municipal area.
   IV. The chairpersons of committees (other than wards committees).
3. **Wards Committees:** There shall be constituted a wards committee, consisting of one or more wards, within the territorial area of a municipality having population of three lakhs or more. The state legislature may make provision with respect to the composition and the territorial area of a wards committee and the manner in which the seats in a wards committee shall be filled. It may also make any provision for the constitution of committees in addition to the wards committees.
4. **Reservation of Seats:** The Act provides for the reservation of seats for the scheduled castes and the scheduled tribes in every municipality in propor-tion of their population to the total population in the municipal area. Further, it provides for the reservation of not less than one-third of the total number of seats for women (including the number of seats reserved for women belonging to the SCs and the STs).

   The state legislature may provide for the manner of reservation of offices of chairpersons in the municipalities for the SCs, the STs and the women. It may also make any provision for the reservation of seats in any municipality or offices of chairpersons in municipalities in favour of backward classes.
5. **Duration of Municipalities:** The Act provides for a five-year term of office for every municipality. However, it can be dissolved before the completion of its term. Further, the fresh election to constitute a

municipality shall be completed (*i*) before the expiry of its duration of five years; or (*ii*) in case of dissolution, before the expiry of a period of six months from the date of its dissolution.

6. **Disqualifications:** A person shall be disqualified for being chosen as or for being a member of a municipality if he is so disqualified
   (*i*) under any law for the time being in force for the purposes of elections to the legislature of the state concerned; or
   (*ii*) under any law made by the state legislature.

   However, no person shall be disqualified on the ground that he is less than 25 years of age if he has attained the age of 21 years. Further, all questions of disqualifications shall be referred to such authority as the state legislature determines.
7. **State Election Commission:** The superintendence, direction and control of the preparation of electoral rolls and the conduct of all elections of the municipalities shall be vested in the State Election Commission.
8. **Powers and Functions:** The state legislature may endow the municipalities with such powers and authority as may be necessary to enable them to function as institutions of self-government. Such a scheme may contain provisions for the devolution of powers and responsibilities upon municipalities at the appropriate level with respect to (*i*) the preparation of plans for economic development and social justice; (*ii*) the implementation of schemes for economic development and social justice as may be entrusted to them including those in relation to the 18 matters listed in the Twelfth Schedule.
9. **Finances:** The state legislature may (*i*) authorise a municipality to levy, collect and appropriate taxes, duties, tolls and fees; (*ii*) assign to a muicipality taxes, duties, tolls and fees levied and collected by state government; (*iii*) provide for making grants-in-aid to the municipalities from the Consolidated Found of the state; and (*iv*) provide for constitution of funds for crediting all moneys of the municipalities.
10. **Finance Commission:** The Finance commission (which is constituted for the Panchayats) shall also, for evey five years, review the financial position of municipalities and make recommendation to the Governor as to:
    (*i*) The principles which should govern:
       (*a*) The distribution between the state and the municipalities, the net proceeds of the taxes, duties, tolls and fee levied by the state.
       (*b*) The determination of the taxes, duties, tolls and fees which may be assigned to the municipalities.
       (*c*) The grants-in-aid to municipalities from the Consolidated Fund of the state.
    (*ii*) The measures needed to improve the financial position of the municipalities.
    (*iii*) Any other matter referred to the Finance Commission by the Governor in the interests of sound finance of municipalities.

    The Governor shall place the recommendations of the Commission along with the action taken report before the state legislautre.

    The Central Finance Commission shall also suggest the measures needed to augment the Consolidated Fund of a state to supplement the resources of the municipalities in the state (on the basis of the recommendations made by the Finance Commission of the state).
11. **Audit of Accounts:** The state legislature may make provisions with respect to the maintenance of accounts by municipalities and the auditing of such accounts.

    Application to Union Territories: The President of India may direct that the provisions of this Act shall apply to any union territory subject to such exceptions and modifications as he may specify.

12. **Areas Kept Out:** The Act does not apply to the scheduled areas and tribal areas referred in Article 244 of the Indian Constitution. It shall also not affect the functions and powers of the Darjeeling Gorkha Hill Council of the West Bengal.

13. **District Planning Committee:** Every state shall constitute at the district level, a District Planning Committee to consolidate tha plans prepared by Panchayats and municipalities in the district, and to prepare a draft development plan for the district as a whole. The state legislature may make provision with respect to the following points.

    (*i*) The composition of such committees;

    (*ii*) The manner of election of members of such committees;

    (*iii*) The functions of such committees in relation to district planning; and

    (*iv*) The manner of the election of the chairpersons of such committees.

    The Act lays down that four-fifths of the members of a District Planning Committee should be elected by the elected members of the district panchayat and municipalities in the district from amongst themselves. The representation of these members in the committee should be in proportion to the ratio between the rural and urban populations in the district.

    The chairpersons of such committees shall forward the development plan to the state government.

14. **Metropolitan Planning Committee:** Every metropolitan area shall have a Metropolitan Planning Committee to prepare a draft development plan. Metropolitan area means an area having a population of 10 lakhs or more, comprised in one or more districts and consisting of two or more municipalities or Panchayats or other contiguous areas. The state legislature may make provisions with respect to:

    (*i*) The composition of such committees;

    (*ii*) The manner of election of members to such committees;

    (*iii*) The representation in such committees of the Central Government, state government and other organisations;

    (*iv*) The functions of such committees in relation to planning and coordination for the metropolitan area;

    (*v*) The manner of election of chair persons of such committees.

    The Act lays down that two-thirds of the members of a Metropolitan Planning Committee should be elected by the elected members of the municipalities and chair-persons of the panchayats in the metropolitan area from amongst themselves. The representation of these members in the committee should be in proportion to the ratio between the population of the municipalities and the panchayats in that metropolitan area.

    The chairpersons of such committees shall forward the development plan to the state government.

15. **Continuance of Existing Laws and Municipalities:** All the state laws relating to municipalities shall continue to be in force until the expiry of one year from the commencement of this Act. In other words, the states have to adopt the new system of municipalities based on this Act within the maximum period of one year from 1st June 1993, which is the date of commencement of this Act. However, all municipalities existing immediately before the commencement of this Act shall continue till the expiry of their term, unless dissolved by the state legislature sooner.

TWELFTH SCHEDULE

It contains the following 18 functional items placed within the purview of municipalities.

(*i*) Urban planning including town planning

(*ii*) Regulation of land use and construction of buildings

(*iii*) Planning for economic and social development
(*iv*) Roads and bridges
(*v*) Water supply for domestic, industrial and commercial purposes
(*vi*) Public health, sanitation, conservancy and solid waste management
(*vii*) Fire services
(*viii*) Urban forestry, protection of the environment and promotion of ecological aspects
(*ix*) Safeguarding the interests of weaker sections of society, including the handicapped and mentally retarded
(*x*) Slum improvement and upgradation
(*xi*) Urban poverty alleviation
(*xii*) Provision of urban amenities and facilities such as parks, gardens, playgrounds
(*xiii*) Promotion of cultural, educational and aesthetic aspects
(*xiv*) Burials and burial grounds, cremations, cremation grounds and electric crematoriums
(*xv*) Cattle ponds, prevention of cruelty to animals
(*xvi*) Vital statistics including registration of births and deaths
(*xvii*) Public amenities including street lighting, parking lots, bus stops and public conveniences
(*xviii*) Regulation of slaughter houses and tanneries

TYPES

The following eight types of urban local bodies are created in India for the administration of urban areas:

1. Municipal Corporation
2. Municipality
3. Notified Area Committee
4. Town Area Committee
5. Cantonment Board
6. Township
7. Port Trust
8. Special Purpose Agency

Municipal Corporation: Municipal corporations are created for the administration of big cities like Delhi, Mumbai, Kolkata, Hyderabad, Bangalore and others. They are established in the states by the acts of the concerned state legislatures, and in the union territories by the acts of the Parliament of India. There may be one common act for the municipal corporation or a separate act for each municipal corporation.

A municipal corporation has three authorities, namely, the Council, the Standing Committees and the Commissioner.

The Corporation Council consists of the Councillors directly elected by the people, as well as a few nominated persons having knowledge or experience of municipal administration. In brief, the composition of Council including the reservation for SCs, STs and women in governed by the 74th Constitutional Amendment Act.

The Corporation Council is headed by a Mayor. He is assisted by a Deputy Mayor. He is elected in majority of the states for a one year renewable term. He is basically an ornamental figure and a formal head of the corporation. His main function is to preside over the meetings of the Council which is the deliberative and legislative wing of the corporation.

The Standing Committees are created to facilitate the working of the corporation which is too large in size. The deal with public works, education, health, taxation, finance and so on. They take decisions in their fields.

The Municipal Commissioner is responsible for the implementation of the decisions taken by the Council and its Standing Committees. Thus, he is the chief executive authority of the corportion. He is appointed by the state government and is generally a member of the IAS.

Municipality: The municipalities are established for administration of towns and smaller cities. Like the corporations, they are also set up in the states by the acts of the concerned state legislatures and in the union territory by the acts of the Parliament of India. They are also known by various other names like Municipal Council,

Municipal Committee, Municipal Board, Borough Municipality, City Municipality and others.

Like a municipal corporation, a municipality also has three authorities, namely, the Council, the Standing Committees and the Chief Executive Officer.

The composition of the Council including the reservation of seats for SCs, STs and women is governed by the 74th Constitutional Amendment Act. The council is the deliberative and legislative wing of the municipality.

The Council is headed by a President/Chairman. He is assisted by a Vice-President/Vice-Chairman. Unlike the Mayor of a municipal corporation, he plays a significant role and is the pivot of the municipal administration. Apart from presiding over the meetings of the Council, he enjoys executive powers.

The Standing Committees are created to facilitate the working of the Council. They deal with public works, taxation, health, finance and so on.

The Chief Executive Officer/Chief Municipal Officer is responsible for day-to-day general administration of the municipality. He is appointed by the state government.

Notified Area Committee: A notified area committee is created for the administration of two types of areas—a fast developing town due to industrialisation, and a town which does not yet fulfil all the conditions necessary for the constitution of a municipality, but which otherwise is considered important by the state government. Since it is established by a notification in the government gazette, it called as notified area committee. Though it functions within the framework of the State Municipal Act, only these provision of the Act apply to it which are notified in the government gazette by which it is created. It may also be entrusted to exercise powers under any other act. Its powers are almost equivalent to those of a municipality. But unlike the municipality, it is an entirely nominated body, that is, all the members of a notified area committee including the chairman are nominated by the state government. Thus, it is neither an elected body nor a statutory body.

Town Area Committee: A town area committee is set up for the administration of a small town. It is a semi municipal authority and is entrusted with a limited number of civic functions like drainage, roads, street lighting, conservancy. It is created by a separate act of a state legislature. Its composition, functions and other matters are governed by the same act. It may be wholly elected or wholly nominated by the state government, or partly elected and partly nominated. The Rural-Urban Relationship Committee (1963-66) headed by A.P. Jain recommended that small town area committees should be merged with the Panchayati Raj institutions to avoid multiplicity in the pattern of local bodies.

Cantonment Board: A cantonment board is established for municipal administration for civilian population in the cantonment area. It is a delimited area where the military forces and troops are permanently stationed. It is set up under the Cantonments Act of 1924—a legislation enacted by the Central Government. It works under the administrative control of the Defence Ministry of the Central Government. Thus, unlike other types of urban local bodies which are created and administered by the state government, a cantonment board is created as well as administered by the Central Government.

At present, there are 62 cantonment boards in the country. They are grouped into the following three classes.

1. **Class I:** Civilian population is more than 10000.
2. **Class II:** Civilian population is between 2500 and 10000.
3. **Class III:** Civilian population is less than 2500.

A cantonment board consists of partly elected and partly nominated members. The elected members hold office for a term of three years while the nominated members (*i.e.,* ex-officio members) continue so long as they hold the office in that station. The military officer commanding the station is the ex-officio president of the board and presides over its meetings. The Vice-President of the board is elected by the elected members from amongst themselves for a term of three years. The Class I cantonment board consists of the following members.

1. A military officer commanding the station.
2. An executive engineer in the cantonment
3. A health officer in the cantonment
4. A first class magistrate nominated by the district magistrate
5. Four military officers nominated by the officer commanding the station
6. Seven members elected by the people of the cantonment area

The functions performed by a cantonment board are similar to those of a municipality. These are statutorily categorised into obligatory functions and discretionary functions. The sources of income include both, tax revenue and non-tax revenue.

The executive officer of the cantonment board is appointed by the President of India. He implements all the resolutions and decisions of the board and its committees. He belongs to the central cadre established for the purpose.

Special Purpose Agency: In addition to the area-based urban bodies (or multipurpose agencies, that is, municipal corporations, municipalities, notified area committees, town area committees, cantonment boards, townships and port trusts), the state governments have set up certain agencies to undertake designated activities or specific functions which legitimately, belong to the domain of municipal corporations or municipalities or other local urban governments. In other words, these are function-based and not area based. They are known as 'single purpose' or 'uni-purpose' or 'special purpose' agencies or 'functional' local bodies. Some such bodies are:

1. Town Improvement Trusts
2. Urban Development Authorities
3. Water Supply and Sewerage Boards
4. Housing Boards
5. Pollution Control Boards
6. Electricity Supply Boards
7. City Transport Boards, and so on.

These functional local bodies are established as statutory bodies by an act of state legislature or as departments by an executive resolution. They function as autonomous bodies and deal with the functions alloted to them independently of the local urban government, that is, municipal corporations or municipalities and so forth. Thus, they are not subordinate agencies of the local municipal bodies.

Township: This type of urban government is established by the large public enterprises to provide civic amenities to its staff and workers who live in the housing colonies built near the plants. The enterprise appoints a Town Administrator to look after the administration of the township. He is assisted by some engineers and other technical and non-technical staff. Thus, the township form of urban government has no elected members. In fact, it is an extension of the bureaucratic structure of the enterprise.

Port Trust: The port trust are established in the port areas like Mumbai, Kolkata, Chennai and so on , for two purposes: *(i)* to manage and protect the ports; and *(ii)* to provide civil amenities. A port trust is created by an Act of Parliament. It consists of both elected and nominated members. Its Chairman is an official. Its civic functions are more or less similar to those of a Municipality.

MUNICIPAL PERSONNEL

There are three types of municipal personnel systems in India. The personnel working in the urban governments may belong to any one or all the three types. These are:

1. **Separate Personnel System :** Under this system, each local body appoints, administers, and controls its own personnel. They are not transferable to other local bodies. It is the most widely prevalent system. This system upholds the principle of local autonomy and promotes undivided loyalty.
2. **Unfied Personnel System :** In this system, the state government appoints, administers,

and controls the municipal personnel. In other words, state-wise services (cadres) are created for all the urban bodies in the state. They are transferable between the local bodies in the state. This system is prevalent in Andhra Pradesh, Tamil Nadu, Uttar Pradesh, Rajasthan, Madhya Pradesh and so on.

3. **Integrated Personnel System :** Under this system, the personnel of the state government and those of the local bodies form part of the same service. In other words, the municipal personnel are the members of the state services. They are transferable not only between the local bodies in the state but also between local bodies and departments of state government. Thus, there is no distinction between local civil service and state civil service. This system is prevalent in Orissa, Bihar, Karnataka, Punjab, Haryana and others.

The various national level institutions providing training to the municipal personnel are:

1. All-India Institute of Local Self-Government (Bombay) constituted in 1927. It is a private registered society.
2. Centre for Urban and Environmental studies (New Delhi) set up in 1967 on the recommendation of Nur-ud-din Ahmed Committee on Training of Municipal Employees (1963-1965).
3. Regional Centres for Urban and Environmental Studies (Kolkata, Lucknow, Hyderabad and Mumbai) set up in 1968 on the recommen-dation of Nur-ud-din Ahmed committee on Training of Municipal Employees (1963-1965).
4. National Institute of Urban Affairs, established in 1976.
5. Human settlement management institute established in 1985.

CENTRAL COUNCIL OF LOCAL GOVERNMENT

The Central Council of Local Government was set up in 1945. It was constituted under Article 263 of the constitution of India by an order of the President of India. Originally, it was known as the Central Council of Local Self-Government. However, the term 'self-government' was found to be suparfluous and hence was replaced by the term 'government' in the 1980s. Till 1958, it dealt with both urban as well as rural local governments, but after 1958 it has been dealing with matters of urban local government only.

The Council is a advisory body. It consists of the Minister for Urban Development in the Government of India and the ministers for local self government in states. The union minister acts as the Chairman of the Council.

The Council performs the following functions with regard to local government:

(*i*) Considering and recommending the policy matters.

(*ii*) Making proposals for legislation.

(*iii*) Examining the possibility of cooperation between the centre and the states.

(*iv*) Drawing up a common programme of action

(*v*) Recommending Central financial assistance

(*vi*) Reviewing the work done by the local bodies with the central financial assistance.

15

POLITICAL PARTIES

A political party is an organised group of people sharing common policy preferences and programmes formed for the purpose of acquiring and retaining government power by electoral or other means.

- They aim to exercise government power
- They have formal membership
- They focus on broad issues
- They show strong ideological identity

Functions of Indian Political Parties

1. Unify, simplify and stabilize the political process.
2. Provide coherence to divisive social structures.
3. Provide link between citizen and Government (most imp.) representation.
4. Provide training ground for leadership.
5. Educate, instruct and activate the electorate i.e. function of interest, articulation and aggregation.
6. Perform the task of socialization and mobilization.
7. Form Government (more important in Parliamentary democracy).
8. Provide representation

Constitutional Provision

In the constitution of India no mention was made of the political parties. It was made in a limited way in The Representation of People's Act 1950, 1951 and Election Commission : power to register political parties. A mention of parties came in the Fourth schedule in the context of defections.

Phases of Party System

1. One party dominant Phase or Congress system (Rajni Kothari), predominant party system (Sartori), 1952-1967
2. Trend towards two party system, 1977-1980
3. Hegemonic Dominance, 1980-1989
4. Multi-party system and Coalition era, 1989 onwards

NATIONAL AND REGIONAL PARTIES

According to the Election symbols (Reservation and allotment) order, 1968, a political party shall be created as a recognised political party in a state if, either of the conditions are fulfilled.

A. That such a party :
   (i) has been engaged in political activity continuously for 5 years.
   (ii) at election to Lok Sabha or Legislative Assembly, has returned, member to Lok Sabha one member for every 25 members of that House elected from that state or at least one member to Legislative Assembly for every thirty members of the Assembly.

B. That the total number of the votes polled by candidates set up by the party in the state for Lok Sabha or Legislative Assembly is not less than 4% of the total number of valid votes polled by all candidates in the state.

A party fulfilling either A or B is a state party.

A party recognised as state party at least in four states is recognised as a national party.

At present, there are **six political parties recognised as National parties**. They are:

(1) Indian National Congress, (2) Communist Party of India (Marxist), (3) Bhartiya Janata Party, (4) Bahujan Samaj Party, (5) Nationalist Congress Party, (6) National People's Party.

There are **58 parties recognised as State parties** at present. The number of recognised parties keeps on changing on the basis of their performance in the elections.

National and State Parties at the time of different General Elections*

Election year	National Parties	State Parties
1952	14	60
1957	4	12
1962	—	16
1967	—	21
1971	8	17
1977	5	18
1980	6	19
1984	7	19
1989	8	20
1998	7	48

***See appendix for rest list**

SOME IMPORTANT PARTIES

Congress

- Division in 1969 into two-Congress (R) led by Mrs. Gandhi and
  Congress (O) led by Mr. Morarji Desai
- Congress (R) got divided in 1978 into-Congress (I) led by Mrs. Gandhi
  Congress (S) led by Swarn Singh
- 1994-Arjun Singh and N.D. Tiwari formed Indira Congress
- 1999-Sharad Pawar, Tariq Anwar and P.A. Sangma formed Nationalist Congress Party (NCP)
- More a pragmatic party than ideologically committed, a centrist party.

Janata Party

- Formed out of conglomeration of five parties (1977)
- Cong (O), Socialist party, Bhartiya Lok Dal, Jan Sangh and Congress for Democracy were its constituents
- tilt was towards farming classes.
- Member of Lok Dal and Socialist Party came out of Janata Party on the issue of dual membership of Jan Sangh.

Janata Dal

- Formed out of merger of Janata Party, Lok Dal and Janata Morcha in 1998
- Became a part of National Front a coalition of seven parties
- In 1990 Samajwadi Janata Party was formed
- In 1992 Janata Dal (A) led by Ajit Singh was formed
- In 1994 Samata Party was formed
- In 1997 RJD was formed
- In 1998 BJD was formed
- All factions of Janata Dal rely on regional caste based support and are dominated by single individuals.

  RJD : Laloo Prasad Yadav

  SP : Mulayam Singh Yadav

Bhartiya Janata Party

- Founded in 1980
- Majority was erstwhile Jan Sangh member which propounded, one country, one nation, one culture and rule of law.
- Claimed its ideology as Gandhian Socialism
- In due course of time opted for Liberalised Swadeshi
- Emphasis on cultural Nationalism

Communist Parties

- Got divided in 1964 into CPI & CPI (M)
- In 1957-absolute majority in Kerala (first time)

CPI

- Remained ally of Congress till 1977 elections
- Joined coalition at Centre in 1966
- Part of United Progressive Alliance (2004)

CPI (M)

- Wanted to develop people's democracy

- In 1982 the party even decided to include BJP to build anti-authoritarian fronts
- Critical of liberalisation policy
- CPI (M) has small following in Hindi belt.

BSP

- Origin in All India Backward and Minorities Communities Employees Federation-1978
- DS-4-Dalit Shoshit Samaj Sangharsh Samiti 1981
- Isolationist in the beginning
- It was a personality centred party

EVALUATION OF INDIAN PARTY SYSTEM

Political parties are an inevitable ingredient of representative government. They provide a link between the people and the government. Perhaps, this led **Prof. Laski** to remark that "there is no alternative to party government, save dictatorship in any state of the modern size." He adds that "they are inevitable in a democracy."

India has witnessed one party dominant system, bi-party tendencies and a multiparty system. From 1989 to 1996 the three parties that remained prominent were INC, JD, BJP. But, defections and break ups in JD created a number of regional, personality based factions of erstwhile Janata Dal. There occurred split in the Congress and Nationalist Congress was formed. BJP being a nationalist, Hindu revivalist party remained intact but could not manage required strength in the formation of Government. These factors, together with sizeable strength of left in certain regions have led to different interactional configuration among the parties.

1989-1991 : 1. National Front Government led by V.P. Singh supported by left parties and BJP was formed.
2. Samajwadi Janata Dal Government led by Chandrashekhar was formed.

1991-1996 : Congress Government with the support of left and Janata Dal.

1996-1998 : 1. 13 days minority government led by Vajpayee was formed.
2. Deve Gowda with Congress support formed Government
3. I.K. Gujral became the PM

1998-1999 : BJP with her alliance formed the Government which lasted only for 13 months.

1999-2004 : NDA government completed its full term

2004 : UPA government at the centre

2009 : UPA government at the centre

2014 : NDA government at the centre

2019 : NDA government at the centre

The contemporary reality of Indian political system is a typical experience. Defection and confrontation have plagued all parties. But, what is ironical is that even foes become friends in the power sharing. The electoral behaviour of people does not seem to reflect any commitment to the party or its ideological base. Rather, they reflect the failure of political parties to deliver goods. Despite 50 years of governance, there has not arised a stable and sustained party system. From the above, following trends can be noticed

- The ruling parties are more prone to lose power on account of lack of commitment to deal with basic issues.
- Splinters of Janata Dal are likely to be a regional, caste-based, centred around a personality.
- Influence of left is likely to be confined to Kerala and West Bengal. As a ruling party in these states they need to be sensitive to the outcomes of liberalization.
- There is likely to be moderation of ideological strength in the BJP so as to garner support of anti-Congress parties.
- The ruling and opposition parties in states are likely to rally around either Congress or the BJP.

REGIONAL PARTIES

The development of regional or state based parties in the federal polity is not unusual. In fact, they may precede the national parties. But, in India this trend has been comparatively a late phenomena (with minor exceptions). Congress due to its nationalist legacies remained a major player in the left. But with social differentiation there emerged new pattern of party system. With the emergence of some regional parties by 1962, we are witnessing a chorus of regional players on both sides; ruling and opposition on the national politics.

Some of the factors for the rise of regional parties are

- Decline of ideological commitment and democratic norms in the Congress party.
- Rise of rural middle class or OBC's through the impact of Green Revolution.
- Rise of urban and semi-urban merchant and trading class.
- Fragmentation and defection in major parties like Janata Dal.
- Regional disparity and imbalances giving impetus to the forces of regionalism.

The regional parties have gained ascendence not only at regional or state but also at national level. How far they succeed, depends on their bargaining strength, vis-a-vis party forming government at the centre. If anything, this trend seems to continue for some time.

COALITION GOVERNMENT

A Government formed by joining together of two or more political parties is called Coalition Government. In India, this form of exercise started in 1967 when some of the states went for it. However, with the exception of Kerala and West Bengal its result have not been optimistic. The Centre got the opportunity in 1977, but government fell in two years. From 1989 onwards, there has arisen an era of coalition government at the centre. With exception of Vajpayee government (1999-2004), the experience have not been satisfactory. A serious doubt remains as to whether India can withstand the pressure of coalition politics or could it provide stability. But, of late there seems to be an acceptance in all quarters that coalition is inevitable in a diverse society like India. Some are apprehensive of it for being chaotic and horse trading market place; some visualize it as heralding an era of federalized polity.

16

PRESSURE GROUP

The complexity of political life has witnessed the rise of many groups referred to as pressure groups, interest group or influence groups. They are voluntary organisations, with a particular interest. They do not participate in contest for power in elections. According to **V.O. Key** "pressure groups are non-political groups, though they are engaged in politics, their politics is that of policy." Though they help some parties, they do not fight elections. They are informal, closed and unrecognised associations. They are distinguished from social movements by their greater degree of formal organization. They act as the medium through which the function of articulation is performed in a political system. They constitute links of communication between the citizen and the government. They supply information and supplement in policy formulation. Their role has increased with growing voluntarism, in the era of globalization and liberalization.

They try to build public opinion in their favour and do not seek to capture power but only to influence decisions. As **Arthur Bentley** remarks, "Public policy is the result of interplay of group forces."

Pressure groups is a term applied to those interest groups which use different pressure tactics including extra-constitutional methods to pursue their goals.

Different Views

Prof Finer refers to them as sever anonymous empire and others have called them as invisible government and unofficial government.

Arthur Bentley's 'the process of Government and Human's 'Government process' marked the beginning of group approach to politics.

Marxist View : They see it as a phenomenon characterising capitalism.

In communism, there are to be only trade unions, youth leagues, writers unions, women's committees etc, but they function as sources of originating it. They are thus not autonomous entities.

Gabrial Almond has done indepth analyses of pressure group and classified them as

1. Association
2. Non-Association
3. Institutional
4. Anomic pressure group

Determinants of Pressure Group Politics

1. **Political Institutions :** Whereas in a democratic system, dominant direction of flow is from the groups to the government, in totalitarian system it is just the other way round.

   In Britain, since the cabinet and civil service are more effective rather than the MP's the target are former two. In the U.S. with strong congressional committee system and powerful chairman it is more advantageous to concen-trate on them.

   In France, the administration is the main target.
2. **Party System :** In countries like France and Italy both the parties and interest groups exist as fairly as organised entities but not autonomous systems. The parties control the interest groups in various ways and various degrees. In Britain and U.S.A., the interest groups articulate demands, the political parties play the aggregative role and stands

between interest groups and authoritative policy making agencies. In the third world, neither political parties or interest groups stand very well differentiated. They are powerful where political system are decentralised and political discipline is weak.

In multi party systems, pressure groups have worked effectively among the legislators.

3. **Political Culture :** American political culture shows greater tolerance and acceptability of the interest groups, compared to the European democratic systems.

   French political system has allowed more direct action and groups even resorting to violence.

   Germany is more rigid and authoritarian.

4. Issue or problem which an interest group is projecting also shapes the character of pressure group dynamics.

Thus every interest group, by its own nature and characteristics, employs different approaches, methods and tactics. Thus there exist what Miliband calls an 'imperfect competition' between different groups in a liberal democracy.

Methods used by Pressure Groups

1. **Lobbying :** A political technique whereby groups send representations to the legislators or officials of government departments in order to influence public policy in favour of themselves.
2. Press and media networks are used by them.
3. By aligning with the political party.
4. By physical demonstrations and even resorting to violence.
5. By helping the legislators in winning election and attaining political power.

Functions of Pressure Groups

1. Interest articulation
2. A form of linkage between Government and the masses
3. A means of communication in the political system
4. Create and deepen political consciousness in the society.
5. Nurseries of political leadership
6. Agency for social solidarity and integration.

Origin and Evolution of Pressure Group

The unification of the country and introduction of western education provided impetus to mushrooming of pressure groups in India. Some of them include, Atmiya Sabha, Brahmo Sabha, British Indian Association, Bombay Association etc. Even Indian National Congress and the Muslim League started its career as an interest group.

Types of Pressure Groups

1. **Institutional Interest Groups :** According to **Almond and Powell** "institutional interest groups are found within such organisations as political parties, legislatures, armies, bureaucracies, and churches." They attempt to exert influence or pressure through the machinery of government itself. For example, Choc, CEC, Bureaucracy, Army etc.
2. **Association Interest Group :** These groups are formed by people sharing professional interests. They are also referred to as protective or functional groups. In India, there are two kinds of associational interest groups : occupational and community. There include Business organisations (such as CII and FICCI), trade Unions (such as AITUC), Peasant organisations (such as BKU), etc.
3. **Social or Identity Based Group :** These are groups based on kinship, ethnic, religious or caste affiliations. Their distinguishing characteristic is **informal** interest articulation. Some of them turned into political parties. For example, Anti Brahmin Movement turned into DK and DMK. Scheduled caste federation turned into Republican Party.
4. **Ad-hoc Group :** Group that are organised for a specific purpose and continue for a specific period of time.

Characteristics of Indian Pressure Groups

Pressure groups in India display the following characteristics :

1. The pressure groups are primarily organised on the basis of caste; community, religion and region.
2. According to **Myron Weiner**, the majority of the pressure groups in India are controlled by or affiliated with political parties.
3. Pressure groups in India play a limited role in the formulation of public policies.
4. The professional pressure groups enjoy relative autonomy than the political parties.
5. They often resort to violence and strikes/hartals to achieve their objectives.
6. They mainly target the bureaucracy and administrative establishments.

Dynamics of Pressure Group

Traditional linkages and primordial loyalties remain a constitutive factor in pressure group politics in India. Most of them are linked to some or the other party and called 'parties behind the parties.' Their importance have grown with mounting pressure on the political system and fragmentation of dominant party system. However, their role has not been praiseworthy. They have often created chaotic situation and paralysed the fate of governments. But, under contemporary trends of liberalization the pressure groups are bound to take a fresh look. They are expected of rising above vested interest and promote the interests that are hailed as genuine and commensurate with ethos of the polity. The pressure groups have lost their credibility and popular sympathy due to their negative role. However, some of the pressure groups like the FICCI have adopted positive outlook to fulfil the interest of their members.

However, the pressure groups in India have not only influenced the formulation of public policies but also the whole political process. Many times, they have forced the government to consider their demands and genuine problems. In a way, they have acted as an effective limitations on government's arbitrariness..

17

ELECTIONS IN INDIA

India has a long tradition of having procedure of election for choosing a person to an office or otherwise. But, it has become a celebrated word in recent times. The spread of the ideal of democracy as the most human form of government has forced even totalitarian and authoritarian system to accommodate the mechanism of elections. Perhaps, every political system operationalize the mechanism of elections to project its legitimacy.

Elections comprises a system of rules and procedures whereby a person or group of persons are chosen to perform some task on the part of the choosers. But, there is no unanimity on the role of election. For, in authoritarian regimes they are limited to ensuring the maintenance of status-quo, in democratic system they are change oriented.

Role of Elections

If democratic norms are observed, election can be helpful in

- Political Socialization and political participation
- Providing leaders for political process
- Ensuring legitimate government
- Political education of the masses
- Resolving political conflict by peaceful means
- Peaceful transfer of power

It is by virtue of its significant functions that **S.M. Lipset** hailed elections as the "expression of democratic class struggle."

ELECTION COMMISSION

A three member commission entrusted with the task of supervising and conducting elections. It consists of a Chief Election Commissioner and two Election Commissioners.

Term : Every Election Commissioner has a term of six years from the date he/she assumes office or till he attains the age of 65 years (whichever is earlier).

Safeguard : The Chief Election commissioner cannot be removed from his office, except in a like manner and on like grounds as a judge of the Supreme Court. All the three members are entitled to the same salary and other facilities, as are provided to a judge of the Supreme Court.

Functions/Powers

1. Prepare, revise and maintain the voter's list.
2. Delimitation of Constituencies.
3. Advises the President and Governor regarding electoral matters.
4. Determine criteria for recognizing political parties.
5. Settle election disputes.

Electoral Provisions in Indian Constitution

Apart from **Article 324-329** (dealing exclusively) there are provision in the Acts of Parliament. Elections are explicitly mentioned in **Part XV** of the Constitution.

Article 324 : Provides for a Election Commission to supervise, control and direct the elections to the office of President, Vice President, Parliament and State Legislatures.

President has been conferred the power to increase or decrease the number of election commissioners.

Article 325 : Provides for one general electoral roll.

Article 326 : Provides for Adult suffrage i.e. equal right to vote to persons of 18 years age.

Article 327 : The legislative power as regards the process of election is vested in the Parliament.

Article 328 : Confers similar powers to the state legislatures.

Article 329 : Prohibits the courts to enquire into validity of law as regards delimitation of constituencies. It also lays down disputes regarding election can be called into question only after declaration of result.

Besides these constitutional provisions, there are electoral laws : **Representation of People Act 1950 and 1951. Presidential and Vice Presidential Act 1952, Registration of Electors Rules 1960, Conduct of Election Rules 1961, Election Symbol Order, 1968 etc.**

CHIEF ELECTION COMMISSIONERS*

S.No.	Name	Tenure		
1.	Sukumar Sen	21 March, 1950	–	19 Dec., 1958
2.	K.V.K. Sundaram	19 Dec., 1958	–	30 Sep., 1967
3.	S.P. Sen Verma	30 Sep., 1967	–	30 Sep., 1972
4.	Dr. Nagendra Singh	30 Sep. 1972	–	6 Feb.,1973
5.	T. Swaminathan	6 Feb., 1973	–	18 June, 1977
6.	S.L. Shakdhar	18 June, 1977	–	18 June, 1982
7.	R.K. Trivedi	18 June, 1982	–	31 Dec., 1985
8.	R.V.S. Perishastri	1 Jan., 1986	–	15 Nov., 1990
9.	V.S. Rama Devi	15 Nov., 1990	–	12 Dec., 1990
10.	T.N. Seshan	12 Dec., 1990	–	11 Dec., 1997
11.	M.S. Gill	12 Dec., 1997	–	12 June, 2001
12.	J.M. Lyngdoh	14 June, 2001	–	7 Feb., 2004
13.	T.S. Krishnamurthy	8 Feb., 2004	–	15 May, 2005
14.	B.B. Tandon	15 May, 2005	–	29 June, 2006
15.	N. Gopalaswami	30 June, 2006	–	20 April, 2009
16.	Navin Chawla	21 April, 2009	–	29 July, 2010
17.	S.Y. Quraishi	30 July, 2010	–	10 June, 2012

See appendix for rest list

Electoral Dynamics

Elections are one of the most central political process in India. All sections of the society remain entangled with the electoral politics. That is why **D.L. Seth** observes that elections "can not be ignored while formulating any perspective of the Indian political system."

The change in political milieu from the one party dominion phase to multiparty coalition era is reflection of changing allegiance of people expressed through elections. Taken in this perspective, elections have become tool for analysis of social change, democratic transformation and legitimacy of government.

However, the expediency with which elections are held and practices which are followed during the elections belief such commitments. According to **Prof. Sushila Kaushik**, "more than just important political events, they have been a kind of national festival or tamasha, a source of entertainment..." The electoral outcomes are fragmented on the basis of caste, creed, region and religion. Most often electoral outcomes reflects that ideology has taken a back seat. Common national issues seldom become a part of electoral campaigns.

The contradictions of modernization and development, together with frequency of elections have robbed the parties of genuine issues. As a result, hitherto dormant primordial loyalties and vested interests have come to the fore. Regional and linguistic resources are exploited for electoral gains. The sudden outburst of violence and malpractices of numerous kinds have become an integral part of electoral process. Even the bureaucracy and military seems to serve their political masters or caste directors. Sudden influx of media barons, former bureaucrats, big industrialists and liquor mafias highlights the importance of elections in India.

ELECTORAL REFORMS

In recent times, India's credibility of being the largest democracy has been maligned due to the manner in which electoral politics is played here. In place of awakened, service spirited leadership, criminals and vested interests are being elected. Use of state machinery by the ruling party, selection of candidates with huge surplus of wealth, booth capturing, rigging, electoral violence, politicization of caste and religion are some prominent factors that have put question mark on fair electoral process.

The events during elections are but one aspect of electoral malpractices. There remains other crucial factors that affect the wider society as well. **N.N. Vohra Committee** (1993) reported that, "CBI has reported that all over India, Crime syndicates have become law unto themselves. The means between criminal gangs, police, bureaucracy and politicians has come out clearly in various parts of the country. The existing criminal justice system, which was essentially designed to deal with the individual offences/crimes, is unable to deal with the activities of the mafia."

A four member panel during 1998 Lok Sabha election, consisting of justice Kuldip Singh, Madhav Godbole, C. Subramanium and Swami Agnivesh indicated that 72 candidates had criminal records.

SOME FACTS ABOUT 2024 ELECTIONS

Party	Seats won
Bharatiya Janata Party	240
Indian National Congress	99
Dravida Munnetra Kazhagam	22
All India Trinamool Congress	29
Samajwadi Party	37
Shiv Sena	16
Janata Dal (United)	12
Telugu Desam Party	16
Nationalist Congress Party	9
Communist Party of India (Marxist)	4

History of Electoral Reforms

The talks for reform of electoral system is not a recent event. **Tarkunde Committee** was set up in 1975 by Jai Prakash Narayan. Similarly **Dinesh Goswami Committee** (1990) and **Indrajeet Gupta Committee** (1998) also proposed reforms. The Law Commission (1999) suggested a comprehensive reform in electoral and party system.

Measures of Electoral Reform

Some of the measures include

1. The election commission should be entrusted full disciplinary executive authority during polling. To ensure that the institution acts as a federal agency, the election commissioners must be appointed by the union executive in consultation with the Chief Justice of India and the leader of opposition in the Lok Sabha, subject to ratification by the Rajya Sabha.
2. There should be regular elections in the party and they should show respect to democratic norms. They should maintain transparency in their income and expenditure.
3. To some extent, state funding of election can be worked out, as suggested by Indrajeet Gupta Committee.
4. There should be periodic rotation of reserved seats for schedule castes and scheduled tribes.
5. A working formula must be outlined to give special representation to the women.

18

ROLE OF CASTE AND GENDER IN INDIAN POLITICS

ROLE OF CASTE IN INDIAN POLITICS

Among the major divisive forces affecting the polity, caste remains the formidable one. It refers to an ascriptive system of status and hierarchy. Its chief characteristics are hierarchy, commensality, restrictions on marriage and hereditary occupation. Its dominance is observed by **M.N. Srinivas** ''Caste is so tactly and so completely accepted by all, including those most vocal in condemning it, that it is everywhere the unit of social action.''

Although British gained control over India by playing one caste or community against the other, their system of education and administration helped in individualizing the Indian society. But, while structural and functional aspects underwent transformation, political dimension striked its root. After the Independence, caste began to acquire new turn in Indian politics. Speaking about the interaction between caste and politics, **Rajni Kothari** points out three dimension.

Firstly, In spite of being a stratification system, caste have strived for social mobility.

Secondly, Caste system is not only based on birth but also controls and determines occupational and economic roles.

Thirdly, It is not politics that gets caste-ridden, it is caste that gets politicized.

ROLE OF GENDER IN INDIAN POLITICS

Natural division between male and female has its manifestation under the term sex but its social implication is espoused under the term 'Gender.' The confinement, seclusion, subjugation of women for centuries have come under attack in recent times. There have been persistent questioning of according inferior status to women. Such developments are a manifestation of growth of rational outlook and spread of ideas like democracy, equality and liberty. Moreover, it also reflects wide realization as to how humanity can progress when it denigrates half of its population to an inferior status?

In particular, 20th century would go down in history as an epoch of promoting gender justice by internationalizing struggles for equality of women. Introduction of universal franchise in almost all nations and efforts of U.N. are noteworthy in this regard. Such development has true implications in India also.

Position of Indian Women

After a brief spell of equality of sexes in the vedic period, there began deterioration in status of women. During the medieval age purdah became a custom among muslim and sati became prevalent among Hindus. Patriarchal norms were expressed through cultural metaphors. British system of education together with liberal sentiments led to reformist movement. Organization and persons took cognizance of injustices meted out to women. Social legislation, viz. Abolition of Sati (1829) Widow Remarriage Act (1856), Civil Marriage Act (1872) were important steps in this regard. The Nationalist Movement and Gandhiji's call dragged women into the mainstream of Indian politics. **All India women's conference** was organized in 1927.

After independence a number of steps were taken to ensure equality and dignity of women and free them from the clutches of unjustified subjugation. These include :

Constitutional Provisions

Article 14 : provides that the state shall not delay to any person equality before the law or equal protection of law.

Article 15 : prohibits discrimination on grounds such as caste, religion and sex.

Article 16 : provides for equality of opportunity in matters relating to public employment.

Article 16(4) : empowers the state to make special provisions for women and children.

These provisions are justifiable.

Article 39(a) : equal right to and adequate means of livelihood.

Article 39(c) : equal pay for equal work for both; men and women.

Article 42 : make provisions for just and human conditions of work and maternity relief.

42 Amendment Part IV A Article 51A imposes a **fundamental duty to renounce practices derogatory to the dignity of women.**

The 73rd and 74th Amendment Act heralded a new era by reserving 1/3 seats at all levels of rural and urban local self government for women.

Enactments

Special Marriage Act 1954

Hindu Marriage Act 1955

Hindu Maintenance and Adoption Act 1956

Dowry Prohibition Act 1961

Equal Remuneration Act 1976

Child Marriage Restraint (Amendment) Act 1978

Dowry Prohibition (Amendment) Act 1984.

Judiciary has also been active as shown in the Shah Bano case (1982)

The Protection of Women from Domestic Violence Act, 2005 came into force on October 26, 2006.

Other Measures

Social Welfare Board was constituted in 1953 to grant aid, promote welfare and development services for women.

In 1985 a separate department of women and child development was set up at the centre.

In 1986 National Policy on Education outlined several features for women's education.

In 1987 programme of support to training cum employment for women was started.

In 1990 Parliament enacted a law to create National Commission for women. It came into existence in 1992.

In 1995 Indira Mahila Yojna was started with the aim of organizing women at grassroots level.

In 2001 National Policy for Empowerment of women was launched.

NATIONAL COMMISSION FOR WOMEN

- Statutory body created in 1992
- Consists of a Chairman nominated by the Government.
- There are 5 other members and a member secretary.
- It is vested with power of civil court.

Functions

1. To investigate and examine all matters relating to safeguards for women.
2. Make recommendation for effective implementation of safeguards.
3. Review the existing provision of the Constitution.
4. Call for special studies or investigations into specific problems.

DALITS AND INDIAN POLITICS

The category 'Dalits' includes the castes who fall outside the Varna system. They are also called by various names; such as outcastes, untouchables or achuts. They are marginalised sections whose major source of frustration relates to individual behaviour, norms of the society and state apparatus. Though their position has improved due to constitutional provisions, welfare policies and positive discrimination measures, a firm commitment is required to hinder the hindrances in ensuring equality.

Constitutional Provisions

1. **Article 341** deals with the criteria for identification of scheduled castes. **Article 342** deals with Scheduled Tribes.
2. **Article 17** abolished practice of untouchability in any form.
3. **Articles 14, 15 ,16 and 16(4)** place them in equal position with other members and entrust state to make special provisions.
4. **Article 38** enjoins the state to promote the welfare of people by ensuring justice in society.
5. **Article 46** entrusts the state to promote the educational and economic interests of scheduled caste.
6. 65th Amendment Act, 1990 provided for **National Commission** for SCs and STs. But, recently there has been bifurcation of the commission to deal exclusively with one category.

Legal Enactments

1. Untouchability offences Act 1955.
2. Protection of Civil Rights Act 1975.
3. SC and ST (Prevention of Atrocities) Act 1989.

Development Measures

1. Book Bank Scheme
2. Girls Hostel and Boys Hostel Schemes
3. Coaching
4. Scheduled Caste Development Corporation
5. Separate plan of Action for Primitive Tribe
6. Tribal sub plan strategy to provide legal and administrative support and promote their development.

It is to be noted that mere constitutional provisions or legal safeguards are not adequate in themselves. As **Ambedkar** observed "on 26th January 1950, we are going to enter into a life of contradictions. In political life we will have equality and in social and economic structure, continue to deny the principle of one man one vote... if we continue to deny it for long, we shall do so only by pushing our political democracy in peril. We must remove this contradictions at the earliest possible moment or else those who suffer from inequality will blow up the structure of political democracy."

REGIONAL ISSUES

For a multiculturally diverse and complex country like India, regional affiliations are but natural phenomena. What is of crucial concern is that it has often been a major stumbling block in the task of national integration. But there are others who feel that the urge of regional affiliation is not essentially antithetical to the urge for national unity. Nevertheless, they are unavoidable in a vast country like India. It is upto the policy makers and leadership as to how best they tackle it.

Region and Regionalism

Region connotes a definite territorial area including particular language or languages, caste, ethnic groups etc. It is primarily a social fact.

Regionalism essentially means affiliations and obligations towards a region or a state above and beyond those towards the country as a whole. At the base of it lies a sense of identity.

Even though the British provided opportunity for unification of all the territorial units by their system of administrations, they promoted prejudices on the basis of language, culture, caste or religion.

Major Causes for Regionalism

1. Apprehension on the part of linguistic ethnic or religious minorities in view of uniform system of administration and policies. Many of these groups dominant in specific region, became suspicious as to whether their cultural ties, ethos and symbols would be taken care by the Indian state. Perhaps, this explains the fact that most regional forces have striked roots in non-Hindi belt (Tamil Nadu, Andhra etc.).

2. Uneven pattern of socio-eonomic development have created regional disparities. What is more worst is the naming of these states as BIMARU (Bihar, Madhya Pradesh, Rajasthan and Uttar Pradesh) etc. The categorisation and sub-categorisation of the states on the basis of socio-economic indicators have generated resentment against the central leadership.
3. The elitist character of leadership and unwarranted intervention by the centre in the affairs of the state have rendered the state vulnerable to regional forces. The strategic political calculations at the centre and failure of regional political parties to bargain with them have also been a cause of concern.

PROBLEMS OF NATION BUILDING AND NATIONAL INTEGRATION

The fundamental basis of any country lies on its unity and integrity. It is the national unity that acts a bulwork against forces of domination and exploitation. It also assures peace, prosperity and progress. Consequently every country state aims to strengthen its unity and attain leverage in enjoying the benefits of human civilization.

India that is Bharat is a country with diversity. There exist differences between people on the basis of caste, creed, colour, language, ethos, way of life and religious affiliations. However, many of these issues need not affect the society as long as people abide by the norms and values committed to a broader identity say; a nation. But that is not the case in India. India is still a nation in the making. As **Rajni Kothari** observes, "the problem of national integration is the fundamental problem of political development".

Major Obstacles to the Process of National Integration

In essence, there are certain major aspects of the problem. They are as under :

Firstly, Communalism continues to be a major stumbling block in achieving national integration. The policy of 'divide and rule' used by British to serve their interest, continues to plague Indian society in more robust forms. The frequency of communal riots. Godhra riots and many smaller ones severely damage the prospect for national integration.

Secondly, Regionalism and subregionalism, continue to affect India. It is true that a multicultural society like India can not aspire to be a homogeneous one, but the fissiparous demands add to the woes of the polity.

Thirdly, Politics of populism exploits the inherent structural dimensions of Indian Society. The use of caste, creed, colour or sex as a tool to mobilize votes continues to be a black spot on the political process.

Fourthly, Poverty and illiteracy have continuously created apathy among Indian nationals. They have shown disenchantment with the polity and remain preoccupied either with their conventional ethos and way of life or turn to violent methods. Story of tribes and Naxals speaks volumes about their either anti or non-Indian stands.

Fifthly, Politics of violence and movements centred around sectarian goals damages not only the political propriety but also a belief in the strength of the nation. Anarchy and political turmoil created by these forces hinder the pace of unity and integration.

Sixthly, The inadequate distribution of goods and services continues to result in creating disillusionment among crores of people who have till now owed allegiance to the nation.

Measures/Suggestions for National Integration

Under these background, following measures, can be recommended to overcome problems in the way of achieving national integration. These are as follows:

Firstly, Changing focus and dimensions of political policies by making it more attuned to general rather than sectoral claims. Government need to shed complacency in delivering to genuine claims so that general people could feel some correspondence with the nation.

Secondly, Ensuring favourable conditions under which every section of the society could enjoy or share larger benefits of the society. This could be done by ensuring balanced economic development, strengthening transport and communication, increasing employment and alike.

Thirdly, National viability should be the criteria on which regional issues must be dealt.

Fourthly, Promoting secular ethos through civil society institutions, intellectuals and the mass media by giving financial assistance to hold seminars, symposium, cultural contacts etc.

Fifthly, Dealing firmly with subversive and anti-national forces. So that people would feel a kind of 'awe' towards the nation.

Sixthly, Institute mechanisms to ensure secularism, achieve social justice and discourage populism by activating different wings of the society.

19

ADMINISTRATIVE CORRUPTION

ADMINISTRATIVE CORRUPTION

Corruption affects every society in some or the other way. But, in developing societies like India, it has assumed such tendencies that many other problems have become dependent on it. In fact, the whole programme of development has been serverely paralysed by bureaucratic malpractices. Today, no country can claim to be completely free from corruption, but every country tries to keep it at bare minimum level so that it does not affect much.

The concept of corruption is closely integrated with the concept of integrity. It implies honesty and uprightness of character in conducting administrative tasks. It relates to the aspect of ethics and morality which is underlined in the name of science and rationality. On the contrary, the Bureaucracy has often been engaged in scramble for grabbing whatever they can get through means more often foul than fair.

While large sections of the society are far from meeting their basic human needs inspite of a life time of sweat and tears, some people's greed is apparantly unlimited. Everyone seems to be in a hurry to find the key to short-cuts at the expense of others.

India adopted a British model described as 'Steel frame' of administration. But, no thought was paid as to how an institution geared to serve the interests of colonial masters could be an instrument of change and development. No attention was paid to revive and rejunivate the age-old system of Panchayats which delivered Civil as well as Criminal justice in India.

During the early days of British administration, corruption was mainly confined to lower levels. The second world war period provided opportunities wherein corruption engulfed the entire machinery of administration. A number of war related civil work provided impetus to rising instances of corruption in the departments of central and state government.

There was continuity in the ethos and practices of administration as far as corruption was concerned. If anything, there was rise in such instances. **Santhanam Committee Report** (1964) observed "we heard from all sides that corruption in recent years spread even to those levels of administration from which it was conspicuously absent in the past."

This continuity could be explained partly in terms of increasing role of state in reconstruction and development, partly in terms of social structure of the machinery. The elitist life style of the Bureaucrats turned them to engage in easy money making exercises. Lack of technical expertise on the part of leadership strengthened this trend. When the leadership realized the corrupt network, they themselves became part of it. The nexus between public servants and the corrupt politicians devalued the aspect of honesty and integrity from the realm of public life. Very soon the vigilance, policing, grievance redressal machinery was also under its ambit. In recent times, Vohra Committee on criminalization of politics found an unhealthy nexus between politicians, bureaucrats and criminals operating as law unto themselves.

Causes for Rising Corruption

The main reason for growing corruption.

1. Lack of requisite political will to institute strict legislation to combat corruption.

Moreover, they need avoid giving patronage to a selective few bureaucrats to serve their political interests.

2. Growth of bureaucratic machinery in the realm of law and order maintenance has been another crucial point. The poor, ignorant masses are often seen victimised by policemen to give money even for registration of cases.
3. The scheme of transfer and posting of IAS/IPS officials at the behest of leadership has politicized bureaucracy.
4. The escalating cost of elections and frequency with which Indian celebrate this festival also complicates the issue.
5. The coalition government at the centre rendered the cabinet succumb to pressure of regional players. Every party wants its own administrative lieutenants to be accorded new heights in the administrative machinery.
6. Discretionary powers allowed to ministers in matters like allotment of plots of land, houses, shops, petrol pumps, gas, telephone booth, reservation of seats in Railways or Airways.
7. Lack of adequate and efficient vigilance machinery has also promoted corruption in the sense that when people see their colleagues appropriating wealth without any problem, they are also tempted to do the same.

Modes of Corruption

Corruption need not necessarily be in the form of money. The Central Vigilance Commission has identified following twenty-seven modes of corruption.

1. Acceptance of substandard stores/works.
2. Misappropriation of public money and misappropriation of stores.
3. Incurring pecuniary obligations of persons with whom the public servants have official dealings.
4. Borrowings money from contractors/firms having official dealings with officers.
5. Showing favours to contractors and firms.
6. Claiming of false travelling allowance, house rent, etc.
7. Possession of disproportionate assets.
8. Causing loss to government by negligence or otherwise.
9. Purchase of immovable property, etc. without prior permission or intimation.
10. Abuse of official position/powers.
11. Acceptance of illegal gratification in recruitments, postings, transfers and promotions.
12. Misuse of government employees for personal work.
13. Production of forged certificates of age, of birth of community, etc.
14. Irregularities in the reservation of seats by Rail and by Air.
15. Non-delivery of money orders, insured covers, value payable parcels, etc.
16. Replacement of new postal stamps by used ones.
17. Irregularity in grant of import and export licences.
18. Misuse of imported and allotted quotas by various firms with the connivance of the public servants.
19. Irregularity in the grant of telephone connections.
20. Moral turpitude.
21. Acceptance of gifts.
22. Under assessments of income tax, estate duty, etc., for pecuniary gain.
23. Misuse of advances sanctioned for purchase of scooters and cars.
24. Abnormal delay in settlement of compensation claims to displaced persons.
25. Wrong assessment of claims of displaced persons.
26. Cheating in connection with the sale and purchase of plots for residential purposes.
27. Unauthorized occupation and subletting of government quarters.

Existing Legal Framework

The Prevention of Corruption Act 1947 defines the scope of corruption in regard to public servant as follows :

"A public servant is said to commit the offence of criminal misconduct in the discharge of his duty—

1. If he habitually accepts or obtains or agrees to accept for himself or attempts to obtain from any person, any gratification (other than legal remuneration) as a motive or reward as mentioned in Section 161 of the Indian Penal Code ;
2. If he habitually accepts or obtains or agrees to accept or attempts to obtain for himself or for any other person, any valuable thing without consideration or for a consideration which he knows to be inadequate from any person whom he knows to have been, or to be likely to be concerned in any proceeding or business transacted or about to be transacted by him, or having connection with the official functions of himself or of any public servant to whom he is subordinate, or from any person whom he knows to be interested in or related to the person concerned;
3. If he dishonestly or fraudulently misappropriates or, otherwise abuses his position as a public servant, obtains for himself or any other person any valuable thing or pecuniary advantage."

Corruption in Liberalized Economy

Under the aegis of liberalization strategy there is talk of 'less of Government.' But it does not complete withdrawal of state. Rather, it has still an important role to play in the area of infrastructure (Road, power, petroleum etc.) building and regulatory mechanisms. Moreover, market can not be panacea of all evils. Under this background following measures can be recommended to check administrative corruption.

Measures to Check Corruption

1. Government can selectively withdraw from the areas of over regulation provide scope for corruption. Moreover, personnel of good career record and integrity be preferred in heading an inspection team.
2. Downsizing the administrative machinery would ensure better efficiency and integrity.
3. There should be greater transparency in administration. Right to information is better step in this regard.
4. Proper backing of administrative reforms by electoral and political reforms because they have increasingly become integrated.
5. Slackening the power of politicians in transfer and posting of bureaucrats will ensure discipline and integrity in them. It will also influence them to act in a way that is not solely political.
6. Effectively empowering bodies like Central Vigilance Commission, which is a statutory body. It conducts its investigation through CBI.
7. Set up institution of Lok Pal to investigate alleged cases of corruption against political leaders at the union level. This step was recommended by Administrative Reform Commission. Despite claiming commitment to Lok Pal Bill, the political leadership is reluctant to give it a statutory status.

Central Vigilance Commission

Central Vigilance Commission (CVC) is the key institution to check corruption in the administration of the country. It was created in 1964 but has received statutory status very recently. The Central Bureau of Investigation is the investigating arm of CVC. It is headed by Chief Vigilance Commissioner.

It consists of a CVC and not more than three members appointed by the President of India on the recommendations of a high powered committee under the chairmanship of the Prime Minister, with the Home Minister and the leader of the opposition in the Lok Sabha as members. The Vigilance Commissioner shall have a fixed tenure of 4 years subject to the upper age limit of 65 years.

The Central Vigilance Commissioner can be removed in the same manner as provided for the removal of the Chairman of UPSC. After retirement, he is not eligible for any futher employment under the Central Government or state government.

The Central Vigilance Commission (CVC) Act, 2003 confers a statutory status on the Central Vigilance Commission (CVC) to exercise superintendence over the function by the Central Bureau of Investigation (CBI). The Act authorises the CVC to probe offences committed by Central government officials, corporations, societies and local authorities. The Act lays down that the Central Vigilance Commissioner and other vigilance commissioners be appointed by a three member panel consisting of the Prime Minister, the home minister and the leader of the opposition in the Lok Sabha.

Ombudsman

A Swedish institution to redress public grievances. It embodies suo-motu power to start investigation. According to Donald C. Rowat, the institution of Ombudsman represents a "bulwork of democratic government against the tyranny of officialdom.'' In India, Lokpal and Lokayukta are Ombudsman like institutions.

Lok Pal

The institution of Lok Pal, though promised on many occasions, never came into practice. Its novel feature is that it brings even the Prime Minister under the sphere of its enquiry. Moreover it is to have its own administrative staff to carry on its investigations. It was firstly suggested by Administrative Reform Commission, 1966. It is a grievance redressing institution.

On March 19, 2019 Justice Pinaki Chandra Ghosh was appointed as India's first Lokpal along with eight other members. The appointment itself was made five years after the Lokpal and Lokayukta Act was passed in 2013 to investigate cases of corruption against certain categories of public servants. An institution of similar kind called Lokayukta came up in some states. It conducts investigation charges against Chief Minister and other Ministers at the State level. Lokayuktas are responsible to the state legislature.

Lokayuktas*

State	Created in
1. Odisha	1970
2. Maharashtra	1971
3. Rajasthan	1973
4. Bihar	1974
5. Uttar Pradesh	1975
6. Madhya Pradesh	1981
7. Andhra Pradesh	1983
8. Himachal Pradesh	1983
9. Karnataka	1985
10. Assam	1985
11. Gujarat	1986
12. Punjab	1995
13. Delhi	1995
14. Kerala	1999
15. Jharkhand	2001

**See appendix for rest list*

Central Bureau of Investigation

The Central Bureau of Investigation (CBI) was set up in 1963. The CBI is the main investigating agency of the Central Government. It plays an important role in preventing corruption and main-taining integrity in administration. It also provides assistance to the Central Vigilance Commission.

The Functions of CBI are:

1. To investigate cases of corruption, bribery and misconduct of the Central government employees.
2. To investigate cases relating to infringe-ment of fiscal and economic laws.
3. To investigate serious crimes committed by organised gangs of professional criminals.
4. To coordinate and assist other anti corruption agencies.

ADMINISTRATIVE REFORM

Like many other institutions, India adopted the administrative machinery from United Kingdom. However, while other institutions helped in ensuring democracy and development, bureaucracy became reluctant to deliver in achieving those

Various Administrative Reform Committees and their Recommendations

	Year	Name	Recommendation/purpose
I	1949	N. Gopal Swamy Iyenger Committee	Recommended reorganisation of Head Offices
II	1950	A.W. Gorewala Committee	To review the working of public administration in the task of development
III	1952	P.H. Appleby Committee	To do a survey of Administration in India
IV	1956	P.H. Appleby Committee	To review the working of industrial enterprises
V	1955-57	J.B. Kriplani Committee	To examine the issue of corruption in Indian Railways
VI	1956	A. Ramaswamy Muddaliar Committee	To outline the criteria of merit for civil servants
VII	1964	K. Santhanam Committee	To examine the working of Indian Administration in total
VIII	1976	D.S. Kothari Committee	Concerned with process of recruitment of civil servants
IX	1989	Satish Chandra Committee	Recommended broad changes in Civil Service Examinations
X	1997	N.N. Vohra Committee	To examine the issue of corruption
XI	1998	P.C. Jain Committee	To examine the operational aspect of administrative law
XII	2000	Y.K. Alagh Committee	To examine civil services Examination
XIII	2004	P.C. Hota Committee	To examine civil services Examination
XIV	2005	Second Administrative Reforms Commission	To prepare a detailed blueprint for revamping the public administrative system.

objectives. Instead, it developed vested interest in maintaining status-quo, revised as an agency of change and transformation, bureaucracy itself became a major stumbling block in this direction.

Administrative Structure

The administrative system which has been alien to a country failed to deliver the goods. In due course of time, it complicated other problems as well. The whole edifice of development became paralysed. The alien nature of administrative system was most potent cause of its drawbacks. While adopting a alien model; socio-economic milieu, political structure, ethical orientations of the society were not taken into consideration. Moreover, it provided a lucid opportunity to a minority of privilged, affluent, english educated stalwart to command the administrative system. As a result the administrators became a class for themselves seeking to maximize gains for themselves without any consideration for the society.

Integrated Reform : Despite claims and counter claims of reform, the administrative system continues to suffer from severe lacunae. The failure of reforms are partly due to failure to integrate the aspect of administrative reform with political and electoral reform and partly on account of weak enforcement agencies to combat the aspect of corruption.

It is ironical as to how one can expect that the administration, the whole edifice of which is built on corruption and ethos of power, would easily give upto demands of reform. Such changes demand strict legal/statutory provisions, strong law enforcement and investigating agencies, system of reward and penalty for acts of bureaucrats etc. But, most important of them all is the desire and a firm commitment on the part of political leadership.

Specific Measures for Administrative Reform

1. To promote total transparency in the functioning of government at all levels such as right to information Act. Moreover, the officials and people providing important information be provided protection through measures like 'Whistleblower Act.' The area of 'Secrecy' and 'Confidential' information must be redefined with reference to their rational basis and their actual consequences.
2. The delay in decision making should be checked. There should be mandatory time frame for decision making. The contingent and arbitrary elements must be eliminated with proper care.
3. To enforce accountability of administrators the committee system should be abolished because it dilutes the responsibility of individual members.
4. Corruption related cases should be speedily disposed. This could be ensured by deciding a time limit for all stages from receipt of complaint to the final disposal.
5. There should be across the country transfer/ posting provision for civil servants. This would be contrary to alignment of political-bureaucratic criminal nexus on grounds of caste, colour, religion, region or language. It will also ensure accountability and integrity in officer because he will not be able to develop vested interest.
6. The election commission should be made a quasi-judical administrative body charged with all tasks of conducting election. It should be given full power to ensure free and fair election. This will ensure that only true representatives are elected and politics is not maligned in its sacred ceremony of elections.
7. There is an urgent need to check the growing infiltration of big business houses in the power structure. Money has rendered the power of true leaders obsolete. The cost of elections should be minimised and even state funding could be promoted to some extent. This will break the alliance growing between capitalists and bureaucrats.
8. To broaden the social base of bureaucracy, hitherto neglected, poor section should be empowered. The tribal, women, Dalits and economically weaker section should be provided educational facilities and reservation in government services. This will ward off tension and fill the gulf that has developed between rich and the poor.
9. The regulatory role of the state should of selectively and gradually withdrawn. It will break the coalition that have often damaged the national interest than serving it.
10. Decentralization of decision making administrative structure. The 73rd and 74th Amendment have heralded a new era, but have to go a long way in ensuring effective participation of the people. Today, they are marred by violence, social polarization, enmity and orthodoxy.
11. Empowering the investigating agencies to check administrative corruption. CVC getting a statutory status and power to monitor the work of investigating agencies is an enthusiastic step. But, there remains problems as regards proposal to start *suo-motu* investigation against higher officials.

12. There is an urgent need to enact the Lok Pal Bill. It will bring the ministers under a scanner. This will have double impact : on the one land it will restrain the corrupt politicians to engage in fish trading and secondly, it will also restrict corruption racket below them. For, civil servants can not dare to do from what their masters have been banned.

13. To check the nexus between corrupt politicians-bureaucrats and the criminals, there should be an amendment in the Representation of people's Act. On the basis of national consensus some educational qualification be prescribed for them. Moreover, some strict provision should be introduced, so that they never engage in violent, corrupt or shameful acts.

THEORIES OF INTERNATIONAL RELATIONS

THE REALIST THEORY

According to Erich Kauffman ''the essence of state was Machtentfaltung development, increase and display of power.''

Similar sentiments have been echoed by a number of scholars. However, Hans Morgenthau was the first to develop a realist theory in '*Politics Among Nations*.' His work came after the second world war and gave a big impetus to theoretical studies of international relations. As **U.R. Ghai** observes ''His realist view of international politics-a struggle for power among nations which could be analyzed as interest defined in terms of power-not only provided a strong alternative to utopion idealism but also acted as an important invigorator for undertaking studies of international relations.'' Similar observation has been made by **Kenneth W. Thompson** ''Much of the literature of international politics is a dialogue, explicit or not between Moregenthau and his critics''. Other scholars emphasizing the concept of power in the field of international relations include **E.H. Carr, George Schwarzen Berger, Qunicy Wright and Martin Wright**. However, as **Prof. Mohinder Kumar** observes ''even among the realist writers, Hans Morgenthau occupies the most prominent place'' or as **Ghazi A.R. Al Gosaibi** says 'Realism and Morgenthauism have been synonymous.''

Basis of Realist Theory

This approach focuses on units of interaction in the International relations. It is called realism because it emphasizes the **importance of national interest and power as a means to attain or further those interest**. Each nation is continuously involved in a struggle for power with other nations. The objective always is to secure national interest by means of power. This, according to Morgenthau, is a natural and incontrovertible fact of relations among nations and hence very crucial for the understanding of international politics.

Hence, this is also called power approach defined by Morgenthau as ''**man's control over the minds and actions of other men**.''

Six Principles of Political Realism

Morgenthau elaborates his theory of Political Realism by his six principles. These are mentioned under following heads :

1. **Politics governed by objective laws based on Human nature :** According to Morgenthau man moves by laws which are 'eternal.' ''These laws are impervious to human preferences and as such cannot be refuted and challenged.'' Consequently, the aim should be to ascertain facts and interpret them through our reason. The human nature necessarily does not change. They can be collected as facts from the history through empirical and logical devices. But, he contends that it must be rational, as he remarks ''It is the testing of rational hypothesis against the actual facts and their consequences that give meaning to facts of international politics and makes a theory of politics possible.'' Thus, the first principle of Morgenthau's Realist Theory of international politics holds that politics is governed by some objective laws which have their roots in human nature. By understanding these objective laws one can understand and study International Politics.

For knowing these objective laws one has to study the history of human relations. By doing this we can formulate an empirical and logical theory of International Politics.

2. **National Interest defined in terms of power :** In the words of Morgenthau "The main sign-post that helps political realism to find its way through the landscape of international politics is the concept of interest defined in terms of power. This concept provides the link between reason trying to understand international politics and the facts to be understood." This aspect offer difference between domestic politics and international politics. It assumes that the statesman think and act in terms of interest defined as power, and support it with historical evidences. Consequently, political Realism as less concerned with ideological preferences and motives. It is the aspect of success that predominates foreign policy perceptions. However, the **values are not altogether sidelined.** As Morgenthau observes "political realism contains not only a theoretical but also a normative element. It knows that political reality is replete with contigencies and systematic irrationalities and points to the typical influences they exert upon foreign policy. Yet, it shares with all social theories the need to stress the rational elements of political reality, for it is these rational elements that make reality intelligible for theory... political realism considers a rational foreign policy to be good foreign policy; for only a rational foreign policy minimizes risks and maximizes benefits and, hence complies both with moral precept of prudence and the political requirement of success."

3. **No fixed or unchanging meaning of Interest :** Political realism takes a **dynamic view** of interest. It changes with the change in environment. Similarly, the power of a nation also undergoes changes so as to secure national interest. It exhorts periodic analysis of national interest defined in terms of power, as Morgenthau points out "it is the function of political science to stress the importance of power when times tend to deprecate it, and it must point out limitations of power when time tend to power the monistic concept of power." For change can be brought about by "workman like manipulation of the perennial forces that have shaped that past as they will future."

4. **Inapplicability of Abstract Moral Principles :** Although political realism realizes the importance of morality, but holds that universal moral principles cannot be applied to the actions of states. The primary function of a state is to satisfy and protect its national interest. As such, it can not be expected to observe the same standard of morality for all time to come. Whatever accommodation to the aspect of morality is granted, it is within the notion of prudence. As Morgenthau observes "there are to be no political morality, without prudence, that is without consideration of political consequences of seemingly moral action. Realism, then, considers prudence—the weighing of the consequences of alternative political actions—to be the supreme virtue in politics." Realism maintains that universal moral principles cannot be applied to the actions of states, but that these must be filtered through the concrete circumstances of time and place and then applied to actions of states.

5. **Difference between Moral Aspiration of a nation and Universal Moral Laws :** Political realism believes that the moral laws that govern the universe do not apply to the action of states. The national interests of nation are not based on universally applied moral principles. Their actions are always based upon national interests as conceived in terms of power. The policy of a nation as such cannot be equated and should not be confused with universal moral principles. It is only in appearance and not in reality that the policy of a nation accepts and follows universal moral principles. As such the true nature and content of the policy of a nation

can be understood only through an understanding of its national interest. ''The concept of interest acts as a deterrent force against both moral excesses and political expendiencies which nations, often resort to in the name of morality.''

6. **Autonomy of the ''Politics'' :** According to Morgenthau ''A political realist always thinks in terms of interest defined as power, as an economist thinks of interest defined as wealth; the lawyer, of the conformity of action with legal rules and the moralist, of the conformity of action with moral principles.''

It does not mean that there are no other alternatives, but it assumes that they are all subsumed under the notion of 'political.' It is this autonomy of the political that distinguish realist from the legalistic and moralistic approach to the international relation. It stands for political standards of political actions and subordinate all other standard to the political action.

Assumptions of Realist Theory : Prof. Mohinder Kumar in his ''Theoretical Aspects of International Politics'' has identified three basic assumptions on which Morgenthau's Political Realism is based; These are

Firstly, The statesmens desire to pursue their national interest.

Secondly, The interest of every nation lies in the expansion of its influence, territorial, economic, political and cultural.

Thirdly, States use their power, which is also defined as influence, in the protection and furtherance of their interests.

According to Morgenthau **power is most fundamental of all political activity**. As he says ''all permeating fact which is the essence of human existence.'' Power is ''**Control of man over man**.'' ''Political power is a **psychological relation** between those who exercise it and those over whom it is exercised.'' It is primarily an end but can also be a means to other ends. Since the national interest does not remain static, the possession and expansion of power remain essential to safeguard national interests. Every political action seeks to keep power, to increase it, or to demonstrate it.

A GRAPHIC REPRESENTATION OF REALIST THEORY GIVEN BY U.R. GHAI

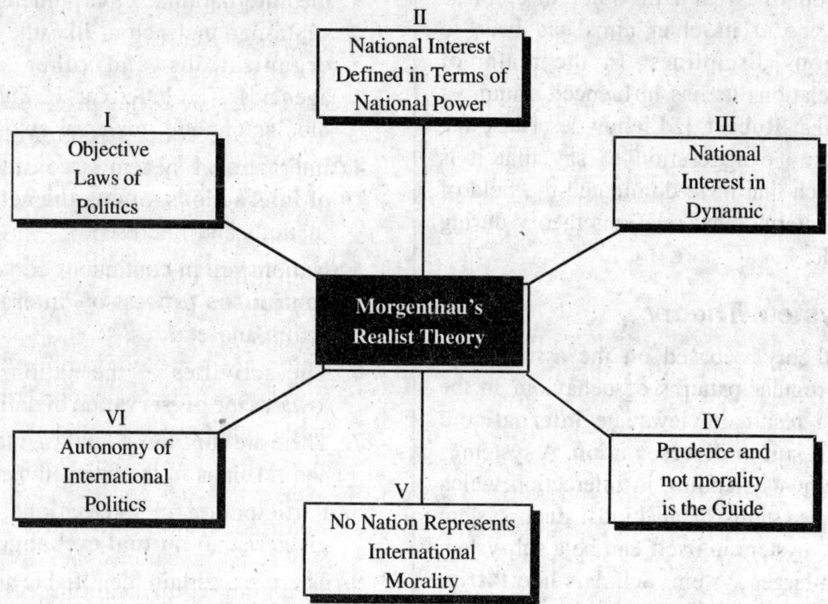

Source: U.R. Ghai ''International Politics''

SCIENTIFIC THEORIES

According to **U.R. Ghai** "The Scientific theory or the Behavioural theory to the study of International Politics is a broad and convenient term to refer to all the modern approaches which accept the use of empirical analysis-involving quantification, and statistical analysis, for arriving at tested valid generalisation about the behaviour of states in international relations. It advocates the study of international relations through the use of scientific method."

They are as follows

1. THE SYSTEMS THEORY
2. DECISION MAKING THEORY
3. GAME THEORY
4. COMMUNICATION THEORY
5. BARGAINING THEORY

SYSTEMS THEORY

The systems theory to the international relations is a contribution, chiefly made by **Mortan Kaplan.** It is an outcome of behavioural revolution in social sciences after the end of second world war. It is interdisciplinary and seeks to use data and information from the realm of other disciplines. Consequently one of its chief aims had been to integrate various disciplines. In the realm of international relations its has influenced a number of researches that **Robert J. Lieber** describes that "It would be no exaggeration to say that it is systems approach that have dominated the field of broad gauged international relations theory during the past decade."

Basis of System Theory

The systems theory is based on the assumptions that there are regular patterns of behaviour in the structure. As a result, it views the **international system as the result of diverse action**. A system is a group of elements standing in interaction which are common to systems of all kinds. Each system besides being a system in itself can be a subsystem in relation to a larger system. Scholars like **Pitrim Sarokin and Charles McCelland** subscribe to the general systems approach, while **Rosenon and Harold Guetzkow** advocate partial system approach.

U.R. Ghai in his "*International Politics*" has listed following main assumptions of the systems theory.

1. **International System is not International Political System :** When the concept of 'system' is used in the context of International Politics it is, taken to mean International System and not International Political System. It cannot be described as International Political System because it does not allocate authoritative values. International units or actors are sovereign states and as such no International actor or agency can authoritatively implement values over them. Hence, it cannot be described as International Political System.
2. **International Actors and National Actors :** What are known as international actors are basically the national actors acting in the international environment.
3. **National and Supra-National Actors :** The international actors can be classified into two main parts—(i) the national actors acting in the international environment, and (ii) the supra-national actors like the UN, regional organisations and other international agencies. The latter can be sub-classified as bloc actors and universal actors.
4. International system is constituted by **a set of interactions among the actors** or entities (nations and interests).
5. Nations are in continuous contact. There is a **continuous process of interactions** among actors and entities.
6. The activities of the nations are directed towards the **preservation of national interests.**
7. There are **continuous and regular interactions** and relations in the international environment.
8. Participation in international environment gives rise to **mutual exchanges.**
9. There are certain identifiable and describable **regularities** in the patterns of interacting among nations.

10. The use of concept of system for describing or **explaining or analysing international politics** can greatly enrich our understanding of the phenomena, which can further help us in theory-building in international relations.

11. All systems analysis distinguish units (or actors), structures, processes, and context (or environment) as major elements in every system. These elements are considered as major factors in terms of which all substantive phenomena are explained.

Morton Kaplan

Morton Kaplan is the most outstanding exponent of the systems theory. In his opinion, the international system is the most important of all the systems. But, it is **not a political system**. Its aim is "to examine both what happens to the international system as changes occur inside the systems of the international actor and how the behaviour of the international actors is modified as the international system undergoes changes."

Models of International System

Kaplan classifies **six models** of international system in his work "*System and Process in International Politics*."

1. The Balance of Power System
2. The Loose Bi-polar System
3. The Tight Bi-polar System
4. The Universal System
5. The Hierarchical System
6. The Unit Veto System

1. Balance of Power System: This system corresponds to the one that operated in 18th and 19th century Europe. It is marked by five or six essential actors. It operates on the basis of six principles.

Firstly, Each actor should increase its capabilities through negotiations and not through war.

Secondly, Each actor is prepared to fight rather than pass on an opportunity to increase capabilities.

Thirdly, No actor is to be eliminated from the system.

Fourthly, An actor or a group of actors acts to oppose any other group or single actor that tends to assume unduly powerful position and predominance with respect to the rest of the system.

Fifthly, Attempts are made to check the actors who try to follow supranational organising principles.

Sixthly, The defeated or constrained essential actors are permitted to re-enter the system as acceptable role partners.

The following conditions can unstabilize the balance of Power system.

1. Arbitrary acts by an essential actor
2. Intention of essential actor towards formation of Supranational organization
3. Failure in the decision making system of essential actors.
4. World War

Setting in of unstability can lead to transformation of the balance of power system. Kaplan thinks that the most likely transformation of the balance of power system is **into a bipolar system**. It may be either loose bipolar system or tight bipolar system.

2. **Loose Bipolar System:** This system is characterised by the existence of two super powers. They are surrounded by a group of smaller powers. There exists two respective competing blocs or groups. However the existence of some **non-member bloc actors** like non-aligned states and Universal actors makes the power of the two major actors loose. It resembles the **cold war, model**. As such, there exists considerable degree of instability. **Prof. Mohinder Kumar** has highlighted three differences between Loose bipolar system and balance of power system. These are

"**Firstly,** Supranational as well as national actors participate in the loose bipolar system.

Secondly, Supranational actors are divided into a subclass of bloc actors like NATO and Warsaw pact countries and a universal actor like the United Nations.

Thirdly, The norms of the system among the actors differ according to their roles."

3. **Tight Bipolar System:** This system is characterized by the existence of two power blocs, there are two super powers leading each bloc. There are **no non-member national actor**. Either there does not exist the universal actor or there is loss of its role. In such a system as Mohinder Kumar points out "stability will be guaranteed only when both the power blocs are hierarchically organized".

4. **Universal System:** This system resemble a federal organization wherein nation states acts as units working through a universal actor. The international organization will perform a wide range of functions, viz; judicial, administrative, political and economic. However, there are chances of instability arising out of lack of absolute power at the hands of universal actor.

5. **Hierarchical System:** This system is characterized by complete integration of whole world. If this system comes in through conquest, it is a directive system, but if it comes through democratic means, it is a non-directive system.

6. **Unit Veto System:** This system is characterised by existence of many actors each possessing capacity of destroying the other. There does not exist any universal system. It can develop from any other international system.

New Models of International Systems

However, in view of changing international situation, Kaplan came up with four new categories of international system. These are

1. Very loose Bipolar System
2. Detente System
3. Unstable Bloc System
4. Incomplete Nuclear Diffusion System

1. **Very loose Bipolar System :** This system is marked by a **continuous quest at arms control and accommodation.** The structure of the two blocs are weak. Consequently both compete to attain leverage in international relations.

2. **Detente System :** This system is characterized

by the existence of two super powers each competing with each other without assuming any dimension of a serious conflict.

3. **Unstable Bloc System :** This system is characterized by existence of two super powers wherein each of them will be increasingly suspicious of one another.
4. **Incomplete Nuclear Diffusion System :** This system is characterized by the existence of a number of nuclear powers apart from the super powers.

DECISION MAKING THEORY

In recent times, decision making theories have come to occupy significant place in the realm of international relations. It seeks to study relations among nations by analyzing the foreign policy decisions of various nations. Some of the important advocates, include; **Richard Snyder**, **H.W. Bruck** and **Burton Spain**. Some of the other advocates include, **James Bates**, **James March**, **Ward Edwards** etc.

Main Features

Prof. Mohinder Kumar has highlighted some of the important features of decision making theory :

1. Emphasis on foreign policy decisions made by decision makers.
2. Emphasis on perception of the decision makers about the international relations.
3. Focus on actions of states through the actions of decision makers.
4. Emphasis on identifying the causes of actions through decision making process.

Richard Snyder treats decision making as a process, having following components :

1. Spheres of Competence
2. Communication and Information
3. Motivation

He also focuses on aspects that affect the decision making process. They may result either from inside the decision making system or from outside.

GAME THEORY

The game theory to international relations is comparatively a recent phenomenon. Developed in the domain of **mathematics and economics**, it has come to occupy significant place in the realm of international relations. In essence, it provides models for studying games of politics among nations.

Main advocates of Game Theory :

	Name	Work
1.	Martin Shubik	*Game Theory and Related Approaches to Political Behaviour*
2.	Thomas Schelling	*The Strategy of Conflicts*
3.	Neumann and Morgenstern	*Theory of Games and Economics Behaviour.*
4.	Karl Deutsch	*Game Theory and Politics.*

Different Views of Game Theory

Martin Shubik : "Mathematical model for the study of some aspects of decision-making in situations involving the possibilities of conflict or cooperation. It deals with the processes in which the individual decision unit has only partial control over the strategic factors affecting its environment. The decision unit may be an individual, a firm, a government or any formal or informal institution".

Charlesworth : "Game theory operates on the assumption that political process is the confrontation like a chess game or contest between two merchants or the manoeuvres of rival political candidates or the counter actions of opposed diplomats."

Mohinder Kumar : "'Game' is an analytic device. It attempts to answer the questions what action is rational in which situation".

Important Components of Game Theory :

There are five important concepts in the game theory. They are as follows :

1. **STRATEGY :** It signifies skilful plan of the previously decided set of moves to be taken as and when the expected moves of the other side requires them. By taking account of

potential behaviour of the opponents, it intends to play against expected action of opponents.

2. **OPPONENT :** It is the second important ingredient of the game theory.
3. **PAY OFF :** It refers to 'what game is worth at the end'. A win means maximum pay off, a drawn or even game stands for second best pay off and a defeat, the third best pay off.
4. **RULES :** It refers to the laws which actors observe in international relations. They are such that the equation between the players are either loss or gain.
5. **INFORMATION :** It is the fifth important component of the game theory.

Dynamics of the Game Theory

The game theory treats nations as players who compete in the international arena to fulfil their national interest. As **Mohinder Kumar** observes "The objective is to discover how the imposed rules, conditions and choices affect the process of foreign policy making. The idea is to discover how these rules and conditions affect the process of interaction, communications, war and so on".

Models of the Game Theory

The following models are popular in the Game Theory :

1. **Zero-sum two person game :** marked by the existence of only two players wherein the gains of one are always equal to the loss of the other.
2. **Non-zero-sum two person game :** marked by the existence of two or more persons in the game wherein the gain of one participant need not be equal to the loss of the other.
3. **Zero-sum-n-person games :** marked by the existence of more than two players in the game, wherein the pay off is shared.
4. **Non-zero-sum-n-person games :** marked by the existence of more than two players in the game, wherein new arrangements come to operate. For example they may act through coalition and "it may become" as Martin Shubik remarks "a game within-n-game, in which players exercise rules (apply resources) in order to enforce agreements and keep less advantaged member from breaking away in response to higher bids from adversary players".

"Chicken Game" and "Prisoner's Dilemma"

In "The Strategy of Conflict", Schelling has forwarded the concept of 'mixed motive game' and used it to the study of limited war, deterrence and arms control.

The two other models of game theory are 'chicken game' and 'prisoners dilemma'. These models are based on unpredictability of outcomes. As **Mohinder Kumar** observes, "The principal characteristic of the chicken game situation is that inspite of not being able to know the intentions of its opponent, a nation can adopt such a course of action as would guarantee its own interests if only it does not mind its opponent also benefiting from that course of action". However in case of prisoners dilemma it is assumed that rational or irrational course of action have no significance in International Relations. Rather, a country acts as the presumption of its opponents threats.

COMMUNICATION THEORY

The Communication Theory of international relations has been a systematic outcome of concepts drawn from the cybernetics and communication theory. Cybernetic is the study of informations self regulating systems and physiology of the nervous system. The name of **Nobert Weiver** and **Arhby** are originally associated with this theory. However its introduction into the realm of political science has been achieved by **Karl Deutsch**.

Main Theme : The communication theory of international relation emphasize the role played by communication. It visualizes **politics as a process of steering, coordination and control**. The focus is on the decision making apparatus which itself is a bundle of numerous information networks. As such, it is itself a 'self-adjusting and self-regulating mechanism".

Deutsch's Contribution

Karl Deutsch in his works "*The Nerves of Government*" and "*Nationalism and Social Communication*" puts forward his communication theory. **Charles** McClelland is another exponent of this theory.

Karl Deutsch looks at political system as a network of communication channels and government as steering and coordinating agency that leads human efforts towards attainment of a set of goals. He lays more emphasis on the aspect of steering and coordination than on final attainment of goal.

Karl Deutsch, holds that the flow of information in a political system occurs at three levels :

Firstly, it occurs between the political system and its environment.

Secondly, it occurs between two or more political systems.

Thirdly, it occurs within the political system itself.

Different concepts involved in communication theory :

Influenced by the domain of communication theory and cybernetics, it is but natural for the communication theory to have many concepts.

1. **Concepts relating to structural aspect :**
   (a) **Receptors :** means receipt of information by structures.
   (b) **Data processing units :** that process data.
   (c) **Memory value complex :** that relate data with values.
   (d) **Effectors :** concerned with implementing the decisions and feeding information.
2. **Concepts relating to process :** It relates to the flow of information in the political system. It involves
   (a) **Load :** denotes the amount of information in a system.
   (b) **Load capacity :** denotes channels of communication and available factors like responsiveness, fidelity, distortion.
   (c) **Recall :** denotes capacity to bring forward past experiences.
   (d) **Combinatorial capacity :** Combine informations and implement them in a way so as to make and implement decisions having positive consequences.
   (e) **Lag :** denotes delay in receiving information about the action taken.
   (f) **Gain :** positive endorsement of decisions by the system.
   (g) **Lead :** denotes ability to predict future events.

The basic highlight of this theory is that information can be quantified and the channels can be evaluated in qualitative terms. By doing so the theory enable the political system to evaluate its goals and learn by experience. The notion of feed- back enables a system to attain information about its actions.

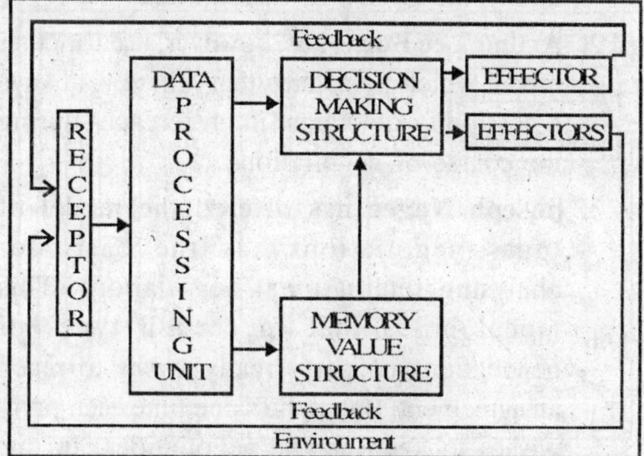

Deutsch's Communication Model

BARGAINING THEORY

The bargaining theory is an extension of the game theory. As **Joseph Frankel** observes, "The theory of (international) bargaining is an application of the theory of games to international negotiations, or, to put it in the terminology of the theory of games, the analysis of threats and deterrence and promises in mixed-motive-game-strategies".

Main advocates of Bargaining Theory :

1. Thomas Schelling—*The Strategy of Conflict.*

2. John C. Harsawyl—*Bargaining in Ignorance of the Opponent's Utility Function.*
3. O.R. Young—*Politics of Force : Bargaining in International Crises.*
4. Others include, J.F. Nash, Roger Fishur, Arthur Lee Burns etc.

The bargaining theory to international relations is used to study the process of negotiations. **U.R. Ghai** has outlined following dimensions of bargaining theory.

1. **Thomas Schelling** has used the 'Tacit Bargaining' as the model for studying communications among nations which have shared, rather than divergent, interests. Another scholar has used a different model for studying negotiations which hold that preference schedules of negotiating parties remain constant. This model assumes that it is never rational to change one's preferences during the course of negotiation.
2. **Arthur Lee Burns** has, however, used another model which postulates that "there is always a possibility of change in preferences during the course of negotiations.
3. **Joseph Nogee** has offered the model of 'quasi-negotiations" as the basis for analysing international negotiations. This model holds that in certain types of negotiations no party really wants to reach an agreement. But at the same time each party wishes to keep up the negotiations. In this type each party keeps on negotiating with the other on the basis of a widely publicised plan or formula. The plan contains many, almost all provisions which the other party can readily accept. However, there is included one or two such clauses or provisions called **"Joker clause or provisions"**, which are least acceptable, or which can never be accepted by the other party. The plan is offered as one piece plan or package deal that can be accepted or rejected in toto. The disarmament talks can certainly be analysed with the help of this model.''

IDEOLOGY, POWER AND INTEREST

IDEOLOGY

Ideology retains a place of crucial importance in the realm of international relations. It is considered a realist element in international politics because it influences the power. It has also been alleged that ideology not only creates a situation of conflict and confrontations but even wars are result of ideology. World War I and World War II were outcome of competition between two ideologies. As such it becomes expedient to study the role of ideology in international relations.

Definitions

1. **Schleicher :** "An ideology is a system of abstract ideas held by an individual (or group) which purports to explain reality, expresses value goals, and contains programmes of action for the rejection or attainment of the kind of social order in which its proponents believe the goals can best be realised.''
2. **Snyder and Wilson :** "A cluster of ideas about life, society or government, which originate, in most cases, as consciously advocated dogmatically asserted social, political or religious slogans or battle cries and which through continuous usage and preachings gradually become the characteristic belief or dogmas of a particular group, party or nationality".
3. **Sterling :** "Ideology is a set of ideas that purports to give meaning to the past, to explain the present and to prognosticate the future. It necessarily couples these explanatory and predictive functions with a series of value judgements, ideology distinguishes between what has been good and what has been evil in the past, it decrees what kind of behaviour is virtuous in the present and it prescribes desirable objectives for the future and the means to achieve them."
4. **Morgenthau :** "Ideologies are a cover to conceal the true nature of political actions...

It is the very nature of politics to compel the actor on the political scene to use ideologies in order to disguise goals of his action".

5. **Karl Manneheim :** "Ideology refers to the particular ideologies which are used by nations for securing the goals of their national interests. These are in the form of simple, legal, ethical or biological principles such as justice, equality, fraternity...."

Role

The role and impact of ideology in international relations can be summarized as follows :

Firstly; ideology organizes and strengthens unorganized activities.

Secondly; ideology promotes unity in a country of multiple nationalities and strengthens its military power.

Thirdly; ideology makes the foreign policy very rigid.

Fourthly; ideology gives effect to expansionist tendencies which often culminates in the outbreak of war.

Fifthly; ideology with conservative element is often seen to garner broader support than a rational one.

POWER

The concept of power is one of the crucial ingredient of international politics. As U.R. Ghai and V. Ghai observes "Because of the absence of any sovereign or fully powerful centralised international machinery for the authoritative allocation of values among the nations, and because of the sovereign status of each nation-state the securing of national interest is always done by the use of power". As it plays a vital role in the conduct of relations among nations, its study remains a significant aspect of international relations. However, the flexibility with which the term is used remains a problematic task in the study of power. Nevertheless, "The problem of power", writes **Frankel**, "enters into all types of international relations—wars, competition, and cooperation, all involve power.... A state which is devoid of resources and organization can neither compete nor cooperate successfully with other states".

Definitions

Hans Morgenthau : "Power is a psychological relationship between those who exercise it and over whom it is exercised. It is man's control over actions and minds of other men".

Charles Schleicher : "Power is the ability to exercise such control to make others do what they otherwise would not do by rewarding or promising to reward them, or by depriving or threatening to deprive them of something they value".

Frankel : "Power is a relational phenomenon that denotes capacity to produce intended benefits".

Schwarzenberger : "Power is the capacity to impose one's will on others by reliance on effective sanctions in case of non-compliance".

Bachrach and Baratz : "Coercion is the essence of power".

Vermon Van Dyke : "Coercive influence, distinguishing from pervasive influence".

Mohinder Kumar : "Ability or capacity to control others and get them to do what one wants them to do and also to see that they do not do what one does not act or want than to do".

In the realm of international relations, one is essentially concerned with the national power.

Definitions of National Power

Kingsley David : "the ability to control the behaviour of other states in accordance with one's own will".

Organski : "ability of a nation to influence the behaviour of others in accordance with its own ends".

Hartman : "ability of a nation to fulfil its national goals".

Mohinder Kumar : "the ability of a state to make its will prevail and enforce respect and command obedience from other states".

Important works :

Hans Morgenthau	—	*"Politics Among Nations.*
	—	*"Power and Ideology in International Relations".*
	—	*The Decline of Democratic Politics.*
Vernon Van Dyke	—	*"International Politics.*
Organski	—	*World Politics.*
Bertrand Russell	—	*Power : A New Social Analysis.*
H. Spront and Murgarst Spront	—	*Foundations of National Power.*
Charles McClelland	—	*Theory and International System.*
I.L.Claude (Jr.)	—	*Power and International Relations.*
William Riker	—	*"Some ambiguities in the Notion of Power".*

Forms of Power : Broadly, power can be characterized into three forms. These are as follows:

1. Economic Power
2. Military Power
3. Psychological Power

Economic Power : This form of power is the most crucial constituent of power in contemporary time. It signifies the ability of a nation to fulfil its own requirements and also to control the behaviour of other states by enabling or prohibiting access to goods and services. Its importance is highlighted by **Palmer and Perkins,** "Economic power is inseparable from military power, for it is one of its basic components, to say that under conditions of modern warfare economic power is military power is only a slight exaggeration". The multipolarity of contemporary world is exclusively due to ascendance of economic giants like Germany, Japan and South East Asian countries. Lack of economic power remains a major factor for lower power position of third world countries. The economic power of a country is calculated in terms of raw material, natural resources, industrial out put, technological advancement, favourable balance of trade, modern and speedy means of transportation and alike.

Military Power : This form of power has remained the most important form of power for a long time. Its major objective is to secure a nation from outside forces. It remains a crucial ingredient for a country's victory in a war with other states. Its importance has been highlighted by E.H. Carr "Every act of the state, in its power aspect, is directed towards war, not as a desirable weapon but as a weapon which it may require in the last resort". In the same vein, Palmer and Perkins says "The paramount importance of military power lies in the fact that it is the end-argument, the last word and the final court of appeal". As a matter of fact, no state can attain the status of a super power without being a military power. For example, even though Japan and Germany are big economic powers, they are not accorded the status of a super power or great powers because of their being weak military powers. Nevertheless, the states can not solely rely on the military power. It has to be supplemented by other forms of power.

Psychological Power : This form of power has its own utility in the realm of international relations. According to **Schleicher** "Psychological power consists of symbolic devices which appeal to the minds and emotion of men". Propaganda and persuasive negotiations are important ingredient of psychological power. Its obvious advantages are : ward off escalation of conflict, uplift national morale, cost effective and alike. Its importance has increased in recent times. As **Ghai and Ghai** observes "The improvement in the means of communication and increased role of mass media and public opinion on foreign policy, the emergence of open and conference diplomacy, the change in the character of war from limited war to total war, the popularities of alternative ideologies and the development of group loyalties conflicting within the main sphere of loyalty to the state, have been the factors which have increased the role of propaganda international relations".

Main Methods of Acquiring Power

The main methods through which states seek to secure and exercise power are

1. Persuasion

2. Rewards
3. Punishments
4. Force

Persuasion : Persuasion is one of the most common and easiest methods of exercising power in international relations. It is done by influencing other nations through arguments with a view to convince them that they adopt a particular course of behaviour. This is used mostly by diplomats in securing support for foreign policy issues. It is used mostly by smaller powers. However, the extent of its success invariably depends on other forms of power.

Rewards : Rewards are another most important method of exercising power. It can be material, economic and political. Various kinds of economic aid and grants in aid helps in winning support and inducing a change in the behaviour of other states. Similarly, conferring honours to people of other states also helps as psychological rewards intended to keep the other states friendly and cooperative.

Punishment : The method of punishment is closely related to reward. For, an attempt to withhold a reward is also a punishment. Speaking about efficacy of punishment as a method of power, **Mohinder Kumar** says "The most effective punishment is the one which is never meted out because the very threat of it should succeed in preventing the action of which the punisher disapproves and in getting a promise of an action or behaviour which the punisher desire".

Force : The force is the ultimate method of exercising power. It is closely related to punishment. But, the difference between force and punishment is the actual use of force versus the threat of use of force. War is the extreme form of exercise of force and is usually adopted as a last resort to exercise power.

Elements of Power : Determinants of Power

The ability of nation to use power depends upon different factors but no single factor is entirely responsible for the growth of national power. Moreover, mere existence of various elements does not make a nation powerful. It is the ability to skilfully harness and use these factors that leads to national power.

Different Classification of Elements of Power

According to **Morgenthau** : Permanent and Temporary.

According to **Organski** : Natural and Social.

According to **Palmer and Perkins** : Tangible and Intangible.

Broadly speaking there are following elements of power :

1. Geography
2. Natural Resources
3. Population
4. Economic Development
5. National Morale
6. Ideology
7. Political Structure
8. Military Preparedness
9. Leadership

(1) Geography : Among the geographical elements of power size, location, climate, topography and boundary are important ones. The exponents of geographical elements include.

Exponent	Work
⇒ Halford J. Mackinder	Democratic Ideals and Reality.
⇒ N.J. Spykman	The Geography of Peace.
⇒ A.E. Moodie	Geography Behind Politics.

(a) Size : The large size of a country enables it to accommodate large population. It can also be a source of large and varied natural resources. The military advantages of a country's size was even acknowledged by Hitler. A large size can help the country to defend itself. It was the largeness of size that enabled China to defeat Japan and Russia to defeat the armies of Napoleon and Hitler. As **Mohinder Kumar** observes, "In a time of war a large country can retreat and yet have space left in which to mobilize power and prepare for counter-attack." It enables location of strategic industries at safer places away from easy targets of attack from enemy.

(b) Location : England's supremacy in sea was perhaps due to its location. A favourable location can be a strength to a nation's power and an unfavourable location can hinder such prospects. Land locked countries often suffer in prospects for power in comparison to a country's location along sea.

(c) Climate : The role of climate in a nation's power is emphasized by **Stephen B. Jones** in his article "*The power Inventory and National Strategy*" and **Nicolos J. Spykman** in his "*Geography and Foreign Policy*". Generally it is assumed that extreme climate are not favourable for a nation's power. As **Mohinder Kumar** observes "A country must have a temperate climate to be a major power because it is climate which conditions its population to engage in the kind of activity required for a modern industrial nation".

(d) Topography : It constitutes the existence of geographical/physical features in a state. Natural boundaries have a decisive importance in determining the power of a state. For example the Himalayas in India, Pyrenese in Spain, English Channel in England provide strength and security to these countries. However, these features are not exclusive in themselves. They have to be adequately garrisoned and vigilance must be kept along these fronts.

(e) Boundary : Boundary disputes and conflict have been a major irritant in securing harmonious relation between two countries. Consequently, if boundaries are well defined and clearly marked, they can be a significant factor in nations power.

A severe limitation of geographical elements of power is highlighted by **Padelford and Lincoln**, who observe "The astronomical impact of technology in areas such as communication, air mobility, ICBM (Inter Continental Ballistic Missile) systems, nuclear weaponry, intelligence gathering, and satellite has drastically collapsed the strategic (Geographic) obstacles to the projections of national power". In today's world, geography does not remain an independent variable of national power. Its role must be examined in relation to other factors. As **Robert Richow** remarks "Although it is well to recognise the contribution of geography to the destiny of state, it is well also not to over-rate it. Men are not trees wholly at the mercy of the environment. Instead men may perversely thrive on obstacles.... A nation without a coast or good harbour can hardly become a sea power by the same token it is more than rain, sunshine to make crops-some one has to cultivate the soil".

(2) Natural Resources : Natural resources remain a crucial element of a nations power. They have crucial significance for economic as well as military power of a nation. As **Mohinder Kumar** observes "A strong nation without resources can obtain them by one or the other method of power, whereas a weak nation even with abundant resources is likely to lose not only its resources but even its freedom. History is full of examples to show the lack of natural resource limiting the power of a nation. Deposits of oil in the Arab States remain the most crucial element of their power in international relations. Likewise, the self-sufficiency of United States in respect of key materials has contributed to its industrial and military strength. However, the existence of raw materials/natural resources can not be the sole guarantee of a nations power. The ability to exploit the raw materials is a factor, almost as important as the existence of raw materials.

Apart from raw materials, food is also an important ingredient of national power. As Morgenthau observes, "Nations self sufficient in food are better placed than nations which import food". The problem of food shortage has remained a big handicap for the developing countries. They have to depend upon grants and import which limits their own power.

(3) Population : Population plays a crucial role in the power of a country. As **Mussolini** observed "Let us be frank with ourselves. What are 40 million Italians compared with 90 million Germans and 200 million Slaves". Its implication is also acknowledged by Voltaire, who observed that "God is always on the side of the biggest battalions". Role of population has been highlighted by **Organski** and **Davis** in their "*Population and International Relations*".

The obvious advantages of population are that it can provide basis to military power, help build sound and progressive economy through labour force, it can be a source of other material and psychological advantages. However, a large population by itself, is no guarantee for a nations power. An illiterate population without the knowledge of modern methods is a poor base of power. Its contribution to military or economic power as **Mohinder Kumar** observes "depends upon many factors, particularly, upon the degree to which a nation has industrialized and modernized its military forces and productive machinery". Similarly, **Palmer** and **Perkin's** remarked "Large population may be a source of weakness or a source of strength in the modern world. The test is whether or not a state can utilize its human resources effectively, can support them at tolerable standards of living, and can provide constructive outlet for their talents and energies. In developed countries, large numbers are usually a source of strength, whereas in underdeveloped countries the opposite is usually the case".

(4) Economic Development : The level of economic development and effective economic organization have remained a factor of pivotal importance for a nation's power. This has become more pronounced than ever. On the one hand it supplements military power, on the other hand it provide basis for welfare and prosperity of the people. A nation which produces surplus of production uses it in many ways. It can act as means of persuasion and punishment giving the nation a leverage in international relations. Even Morgenthau acknowledged the role of advanced industries, as he remarked "The technology of modern warfare and communications has made the over-all development of heavy industries an indispensable element of national power. The quality and productive capacity of the industrial plant, the know-how of the working man, the skill of the engineer, the inventive genius of the scientist, the managerial organization-are those factors upon which industrial capacity of a nation and hence its power depends".

(5) National Morale : National morale is an important element of national power.

Definitions of National Morale.

Morgenthau : "the degree of determination with which a nation supports the foreign policies of its government in peace and war, it permeates all activities of a nation, its agriculture and industrial productions as well as its military establishments and diplomatic service".

Frankel : "the extent to which the people support their leaders, believe in the superiority of their state and in the rightness of their cause".

Mohinder Kumar : "the sum-total of the individual qualities of men in a nation in the form of their willingness to put the nation's welfare above their own personal welfare".

National morale is based on people's willingness to sacrifice. As such, it can be a great ingredient in nation's power.

(6) Ideology : Ideology has a great role in nation's power. History provides ample proof as to how the ideology of communism and nationalism have affected the power positions of nations. The role of ideology as an element of national power has been emphasised by **V.V. Dyke**, who observes "To be strong, a government must stand for ideas which command support at least at home, and it will be stronger if they also command support abroad". A broad analysis of ideological elements of power has been undertaken by **Bertrand Russell** in his "*Power : A New Social Analysis*".

However, the ideology can be both; positive and negative source for a nation's power. If it can minister power, it can also weaken states. Nazism weakened Hitler's Germany and Fascism did the same to Mussolini's Italy.

(7) Political Structure : Like other elements of power, political structure also serves as an element of power. Moreover, it acquires crucial importance in view of its being an agency for steering and coordination. A well organized, efficient government always remains a strength for a nation. As **V.V. Dyke** observes "Effectiveness of government organization and administration within a state is another element of national power. It is required for a judicious and proper use of resources and exercise of power. Government alone can effectively mobilise the elements of national power and thereby increase it. Lack of effective and well organized government can seriously limit the power of a state". The contemporary experiences reveal that democratic governments serve as a better ingredient of power than dictatorial ones. The democratic governments have been able to harness power that have been durable and effective in international relationships.

(8) Military Preparedness : It remains a crucial element of national power. According to **Robinson**, "Military preparedness is the most important and tangible factor capable of supporting the foreign policy and promoting national interest". The methods of war and quantity and quality of arms, ammunition and soldiers have vibrant impact on nations power. A country with high degree of warfare techniques has obvious advantages. The advent of nuclear bombs and inter continental missile technology have completely altered the domain of power equations. Similarly, skilled, trained, experienced, dedicated, energetic and disciplined military leadership help in effective use of available weapons, equipment and manpower.

(9) Leadership : The quality and wisdom of leadership is an invaluable element of power. For, other factors remain irrelevant; if they are not utilized effectively and efficiently. **Sprout** and **Sprout** in "*Foundations of National Power*" have pointed out the advantages of a wise and strengthful leadership. Similarly, **M.R. Singer** in his "*Weak States in a World of Powers*" argues that leadership is inevitably connected to the strength of a nation. A mature leadership can be source of power, as **V.V. Dyke** observes "Political leadership determines in what proportion to allocate resources between military and civilian programmes, that is, how great the military power should be. They allocate appropriations among the branches of the armed services. They determine when to seek alliances, with which states and on what terms!"

Limitations of Power

The international relations among the states are often accompanied by the mechanics of power. But, the nations power are not absolute. They are limited by a number of factors.

1. **Balance of Power :** By this principle, sizeable restriction is placed on the power of a state. The existence of a number of powers in the international arena automatically limits the power.
2. **International Law :** International law operates as a body of rules having binding character on the nation states. As such, it limits the power of nation.
3. **International Morality :** A set of norms valued by the international society also acts as limitation of power. Even though they are neither codified, nor binding, they enjoy great sanctity. Certain values like peace, equality, mutual respect etc. remain core element of international relations.
4. **International Organizations :** Agency like U.N. remains a check on growing preponderance of power. Through its activities it checks and balances power of nations in the international relations.
5. **World Public Opinion :** This aspect has acquired prominence in recent times like the anti-Vietnam war protests and peace movements have revealed what people can do in international relations. States can no longer remain aloof from the public opinion.
6. **Collective Security :** A principle that emphasises that international peace and security is the common objective of all nations, has limited quest for power.

NATIONAL INTEREST

National interest is one of the crucial ingredients of international relations. It often acquires a central focus of enquiry because the interaction of each nation in the international arena is primarily based on its national interests.

Main works

Charles A. Beard—*The Idea of National Interest : An Analytical study of American Foreign Policy.*

J.N. Rosenau—*National Interest.*

Joseph Frankel—*National Interest.*

Kenneth Waltz—*Man, the State, and War.*

Hans Morgenthau—*Dilemmas of Politics. In Defence of the National Interest.*

According to **Charles A. Beard** the history of the concept of national interest goes back to the time when the evolution of the modern state system took place. However, the term underwent modifications so much that there is hardly any unanimity among the scholars.

Definitions

Charles Lerche and Abdul Said, "The general, long term and continuing purpose which the state, the nation, and the government all see themselves as serving".

Vernon Von Dyke, "That which states seek to protect or achieve in relation to each other. It means desires in the part of sovereign states".

Morgenthau, "The concept of national interest is similar to the general principles of the constitution".

Mohinder Kumar, "The application of a generalized value-synthesis to the overall international situation in which a state has to formulate and execute its foreign policy".

"Objectivist and Subjectivist"

Joseph Frankel divides different approaches defining national interest into two categories. These are called objectivist and subjectivist. The objectivist views national interest as a concept which can be defined or examined with the help of some objectively definable criteria. The subjectivist seeks to interpret national interest as a "constantly changing pluralistic set of subjective references".

Components/Ingredient of National Interest

Even though national interest of a country is dynamic affair, they are components of two sets of factors, viz., vital components or permanent components and non-vital or temporary components.

Vital Components of National Interest

There are different views as to which variables account for the vital components of national interest. They are also described as the goals.

Hans Morgenthau : To secure identity, viz., physical, political and cultural.

Vernon Von Dyke : Allocates primacy to security and self-preservation for whose sake states even go to war. In brief he includes preservation of territorial integrity, sovereign equality, political system and political culture security.

Mohinder Kumar : To protect and preserve independence of territorial integrity. But he also observes that "since the second world war, the economic, psychological and ideological aspect has been gaining in importance as far as the character of vital national interest is concerned".

Non-vital Component of National Interest

Non-vital national interests are those determined by circumstances or necessity. They are called objectives. **V.V. Dyke** includes Prosperity, Peace, Ideology, Justice, Prestige, Aggrandisement and Power in this category. According to **Mohinder Kumar** "The objectives that nations normally seek to pursue are : the material welfare of the people, the safeguarding of prestige, the protection of ideology, and the acquisition and enhancement of power".

Instruments/Methods for the Promotion of National Interest

The common methods of protecting and promoting national interests are as follows :

1. Diplomacy
2. Propaganda
3. Alliances and Treaties
4. Economic Aid and Loans
5. Coercive Means

Diplomacy : Diplomacy has been regarded as a means for securing the national interest for a long time and it still constitutes the most effective means for this purpose. Generally diplomatic negotiations are used to reconcile the conflicting claims. Though, diplomacy is regarded as a universal aspect of international life, it is by no means successful in achieving every end.

Propaganda : Propaganda means the art of convincing others to accept the desired course of action. As Frankel says "propaganda is systematic attempt to affect the minds, emotions and actions of a given group for a specific public purpose".

Almost every regime seeks to maximize its national interests by resorting to technique of propaganda. Hitler and Mussolini made use of it to enhance their influence in Europe.

Alliances and Treaties : In order to protect and promote their national interest, almost every state enter into alliances and treaties. Famous military alliances like NATO and Warsaw pact were entered into by countries to protect their interests.

Economic Aid and Loan : The division of world into the rich and poor has made the latter more vulnerable. The rich countries often use economic aid and loan to promote their interests vis-a-vis the poor states. Marshal Plan started in 1948 by U.S.A. is eloquent testimony to this aspect of international relations.

Coercive Measures : Some of the important coercive measures of national interest are as follows: Intervention, embargoes, boycotts, non-intercourse, reprisals, retortion. Though war and aggression are regarded as illegal means, most often nations resort to war as a means securing national interest.

CONFLICTS AND CONFLICT RESOLUTION

In the realm of international relations, almost every state seeks to fulfil its national interest. Consequently, the existence of conflict and the emergence of dispute is permanent phenomenon of the international relations. These conflicts are in no way congenial to the international society. Some of the important factors giving rise to international conflicts are, ideology, military alliances, economic system and alike.

Methods of Conflict Resolution

Broadly speaking, there are two methods of conflict resolution

(I) Peaceful means

(II) Forceful means

I. Peaceful Means of Conflict Resolution

It is also called pacific settlement of international disputes. **Article 33 of the United Nations Charter** explicitly states that "any dispute endangering international peace and security would at first be tried to be resolved through negotiations, arbitration, judicial remedy and several other such means". Negatively it implies use of all methods of conflict resolution where there is no involvement of use of force. There are following methods of pacific settlement of international disputes.

(1) Negotiations : It is the most simplest of all methods of peaceful settlement of international disputes. The provisions in **Article 40 of the UN Charter** also specifically focuses on this aspect before taking help from the Security Council. However, it may not always result in resolving the conflict. As **Schleicher** points out "is one which may or may not result in binding action and whose effectiveness depends on their contribution to a meeting of mind".

(2) Conciliation : It implies settlement of disputes by referring them to a conciliator or a Commission. As **Oppenheim** observes "the process of settling a dispute by referring it to a commission or persons whose task is to elucidate the facts and proposals for settlement, but which does not have the binding character". United Nations also used the instrument to resolve Kashmir dispute between India and Pakistan.

(3) Mediation : It implies effort by a third state to resolve dispute between two states amicably. **Article 4 of the Hague Conference** specifically mentions mediation as "reconciling the opposing claims and appeasing the feelings of resentment which may have arisen between the states at variance". The art of mediation may be performed by a person or an institution. In 1947 the role played by United Nations Security in Indonesia was more than that of a negotiator.

(4) Enquiry : It implies investigation by a third party into the competing claims of the states. But, the judgement is binding on the parties. Its birth can be traced to Hague Conference (1899). This method has been used to resolve those international conflicts which were limited to facts. In 1931 League of Nations constituted little commission to enquire into disputes in Manchuria.

(5) Arbitration : It refers to settlement of a dispute by an umpire, a commission or a tribunal (other than International Court of Justice) whose decisions are binding on the parties. As **Oppenheim** observes "Arbitration means the determination of a difference between states through a legal decision of one or more umpires or of a tribunal, other than the International Court of Justice chosen by the Parties".

(6) Judicial Settlement or Adjudication : It refers to a process of settlement of dispute by the International Court of Justice. Its judges are appointed by the United Nations General Assembly and the Security Council. It adjudicates on the principles of law, equality and justice. Its judgements are binding on the parties. Some of the important examples are dispute between Britain and Palestine (1929), Germany and Poland (1927).

(7) Role of League of Nations and United Nations : Covenant of the League mentioned various provisions relating to the pacific settlement of international disputes. Similarly UN Charter has also devised means by which disputes could be settled peacefully. **Chapter 6 containing 6 Articles,** specifically deals with these aspects. **Article 33** provides that "the parties to any dispute, the continuation of which is likely to endanger the maintenance of international peace and security, shall first of all, seek a solution by negotiation, mediation, conciliation, arbitration, judicial settlement, resort to regional agencies or arrangements, or other peaceful means of their own choice. The Security Council shall, when it deems necessary, call upon the parties to settle their disputes by such means". If the disputes are not resolved peacefully, the Security Council retains the power of imposing sanctions and military intervention.

II. Forceful Means

Forceful means of settlement of international disputes are used when the peaceful means fail to resolve the issues. According to **Oppenheim** "forceful means are those in which there is some element of force. One state uses it to ensure that the other state accept the terms of settlement". The forceful methods are as follows :

1. **Counteraction :** Despite being a forceful means, it is not a means to damage the other state. For example, it includes severing political relations and ending other relations with the enemy. India has used this method against the racial policies of South Africa and anti-India activity promoted by Pakistan.
2. **Retaliation :** According to Brailey it means "seizing property and person.'' Though UN charter declares it to be an illegal method, most often states use it.
3. **Peaceful Seizure :** This method is used by powerful states against the weaker ones through naval forces.
4. **Intervention :** It means interference by a third party in dispute between two states. The interventionist state makes its recommendations binding on the parties in terms of its power. USA intervened in resolving crisis in Yugoslavia (1997) by resorting to this method.
5. **UN Charter and Forceful Methods : Chapter 7 of UN Charter** specifically deals with the forceful methods.

Section 39—Security Council can enquire into questions relating to international peace and security.

Section 40, 41—Security Council can impose economic sanctions and recommend measures for severing diplomatic relations.

Section 42—Authorises use of army in settling disputes.

There are various methods of conflict resolution in international politics. The international society has struggled to evolve effective mechanism to resolve conflicts. Though peaceful and forceful means help in resolving and slackening the intensity of conflict, very often political stake of big powers malign the democratic norms. The arbitrary use of force by third party remains a hallmark of twentieth century. The issue of Gulf War (1990) and Iraq (2003) are eloquent testimony of big power hegemony. The international society must outline new mechanism which are genuinely fair and acceptable to the majority.

NATION-STATE SYSTEM

Nation-state have remained one of the fundamental units of interaction in the international system. But, today their relevance is being questioned in the realm of international relations. While some scholars have labelled 'end of the nation-state system', others have visualized the 'decline of nation-state'. Such apprehensions are due to the persistent global changes in the nineteenth and twentieth century that have affected the nation state. The rise of nationalism, application of science and technology to the conduct of warfare and rise of ideological principles and political doctrines played a crucial role in the evolution of nation state system. However, in recent times writers like **John Herz** and **Kenneth Boulding** denounce the relevance of nation state system in contemporary times.

Reasons for Decline

U.R. Ghai in his "*International Politics* : *Theory* and *Practice*" has listed following factors giving "setbacks for the traditional state centric international system :

(1) Increased Interdependence : The age of mass production resulting from advances registered in scientific, technological and industrial spheres, the consequent possibility of meeting the increased demands for socio-economic welfare of the people, the communications revolution, increased mobility of the people all over the globe, etc. have all combined to provide for increased and ever increasing international interdependence. This has compelled the nation-states to enter into increased international intercourse. Each nation-state finds itself now interdependent upon others just as others depend upon it. The rich states are dependent upon the poor for purchasing raw materials and selling the finished products and the poor states cannot meet the demands of their populations without depending upon the rich states.

(2) Nationalistic Universalism : In this age of internationalism, the nation-state finds it essential to formulate the goals of its national interests in such a way as can help the achievement of universally recognised objectives of international relations. Even the powerful actors, including the two super powers, now find it impossible to ignore the need for efforts towards arms control and disarmament even while these continue to remain involved in an arms race.

(3) Trends towards International (regional) Integration : The economic integration of Western European states (with single European currency and banking system), the attempt at regional economic/integration of the ASEAN states, the emergence of SAARC, the emergence of a large number of regional organisations–defence oriented as well as a functional, the rise of a large number of global organisations actively engaged in promoting socio-economic cultural cooperation among the nation-states, the stability of the United Nations and an increasing realisation about its utility as a shared organisation, the trend towards institutionalisation of bilateral as well as regional relations, the strength of the international movements like Afro-Asian solidarity movement and Non-aligned Movement, the consolidation of the Third World, the growing signs of an European Union consisting of both Western and Eastern European nations etc., all such developments indicate the increased community consciousness among the people of the World. The national boundaries are no longer regarded absolutely sacred and essential for human well being. Such a feeling has played an important role in diluting nationalism in favour of internationalism or at least universalistic nationalism.

(4) The Nuclear Age and its Impact : The emergence of the nuclear weapons has seriously affected the nation-state. A modern nation-state finds itself incapable of providing security to its people from a possible nuclear war. The non-nuclear states today find themselves defenceless against the threats of a nuclear war. The nuclear powers have the means, rather the overkill capacity, and yet they find it difficult to use it to securing their desired goals.

(5) Limitations on National Power : Rise of World Public Opinion, codification of International Law and its increased role; a strong movement in favour of disarmament and arms control etc., have been a source of big limitation on the national power of a state in contemporary era of international relations. The nation-state finds it very difficult, if not impossible, to achieve its desired goals of national interests by the use of force/war in international relations.

(6) The Erosion of the concept of sovereign Equality of the Nation-states : In contemporary times the U.S.A., Russia, Britain, France and China as nuclear powers holding the veto power in the U.N. Security Council, Japan and Germany as the two new economically and technologically advanced states and other four or five local leviathans are the main actors. Most of the smaller states are either totally or partially dependent upon the rich, developed and powerful nations. The control that the U.S.A. enjoys over international economic institutions clearly gives it an edge over other states. Hence equality of all nation-states has not been an operational principle. It is true only in theory.

(7) Rise of several powerful Non-state Actors: The rise of several powerful non-state actors like the Multinational Corporations, has still adversely affected the nation-state system. These non-state actors, called as transnational, non-government, or multinational actors, are formed by private companies or people living in different parts of the world for carrying out a particular trade or production and distribution of goods and services. These are not formally associated with the governments of the states whose people/companies join hands to establish them.

Future of Nation-State System

The main advocates declaring decline of nation-state system are John Herz and Kenneth Boulding. **Herz** visualizes the changes in the sense that the principle of territoriality and sovereignty appear to be undergoing a transition. Boulding derives the similar conclusion from the advent of nuclear weapons. As he says "every nation can destroy any other nation but without being able to prevent its own destruction. Everywhere is now accessible to everybody, there are no nooks, corners or retreats left, and no singly protected centres of national power. The great continental heartlands are as exposed to aerial warfare as are the coasts to naval bombardment". In essence, the crux of Herz-Boulding argument is that the nation-state can no longer perform the vital function of defence.

There has occurred vital changes in the Nation-state system. Revolution in the realm of information technology, advent of atomic weapons, total war, growing interdependence and rise of non-state actors have given big jolt to the traditional nation-state system. As **Mohinder Kumar** has observed "It is this change in the nature of the state system which has brought about a change in the entire character of the units that join interaction process of international politics. Instead of states, groups of states now deal with one another and sometimes we find that the policies of several nations are uniform on varied issues."

However, this does not mean the end of nation-state system. Even **Herz** accepts that the nation-state system will continue in some form. **Mohinder Kumar** observes that "continuance of the nation-state is the unavoidable consequence of the process of decolonization on the one hand and of modernization on the other". The doctrine of sovereignty and nationalism may get modified with changing circumstances but, the nation states are flexible enough to enable themselves to retain their viability in the everchanging world. They continue to be the basic unit of interaction in the international politics and retain considerable influence.

Challenges to Nation-State System

The pivotal role of nation-state since the time of Machiavelli has been to maintain its security. However, in recent times a serious question mark has been raised against this role. The reasons are as follows :

Firstly, The problem of international terrorism.

Secondly, The issue of development and economy.

Thirdly, Rise of unilateral world centred around U.S.A.

Fourthly, Trend towards globalization and liberalization creating large scale socio-political, cultural changes as well.

Fifthly, Natural disasters and problem of reconstruction and rehabilitation.

Sixthly, Nuclear proliferation and chemical arsenals.

ARMS AND ARMS CONTROL

Arms have remained a crucial (if not the sole) cause of destructive wars that the late twentieth century witnessed. The race for armaments and claims for arms control or disarmament have become a bone of contention between many regimes. As **M.R. Srinivasan** observes "The United States and Britain justified war in Iraq on the ground that its ousted President, Saddam Hussein, possessed Weapons of Mass Destruction (WMD) and that he would not hesitate to use them against the coalition forces".

According to **Schelicher** "Arms control is used by some writers as a generic term to include any kind of cooperation with respect to armaments which could curtail the arms race, reduce the probability of war, or limit the scope and violence. It includes unilateral decisions of states, informal understanding among them and formally negotiated and institutionalized agreements. The stress is on reducing the incentives rather than the capacity for war. Arms control entails the limitation of certain types of weaponry or reduction of armaments". Arms control indicates reduction and control of armament. Disarmament is concerned with appeal to continue efforts for continuous reduction of armaments. It is concerned with reduction of severe dangers occurring out of arms race. However, it must be noted that the two are complementary. Arms control is essentially a move towards disarmament.

Various efforts at arms control can be studied under following heads.

(1) Hague Conference of 1899 and 1907 : First Hague Conference (1899) emphasized on the need to reduce military expenditure and recommended measures for the material and moral welfare of people. The Second Hague Conference (1907) came to the conclusion that disarmament is impracticable in the contemporary phase of arms race.

(2) Washington Conference 1922 : The main aim of the Conference was to fix the naval strength of some countries. Seven treaties were signed and "Nine Power Treaty Limiting Naval Arrangement" was the most important one.

(3) Geneva Conference 1932 : There were 61 participants in the conference. It prohibited certain forms of warfare like dropping bombs from aeroplanes or baloons, use of bacterial or chemical weapons. It also emphasized on the necessity of arms limitation, international supervision of arms business and the publication of arms budget.

(4) Provisions of UN Charter 1948 : To eradicate the evil perpetuated by arms race, various provisions were included in the Charter itself. **Article 11, Article 25 and Article 47** specifically deal with the power of General Assembly and Security Council in making efforts towards arms control and disarmament.

(5) Disarmament Commission 1952 : United Nations General Assembly created a Disarmament Commission in 1952 to outline a framework for the regulation of conventional as well as atomic weapons.

Besides these, there were a number of conferences and meetings that sought to promote the arms control. This led to a number of arms control regime symbolized under treaties and conventions. They are discussed under following headings.

(a) Partial Test Ban Treaty (PTBT) : In 1963 PTBT was signed by Britain, Soviet Union and America. The main provisions were

— prohibited nuclear test in territorial atmosphere, outerspace and underwater.

— prohibited states from undertaking any nuclear test in territorial water and high seas.

— to prohibit other states from carrying such tests.

China and France evaded the requests to sign the treaty and it failed to make any major breakthrough because nuclear powers continued with underground testing of nuclear weapons.

(b) Nuclear Non-Proliferation Treaty (NPT) : NPT agreement of July **1968**, signed simultaneously at London, Moscow and Washington emphasized on

— non-assistance to states not possessing nuclear weapons, in obtaining or producing them.

— giving protection to non-nuclear states in case they were subjected to nuclear attack.

— giving material and information to signatories for peaceful use of nuclear energy.

— accept inspections and supervision by IAEA (International Atomic Energy Agency).

However, the treaty do not envisages any programme of disarmament. **India, Israel and Pakistan have not signed** it on account of what they view as 'discriminatory provisions'. The Treaty has been **extended indefinitely in 1995** by a consensus vote of 174 at UN headquarters in New York.

(c) Strategic Arms Limitations Treaty (SALT): SALT was an outcome of negotiations between **two Great powers** to curtail the manufacture of strategic missiles. SALT (I) was signed in 1972 and SALT (II) was signed in 1979.

Anti-Ballistic Missile Treaty (ABM) was the most important outcome of SALT I. Another important treaty was Interim Agreement and Protocol on Limitation of Strategic offensive weapons.

SALT II treaty set limit on the number of launchers.

(d) Strategic Arms Reduction Treaty (START) : The discussion for START started in Geneva in 1982. American President's (Reagan) insistance of reduction rather than limitation in existing stockpiles of weapons paved way for this treaty. The treaty was finally agreed in 1991. By the terms of the treaty Soviet Union was to reduce arsenal of nuclear warheads and bombs from 11,000 to 8,000. U.S.A. was to reduce then from 12,000 to 10,000.

(e) Chemical Weapons Convention (CWC) : CWC came into effect from **1997** and prohibits development, stockpiling and use of chemical weapons. It also calls for destruction of existing stockpile of chemical weapons. The member states are debarred from aiding third world countries in developing these weapons. They are also obliged to annually report to Central Secretariat at Hague on the production, capacity, location and other information of their chemical stockpiles.

(f) Comprehensive Test Ban Treaty (CTBT) : The treaty came for signature in **1996** with objective of banning all nuclear tests in future by preventing both the horizontal and vertical proliferation and cutting of the production of fissile material. However the treaty neither presents a time bound programme of total nuclear disarmament, nor does it prohibits laboratory testing and computer simulating. Moreover, the verification provisions of the treaty are highly objectionable. The Article XV of the treaty having provision of "Entry Into Force" infringes with the sovereignty of the member states.

21

MISCELLANEOUS

END OF COLD WAR, GLOBALISATION AND POLITICAL ECONOMY OF INTERNATIONAL RELATIONS IN THE CONTEMPORARY WORLD

The cold war that ravaged the world from 1945 to 1990 was marked by a continuous rivalry and confrontations between the two power blocs with the third force of non-aligned countries virtually insignificant in the international arena. The process of end of cold war started in the second half of the 1980's. The leadership of the two blocs softened their stands and became more conciliatory and accommodative of each others posture.

Major Land Marks in the End of Cold War

- **Malta Summit**, 1984—First sign of political cooperation between US and USSR.
- Dismantling of **Berlin Wall,** 1989 and Unification of Germany 1990
- **Washington Summit,** 1990—A number of steps at disarmament.
- NATO Summit at London, 1990—**Formal announcement of end of cold war by NATO** states.
- End of WARSAW Pact in 1991.
- Disintegration of the U.S.S.R. 1991—Gave a final burial to the end of cold war.
- Afghan Treaty in 1991 whereby U.S.A. and U.S.S.R. agreed to establish peace in the region.

Implications/Significance of End of Cold War

The end of cold war indicated following trends in the international relations.

Firstly; It indicated a growing interdependence among states free from military alliances and confrontations.

Secondly; Renewed commitment to United Nations and its working.

Thirdly; Emergence of a new kind of world order with trends towards integration of economies.

Fourthly; Renewed emphasis on arms control and disarmament through common efforts.

Fifthly; Focus on issues of development, environment protection, hunger, disease, human right and other social issues.

Sixthly; World wide wave of democratization and protection of human rights.

Seventhly; Declining intensity as well as instances of conflict and confrontations and limiting their range to regional or local levels.

Eighthly; growing hegemony of western values and institutions in the emerging global order at the cost of other equally legitimate values and ideals.

GLOBALIZATION

The term globalization is a recent entrant in the realm of discourses on politics and society. In essence, it is a process of worldwide integration of economies. Though economic contracts between the nations have been evident since the time immemorial, an ideal globalization is comparatively a new phenomenon. The accumulatively effect of revolutions in science and technologies has given effect to this trend. As **Andrew Heywood** has observed "It is a product of technological revolution. Its is connectivity ..... There is no escape from it."

In its politic-economy manifestation, Globalization has also been labelled as a cyber capitalism, mediated through communication technology and media networks wherein capital moves on a global scale. However, much of the apprehensions flow from the prospect of social and cultural integration endangering local customs and traditions. The paradoxical position of globalization has been best underlined by Andrew Heywood who points out that "Supporters of globalization, sometimes called globalists, usually argue that capitalism tends towards general prosperity, and widening opportunities, in which case global capitalism will allow these benefits to be enjoyed by more people in more countries. Opponents of globalization, on the other hand, tend to associate capitalism with inequality and exploitation, in which case global capitalism will simply generate new forms of misery and injustice''.

Different Views on Globalization

Anthony Giddens, "intensification of worldwide social relations which link distant localities in such a way that local happenings are shaped by the events occurring many miles away and vice versa".

Held and McGrew, "globalization refers to a historical process which transforms the spatial organization of social relations and transactions, generating transcontinental or inter-regional networks of interaction and the exercise of power".

Scholte, "globalization is linked to the growth of 'superterritorial' relations between people, a reconfiguration of social space in which territory matters less because an increasing range of connections have a 'transworld' or 'transborder' character".

Andrew Heywood, "globalization is the emergence of a complex web of interconnectedness that means that our lives are increasingly shaped by events that occur, and decisions that are made, at a great distance from us .... it highlights the deepening as well as the broadening of the political process, in the sense that local, national and global events (or perhaps local, regional, national, International and global events) constantly interact."

Globalization marks a new wave of capitalism wherein capital flows in the role of market for generating financial assets. The Global institutions govern the mechanics of trade and commerce.

Economic relations between the states in contemporary period is being carried on within the purview of following institutions.

1. World Bank.
2. International Monetary Fund.
3. World Trade Organization.

(I) WORLD BANK

World Bank, also called **International Bank for Reconstruction and Development** was created in 1945 and started functioning in June, 1946. It functions through two agencies. **Firstly**, there is **International Development Association** (IDA), established in 1960 and **Secondly**, there is **International Finance Corporation** (IFC), established in 1956.

It provides long term financial assistance to member countries in their task of reconstruction and development. Every member country is liable to contribute towards the Bank in terms of its GDP or contribution in the world trade. There are 180 members of the World Bank. While International Development Association generally provides loan to the states for investment in social sectors, International Finance Corporation is more concerned with lending assistance to the private sector of the member countries. Members of the IMF can only be the members of the World Bank.

Objectives of World Bank

According to the Clause I of the Agreement made at the time of establishment of World Bank, it was assigned the following objectives:

1. To provide long-run capital to member countries for economic reconstruction and development. World Bank provides capital mainly for following purposes :
   (*a*) To finance productive efforts according to peace time requirements.
   (*b*) To develop resources and production facilities in underdeveloped countries.
2. To induce long-run capital investment for assuring BOP equilibrium and balanced

development of international trade (This objective was adopted to increase the productivity of member countries and to improve economic conditions and standard of living among them).

3. To promote capital investment in member countries by following ways :
   (*a*) To provide guarantee on private loans or capital investment.
   (*b*) If private capital is not available even after providing guarantee, then IBRD provides loans for productive activities on considerate conditions.
4. To provide guarantee for loans granted to small and large units and other projects of member countries.
5. To ensure the implementation of development projects so as to bring about a smooth transference from a war-time to peace economy.

International Finance Corporation

World Bank established IFC in July 1956. This corporation provides loan to private industries of developing nations without any government guarantee and also promotes the additional capital investment in these countries. Thus, the main work of IFC is to ensure the financial support to private sector in developing countries.

Its main objectives are as follows :

1. To provide loans to private sector.
2. To co-ordinate capital and management.
3. To induce capitalist countries to invest in developing countries.

International Development Association

IDA is an associate institution of World Bank established on September 24, 1960.

It provides soft loans to member states. The repayment period is very long say, 40 to 50 years. These loans are primarily aimed at creating **"Social Capital"**.

Some of the Important Programmes

1. **Structural Adjustment Lending (SAL) :** Started in 1980's to support programmes of specific policy changes and institutional reforms so as to tide over the deteriorating economic conditions.
2. **Special Action Programme (SAP) :** Started in 1983 to increase assistance to countries in view of global recession.
3. **B-Lan Pilot Programme :** Started in 1983.

(II) INTERNATIONAL MONETARY FUND (IMF)

It was established on December 27, 1945 to promote international monetary co-operation. It is a specialized agency of the United Nations. Its purpose is to help the member states in balance of payment crises and ensure international monetary stability.

Structure of IMF

- A Board of Governors
- An Executive Board
- Managing Director
- The Staff.

The IMF finances its activities by lending from the countries. The borrowing countries are obliged to follow **Structural Adjustment Programme (SAP)** which includes cutting down subsidies, encouraging private investments and devaluation of currencies. IMF also provides assistance under **Compensatory Contingency Fund Facility** (CCFF) in view of contingent situations. **Special Drawing Rights** (SDR) are designed to help a member country to meet the problem of Balance of Payment.

Objectives of IMF

According to 'Articles of Agreement' of the IMF, its main objectives are as follows:

1. To promote international monetary co-operation.
2. To ensure balanced international trade.
3. To ensure exhange rate stability.
4. To eliminate or to minimize exchange restrictions by promoting the system of multi-lateral payments.
5. To grant economic assistance to member countries for eliminating the adverse imbalance in balance of payments.

6. To minimize imbalances in quantum and duration of international trade.

(III) WORLD TRADE ORGANIZATION (WTO)

WTO was created in 1995 at the Uruguay round of GATT (General Agreement on Trade and Tariff) negotiations. It implements 28 treaties related with the international trade. It is the "**watch dog**" of world trade. It has 164 members. The purpose of WTO is to promote free trade by reducing barriers like duties and quotas. Its headquarters is at **Geneva**. There are two committees—**Dispute Settlement Body** and **Trade Policy Review Body** that play significant role in the organization.

Various Dimensions of WTOs Programmes

1. **Trade Related Intellectual Property Right (TRIPS)** : To enforce Patent laws commensurate with WTO.
2. **Trade Related Investment Measures (TRIMS):** To remove quantitative restrictions and ensure equal treatment of foreign investors.
3. **General Agreement on Trade in Services (GATS)**
4. **Multi Fibre Agreement (MFN)** : To phase out or dismantle restrictions or quotas.
5. **General Agreement on reduction of Average level of import duties.**
6. **Agreement on Agriculture** : To ensure market access, reduce subsidies and patenting of seeds and plant varieties.

Objectives of WTO

1. To improve standard of living of people in the members countries.
2. To ensure full employment and broad increase in effective demand.
3. To enlarge production and trade of goods.

The above three objectives were also included in GATT, but WTO also included some other objectives which are :

4. To enlarge production and trade of services.
5. To ensure optimum utilisation of world resources.
6. To accept the concept of sustainable development.
7. To protect environment.

Functions of WTO

1. To provide facilities for implementation, administration and operation of multilateral and bilateral agreements of the world trade.
2. To provide a platform to member countries to decide future strategies related to trade and tariff.
3. To administer the rules and processes related to dispute settlement.
4. To implement rules and provisions related to trade policy review mechanism.
5. To assist IMF and IBRD for establishing coherence in universel economic policy determination.
6. To ensure the optimum use of world resources.

Conferences of WTO*

Ist	Singapore	1996
IInd	Geneva	1998
IIIrd	Seattle	2000
IVth	Doha	2001
Vth	Cancun	2003

See appendix for rest list

The implications of contemporary changes in international trade is crucial in relation to India. Globalization has integrated Indian economy with the other nations economy. India seeks to benefit from the mechanisms of world trade by enhancing its cooperation with other countries. Though it remains to be seen as to how far globalization confers benefit on Indian economy but recent experience do not reveal a better picture. The liberalization of Indian economy and downsizing of public sector have led to increase in unemployment. New forms of exploitation have started wherein poor, illiterate masses are getting trapped. Multinational corporations are gaining control over Indian markets by destroying the traditional Indian market. Consequently, its consequences must be cautiously examined by leadership and the intelligentia. **Joseph Stiglitz** in his **"Globalization and Its Discontents"** highlights the economic and financial turmoil brought about by Globalization in a decade. According to him the culprit is "Washington consensus" at the U.S. Treasury and the IMF that has pushed the rest of the world to open too quickly and which has "pushed austerity on poor countries that instead needed stimulus". In his opinion, globalization can work only if the IMF is less aggressive in pushing countries to open their markets, and if countries themselves focus on social sectors.

DETERMINANTS AND COMPULSIONS OF INDIA'S FOREIGN POLICY

According to J.N. Dixit ''Foreign policy of a country is a statement of what it stands for and the role that it takes upon itself and projects to the world at large.'' It is seldom static. Rather it remains in a state of constant flux. Nevertheless, there are crucial ingredients that remain significant for longer times. The factors that have influenced the determination of India's foreign policy are as follows.

FACTORS AFFECTING INDIA'S FOREIGN POLICY

Geographical Location

Rightly remarked by Napoleon Bonaparte ''Any country's foreign policy is determined by its geography.'' India's location between middle-east, south-east Asia and far-east obliged her to engage in the events of the region. Natural frontiers in the form of Himalayas in the north and Indian ocean and Bay of Bengal on the three sides has considerably influenced its foreign policy.

Historical Traditions

India's commitment to peace from time immemorial have significantly influenced the foreign policy. Her experience of colonialism in the modern period promoted India to take a firm stand on any form of imperialism. There has been constant emphasis on the aspect of world peace and spirit of brotherhood among nations because of the fact that Indians still pin faith in the dictum ''Vasudhaiva Kutumbakam.''

Impact of Ideology

Gandhi's ideas of peace and non-violence is crucially important. Nehru concretised the ideas of Gandhi into pragmatic form and channelled them into foreign policy. It was only because of rich intellectual heritage of Indian leadership that India chose to have an independent stance on her relations with other nations. Non-alignment, mixed economy etc. are outcome of ideological base provided by Indian leaders.

Economic Condition

The stagnant economy at the time of independence profoundly affected India's foreign policy. The problems of poverty, health, scarcity that was outcome of British imperialism convinced the country of futility of alignments. Instead, it chose to welcome assistance from all the countries.

Security, Defence

After independence India inherited a weak defence system. Her military was organized on British pattern, geared to serve the interest of an alien country. It was plagued by maladministration, lack of equipments and up to date technical know how. Lack of capital to modernize the army led India to pursue her economic interests at the cost of security issues. However, with the passage of time, India took cognizance of this lacunae in her security. Today Indian army is one of the ablest and strongest armies in the world.

Cold War

The politics of cold war and the polarization of the world into two camps remained a dominant feature of international politics when India became independent. Under such circumstances, India opted to remain outside the blocs and pursue a policy of non-alignment. In fact, this stand was soon emulated by a large number of newly emerging independent countries from Asia and Africa. Though India remained outside bloc politics, it welcomed aid and assistance from both the blocs and helped in slackening tension between them.

Influence by above cited factors, India's foreign policy stance outlined following principles and objectives.

MAIN PRINCIPLES AND OBJECTIVES OF INDIA'S FOREIGN POLICY

Principles

They are in the form of guidelines to the policy makers through which India carries out its foreign relations. In essence, they are the means through which national interest is sought to be protected and promoted.

(*i*) **Non-Alignment:** It is India's gift to the world and has been one of the main principles which has remained integral part of India's foreign policy even after the end of cold war. The vitality of non-alignment can be realized from the fact that it has not only helped in securing friendship and cooperation, promoting world peace, etc; but ensured independence on foreign policy issues. India and NAM countries played a vital role in cold war politics by acting as a third force to reduce the tension.

(*ii*) **Opposition to Colonialism and Imperialism:** Being subjected to colonial subjugation for about 200 years, India firmly stand in opposition to any form of colonialism and imperialism. It is with this line of thinking that India played a major role in liberating the newly independent countries of Asia and Africa from colonial shackles.

(*iii*) **Supporting U.N. in Achieving World Peace:** India is one of the founding members of the UN (1945). She has played a major role in its instrumentality to achieve world peace. She has always advocated that resolution of international disputes be done under the purview of U.N.

(*iv*) **Fairness of Means:** Inspired by the ideas of Gandhi, India has always emphasised that fair means should be used in the resolution of international disputes. She has advocated use of peaceful and non-violent methods and opposes war, aggression and power politics. Panchsheel is an outgrowth of this line of thinking.

(*v*) **Friendship with All Countries:** Without being committed to military alliances, India has opted for cultivating friendly relations with other countries. For this purpose she has concluded treaties and bilateral agreements in the fields of politics, economy, culture or science and technology.

Objectives

Objectives of India's foreign policy are in the nature of goals that it seeks to promote. They are not static but are influenced by time and space.

(*i*) **Protection and Preservation of Territorial Integrity:** This protection and preservation of territorial integrity has been one of the foremost objectives of India's foreign policy. Priority assigned to this aspect was made clear as early as Bandung Conference (1947). It said, "India and other countries had been used as a pawn by other nations in their international games; now that they were emerging into independence, it was a good reminder to those nations that the newly-independent nations proposed to stand on their own feet and must be free to decide their own policies and play their part in the maintenance of peace." The country does not want interference in the internal affairs of other country.

(*ii*) **Independence in Foreign Policy:** Being a scapegoat of colonial exploitation, India is firmly committed to the word 'Independence.' She favours independence in foreign police making without being subjected to dictation by big power. Her policy of non-alignment is geared to achieve the objective that India retains full autonomy on foreign policy issues.

THE RELEVANCE OF NON-ALIGNMENT

Today the world is no longer bipolar. But there is also no consensus about the nature of its configuration. Some writers feel that it is unipolar with the U.S. being the sole Super Power. Other writers argue that it is multipolar with the European Union, Japan, Russia and China being important centres of power together with the U.S. Still others have referred to it as "uni-cum-multipolar. Whatever the terminology, that may be used, there is no doubt that the U.S. and the G-8 powers together are in a position to work in concert and manage the rest of the world. There has arisen what has been called the new Northern concert of Powers. Within this global scenario, the practice of nonalignment becomes difficult because there is no longer the space for maneuvering nor does there exist the intermediatory role. Nevertheless, there is a vital need for its practice, precisely because the developing countries of the South need to assert their independence and act together, if they are not to be totally overwhelmed by the North. The imperatives for a revitalized Non-aligned Movement springs from many sources. For the developing countries this multipolarity presents an uncertain, complex and gloomy environment in which there may not be many new opportunities, but increased vulnerability. At present there seems to be no change of the developing countries being able to exploit the differences that are seen among the major economic powers. Of course, the situation may change in the medium or long-term.

The Third World countries are also being pressurised to agree to all the demand of the developed world on the question of opening of markets and intellectual property rights, even though the fact of the matter is that trends towards protectionism are rising in the developed countries at the time when most of the developing countries are seriously reforming their economies and providing for market deregulation. So also is the impression being fostered that the Third World is somehow responsible for environmental pollution when actually it is the wanton wastage of resources by the Northern countries that has been the chief source of environmental degradation. The Northern governments are bent upon maintaining their unsustainable production and consumption systems. At the same time, they expect the Southern governments to make all the adjustments and sacrifices necessary to keep the environment safe for the North. Now the prospects of the North imposing sanctions and other punitive measures on the South in the name of environmental protection looms large before us.

Thirdly, there is a tendency on the part of the developed countries to impose stringent restrictions on the transfer of technology to the developing countries. The ever-growing list of items subjected to the so-called dual use restrictions effectively threatens to deprive the developing countries of the fruits of technological progress in many key areas. Such restrictions have come to cover everything from computers to machine tools,to specialised alloys to chemicals and even to medical equipment. They are imposed in the name of preventing proliferation even though the major responsibility for proliferation often rests with the very countries that are imposing the restrictions. This is extremely unfair.

Fourthly, the world continues to be divided into the nuclear 'haves' and 'have-nots'. The nuclear 'haves' seem to be determined to retain their arsenals of the nuclear weapons, albeit on a reduced scale and to prevent others from acquiring such weapons. The irony is that the targets of nuclear weapons are now the countries of the Third World as these are being looked upon as the main threat to the security of the nuclear-weapons powers. Instead of being discarded after the end of the Cold War, deterrence is being retained and honed for being used discriminately against the countries of the Third World. The countries of the Third World are now under tremendous pressure to desist from developing weapons of mass destruction and to reduce their alleged excessive military expenditure.

Fifthly, instead of revitalising multilaterialism under the United Nations, the new alliance headed by the United States has successfully mounted an all out campaign to destroy the multilateral character of the world body to alter its agenda and to undermine its functioning to certain areas. Hard-core economic issues like the removal of poverty, developmental plans, trade, money, finance and debt have been taken off the agenda of the United Nations and transferred to the International Monetary Fund (IMF), the World Bank and the General Agreement on Trade and Tariffs (GATT), over which they have greater control and which permit them to use cross-conditionalities and cross-relation. Organisation forming part of the UN family are being held in leash through denial of the finances due to them. And in the UN Security Council, it is the permanent members which, acting in close cooperation, take all the decisions affecting world peace and security. There are a number of ad hoc discriminatory regimes aimed at preventing the proliferation of weapons of mass destruction. These include regimes for chemical weapons (the 'Australian Club), nuclear weapons "London Supplier Group" (LSG) and Missiles (the Missile Technology Control Regimes, or MTCR). The lists of dual purpose technologies, substances and equipment which cannot be exported to the countries of the Third World under these regimes are so extensive as to have the effect of freezing the technological and industrial development of the developing countries in those vital areas. It is also very difficult to judge whether the restrictions applied in any particular case are motivated by the commercial consideration of preventing the country concerned from developing competitive capacity or by the consideration of ensuring nonproliferation. These regimes have no sanction of international law. As they are outside the United Nations and their membership is restricted, they have the effect of undermining multilateralism.

All the Third World countries are facing today the threat of the disintegration of nation-states.The examples are Czechoslovakia, Ethiopia, the former Soviet Union and Yugoslavia. Being sure of their own national integrity, which is underpinned by their military power or that of their allies and in view of their own relative political stability and economic prosperity, the countries of the new alliances have started espousing causes and championing principles aimed to encourage fissiparous tendencies in those countries of the Third World where the economic and political situation is far from stable. This may lead to further disintegration of nation-states ; recently discovered enthusiasm of the new alliance for self determination use its political and economic leverage to interfere in the affairs of other states in the name of human rights and good governance and the sanctions that it has successfully sought for intervention in other countries on humanitarian grounds-are all pointers in this direction. Sovereignty, of late, has never been absolute, but now it is being subjected to further curtailment and abridgement. Then, there is a trend at present in the field of trade to resort increasingly to unilateral and bilateral coercive measures as exemplified in the application of the Special and Super 301 of the US Trade and Competitiveness Act, to negotiate reciprocal access to markets and to use cross-retaliation. This practice has not been stopped even after signing the GATT Treaty at Marrakesh by 115 countries including America in April,1994. Moreover, the attempt by the developed countries to raise new issues not directly, linked to trade, such as labour standards, social conditions and environment at the recently concluded GATT Treaty clearly proves that the newly formed world trading system is not likely to serve any better the interests of the developing countries.

The above analysis shows that with the end of the Cold War, the threat to and pressure on the independence of the non-aligned countries have assumed new forms. The present negative trends in the world are contrary to the aims and objectives of the Non-aligned Movements for a just, equitable and democratic world order. None of the NAM countries or group of countries, however, big or rich they may be, can face these new realities alone. Hence, the countries of NAM must continue to stay and act together for common thought and action. But question is how to bell the cat? The answer is the non-aligned countries can reverse the above negative trends by three important ways: (a) reforming and strengthening the United Nations; (b) encouraging South-South Cooperation; and (c) consolidating the Movement through necessary reforms.

Thus the realities of current global politics make non-alignment equally relevant today for the developing countries of the world as it was during the Cold War period.However, while Non-alignment continues to be relevant, the role of the Non-aligned Movement in current global affairs has been somewhat declining. The NAM could not first prevent the conflict between two of its members-Iraq and Kuwait and neither could it play an effective role in the subsequent Gulf crises. Nor could it halt the civil war in Yugoslavia, itself an important member.

One of the reasons for its inefficiency is that today the NAM is faced with serious internal problems. Some of these include the membership criteria which is too liberal and often violated, the lack of self discipline amongst its members, the weaknesses in the method of consensus and the absence of any mechanism for monitoring of global events.

INDIA'S NUCLEAR POLICY

India has been a firm believer in principle of peaceful co-existence and oppose any form of arms race or nuclear proliferation that endanger the prospects for peace or threaten the security of any nation. In early years she strongly condemned nuclear attack on Hiroshima and Nagasaki and stood for use of nuclear energy only for peaceful purposes. But frustrations on foreign policy issues, changing international climate and threats from nearby countries led India to embark on path of nuclear weaponisation.

India's Nuclear Weaponization

It may seem ironical as to why a firm champion of programme for complete elimination of the nuclear weapons chose to opt for nuclear weaponisation. The reasons are :

- **Sino-Indian conflict** even after slogans of Hindi-Chini Bhai-Bhai.
- **Chinese nuclear explosions** from 1964 onwards and her meaning posture during Indo-Pak war (1965).
- **Pakistan's clandestine nuclear weaponisation** and threat by military rulers to use it against India.
- **Changing international environment** that showed that countries who became nuclear powers were not sidelined if they could withstand some pressure. **China and France tested their weapons** as late as signing treaties on disarmament and non-proliferation.
- Gradual evolution of discriminatory non-proliferation regimes convinced India of **hegemonistic designs of big power**.

Nuclear Tests

First Nuclear Test—1974-Pokhran

Second Nuclear Test—1998-Pokhran

There are five nuclear tests including two sub-kilotons nuclear tests.

International Response

Test were followed by wide expressed anguish, particularly by Japan, U.S.A., Australia, E.U., New Zealand. But, India was able to tide over pulls and pressure. It was able to convince the world that nuclear tests were expedient in the interest of peace and security in the region. Moreover, India made it clear that she did not want to enter into race for nuclear armaments and would actively participate in any endeavour at disarmament provided they are free from ambiguities and biases in favour of a privileged few.

INDIA'S NUCLEAR DOCTRINE

India's nuclear that has been an outcome of India's nuclear tests in May 1998 is still in the process of evolution. The main points of India's nuclear policy can be summarized as follows :

- **Maintain Minimum Nuclear Deterrence :** India has made it clear that the purpose of India's nuclear weaponisation programme is to prevent blackmailing by other states. It is not aimed at arms race.
- **No first Use of Nuclear Weapons :** India has unilaterally declared that it will not be the country to use weapons at first instance. It will retaliate only if attacked by nuclear weapons. To deal with such eventualities, India has strengthened its command control mechanism which can strike within 24 hours and is capable of inflicting unacceptable damage.
- India will continue to **co-operate in efforts at disarmament** and endeavour for world peace.
- India's nuclear weaponisation is under the control of **National Security Council** with PM at the top of the hierarchy.
- **No use of nuclear weapons against non-nuclear weapon states.** However, in case of attack by nuclear or biological weapon, India

will retain the option of retaliating with nuclear weapons.

- Nuclear retaliation to a first strike will be massive and designed to inflict unacceptable damage.

SIGNIFICANCE OF NUCLEAR TESTS

India's nuclear tests in 1998 have been hailed as thumping mark in nuclear energy programme. It has underlined :

- India's **independence on foreign policy issues** which has hitherto been undermined by threats from Pakistan and China.
- India's **self-reliance** without being dependent on outside powers for security and integrity of the Nation.
- The technical know-how of Indian scientists whose **temper and morale** had hitherto been downplayed due to persistence postponement of ground testings. They have got due recognition of their persistence work.
- **Uplifted the confidence and morale** of people who felt being let down when there were persistent threats and blackmailing from close door neighbours.
- Shown the world that even if the world is discriminatory in its approach towards issues of vital interests, India has adequate resources and competent man-power to **promote and protect its national interests.**

INDIA'S STAND ON DISARMAMENT TREATIES

It is with this line of thinking that India has taken its stand on CTBT and NPT.

INDIA AND NPT

NPT or Non-Proliferation Treaty was proposed by the two super powers at **Geneva conference** (1967). From then on, a number of rounds of negotiations have taken place, but India has refused to sign it on the following grounds.

- **NPT is against the provisions of disarmament** advocated by United Nations.
- **NPT is discriminatory treaty** that seeks to maintain differences between Nuclear power and non-nuclear powers.
- NPT has no provision by which security of India could be secured from the mighty China.
- NPT is favourable for countries who can use nuclear weapons.

Not only India, but even **Italy, Brazil, Argentina, Nigeria have refused to sign NPT** because of discriminatory provisions.

INDIA AND CTBT

CTBT or Comprehensive Test Ban Treaty was prepared by a committee of the conference on Disarmament (1994) and **adopted by UN General Assembly (1996)** despite opposition from India, Bhutan and Libya.

Article 1 of the treaty prohibits states from nuclear weapons tests explosion or any other nuclear explosion at any place under its jurisdiction or control. India opposes it on the ground that it is discriminatory and merely an extension of the discriminatory NPT system. There are substantial grounds because of which India opposes CTBT.

- Does **not have any provision for time bound** nuclear disarmament.
- Does **not prohibit sub-critical testings** and computer simulation methods for refinement and modification of nuclear armaments.
- More inclined to maintain the status-quo rather than having any commitment to complete disarmament.
- It is intended to **perpetuate monopolistic hold** of big powers on nuclear weapons and their delivery system.

In fact, India's opposition to CTBT is grounded in response to the public opinion and reflect the national consensus. But, in future India can opt to become a party to CTBT because she has already acquired the arsenal and sophistication in its delivery system. Moreover, it will send a better signal to the world and will be in tune with our commitment to world peace.

NCA-Nuclear Command Authority

The deadlocks and delay in finalizing the India's nuclear command authority were finally settled in Jan, 2003. The out come was nuclear command Authority.

The constitution of nuclear command Authority is as follows :

I. Political Council
- headed by PM
- includes Home Minister, Defence Minister and Finance Minister.
- solely responsible for authorising the use of nuclear weapons

II. Executive Council
- headed by National Security Advisor
- provide inputs/information for decision making
- execute directives of the political council

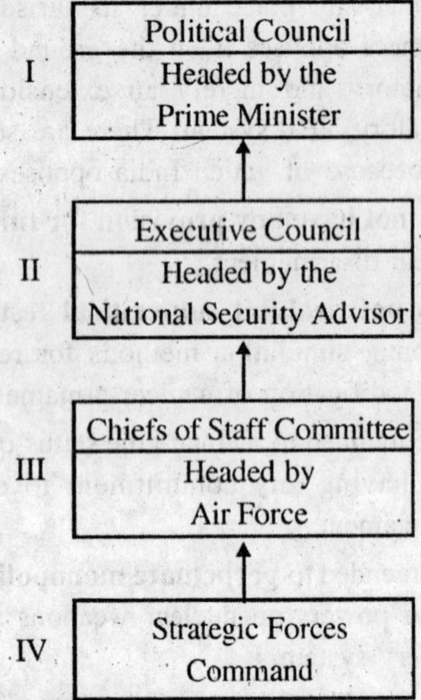

III. Chief of staff
- act as link between and provide military advice to other agencies

IV. Strategic Process Command
- custodian of nuclear weapons and delivery system.
- administer the nuclear force.

FACTS AND DEFINITION

PTBT

Partial Test Ban Treaty that came up for signature in 1963, prohibits testing of atomic bombs in the air, ocean or land but not underground testing. India is signatory to this treaty.

Minimum Nuclear Deterrence

A component of Indian nuclear policy by which she has committed herself to such a stockpile of nuclear weapons by which she can retaliate in case of attack and inflict heavy damage on the enemy.

INDO-PAK RELATIONS

Ever since the partition of country into India and Pakistan, the two states have been often engaged in some sort of tension and conflicts that culminated in three wars. The main causes of the strained relations have been as under :

Major Irritants in Indo-Pak Relations

(a) Refugees-sent after the partition.

(b) Distribution of assets and properties at the time of partition.

(c) Sharing of river water from tributries of Indus.

(d) Status of Kashmir.

(e) Border disputes-stand on LOC (Line of Control).

(f) Infiltration by Pakistani insurgents.

(g) Pakistan's aggressive posture; evident in attaining membership of SEATO, CENTO nuclear programmes, military strength, activities of ISI etc.

(h) Pakistan's close proximity to China and surrender of a large tract of Indian territory under its occupation.

(i) Pakistan's scepticism with India's stance during the revolt of East Pakistan and creation of independent state of Bangladesh. On the contrary India's intervention became a necessity to deal with large influx of refugees.

(j) Islamic state, political instability and dominant military have contributed in building anti-India posture in the minds of people.

(k) Extending support to separatist and terrorist elements to cause severe deadlocks and instability in India.

Major Instances of Conflict

1. 1948-riots
2. 1965 war
3. 1971 war
4. 1999 Kargil war

Steps Taken to Lessen Tensions

- 1966—**Tashkant Agreement**-to normalise the relations between India and Pak, return the property captured in the war etc.
- 1972—**Shimla Agreement**-showed faith in the principles of peaceful co-existence and non-interference, settlement of disputes through negotiations.

  But Soviet's intervention in Afghanistan and U.S. strategic involvement with irritant Pakistan created new hindrance in Indo-Pak relations.
- 1983—Setting up of a **Joint Commission** to increase co-operation in the realm of economy, culture, information and alike.

  But, acquisition of Harpoone missiles, India's insistence on restoration of Democracy in Pakistan, Pakistan's help to Sikh secessionists in Punjab hindered the prospects for peace.
- 1985-86 **six meetings between Rajeev Gandhi and General Zia** led to some slackening of tensions.

  But, suddenly by the end of 1986, the two countries increasingly became suspicious of each other, Rajeev Gandhi postponed his Pakistan trip, Pakistan started supporting terrorists in Punjab.
- 1988 Benazir Bhutto promised to abide by the Shimla Agreement and showed accommodative posture. The two countries agreed to share a number to information about nuclear energy production, fight terrorists, smugglers and drug traffickers.

Contemporary Issues

The period under review witnessed efforts by the Government of India to build cooperative relations with Pakistan that were undermined by continued cross-border terrorism launched from Pakistani soil or from territory under Pakistan's control, large scale ceasefire violations by Pakistani Security Forces coupled with unrelenting efforts to infiltrate terrorists into India from across the Line of Control (LoC)/International Border (IB).

Stalling by Pakistan of the Pathankot Airbase Terror Attack investigation and the Mumbai Terror Attack trial in Pakistan were major hindrances in normalizing of ties between the two countries.

The cross border terrorism emanating from Pakistan affected the wider region and denied a conducive environment for the SAARC Summit to be held as scheduled for November 2016 at Islamabad. Indian diplomacy was successful in highlighting Pakistan's role in supporting terror in Jammu and Kashmir and in combating its efforts to glorify terrorists.

Mr.Sartaj Aziz, Foreign Affairs Adviser to Pakistan Prime Minister led the Pakistan delegation to the Sixth Ministerial Conference of the Heart of Asia Istanbul Process on Afghanistan in Amritsar on 4 December 2016.

Future Issues

For the time to come following issues will shape Indo-Pak relations.

1. Insurgency in Kashmir backed by ISI.
2. Economic contacts, SAFTA, gas pipeline from Iran etc.
3. Growing stature of India in the region as well as world.
4. Military manoeuvres and arms race.
5. Rising popularity of conservative section in Pakistan political circles as evident in last election.

Though Pakistan seems to break all roads to peace in the last 78 years, India can not hope to benefit the least from being accommodative. It needs to shed complacency of not being decisive at crucial moments. It can do so only by manoeuvering economic, military and political strengths in international arena.

Kashmir Issue in Indo-Pak Relation

Jammu and Kashmir in the northernmost territory of Indian Union was under the control of Maharaja Hari Singh at the time of independence. The delay caused by Maharaja to take a firm stand on the status of Kashmir provided opportunity to Pakistan to attack it, on 15 October, 1947. Soon afterward the **Maharaja signed the instrument of accession in favour of India, on 26 October, 1947**. It was later ratified by the legislature of the State and J and K became a part of Indian Union.

But, Pakistan has never accepted Kashmir to be the part of India and promoted insurgency backed by its military and ISI. This issue has been one of the main causes of confrontation between two states even though the accession of the state was fully in line with provision of Government of India Act 1947 that provided for organization of the Indian Union.

UN Commission on India and Pakistan

Soon after reference of Kashmir question to the Security Council of U.N. by India, a commission named UNCIP was appointed which recommended among other things, a plebiscite in Kashmir. But, it was a failure which it accepted in its final report.

Later on there were **Mc Nanghton plan, Dixon Proposal** (1954) and **Graham Mission** to solve the issue but they also failed and efforts were made at Bilateral Negotiations.

Simla Agreement

Signed between Indian Prime Minister Indira Gandhi and Pakistani President Z.A. Bhutto in 1972. It showed commitment in resolving conflict and confrontation that had hitherto marred their relations and work for promotion of friendly and harmonious relations. India's success was noteworthy, for it was able to acquire control over some strategic positions like Kargil.

INDO-SRI LANKA RELATIONS

India is Sri Lanka's closest neighbour. The relationship between the two countries is more than 2,500 years old and both sides have built upon a legacy of intellectual, cultural, religious and linguistic intercourse. In recent years, the relationship has been marked by the contacts at the highest political level, growing trade and investment, cooperation in the fields of education, culture and defence, as well as a broad understanding on major issues of international interest.

India-Sri Lanka relations were marked by regular high level exchanges, accelerated progress on projects and a synergy in objectives relating to maintenance of peace and security in the Indian Ocean. The year also saw a number of Ministerial level visits between the countries in furtherance of the direction given at the highest political levels. Sri Lanka continued to be India's largest trading partner in SAARC while India remained Sri Lanka's largest trading partner globally. India is also amongst the top four investors in Sri Lanka with cumulative investments of over US$ 1 billion since 2003.

Concerted focus continued on developmental assistance to Sri Lanka and India's commitments aggregated Rs. 2,300 crore as grant assistance and Rs. 12,900 crore as Lines of Credit. Further synergies were built between the two countries on issues relating to defence and security including maritime safety and security issues in the Indian Ocean. India now offers more than 700 scholarship slots annually to Sri Lankan students, apart from the 370 slots offered under the Indian Technical and Economic Cooperation Scheme and the Colombo Plan.

IOR: India intensified its engagement with member countries of Indian Ocean Rim Association (IORA) in preparation for the 1st IORA Summit on 7 March 2017 in Indonesia and the 20th Anniversary of IORA in 2017. Ahead of the 1st IORA Summit, India announced several initiatives covering diverse sectors including Water, Renewable Energy, Women's Empowerment and Maritime Security.

Seychelles: India-Seychelles relationship continued its focus on development partnership, capacity building programmes, maritime security cooperation and cultural exchanges. Particular emphasis was given to capacity building in fields of Blue Economy, defence, renewable energy, connectivity and health. Seychelles continued utilization of the US$ 25 million grant extended by India to procure critical stock of medicines, medical equipment, police uniforms, police vehicles, etc. The Seychelles-India Day held in October every year was declared a "national event" by the Government of Seychelles and a commemorative stamp was released to mark the occasion. Defence and security synergies further consolidated with enhanced exchanges and continuing surveillance of Seychelles EEZ by Indian naval ships.

INDO-BANGLADESH RELATIONS

India-Bangladesh ties have witnessed a high trajectory sustained by high level interaction between the two countries which continued in 2016-17. Prime Minister of Bangladesh Sheikh Hasina visited India in October 2016 for the BRICS-BIMSTEC Outreach Summit in Goa. MoS for External Affairs Shri M. J. Akbar led the Indian delegation for the 9th Summit Meeting of Global Forum on Migration & Development (GFMD) held in Dhaka in December 2016. The year saw signing of an amendment to the Extradition Treaty during the visit of Home Minister of Bangladesh in July 2016. An important development was the visit of Defence Minister Shri Manohar Parrikar to Bangladesh in November-December 2016 which was the first visit by an Indian Defence Minister since 1971.

This was in addition to mil-to-mil exchanges which saw intensification during the year. India-Bangladesh bilateral trade has grown steadily over the last few years with total trade in the last five years (from FY 2011-12 to FY 2015-16) growing by more than 17%. Connectivity through Rail, Road, Inland waterways, and Coastal shipping remained a key focus area for the two countries and a number of meetings related to these were held to advance specific projects in these areas. The fourth railway line between the two countries through Radhikapur- Birol is now ready. The year also saw inauguration of the Petrapole Integrated Check Post (ICP) to facilitate cross-border movement of people and goods in July 2016, and Phulbari-Banglabandha immigration check-post in February 2016.

The two countries identified 11 projects to be executed under the credit line of US$ 2 Billion offered in 2015. After Sheikh Hasina deportation, the tensions between the two countries reduced after a diplomatic visit by India's foreign secretary. He called on the advisor in-chief Muhammad Yunus and the metting concluded on a positive note.

INDO-NEPAL RELATIONS

The Kingdom of Nepal was founded in 1789 by Prithvi Narayan Shah. It has common borders with India and China. It is significant factor for India's security interests in the northern frontier. So, Indian government have adopted policies that ensure political and economic stability of the tiny kingdom.

Major Irritants

There remains certain areas where strain in relationship was clearly visible. For instance

- Nepal's insistence on changes in Indo-Nepal Peace and Friendship Treaty of 1950.
- Use of Indian land by terrorists from Nepal for their activities in Nepal.
- Problem faced by Nepalese in Assam and Darjeeling district of West Bengal.
- Treatment meted out to the Indian citizens in Nepal in recent times.
- Nepal's tilt in favour of China to get economic and military support from China.
- Strong Maoist base in Nepal fostering anti-India sentiments.
- Use of Nepal's territory by Pakistani terrorist as evident in IC-814 hijacking and smuggling of weapons and narcotics through Bihar and U.P.

India-Nepal friendship and cooperation is characterized by open borders, age-old people-to-people ties and multi-faceted socio-economic interaction. The relationship derives its strength from shared history, common cultural ethos, trade and economic partnership and intense people to people contacts. The Year 2016 witnessed a number of high-level exchanges, which further strengthened bilateral ties in all spheres. Rashtrapatiji paid a State visit to Nepal in November 2016, after a gap of about 18 years. PM of Nepal paid a State visit to India in September 2016. With the launch of "Operation Maitri", India was at the forefront of international efforts to assist in post earthquake relief and rehabilitation efforts.

India has committed US$ 1 billion in assistance to Nepal for post-earthquake reconstruction, including US$ 250 million grant-in-aid and US$ 750 million in Lines of Credit. Out of US$ 250 million, an amount of US$ 100 million has been allocated for reconstruction of 50,000 houses in Nepal and US$ 50 million each has been allocated for reconstruction/repair in health, education and cultural heritage sectors. Developmental partnership is one of the main pillars of India-Nepal bilateral cooperation. A number of economic and connectivity projects are in different phases of implementation. Small Development Projects like roads, bridges, irrigation and energy are benefiting the local communities in Nepal. Under the Lines of Credit amounting to over US$ 900 million extended by Government of India, a number of projects are in different phases of implementation. India and Nepal have robust cooperation in the area of capacity building and human resource development. India offers around 3000 scholarships to Nepalese students every year, providing opportunities to study in Nepal and in India. More than 250 scholarships are offered annually for Government and non-Government employees of Nepal for training in technical institutes in India under ITEC programme.

Mahakali Treaty

A treaty signed between India and Nepal in 1996 by which India acknowledged Nepal's right to use water from Mahakali river and the benefits accruing out of any project on this river.

INDO-CHINA RELATIONS

China is a mighty nation situated in the north of India. The two countries have ties and interactions since the ancient times. It was in the reign Chandragupta II and Harshavardhana that the famous Chinese traveller Fa-Hiuen and Hiuen Tsang came to India. A large number of Chinese students were regular visitor of Nalanda University. In modern times, the relationship between the two countries have been mostly strained. Despite India's sympathies with the newly formed communist government (1950) and its endeavour to promote the cause of communist China's membership in the U.N. China continues to be a threat in Indian perspective.

Major Issues between India and China

Panchsheel : An agreement signed between **Nehru and Chou-en-Lai** in 1954 that sought to govern the relationship between India and China on the basis of five principles :

- Mutual respect for each other's territorial integrity and sovereignty
- Mutual non-aggression
- Mutual non-interference in each other's internal affairs.
- Equality and mutual benefits
- Peaceful co-existence

It guided the basis of relationship between 1954-57, marked by numerous visits and exchanges. This period (3 years) is described as years of Sino-Indian honeymoon. India supported China's membership in U.N. and China replied by its stand on Goa.

Issue of Tibet : It has been a bone of contention between India and China since 1950, when the Chinese government prepared plans to annex it. India on the other hand insisted that China should respect the right to self-rule and settle the issue by holding negotiations with Dalai Lama. But, China captured Tibet and declared it as an integral part of its territory. A Sino-Tibetan Agreement was signed in 1951 between Dalai Lama and Chinese government by which China was to have control over external affairs, trade and communications station and army, but not to interfere in internal affairs. India, in the midst of panchsheel agreement did not act seriously.

Later on Chinese aggressive policies led to flight of people into India. Even Dalai Lama continues to live in exile. India strongly resented to China's stance on Tibet and sided with the Tibetans in their demand for autonomy.

In recent years, China's softening stance on Tibet and implicitly recognising Sikkim as a part of Indian Union has led to change in India's stance on Tibet. It has become more accommodative of Chinese presence in Tibet.

Boundary Dispute : Although the boundary dispute between India and China became stumbling block in the relations only in 1957; its signs could be traced to 1954 when Chinese maps showed parts of Indian territory as its own. In the meantime, Chinese soldiers intruded into Indian territory. India's protest was met with the response that 'the Sino-Indian boundary has never been formally delimited.' China's intrusion continued and in 1962 they crossed the McMahon Line. This marked the start of war and India faced massive defeat in NEFA.

India has repeatedly stressed restoration of status quo-ante. But, China showed not only reluctance but even captured more land (1986- Arunachal Pradesh). As of now, the discussions are mainly paralyzed due to ambiguities on 600 km middle sector of the line of actual control.

On July 12, 2017 China signalled its intent to end the standoff between Indian and Chinese troops in the Dokalam area at an early date, if Indian forces withdraw to what it called the "Indian side of the boundary". The standoff has been continuing since first week of June 2017, adding tension to the Sino-Indian relations. Dokalam is the Bhutanese name of the region which is recognised by India as Doka La. China claims it as part of its Donglang region. Doka La is also India's last military post on the tri-junction of its boundary with Bhutan and China.

Relation in Post Indo-China War Period

From 1962 to 1971, India and China remained apart. Meanwhile, China came closer to Pakistan and created a situation wherein Pakistan attacked India in 1965. Left with limited option and on account of eagerness shown by former Soviet Union, India signed Tready of Peace, Friendship and Cooperation with Soviets. This horrified China and she became bitter critic of India in East Pakistan crisis and supporter of Pakistan on the issue of Kashmir. India's Peaceful Nuclear Explosion (1974) and Sikkim's accession to Indian Union (1975) aggravated China's anger. Though, the leadership of the two countries expressed desire to restore harmony in their bilateral relation, it was only after K.R. Narayanan was appointed India's Ambassader to China that something concrete was achieved. Sudden fall of Janata government hampered the prospects for good relations because initially Chinese continued to see Mrs. Gandhi with apprehension. But, as result of her assurance, trade and cultural contacts increased.

Soon after, political deadlocks arose on account of :

- India''s stance on Soviets presence in Afghanistan.
- India's support for Vietnam against Chinese action.
- India's apprehension over opening of Karakoram pass in POK. (Pakistan Occupied Kashmir)
- Boundary dispute continued to be a major irritant.

Nevertheless, the economic relationship continued to grow and there was exchange of visits by high level dignitaries of the two countries.

Contemporary Issues

Increased interactions and engagements across all levels continued to provide positive momentum to the India-China bilateral relations during 2016. The G-20 Summit in China and the BRICS Summit in India provided opportunities for enhanced interaction at the leadership level and also exchanges at the working level between the two countries across the political, economic, security and cultural sphere.

Expanding interactions at the summit level, President Shri Pranab Mukherjee paid a State Visit to China in May 2016 and travelled to Guangzhou and Beijing. Prime Minister Shri Narendra Modi met President Xi Jinping on several occasions on the sidelines of multilateral events (SCO Summit in Tashkent in June 2016, G-20 Summit in Hangzhou in September 2016, and BRICS Summit in Goa in October 2016). Other important visits during the course of the year included visit of Raksha Mantri in April 2016. Visits from the Chinese side included Foreign Minister Wang Yi in August 2016 and Mr. Meng Jianzhu, Secretary of the Central Political and Legal Affairs Commission of the Communist Party of China in November 2016. Exchanges under a variety of bilateral dialogue mechanisms also continued at a steady pace.

INDIA-U.S.A. RELATIONS

India's foreign policy issues with USA in initial years were determined by

- Policy of non-alignment in the context of cold war.
- It welcomed aid and support from both, eastern and western blocks, without being aligned with any one of them.
- Ideal of Democracy, that have been cherished by both the countries.
- Frustrations due to debacle over Kashmir issues in U.N. where India expected US to support her.
- Stand taken by the two countries on Korean Crisis (1950).
- Military alliances like SEATO and CENTO wherein Pakistan became a member.

Compromise and Conflicts : While in the political field, there were serious differences between the two countries; United States continued to provide foodgrains, technical cooperation and aid to tide over mounting food-shortage. Under PL 480 programme, USA agreed to provide foodgrains against rupee payment. Even they provided money for atomic plant at Tarapore.

Following factors strained the bilateral **relationship in 1960's and 1970's**.

- US bombing of North Vietnam (1965).
- War between India and Pakistan where US sided with Pakistan (1965).
- Tashkent Conference showed growing Soviet influence in the area and angered the Americans.
- Indo-Pak war (1971) where USA even threatened to enter Bay of Bengal with its own ships, against India.
- Indo-Soviet Treaty of Peace, Friendship and Coopertion (1971).
- India's peaceful Nuclear explosion (1974) at Pokhran.
- National Emergency (1975-1977) in India.

But, there was some respite in tension due to changed international climate; end of Vietnam war, detente between USA and Soviet Union. US Secretary of State's (Henry Kissinger) visit marked some improvement. Soon it was starined due to India's refusal to sign Non-Proliferation Treaty (NPT).

During **1980's** despite change in leadership in both the countries and their (Indira Gandhi and Ronald Reagan) endeavour to evolve friendly and co-operative relationship, there was serious differences on account of :

- India's stance on Soviet's presence in Afghanistan.
- U.S. supply of arms to Pakistan.
- US refusal to supply fuel for Tarapore atomic plant on the gound of not being a signatory to NPT.
- Military base at Diego-Garcia and growing presence of USA in the Indian Ocean.
- US's threat to use Super 301 law for being unfair trade partner.

Big Leap Forward

From 1990 onwards there was initiation of effort to improve relation between the two countries. While, USA acknowledged Pakistan's aid to terrorism in India and softened its stance on

Kashmir; India responded by providing strategic support in the Gulf war (1990-91).

The end of Cold war and disintegration of the Soviet Union further helped in strengthening this trend. But, some of the hitherto dormant issues came to the forefront and irritated the pace of cordial bilateral relationship. These includes

- U.S.A's insistance to India to sign NPT and refusing her plea of security threat from neighbours.
- Alleged violations of Human Rights by India in dealing with secessionist movement in Punjab and North East.
- Issues of democratization of UN, NIEO, nuclear disarmament etc.

Recent Development

India and the United States continued their intensive engagement, as strategic partners, in a broad range of sectors including defence, security & counter-terrorism, civil nuclear cooperation, trade and investment, science & technology, energy, health, education and people-to-people ties. Summit-level interactions continued to lend momentum to bilateral ties.

Prime Minister visited the US in June 2016 during which there were significant and concrete outcomes in key areas of cooperation such as civil nuclear; clean energy; defence and security; politico-strategic engagement; economy and people-to-people ties.

PM's historic address to the Joint Meeting of the US Congress, the first foreign leader to do so in 2016, demonstrated the bipartisan support for India- US relations. Prime Minister and President Barack Obama also met on several occasions on the margins of multilateral summits.

During the year, there were major exchanges at political and functional levels in various sectors including in trade and economy, energy, defence, cyber security, counter-terrorism, climate change and others, which culminated in the second India-US Strategic and Commercial Dialogue (S&CD) held in New Delhi in August 2016. S&CD is the most comprehensive mechanism for discussion and deliberation on the bilateral agenda of cooperation in different fields.

There were also regular exchanges on bilateral, regional and global issues. These included Strategic Security Dialogue, Maritime Security Dialogue, Policy Planning Dialogue, India-USAfghanistan Trilateral Dialogue and India-US-Japan Trilateral Dialogue.

Defence and Security cooperation was a key component of the bilateral strategic engagement during this period. The signing of Logistics Exchange Memorandum of Agreement (LEMOA); recognition of India as a Major Defence Partner of the US; and the Understanding reached regarding US export control policy towards India in recognition of India as a "Major Defense Partner" of the US were some of the major achievements in the bilateral defence partnership in 2016. Both sides finalized a roadmap for implementation of the Joint Strategic Vision for Asia Pacific and Indian Ocean Region. In the area of counter-terrorism cooperation, an agreement for the exchange of terrorist screening information was signed.

Other notable inter-governmental documents concluded during the year included the Technical Arrangement between the Indian Navy and the United States Navy concerning Unclassified Maritime Information Sharing, an MoU to enable India's entry into the Global Entry Program, the Framework for India-US Cyber Relationship, MoU on Energy Security, Clean Energy and Climate Change, MoU on Cooperation in Gas Hydrates and MoU on Wildlife Conservation and Combating Wildlife Trafficking.

Also, several bilateral initiatives in the area of clean energy were announced during the year. Several initiatives were taken to support people-to-people contacts including an agreement to open new Consulates.

The bilateral economic and commercial relations remained robust during 2016. The United States continued to be a major destination for India's exports of goods and services.

Following the elections in the US, Prime Minister sent a congratulatory message to President-Elect Donald Trump on his election and also had a telephone conversation with him. There have been other high-level contacts with the members of the new administration. The bipartisan support for the relationship will help maintain the upward trajectory of India-US relations.

PROBLEMS AND PROSPECTS OF INDO-U.S. RELATIONS

- **Issue of India's signing the CTBT :** For the time being, U.S. is unlikely to force India to sign the treaty because of its engagement in Iraq and war on terror etc. Even India can think of signing it after acquiring minimum Nuclear Deterrence.
- **Issue of India's membership in UN Security Council :** The big powers led by US are likely to allow membership to other countries and even India but without veto power. India can lobby with third world countries and other new entrants either for abolishing veto power or entrusting it to every permanent member. If done otherwise, it is tantamount to the principle of equality and democratisation of the world body for which India stands.
- **Military deal between Pakistan and U.S. :** India should realize that it can not benefit from assertive posture against defence deals between US and Pakistan. A sizeable section of American power elite requires market for the defence product and pakistan is a lucrative outlet. Moreover, US in its Osama hunt can not sideline Pakistan. It is also beneficial in India's interest that Pakistan remains under the American control. For, military, ISI, fundamentalist may endanger the prospects for peace in the region. Instead, India should build its relationship on its own ground and stature that has been increasingly becoming significant in Indo-U.S. ties.
- As regards multilateral agencies like IMF and WTO, India and U.S. can come into confrontations. For, protectionist measures, patent laws, etc tilt is in favour of U.S. business establishment. But, India can hope to benefit by widening its coordination with newly emerging economic giants.
- In geo-strategic calculations the two countries interests seem to be converging on account of culturally diverse countries with democratic institutions. Their socio-economic milieu and ethical perception are likely to stimulate foreign policy orientation that remains committed to Democracy as an Ideal.

INDIA'S ROLE IN UNITED NATIONS

United Nations came into existence on October 24, 1945 to **'save the future from scourge of war'**. India has been one of the **51 original members** of the organization. India's foreign policy perspective have always been in tune with the objectives of the organization and it has actively participated in the activities of the world body. On account of its size and population, India has remained an important member and this fact is recognized even by the organization.

India's Participation in U.N. Programmes

India's endeavour to fulfil its role can be summarized as under.

- Commitment to objectives of organization by incorporating them in the constitution (Article 51) or various treaties, declarations and agreements.
- Favoured Universalisation and Democratization of United Nations by admitting new states and giving them say on matters of common and collective interests. It was due to India's effort that communist China became a member of UN in 1971.
- India raised voice against colonialism and helped in constitution of a committee of General Assembly for this purpose.
- India has shown commitment on issues of Disarmament, discussed within the preview of UN provided they are not discriminatory. In fact, India supports comprehensive disarmament in a planned way which can effectively put an end to arms race.

- As regard its financial obligation, India has shown discipline. While some of the big powers are often reluctant in fulfilling their liabilities, India has never defaulted.
- India has played significant role in various peace keeping operations taken under the auspices of U.N. For example in Korea, Indo-China, Congo, Gaza, Cyprus etc. her role was widely praised. But, experience in Sierra-Leone led India to advocate some modification in the peace keeping exercise. Thereafter, the Security Council passed a resolution which sought to strengthen the partnership between the troops contributors, the Council and the Secretariat.
- India presented a case for New International Economic Order (NIEO) for the developing countries in U.N. which led to adoption of a resolution for this purpose in General Assembly (1974).
- A large number of Indian personnel have rendered valuable services to different agencies of U.N. For instance,

→ Mrs. Vijay Lakshmi Pandit – President of General Assembly

Maulana Abul Kalam Azad and Dr. S. Radhakrishnan – Chairman of UNESCO

Mrs. Rajkumari Amrit Kaur – Chairperson of WHO

V.R. Sen – President of FAO

Reform of UN and India's Case for Permanent Membership of The Security Council

Since its formation, India has stood for the democratization of UN and effective implementation of its programmes and policies. But, it is only recently that there has been wider acknowledgement of the need to reform the organization. Such changes are partly a manifestation of changes in international milieu and also a reflection of new issues that are being confronted by member states.

Agenda for Reform

India's suggestions revolve round following claims.

- To increase the number of members of the security council, in view of the increasing membership of the UN from 51 to 192. It should be widened so as to include either 21 or 27 members.
- To increase the number of permanent members of the security council only countries who have enthusiastically fulfilled their obligations in achieving the objectives of the organization should be included in this category.
- To grant membership to countries representing continents and having democratic institutions viz; Nigeria, Brazil and India. Moreover membership should also be granted to two fastly growing eocnomies like Germany and Japan.
- To reform the security council so as to make it fully deliberative democratic body; not an instrument of big power interests.
- Security Council is the instrument arm of the UN. So, its strengthening and democratisation are necessary for its vitality in the newly emerging world order.
- To empower the new member with veto power or to propose a scheme whereby the power be withdrawn from all the members.

Though the talks for reform have remained dormant from 1992 onwards; there has emerged a renewed interests in it. Even the Secretary General in his speech has clearly outlined a proposal for reform.

India's Claims

India's case for permanent membership of the security council rests on following grounds :

- India has been a founding member of UN and done its best in fulling the role expected of it.
- India is the largest democracy and a fastly growing economy.
- India has fulfilled it financial obligations on time without any default.

- India has genuinely pursued a policy of national interest which has seldom threatened the security and integrity of any other state.

Recently Group of 4 consisting India, Brazil, Japan and Germany has intensified efforts to reform the Security Council. In May 2005, G. 4 proposed inclusion of six new permanent and four new non permanent members.

However, reports from Washington saying inclusion of two permanent members, one of which will be Japan seems to split the group. India is of the opinion that it fulfills all the conditionalities mentioned by Nicholas Burns, (U.S. under secretary of state).

But, it remains to be seen whether India is able to garner the required support to achieve permanent membership of the council.

FACTS AND DEFINITION

Peace Keeping Operation

Exercise undertaken by UN authorized forces to maintain peace in region, where violence has broken out. It has been one of the main engagement of UN over the last 60 years.

Veto Power

Power of the permanent members of the security council by which they can withhold decisions of the council on any matter that comes before it. It is an absolute power exercised by an individual country.

Security Council

Most important instrumental organ of the United Nations that carries out its functions as an executive agency. There are five permanent and ten non-permanent members in the Council.

General Assembly

An organ of the United Nations where all the member states are represented. It is merely a deliberative body and has to depend on security council for carrying out the decisions taken by it.

INDIA AND SAARC

SAARC or "**South Asian Association for Regional Co-operation**" was formed in December, 1985 at **Dhaka. India, Pakistan Nepal, Bhutan, Bangladesh, Sri Lanka and Maldives** are its founding members. Afghanistan became its 8th member in 2007.

SAARC is the first systematic organizational output of efforts at regional level among member states of South Asia.

The original idea was put forth by President Zia-ur-Rahman of Bangladesh.

Objectives of SAARC

- Promote welfare of the people
- Promote mutual trust and understanding
- Accelerate economic growth
- Collaborate with regional and international organisations with similar objectives
- Collaborate in socio-economic, cultural and scientific fields

But, it also showed commitment to non-interference in internal affairs and respect for the sovereignty, equality and territorial integrity of member states.

It emphasised that decision must be taken on the basis of consensus leaving aside bilateral or contentious issues.

Areas of Cooperation

SAARC countries have identified some areas of cooperation.

The 11 stated areas of cooperation are agriculture and forestry, health and population, meteorology, rural development; telecommunications; transport; science and technology; postal services; sports, arts, and culture; women in development; and drug trafficking and abuse. Other concerns, such as tourism and terrorism, however, have also been targeted.

The charter stipulates that decisions are unanimous and that "bilateral and contentious issues" are to be avoided.

SAARC SUMMITS*

S.No.	Year	Place
I	1985	Dhaka
II	1986	Bangalore
III	1987	Kathmandu
IV	1988	Islamabad
V	1990	Male
VI	1991	Colombo
VII	1993	Dhaka
VIII	1995	New Delhi
IX	1997	Male
X	1998	Colombo
XI	2002	Kathmandu
XII	2004	Islamabad
XIII	2005	Dhaka
XIV	2007	New Delhi
XV	2008	Colombo

See appendix for rest list

SAARC IMPORTANT YEARS

Year for Girl Child	1990
Year for House	1991
Year for Environment	1992
Year for Handicapped	1993
Year for Poverty Removal	1995
Year for Literacy	1996
Year of Participatory Governance	1997
Year of Biodiversity	1999
Year of Contribution of Youth to Environment	2002-03
SAARC Awareness Year for TB and HIV/AIDS	2004,
South Asia Tourism Year	2006
Green South Asia Year	2007

Social Charter : The charter deals with poverty alleviation, health issues, education, human resource development and youth mobilisation, promotion of the status of women, promotion of the rights and well being of the child, population stabilisation and drug addiction, rehabilitation and reintegration.

The charter urges all the member-states to attach importance to social development and economic growth. It stresses that legislative, executive and administrative frameworks should be provided for the progressive realisation of social and economic goals. It asks the SAARC states to maintain a social policy and strategy to ensure an overall and balanced social uplift of their people.

India's Role

India realizes the importance the regional organizations are to play in foreseeble future. Since its formation, India has played vital role and at times as a 'big brother' in establishing cooperation between members.

In later years SAARC sought to tackle issues such as women's participation, drug trafficking, tackling terrorism etc. It urged resumption of North-South dialogue to normalise the distribution of world trade, titled in favour of the developed countries. It established Food Security Reserves (1988) and adopted convention on Narcotic drugs (1990).

DESIGNATED SAARCH DECADES

1991-2000	SAARC Decade of the Girld Child
2001-2010	SAARC Decade the Rights of the Child
2006-2015	SAARC Decade of Poeverty Alleviation
2010-2020	SAARC Decade of Intra-regional Connectivity

SAFTA : South Asian Free Trade Area

The members of SAARC at its **12th summit** held in **Islamabad** (2004) signed a historic Agreement on Free Trade by agreeing to create a South Asian Free Trade Area by 2006. It plans to establish a **system of common market, currency and free**

flow of goods and services between the member states. Nevertheless the agreement puts faith in preferential treatment of Least Developed Countries. The scheme encompasses two stages. Firstly the scheme will begin from 2006. Secondly the member states will subsequently reduce tariffs from 0 to 5% till 2015. The member states are not bound to abide by the terms of the agreement and are left free to pull out of the treaty at any time, after it comes into force from January 1, 2006.

The SAFTA Agreement

The agreement on South Asian Free Trade Area (SAFTA) came into effect from January 1, 2006, ushering in an era of free trade in goods among the seven South Asian Association for Regional Cooperation (SAARC) member-countries. It paves the way for a full-fledged South Asia economic union in the future.

As per the agreement terms, India, Pakistan and Sri Lanka have to scale down their customs duties to the level of 0-5 percent by 2013. On the other hand, the four "least developed" members in the SAARC group—Bangladesh, Maldives, Nepal and Bhutan—are expected to follow suit by 2018.

India, being the larger economy among the seven members, has to provide certain concessions to the four least developed countries (LDCs). This would include a compensation mechanism for the revenue loss that they may incur owing to the cut in their import duties.

As per the agreement provisions, the trade liberalisation programme would not be applicable to the tariff lines included in the 'sensitive' list of items. Accordingly, India, which ratified the agreement at the Cabinet meeting on December 29, 2005, has finalised two lists for the purpose. For Pakistan and Sri Lanka, it has prepared a list containing 884 items, while that for Bangladesh, Nepal, Bhutan and Maldives, the list contains 763 items. The four LDCs within the SAARC have to be provided technical assistance by the other three members in training of human resources, improvement of the legal system and administration, custom procedures and trade facilitation.

Problems Facing the Organization

The primary idea of setting up SAARC was to promote economic, social and cultural development and to strengthen collective self reliance through joint action. The disputed bilateral issues were to be sidelined from SAARC deliberations. The coopera-tion was to be based on the principles of sovereign equality of member states, territorial integrity, political independence, non-interference in the internal matters of other states and mutual benefits.

However, the reality is somewhat different. Its progress on many issues have been slow and marred by confrontations among member states. Economic disparity and unbalanced development acts is a major hindrance in realizing the potential of the organization. The commercial rivalries and conflicting interests often paralyze the prospects for moving ahead. The growing stature of India is also a cause of apprehension among some members. The organization has failed to evolve in ASFAN way. Nevertheless, the move towards SAFTA, declining hostility between India and Pakistan growing acknowledgement of fair Indian stand, seems to move the organization ahead with renewed vigour and commitment.

FACTS AND DEFINITION

Indo-Pak Relation in the Context of SAARC

There is no denying the fact that escalated tension and conflict between India and Pakistan have severely hampered the prospects of SAARC. The futility of Kargil war and infiltration in Kashmir have become more than evident. At its best, the member states have interest in ensuring a cordial relation not only in economic realm but also political one. Because, an organization can not hope to benefit the least, if two of its members are continuously engaged in strife and tension.

INDIA AND ASEAN

ASEAN or ''*Association of South-East Asian Nations*'' was formed in **1967 by Indonesia, Malaysia, Philippine, Singapore and Thailand** with the main aim of guiding economic progress and promote economic stability in the region. Later on, **Brunei** (1984), **Vietnam** (1995), **Laos** and **Myanmar** (1997), **Cambodia** (1999) became its members. **India became full dialogue partner**. India became summit level partner in 2002.

India's interaction with ASEAN began as part of India's **'Look East'** policy when India became a partner in the sectoral dialogue in 1992. This was upgraded to a full dialogue partnership in 1995. In 1996, India became a member of the **ASEAN Regional Forum** which is an international group for security-related consultations.

India had cordial relations with ASEAN countries— Indonesia, Malaysia and Singapore till the mid 1960s. There was some disruption during the Cold War when ASEAN supported America's war against Vietnam. After the Cold War (especially after India's improved relations with the US and China) India and ASEAN have moved closer. India is now in a position to offer investments in IT and pharma technologies to ASEAN. Moreover, Japan, ASEAN, China, India and South Korea (JACIK) are working on a free trade arrangement in the framework of ASEAN + 1. A research at RIS showed that JACIK has 14 of the world's largest and fastest growing economies with half the world's population (3 billion) and a GNP of over $ 7.2 trillion and a combined official reserves of about $ 800 million—more than that of EU and the US put together.

There are now 14 non-ASEAN members in the ARF besides the ten ASEAN members. The member countries of ARF are Australia, Brunei, Canada, China, EU, Indonesia, Japan, Laos, Malaysia, New Zealand, Papua New Guinea, Philippines, South Korea, Russia, Singapore, Thailand, US, Vietnam, all of which joined ARF in 1994; Cambodia joined in 1995; India and Myanmar in 1996; Mongolia in 1999; North Korea in 2000; and Pakistan in 2004.

Aims and Purposes

As set out in the ASEAN Declaration, the aims and purposes of ASEAN are:

1. To accelerate the economic growth, social progress and cultural development in the region through joint endeavours in the spirit of equality and partnership in order to strengthen the foundation for a prosperous and peaceful community of Southeast Asian Nations;
2. To promote regional peace and stability through abiding respect for justice and the rule of law in the relationship among countries of the region and adherence to the principles of the United Nations Charter;
3. To promote active collaboration and mutual assistance on matters of common interest in the economic, social, cultural, technical, scientific and administrative fields;
4. To provide assistance to each other in the form of training and research facilities in the educational, professional, technical and administrative spheres;
5. To collaborate more effectively for the greater utilisation of their agriculture and industries, the expansion of their trade, including the study of the problems of international commodity trade, the improvement of their transportation and communications facilities and the raising of the living standards of their peoples;
6. To promote Southeast Asian studies; and
7. To maintain close and beneficial cooperation with existing international and regional organisations with similar aims and purposes, and explore all avenues for even closer cooperation among themselves.

India's Role

India realizes the importance of South-East Asian giants in today's economic scenario. Moreover, India's history and its political role over the years have yielded strong ties with the region. India has, in recent times, adopted a **Look Act Policy** whereby it has attempted to widen its basis of co-operation in a number of areas with these countries. Different projects entered into by individual countries, with India are expected to benefit the region as a whole. For example, a road project between India, Myanmar and Thailand is expected to link a number of areas.

At Hanoi (1998) meet, India proposed to strengthen the ties with ASEAN. It showed interest to participate in **'Initiative for ASEAN integration'** programme. India is also providing scholarship to 100 students for six weeks in IT programme to students of ASEAN countries. Similarly, AIDA-**ASEAN India Digital Archive**, is formed to enable the two sides to share information on linguistic, cultural and scientific fronts.

In recent times, the Mekong-Ganga cooperation (2000) marks a new phase in India's relations with Myanmar, Thailand, Cambodia, Laos and Vietnam. It has sought to facilitate communication and transportation links to enable the people to have artistic and cultural interactions.

It has been realized that India can take up multifarious activities in consonance with ASEAN to further **anti-terrorist declaration** issued in 2001. Exchange of information will be a very vital constituent of this cooperation. The meet also analyzed the intricate relationship between abject poverty which reinforces alienation and terrorism. They considered financial and economic debacle as most boggling issue for South-East Asia.

The ASEAN summit (2003) at Bali was marked for two pacts that an ASEAN signed—one with China, and the other with India called Treaty of Amity and Cooperation.

India and ASEAN signed three accords on cooperation at Bali on October 8, 2003. The accords were a framework agreement towards a free trade area (FTA) by 2011, a joint declaration against terrorism, and New Delhi's accession to the ASEAN Treaty of Amity and Cooperation (TAC). The documents were signed when the ASEAN-10 met for a formal ASEAN+ India summit.

ASEAN SUMMITS*

S. No.	Year	Place
I	1976	Bali
II	1977	Kuala Lumpur
III	1987	Mamia
IV	1992	Singapore
V	1995	Bangkok
VI	1998	Hanoi
VII	2001	Jakarta
VIII	2002	Phonon Penh
IX	2003	Bali
X	2004	Laos
XI	2005	Kuala Lumpur
XII	January, 2007	Cebu
XIII	November, 2007	Singapore
XIV	February, 2009	Cha-Am (Thailand)
XV	October, 2009	Cha-Am Hua Hin (Thailand)
XVI	April, 2010	Hanoi (Vietnam)
XVII	October 2010	Hanoi (Vietnam)
XVIII	May 2011	Jakarta (Indonesia)
XIX	November, 2011	Bali (Indonesia)
XX	April, 2012	Phnom Penh (Cambodia)
XXI	November, 2012	Phnom Penh (Cambodia)
XXII	April, 2013	Bandar Seri Begawan (Brunei)
XXIII	October, 2013	Bandar Seri Begawan (Brunei)
XXIV	May, 2014	Nay Pyi Taw (Myanmar)
XXV	November, 2014	Nay Pyi Taw (Myanmar)
XXVI	April, 2015	Kuala Lumpur & Langkawi (Malaysia)
XXVII	November, 2015	Kuala Lumpur & Langkawi (Malaysia)
XXVIII	September, 2016	Vientiane (Laos)
XXIX	September, 2016	Vientiane (Laos)
XXX	April, 2017	Manila (Philippines)

See appendix for rest list

India's relationship with ASEAN has got momentum due to six per cent growth rate of GDP achieved by India while many ASEAN countries are still recovering from the crisis of their economies in 1998.

The Cebu ASEAN Summit: The theme of 2007 summit was "One Sharing And Caring Community."

After discussion and deliberations on a diverse range of issues, leaders of ASEAN signed the Cebu Declaration Towards One Caring And Sharing Community and committed to promote a socially prosperous community within the region. The Cebu Declaration cited the need to reduce poverty, protect the rights of children and women, improve education and cherish the environment on their way to the economic integration by 2015. The document reaffirmed the ASEAN countries' commitment to realise the Millennium Development Goals (MDGs) of the United Nations as part of their efforts of socio-cultural community building. The Heads of 10 countries also agreed to rely on the ASEAN Sectoral Ministerial bodies to achieve the goals of their collective social welfare with clear timelines.

Leaders from the 10-member Association considered moving the bloc into a more "rules-based" community at the concluding session of the summit on January 15, 2007. ASEAN leaders adopted the Convention on Counter Terrorism, a historic pact that enables member countries' anti-terror units to track movements of suspicious money or people throughout the region, and to allow for the extradition of terror suspects. The convention is the first and a legally binding one on anti-terrorism.

FACTS AND DEFINITION

LOOK-EAST POLICY

It is an Indian foreign policy stance by which the country is planning to widen its ambit of co-operation with the South-East Asian Nations in view of gaining ascendance of Malaysia, South Korea and Indonesia. Mekong Ganga project and Road link between India and Thailand are part of this re-orientation in Indian foreign policy.

BIMSTEC

(Bangladesh, India, Myanmar, Sri Lanka, Thailand Economic, Cooperation) BIMSTEC is a subregional organization formed on 6 June, **1997** at **Bangkok**. It started with four original members—**Bangladesh, India, Sri Lanka and Thailand**, Myanmar joined later in the same year. In 2004, **Nepal** and **Bhutan** also became its members. The minister of state of foreign affairs and trade ministers meet at regular intervals to supervise the cooperative effort. The organization is seen as a reliable **bridge between SAARC and ASEAN** because members of both the organizations are present in BIMSTEC.

The organization seeks to promote the socio-economic development and create an environment of cooperation in various fields so as to enhance the livelihood of people in the region. Its main areas of cooperation comprises sectors of energy, tourism and infrastructure. It has a cooperative work programme in six key sectors :

- Trade and investment
- Technology
- Transport and Communication
- Energy
- Tourism
- Fisheries

The members of BIMSTEC came to an **agreement on Free Trade Area in Phuket** (Thailand) on 8 Feb., 2004.

For the first time in the seven year history of the organization, the heads of government and states met at the Bangkok Summit in 2004. The BIMSTEC was **renamed as Bay of Bengal Initiative for Multi-Sectoral Technical and Economic Cooperation.**

MEKONG-GANGA COOPERATION

A cooperation of six member states : **India, Myanmar, Thailand, Laos, Cambodia** and **Vietnam** to promote the sphere of tourism, culture and education. It aims at "**strengthening traditional bonds of Friendship**". It seeks to increase movement and transportation of goods and people between member states, create infrastructure and participate in poverty eradication in the area.

INDIA AND EUROPEAN UNION

European Union or EU is a group of European nations committed to economic union and greater political integration. It came into existence in 1993 and its headquarter is at **Brussels**. The six original members include; Belgium, France, Netherlands, Italy, Luxemburg and West Germany. Later on following countries joined EU.

In 1973 UK, Denmark and Ireland

In 1981 Greece

In 1986 Spain and Portugal

In 1995 Austria, Finland and Sweden.

Twelve member of the EU changed over to **common currency from Jan. 1, 2002** In May 2005, thirteen new members joined the organizations. Total strength has gone to 25.

Institutions

EU operates through following institutions :

(i) The Council having representative from each state (usually the foreign minister).

(ii) The Council of Ministers is a deliberative but not a legislative body.

(iii) The European Court of Justice at Luxemburg can decide cases and its judgements are binding.

(iv) Economic and Social Committee is a advisory body.

EU has serious implications for Indian entrepreneurs. The advent of Euro has simplified trading procedures and provided a common market. It has resulted in cost effective tradings. However, it also has negative implications in the sense that Euro is competing with dollar in the international financial market which may hamper the prospect of Indian business if deflation of Euro occurs. Nevertheless, the trend towards integration in Europe has provided a model to the world to emulate.

The first India – EU summit was held at Lisbon in Portugal (2000). In the fifth Summit held at **Hague (2005)** the two sides showed keen interest in renewing their commitment to increase market access and create an enabling economic environment. Apart from economic cooperation, the two sides pledged to combat terrorism and enhance collective action against proliferation of weapons of mass destruction. For this, they outlined five point action plan. They also pledged to continue their effort in reconstruction of Afghanistan and Iraq.

INDIA AND G-8 (G-7 + 1)

It is a group of eight major industrial economies of the world. Its members are **United States, Japan, Germany, France, Britain, Italy, Canada and Russia.** Russia became a full fledged member at Denver Summit, 1997. At present Russia is not a member of this group. It seeks to discuss and outline strategies to deal with major economic and political issues. It works in close association with the international financial institutions.

G-8 Annual Summit*

S.No.	Year	Host Country
1st	1975	France
2nd	1976	U.S.A.
3rd	1977	U.K.
4th	1978	West Germany
5th	1979	Japan
6th	1980	Italy
7th	1981	Canada
8th	1982	France
9th	1983	U.S.A.
10th	1984	U.K.
11th	1985	West Garmany
12th	1986	Japan
13th	1987	Italy
14th	1988	Canada
15th	1989	France
16th	1990	U.S.A.
17th	1991	U.K.
18th	1992	Garmany
19th	1993	Japan
20th	1994	Italy
21st	1995	Canada
22nd	1996	France
23rd	1997	U.S.A.

S.No.	Year	Host Country
24th	1998	U.K.
25th	1999	Garmany
26th	2000	Japan
27th	2001	Italy
28th	2002	Canada
29th	2003	France
30th	2004	U.S.A.
31th	2005	U.K.
32nd	2006	Russia
33rd	2007	Germany
34th	2008	Japan
35th	2009	Italy
36th	2010	Canada
37th	2011	France
38th	2012	U.S.A.
39th	2013	U.K.
40th	2014	Belgium

See appendix for rest list

INDIA AND INDIAN OCEAN

Strategic importance of territorial location of a country can not be over emphasized. But, this become more so when one talks about Indian Ocean. It is the main route between East and West, witnessing transactions of varied products, particularly oil. Political turbulance and confrontations between big powers has led to a situation where demands have been made to make the Indian ocean as a peace zone. India stands on the front to champion the cause of peace and stability in the Indian Ocean (1975) because of its strategic as well as normative presumptions.

Causes

- Presence of big powers in Indian Ocean area
- Military base at Diego Garcia-America
- Soviet Ships armed with Nuclear Weapons
- Chinese presence at Cocco Islands
- French intervention from T.Union Island.

Various Measures

Efforts at declaring Indian Ocean a 'Peace Zone' include

- 1964-Sri Lanka suggested for it-NAM summit
- 1970-NAM summit at Lusaka
- 1971-UN-General Assembly adopted a resolution
- 1993-UN-General Assembly passed the resolution

Basis of India's claim

India took upon itself the task of ensuring peace in Indian Ocean area because

- It is a South Asia country, surrounded by Indian Ocean on two sides.
- It is in line with India's policy of non-alignment and peaceful co-existence.
- It may create a situation of arms race and fearness among the countries lying in the vicinity of military bases or site of confrontations.
- It threatens the territorial integrity and sovereignty of neighbouring countries.

Indian Ocean Rim Association for Regional Co-operation

In recent times **Mauritius** along with India and thirteen other states formed "Indian Ocean Rim Association for Regional co-operation" to promote cooperation among the countries lying in the zone. It has been named M.T signifying the number of founding members. Its major objectives are

- To promote the welfare and living standard.
- To promote sustainable development.
- To enhance economic cooperation.
- To help on knowledge front.
- To increase communication.
- To promote trade and commerce.

MULTIPLE CHOICE QUESTIONS

1. Indian Federation closely resembles
(*a*) U.S.A. (*b*) Canada
(*c*) Australia (*d*) Nigeria

2. Which of the following countries have separate constitutions for state?
1. The USA 2. Australia
3. Germany 4. Canada
Select the correct answer using the codes given below:
(*a*) 1, 2, 3, 4 (*b*) 2 and 3
(*c*) 3 and 4 (*d*) 1, 2, 3

3. Match the following:

	Books		Authors
A.	The American Residency	1.	Woodrow Wilson
B.	Democracy in America	2.	Harold J. Laski
C.	The American Commonwealth	3.	James Bryce
D.	Congressional Government	4.	De Tocqueville

Codes:

	A	B	C	D
(*a*)	4	2	3	1
(*b*)	4	2	1	3
(*c*)	2	4	3	1
(*d*)	2	4	1	3

4. Which of the following federation does not empowers its higher court to have judicial review?
(*a*) India (*b*) Former U.S.S.R.
(*c*) The U.S.A. (*d*) Canada

5. Which of the following countries has/ had single citizenship?
(*a*) The U.S.A. (*b*) Australia
(*c*) Former U.S.S.R. (*d*) Nigeria

6. The method of elections of Rajya Sabha on the basis of Proportional Representation is borrowed from which country.
(*a*) U.S.A. (*b*) Australia
(*c*) South Africa (*d*) Ireland

7. Who had said the following: "Natural Rights Theory is non-sense upon stiffs"?
(*a*) Bentham (*b*) Locke
(*c*) Mill (*d*) Cephalus

8. Who has given this definition of democracy, "Democracy is a form of government in which the governing body is a comparatively large fraction of the entire nation"?
(*a*) Machperson (*b*) Dicey
(*c*) Rousseau (*d*) Pt. Nehru

9. Who has given the Normative Theory of Democracy?
(*a*) Aron (*b*) Roberts Michells
(*c*) Rousseau (*d*) C.Macpherson

10. Which is not correct according to Legal Theory of Representation?
(*a*) Suffrage is a political right granted by the state.
(*b*) Suffrage is decided by political expediency.
(*c*) Voting is a private function.
(*d*) Electorate is an organ of government.

11. Match the following:

	List I		List II
A.	Single Transfe-reable Vote System	1.	G.D.H.Cole
B.	Instructed Representation	2.	Carl Andrae
C.	Public Voting	3.	J.S.Mill
D.	Functional Representation	4.	Montesquie

Codes:

	A	B	C	D
(*a*)	2	3	4	1
(*b*)	2	1	3	4
(*c*)	3	1	4	2
(*d*)	1	2	3	4

12. "Party is the Vanguard of the revolution for the working class" Who said it?
(*a*) Marx (*b*) Bhukasin
(*c*) Lenin (*d*) Bhagat Singh

13. Hegel saw civil society as a demain of
(*a*) Particularity (*b*) Freedom
(*c*) Universality (*d*) Harmony

14. Match the following:

	List I		**List II**
A.	Thomas Hobbes	1.	Monarchical Absolutism
B.	John Austin	2.	Parliamentary Sovereignty
C.	Rousseau	3.	Popular Sovereignty
D.	Bodin	4.	Sovereign Monarchy

Codes:

	A	B	C	D
(*a*)	1	2	3	4
(*b*)	4	1	3	2
(*c*)	2	1	4	3
(*d*)	3	1	2	4

15. Match books with the correct authors:

	Authors		**Books**
A.	Pareto	1.	State and Revolution
B.	Walter Lippman	2.	Mind and Society
C.	VI Lenin	3.	Public Opinion
D.	Mosca	4.	The Ruling Class

Codes:

	A	B	C	D
(*a*)	2	3	1	4
(*b*)	1	2	3	4
(*c*)	2	1	3	4
(*d*)	3	2	1	4

16. A Welfare State means
(*a*) a fully egalitarian society.
(*b*) abolition of private property.
(*c*) a system which combines right to personal property.
(*d*) state ownership of means of production.

17. The most important function of the Welfare State is the creation of conditions which ensures
(*a*) fair elections
(*b*) freedom of expression
(*c*) social justice
(*d*) liberty

18. According to Hobbes man may resist sovereign if he fails to provide
(*a*) Justice (*b*) Security
(*c*) Welfare (*d*) Equality

19. Which of the followings are characteristics of a political system?
1. Political system not only consist of the legal structures but also include all the social structures.
2. If one component of the whole system changes, it has its impact on other component of the system.
3. The boundaries of political system are subjected to large fluctuation indifferent environment.
4. Changes in the political system do not affect the outcome of the political activity.

(*a*) 1 and 4 (*b*) 1, 2 and 3
(*c*) Only 1 (*d*) None of the above

20. Who have the view that 'Politics is about Power'?
1. Marxist 2. Feminist
3. Liberal 4. Conservatives

(*a*) 1 and 2 (*b*) 3 and 4
(*c*) 1 and 4 (*d*) 2 and 3

21. Which of the following is rejected by Hobbes as the founder of the state?
(*a*) The view that might is right.
(*b*) Individualism
(*c*) Concept of authorization.
(*d*) Rational self-preservation as the ground for social contract.

22. Who among the following were members of the Fabian Society established in 1883?
1. Bertrand Russell
2. Harold J. Laski
3. George Bernard Shaw

4. H.G.Wells

Select the correct answer using the codes given below:

(*a*) 1, 2 and 4 (*b*) 1 and 2
(*c*) 1 and 3 (*d*) 2 and 4

23. Correctly match the authors with books:

Authors	**Books**
A. Oppenheim	1. Arthashastra
B. Kautilya	2. Law of Free Monarchies
C. James I	3. Physics and Politics
D. Bagehot	4. The State

Codes:

	A	B	C	D
(*a*)	4	1	2	3
(*b*)	1	2	3	4
(*c*)	4	1	3	2
(*d*)	3	2	1	4

24. According to Locke the supreme power of the Commonwealth is

(*a*) executive power
(*b*) legislative power
(*c*) judicial power
(*d*) combination of all above

25. Who among the following scholars argues that the electoral system determines the nature of the party system?

(*a*) Michels (*b*) Duverger
(*c*) Schumpeter (*d*) Weber

26. Which of the following is not the role of pressure groups?

(*a*) To contest elections to promote their interest.
(*b*) To help candidate favourable to them elected.
(*c*) To patronize legislatures to secure their help in furthering their cause.
(*d*) To try to influence public opinion and enlist its support.

27. Who does not belong to Idealistic Theory?

(*a*) Bosanquet (*b*) Kant
(*c*) Fichte (*d*) Bentham

28. Who had said the following statement, "Over himself, over his own body and mind, the individual is sovereign".

(*a*) Marx (*b*) J.S. Mill
(*c*) Bentham (*d*) Montesquieu

29. The three sources of Marx's thought are

(*a*) German Philosophy, Russian Anarchism, and French Socialism.
(*b*) German Philosophy, French Economy and British Socialism.
(*c*) German Philosophy, British Economics and French Socialism.
(*d*) Utopia Socialism, French Revolution and Tsarist Autonomy.

30. Who was the first person to study Pressure Group systematically?

(*a*) A.F.Bentley (*b*) Laski
(*c*) Gramsci (*d*) Pareto

31. Whose name is associated with Distributive Justice?

(*a*) Rawls (*b*) Plato
(*c*) Aristotle (*d*) Hayek

32. Match the following:

List I	**List II**
A. Hayek	1. Utilitarism
B. Robert Nozick	2. Philosophical basis of freedom
C. Lenin	3. Fundamental Rights
D. Bentham	4. Imperialism

Codes:

	A	B	C	D
(*a*)	3	2	4	1
(*b*)	4	1	3	2
(*c*)	1	2	3	4
(*d*)	4	3	2	1

33. In which one of the following schools of thought, is law supposed to be antithetical to liberty?

(*a*) Democratic School
(*b*) Classical Liberal School
(*c*) Socialist School
(*d*) The Collectivist School

34. Whose name is associated with Social Democracy?

(*a*) Sidney and Beatrice Webb
(*b*) G.D.H. Cole
(*c*) Sartori
(*d*) Tocqueville

35. Who in the followings are not the supporter of elitism?
(*a*) Pareto (*b*) Mosca
(*c*) Schumpeter (*d*) Sydney Webb

36. The Austinian theory attributes to the sovereign as
(*a*) Moral Omnipotence
(*b*) Political Supremacy
(*c*) Absolute Judicial Authority
(*d*) The power of Political Legitimation

37. Fascism is opposed to
1. Individualism
2. International Socialism
3. Liberalism
4. Parliamentary Democracy

Select the correct answer using codes given below:
(*a*) 1 and 2 (*b*) 1, 3 and 4
(*c*) 4 and 2 (*d*) All the above

38. Who said, "The state exist for individuals, individuals do not exist for the state"?
(*a*) MacIver (*b*) C.M.Joad
(*c*) Rawls (*d*) Green

39. Who opposed capitalism as it is based on exploitation of human labour which to him was voilence?
(*a*) Marx (*b*) Fiedel Castro
(*c*) Mao Tse-Tung (*d*) Mahatma Gandhi

40. Which of the following are the characteristics of socialism?
1. An egalitarian society.
2. Satisfaction of basic needs.
3. Ideal of Service
4. Nationalisation of Industries completely

Select the correct answer using the codes given below:
(*a*) 1 and 4 (*b*) 1, 3 and 4
(*c*) 1, 2, 3 (*d*) only 4

41. What distinguishes between modern liberalism and classical one?
(*a*) The concept of socialist planning
(*b*) Egalitarianism
(*c*) Liberatarianism
(*d*) Corporation

42. Match the following:

	List I		List II
A.	Rocco	1.	Syndicalism
B.	Pouget	2.	Fascism
C.	Gramsci	3.	Hagemony
D.	Bentham	4.	Utilitarianism Republican

Codes:

	A	B	C	D
(*a*)	4	2	1	3
(*b*)	2	1	3	4
(*c*)	1	4	2	3
(*d*)	4	1	3	2

43. Who said that fascism is an exceptional phenomena of a particular epoch?
(*a*) Gandhi (*b*) Marx
(*c*) Nettle (*d*) Lasswell

44. Which of the following statements represent dilemmas of modern democracy?
1. Self-government, in effects means government by elected representative.
2. Controlled and regulated political process.
3. Political structures functions under cross pressure.
4. Bureaucracy's operational accountability negates participatory exception.

Select the correct answer using the codes given below:
(*a*) 1 and 2 (*b*) 2 and 3
(*c*) 3 and 4 (*d*) All the above

45. Which among the following does not come under pressure group?
(*a*) Trade Union
(*b*) Student Union
(*c*) Friendship Organisation
(*d*) Peasant Organisation

46. Who has given the concept of invisible hands?
(*a*) Adam Smith (*b*) Bentham
(*c*) Locke (*d*) Rawls

47. Given below are two statements, one is Assertion (A) other is Reason (R):
Assertion (A): Political participation does not necessarily mean playing of an equal part by all.
Reason (R): Greater political awareness and increasing opportunities lead to equalitarian political participation.
(*a*) Both A and R are true and R is the correct explanation of A.

(*b*) Both A and R are true but R is not the correct explanation of A.
(*c*) A is true but R is false.
(*d*) A is false but R is true.

48. Which one of the following is an essential pre-requisite for constitutionalism?
(*a*) Limited Government
(*b*) Division of Power
(*c*) A Written Constitution
(*d*) Guarantee of Fundamental Rights

49. For explaining which one of the following phenomena does one normally use 'Centre-Periphery' framework of reference?
(*a*) Under representation
(*b*) Loose federation
(*c*) Market economy
(*d*) Under development

50. Marxist theory maintains that in the highest phase of development, the society will adopt the principle of
(*a*) from each according to his ability, to each according to his need.
(*b*) from each according to his ability, to each according to his work.
(*c*) he who does not work, neither shall eat.
(*d*) that government is the best which govern the least.

51. Which type of socialism believes that 'State is an instrument of reform'?
(*a*) Utopian Socialism
(*b*) Syndicalism
(*c*) Guild Socialism
(*d*) Fabian Socialism

52. "The state exist merely because crime exists and its principal function is to protect and restrain, not to foster and promote". The above statement reflects which idea?
(*a*) Liberalism (*b*) Socialism
(*c*) Anarchism (*d*) Fascism

53. The similarity between Fabian Socialism and Marxian Socialism lies in the fact that both
(*a*) support the Materialistic Interpretation of History.
(*b*) believe in the theory of Class Struggle.
(*c*) support common ownership of the basic mean of production.
(*d*) believe in the theory of Surplus Value.

54. Which is not related with Fascism?
(*a*) The state is a mean.
(*b*) Rejection of liberty.
(*c*) Authoritarian character of the state.
(*d*) Rejection of liberalism.

55. Who believe that property is an obstacle in realisation of God?
(*a*) Bentham (*b*) Hegel
(*c*) Louis Blance (*d*) Gandhi

56. Match the following:

	List I		**List II**
A.	Stateless Society	1.	Monopoly of legitimate violence
B.	City-State	2.	No public cohesive Institution
C.	Withering away of the state	3.	No distinction between state and society
D.	De jure State	4.	End of alienation

Codes:

	A	B	C	D
(*a*)	2	3	4	1
(*b*)	1	2	3	4
(*c*)	4	1	2	3
(*d*)	3	2	4	1

57. Awami League is a political party of which country?
(*a*) Pakistan (*b*) Iran
(*c*) Bangladesh (*d*) Maldives

58. "Parties are formed by man to express his combative instincts". This statement reflect which theory of the origin of party?
(*a*) Human Nature Theory
(*b*) Environment Theory
(*c*) Interest Theory
(*d*) Marxist Theory

59. Of the various indices of Public Opinion in democracy, the least important is
(*a*) trend study of voting behaviour.
(*b*) freedom of the press.
(*c*) multiparty system.
(*d*) responsive behaviour of authorities.

60. Who is the first person to undertaken the study of pressure group systematically?
(*a*) Mosca (*b*) Kant
(*c*) A.F. Bentley (*d*) Sir James

61. Which one of the following functions pertain only to political party and not to pressure group?
(*a*) Collecting money for the organisation.
(*b*) Contesting political elections with own symbol.
(*c*) Organizing public meeting and rallies.
(*d*) Publishing pamphlets and leaflets.

62. Who had said that, "Public Opinion is the voice of the interested spectators of actions"?
(*a*) Walter Lippman
(*b*) Bluntchli
(*c*) Robert Michels
(*d*) V.O. Key

63. Which amendment of the Constitution of India lowered the voting age of elections from 21 years to 18 years?
(*a*) 61st Amendment
(*b*) 42nd Amendment
(*c*) 84th Amendment
(*d*) 91st Amendment

64. The feature which is present in the Presidential system but lacking in the Parliamentary system is the
(*a*) distinction between real and nominal executive.
(*b*) fixed tenure of chief executive.
(*c*) formation of the executive from the members of legislative.
(*d*) responsibility of the executive to legislature.

65. Which one of the following function is not the concern of local government?
(*a*) Public health
(*b*) Sanitation
(*c*) Public Utility Service
(*d*) Maintenance of Public Order

66. The practice of appointing government servants from, and by the political parties victorious at the polls results belong to
(*a*) Filibuster (*b*) Gerrymander
(*c*) Log rolling (*d*) Spoils system

67. For which type of government the notion "Fusion of Power", is used?
(*a*) Presidential (*b*) Parliamentarian
(*c*) Authoritarian (*d*) Mixed

68. Under a Cabinet form of Government, the Cabinet generally remain in office
(*a*) for a fixed term.
(*b*) so long as it enjoys the confidence of the popular chamber of legislature.
(*c*) so long as it enjoy the confidence of the head of the state.
(*d*) so long as it enjoys confidence of the electorate.

69. Which of the following principles distinguishes the Cabinet system from the Presidential System?
(*a*) Fixed tenure of government.
(*b*) Judicial Review.
(*c*) The relationship of the legislature with the executive.
(*d*) The concentration or division of governmental power.

70. Who said, "As a political process the Constitution can be described as analogous to the rule of a game insuring fair play"?
(*a*) Bouvier
(*b*) Lord Bryce
(*c*) Friedrich
(*d*) K.C. Wheare

71. On which date the first revolt of Indian Independence started in 1857?
(*a*) 11th May 1857
(*b*) 9th May 1857
(*c*) 10th May 1857
(*d*) 15th May 1857

72. Who first used the word 'Swaraj', in context of Self-rule?
(*a*) Dadabhai Naroji
(*b*) Gopal Krishna Gokhale
(*c*) Bal Gangadhar Tilak
(*d*) Lala Lajpat Rai

73. The Partition of Bengal scheme was basically worked out by
(*a*) H.H. Risley (*b*) Lord Curzon
(*c*) Lord Ripon (*d*) Elizabeth

74. In which year the British Government enacted first Statute for the governance of India?
(*a*) 1858 (*b*) 1857
(*c*) 1874 (*d*) 1909

75. In which 'Government of India Act' the word 'Federation' was first placed?
(*a*) 1935 (*b*) 1919
(*c*) 1929 (*d*) 1942

76. According to Constitution of India, a new All India Service can be instituted with the initiative taken by
(*a*) the Inter-State Council
(*b*) more than 2/3rd of the State
(*c*) Lok Sabha
(*d*) Rajya Sabha

77. Who termed Indian constitution as 'Quasi-Federal'?
(*a*) K.C. Wheare
(*b*) Granville Austin
(*c*) C. Rajgopalachari
(*d*) Subhas Kashyap

78. Which is not a part in the impeachment of the President?
(*a*) The resolution must be signed by 1/4th of the members of the house in which it is brought.
(*b*) It should be passed by 2/3rd majority.
(*c*) Prior notice of 1 month should be given before presenting the resolution.
(*d*) The Second House act as a investigative house.

79. Which one of the following Prime Minister did NOT head a minority government?
(*a*) I.K. Gujral (*b*) V.P. Singh
(*c*) Chandrashekhar (*d*) Morarji Desai

80. Following are two statements, one is Assertion (A) and other is Reason (R):
Assertion (A): Money Bill cannot be introduced in the Councils of State (Rajya Sabha).
Reason (R): Finance Minister belongs only to the House of the People (Lok Sabha).
(*a*) 'A' is true and R is the correct explanation of A.
(*b*) 'A' is true but R is not a correct explanation of A.
(*c*) Both A and R are true.
(*d*) A is false but R is true.

81. Match the following:

	List I		List II
A.	Article 14	1.	Attorney-General of India
B.	Article 54	2.	Qualification for membership of Parliament
C.	Article 84	3.	Election of President
D.	Article 76	4.	Equality before Law

Codes:

	A	B	C	D
(*a*)	4	3	2	1
(*b*)	4	1	2	3
(*c*)	4	1	3	2
(*d*)	1	2	3	4

82. For which state in India there was a separate constitution?
(*a*) Sikkim
(*b*) Jammu and Kashmir
(*c*) Nagaland
(*d*) Tamil Nadu

83. There is no constitutional provision for reward of titles, so a prominent member of the Constituent Assembly refused to accept it. He was
(*a*) K.M. Munshi
(*b*) H.N. Kunzru
(*c*) B.R. Ambedkar
(*d*) R.S. Muddaliar

84. Which is NOT true for Budget?
(*a*) It will be presented only in Lower House.
(*b*) Upper House cannot disapprove it.
(*c*) Budget is referred as 'Annual Financial Statement'
(*d*) It mentioned in Article 110

85. Which is NOT a characteristic of Indian Federation?
(*a*) Unitary Government
(*b*) Distribution of Power
(*c*) Supremacy of the Constitution
(*d*) Final power rest with Judiciary to interpret the constitution.

86. Who called Indian constitution as "Unitary as well as the federal according to the requirements of time and circumstances".

(*a*) D.D. Basu (*b*) B.R. Ambedkar
(*c*) Iver Jennings (*d*) Austin

87. Match the followings:

	List I		**List II**
A.	Madhya Pradesh	1.	Anchalik Parishad
B.	West Bengal	2.	Janapad Panchayat
C.	Uttar Pradesh	3.	Taluka Panchayat
D.	Gujarat	4.	Kshetra Samiti

Codes:

	A	B	C	D
(*a*)	1	2	3	4
(*b*)	1	2	4	3
(*c*)	2	1	4	3
(*d*)	2	1	3	4

88. Who can decide that whether a Bill is a Money Bill?
(*a*) Speaker of Lok Sabha
(*b*) Finance Minister
(*c*) The President of India
(*d*) The Prime Minister

89. Which are those Fundamental Right containing in different Articles given only to the citizens?
(*a*) 14, 16, 17
(*b*) 15, 16, 19
(*c*) 17, 15, 16
(*d*) 15, 16, 24

90. Right to property is removed from the group of Fundamental Rights in which amendment?
(*a*) 42nd Amendment
(*b*) 43rd Amendment
(*c*) 44th Amendment
(*d*) 46th Amendment

91. Which of the following are the Fundamental Duties mentioned in the Constitution of India?
1. To follow the principle of morality.
2. To uphold and protect sovereignty, unity and integrity of India.
3. To value and protect the rich heritage of our composite culture.
4. To safeguard public property and to adjure violence.

Select the correct answer using the codes given below:
(*a*) 1, 2, 3 and 4 (*b*) 1 and 4
(*c*) 1, 2 and 3 (*d*) 2, 3, 4

92. Which does not apply to the U.S.A.'s Constitution?
(*a*) It has one set of Judiciary.
(*b*) It has a written constitution.
(*c*) It has separate Constitution for State.
(*d*) It follows dual citizenship.

93. Directive Principles of Sate Policy in Indian Constitution is taken from
(*a*) Ireland (*b*) Australia
(*c*) The USA (*d*) Canada

94. Which one of the following statements correctly explains the meaning of 'Checks and Balance' in the Presidential System of the USA?
(*a*) Checking the growing power of the federal government and balancing it against the power of states.
(*b*) Checking the growing authority of the state and balancing it against the rights and liberties of the people.
(*c*) The functions of the legislature, executive and Judiciary acting as a check on one another, creating smooth functioning of government.
(*d*) The power of Supreme Court in respect to judicial review is kept in check.

95. Which one of the following documents first declared that men are created equal?
(*a*) Magna Carta
(*b*) U.S. Declaration of Independence
(*c*) Declaration of Rights of Man, 1789
(*d*) Constitution of India

96. Which country has the weakest Second Chamber in the world?
(*a*) Nigeria (*b*) France
(*c*) Canada (*d*) Former USSR

97. In which country 'Standerat' is the name given to the Upper House?
(*a*) Switzerland (*b*) Canada
(*c*) Australia (*d*) Nigeria

98. What procedure is to be followed for amending Australian Constitution?
(*a*) By 2/3rd Majority of Parliament
(*b*) By Referendum
(*c*) By 50% vote of governors
(*d*) By a simple majority

99. Soviet Federal Structure was based upon
1. voluntary association of constituents.
2. democratic Centralism.
3. right to freely secede from Union.
4. inviolability of territorial integrity of constituent republics.

(*a*) 1, 2, 3, 4
(*b*) 1 and 2
(*c*) 3 and 4
(*d*) 1, 2 and 3

100. Which of the following pair is NOT correctly matched?
(*a*) Former U.S.S.R. : Republics
(*b*) Germany : Cantons
(*c*) India : States
(*d*) U.S.A. : States

101. Match the ideas on the relationship between ethics and politics given in List-I with their progenitors given in List-II and mark the correct answer from the codes given below the Lists

List-I	List-II
A. Politicsis a sub-division of ethics	1. Catlin
B. Ethics prescribes as to which among the serveral courses are desirable while politics prescribes which among the several are feasible	2. Merriam, Lasswell and Margen
C. Politics need to be freed of all ethical considerations.	3. Plato

Codes:

	A	B	C
(*a*)	3	2	1
(*b*)	1	2	3
(*c*)	1	3	2
(*d*)	3	1	2

102. Aristotle is rightly regarded as 'the father of political science' because:
(*a*) Prior to him, political thinking was virtually absent in the world.
(*b*) He combined the 'practical' and 'theoretical' facets of politics
(*c*) It was he who first brought to bear on political phenomena the patient analysis and unbiased research which are the proper marks and virtues of scientific inquiry.
(*d*) It was he who made the first effort to grant political science the shape of a separate academic discipline.

103. Consider the following statements:
1. Politics must promote individual and common well – being
2. State exists for the people and not the people for the state.
3. Man as an individual is the centre of the study of politics. Each individual becomes a member of society to further his own interests. Different individuals seek their interests as members of different groups.
4. Politics is essentially an instrument of conflict – resolution.

Which of the above – encapsulate the liberal view of politics?
(*a*) Only 3 (*b*) 1 and 2
(*c*) 3 and 4 (*d*) 1, 2, 3, and 4

104. "The ultimate cause of all social changes and political revolutions are to be sought not in the minds of men, in their increasing insight in to eternal truth and Justice but in changes in the mode of production and exchange"– Engels.

The above statement reflects:
(*a*) Disjunction between political science and economics.
(*b*) Harmony between psychology and political science.
(*c*) Complementary nature of relationship between political science and economics.
(*d*) Contradiction between political science and psychology.

105. Consider the following statement:
" .... the notion of politics does not come from heaven. It does not come Oak trees. It is

not a gift of any angel. It is a human venture centred in man and created by man".

The above statement is made by:

(*a*) Ramsay Mcdonald
(*b*) Heinz Eulau
(*c*) Robert A. Dahl
(*d*) Aristotle

106. Political science first began with the Greeks. Which of the following are true in this context?

1. The term 'politics' is derived from the Greek term 'Polis' which mean the 'city-state' and political science in Greece was treated as the Science of the city state.
2. Greeks were highly politically conscious compared to the people of other contemporary civilizations. So they were the first to generate knowledge on politics.
3. Although Greece was a small country it was a land of enlightenment in ancient Europe. Almost all branches of knowledge originated in Greece.
4. Politics in ancient Greece emerged as an instrument to serve as a moral guide to the ruling section of the society.

Select the correct answer from below:

(*a*) 1 and 2
(*b*) 1,3 and 4
(*c*) 1 and 4
(*d*) 1, 2 and 3

107. Which of the following are valid in the context of the growth of political science as a discipline?

1. The traditional understanding of political science, as the study of state and government, remained valid until the dawn of the twentieth century.
2. New researches and employment of new methodologies made the traditional understanding of politics completely redundant.
3. By the beginning of the twentieth century, other social sciences began to flourish on their own, whereas political science which was described as master science by Aristotle remained confined to the study of government with a heavy thrust on legal aspects.
4. In view of the intellectual stagnation in political science new academic beginnings were sought to be made by political scientists led by George Catlin, Charles Merraim, Almond, Powell, G. Bingham and others in the early twentieth century.

Select the correct answer from the following:

(*a*) 1 and 2
(*b*) 2 and 3
(*c*) 1, 3 and 4
(*d*) 1, 2 and 4

108. Who among the following emphasised the element of 'power' in the study of politics?

(*a*) Machiavelli, Locke and Bentham
(*b*) Machiavelli, Hobbes and Max Weber
(*c*) Hobbes, Rousseau and Hegel
(*d*) Hobbes, Rousseau and Mortan Kaplan

109. In the course of the growth of political science, American scholars have focussed their attention on:

(*a*) Modelling political science after the fashion of physical sciences
(*b*) Replacing the social content of political science with mathematical tools
(*c*) Search for more comprehensive scope, for realism, for precision and for intellectual order
(*d*) Breaking, the integrity of political science as a discipline into several sub-disciplines like political geography etc

110. According to Marx, State is:

(*a*) a devise to enhance class contradictions
(*b*) an instrument of class domination
(*c*) a mode of ensuring social harmony
(*d*) a process aimed at welfare of the dominant class

ANSWER

1	2	3	4	5	6	7	8	9	10
(*b*)	(*d*)	(*c*)	(*b*)	(*c*)	(*c*)	(*a*)	(*b*)	(*d*)	(*c*)
11	**12**	**13**	**14**	**15**	**16**	**17**	**18**	**19**	**20**
(*b*)	(*c*)	(*c*)	(*a*)	(*a*)	(*c*)	(*c*)	(*b*)	(*b*)	(*a*)
21	**22**	**23**	**24**	**25**	**26**	**27**	**28**	**29**	**30**
(*a*)	(*a*)	(*a*)	(*b*)	(*a*)	(*a*)	(*d*)	(*b*)	(*d*)	(*a*)
31	**32**	**33**	**34**	**35**	**36**	**37**	**38**	**39**	**40**
(*a*)	(*a*)	(*d*)	(*d*)	(*d*)	(*b*)	(*d*)	(*b*)	(*d*)	(*c*)
41	**42**	**43**	**44**	**45**	**46**	**47**	**48**	**49**	**50**
(*c*)	(*b*)	(*c*)	(*b*)	(*c*)	(*a*)	(*a*)	(*a*)	(*d*)	(*a*)
51	**52**	**53**	**54**	**55**	**56**	**57**	**58**	**59**	**60**
(*d*)	(*a*)	(*c*)	(*a*)	(*d*)	(*a*)	(*c*)	(*a*)	(*d*)	(*c*)
61	**62**	**63**	**64**	**65**	**66**	**67**	**68**	**69**	**70**
(*b*)	(*a*)	(*a*)	(*c*)	(*d*)	(*d*)	(*b*)	(*b*)	(*c*)	(*c*)
71	**72**	**73**	**74**	**75**	**76**	**77**	**78**	**79**	**80**
(*c*)	(*a*)	(*a*)	(*a*)	(*a*)	(*d*)	(*a*)	(*c*)	(*d*)	(*a*)
81	**82**	**83**	**84**	**85**	**86**	**87**	**88**	**89**	**90**
(*a*)	(*b*)	(*a*)	(*d*)	(*a*)	(*b*)	(*d*)	(*a*)	(*b*)	(*c*)
91	**92**	**93**	**94**	**95**	**96**	**97**	**98**	**99**	**100**
(*d*)	(*a*)	(*a*)	(*c*)	(*b*)	(*c*)	(*a*)	(*b*)	(*d*)	(*b*)
101	**102**	**103**	**104**	**105**	**106**	**107**	**108**	**109**	**110**
(*d*)	(*c*)	(*d*)	(*c*)	(*d*)	(*b*)	(*c*)	(*b*)	(*c*)	(*b*)

2502

APPENDIX

PRESIDENTS AND THEIR TENURE

S.No.	Name	Tenure
14.	Dr. A.P.J. Abdul Kalam	25 July 2002 – 25 July 2007
15.	Smt. Pratibha D.S. Patil	25 July 2007 – 25 July 2012
16.	Pranab Mukherjee	25 July 2012 – 25 July 2017
17.	Ram Nath Kovind	25 July 2017 – 25 July 2022
18.	Droupadi Murmu	25 July, 2022 – ....

Vice Presidents of India

Name	Tenure	Name	Tenure
11. Bhairon Singh Sekhawat	2002 - 2007	14. Jagdeep Dhankhar	2022 - 2025
12. Md. Hamid Ansari	2007 - 2017	15. C.P. Radhakrishnan	2025 - ....
13. M. Venkaiah Naidu	2017 - 2022		

PRIME MINISTERS OF INDIA

Name	Party	Tenure
A.B. Vajpayee	BJP	19 March, 1998 – 13 Oct., 1999
A.B. Vajpayee	BJP	13 Oct., 1999 – 22 May, 2004
Dr. Manmohan Singh	Congress	22 May, 2004 – 26 May, 2014
Narendra Modi	BJP	26 May, 2014 – ....

DURATION OF DIFFERENT LOK SABHAS

Term	DATE From	DATE To
Fourteenth Lok Sabha	17 May, 2004	18 May, 2009
Fifteenth Lok Sabha	23 May, 2009	18 May, 2014
Sixteenth Lok Sabha	18 May, 2014	19 May, 2019
Seventeenth Lok Sabha	19 May, 2019	1 June, 2024
Eighteenth Lok Sabha	1 June, 2024	.....

SPEAKERS OF LOK SABHA

S.No.	Name	Tenure		
18.	Manohar Joshi	10 May, 2002	–	February, 2004
19.	Somnath Chatterjee	4 June, 2004	–	31 May, 2009
20.	Meira Kumar	1 June, 2009	–	4 June, 2014
21.	Sumitra Mahajan	5 June, 2014	–	17 June, 2019
22.	Om Birla	19 June, 2019	–	.....

Chief Justices of India

S.No.	*Name*	*Tenure*		
41.	R.M. Lodha	27 April, 2014	–	27 September, 2014
42.	H.L. Dattu	28 September, 2014	–	2 December, 2015
43.	T.S. Thakur	3 December, 2015	–	3 January, 2017
44.	J.S. Khehar	4 January, 2017	–	27 August, 2017
45.	Dipak Misra	28 August, 2017	–	2 October, 2018
46.	Ranjan Gogoi	3 October, 2018	–	17 November, 2019
47.	S.A. Bobde	18 November, 2019	–	23 April, 2021
48.	N.V. Ramana	23 April, 2021	–	26 August, 2022
49.	U.U. Lalit	27 August, 2022	–	8 November, 2022
50.	D.Y. Chandrachud	9 November, 2022	–	10 November, 2024
51.	Sanjiv Khanna	11 November, 2024	–	13 May, 2025
52.	B.R. Gavai	14 May, 2025	–	23 November, 2025
53.	Surya Kant	24 November, 2025	–	......

National and State Parties at the time of different General Elections

Election year	National Parties	State Parties
2000	5	50
2004	6	45
2009	7	40
2014	7	49
2019	7	50
2024	6	58

CHIEF ELECTION COMMISSIONERS

S.No.	Name	Tenure		
18.	V.S. Sampath	11 June, 2012	–	15 January, 2015
19.	H.S. Brahma	16 January, 2015	–	18 April, 2015
20.	Nasim Zaidi	19 April, 2015	–	5 July, 2017
21.	Achal Kumar Joti	6 July, 2017	–	22 January, 2018
22.	O.P. Rawat	23 January, 2018	–	1 December, 2018
23.	Sunil Arora	2 December, 2018	–	12 April, 2021
24.	Sushil Chandra	13 April, 2021	–	14 May, 2022
25.	Rajiv Kumar	15 May, 2022	–	18 February, 2025
26.	Gyanesh Kumar	19 February, 2025	–	......

Lokayuktas

State	Created in
16. Haryana	2002
17. Chhattisgarh	2002
18. Uttarakhand	2002
19. Jammu & Kashmir	2002
20. West Bengal	2003
21. Tripura	2008
22. Goa	2011

Conferences of WTO

VIth	Hong Kong	2005
VIIth	Geneva	2009
VIIIth	Geneva	2011
IXth	Bali	2013
Xth	Nairobi	2015
XIth	Buenos Aires	2017
XIIth	Geneva	2022
XIIIth	Abu Dhabi	2024

SAARC SUMMITS

S.No.	Year	Place
XVI	2010	Thimphu
XVII	2011	Addu (Maldives)
XVIII	2014	Kathmandu (Nepal)
XIX	2016	Islamabad (Pakistan) (cancelled)

ASEAN SUMMITS*

S. No.	Year	Place
XXXI	Nov., 2017	Manila (Philippines)
XXXII	April, 2018	Singapore
XXXIII	Nov., 2018	Singapore
XXXIV	June, 2019	Bangkok
XXXV	Nov., 2019	Bangkok
XXXVI	June, 2020	Hanoi
XXXVII	Nov., 2020	Hanoi
XXXVIII & XXXIX	Oct., 2021	Bandar Seri Begawan
XXXX & XXXXI	Nov. 2022	Phnom Penh
XXXXII	May 2023	Labuan Bajo
XXXXIII	Sept. 2023	Jakarta
XXXXIV & XXXXV	Oct. 2024	Vientiane
XXXXVI	May, 2025	Kuala Lumpur
XXXXVII	Oct., 2025	Kuala Lumpur

G-7 Annual Summit

S.No.	Year	Host Country
41st	2015	Germany
42nd	2016	Japan
43rd	2017	Italy
44th	2018	Canada
45th	2019	France
46th	cancelled	
47th	2021	UK
48th	2022	Germany
49th	2023	Japan
50th	2024	Italy
51st	2025	Canada

YOUR SPACE